Corrupting Luxury in Ancient Greek Literature

Corrupting Luxury in Ancient Greek Literature

Robert J. Gorman
Vanessa B. Gorman

UNIVERSITY OF MICHIGAN PRESS

ANN ARBOR

Published in the United States of America by
University of Michigan Press
Manufactured in the United States of America
♾ Printed on acid-free paper

2017   2016   2015   2014   4   3   2   1

A CIP catalog record for this book is available from the British Library.

Library of Congress Cataloging-in-Publication Data

Gorman, Robert (Robert Joseph)

Corrupting luxury in ancient Greek literature / Robert J. Gorman, Vanessa B Gorman.
      pages   cm
   Includes bibliographical references and index.
   ISBN 978-0-472-07229-3 (hardback : acid-free paper)—ISBN 978-0-472-05229-5 (paperback : acid-free paper)—ISBN 978-0-472-12046-8 (e-book)
      1. Greek literature—History and criticism.   2. Luxury in literature.   3. Literature and morals—Greece.   4. Literature and society—Greece. I. Gorman, Vanessa B., 1963– author. II. Title.
PA3009.G67   2014
880.9'355—dc23
                                                          2014018816

Viridiann Gorman and Lettie Barrett,
μητράσιν ἐπιμελεστάταις

Contents

Introduction

"When did it become a bad thing to have stuff?" That question, asked more than a decade ago, has served as the inspiration for this book. In the epics of Homer, valor and manliness are exemplified in possessing captured armor, hosting lavish feasts, and owning a majestic house populated by slaves and henchmen. Yet Sybaris remains to the modern day as the paradigm of a city destroyed because of its luxury. It has become a widely accepted truism of Western culture that luxury corrupts. We see this sentiment expressed in news editorials and in novels, and it is a favorite theme of moralistic literature both ancient and modern. It is usually assumed that the idea of corrupting luxury dates back to the Classical era, that it is a Natural Truth. Though it does not appear in Homer, scholars generally see it established in Herodotus at the very latest and thereafter pervasive in Greek literature.

We have begun our search for the origins of the thesis of corrupting or pernicious luxury by investigating the story of Sybaris. In Chapter 1, we have collected all of the relevant evidence for the city, in literature and in archaeology. Our findings are surprising, to us as much as to anyone else. We have learned that the excavations and explorations carried out thus far do not support the view that the physical city was a particularly substantial site— certainly not obviously the head of a large empire of dependents, described in the literature as being able to field an army of three hundred thousand men. As for the literary material, there is not a single securely attested piece of Classical evidence that interprets the destruction of the city to be the result of the luxury of its inhabitants. This discovery made us question the significance of the theme of pernicious luxury in Greek thought more generally.

With the cautionary lesson of Sybaris fresh in our minds, we have set out to locate the origin of the idea that luxury corrupts and even destroys. We have investigated Archaic and Classical Greek literature in order to establish the vocabulary of luxury. We have used close textual readings in order to determine precise meanings and connotations of each pertinent word. In the course of our study, we have come to focus on τρυφή, as the key term and also in order to narrow our investigation within reasonable limits. It is as close to a general word for luxury as one can find in the Greek language, and it is hopelessly mistranslated. We conclude that the term is not simply a vague expression that can be rendered "softness," "delicacy," or "wantonness" (*LSJ*). Instead, τρυφή designates a kind of relationship in which the possessor expects that his or her wants will be attended to and fulfilled by others. It is a majesty or dignity, often characteristic of kings and of elite women. In short, τρυφή is a psychological attitude of material entitlement, which is attended by, but not defined as, the physical paraphernalia of luxury. Also noteworthy is the secondary conclusion that, in the Classical literature, there are no necessarily negative connotations to the word. It can be a neutral quality or a good one. Its negative valorization is a matter of degree: taken to excess, it can degenerate in one of two contrary directions. A person may emphasize τρυφή to such an extent that he foregoes military training, and thus become soft and unwarlike. On quite the opposite tack, τρυφή may become so pronounced that a person may expect to be taken care of by people who do not owe her service or devotion; she may become angry and violent when she does not get the attention which she thinks she is due. Thus arises a hubris that easily accompanies τρυφή. Neither enervation nor violence comes as a necessary result of τρυφή: they only ensue from certain circumstances, symptomatic of a degeneration into an extreme.

Herodotus occupies an entire chapter to himself (Chapter 2). So many scholars accept the theme of corrupting luxury as fundamental to his work that we felt we needed to address their arguments square on, despite the fact that the word τρυφή occurs nowhere in Herodotus. Our thinking is thus: in order to argue that Herodotus consistently employs a subtext that luxury is pernicious, that theme must be clearly established in the literature of his era. Since we have already determined that it is not, then Herodotus must himself make the argument explicitly. It is a classic chicken-and-egg situation. If the thesis is to be read into Herodotus from the context of the remainder of Classical literature, then it must be explicit in that literature. But if it is going to be assumed in the other literature on the basis of the words of Herodotus, then it must be unequivocally expressed in Herodotus. It is our argument that the theme of corrupting luxury cannot be found unambiguously articulated in extant Classical Greek literature, including Herodotus.

Yet, surely, if not in Classical literature, we can all agree that the theme of pernicious luxury is rampant in the Hellenistic writers? Here again, an analysis of the texts themselves has raised a series of red flags. Nearly all of the Hellenistic fragments that contain moralistic attitudes are preserved in one cover text, Athenaeus. To understand their reliability, we have to establish the purpose and methods of Athenaeus (Chapter 3). We have studied the extant citations, which reveal that Athenaeus has a habit of playful manipulation of the sense and even the wording of his sources. Then we offer a method to develop data which may help to assess the accuracy of citations from lost originals by examining the diction of these so-called fragments along two axes. First, one must analyze the language of a given quotation and its framing context horizontally, as it were, and map the results against Athenaeus's usage more generally. Then, vertically, one must seek instances of similar material in extant authors from Homer through the early Christian writers, looking for earliest occurrences, frequency of use over time, particular idioms, changing meaning, and also the historical development of metaphorical uses. After demonstrating the usefulness of this method of word-by-word and phrase-by-phrase treatment of citation and cover text, we have applied that method to the most important Hellenistic fragments featuring τρυφή and critique the language and content of each (Chapter 4). We conclude that the moralistic terminology of the fragments is far more likely to belong to Athenaeus than to his sources. In other words, instead of presenting the originals accurately, he reinterprets his sources, inserting τρυφή as a cause and adding expressions of moral disapproval where none existed in the original text. Thus the Hellenistic testimony for pernicious luxury in general, as well as for the specific example of Sybaris, is found to be specious, to a large extent the result of Athenaeus's technique of projecting that theme onto earlier authors.

The final chapter (Chapter 5) situates the origin of the concept of pernicious luxury where it belongs, in the Roman tradition of moralistic historiography. It is accepted as commonplace that the earliest extant Latin prose authors regularly color their accounts with a heavy-handed moral agenda. Thus Cicero, Sallust, and Livy all iterate the theme of the corruption of plain and rustic Romans by the introduction of wealth and luxury. This idea is taken up in the Greek literature written under Rome, gradually becoming a stock feature of the historical and moralistic writers of the early Roman empire, so that a pattern develops whereby τρυφή itself causes hubris, excess, and eventually either corruption or ruin. In the course of this development, the two Classical threads—soft τρυφή and hubristic τρυφή—are ultimately combined into the same, contradictory thesis that τρυφή can make someone both effeminate and violent at the same time, a representation we see depicted frequently in Athenaeus. By the onset of the Christian period, the word τρυφή becomes a kind of catchall cliché for sin and vice.

Thus this work has two main theses. The first is that the theme of pernicious luxury is not a Classical or Hellenistic invention, nor is it a Natural Truth. Rather, it is derived from the Late Republican Latin prose historiography that developed concurrently with Rome's growing empire. It is introduced from that genre into the Greek writers of the era, who adapt it to their Hellenic terminology. The second thesis is methodological. We lay down a strategy to interpret the reliability of fragments of earlier authors found in cover texts such as Athenaeus, by examining the phrasing in great detail along synchronic and diachronic lines. We conclude that the language of moral censure derives from an Athenaean reworking of earlier Greek authors.

This work presents the history of an idea, not an investigation of *realia*. We do not write about the things that the ancients possessed, but rather concentrate entirely on their concept of the morality of the possession and enjoyment of wealth—what we may call the lifestyle of luxury. With such an enormous topic, we cannot be all-encompassing in the space of one volume, nor can we pretend to be proficient authorities on nine hundred years' worth of Greek authors and genres. We do not address all the bibliography on every passage and every author. Instead, we have attempted to lay down as our starting point the generally accepted view on a given matter, using the most recent studies on a subject and the established standard works. At times it may seem that we treat individual passages too superficially or focus too narrowly on the significance of the one word, τρυφή. Some sharp emphasis is necessary in order to avoid a mushroom-cloud of disorganized ramble. The fact is that what we have done for τρυφή, we hope that others will do for other aspects of the topic.

We respect and applaud the scholarship of preceding classicists who have laid the groundwork for any study such as this. If we have been able to make advances and offer improvements to their work, that is largely the result of changing technology. Today we have practical capabilities that were unknown even a few decades ago and that continue to improve at a remarkable rate. The philological method that we employ was impossible just a few years ago; it has only become feasible with the advent of electronic databases with increasingly fast search engines, notably the *Perseus Project* and the *Thesaurus Linguae Graecae*. Even now, it is no small task, once thousands of relevant passages have been isolated, to try to determine the specific meaning of a given word or to differentiate metaphorical from literal uses of a phrase and judge how usage changes over the centuries. Doing so for many different words and phrases has been arduous but, through this expansion of the digital tools available to study texts and through sheer legwork, we have often come to conclusions far different from those of our predecessors. We believe the method that we have adopted has made the data and reasoning upon which those conclusions rest transparent and readily open to critical evaluation. We would like our work to inspire specialists in particular authors and subfields to apply this methodology to create more accurate collections of fragmentary authors and thus a better understanding of the ancient world.

We should say a few words about our approach. First, we are very much philologists, shaped by the likes of A. John Graham and Martin Ostwald. We make no apologies for the accumulation of painstaking analyses of diction and argument that guide our research: we try first and foremost to report what the ancients actually said, and not what we wish to read into their words as subtext. With this in mind, we have avoided translating the word τρυφή, since there is no good English equivalent that contains the nuances of the Greek, and we prefer not to nudge the reader one way or another through even a provisional translation. We should also point out that we rarely use sources to lay down general proposals unless those sources have been directly transmitted, since we prefer, when establishing the most basic contours of a phenomenon, to avoid the tangled issues of authenticity that accompany fragments, excerpts, and epitomes by standing on our best possible testimony. Since our approach to the evidence does bring us into disagreement with many previous lines of thinking, we favor establishing our argument in a positive fashion, and therefore spend a minimum of time contending with standard views.[1] Those positions are usually very reasonably and intelligently argued, but their foundation is often laid on what we think we can prove is unreliable evidence. We hope that many of those

---

1. A major exception to this approach is the chapter on Herodotus, where we feel it is necessary to answer pervasive, persistent arguments about what he does and does not say about luxury.

same scholars will read our work and find it a valuable contribution to a fascinating subject and a healthy counterpoise to the scholarly orthodoxy.

We thank the many people who have contributed directly and indirectly to this venture. Since it is not feasible to mention by name all those to whom we feel gratitude, we would like to say simply that we appreciate the support of our colleagues in the Department of Classics and Religious Studies and the Department of History, as well as the members of the Pre-Modern reading group at the University of Nebraska–Lincoln; the receptive audiences at various annual meetings of both the American Philological Association and the Association of Ancient Historians; Monica Berti, who read several chapters; the people at the University of Michigan Press, particularly Ellen Bauerle, as accommodating and supportive an editor as one could desire; and the anonymous readers of our manuscript, whose comments were both thorough and valuable. Of course, we thank our students, our families, and friends for their forbearance in the course of this long project, during which we no doubt often seemed to be heedlessly dedicated to our own ἰδία τρυφή.

CHAPTER 1

Luxury and Corruption

The Problem of Sybaris

Anyone familiar with the literary sources for the history of archaic Sybaris must recognize that they are unusually rife with fiction.[1] The prosperity and luxurious lifestyle of the Sybarites was a favorite target for the imaginative detail. We hear, for example, of vineyards so rich that the wine was piped into the city for both local use and export. Roads out of the city were roofed over. Human dwarves were kept as pets. The notorious Smindyrides journeyed abroad with a thousand cooks and found sleeping on a bed of rose petals too harsh for his delicate constitution. In the face of such a malleable tradition, scholars have scrutinized the evidence with due caution, identifying many of the influences that led to the development of its more dubious aspects.[2] In separating wheat from chaff, scholars naturally differ, but a broad consensus has developed. And perhaps the most firmly accepted facts about the archaic city—other than its destruction by the Crotoniates c. 510 BCE—concern an extension of political power unique in the Greek world of the sixth century.

---

1. Portions of the material on Sybaris appeared earlier in Gorman and Gorman 2007.
2. Ampolo 1993, esp. 213–22. There are, however, surprising examples of credulity. Relying on one passage (Athen. 12.519d = Timaeus, *FGrH* 566 F 60), Zancani Montuoro (1982a) deduces that Sybaris produced wine sufficient in quantity and quality for export, and this in spite of her admission that among the tens of thousands of extant *bolli* identifying the point of origin for wines, none had been reliably referred to Sybaris. Because Phylarchus relates (Athenaeus 12.521e = Phylarchus, *FGrH* 81 F 45) that the Sybarite magistrates dreamed that Hera vomited bile into the "middle of the agora," Camassa (1993, 580) argues that Sybaris's Heraion was adjacent to the marketplace. And Bugno (1999) finds in the notorious mantel of Alcisthenes (Athen. 12.541a = Ps.-Arist., *Mir.* 838a) support for his thesis of a connection between Sybaris and Persia.

Our sources tell us that, relying on its great wealth, Sybaris became preeminent among the Western Greeks, and, more intriguingly, that it reached these heights as much by sharing power as by imposing it. Strabo and Diodorus Siculus supply the principal evidence. The geographer tells of what seems to be a rather complexly organized hegemony:

τοσοῦτον δ᾽ εὐτυχίᾳ διήνεγκεν ἡ πόλις αὕτη τὸ παλαιὸν ὥστε τεττάρων μὲν ἐθνῶν τῶν πλησίον ἐπῆρξε, πέντε δὲ καὶ εἴκοσι πόλεις ὑπηκόους ἔσχε, τριάκοντα δὲ μυριάσιν ἀνδρῶν ἐπὶ Κροτωνιάτας ἐστράτευσεν.

[In the old days, this city excelled in its prosperity so much that it controlled four tribes of its neighbors and had subjected twenty-five cities and put three hundred thousand men in the field against the Crotoniates.] (Strabo 6.1.13)

Diodorus, for his part, indicates that a good number of those under the Sybarite domination had the rights of citizens.

πολλοῖς δὲ μεταδιδόντες τῆς πολιτείας ἐπὶ τοσοῦτο προέβησαν, ὥστε δόξαι πολὺ προέχειν τῶν κατὰ τὴν Ἰταλίαν οἰκούντων, πολυανθρωπίᾳ τε τοσοῦτο διήνεγκαν, ὥστε τὴν πόλιν ἔχειν πολιτῶν τριάκοντα μυριάδας.

[Sharing citizenship with many, they reached such a point that they seemed to far outdo all the Greeks in Italy and they so excelled in size of population that they had a city of three hundred thousand citizens.] (Diod. Sic. 12.9.2)

As one might expect, scholars have tried to make the most of these tantalizing details. In the arrangement of its empire, Sybaris is seen as a strange anachronism, whose innovative spirit is more in tune with the Hellenistic than with Archaic and Classical *poleis*. Explanations for the "liberalità sibaritica" which gave citizenship to subjects have been sought in sources as diverse as the influence of Lydio-Persian Asia Minor and the πατρίος πολιτεία of the Achaean homeland.[3] Yet, in spite of such differences of interpretation, scholars are prac-

---

3.   Bugno (1999, 19–22) argues that Sybaris had to look to the East and particularly to Persia for a model of an empire that included *ethnē* and *poleis* of diverse status. Ampolo (1993, 242–44) draws a parallel between the liberality with which the Hellenistic Achaean League granted citizenship and the πολυανθρωπία of the Sybarites, concluding that the political organization of Sybaris's subject tribes and cities owed much to traditional Achaean institutions.

tically unanimous in accepting the testimony of Diodorus and Strabo as accurate in regard to the organization of the Sybarite hegemony and the city's extravagance in the matter πολιτεία.

This evidence on the empire of the Sybarites should be treated with greater skepticism. Although they lack the obvious flights of fancy that identify many of the stories about Sybaris as fictions, these two passages bear the marks of what we might for convenience call the τρυφή tradition, the strain of popular moralizing that emphasized the ruinous effect of luxury on individual and community. While those working closely with these texts have recognized that the information they contain was, in earlier stages of the transmission, associated with the τρυφή tradition—indeed, that association is thought to have been necessary to that transmission—nevertheless, they have underestimated the extent to which the workings of that tradition have compromised the integrity of what appear to be soberly related historical facts. Furthermore, proponents of this line of interpretation seriously overestimate the antiquity of the τρυφή tradition itself.

As is true for many Archaic cities, most of the evidence for early Sybaris reaches us only through authors of the Hellenistic or Roman period. Attempts to reconstruct details of its history in this period are careful to delineate a probable chain of transmission by which genuine data on Sybarite *Realien* could reach a late source. The description of the basic elements of this transmission has become practically standardized in the relevant scholarship: Croton's capture and demolition c. 510 BCE of Sybaris, a community renowned for its extraordinary wealth, shocked the Greek world. The destruction of such a city at the hands of fellow Greeks constituted a horrifying catastrophe that demanded explanation. The Crotoniates, under Pythagorean influence, developed stories which met that need, and which, needless to say, put the responsibility for the fall of Sybaris squarely on the Sybarites themselves.[4] These explanations might focus on different aspects of Sybarite behavior—for instance, the internal politics of tyranny or the external politics of commercial rivalry—but were variations on the same theme: Sybaris was "la città dell'eccesso." The great riches of Sybaris had brought it to τρυφή, a kind of morally debilitating luxury, which in turn led to an overweening hubris, offensive to divine as well as human sensibilities. The punishment by god and man was swift and just.

While the Crotoniates circulated these stories to deflect any blame from

---

4.   García 2002, 2010.

themselves, there were unexpected consequences. It is assumed that the Crotoniates were well informed about the details of Sybarite society and used this
information to make their version of events plausible. In this way the exaggerated depictions of τρυφή at Sybaris allowed these tales to serve as a kind of
vector for the historical facts associated with unrestrained luxury and license.
After the Persian Wars, it is thought, Greek tastes turned away from the Orien-
talizing delicacy and refinement of the Archaic period to a new Laconian austerity. The resonance between changing *mores* and the traditions hostile to
Sybaris allowed these stories to survive to reach the hands of the earliest historians of the Western Greeks (principally Antiochus of Syracuse) in the last
quarter of the fifth century.

Next, the moralizing tendencies of fourth-century historiography made
Sybaris a favorite *exemplum* for several authors. Of particular significance was
Timaeus of Tauromenium. His *Sicilian History* in thirty-eight books became
the standard authority on the Italian Greeks, and inclusion in this work ensured
that the Sybaris tradition might reach our era, since Timaeus was a chief source
for Diodorus Siculus and Athenaeus of Naucratis, to name only the two most
important surviving witnesses. Thus, it was the emphasis on Sybarite τρυφή—
especially as a cause of community-wide moral collapse and unforgivable acts
of hubris—that was largely responsible for the transmission of historical data
such as those in the passages quoted above.

Such is the *communis opinio*. However, a reexamination of the full range of
evidence on Archaic Sybaris shows that this reconstruction is to a great degree
untenable.

In the first place, it is taken to be an incontrovertible fact of our literary
evidence that by the last decades of the sixth century Sybaris was unusually
prosperous in both men and goods. Modern scholarship insists upon this point,
holding to the presumption that it was the sudden and paradoxical character of
the Italian city's collapse that secured a place for its story in the collective memory of the Greeks. Not just in the West, but in cities throughout the Greek world
the question was asked, "How could such a flourishing community disappear
so abruptly?" The answer given was the decadence of τρυφή, and the fall of
Sybaris became a favorite cautionary tale for centuries.

In view of the very basic importance that the great wealth of Sybaris has for
the reconstruction of the ancient historiography of that city, it may come as
something of a surprise that the evidence for that "fact" is not nearly as strong
as commonly assumed. For substantiation of the actual wealth and size of the

city, as distinct from the ancient traditions about it, we must turn to archaeology. In the 1960s, heroic efforts led to the discovery of the site of Sybaris and
excavations were soon set in motion.[5] However, the superposition of the later
foundations of Thurii and Copia, as well as difficulties presented by the water
table, make the investigation of Archaic Sybaris an extremely delicate and expensive task. As a result, we know far too little about the early city to offer any
firm conclusions. Nevertheless, we may note that the data so far published
would not cause us to be confident of the unusual claims of prosperity for Sybaris, if the literary tradition were silent on this point.

Perhaps the best archaeological indication for Sybarite affluence is the extent of the city. Sybaris was of an unusual shape: it was situated on a narrow
ribbon of dune running parallel to the Ionian Sea. Two sectors of the excavation, Parco del Cavallo and Stombi, both give evidence of habitation in the first
generation of the city, though the areas in question are 1800 meters apart. While
it cannot be proven that there was a continuous area of habitation between
Parco del Cavallo and Stombi, it is not unlikely.[6]

On the other hand, the archaeological finds, even taking into account their
exiguous state, show surprising gaps for a city of fabulous wealth. In his study
of Sybarite artistic production, Croissant feels the need to apologize for offering
conclusions that will disappoint expectations. To be sure, he says, we would
expect a center of economic power to be correspondingly advanced culturally.
But history shows us examples where this connection does not hold, and we
must count Sybaris as one of these: neither in ceramics not in plastics does
Croissant find evidence for significant creative activity.[7]

In a similar fashion, Guzzo's investigation of the effects of the fall of Sybaris
yields paradoxical results. While some scholars have found in this event the
source of an economic dislocation that could be linked with the fall of the Tar-
quinii at Rome, Guzzo notes that the disappearance of Sybaris caused little

---

5. For details of the search and discovery, see Rainey 1969. Excavation reports: Guzzo 1976, 1981a,
    1981b, 1982, 1992a, 1992b, 1993, 1997; Stazio and Ceccoli 1993; Greco 2004, 2005, 2006; Spagnoli
    2006. For a history of attempts to discover the site, see Kleibrink 2001.
6. Guzzo 1982, 243. The chief argument in favor of a densely developed site is the occupation, begin-
    ning c. 650 BCE, of the area in the eastern part of the city known as the Prolungamento Strada. Here
    the ground consisted of new *terra firma* from fluvial deposits. It is assumed that such land would not
    have been used until older areas were already filled up.
7. Croissant 1993. He must address these concerns because, relying on the literary traditions, he be-
    lieves that the economic wealth of Sybaris is incontestable. Thus he is ready to interpret the presence
    of imports, such as fragments of large, high quality, black figure vases as confirming the prosperity of
    Sybaris (542).

measurable change, even in nearby cities.[8] Such lack of influence is quite unexpected for one of the richest cities of its time. Indeed, Guzzo argues that the contrast between his conclusions and the traditional view indicates the need to give up abstract speculations about the economy of the area and to rely instead on systematic research on the ground in the isthmus of Sybaris.[9] In a later study, Guzzo himself details the pertinent archaeological evidence for the eighth and seventh centuries: Sybaris had an "economia composita" consisting of the agricultural cultivation of the nearby countryside, the "drenaggio capillare" of the resources of the larger hinterland toward the city, and its position as a port of call along trans-Mediterranean sea routes. Such a combination did not allow "immediate e notevoli accumulazioni."[10] The wealth of Sybaris must have been a phenomenon limited to the sixth century, and as such, outside the bounds of Guzzo's examination.[11] In view of this rather meager and ambiguous data, it seems best to answer inquiries about the actual strength of the Sybarite economy with a cautious *non liquet*.[12]

The literary evidence on Sybaris is much more ample, but here again its effect is not what we are led to expect by the widespread insistence on the wealth of the city as the most basic and well established truth in its history. In fact, a careful survey of all of this evidence leads to the rather startling conclusion that the first explicit and reliably datable statements about the unusual wealth of Sybaris come as late as the first century BCE. Diodorus Siculus, for example, reports:

---

8. "Il commercio greco con l'Etruria continua su livelli quasi costati dopo il 510. . . . la scomparsa di Sibari ha provocato scarsi effetti solo nelle città a lei più vicine" (Guzzo 1976, 55). On the other hand, small communities within and near the boundaries of the Sybarite territory itself (i.e., Amendolara, Francavilla, Torre Mordillo, and Scalea-Petrosa) were abandoned upon the destruction of the city (Guzzo 1982, 244).

9. Guzzo 1976, 56.

10. Guzzo 1982, 249–50.

11. As hard evidence of the wealth of the city, Guzzo (1982, 250) cites Sybaris's first Olympic victor in 616 and a pectoral in gold and silver found in the excavations and dated to the end of the seventh century.

12. Kleibrink (2001) argues for an Achaean dominance in the area starting only in the second half of the seventh century, and describes some of the claims made by archaeologists that are clearly supported more by literary than physical sources. E.g., (42): "Guzzo's publications on the *Sibiritide* are very stimulating for the study of this area, but at times they seem to be too partial to the Achaians. It seems the colonial theories of the 19th and 20th centuries strongly influenced his work." She summarizes (40): "However, archaeological evidence for the domination of the Achaians in the *Siritide/Metapontino* is usually dated no earlier than the second half of the 7th c. BC. . . . [T]he first half of the 7th c. BC, except for Francavilla Marittima, is archaeologically largely unattested anywhere in the *Sibaritide*, the site of Sibari itself included." In response, Guzzo 2003.

συνέβη ταύτην λαβεῖν ταχεῖαν αὔξησιν διὰ τὴν ἀρετὴν τῆς χώρας. . . . οἱ κατοικισθέντες νεμόμενοι πολλὴν καὶ καρποφόρον χώραν μεγάλους ἐκτήσαντο πλούτους. πολλοῖς δὲ μεταδιδόντες τῆς πολιτείας . . .

[It achieved rapid growth because of the excellence of the land. . . . The inhabitants, sharing a large and fertile country, gained possession of great riches. Sharing citizenship with many. . . .] (Diod. Sic. 12.9.1–2)

To be sure, earlier texts do mention wealthy individuals or small groups of Sybarites, and it is possible to presume that such instances imply a more general prosperity,[13] but it is nonetheless necessary to recognize that the idea of Sybaris as a city of wealth and luxury is at most an implication, not a datum, of the evidence dating earlier than the first century CE.

The supposition that the destruction of Sybaris caused an "eco vastissima"[14] of shock and consternation throughout the Greek world likewise rests on an uncertain basis. The chief evidence for this view is the testimony of Herodotus that the Milesians adopted public marks of grief when they learned of the capture of Sybaris, a gesture the Sybarites did not reciprocate when the Persians razed Miletus a few years later (Hdt. 6.21). Even if we accept the historicity of the unusually close relationship between Miletus and Sybaris,[15] there is reason to be suspicious about this particular episode. The point of the story is clear: to make the behavior of the Sybarites look bad when compared to actions of the

---

13. The most notable individuals are Alcisthenes, who dedicated a fabulous garment later worth one hundred and fifty talents, and the famous Smindyrides. Timaeus relates a joke to the effect that there were certain Sybarites who so despised work that they found it painful to see it done or even hear about it; this anecdote has been taken to indicate the existence of "a capitalist system" and a group of idle rich who lived from the exploitation of the "lower classes" (Sartori 1960, 153–54). Other examples that seem to indicate widespread wealth at Sybaris are commonly referred to the authority of Timaeus, but this evidence comes mainly from Athenaeus and is extremely problematic. See the discussions, below, of Alcisthenes (pp. 201–2), Smindyrides (pp. 191–92), and Timaeus's fragments on Sybaris (pp. 318–23).

14. Ampolo 1993, 218. Rutter (1973, 169), who usually displays a prudent caution in interpreting the literary sources on Sybaris, claims that in spite of exaggeration in the sources about certain aspects of Archaic Sybaris, "there is no doubt . . . that the repercussions of its fall were considerable, not only in Italy, but in distant parts of the Greek world." Zancani Montuoro (1980, 149) writes of a sensational event in the ancient world which provoked astonishment as word of the disaster spread.

15. Ceramic imports from the Greek east begin to appear at Sybaris c. 625 BCE; these products include Wild Goat Style oinochoes, Chian calices, and cups of a Samian type. An Ionian trade connection of some sort is therefore not in doubt. On the other hand, no close link with Miletus in particular has been established from the material evidence; for example, Ionian influence appears in Sybarite plastic arts beginning c. 575, but Samos is a more important source than Miletus (Croissant 1993, 551–52).

Milesians and then of the Athenians, who took the fall of Miletus as a domestic evil. We can therefore be confident that this tradition reached Herodotus from sources hostile to Sybaris, most probably from the Crotoniates themselves. That Herodotus had access to such sources is clear from 5.44–45, where he contrasts Sybarite and Crotoniate versions of the contribution of the Spartan Dorieus to the fall of the city.[16] A story transmitted by the Crotoniates that puts their enemies in a bad light might well be a Crotoniate invention. The claim was made that the sack of Sybaris was an event so sensational as to demand justification, which the Crotoniates promptly provided in a mixture of fact and fiction. But it would indeed be imprudent to overlook the possibility that this claim is based on evidence that could itself be an instance of Crotoniate propaganda.[17] Emphasizing the Milesian reaction to the fall of Sybaris would highlight Sybarite indifference when the tables were turned. Furthermore, if this passage is to be taken at face value, it remains insufficient to establish a general or even common reaction of shock among the Greeks. Herodotus indicates that the grief of the Milesians was a special case with a specific cause: the unusual closeness between the Ionian and the Italian city (Hdt. 6.21).

The common view that the great wealth of Sybaris evoked a correspondingly great outpouring of distress when the city fell is not, it appears, firmly anchored in the ancient evidence. What then may we say about the explanations intended to answer that distress? An examination of the ancient traditions on Sybaris which focuses on the role of τρυφή and hubris in its ruin gives results which likewise undermine the prevailing interpretation. In the following discussion we will present the evidence in approximate chronological order, with one major exception: prose fragments transmitted by Athenaeus—by far

---

16. Herodotus 5.44.1 first gives the Sybarite version (ὡς λέγουσι Συβαρῖται), according to which the Crotoniates grew exceedingly fearful at the impending attack by Sybaris and begged for the help of Dorieus and his Spartans. He follows this with the Crotoniate view (Κροτωνιῆται δὲ . . . φασί, 5.44.2) that the only foreigner to aid them was the Elian seer Kallias. The fact that the Sybarite leader Telys is called βασιλέα in the first version and τυράννου in the second further supports the idea that Herodotus had access to two separate sources for these events, one Sybarite, the other, Crotoniate.

17. Notwithstanding the obvious problem with this passage, the special friendship between Sybaris and Miletus is another of the elementary "facts" about Sybaris that are almost universally accepted. It has been made to bear the weight of complex and wide-ranging theories. Lepore (1980, 1334–36) argues that the concept of *Magna Graecia* was anticipated in the idea of "Italy" developed by Hecataeus of Miletus. Hecataeus, relying on the reports of Milesian sailors returned from Sybaris, saw that part of the world from the perspective of the Sybarites. Italy represented for him "un nuovo mondo unitario" which was coextensive with the territory dominated by the Sybarites. Nenci (1983, 1020–23) makes a case that the concept of τρυφή itself developed under the influence of Hecataeus and the periegetic tradition, and that the word τρυφή was coined at Miletus among the lower classes in the seventh to sixth centuries BCE. A chief premise in Nenci's argument consists in the "very close connections with Sybaris," a city whose name was a veritable synonym for τρυφή.

the most important source for ancient views of τρυφή—will be handled in great detail in Chapter 4, since this author offers particular problems that must be dealt with most judiciously.

The earliest name associated with relevant material is that of Epicharmus, the Sicilian comic poet active in the first quarter of the fifth century. The *Suda* (Σ 1271) attributes Συβάρεια ἐπιφθέγματα to him. The content of these sayings is unknown, but the conjecture that they are passages taken from his plays is not unlikely.[18] Ampolo assumes a connection between the ἐπιφθέγματα and the γέλοιον Συβαριτικόν of Aristophanes *Wasps* 1259.[19] This comedy presents two such γέλοια. At 1427–31, Philocleon relates that a Sybarite man fell from his chariot and hurt his head, whereupon a friend told him to stick to the business he knew. A few lines later (1435–40), the subject is a woman of Sybaris who, upon breaking a jar, passed a suitable witticism. There is here no unambiguous relevance to τρυφή, hubris, or a justification for the sack of Sybaris.

Other early evidence, however, may possibly hint at Sybarite decadence. Many scholars see Hippys of Regium at the root of our historical traditions about Sybaris. The Suda (I 591) makes Hippys a contemporary of the Persians Wars, but among modern historians there is little that is not in dispute about this shadowy figure. Pearson believes that, because Hippys is not cited by Diodorus Siculus, Dionysius of Halicarnassus, Strabo, or Pausanias, "there are good reasons for doubting his real existence and adding his name to the list of imaginary writers whose works were invented in Hellenistic times."[20] Other experts hold fast to idea that Hippys was the first important historian of the West.[21] Be that as it may, Zenobius (3.42) cites Hippys in connection with the foundation of Croton. A certain Myscellus, sent by the Pythia as the *oikist* for that city, earned Apollo's rebuke because he preferred the site of Sybaris.

This same story appears in fuller form in Strabo, where it is attributed to the historian Antiochus of Syracuse, a younger contemporary of Herodotus.

---

18. Testimony on Epicharmus is notoriously difficult to evaluate, given the number of forgeries extant under his name already in the fifth century; cf. Cassio 1985. Bernhardt (2003, 51–67) argues that Epicharmus contributed to early versions of the legend of Sybaris, a view opposed by Dalby (2007, 165). See also Gorman and Gorman 2007.
19. From the suggestion of the scholia to this passage, Ampolo (1993, 214) concludes that a Sybaritic γέλοιον differs from an Aesopic one through the use of human rather than animal protagonists, while Ampolo argues that historical personages may have appeared in these stories.
20. Pearson 1987, 8; he also discusses several other reasons for caution, such as Hippys's dating by Olympiads, generally thought to have originated in Timaeus's day.
21. Pearson follows Wilamowitz and Jacoby in his skepticism. Believers include De Sanctis and Momigliano. For references see Pearson 1987, 8 n. 23; Spoerri 1979.

φησὶ δ᾽ Ἀντίοχος, τοῦ θεοῦ χρήσαντος Ἀχαιοῖς Κρότωνα κτίζειν, ἀπελθεῖν
Μύσκελλον κατασκεψόμενον τὸν τόπον, ἰδόντα δ᾽ ἐκτισμένην ἤδη Σύβαριν . . .
κρῖναι ταύτην ἀμείνω· ἐπανερέσθαι δ᾽ οὖν ἀπιόντα τὸν θεὸν εἰ λῶον εἴη ταύτην
ἀντ᾽ ἐκείνης κτίζειν.

[Antiochus says that when the god had ordered the Achaeans to found Croton,
Myscellus went to scout out the place, but when he saw Sybaris already founded,
. . . he judged this city to be better. So he went back and asked the god whether
it would be preferable to colonize this city instead of that one.] (Strabo 6.1.12)

In this passage the idea that Sybaris is better than Croton may be a hint that
Antiochus—and Hippys, who is assumed to be his source—was aware of the
tradition that identified τρυφή and hubris as the cause of Sybaris's downfall.

As we have seen in Diodorus Siculus 12.9.1, the great riches of the Sybarites
were acquired "because of the excellence of the land."[22] This phrase is significant, because we elsewhere find this or related wording in an explicit context of
τρυφή. Athenaeus 12.528b (= Polyb. 7.1.1–3) relates that διὰ τὴν ἀρετὴν τῆς γῆς
the people of Campania fell into τρυφή during the war with Hannibal. Diodorus himself, in a discussion of Etruria, makes the same point: συνεβάλετο δ᾽
αὐτοῖς πρὸς τὴν τρυφὴν οὐκ ἐλάχιστον καὶ ἡ τῆς χώρας ἀρετή ("The excellence
of the countryside made not the smallest contribution toward their *truphē*,"
Diod. Sic. 5.40.5).

Given the later existence of a clear connection in thought between a fertile
χώρα and luxury,[23] it may just be possible to see in Antiochus's κρῖναι ταύτην
ἀμείνω a pale but discernible reflection of this idea. It would however be imprudent to insist upon this point. The Myscellus tradition may be the product of
circumstances of the fifth century unconnected with the need to explain the
destruction of Sybaris. In the sixty-five years that followed this event, several
attempts were made to reestablish an independent settlement in the Sybaritide,
including the famous pan-Hellenic foundation of Thurii in 446/5 BCE. The desire to emphasize its ancient autonomy from Croton would certainly have been

---

22. Diodorus, too, knows the story of Myscellus: ὁ Μύσκελλος τὴν περὶ τὴν Σύβαριν χώραν θαυμάσας
    ἐβούλετο κτίσαι ("Myscellus marveled at the countryside around Sybaris and wanted to colonize it."
    Diod. Sic. 8.17.2). Here it is noteworthy that the χώρα is explicitly identified as the feature of the
    Sybaritide that catches Myscellus's eye.
23. The text of Diodorus alone offers further parallels at 3.42.2 (Phoenicia), 5.10.2 (the Liparic islands)
    and 34/35.2.26 (Sicily at the time of the slave revolt). See the section on Diodorus in Chapter 5.

sufficient to give rise to this oracle story.[24] In the terms of this narrative, just as Myscellus must express his preference for the Sybaritide in order to provoke the Pythia's sharp distinction between the land of Sybaris and Croton, so must Myscellus's preference be given motivation. Thus some such detail as the excellence of the χώρα is inherently necessary and may be generated by narrative processes alone.[25] Even setting aside narrative considerations, no allusion to τρυφή and hubris is necessary, since the possibility that Sybaris was later seen as wealthy does not require that it was also seen as decadent.

It is important to have a clear understanding of Antiochus's evidence on Sybaris, because this writer is thought to have played a crucial role in the transmission of the traditions of Sybarite decadence. In this view Antiochus served as the principal intermediary between the obscure Hippys (or some other, unknown source) and Timaeus and other widely read historians of the West. Antiochus's history of Sicily and Italy was a work of some influence; it was known to Diodorus, and fragments are preserved by Strabo and Dionysius. It is therefore plausible that Antiochus could have been responsible for passing on the Sybarite τρυφή stories. However, the Myscellus passage is the only fragment of Antiochus in which an allusion to Sybarite τρυφή may be argued,[26] and the connection is so tenuous that Antiochus's role in this matter must remain speculation.

For the remaining fifth-century evidence on Sybaris, the connection to luxury is somewhat stronger, though still not explicit or of general scope. Most important is Herodotus 6.127, where he relates the story of the competition for the hand of Agariste, the daughter of Cleisthenes, tyrant of Sicyon. Wishing to marry Agariste to the best man in Greece, Cleisthenes invited all who desired to prove themselves to come as suitors. Among those who accepted the chal-

---

24. Bugno (1999, 27–28 n.19) thinks that the traditions of Hippys and Antiochus arose after 510 in the context of the dispute between the Crotoniates and the former Sybarites over control of the area in question.

25. Bugno (1999, 9) believes that the passage as cited by Strabo is resumptive, and that Antiochus's version was rich in details. He insists (10) that the idea of the fertility of the χώρα must be rooted in a Sybarite tradition dating back to the sixth century. This is a difficult proposition to defend, even if Bugno would not accept our argument that Sybaris's marvelous χώρα may be an integral feature of the story of the oracle and so created out of the same act of fiction as the Pythia's words. It is established that, by the time of Diodorus, unusually fertile land was seen as a contributing cause of τρυφή and that, by the same period, Sybaris was closely associated with τρυφή. Given that our sources for the Myscellus story are all from the first century BCE or later, there is the possibility that the depiction of Sybaris in the oracle story was affected by views on τρυφή current at the time of the transmitting authors.

26. Strabo (6.1.15) cites the authority of Antiochus for the tradition that the Sybarites persuaded certain Achaeans to settle at Metapontium after the original colony had been destroyed by Samnites.

lenge was a certain Sybarite named Smindyrides, ὃς ἐπὶ πλεῖστον δὴ χλιδῆς εἷς ἀνὴρ ἀπίκετο ("who was a man who had come into the greatest amount of *chlidē*"). This passage is influential, since Smindyrides eventually became an avatar of hedonism and τρυφή. Aristotle and Theophrastus connect him with the life of pleasure, and elaborated, surely embroidered, accounts of his τρυφή are given much later by Athenaeus and Aelian. The word χλιδή is only used this one time in the *Histories*, so its meaning is not entirely clear from this context; yet, whatever its precise meaning (and we will discuss this more below), it is unlikely that χλιδή has the derogatory sense appropriate to link it with a justification for the destruction of Sybaris. Herodotus himself associates Smindyrides not with that city's end, but with its zenith.[27] This passage, then, is evidence of a tradition putting χλιδή—not τρυφή—into the hands of one man at Sybaris; it is not necessarily an indication of unusual wealth in the city at large. Nor does Smindyrides' penchant for χλιδή clearly imply even his own individual decadence, since Herodotus reports that he was among those who competed in wrestling and running to be chosen as the "best man in Greece."

While Herodotus is interested in the individual characteristics of the suitors and does not necessarily present Smindyrides as a representative Sybarite, two passages from Aristophanes are taken to indicate a more general association between Sybaris and τρυφή. In the *Peace*, the protagonist Trygaeus explains to the chorus the pleasures that will be possible once they lay hands on the goddess Eirene.

> εἰς πανηγύρεις θεωρεῖν,
> ἑστιᾶσθαι, κότταβίζειν,
> συβαριάζειν,[28]
> ἰοῦ ἰοῦ κεκραγέναι
>
> [... to go to festivals,
> to feast, to play cottabus,
> to act the Sybarite,
> to shout "Io, Io."]
> (Ar., *Pax* 342–45)

---

27. ἡ δὲ Σύβαρις ἤκμαζε τοῦτον τὸν χρόνον μάλιστα ("At this time Sybaris was especially flourishing," Hdt. 6.127.1).
28. The MSS have the unmetrical συβαρίζειν, corrected by Meinike.

Apparently the Athenian audience thought of Sybaris as a place of feasting and fun, if the poet could use the bare verb συβαριάζειν in such a context and expect to be understood.[29] The exact meaning of the term is unclear.[30] Fragment 225.3 KA, from Aristophanes' *Banqueters* is no more informative, speaking of Συβαριτίδας τ' εὐωχίας ("Sybarite feasts"). Immoderate indulgence in feasting and entertainment comes to be seen as one aspect of τρυφή, and these two passages may indeed be the first plausible indications of the tradition that made Sybaris a center of that vice. Yet we must note that the idea of mortal decadence is still missing from the picture. Whatever precisely it may mean, συβαριάζειν belongs to a list of advantages of peace that are clearly benign. The "Sybarite feasts" of Aristophanes, frag. 225 KA, on the other hand, do seem to have been spoken of with disapproval,[31] but again the misbehavior is hardly of a caliber to justify divine retribution.

We may sum up the fifth-century evidence in this way: the Sybaritide was better than the land around Croton; one of the city's leading men was unique for the ostentatiousness of his display of wealth; a certain festive behavior could be called συβαριάζειν; and feasts could be described as "Sybarite." Thus it may be possible to recognize faint traces of a tradition which associated Sybaris with wealth and pleasure, although this interpretation is not self-evident. On the other hand, we find no indication—nor even a firm hint—that any degree of prosperity which Sybaris may have enjoyed contributed to its demoralization and destruction.[32]

---

29. Ampolo (1993, 215) believes that the context makes clear that the meaning of συβαριάζειν was already current.

30. The scholia's surmise that Aristophanes has in mind the "extravagant table" (τραπέζῃ πολυτελεῖ) of the Sybarites is of little value, given Sybaris's subsequent reputation. It would, however, be careless to dismiss out of hand the other suggestion of the scholiast, namely that συβαριάζειν refers rather to τὰ συβάρεια ἐπιφθέγματα. We have seen above how at *Vesp.* 1259 the "Sybarite joke" is included among the repertoire of the sophisticated symposiast. If this suggestion is correct, συβαριάζειν would be close in meaning to the immediately preceding κοτταβίζειν, and συβαριάζειν would not be translated "act the Sybarite," but "tell tales about Sybarites."

31. οὐ γὰρ ἔμαθε ταῦτ' ἐμοῦ πέμποντος, ἀλλὰ μᾶλλον πίνειν, ἔπειτ' ᾄδειν κακῶς, Συρακοσίαν τράπεζαν, Συβαρίτιδάς τ' εὐωχίας... ("He didn't learn what I sent him to learn, but rather to drink and to sing dirty songs, . . . a Syracusan table and Sybarite feasts.")

32. The remaining evidence from this period is consistent with that offered by Aristophanes. A pertinent line of the comic poet Phrynichus (frag. 64 KA, from the last quarter of the fifth century) has survived: πολὺς δὲ συβαριασμὸς αὐλητῶν τότ' ἦν ("then there was much Sybarism from the flute-players"). A sympotic context seems likely, since the scholiast cites Phrynichus to elucidate *Pax* 344. The relevance of a fragment of the comedy *Thuriopersai* of Metagenes (from the last decade of the fifth century) has recently been recognized by Lombardo (1983, 325–28). In this passage, the poet praises the rivers of the Sybaritide, which flow with κῦμα ναστῶν καὶ κρεῶν / ἑφθῶν τε βατίδων εἰλυομένων αὐτόσε ("a wave of cakes and meat and boiled fish already wrapped, ready to eat," Metagenes 6.3–4KA). Clearly the stereotype of the Συβαρῖτις εὐωχία had been transferred to the more recent colony of Thurii. Once again, there is no sign of a theme of retribution.

Several fourth-century authors provide information that must be included in any evaluation of traditions of Sybarite τρυφή, and we have noted above that the interest of moralizing fourth-century historians in τρυφή is assumed by scholars as a principal cause for the survival of the stories about Sybaris.[33] Of the pertinent material, *only* the evidence of Aristotle is independent of Athenaeus. *Eudemian Ethics* 1.1216a17 reintroduces Smindyrides, who by this time seems to have become, alongside of Sardanapalus of Assyria, a symbol of the hedonistic lifestyle. This passage tells us no more than does Hdt. 6.127 about the reputation of Sybaris in general. However, the present context makes it very unlikely that Aristotle saw Smindyrides as an example of a morally vicious luxury. In this part of the *Eudemian Ethics*, Aristotle set the stage for his investigation by identifying the three modes of life that could be supported by reason. Φρόνησις, ἀρετή, and ἡδονή provide the respective justifications for these βίοι, since they "were the three greatest goods for human beings" (τριῶν ὄντων . . . ἀγαθῶν ὡς μεγίστων τοῖς ἀνθρώποις, Arist., *Eth. Eud.* 1215a33–34). Lest anyone suspect that Aristotle might be guilty of the muddled thinking that he here ascribes to the many, he emphasizes that the ἡδονή he has in mind as a human good is not a low and slavish kind. Thus the life of pleasure (βίος ἀπολαυστικός) which Smindyrides represents here for Aristotle is explicitly removed from the range of evils in which we might expect to find τρυφή.[34] Accordingly, one should not insist that the role of Smindyrides as representative of hedonism at *Eth. Eud.* 1216a17 indicates a familiarity with Sybarite τρυφή traditions in the mid-fourth century.[35]

---

33. Ampolo (1993, 231–22) gives the clearest example of this view. He is detailed in his discussion of how "facts" about Sybarite lifestyle became historiographically significant in the fifth century, in order to explain the sudden and unexpected destruction of the wealthy and powerful city. Subsequently, the perpetuation of the tradition of Sybarite decadence was driven by other "narrative demands" (215), as, for example, Timaeus's interest in what Ampolo jokingly calls the "International of soft peoples." The great and self-evident interest of the Hellenistic writers in the moral dimensions of luxury has been a *topos* of the scholarship at least since Passerini 1934.

34. In the corresponding section of the *Nicomachaean Ethics*, Aristotle takes a much harsher view of pleasure: τὸ γὰρ ἀγαθὸν καὶ τὴν εὐδαιμονίαν οὐκ ἀλόγως ἐοίκασιν ἐκ τῶν βίων ὑπολαμβάνειν οἱ μὲν πολλοὶ καὶ φορτικώτατοι τὴν ἡδονήν· . . . οἱ μὲν οὖν πολλοὶ παντελῶς ἀνδραποδώδεις φαίνονται βοσκημάτων βίον προαιρούμενοι, τυγχάνουσι δὲ λόγου διὰ τὸ πολλοὺς τῶν ἐν ταῖς ἐξουσίαις ὁμοπαθεῖν Σαρδαναπάλλῳ ("The many and the more common folk seem not without reason to fix upon, of the different lives, pleasure as the Good and Happiness. . . . Well, the many seem utterly slavish, preferring the life of cattle, but they have reason because of the fact that many of those in power feel the same as Sardanapalus." Arist., *Eth. Nic.* 1095b14–22). Because of the reference is to τῶν ἐν ταῖς ἐξουσίαις, mention of Smindyrides would be inappropriate.

35. One may perhaps advance a stronger claim: Herodotus has made Smindyrides the most prominent exponent of what would later become widely accepted as the typical Sybarite lifestyle (ἐπὶ πλεῖστον δὴ χλιδῆς . . . ἀπίκετο). If the view of Sybaris as the home of τρυφή was prevalent in Aristotle's day, it is quite difficult to see how the character Smindyrides would not have been already deeply implicated in the exaggerated τρυφή stories (as was clearly the case by the first century, as we will see below).

The *Politics* is of particular interest to us, for, while analyzing the causes of civil discord, Aristotle alludes to the fall of Sybaris:

διὸ ὅσοι ἤδη συνοίκους ἐδέξαντο ἢ ἐποίκους, οἱ πλεῖστοι διεστασίασαν· οἷον Τροιζηνίοις Ἀχαιοὶ συνῴκησαν Σύβαριν, εἶτα πλείους οἱ Ἀχαιοὶ γενόμενοι ἐξέβαλον τοὺς Τροιζηνίους, ὅθεν τὸ ἄγος συνέβη τοῖς Συβαρίταις.

[For that reason most of the communities that have accepted joint colonists or additional colonists have fallen apart in civil war. For example, the Achaeans colonized Sybaris jointly with the Troezenians and then, when the Achaeans grew more numerous, they expelled the Troezenians. From this the curse befell the Sybarites.] (Arist., *Pol.* 5.1303a27–33)

It is natural to take τὸ ἄγος as a reference to the destruction of the city c. 510.[36] Apparently it is Aristotle's understanding that, in the course of their conflict with the Troezenians, the Achaean Sybarites committed some heinous act that subjected them to divine anger and subsequent punishment. At first glance, this view would seem in harmony with the modern *communis opinio*, according to which τρυφή engenders self-destructive hubris. Further consideration reveals a chronological difficulty. Aristotle seems to set the Sybarite *stasis* in a time frame following closely upon the foundation of the colony.[37] By contrast, the hubristic acts related in the τρυφή tradition seem for the most part to occur, where chronology is specified, in the last years before the city's fall.[38] Perhaps, then, *Pol.* 1303a27–33 reflects a tradition in which the fall of Sybaris was due to certain acts that were not based on τρυφή. In any case, one must admit that, even taken

---

Eth. Eud. 1.1216a17 might indicate, then, that Aristotle did not know such stories. However, it is best not to insist on this point, because we have seen that at *Eth. Nic.* 1095b22, Sardanapalus stands for a life of pleasure fit for beasts. Perhaps, then, the expurgated ἡδονή of *Eudemian Ethics* is a case of special pleading in which Aristotle counteracts the generally held perception of Sardanapalus and Smindyrides. The matter is unclear.

36. So Ampolo 1993, 218 n.12.
37. Such is the implication of the words that immediately precede Aristotle's reference to the Achaeans and Troezenians at Sybaris: στασιωτικὸν δὲ καὶ τὸ μὴ ὁμόφυλον, ἕως ἂν συμπνεύσῃ· ὥσπερ γὰρ οὐδ' ἐκ τοῦ τυχόντος πλήθους πόλις γίγνεται, οὕτως οὐδ' ἐν τῷ τυχόντι χρόνῳ ("A community not from the same stock is prone to discord, until they become of one mind. For as a city is not made of any chance number, nor is it made in some chance period of time." Arist., *Pol.* 5.1303a26–28). Aristotle will not fix the number of years that would turn a polymorphous group of colonists into a polis, but it is nonetheless clear that *some* length of time would bring about this change. It is unlikely that he is thinking in terms of centuries.
38. So Phylarchus (*FGrH* 81 F 45) and Heraclides Ponticus (frag. 49 Wehrli) are both said by Athenaeus (12.521e) to have reported the murder of Crotoniate ambassadors during the rule of Telys, who led the war against Croton according to Herodotus 5.44–45.

together, this passage and the reference to the βίος ἀπολαυστικός of Smindy-rides do not suffice to show that Aristotle knew of the τρυφή and hubris stories about Sybaris.[39]

No pertinent evidence survives via direct manuscript tradition from the period between Aristotle and the first century BCE. It would therefore seem appropriate at this point in our chronological account to discuss the many fragments of Hellenistic writers that apparently constitute clear evidence of the view that the fall of Sybaris was due to the immorality of its inhabitants. However, the transmission of these fragments, and most particularly, the part played in this process by the *Deipnosophistae* of Athenaeus of Naucratis, requires detailed study. We undertake this investigation in Chapters 3 and 4, where we develop arguments which cast doubt on all the Hellenistic fragments pertaining to Sybarite decadence. Meanwhile, we will limit our preliminary evaluation of the evidence to directly transmitted material.

Thus the next text chronologically is from the periegetical work in iambic verse that was once mistakenly ascribed to Scymnus of Chios, and is generally dated to c. 100–90 BCE. Verses 340–60 treat Sybaris:

> ... Σύβαρις, Ἀχαιῶν ἐπιφανὴς ἀποικία,
> δέκα μυριάδας ἔχουσα τῶν ἀστῶν σχεδόν
> περιουσίᾳ πλείστῃ τε κεχορηγημένη·
> οἳ δὴ παρεξαρθέντες οὐκ ἀνθρωπίνως
> αὔτανδρον ἐξέφθειραν ἐπιφανῆ πόλιν,
> τἀγαθὰ τὰ λίαν μὴ μαθόντες εὖ φέρειν.
> Λέγεται γὰρ αὐτοὺς μήτε τοῖς νόμοις ἔτι
> τοῖς τοῦ Ζαλεύκου τἀκόλουθα συντελεῖν,
> τρυφὴν δὲ καὶ ῥάθυμον ἑλομένους βίον
> χρόνῳ προελθεῖν εἰς ὕβριν τε καὶ κόρον,
>
> . . . .
> Κροτωνιᾶται πλησίον δὲ κείμενοι
> κατὰ κράτος αὐτοὺς ᾖραν ἐν βραχεῖ χρόνῳ
> τὰ πάντα διαμείναντας ἀπταίστως ἔτη
> ὡς ἑκατὸν ἐνενήκοντα πρὸς τοῖς εἴκοσι.

---

39. We here omit detailed discussion of the Pseudo-Aristotelian *Mir.* 96.838a15–26, where we are told of the fabulous cloak of Alcisthenes. See our discussion in Chapter 3, below (pp. 201–2).

[Sybaris, the famous colony of the Achaeans, possessing nearly one hundred thousand townspeople and furnished with a great deal of wealth. Exalting themselves as human beings should not, they destroyed their famous city and all its people, for they had not learned to handle good fortune well. The story is that they no longer acted in harmony with the laws of Zaleucus, but choosing *truphē* and the easy life, in time advanced to hubris and excess.... The Crotoniates, their neighbors, did away with them by force in a short time. Altogether they had lasted without a stumble two hundred and ten years.] (Ps.-Scymn. 340–49, 357–60)

For the first time in extant literature, this passage clearly and explicitly offers a moral cause for the fall of Sybaris: τρυφή and hubris. It is indisputable evidence for the τρυφή tradition that is thought to have carried with it the "facts" about the Sybarite Empire related in Diodorus and Strabo. However, Ps.-Scymnus 340–60 does not so much corroborate as complement the testimony of Diodorus and Strabo, since it is generally accepted that all three passages derive from the same source.[40] Thus the Ps.-Scymnus passage adds nothing to help settle the question of the genuineness of the historical information associated with this complex of texts. But it does set a *terminus ante quem* for the development of this particular pattern of destruction and it reveals a more elaborate schema of Sybarite moral degeneration than can be found in the other two authors: τρυφή leads to κόρος and ὕβρις, which may bring destruction.

By the beginning of the Common Era, this progression seems to have become something of a commonplace. For Philo Judaeus, the Sybarites represent

---

40. The common provenance of these passages is widely recognized. Beyond coincidence seems, for example, the correlative structure τοσοῦτο ... ὥστε introducing the τριάκοντα μυριάδες in both Strabo and Diodorus. Furthermore, Diodorus also mentioned the three hundred thousand Sybarites in the fragmentary Book 10: ὅτι οἱ Συβαρῖται μετὰ τριάκοντα μυριάδων ἐκ στρατεύσαντες ἐπὶ τοὺς Κροτωνιάτας καὶ πόλεμον ἄδικον ἐπανελόμενοι τοῖς ὅλοις ἔπταισαν, καὶ τὴν εὐδαιμονίαν οὐκ ἐνεγκόντες ἐπιδεξίως ἱκανὸν παράδειγμα τὴν ἰδίαν ἀπώλειαν κατέλιπον τοῦ πολὺ μᾶλλον δεῖν προσέχειν ἐν ταῖς ἰδίαις εὐτυχίαις ἤπερ ἐν ταῖς ταλαιπωρίαις ("The Sybarites taking the field with three hundred thousand men against Croton and undertaking an unjust war, took a fall with everything. Unable to bear their good fortune properly, they left behind their own destruction as a suitable lesson that it is much more necessary to be on one's guard in prosperity than in hard times." Diod. Sic. 10.23.1). While the number of Sybarites indicates a common source with Diod. Sic. 12.9.1, similarities such as Diodorus's τὴν εὐδαιμονίαν οὐκ ἐνεγκόντες ἐπιδεξίως and ἔπταισαν to Ps.-Scymnus's τἀγαθὰ τὰ λίαν μὴ μαθόντες εὖ φέρειν and ἀπταίστως point to a common source for Diod. Sic. 10.23.1 and Ps.-Scymnus. Again, we may compare Strabo directly to Ps.-Scymnus: αὐτανδρον ἐξέφθειραν ἐπιφανῆ πόλιν ... τρυφὴν δὲ καὶ ῥάθυμον ἑλομένους βίον ... προελθεῖν εἰς ὕβριν τε καὶ κόρον, and ἐν βραχεῖ χρόνῳ (Ps.-Scymnus 344, 348–49, 358); ὑπὸ μέντοι τρυφῆς καὶ ὕβρεως ἅπασαν τὴν εὐδαιμονίαν ἀφῃρέθησαν and ἐν ἡμέραις ἑβδομήκοντα (Strabo 6.1.13). An allusion to τρυφή and hubris may be seen in Diodorus's πόλεμον ἄδικον ἐπανελόμενοι.

dedication to food, wine, and sex, indulgences that naturally lead to hubris.[41] Dio Chrysostom, speaking of the effects of τρυφή, claimed that the more Sybaris luxuriated, the quicker it was destroyed.[42] Plutarch, in addition to recounting stories of Sybarite τρυφή familiar from elsewhere, adds the intriguing point that Sybaris owed "three destructions" to the anger of Hera.[43] Cassius Dio (*Hist. Rom.* 57.18.4–5) refers to a Sibylline prophecy that stasis and ἁ Συβαρῖτις ἀφροσύνα would destroy the Romans. Aelian is also indirect: the author will pass over as too well known that Sybarite τρυφή was αἰτίαν τῆς ἀπωλείας. Rather, he recounts the more obscure case of Colophon, where culinary extravagance led to hubris (Aelian, *VH* 1.19). But after the middle of the third century CE, evidence for any kind of detailed knowledge about Sybaris as historical or moral exemplar largely disappeared. Reference to the luxury of the Sybarites was reduced to the adjective Συβαριτικός (especially in the phrase τράπεζα Συβαριτική), except for the occasional appearance in the lexicographers of one of the familiar anecdotes.

We have seen that, before the beginning of the first century BCE, there is no direct evidence for a narrative in which Sybaris was destroyed because of its τρυφή. Yet that same theme was a commonplace in the Roman era. This distribution of the evidence may be surprising, given Sybaris's status as a watchword for the corrosive effects of immoderate wealth. Perhaps more surprising still will be the claim advanced in this book that the pattern of material on Sybarite decadence is not the result of accidents of transmission. Rather, the case of Sybaris epitomizes the development of the idea of pernicious luxury. We argue that the view in question—that an opulent lifestyle naturally led to the ruin of

---

41. Philo, *Spec.* 3.43–44: ἀλλὰ γὰρ ἔνιοι τὰς Συβαριτῶν καὶ τὰς ἔτι λαγνιστέρων ἐπιθυμίας ζηλώσαντες τὸ μὲν πρῶτον ὀψοφαγίαις καὶ οἰνοφλυγίαις καὶ ταῖς ἄλλαις ταῖς γαστρὸς καὶ τῶν μετὰ γαστέρα ἡδοναῖς ἐνησκήθησαν, εἶτα δὲ κορεσθέντες ἐξύβρισαν—ὕβριν γὰρ κόρος γεννᾶν πέφυκεν—, ὡς ὑπὸ φρενοβλαβείας λυττᾶν καὶ ἐπιμεμηνέναι μηκέτ᾽ ἀνθρώποις εἴτ᾽ ἄρρεσιν εἴτε θηλείαις ἀλλὰ καὶ ἀλόγοις ζῴοις ("Some, emulating the desires of the Sybarites and people even more lecherous, in the first place were practiced in gourmandizing and drinking and the other pleasures of the belly and the parts below the belly; then becoming sated they became hubristic—for excess naturally produces hubris—so that they were out of their heads with madness and went crazy no longer for human beings, whether male or female, but for dumb animals.").

42. Dio Chrys., *Or.* 33.25: οὐ Σύβαρις μὲν ὅσῳ μάλιστα ἐτρύφησεν, τοσούτῳ θᾶττον ἀπώλετο.

43. Plut., *Pel.* 1.5–6, tells how the Sybarites did not wonder that the Spartans face death fearlessly, since the Spartan way of life is so unattractive (also at Diodorus 8.18 and Athenaeus 4.138b–d). Plut., *Mor.* 147e5, reports the tale that the Sybarite women were given a year's notice when invited to feasts, so they could properly prepare (*sim.* in Phylarchus, *FGrH* 81 F 45, as quoted at Athenaeus 12.521c). The "three destructions" of Sybaris are at Plut., *Mor.* 557c: Συβαρίταις δὲ φράζων ἀπόλυσιν τῶν κακῶν, ὅταν τρισὶν ὀλέθροις ἱλάσωνται τὸ μήνιμα τῆς Λευκαδίας Ἥρας ("Holding out to the Sybarites a deliverance from evils, when they would propitiate the anger of Hera Leucas with three destructions").

individuals and communities—was of no historiographical importance before the Roman era. The story of the fall of Sybaris, then, is indeed highly illustrative of the role of τρυφή as a historical force, although its effect is counter to the accepted view. We will return to Sybaris, the icon of the fruits of decadence, at the end of our study, but now let us undertake a general examination for the concept of pernicious luxury in Greek thought.

The Vocabulary of Luxury

It is natural that we begin this inquiry into the moral dimension of luxury by carefully explicating the ancient vocabulary which is regularly advanced as key evidence that, by the fifth century, the Greeks widely believed that an opulent lifestyle was debilitating in and of itself. "Luxury" is a tricky term. It has no exact equivalent in Greek, nor does it have precise implications in English. Because of this vagueness, slippery arguments have developed, equating words that are not synonyms, or resting too much weight on something whose precise meaning is assumed rather than established from the surviving texts.

For example, one might easily object that Solon has already established the self-same chain by which luxury causes moral ruin, so it is worthwhile to look closely at the words of the Lawgiver. There, a significant distinction can be noted. Solon says:

τίκτει γὰρ κόρος ὕβριν, ὅταν πολὺς ὄλβος ἕπηται ἀνθρώποις ὁπόσοις μὴ νόος ἄρτιος ᾖ.

[handwritten: excessive pride]
[handwritten: when people become excessively wealthy → causing corruption of oneself]

[Excess breeds hubris, whenever great prosperity attends upon people whose minds are not right.] (Solon, frag. 6.3–4 West)

Solon makes it absolutely clear that his emphasis is on κόρος and ὕβρις manifested in the *acquisition* of wealth, not its enjoyment.[44] For when he speaks about the enjoyment of luxury, he expresses approval:

[handwritten: statement regarding negativity toward the way one acquires wealth]

ἴσόν τοι πλουτέουσιν, ὅτῳ πολὺς ἄργυρός ἐστι
καὶ χρυσὸς καὶ γῆς πυροφόρου πεδία

---

44. For Solon's striking use of κόρος as "greed," see Balot 2001, 79–98.

ἵπποι θ᾽ ἡμίονοί τε, καὶ ᾧ μόνα ταῦτα πάρεστι,
    γαστρί τε καὶ πλευραῖς καὶ ποσὶν ἁβρὰ παθεῖν
. . . .
ταῦτ᾽ ἄφενος θνητοῖσι·

[The two are equally rich. One has much silver and gold and fields of wheat-bearing earth and horses and mules. The other has only this: to enjoy fine things with his stomach, sides, and feet. . . . This is abundance for mortals.] (Solon, frag. 24.1–4, 7 West)

This emphasis is equally clear at Solon, frag. 13.9–13 West:

πλοῦτον δ᾽ ὃν μὲν δῶσι θεοί, παραγίγνεται ἀνδρὶ
    ἔμπεδος ἐκ νεάτου πυθμένος ἐς κορυφήν·
ὃν δ᾽ ἄνδρες τιμῶσιν ὑφ᾽ ὕβριος, οὐ κατὰ κόσμον
    ἔρχεται, ἀλλ᾽ ἀδίκοις ἔργμασι πειθόμενος
οὐκ ἐθέλων ἕπεται, ταχέως δ᾽ ἀναμίσγεται ἄτη·

[Wealth that the gods give remains securely established from the bottom to the top. But wealth that men honor with hubris arrives in disorder and remains in attendance unwillingly, persuaded by unjust deeds. Ruin quickly joins the company.]

Frag. 13 ends (lines 71–76) by pointing out that the desire for riches is unbounded and its consequences disastrous.[45] Likewise:

οὐ γὰρ ἐπίστανται κατέχειν κόρον οὐδὲ παρούσας
    εὐφροσύνας κοσμεῖν δαιτὸς ἐν ἡσυχίηι
[lacuna]
    οὔθ᾽ ἱερῶν κτεάνων οὔτέ τι δημοσίων
φειδόμενοι κλέπτουσιν ἀφαρπαγῇ ἄλλοθεν ἄλλος

---

45. Another relevant text is frag. 5. Fisher (1992, 69–82) recognizes the importance to Solon of the proper acquisition of wealth in his discussion of these passages: "Similarly he [Solon] was aware of the dangers of hybristic behaviour from any quarter, but for him, as for the fourth-century orators, *hybris* was especially the crime of the upper class, striving to increase their wealth and enjoy its fruits in contempt of the rights and honour of others" (81). Cf. Lewis 2008, ch. 6.

[For they do not know how to restrain excess nor to put quietly in order the merriment of the present feast. . . . Sparing neither sacred nor public property, they steal greedily, one from one place, one from another.] (Solon, frag. 4.9–10, 12–13 West)[46]

unlike others Solon only criticizes the way one acquires wealth

The focus in Solon's poetry is decidedly on hubris in *obtaining* wealth, not in the lifestyle of luxury. His words cannot be taken as evidence for the early existence of an attitude that luxury was a corrupting force in the lives of men.

With this cautionary tale before us, we can now look one-by-one at the terms most commonly associated with luxury, and determine both their exact meanings and their moral implications in extant Greek literature before the Roman era. With few exceptions, proponents of the importance of the idea of pernicious luxury have paid little attention to the nuances of the relevant terms. The words are all generally taken to mean the same thing, more or less, and all assumed to have negative connotations. For example, Geddes claims, "Greek has a good vocabulary for luxury and all the words are, at any rate by the end of the fifth century, pejorative [sic]: τρυφή, ἁπαλότης, ἁβρότης, χλιδή."[47] Geddes does not offer any particular evidence for this view. In fact, as is not unusual in the scholarship, the negative sense of the luxury words is taken to be self-evident. In contrast, it is our claim, based on a close reading of the primary sources from the Archaic and Classical periods, that these words not only represent different nuanced aspects of wealth and social status, but also that they are not naturally or inherently pejorative and can often be quite positive in their implications.

To begin, for example, with the least important term on Geddes's list, an investigation of ἁπαλός and its compounds[48] indicates that the primary meaning is the softness of skin, whether of feet, necks, babies, or girls, although it can also be used adverbially of laughter. So, for example, at *Iliad* 19.92, the goddess

---

46. Fisher (1992, 72) believes that the missing lines rebuked the rich for the "extravagant, drunken and violent flaunting of their wealth at *symposia* and subsequent *komoi* through the streets." He then connects displays of such "sympotic and komastic *hybris*" (72 n. 115) with the depiction on the so-called Anacreontic vase of κῶμοι of cross-dressing Athenians (206 n. 31). Following a line of analysis initiated by DeVries (1973), Kurke (1992, 98) points out that the dress in question "was not effeminate."

47. Geddes 1987, 31. Under the label "the vocabulary signifying barbarian luxury recurrent in the *Persae*," Hall (1989, 127; cf. 81) lumps together *habros* compounds, *ploutos*, *chrusos*, and *chlidē*. We think one needs to be more wary in generalizing, for example, that any word for wealth or money indicates a luxurious use of resources, rather than, for example, the avaricious acquisition of them.

48. ἁπαλότης does not seem to occur until the fourth century, in spite of Geddes's claim.

Atē has feet that are ἁπαλοί, and at *Odyssey* 22.16, Odysseus shot Antinoos through the throat and the arrow came out ἁπαλοῖο δι᾽ αὐχένος ("through the tender neck").[49] This fairly narrow meaning is reinforced by the compounds that occur, such as ἁπαλόθριξ ("soft-haired," Eur., *Bacch.* 1186), ἁπαλόχροος ("soft-skinned," Hom. *Hymn Aphr.* 5.14, Hes., *Op.* 519), and ἁπαλοτρεφής ("plump," of a roasting hog at *Il.* 21.363). The only usage of any relevance is from Aristophanes' *Pax*, where the chorus sings that they have been transformed from a bitter and angry, hard (σκληρός) man into something softer: ἀλλ᾽ ἁπαλὸν ἄν μ᾽ ἴδοις καὶ πολὺ νεώτερον ("But you may see that I am soft and much younger," 351). Even here it is not certain that a moral sense is intended, since peace has made the chorus feel younger, and one attribute of youth is softness of skin (cf. Ar., *Thesm.* 192). Nonetheless, it is worth noting that in this context Aristophanes contrasts the quality of being ἁπαλός with being δριμύς ("bitter") and δύσκολος ("malcontented"). Thus, any moral implications of the antithesis between "hard" and "soft" are contrary to the usual interpretation: a moral disposition which is ἁπαλός is clearly superior to one which is σκληρός. In sum, ἁπαλός and its compounds seem never to be negative and are never used for wealth or luxury in the fifth century. Thus, they are not applicable to the discussion at hand.

More relevant are χλιδή and its cognates. These terms are often mistranslated to express something particularly voluptuous, sensual, or effeminate. Its primary meaning in the *LSJ* is "delicacy, luxury, effeminacy."[50] Yet the evidence from the Classical era demonstrates that the word has a narrow meaning centered on the concept of ornamentation in the form of gold, fine clothing, beautiful hair, and generally a rich way of life. Χλιδή is associated with objects of gold in Euripides: Andromache and then Hermione are dowered in golden χλιδή (Eur., *Andr.* 2 and 147), and the golden serpent statue left with baby Ion is marked as χλιδή (*Ion* 26). Sophocles has women heaped up with χλιδή (frag. 942.2 *TrGF*), and unlucky χλιδή is associated with profit which is not fairly gained (*OT* 887–88). Likewise we find in Euripides that the χλιδή of Mt. Tmolus flows in gold (*Bacch.* 154) and that Paris came to Sparta with a golden robe and barbarian χλιδή (*IA* 74). Euripides pairs it twice more with robes (*Hel.* 424;

---

49. Skin: Archilochus, frag. 113 Diehl (= 188 West); Theognis 2.1341; Ar., *Lys.* 418, *Thesm.* 192. Feet: Hom. *Hymn Dem.* 2.287; Hom. *Hymn Herm.* 4.273; Hes., *Theog.* 3. Neck: Hom., *Il.* 17.49, 22.327. Human or animal babies: Hom., *Il.* 11.115; Eur., *IA* 1286. Girls: Hom. *Hymn Aph.* 5.90; Ar., *Av.* 668, *Eccl.* 902. Laughing: Hom., *Od.* 14.465; Hom. *Hymn Herm.* 4.281.

50. Other meanings given are: wantonness, insolence; of luxuries, fine raiment, costly ornaments, etc.

Rhes. 960) and Aeschylus uses it to refer to couches (*Pers.* 544). At *Phoen.* 224, it describes the hair of maidens, as it also does at frag. 313 (*TrGF*) of Aeschylus. In Soph., *Elec.* 52, Orestes' offering on his father's tomb consists of locks of hair, described as "cut-off χλιδαί," while at 452, Electra's offerings are unworthy: locks of hair not covered with unguent and a very plain girdle, not worked with χλιδαί.[51] In Aesch., *Pers.* 608, Atossa has come in mourning, without carriage or χλιδή, to bring libations for the dead, and at *Prom.* 466, yoked horses are an image of overly rich χλιδή.

With all these well-defined instances at hand, other less-clear examples can best be interpreted along the same vein. Χλιδή is an attribute of a rich upbringing, as at Xen., *Cyr.* 4.5.54, where Cyrus is raised in it, rather than rustically. It is applied particularly to women on a number of occasions (Aesch., *Suppl.* 1003; Eur., *Cyc.* 500; cf. Eur., *Phoen.* 348, for the wedding ceremony). Certain women are raised in χλιδή and become priestesses (Ar., *Lys.* 640), surely a sign of wealth. The three goddesses come to the Judgment of Paris in jest and in χλιδή (Eur., *Tro.* 975), which can naturally be read as referring to beautiful clothing or ornamentation.

Χλιδή and its verbalizations can also refer to the act of showing off nice possessions, well-translated as "revelry." Electra accuses her sister of reveling in the gifts given her by Clytemnestra and Aegisthus, namely the richly spread table and the overflowing life (Soph., *Elec.* 360).[52] The word can be taken further, to imply scornful pride, as at Aesch., *Ag.* 1447, where Cassandra's death has brought to Clytemnestra εὐνῆς παροψώνημα τῆς ἐμῆς χλιδῇ ("an added relish of *chlidē* of my bed"),[53] and at Aesch., *Prom.* 436, where it is paired with αὐθαδία ("willfulness").[54] Most interesting is the passage that occurs later in the same play:

---

51. Finglass 2007, ad loc.: "The opulence of the expression mirrors the luxuriousness of the offering: contrast the meagreness of Electra's hair at 449."
52. A goat revels in his golden beard at Soph., frag. 314.367 (*TrGF*), in a passage reminiscent of the women reveling in their hair.
53. Both Fraenkel ([1950] 1962) and Denniston and Page (1957) are at a loss as to how to treat this line, with Fraenkel arguing that the εὐνῆς must be corrupt, and Denniston and Page accepting χλιδῇ as "surely not corrupt" but questioning the glossed παροψώνημα (suggesting perhaps "πάροψον, ὄμμα" in its place). The interlinear gloss in ms F reads "τὴν ἐκ περιουσίας τρυφήν." Cassandra's body is an ornament for Clytemnestra. If we accept the meaning of "scornful pride," then Clytemnestra is using the object of Cassandra's corpse to exalt in having avenged her own bed and marriage.
54. Cf. Xen., *Symp.* 8.8, "reveling in luxury" (ἁβρότητι χλιδαινομένου). These examples make the metaphorical uses at Aesch., *Suppl.* 833 (where there is a textual problem) and Pind., *Ol.* 10.84 easier to understand.

{Ερ.} χλιδᾶν ἔοικας τοῖς παροῦσι πράγμασιν.
{Πρ.} χλιδῶ; χλιδῶντας ὧδε τοὺς ἐμοὺς ἐγὼ
ἐχθροὺς ἴδοιμι·

[HERMES: You seem to revel in your present woes.
PROMETHEUS: I revel? I wish I could see my enemies reveling so!]
(Aesch., *Prom.* 971–73)

The passage is made more poignant by the dramatic fact that Prometheus, instead of flaunting jewelry, is wearing heavy chains, an unwanted ornamentation
that makes the reference to χλιδή particularly ironic.

There is no fifth-century context in which χλιδή is best taken to mean "effeminacy," "voluptuousness," or "wantonness." Therefore, when its context
leaves its connotations unspecified, it is best not to insist on a reference to a
process of decadence.[55]

For those concerned with the moral position of luxury before the last quarter of the fifth century, ἁβρός and its cognates are of primary importance. They
first appear in fragments of Sappho from the late seventh or early sixth century
BCE and occur occasionally in lyric poetry.[56] Already in its earliest attestations,
it is difficult to assign this root a concrete or primarily physical sense; its uses
are more abstract than the vocabulary of luxury which we have already examined. Thus, the *LSJ* defines the word with terms like "graceful," "delicate,"
"pretty," "dainty," and "luxurious." The item is taken to indicate a negative tone
of weakness and unmanliness, yet some of the earliest uses manifest a very different valuation than these translations would imply.[57] Thus, Kurke, in a study

---

55. Interestingly, χλιδή does not change meaning significantly through the time of Athenaeus. Although
that author does pair it with τρυφή on three occasions (Athen. 6.273b–c, 10.428b, 12.541b–c), his
eight uses of it that are not in direct quotes conform with the meanings established above: 5.212c
(gold litter and purple robes), 10.428b (banqueting and the good life in general), 12.525c *bis* (dyed
garments; bracelets), 12.528b (the hair of maidens), and 15.691c (perfume and unguents). Athen.
6.273b–c is difficult to read, since the reference is to all of the attendants who accompany Smindyrides and could refer to the ornamentation of the procession or the pride he has in it. The remaining
passage (5.191c) extends the meaning of the word, just as Classical authors do, to the idea of "reveling" or "being haughty."

56. Sappho, frags. 2, 44, 58, 100, 128, 140 LP. Cf. Stesich. 211 *PMG*; Alc. 41, 42, 307b LP; Anac. 2/347,
28/373 *PMG*; Semon. 7.57; Thgn. 1.474, 922. In a fragment of Hesiod of doubtful attribution and
attested very late, the word modifies *parthenos*: Steph. Byz. p. 503. 21 Meineke = frag. 339 M-W.

57. One must, of course, recognize that the connotations of English terms like "delicate" and "dainty"
may have altered considerably since the *LSJ* entry was composed. Such semantic drift is a further
obstacle for those who may have tried to understand Greek attitudes toward a luxurious lifestyle
without being in a position to reevaluate the relevant vocabulary in detail.

of the evidence on Archaic ἁβροσύνη, finds that for much of the Archaic period luxury was not linked particularly closely with "the world of women" or with effeminacy, but rather is a political endorsement of aristocratic luxury.[58] Sappho embraces it enthusiastically in the famous line, "I love *habrosunē*" (ἔγω δὲ φίλημμ᾽ ἀβροσύναν, frag. 58.25 LP), and no less a moral authority than Solon speaks with approval of a way of life he calls ἁβρὰ παθεῖν ("to experience *habra*").[59] This passage is not so different from that in Thucydides (1.6.3),[60] whose only use of a relevant cognate is to describe the lifestyle recently abandoned by the older men, the generation of the Marathonomachoi, who, though perhaps "luxurious," would clearly not be called "delicate" in a depreciatory sense. Thus, we would suggest expanding Kurke's conclusions to claim that not even in the fifth century do ἁβρός words come predominately to indicate something properly or improperly effeminate.

Certainly ἁβρός is a favorite term to modify women's gait or beauty,[61] but it would be simplistic to stop its interpretation there, since many passages do not entail daintiness or even femininity. Euripides' applications make it clear that the word doesn't apply to the walk of just *any* women, but rather women (or men) of noble bearing who are demonstrating dignity or noble affectation. In the *Trojan Women*, Cassandra laments her slavery by contrasting it with her former life when she walked through Troy with her *habros* step (τὸν ἁβρὸν . . . πόδα, 506), while at *IA* 1343–44, Clytemnestra compares ἁβρότης favorably to σεμνότης ("dignity" or "solemnity"). The chorus in the *Medea* describes the ancient children of Erechtheus, "fortunate and offspring of the blessed gods," as βαίνοντες ἁβρῶς (830),[62] while Menelaus himself is recognized from afar by the chorus leader precisely because of his bearing: πολὺς ἁβροσύνηι, / δῆλος ὁρᾶσθαι τοῦ Τανταλιδῶν / ἐξ αἵματος ὤν ("abounding in *habrosynē*, clearly

---

58. Kurke 1992, 98–101.
59. Solon, frag. 24.1–4, 7 West, quoted above (pp. 25–26). It is striking that the things Solon most appreciates—high-quality food and apparel—are just the items in whose enjoyment later authors frequently discover effeminizing effects. Note as well that wealth is valorized as the limit of what can give its possessor immediate physical pleasure. Any excess beyond that limit is discounted. Thus, Solon makes the luxurious lifestyle a moral standard by which to restrain the greedy acquisition of wealth. No one need seek more than is required to provide bodily comforts.
60. Cited below (pp. 44–45).
61. Sappho, frag. 128.1 LP (the Graces), 140.1 (Adonis); Semonides, frag. 7.57 West (the woman who is like a mare); Alcaeus 42.8 LP (*Parthenos*); Anacreon, frag. 2.1 Davies (neck and hair); and in a number of other texts too fragmentary to interpret. In the fifth century, we see it used of women at: Soph., *Trach.* 523; Eur., *Med.* 1164, *Hel.* 1528, *IA* 614, *Phoen.* 1485.
62. At Eur., *Tro.* 820 the chorus used the same words to depict Ganymede moving happily about in heaven.

seen as being from the blood of the Tantalids," Eur., *Or.* 349–51).[63] Aeschylus often uses the term to describe the Persian royal women as well as Helen herself, but he is also able to employ the phrase of Lydian men, saying, ἀβροδιαίτων Λυδῶν ὄχλος ("the crowd of Lydians with their *habros*-lifestyle," Aesch., *Pers.* 41–42), where the context makes clear that these Asians are formidable warriors: a few lines later, the cavalry of wealthy Sardis is φοβερὰν ὄψιν προσιδέσθαι ("a frightful sight to behold," 48).[64]

The most striking fifth-century examples of the term used in a positive sense are provided by Pindar. Here, far from indicating any kind of femininity, delicacy, or weakness, ἀβρός stem vocabulary is explicitly associated with virility and success.

ὃς δ᾽ ἀμφ᾽ ἀέθλοις ἢ πολεμίζων ἄρηται κῦδος ἀβρόν,
εὐαγορηθεὶς κέρδος ὕψιστον δέκεται, πολιατᾶν καὶ ξένων γλώσσας ἄωτον.

[He who wins a *habros*-reputation in competitions or in fighting receives the highest gain in being praised, the finest flower of the speech of citizens and strangers alike.] (Pindar, *Isthm.* 1.50–51)

Ἁβρός is paired with κῦδος yet again at *Olympian* 5.7, when Psaumis dedicates it to the daughter of Ocean in winning the mule car team race. The meaning of this phrase is perhaps suggested a few lines later where success in manly endeavors is a product of a combination of "toil and expense."[65] Likewise, at

---

63. West (1987, ad loc.) is disturbed by this line: "I delete this sentence, because it is silly (Menelaus' elegance, whether of gait or apparel, cannot be evidence of his descent) and because *poly* cannot be used to mean 'very' in classical Greek where there is no sense of measurement. . . ." He thinks it is an interpolation from a production which chose to exaggerate the excessive pomp of the situation. We would argue that the line is perfectly appropriate: Menelaus is one of the *kaloi k'agathoi*, and can be recognized as such by his bearing.

64. Also at *Pers.* 135, 541, 543, 1073; *Ag.* 690. Cf. also Soph., *OC* 1339. Hall (1989, 81) takes note of the high concentration of ἀβρός compounds in the *Persians*, but she believes the term here has distinctly negative connotations: it is "untranslatable . . . combining the senses of 'softness', 'delicacy', and 'lack of restraint' . . . In respect of women, goddesses, and even eastern gods it is neutral or even complimentary . . . but in connection with men and cities it is from early times pejorative." Elsewhere Hall (1993, 121) speaks of the term's "suggestions of effeminacy" and refers to ἀβρο- as a "feminizing prefix." She offers no evidence for this supposedly well-established negative sense. In contrast, Garvey (2009, ad loc.) argues for a positive meaning lasting until the second half of the fifth century.

65. αἰεὶ δ᾽ ἀμφ᾽ ἀρεταῖσι πόνος δαπάνα τε μάρναται πρὸς ἔργον / κινδύνῳ κεκαλυμμένον· εὖ δὲ τυχόντες σοφοὶ καὶ πολίταις ἔδοξαν ἔμμεν ("Always, in matters of excellence, toil and expense struggle toward a deed veiled in danger; those achieving it seem to be wise, even to their countrymen," Pind., *Ol.* 5.15–16). The conjunction of πόνος and δαπάνα in this context gains added interest from the fact, as will be apparent in the discussion of the Thucydidean evidence below, that the relationship among toil, luxury, and ἀρετή was a topic of contention in Periclean Athens and later.

Nemean 7.31–32, death may come to all alike, but τιμὰ δὲ γίνεται ὧν θεὸς ἁβρὸν αὔξει λόγον τεθνακότων ("those who have died gain honor if the god increases their *habros*-reputation."[66] In the changing ebb and tide of fortune, *habros*-wealth (πλοῦτον ἁβρὸν) can be the stepping stone to lofty fame (κλέος ὑψηλὸν), such as that of Sarpedon and Nestor (*Pyth.* 3.110–14), or ἁβρότης can be something beyond mere wealth:

ὁ δὲ καλόν τι νέον λαχών
ἁβρότατος ἔπι μεγάλας
ἐξ ἐλπίδος πέταται
ὑποπτέροις ἀνορέαις, ἔχων
κρέσσονα πλούτου μέριμναν.

[He who has won some fine new thing in his great *habrotēs* flies beyond hope on soaring manliness, having a concern greater than wealth.] (Pind., *Pyth.* 8.88–92)

For Pindar, then, ἁβρο- is in every instance redolent of success in areas of achievement which define masculinity.[67] There is no trace of a pejorative sense.

Thus, when faced with a ἁβρός word, one should not assume the presence of the idea of delicacy, which is completely inappropriate for many of the passages we have examined. A better feel for nuance would stress the idea of "luxurious," but even more "refined," "dignified," or "affected." It is enfolded within the spheres of both wealth and status—items that go hand-in-hand in Greek society. How else is the chorus in the *Agamemnon* able to say, ἁβρύνεται γὰρ πᾶς τις εὖ πράσσων πλέον ("For everyone, when he is prosperous, is full of *habros*," Aesch., *Ag.* 1205)?

---

66. Kurke (1992, 111) reads this and other references to ἁβρός as "a profound challenge to the aristocrats in his audience. . . . True luxury, the poet implies, does not consist of beautiful robes, gold ornaments, and scented oils, but rather of the effort and expenditure needed to win and the cost of commissioning a victory ode—since only these latter will bestow immortality." We disagree with Kurke's theory (109) that Pindar is redefining the term "as prestige expenditure that is also public service." In our view, the meaning of ἁβρός has remained consistent.

67. Burton 1962, 190: "It is most unlikely that ἁβρότης (v. 89) should mean the freshness and delicacy of youth. [fn *LSJ* s.v.] Rather, . . . we should take it of the luxury and wealth of the victor's condition of life." Compare also Bacch., *Dithyr.* 4.1–2: Βασιλεῦ τᾶν ἱερᾶν Ἀθανᾶν, / τῶν ἁβροβίων ἄναξ Ἰώνων ("King of Holy Athens, Lord of the Ionians living in *habros*"). Kurke (1992, 108–9) casts these lines in terms of the luxury of having the economic wherewithal to train for future games.

In the last quarter of the fifth century, a new set of terms for luxury, τρυφή and its relatives, began to appear in the literary record. These are the words most widely associated with a putative Greek belief in pernicious luxury and we will concentrate most of our efforts on them for the remainder of this study.

To begin, the word τρυφή is cognate with θρύψις and θρύπτω, which have the root meaning "breaking into pieces." Though far rarer than τρυφή, θρύπτ- occurs earlier, as one might expect from a more physical term. Homer uses it of a shattered sword (*Il.* 3.363) and Aeschylus of breaking off fingers and toes (*Ag.* 1595).[68] The literal use quickly shades into a figurative one. Plato can describe souls that are broken up and shattered by low occupations (συγκεκλασμένοι τε καὶ ἀποτεθρυμμένοι, *Rep.* 6.495e1) and a spurned lover in Aristophanes can describe himself as heartbroken with the word θρύψομαι (*Eq.* 1163; cf. Acts 21:13). It is a short trip to being "shattered by wealth" in Xenophon (διὰ τὸν πλοῦτον διαθρυπτόμενοί, Xen., *Mem.* 4.2.35).[69]

By way of contrast, the cognate term τρυφή and its relations never have the physical meaning of "breaking into pieces." By its first datable occurrence in the *Suppliants* of Euripides, c. 423 BCE, τρυφ- encompasses a more sophisticated abstract idea related to the enjoyment of an easy lifestyle that is not necessarily pejorative. At Euripides, *Ion* 1375–76, the title character laments that he was never able ἐν ἀγκάλαις μητρὸς τρυφῆσαι ("to have *truphē* in a mother's arms"). Similarly neutral meanings are likely elsewhere in Euripides: at *Phoen.* 1491, Antigone speaks of στολίδος κροκόεσσαν ἀνεῖσα τρυφάν ("undoing the saffron *truphē* of my stole"), and in the *IA*, the chorus, telling of the guest list at the wedding of Peleus and Thetis, characterizes "Phrygian Ganymede" as Διὸς / λέκτρων τρύφημα φίλον ("dear *truphē* of Zeus's bed," 1049–50). One may argue that the Greeks would interpret being the τρύφημα of anyone's bed—be it a man's or a

---

68. Fraenkel ([1950] 1962, ad loc.) argues: "ἔθρυπτε must not be altered," while Denniston and Page (1957, ad loc.) believe the line is deeply corrupted. They do not dispute this particular word so much as the emphasis in the story on cutting off hands and feet to the exclusion of other things, like heads, and so suggest a lacuna. Any putative difficulty does not affect our argument. Other physical uses in the Classical era include: Plato, *Crat.* 426e2, *Parm.* 165b4; Dem., *De cor.*18.260.8; Xen., *Ages.* 2.14.4. Every occurrence in Aristotle is physical (*De an.* 419b23, 419b26, 420a8; *Part. an.* 651a35, 694b29; *Gen. corr.* 316b30). Cf. also later authors: Diod. Sic. 1.83.3, 3.16.2; Dion. Hal., *Ant. Rom.* 9.21.4; Strabo 12.8.17, 17.1.36.

69. Hereafter θρύπτω and especially the noun form, θρύψις, are often used in a way indistinguishable from τρυφή, though they will always maintain a parallel, physical and metaphorical meaning of being shattered. Interestingly, in Philo for example (*Cher.* 12), τρυφή and θρύψις are contrasted, because τρυφή is an ease that comforts the soul while θρύψις is a disturbance and agitation. See the discussion in Chapter 5.

god's—as having a clearly negative moral dimension, and that this is exactly the kind of feminization that is generally thought to be connected with luxury. It is certainly possible that Euripides had this connection in mind and is referring to it ironically in the expectation that some in the audience will pick up on it. Nevertheless, the chorus itself, speaking in its dramatic character, is not being ironic, and therefore the *literal* meaning of τρύφημα is at least neutral.

Even in passages where τρυφή seems to bear a negative sense, it is not a question of a general moral or physical weakness or indolence brought on by indulgence in luxury. Euripides gives a broad indication of the word's true meaning in its very first extant occurrence, at *Supp.* 195–218, where Theseus lists all the goods given to humans by the gods, including the powers of reason and speech, crops, protection from the elements, sailing, and prophecy, and then asks:

ἆρ᾽ οὐ τρυφῶμεν, θεοῦ κατασκευὴν βίῳ
δόντος τοιαύτην, οἷσιν οὐκ ἀρκεῖ τάδε;

[Are we not *trupheroi* to whom all this is insufficient, when the god has given us such resources for life?] (Eur., *Supp.* 214–15)

Here τρυφή represents the psychological attitude which consists in not being content with the goods at hand.[70] While such dissatisfaction may be a moral failing, it is by no means indicative of a passive or yielding disposition. In fact, one affected with τρυφή also displays a certain attitude of entitlement: in the fifth-century evidence, τρυφή indicates an expectation that the cause of one's dissatisfaction will be ameliorated.[71] By extension, and more objectively, it can also describe a situation in which this expectation is being met.

Two passages from Euripides make the relevant meanings apparent. Theseus compares the hard lot of mortals to the τρυφή enjoyed by divine Fortune:

γνῶτε τἀνθρώπων κακά·
παλαίσμαθ᾽ ἡμῶν ὁ βίος· εὐτυχοῦσι δὲ

---

70. Collard (1975, s.v.) translates it well: "How can we be so choosy and ungrateful?"

71. Aeschylus uses θρύπτω in a similar vein when he admonishes that people should marry within their class and a poor man ought not to seek a wife among those who are "spoiled because of their wealth and exalted in their birth" (μήτε τῶν πλούτῳ διαθρυπτομένων μήτε τῶν γέννᾳ μεγαλυνομένων, Aesch., *Prom.* 891–92). Cf. Xen., *Mem.* 1.2.25, *Cyr.* 7.2.23.

οἱ μὲν τάχ᾽, οἱ δ᾽ ἐσαῦθις, οἱ δ᾽ ἤδη βροτῶν·
τρυφᾷ δ᾽ ὁ δαίμων· πρός τε γὰρ τοῦ δυστυχοῦς,
ὡς εὐτυχήσῃ, τίμιος γεραίρεται,
ὅ τ᾽ ὄλβιός νιν πνεῦμα δειμαίνων λιπεῖν
ὑψηλὸν αἴρει.

[Acknowledge the evils of mortality: our life is a series of struggles; some men find good fortune quickly, some after a while, others straightaway. But the daemon lives in *truphē*: he is honored and rewarded by the unfortunate man, so that he may become lucky; the prosperous man exalts him to heaven, fearing the favoring breeze may leave.] (Eur., *Supp.* 549–55)

Here the verb τρυφάω denotes not just the objective fact that life is as easy for a god as it is hard for human beings. It also makes a subjective claim about the mental disposition of the daemon: a god expects to have his wishes seen to, while a mortal should expect only trouble and uncertainty.

The willfulness associated with τρυφή may be more important in prompting the choice of this term than any reference to creature comforts per se. At *IA* 1303, in a passage where Iphigenia laments the Judgment of Paris and its ramifications, τρυφάω refers without question to the unshakeable expectations of the three divine competitors:

ἁ μὲν ἐπὶ πόθῳ τρυφῶσα
Κύπρις, ἁ δὲ δορὶ Παλλάς,
Ἥρα δὲ Διὸς ἄνακτος
εὐναῖσι βασιλίσιν,
κρίσιν ἐπὶ στυγνὰν ἔριν . . .

[Cypris, having *truphē* in lust, and Pallas, having *truphē* in the spear, and Hera, having *truphē* in the kingly bed of lord Zeus [came] to the hateful judgment.] (Eur., *IA* 1303–7)

The point of τρυφῶσα is not that the goddesses take delight in their respective attributes, as the *LSJ*'s "run riot" may suggest; each of the contestants assumes that, because of her own powers or status, she will be given the prize.

The directly attested early evidence on τρυφή and cognates is consistent with this interpretation.[72] At *Bacch.* 969, Pentheus uses τρυφάω to describe himself when he hears he will be in his mother's arms. This passage has the added interest of the juxtaposition of τρυφάω and ἁβρότης. With the latter, Pentheus characterizes his situation if he returns from the countryside not on foot, but "carried" (φερόμενος, 968). In the next line, the level of luxury has been heightened: Pentheus recharacterizes his position as involving τρυφή because it will be his mother who carries him (ἐν χερσὶ μητρός), evoking the image of an infant whose every want is seen to by his mother. On our interpretation, Pentheus imagines a move from the deference appropriate for a member of an aristocratic elite to the utterly self-centered willfulness of a child.

In contrast, it may at first seem that *Bacch.* 150 has nothing to do with the psychological dimension of τρυφή when Dionysus is described thus: τρυφερόν <τε> πλόκαμον εἰς αἰθέρα ῥίπτων ("casting his *trupheros*-locks into the air"). Surely, the point may just be the physical softness of the god's hair. Yet the reference may be to the attention required by servants in order to maintain any kind of extravagant coiffure. We will see below other examples of τρυφή used to indicate the care from servants that is involved in opulent cosmetics, hairstyles, and clothing. Developing the idea further, physical attractiveness can be a means for its possessor to get his or her way, and in this passage Dionysus shakes his hair to stimulate his followers to worship. Compare Aristophanes, *Eccl.* 900–905, where a young woman mocks an old one:

μὴ φθόνει ταῖσιν νέαισι.
τὸ τρυφερὸν γὰρ ἐμπέφυκε
τοῖς ἁπαλοῖσι μηροῖς
κἀπὶ τοῖς μήλοις ἐπανθεῖ· σὺ δ᾽, ὦ γραῦ,
παραλέλεξαι κἀντέτριψαι,
τῷ θανάτῳ μέλημα.

[Don't envy young girls. The *trupheron* grows in our soft thighs and blossoms on our melons. You, old woman, have been laid out and anointed an object of attention to Death.]

---

72. The difficulties involved in the interpretation of fragments preclude their use in establishing a nuanced definition.

Though it may refer to the physical softness of breast and thigh (redundantly, in view of ἁπαλοῖσι),[73] τὸ τρυφερόν is better taken to indicate that quality which will enable the young girl to attain her goal: to be taken care of by a man. In contrast, the older woman relies on the allure of know-how to catch a man's attention:

εἴ τις ἀγαθὸν βούλεται παθεῖν τι, παρ᾽ ἐμοὶ χρὴ καθεύδειν.
οὐ γὰρ ἐν νέαις τὸ σοφὸν ἔν-
εστιν, ἀλλ᾽ ἐν ταῖς πεπείροις·

[If anyone wants to have a good time, he should sleep with me. For there is no skill in young girls, but in the ripe ones.] (Ar., *Eccl.* 893–96)

Put another way, while the old woman expects to give care, the young woman expects to receive it, and that expectation and its fulfillment is τρυφή.[74]

That the possession of τρυφή brings with it the expectation that one will be the object of solicitous concern (μέλημα) is confirmed in a passage from Xenophon, where the subject is likewise the field of sexual commerce. Socrates helps the notorious beauty Theodote articulate the intuitions that enable her to live prosperously on the generosity of the men with whom she takes up: . . . ἢ καταμανθάνεις . . . ὅτι δεῖ τὸν μὲν ἐπιμελόμενον ἀσμένως ὑποδέχεσθαι, τὸν δὲ τρυφῶντα ἀποκλείειν (". . . by which you understand that it is necessary to give a warm welcome to the solicitous suitor, but to shut the door on a man of *truphē*," Xen., *Mem.* 3.11.10). Theodote's goal is to attract a man who will take care of her (τὸν ἐπιμελόμενον); ὁ τρυφῶν, on the other hand, will not see to her needs, but demand that she attend to his.[75]

Elsewhere in Aristophanes, τρυφή bears the same sense. At *Nubes* 48,

---

73. Thus Ussher 1973, ad loc. While such a meaning might work in this instance, it clearly does not work for all the other passages containing the word τρυφή, whereas our proposed definition of the word explains this passage coherently and gives it a richer meaning.

74. See the corresponding contrast between ἐπιμέλεια and τρυφή, discussed below. In order to make this passage work at all, Ussher (1973, ad loc.) needs special pleading: "The hag is not here intending to compare herself (as Rogers, van Leeuwen) with the μεῖραξ: she rates her quality against the world."

75. Xenophon uses θρύπτω with the same sense of sexual solicitude at *Symp.* 8.4.3: when Antisthenes confesses his love for Socrates, the philosopher responds "coquettishly" (θρυπτόμενος), telling the man not to bother him right now. The sense must be that he likes the attention, though he pretends otherwise. This same sense of coquettishness is extended to the speaker, who is bursting with desire to perform but pretends to be otherwise, at Plato, *Phdr.* 228c2.

Strepsiades blames his wife—σεμνήν τρυφῶσαν ἐγκεκοισυρωμένην ("grand, full of *truphē*, acting like Coesyra")—for his son's selfish interest in horse racing.[76] At *Vespae* 551, no creature is τρυφερώτερον ἢ δεινότερον ("more full of *truphē* or more terrible") than a juror, since the leading men of the city vie to win his favor. By the same token, an official of the law courts is τρυφερανθείς, because he can set the time for a trial and exclude any juror who comes late (*Vesp.* 688); even dikasts must defer to him.

Our lexicon uses *Lysistrata* 387–430 as the main support for a primary meaning of "wantonness" and "licentiousness" for τρυφ-.[77] However, in this passage, as in the others we have examined, there is no question of a reference to the lack of self-control suggested by the traditional interpretation: the implication is rather the opposite one, that of presumption. Arriving at the Acropolis, where Lysistrata's women have taken over the public treasury and barred the gates, a magistrate describes the situation:

ἆρ᾽ ἐξέλαμψε τῶν γυναικῶν ἡ τρυφὴ
χὠ τυμπανισμὸς χοἰ πυκνοὶ Σαβάζιοι,
ὅ τ᾽ Ἀδωνιασμὸς οὗτος οὑπὶ τῶν τεγῶν,
οὗ ᾽γώ ποτ᾽ ὢν ἤκουον ἐν τἠκκλησίᾳ;

[Has the *truphē* of our women burst forth? The beating of drums and frequent recourse to Bacchus, and the festival of Adonis on the roofs, like the one I heard once in the assembly?] (Ar., *Lys.* 387–90)

The women's activity is τρυφή, not because the magistrate imagines they are involved in some kind of orgiastic rite and so not because they are dancing or drinking or behaving wantonly. The significance of τρυφή is here indicated by the parallel with the festival of Adonis at the time of the debate over the Syracusan expedition. The magistrate has come to the Acropolis to draw funds for the navy (421–22). The women have locked the gates, intent on their own agenda and without regard for the good of the city, just as the wife of Demostra-

---

76.   Dover (1968, ad loc.) notes of σεμνός that "applied to a woman the meaning is almost 'classy' and implies one kind of sex-appeal." He adds that Coesyra "figured in folklore as a *grande dame*" and that all the stories about her extravagances preserved in the scholia were based on guesswork from the text of Aristophanes itself. When Strepsiades is asked at *Nub.* 799 why he lets his son have his way, he says that Pheidippides is big and strong and a descendent of Coesyra.

77.   *LSJ* s.v. τρυφάω, section II: "*to be licentious, run riot, wax wanton*, Ar. *Lys.* 405 etc"; s.v. τρυφή, section II: "*luxuriousness, wantonness*, τῶν γυναικῶν ἡ τ. Ar. *Lys.* 387."

tus danced and shouted for Adonis while her husband supported the launch of the disastrous armada (391–98). The act of putting one's own concerns and pleasures before the national welfare is what the magistrate has in mind when he views the women as engaged in a renewed outbreak of τρυφή. Yet the passage is richly ironic. The audience knows what the magistrate does not: Lysistrata and her companions have embarked on a breathtakingly audacious act of τρυφή. They will use their sexual attractiveness to impose their will on their men and force them to end the war. In this case, the women's τρυφή will demand a heroic degree of self-abnegation and will be carried out for the good of all the Greeks.

Τρυφή has the same significance—"presumptuousness," or the like—a few lines later, even though there the context does refer to sexual promiscuity. The magistrate shows little sympathy for the indignity the old men have suffered at the hands of the women on the citadel. They have only themselves to blame:

ὅταν γὰρ αὐτοὶ ξυμπονηρευώμεθα
ταῖσιν γυναιξὶ καὶ διδάσκωμεν τρυφᾶν,
τοιαῦτ' ἀπ' αὐτῶν βλαστάνει βουλεύματα.

[For whenever we ourselves abet our women in their wickedness and teach them to have *truphē*, they produce such plots as these.] (Ar., *Lys.* 404–6)

Then, in a series of *double entendres,* the magistrate claims that the Athenian men have pandered for their wives, arranging for other men to service them while the husbands are away. Yet, in spite of the allegation that the women of Athens are engaged in sexual impropriety, τρυφᾶν itself need not refer to sexual activity per se. What the women are being taught through the connivance of their husbands is not infidelity and promiscuity. For in that case it would be very difficult to see how τοιαῦτα βουλεύματα—for example, embarrassing the chorus of old men by dowsing them with water, which is the proximate cause of the magistrate's remarks—could be seen as following naturally from the sexual appetite of the city's wives. Rather, they are being taught to expect to get their own way; they are being taught that they can bend their husbands to their will (αὐτοὶ ξυμπονηρευώμεθα), even to the extent that the men become procurers for their own wives. It is little wonder then that the intransigence of the old women's chorus is characterized as τρυφή.

It is noteworthy that in this *Lysistrata* passage, the action of the women in barring the entrance to the Acropolis, which was called τρυφή at 387 and τρυφᾶν at 405, has become ὕβρεως at 425. Indeed, a sharper understanding of τρυφή may help illuminate this controversial term, for certain passages in which hubris is linked with τρυφή are taken as important evidence in the debate over the precise meaning of hubris.

The seminal work on this subject has been done by Fisher, who says:

> *Hybris* is essentially the serious assault on the honour of another, which is likely to cause shame, and lead to anger and attempts at revenge. *Hybris* is often, but by no means necessarily, an act of violence; it is essentially deliberate activity, and the typical motive for such infliction of dishonour is the pleasure of expressing a sense of superiority, rather than compulsion, need or desire for wealth. (Fisher 1992, 1)

The *locus classicus* is found in Aristotle (*Rhet.* 1378b23–35), for whom the typical act of hubris is the gratuitous exploitation by the powerful, especially tyrants, of those considered inferior to them.[78] However, it is certainly possible for subordinates to act hubristically as well, forgetting their place and assaulting the honor of the superior party. On an individual level, hubris is frequently a violent act or a sexual assault, but it can just as easily consist of verbal insults: anything designed to dishonor may fall into the category. Thus, within a state, hubris often provokes disputes and even political unrest: Athens went so far as to pass a law against it, the *graphē hubreos*, which carried any penalty the jury wished to impose, including execution.[79]

While Fisher has argued exhaustively that hubris cannot be understood as has traditionally been done, merely as "arrogance," others press the case that hubris is better seen as a more general moral disposition or even as "a form of unchecked energy."[80] It is noteworthy that in our interpretation, τρυφή is similar to Fisher's view of hubris, in that both are terms for imposing one's will on someone else. If we are correct that the person practicing τρυφή expects someone else to do what s/he wishes, then the two terms can be associated quite naturally when getting one's own way (τρυφή) also involves disrespect (ὕβρις) by expecting to be taken care of by people who have no obligation to serve,

---

78. Fisher 1992, 7–35, esp. 32. Cf. Arist., *VV* 1251a30ff.
79. Fisher 1992, ch. 2.
80. Cairns 1996, 24, on the connection of τρυφή and the idea of hubris as unrestrained energy; *passim* for hubris as a disposition.

people who are equals or superiors rather than attendants. An example occurs at Aristophanes, *Ranae* 21, where Dionysus bemoans the fact that he walks while his slave rides the donkey: εἶτ᾽ οὐχ ὕβρις ταῦτ᾽ ἐστὶ καὶ πολλὴ τρυφή ("Isn't this hubris and much *truphē*?"). The collocation is perfectly appropriate to the circumstances, given that Xanthias is having his physical comfort attended to, a reversal of roles which is in itself also an act of disrespect to his master.[81]

On the other hand, Cairns takes the association of hubris with τρυφή at Euripides, *Troides* 997, as demonstrating that hubris can be "an attitude which affronts other people in general," but is not "intended to dishonour anyone in particular."[82] Hecuba accuses Helen of having run off with Paris, because she was dissatisfied with the resources of Argos: οὐδ᾽ ἦν ἱκανά σοι τὰ Μενέλεω / μέλαθρα ταῖς σαῖς ἐγκαθυβρίζειν τρυφαῖς ("Nor were the halls of Menelaus sufficient for you to be hubristic in your *truphai*," Eur., *Tro.* 996–97). To Cairns, Fisher's explanation that ἐγκαθυβρίζειν refers to Helen's "assertiveness against [her] husband" seems "a rather desperate attempt to maintain his schema."[83] However, we may observe that the presence of ταῖς σαῖς τρυφαῖς may indicate rather that Helen's offensive behavior is to be understood as directed against her servants and underlings, whom she expected to see to her comforts, perhaps to an unreasonable degree. Such an interpretation would be consistent with Hecuba's description of Helen's behavior at Troy:

ἐν τοῖς Ἀλεξάνδρου γὰρ ὕβριζες δόμοις
καὶ προσκυνεῖσθαι βαρβάρων ὕπ᾽ ἤθελες

[You used to be hubristic in Alexander's house and wanted to be bowed to by barbarians.] (Eur., *Tro.* 1020–21)

Perhaps we are meant to recognize a close parallel between the way Helen acted among Paris's household and the way she wished to act in Menelaus's home.

Euripides seems to use τρυφή to include just such a reference to the ministrations of servants in the *Orestes*, when Pylades has suggested that he and Orestes kill Helen:

---

81. Cf. Plato, *Leg.* 6.777e6 (*bis*) and 11.922c3, where he upbraids those masters who treat slaves with θρύψις, as if they were free men, resulting in a situation that is worse for both parties.
82. Cairns 1996, 9.
83. Cairns 1996, 9–10; Fisher 1992, 114.

{Ορ.} καὶ πῶς; ἔχει γὰρ βαρβάρους ὀπάονας.
{Πυ.} τίνας; Φρυγῶν γὰρ οὐδέν᾽ ἂν τρέσαιμ᾽ ἐγώ.
{Ορ.} οἵους ἐνόπτρων καὶ μύρων ἐπιστάτας.
{Πυ.} τρυφὰς γὰρ ἥκει δεῦρ᾽ ἔχουσα Τρωϊκάς;
{Ορ.} ὡς Ἑλλὰς αὐτῇ σμικρὸν οἰκητήριον.
{Πυ.} οὐδὲν τὸ δοῦλον πρὸς τὸ μὴ δοῦλον γένος

[{OR.} "How then? For she has barbarian attendants."
{PY.} "Who? I don't run from Phrygians."
{OR.} "The kind that are stewards of mirrors and perfumes."
{PY.} "Did she bring those Trojan *truphai* here?"
{OR.} "Since Hellas is for her a small house."
{PY.} "The race that slaves is nothing to the one that doesn't."]
(Eur., *Or.* 1110–15)

While it is possible that the phrase τρυφὰς Τρωϊκάς indicates merely the mirrors and perfumes of 1112, it is better to understand also a reference to the Phrygian servants who attend Helen with these items. Such an interpretation provides an easy logical progression in lines 1113–15: "Helen brought servants such as those?" "Greece itself provides her with too small a household." "Anyway, slaves are nothing to free men." If, on the other hand, we take τρυφὰς to refer only to the objects Helen brought from Troy, we are left with a curious aside on the extent of Helen's cosmetic apparatus in the midst of a discussion of her entourage as an obstacle to murder.

To summarize the evidence so far: τρυφή does not indicate a softness that is effeminate or delicate in the sense that it is easily imposed on. It is not weak or yielding. Neither is it a wantonness and lack of self-control. Rather, if it is softness, it is the softness of one who need not toil, languishing in the confident belief that one's needs and desires will be met. It is a softness that willfully controls others.

From this evidence one can see that luxury as a moral concept in the Archaic and early Classical periods is both complex and nuanced. Recognizing this fact is important for putting on a secure foundation any investigation of the historiographical use of the idea of pernicious luxury. It is assumed that Herodotus, for example, in making luxury a force of historical causation, could refer indirectly and ironically to the idea because it was a widely held belief. We have shown that any scholar promoting this interpretation must confront the general evidence with much more care and precision than has been the custom. The evidence of Thucydides is a case in point, for although this historian presents a view of luxury that is markedly different from that claimed for Herodotus, this material is largely ignored in evaluations of the putatively self-evident stand of the earlier historian.[84]

In an important passage, Thucydides outlines three stages of development in the Greek lifestyle:

(1) πᾶσα γὰρ ἡ Ἑλλὰς ἐσιδηροφόρει . . . (3) ἐν τοῖς πρῶτοι δὲ Ἀθηναῖοι τόν τε σίδηρον κατέθεντο καὶ ἀνειμένη τῇ διαίτῃ ἐς τὸ τρυφερώτερον μετέστησαν. καὶ οἱ πρεσβύτεροι αὐτοῖς τῶν εὐδαιμόνων διὰ τὸ ἁβροδίαιτον οὐ πολὺς χρόνος ἐπειδὴ χιτῶνάς τε λινοῦς ἐπαύσαντο φοροῦντες καὶ χρυσῶν τεττίγων ἐνέρσει κρωβύλον ἀναδούμενοι τῶν ἐν τῇ κεφαλῇ τριχῶν . . . (4) μετρίᾳ δ᾽ αὖ ἐσθῆτι καὶ ἐς τὸν νῦν τρόπον πρῶτοι Λακεδαιμόνιοι ἐχρήσαντο καὶ ἐς τὰ ἄλλα πρὸς τοὺς πολλοὺς οἱ τὰ μείζω κεκτημένοι ἰσοδίαιτοι μάλιστα κατέστησαν.

[All of Hellas used to carry swords. . . . Among them, the Athenians were the first to put away the sword and, with lifestyle relaxed, change to a greater degree of *truphē*. And the wealthy old men among them not long ago stopped wearing, owing to their *habros* way of life, linen chitons and binding up their hair in a knot using a clasp made of golden grasshoppers. . . . The Lacedaemonians were the first to dress in the moderate and modern fashion, and in other ways those who were rich tried especially to adopt the same lifestyle as the masses.] (Thuc. 1.6.1–4)

Here custom moves from the rugged to the more luxurious, and then to a place in between the two. Our examination of ἁβροσύνη and τρυφή allows us to see that we need not assume a negative characterization of the Athenian lifestyle:

---

84. Kallet-Marx (1993, e.g., 16) argues that Thucydides separates the concept of wealth from any moral considerations, and that this separation is a revolutionary change from the authors that preceded him. With respect to the Funeral Oration particularly, she says (113), "Nowhere in Thucydides' work, least of all here, is there any sense of uneasiness about wealth, the kind of disquiet that pervades, among numerous other works, Herodotus' *History*." Yet, in the second half of Thucydides' work, she argues, he is actively devaluing display, private expenditure, and even public monuments (Kallet 2001, 292). Of course, there is a significant difference between wealth and luxury, but her argument is that money is neutral when used for the benefit of the city, such as funding the Athenian naval war machine, and bad when used out of personal greed and gain.

the generations favoring τὸ ἁβροδίαιτον included the victors of Marathon.[85] No idea of moral "weakening" or "softening" need be present.[86]

Moreover, a positive view of luxury is clearly on display in the Funeral Oration; Pericles reflects upon the easy living of the Athenians and finds in it a source of their strength.

(2.38.1) καὶ μὴν καὶ τῶν πόνων πλείστας ἀναπαύλας τῇ γνώμῃ ἐπορισάμεθα, . . . νομίζοντες, ἰδίαις δὲ κατασκευαῖς εὐπρεπέσιν, ὧν καθ᾽ ἡμέραν ἡ τέρψις τὸ λυπηρὸν ἐκπλήσσει. (2) ἐπεσέρχεται δὲ διὰ μέγεθος τῆς πόλεως ἐκ πάσης γῆς τὰ πάντα, καὶ ξυμβαίνει ἡμῖν μηδὲν οἰκειοτέρᾳ τῇ ἀπολαύσει τὰ αὐτοῦ ἀγαθὰ γιγνόμενα καρποῦσθαι ἢ καὶ τὰ τῶν ἄλλων ἀνθρώπων. (39.1) . . . καὶ ἐν ταῖς παιδείαις οἱ μὲν ἐπιπόνῳ ἀσκήσει εὐθὺς νέοι ὄντες τὸ ἀνδρεῖον μετέρχονται, ἡμεῖς δὲ ἀνειμένως διαιτώμενοι οὐδὲν ἧσσον ἐπὶ τοὺς ἰσοπαλεῖς κινδύνους χωροῦμεν. . . .

(4) καίτοι εἰ ῥᾳθυμίᾳ μᾶλλον ἢ πόνων μελέτῃ καὶ μὴ μετὰ νόμων τὸ πλέον ἢ τρόπων ἀνδρείας ἐθέλομεν κινδυνεύειν, περιγίγνεται ἡμῖν τοῖς τε μέλλουσιν ἀλγεινοῖς μὴ προκάμνειν, καὶ ἐς αὐτὰ ἐλθοῦσι μὴ ἀτολμοτέρους τῶν αἰεὶ μοχθούντων φαίνεσθαι.

(40.3) . . . κράτιστοι δ᾽ ἂν τὴν ψυχὴν δικαίως κριθεῖεν οἱ τά τε δεινὰ καὶ ἡδέα σαφέστατα γιγνώσκοντες καὶ διὰ ταῦτα μὴ ἀποτρεπόμενοι ἐκ τῶν κινδύνων. . . .

(42.4) τῶνδε δὲ οὔτε πλούτου τις τὴν ἔτι ἀπόλαυσιν προτιμήσας ἐμαλακίσθη . . .

[(2.38.1) In addition we have supplied our minds with a great number of respites from labors, . . . accustomed also to fine personal accoutrements; every day the pleasure from these things drives away our sorrow. (2) Because of the magnitude of our city, all things come in from the whole world, and we enjoy the goods of other people with no less a pleasure of ownership than the goods produced here. (39.1) . . . And as for systems of education, those men already from boyhood go after manliness with a mode of life full of toil, but we, living in a more relaxed fashion, no less approach equal dangers.

---

85. Gomme (ad loc.) cites Ar., *Eq.* 1321–34, where Demos enters the stage dressed as in the age of Aristides and Miltiades: τεττιγοφόρος, τἀρχαίῳ σχήματι λαμπρός ("wearing the cicada, splendid in the old style," 1331); the chorus greets him with praise: τῆς γὰρ πόλεως ἄξια πράττεις καὶ τοῦ 'ν Μαραθῶνι τροπαίου ("your good fortune is worthy of the city and the victory at Marathon," 1334). The τέττιγες are similarly a distinguishing feature of the Μαραθωνομάχαι at Ar., *Nub.* 984–86.

86. For ἐς τὸ τρυφερώτερον μετέστησαν, Classen and Steup (1919, 22–23) suggest "schlugen sie in grössere Weichlichkeit um."

(4) . . . If we are willing to face dangers with an easy mind rather than with practice of hardships, and with bravery more from our characters than our customs, we have the added benefit of not wearying ourselves ahead of time with the coming toils, but of appearing just as spirited as the toilers, when these things really do occur.

(40.3) . . . They would justly be judged the mightiest of spirit who, knowing most clearly both difficulties and pleasures, were not for this reason turned away from dangers. . . .

(42.4) And none of these [war dead], preferring the continuing enjoyment of riches, grew soft.] (Thuc. 2.38.1–42.4)

It is worth quoting from the passage at such length to draw attention to the many expressions used by Thucydides that would later become fixtures in discussions of luxury and decadence: ἀπόλαυσις, καρπόω, ἀνειμένως διαιτάομαι, ῥᾳθυμία, and μαλακίζομαι, and likewise the contrasting terms such as πόνοι, ἀσκήσις, τὸ ἀνδρεῖον, μελέτη, etc. Since behind Pericles' defense of Athenian luxury may be attacks from those who admired Spartan austerity and connected the severe lifestyle with their military prowess, this passage may be evidence for a fifth-century claim that luxury and τὸ ἀνδρεῖον were not well matched.[87] It is definitely evidence for an interpretation according to which the luxuries provided by the city's wealth held advantages, even for a people at war.[88]

The Moral Implications of Τρυφή

pattern of thought

Thus, from the Archaic period through the fifth century there is abundant evidence on the moral valuation of luxury that does not fit with the schema whereby it leads to hubris and then to destruction, an evolution of thought usually attributed to that period by modern scholars. In many passages, ἁβρός and cognates clearly have positive associations, while τρυφή is far from indicating a quality that is passive, weak or lacking self-control. On the other hand, good evidence for the idea that an opulent lifestyle might harm the character is

---

87. That this material is in some sense a "defense of luxury" seems apparent from, among other things, the connection that the phrase ἡμεῖς . . . ἀνειμένως διαιτώμενοι establishes with Thuc. 1.6.3: ἀνειμένῃ τῇ διαίτῃ ἐς τὸ τρυφερώτερον μετέστησαν.

88. In their important examinations of ancient criticism of luxury, both Bernhardt (2003, 138–40) and Kurke (1992) recognize this passage as a positive evaluation of it. Kurke notes that Pericles' sentiments represent "a strong democratic appropriation of aristocratic ἁβροσύνη" (106 n. 60).

much harder to come by.[89] Two recent studies, by Kurke (1992) and Bernhardt (2003) consider the broad context of the Greek attitude toward luxury. Both these authors accept the view that, whatever may have been its positive connotations earlier, by Herodotus's day luxury had "become a dirty word."[90] *Argumenti causa* we will assume that the passages cited in these works represent the best available evidence for the idea of pernicious luxury, and we will address them accordingly.

A fragment of Xenophanes, preserved by Athenaeus, is taken to be the clearest evidence of an Archaic provenance for the belief that excessive luxury can set in motion a process that may bring the destruction of cities:

ἁβροσύνας δὲ μαθόντες ἀνωφελέας παρὰ Λυδῶν
    ὄφρα τυραννίης ἦσαν ἄνευ στυγερῆς,
ἤεσαν εἰς ἀγορὴν παναλουργέα φάρε᾽ ἔχοντες,
    οὐ μείους ὥσπερ χείλιοι ὡς ἐπίπαν,
αὐχαλέοι, χαίτῃσιν †ἀγαλλόμεν† εὐπρεπέεσσιν,
    ἀσκητοῖς ὀδμὴν χρίμασι δευόμενοι.

[Having learned useless *habrosunai* from the Lydians, while they were without hateful tyranny, they proceeded into the marketplace, no less than a thousand in number all told, wearing purple all over, boastful, proud of their comely locks, anointed with unguents of rich perfume.] (Xenophanes, frag. 3 Diehl = Athen. 12.526a–b)

While Xenophanes is undoubtably disparaging of ἁβροσύνας, since they are "useless," and those who parade in them are "boastful," these six verses are not explicit about any ill effects that may be associated with luxury.[91] To be sure, Athenaeus reports that the Colophonians became involved in tyranny and sta-

---

89. Those scholars most insistent on the importance of this concept in Herodotus produce practically no relevant material drawn from outside the *Histories*. See Chapter 2 for a thorough discussion of the Herodotean evidence.

90. Kurke 1992, 98. Both these studies are carefully researched, well argued, and insightfully nuanced. In their reconstructions of the development of the negative moral value of luxury, they differ mainly in that Bernhardt identifies the existence of an Archaic strain of *Luxuskritik* while Kurke argues (correctly, we think) that such an interpretation is based, for the most part, on an anachronistic reading of fragmentary evidence.

91. Bowra (1970, 112–16) interprets these lines as expressing conspicuous consumption by the upper class, an interpretation that will take on greater weight in light of our redefinition of τρύφη; cf. Bowra 1941. For purple as a status symbol, see Reinhold 1970.

sis, and so their city was destroyed, all due to their luxury. However, this material, added in prose in the introduction to this quote, is likely to be an addition by Athenaeus himself.[92] There is no reason to presume that the sentiment derives from Xenophanes (or Phylarchus, who is also cited by name as a source).[93]

The poet Semonides also speaks unfavorably of luxury. Specifically, in his seventh-century BCE *Catalog of Women*, he criticizes the mare as ἁβρή, since she refuses to help with the household chores, but preens and primps all day:

καλὸν μὲν ὢν θέημα τοιαύτη γυνὴ
ἄλλοισι, τῷ δ᾽ ἔχοντι γίνεται κακόν,
ἢν μή τις ἢ τύραννος ἢ σκηπτοῦχος ᾖ,
ὅστις τοιούτοις θυμὸν ἀγλαΐζεται.

[Such a woman is a beautiful sight for others, but an evil for the one who has her, unless he is some tyrant or one who bears a scepter, who delights his spirit in such things.] (Semonides, frag. 7.67–70 West)

Here ἁβροσύνη eats up the resources of a household. Luxury is not in itself an evil, but becomes so for a man of insufficient means.

This exhausts the material from before the fifth century. In a careful discussion of the term, Kurke notes that, besides Xenophanes and Semonides, "the preserved attestations from seventh- and sixth-century poets are *uniformly* positive in their valuations of ἁβροσύνη."[94] The only other evidence offered by Bernhardt is the legend about Sybaris,[95] which discussion we will confront in Chapter 4.

The Persian Wars, it is claimed, formed a watershed in the valuation of luxury. The Greeks turned away from the "effeminizing Eastern luxury" which they associated with the defeated enemy.[96] However, good fifth-century evi-

---

92. He uses the telltale phrase, εἰς τρυφὴν ἐξώκειλαν ("shipwrecking on *truphē*). We will demonstrate in Chapter 3 that this is a very strong indication of Athenaean origin.

93. Kurke (1992, 101), against Nagy (1990), is careful to distinguish between Xenophanes' words and the supplements of Phylarchus and Theopompus. Gorman and Gorman (2007) and Chapters 3 and 4 (below) present evidence which indicates that the link between luxury and the downfall of Colophon quite probably does not stem from these Hellenistic historians, but is an addition made by Athenaeus himself. In spite of Kurke's exemplary caution, more recent scholars such as Granger (2007, 425), still maintain that Xenophanes "criticizes his fellow citizens of Colophon for their effeminate practices."

94. Kurke 1992, 96.

95. Bernhardt 2003, 51–67.

96. So Kurke 1992, 102: "the Persian Wars, which make the Greeks antipathetic to Eastern ways. In the wake of this confrontation, the Greeks choose to construct ἁβροσύνη as effeminizing Eastern luxury."

dence for belief in the effeminizing effect of the oriental lifestyle is difficult to come by. Outside of the text of Herodotus, Kurke's best testimony for this view is the Carpet Scene from Aeschylus's *Agamemnon*.[97] There the king reacts brusquely to Clytemnestra's suggestion that he enter his palace on a path of purple cloths:

καὶ τἄλλα μὴ γυναικὸς ἐν τρόποις ἐμὲ
ἅβρυνε, μηδὲ βαρβάρου φωτὸς δίκην
χαμαιπετὲς βόαμα προσχάνῃς ἐμοί

[As for the rest, don't treat me with ἁβροσύνη in the manner of a woman or gape fawning noises at me, like a barbarian.] (Aesch., *Ag.* 918–20)

Kurke maintains that this passage "reveals quite concisely all the associations of Eastern luxury and effeminacy that cluster around ἁβρός."[98] But it is important to look more closely at just what these associations are. Agamemnon's subsequent words make clear that he is not concerned that indulgence in ἁβροσύνη may bring a loosening of his moral fiber. If he does not want to be treated like a woman or a barbarian, it is not because such behavior is a sign of weakness or indolence:

μηδ᾽ εἵμασι στρώσασ᾽ ἐπίφθονον πόρον
τίθει· θεούς τοι τοῖσδε τιμαλφεῖν χρεών·
ἐν ποικίλοις δὲ θνητὸν ὄντα κάλλεσιν
βαίνειν ἐμοὶ μὲν οὐδαμῶς ἄνευ φόβου.
λέγω κατ᾽ ἄνδρα, μὴ θεόν, σέβειν ἐμέ.
. . . .

       καὶ τὸ μὴ κακῶς φρονεῖν
θεοῦ μέγιστον δῶρον. ὀλβίσαι δὲ χρὴ
βίον τελευτήσαντ᾽ ἐν εὐεστοῖ φίλῃ.

97. As evidence for the Greek reaction against luxury, Kurke also notes that ἁβρ- words appear five times in the *Persae*, four times applied to the Persians or their women. Apparently, her implication is that this context is a sign of the devaluation of luxury. Bernhardt (2003, 127 with n. 38) interprets this evidence differently: "Die Hervorhebung von Reichtum und Luxus der Perser dient im wesentlichen dazu, den Zuschauern die Macht des Grosskönigs vor Augen zu führen, um das Unglück um so grösser in Erscheinung treten zu lassen."
98. Kurke 1992, 102.

[Don't make my path the object of envy by strewing it with carpets. With these it is proper to honor the gods; I think that one who is mortal should not walk on embroidered fineries without fear. I mean you to honor me as a man, not a god. . . . The greatest gift of god is not to lose one's head. To deem a life happy, it is necessary that it end in prosperity.] (Aesch., *Ag.* 921–25, 927–29)

The pattern of thought is a familiar one. In deprecating excessive luxury, Agamemnon seeks to ward off the envy of the gods. Especially at a time of great success and good fortune, it is necessary to remember, with Pindar, that ἄλλοτε δ' ἀλλοῖαι πνοαί / ὑψιπετᾶν ἀνέμων. ὄλβος οὐκ ἐς μακρὸν ἀνδρῶν ἔρχεται / σάος ("the currents of the winds from on high are changeable; the prosperity of men does not come securely or for long." Pind., *Pyth.* 3.104–6).[99] The instance of luxury here can be taken as simply a manifestation—albeit extreme—of ὄλβος: Agamemnon fears not that by this act he will become or appear soft, but that the gods will see him as overweening and will send him misfortune.[100] Consequently, this passage is not solid evidence that luxury could be seen as effeminizing, in the sense of making one passive and unwarlike.[101]

Other putative evidence that eastern barbarians, and the Persians in particular, were enfeebled by luxury comes later, from the fourth century. In the

99. In this poem, the changing winds of fortune may serve as a warning to act appropriately in using *habros* riches (πλοῦτον ἁβρόν, *Pyth.* 3.110). In a similar fashion, at *Pyth.* 8.89–96, Pindar follows mention of the lofty heights one can reach (ἁβρότατος ἔπι μεγάλας, 89) with a reminder that such a state will be short-lived: ἐν δ' ὀλίγῳ βροτῶν / τὸ τερπνὸν αὔξεται· οὕτω δὲ καὶ πίτνει χαμαί ("the delight of mortals grows in a brief time, and thus too it falls to the ground," 92–93). *Pythian* 11 provides a particularly apt parallel. Turning from the failings of Clytemnestra, Pindar discusses the downfall of Agamemnon: ἴσχει τε γὰρ ὄλβος οὐ μείονα φθόνον·/ . . . θάνεν μὲν αὐτὸς ἥρως Ἀτρεΐδας / . . . μάντιν τ' ὄλεσσε κόραν, ἐπεὶ ἀμφ' Ἑλένᾳ πυρωθέντας / Τρώων ἔλυσε δόμους ἁβρότατος ("For prosperity too holds no less envy. . . . The hero, son of Atreus, himself died . . . and he destroyed the girl-prophet when, for Helen's sake, he robbed the burning homes of the Trojans of *habrotēs.*" Pind., *Pyth.* 11.29–34). Since luxury and prosperity may lead to envy (whether human or divine is not made quite clear), Pindar ends the ode by expressing a preference for a more moderate and more fortunate level of ὄλβος: τῶν γὰρ ἀνὰ πόλιν εὑρίσκων τὰ μέσα μακροτέρῳ {σὺν} ὄλβῳ τεθαλότα, μέμφομ' αἶσαν τυραννίδων· ("For discovering that in a city the things in the middle bloom with a longer prosperity, I despise the lot of tyrannies," Pind., *Pyth.* 11.52–53). Clearly, in these passages ἁβρότης is perilous and may be associated with moral transgression, but there is no sign of softness or effeminacy.

100. Fraenkel ([1950] 1962, ad loc.) follows Wilamowitz in deleting line 925 "because it destroys the clear structure of the thought." We would argue that the line is crucial for understanding the meaning of the scene: Agamemnon is unwilling to tempt the envy of the gods.

101. We leave open the question of exactly what Aeschylus meant with the words γυναικὸς ἐν τρόποις and βαρβάρου φωτὸς δίκην. A few lines after Agamemnon's refusal, he notes that, given the same circumstances, Priam would have walked on the cloths. In this case, it seems that a barbarian does not recognize human limits and the danger of divine jealousy. Is it perhaps Aeschylus's implication that women suffer from the same lack of insight?

Philippus, Isocrates calls the Persians μαλακοὺς . . . καὶ πολέμων ἀπείρους καὶ διεφθαρμένους ὑπὸ τῆς τρυφῆς ("soft and inexperienced in wars and corrupted by *truphē*," 5.124). While this passage seems at first glance to establish that τρυφή was a cause of weakness, further consideration indicates that being "corrupted by *truphē*" is not necessarily a synonym for μαλακοὺς: τρυφή might make one incapable in war in quite another way.

Three decades before the *Philippus*, Isocrates had expressed similar sentiments in the *Panegyricus*:

> (151) οἱ δ᾽ ἐν ταῖς μεγίσταις δόξαις ὄντες αὐτῶν ὁμαλῶς μὲν οὐδὲ κοινῶς οὐδὲ πολιτικῶς οὐδεπώποτ᾽ ἐβίωσαν, ἅπαντα δὲ τὸν χρόνον διάγουσιν εἰς μὲν τοὺς ὑβρίζοντες, τοῖς δὲ δουλεύοντες, ὡσανεὶ μάλιστα τὰς φύσεις διαφθαρμένοι, καὶ τὰ μὲν σώματα διὰ τοὺς πλούτους τρυφῶντες, τὰς δὲ ψυχὰς διὰ τὰς μοναρχίας ταπεινὰς καὶ περιδεεῖς ἔχοντες. . . . (152) τοιγαροῦν οἱ καταβαίνοντες αὐτῶν ἐπὶ θάλατταν, οὓς καλοῦσιν σατράπας, οὐ καταισχύνουσιν τὴν ἐκεῖ παίδευσιν, ἀλλ᾽ ἐν τοῖς ἤθεσι τοῖς αὐτοῖς διαμένουσιν, πρὸς μὲν τοὺς φίλους ἀπίστως, πρὸς δὲ τοὺς ἐχθροὺς ἀνάνδρως ἔχοντες, καὶ τὰ μὲν ταπεινῶς, τὰ δ᾽ ὑπερηφάνως ζῶντες, τῶν μὲν συμμάχων καταφρονοῦντες, τοὺς δὲ πολεμίους θεραπεύοντες.

> [(151) Those among them in highest repute have never lived as equals or as respectful members of a community or with the rights of citizens, but all the time they carry on hubristically toward some and in slavery toward others, practically destroying their nature in this way, having *truphē* with respect to their bodies because of their riches, but with souls that are abject and timid because of the monarchy. . . . (152) For example, those who come down to the sea, whom they call satraps, do not put to shame the education they received there, but they remain in the same customs, being untrustworthy to their friends, but unmanly to their enemies, and living now abjectly, now haughtily, now scorning their allies, now attending upon their enemies.] (Isoc. 4.151–52)

The passage is worth quoting in order to draw attention to the structure of the thought. The self-destructive behavior of the Persians is analyzed dichotomously: they are at one and the same time domineering and slavish. Including the examples Isocrates gives in section 153 and taking into account chiastic arrangement, the following series of contrasts can be tabulated:

TABLE 1

εἰς μὲν τοὺς ὑβρίζοντες behaving hubristically	τοῖς δὲ δουλεύοντες behaving slavishly
τὰ μὲν σώματα τρυφῶντες having *truphē* toward their bodies	τὰς δὲ ψυχὰς ταπεινὰς καὶ περιδεεῖς ἔχοντες with souls that are abject and timid
πρὸς μὲν τοὺς φίλους ἀπίστως untrustworthy to their friends	πρὸς δὲ τοὺς ἐχθροὺς ἀνάνδρως ἔχοντες unmanly to their enemies
τὰ δ᾽ ὑπερηφάνως ζῶντες living haughtily	καὶ τὰ μὲν ταπεινῶς living submissively
τῶν μὲν συμμάχων καταφρονοῦντες scorning their allies	τοὺς δὲ πολεμίους θεραπεύοντες attending upon their enemies
τοὺς δ᾽ τὸν μισθὸν ἀπεστέρησαν they robbed them of their pay	τὴν μέν . . . στρατιὰν διέθρεψαν they sustained the army
τοὺς δὲ ὕβριζον they outraged some	καὶ τοῖς μὲν ἑκατὸν τάλαντα διένειμαν they distributed 100 talents to others

For our purposes, it is enough to notice that Isocrates put τρυφή in the same category as hubris. Both involve imposition on other, weaker members of society. Given the carefully constructed contrast and parallelism, it becomes apparent that it would be wrong to translate τὰ σώματα τρυφῶντες as something like "becoming soft in their bodies." Instead, it seems to mean that the Persians were demanding that others see to the concerns of their bodies. When transferred to the field of war, the Persians' education in self-indulgence—whether hubris or bodily τρυφή—is manifested in a demeanor that is ἀπίστως and ὑπερηφάνως: allies are treated as if they were servants.[102] Such an attitude might justify the *Philippus's* description, "ignorant in war" (πολέμων ἀπείρους), but does not imply cowardice or effeminacy. In fact, the *Panegyricus* derives both of these qualities (τὰς ψυχὰς περιδεεῖς ἔχοντες. . . . ἀνάνδρως ἔχοντες) from the Persian constitution. The Persians' μαλακία is caused by living under a monarchical government rather than by lifestyle choices and luxury.[103] Thus, if the *Panegyricus* casts any illumination on Isocrates' description of Persian

---

102. Isocrates illustrates the contempt that the satraps show for the friends of the Persians (τῶν μὲν συμμάχων καταφρονοῦντες) with two specific cases: they expected to be served without offering reciprocal consideration for their attendants (τὸν μισθὸν ἀπεστέρησαν), an attitude we find typical of those τρυφῶντες. Also, they acted with more violence and hubris toward their own helpers than to enemy prisoners of war.

103. Bernhardt (2003, 130) also uses the more detailed *Panegyricus* to explicate the μαλακοὺς εἶναι καὶ πολέμων ἀπείρους καὶ διεφθαρμένους ὑπὸ τῆς τρυφῆς of the *Philippus*. However, while he first recognizes the twofold nature of Isocrates' analysis in the *Panegyricus* ("sowohl in der τρυφή als auch in der monarchischen Staatsform"), he later collapses the distinction between self-assertion and servility and does not consider the possibility of similar nuance in the tripartite expression in the *Philippus*.

degeneracy in the *Philippus* (5.124), it highlights the difference between two components of their military ineffectiveness: μαλακία and τρυφή are quite distinct, and neither is seen as the cause of the other.

The educational ramifications of τρυφή are another aspect that is uppermost in Isocrates' thought when he specifies prerequisites for successful instruction:

τοὺς μὲν γὰρ ἰδιώτας ἐστὶ πολλὰ τὰ παιδεύοντα, μάλιστα μὲν τὸ μὴ τρυφᾶν, ἀλλ᾽ ἀναγκάζεσθαι περὶ τοῦ βίου καθ᾽ ἑκάστην βουλεύεσθαι τὴν ἡμέραν,

[Many things help the education of private citizens, especially not having *truphē*, but being under the necessity of taking thought every day for one's livelihood.] (Isoc. 2.2).

Having one's creature comforts satisfied by others would make the effort required for a serious education seem hardly worthwhile, but Isocrates is also thinking of another effect of luxury. The τρυφῶντες grow accustomed to hearing their every pronouncement meet with approval. Their ideas are not gainsaid, nor is their behavior criticized:

τοῖς δὲ τυράννοις οὐδὲν ὑπάρχει τοιοῦτον, ἀλλ᾽ οὓς ἔδει παιδεύεσθαι μᾶλλον τῶν ἄλλων . . . ἀνουθέτητοι διατελοῦσιν·

[No such circumstances exist for rulers, but they, who ought rather to be educated by others, live on unadmonished.] (Isoc. 2.4).

Plato, too, considers τρυφή to be a key factor in the decadence of the Persian rulers,[104] but, like Isocrates, Plato sees Persian luxury primarily in term of παίδευσις. Cyrus the Great, who was himself poorly educated according to the *Laws*, neglected the training of his children. Instead, he gave this task over to the women and eunuchs of the household:

κωλύουσαι δὲ ὡς οὖσιν ἱκανῶς εὐδαίμοσιν μήτε αὐτοῖς ἐναντιοῦσθαι μηδένα εἰς μηδέν, ἐπαινεῖν τε ἀναγκάζουσαι πάντας τὸ λεγόμενον ἢ πραττόμενον ὑπ᾽ αὐτῶν, ἔθρεψαν τοιούτους τινάς.

---

104. Cf. Bernhardt 2003, 128–29.

[Considering them to be quite perfect, they forbade anyone to contradict them in any way and compelled everyone to applaud whatever they said or did: thus they raised such children.] (Plato, *Leg.* 3.694d)

As a result of this "ruined education" (διεφθαρμένην παιδείαν, 3.694a), the sons of Cyrus were incapable of rule when they inherited the kingdom. Instead, τρυφῆς μεστοὶ καὶ ἀνεπιπληξίας ("full of *truphē* [presumption] and a sense of impunity," 3.695b), they quarreled; Cambyses killed his brother, and then ran mad with drink and was overthrown. The cycle of decadence repeated itself in the persons of Darius and Xerxes. In this passage, we once again find that τρυφή, although it may be a product of a "feminine upbringing" (τροφὴν γυναικείαν, 3.694d-e), does not in itself indicate a kind of soft or unwarlike spirit.[105] It is the expectation of having one's own way, which in Cambyses manifested itself in his inability to tolerate an equal (τῷ ἴσῳ ἀγανακτῶν, 3.695b).[106] Τρυφή here leads to willful murder, not weakness.

Xenophon, for whom Cyrus the Great was a model of virtue, is deeply interested in the idea of Persian decadence. In his opinion, the feeble state of the Persian military in his own day was the result of severe moral decay which began after Cyrus's death (*Cyr.* 8.8.2). This decline was multifaceted: impiety toward the gods—oath-breaking is the chief example—has lost them the trust of allies (*Cyr.* 8.8.3-4); dishonest financial impositions have led the affluent to avoid military service (*Cyr.* 8.8.6); distaste for physical exercise and self-restraint and increased indulgence in luxury brought about a devaluation of military training and a corresponding lack of capable soldiers (8.8.8-26).

In order to grasp clearly Xenophon's understanding of this process of demoralization, it is necessary to note that the various aspects of Persian decline that he cites are parallel to each other. No aspect is said to be more basic than the others; no aspect is referred to as the possible cause of any other.[107] In par-

---

105. Plato does note that, because their education was at the hands of women and eunuchs, the princes did not learn their father's hard skills, such as camping out and campaigning (Plato, *Leg.* 3.695a). Thus, lack of martial experience may be the result of the same education that also produces τρυφή; this fact does not make the latter a cause of the former. Cf. Xen., *Cyr.* 8.8.15-16.

106. Cambyses in turn was despised not for weakness or effeminacy, but because of his stupidity (μωρία, Plato, *Leg.* 3.695b).

107. When Xenophon summarizes his argument in the final chapter of this section, he connects luxury most closely with military weakness. He refers to his discussion of luxury as a proof that the Persians were ἀνανδροτέρους τὰ εἰς τὸν πόλεμον νῦν ἢ πρόσθεν ("more unmanly in war now than before," Xen., *Cyr.* 8.8.27). However, this passage downplays connections between impiety and dishonesty and military impotence that are made explicit in earlier sections, for example: τοιγαροῦν ὅστις ἂν πολεμῇ αὐτοῖς, πᾶσιν ἔξεστιν ἐν τῇ χώρᾳ αὐτῶν ἀναστρέφεσθαι ἄνευ μάχης ὅπως ἂν βούλωνται διὰ

ticular, Xenophon does not see luxury as setting in motion the degeneration of which he complains so strongly. Even more significantly, although Xenophon recognizes that, because of luxury, the contemporary Persians honored bakers, valets, and bath attendants above cavalrymen and charioteers, he does not see this effect as natural or necessary:

ἀλλὰ μὴν καὶ θρυπτικώτεροι πολὺ νῦν ἢ ἐπὶ Κύρου εἰσί. τότε μὲν γὰρ ἔτι τῇ ἐκ Περσῶν παιδείᾳ καὶ ἐγκρατείᾳ ἐχρῶντο, τῇ δὲ Μήδων στολῇ καὶ ἁβρότητι· νῦν δὲ τὴν μὲν ἐκ Περσῶν καρτερίαν περιορῶσιν ἀποσβεννυμένην, τὴν δὲ τῶν Μήδων μαλακίαν διασῴζονται.

[But they are also much more given to *truphē* now than in Cyrus's time. For at that time they still used the training and self-control that came from the Persians, though the garb and affectedness of the Medes. Now, however, allowing the Persian trait of endurance to be extinguished, they preserve the softness of the Medes.] (Xen., *Cyr.* 8.8.15)

Early generations of Persians were able to enjoy a lifestyle of ἁβρότης without giving up their dedication to horseback riding and self-abnegation while in the field.[108]

Unmistakably, then, Xenophon's view of the pernicious workings of luxury is strikingly different than the picture drawn by scholars. While the *Cyropaedia* offers perhaps the clearest evidence in a Classical text for the belief that indulgence in luxury was associated with the lapse of a community into political and martial weakness, it is equally clear that the process of debilitation is contin-

---

τὴν ἐκείνων περὶ μὲν θεοὺς ἀσέβειαν, περὶ δὲ ἀνθρώπους ἀδικίαν ("Therefore it is possible for whoever makes war against them to march about anywhere at all in their country without a battle because of their impiety toward the gods and injustice toward men." Xen., *Cyr.* 8.8.7). And in any case, even in his final recapitulation, there is no indication that Xenophon looks at luxury as more of a cause than a symptom of Persian decline.

108. Xenophon is not entirely consistent in his view of the temporal framework of the Persian moral collapse. Beginning his discussion of this topic, he notes that "when Cyrus died, all things took a turn for the worse" (ἐπεὶ μέντοι Κῦρος ἐτελεύτησεν . . . πάντα δ᾽ ἐπὶ τὸ χεῖρον ἐτρέποντο, Xen., *Cyr.* 8.8.2). There is no doubt, then, that the reign of Cyrus represented a pristine time before the decline. On the other hand, it is unclear whether Xenophon sees the fall as abrupt or gradual. At 8.8.2, he speaks of the righteousness of the "king and his underlings in earlier days" (πρότερον μὲν βασιλεὺς καὶ οἱ ὑπ᾽ αὐτῷ), and the reference seems to be a general one, not limited to Cyrus himself. Similarly, at 8.8.12, we read that the salubrious exercise of hunting was maintained until it was dropped by King Artaxerxes and his followers. In the main, Xenophon gives only the unspecified πρότερον to contrast with an almost equally vague νῦν. It is therefore possible that Xenophon thought that Persian luxury and self-control coexisted for a number of generations.

gent: at one time the Persians were able to be both luxurious and warlike. Then, for some reason, they were not. For Xenophon, luxury did not *in and of itself* produce Persian μαλακία.[109]

Although it concerns the fall of the Medes rather than the Persians, a passage of Aristotle's *Politics* is apt here, because it too presents τρυφή as having a role in historical events, but only in a contingent and secondary fashion. Relating how governments may fall through contempt, he adduces the example of the overthrow of Astyages by Cyrus:

ὡς δυνάμενοι γὰρ καὶ καταφρονοῦντες τοῦ κινδύνου διὰ τὴν δύναμιν ἐπιχειροῦσι ῥᾳδίως, ὥσπερ οἱ στρατηγοῦντες τοῖς μονάρχοις, οἷον Κῦρος Ἀστυάγει καὶ τοῦ βίου καταφρονῶν καὶ τῆς δυνάμεως διὰ τὸ τὴν μὲν δύναμιν ἐξηργηκέναι αὐτὸν δὲ τρυφᾶν.

[As those having power and, because of that power, scorning danger readily make the attempt [i.e., at a coup], like generals against a monarch: for example, Cyrus against Astyages, despising both his life and his power, because his power was neglected and he himself practiced *truphē*.] (Arist., *Pol.* 1312a9–14)

The chief reason given for Cyrus's revolt against his master is that the Persian's position as commander put greater power in his hands than Astyages had at his disposal. It is noteworthy that, to the extent that Aristotle is outlining a general force of historical causation, this principle is the contempt of greater power for lesser; the presence of τρυφή has an ad hoc importance limited here to the case of Cyrus and Astyages. Of course, it is possible to see in this passage an implied link between Astyages' τρυφή and the diminution of his power. Perhaps his lifestyle led him to give insufficient attention to military affairs. Such an interpretation may be correct. As we discuss elsewhere, the validity of this reading would not entail a belief that τρυφή naturally, or even generally, had the effect seen in the example of Astyages.

Criticism of the effects of luxury is not limited to what it had done to the barbarians. This idea had a place in Greek civic life. Kurke, for example, claims that in the context of the rise of the democratic trend of ἰσοδίαιτα ("living in

---

109. Bernhardt (2003, 129) seems to attribute to Xenophon the view that luxury, once adopted even in a limited way, eventually increases from its own momentum: "Die Hang zum Luxus habe nach des Kyros Tod überhandgenommen." However, he offers no evidence that Xenophon believed that luxury would more or less inevitably increase of its own weight.

equality," cf. Thuc. 1.6.4), τρυφή "is stigmatized" as "an antidemocratic attitude."[110] Her best example of this phenomenon is Demosthenes' oration *Against Meidias*, where the speaker stresses how Meidias puts his own pleasures above service to the city:

ἐγὼ δ᾽ ὅσα μὲν τῆς ἰδίας τρυφῆς εἵνεκα Μειδίας καὶ περιουσίας κτᾶται, οὐκ οἶδ᾽ ὅ τι τοὺς πολλοὺς ὑμῶν ὠφελεῖ· ἃ δ᾽ ἐπαιρόμενος τούτοις ὑβρίζει, ἐπὶ πολλοὺς καὶ τοὺς τυχόντας ἡμῶν ἀφικνούμενα ὁρῶ. οὐ δεῖ δὴ τὰ τοιαῦθ᾽ ἑκάστοτε τιμᾶν οὐδὲ θαυμάζειν ὑμᾶς, οὐδὲ τὴν φιλοτιμίαν ἐκ τούτων κρίνειν, εἴ τις οἰκοδομεῖ λαμπρῶς ἢ θεραπαίνας κέκτηται πολλὰς ἢ σκεύη καλά.

[For all the things Meidias possesses for the sake of his private *truphē* and abundance, I don't know what good it has done the majority of you. But I see what hubris he commits, carried away by these things; these acts have affected many of us ordinary people. You need not on each occasion give honor to and marvel at such things, nor assume from them public service, if someone builds a splendid house or possesses many servants or fine furniture.] (Dem. 21.159)

It will be sufficient merely to point out that there is no sign of μαλακία; in contrast, τρυφή is closely associated with hubris.[111] More importantly, if we look closely at this passage, we will see that the "stigmatization" of luxury as τρυφή in the eyes of the Athenian democracy was still very much a work in progress in 353 BCE. It is evident that those actions that in Demosthenes' reasoning constitute τρυφή—building a house that overtops its neighbors, driving here and there with fine horses, strolling through the marketplace with three or four servants—were not viewed in the same way by the Athenian public. As a general rule (ἑκάστοτε), the members of Demosthenes' audience seemed to under-

---

110. Kurke 1992, 104–5. Kurke maintains that, in spite of the fact that the antidemocratic view of luxury must be relatively recent, there is "continuity" between fourth-century criticisms of τρυφή and archaic objections to ἀβροσύνη. However, her view of the content of this archaic strand of moralizing rests on an extremely tenuous basis: an interpretation of fragment 3 of Xenophanes and assumptions about the purpose of sixth-century sumptuary legislation.

111. However, we would not say, as does Bernhardt (2003, 146), that Demosthenes depicts τρυφή as the cause of Meidias's hubris. It is true that a causal relationship is indicated by the phrase ἐπαιρόμενος τούτοις ὑβρίζει ("carried away by these things he does acts of violence"), but the scope of τούτοις is unclear. It certainly refers to Meidias's wealth (ὅσα . . . κτᾶται), but only possibly to the manifestations of τρυφή for which that wealth was used. Rather than looking for a causal nexus between τρυφή and hubris, it might be better to see them as two sides of the same coin: both are attitudes or activities in which one's own wishes become paramount and the personal integrity of others is ignored or violated.

stand behavior such as Medias's as honorable and indicative of public spirit (φιλοτιμίαν). Demosthenes must argue that a luxurious lifestyle does not necesssarily imply civic-mindedness.[112] Apparently, the inherent "opposition of public expenditure and private luxuriance" was not always obvious to the Demos itself.[113]

Demosthenes 19.197 offers particular difficulties for the view that τρυφή equals effeminacy, which in turn equals weakness and μαλακία. There he attacks Aeschines who, at a symposium thrown by one of the Thirty Tyrants, joined in mistreating a captive woman, τινὰ Ὀλυνθίαν γυναῖκα, εὐπρεπῆ μέν, ἐλευθέραν δὲ καὶ σώφρονα ("a certain Olynthian woman, pretty, but freeborn and modest," 19.196). In spite of her modesty, Aeschines and his cronies demanded that she recline with them and entertain them, as if she were a common prostitute. When she demurred, Aeschines accused her of behaving with τρυφή, called for a whip, and gave her a beating. The point of Aeschines' alleged remarks is that the woman had put herself in the wrong by preferring her own comfort and modesty to the pleasures of the men: note that Demosthenes calls the same disposition σωφροσύνη. Once again we see that the self-importance denoted by τρυφή also entails a refusal to accommodate. Thus the quality could easily be an offense to others: Aeschines also characterized the Olynthian woman's reticence as "an act of hubris" (ὕβριν τὸ πρᾶγμα). For Demosthenes, as for the others we have examined, τρυφή is primarily an indulgence in one's wishes and an imposition of one's will.

While weakness is not an integral characteristic of one who exhibits τρυφή, in domestic cases, as among the barbarians, τρυφή may induce μαλακία under the right circumstances. In particular, an attitude in which one expects others to further one's comforts is not conducive to discipline. For this reason, τρυφή is especially dangerous to the young, who may be led to neglect the requisite physical and intellectual exercise. In Book 8 of the *Republic*, Plato identifies this

---

112. Demosthenes' very use of the word τρυφή to categorize Meidias's actions is argumentative and serves to move the jurors toward his own point of view: τρυφή is, on our interpretation, an attitude of self-absorption and self-indulgence. In this respect, it is clearly opposed to φιλοτιμία, which seeks honor from public service. If the former is truly a characteristic of Meidias, then the latter is excluded. All the evidence of the Demosthenic corpus is consistent with the interpretation of τρυφή as an attitude: at 8.34 and 9.4, the speaker predicates τρυφᾶν of the Ecclesia itself, insomuch as it expected its leaders to flatter it and pander to its desires. Similarly, a ship's complement is τρυφῶντας because the men receive high wage and easy duties (Dem. 50.35). At Dem. 42.24, the defendant Phaenippus is criticized as "full of such *truphē*" (τοσαύτης οὗτος τρυφῆς ἐστι μεστός) for giving up his warhorse to purchase a chariot so he would never need to walk anywhere.

113. Kurke (1992, 106) attributes the Athenians' positive view of luxury here to "a tendency in the jurors to be overawed by wealth."

process as contributing to the transition from oligarchy to democracy. Focused too narrowly on money-making, the rulers become unfit for military service, and the city's less well-off soon notice and grow contemptuous. The same happens to the rulers' offspring because of τρυφή:

ἆρ᾽ οὐ τρυφῶντας μὲν τοὺς νέους καὶ ἀπόνους καὶ πρὸς τὰ τοῦ σώματος καὶ πρὸς τὰ τῆς ψυχῆς, μαλακοὺς δὲ καρτερεῖν πρὸς ἡδονάς τε καὶ λύπας καὶ ἀργούς;

[And the young, too, given to *truphē* and not toiling at the things of the body or the mind, but soft and lazy at enduring pleasures and pains?] (Plato, *Rep.* 8.556b–c)

This passage is reminiscent of *Leg.* 3.694–95, examined above, where τρυφή is likewise harmful to the sons of the rulers. There, however, lack of discipline in their luxurious upbringing causes the young to turn violently on each other. Comparison of the two passages reveals that μαλακία is seen as only one possible outcome of a life of τρυφή.[114]

In fact, Plato's depiction of τρυφή as a moral quality is ambiguous and perhaps contradictory. In the *Republic*'s discussion of the tripartite soul in Book 9, Plato's view of τρυφή resembles that of Book 8, in that it is closely associated with a weak and unwarlike disposition:

τρυφὴ δὲ καὶ μαλθακία οὐκ ἐπὶ τῇ αὐτοῦ τούτου χαλάσει τε καὶ ἀνέσει ψέγεται, ὅταν ἐν αὐτῷ δειλίαν ἐμποιῇ;

---

114. The same bifurcation in the effects of τρυφή is seen in Aristotle. On the one hand, he goes much further than Plato, actually making τρυφή a kind of μαλακία: ἡ τρυφὴ μαλακία τίς ἐστιν (*Eth. Nic.* 1150b3). By this he means something quite specific: τρυφή is a species of ἀκράτεια ("incontinence"), a character flaw by which people know the better course of action but cannot abide by their judgment. It is essentially weakness. When the better action is enduring pain, the corresponding failure is labeled a μαλακία. Aristotle understands τρυφή as avoidance of pain and offers this example: ὃς ἕλκει τὸ ἱμάτιον, ἵνα μὴ πονήσῃ τὴν ἀπὸ τοῦ αἴρειν λύπην ("Like one who drags his cloak, so that he may not suffer the pain of lifting it," *Eth. Nic.* 1150b3–4). On the other hand, Aristotle elsewhere uses τρυφή in association with the domineering attitude which we have identified. For example: πρὸς δὲ τούτοις οἱ μὲν ἐν ὑπεροχαῖς εὐτυχημάτων ὄντες, ἰσχύος καὶ πλούτου καὶ φίλων καὶ τῶν ἄλλων τῶν τοιούτων, ἄρχεσθαι οὔτε βούλονται οὔτε ἐπίστανται (καὶ τοῦτ᾽ εὐθὺς οἴκοθεν ὑπάρχει παισὶν οὖσιν· διὰ γὰρ τὴν τρυφὴν οὐδ᾽ ἐν τοῖς διδασκαλείοις ἄρχεσθαι σύνηθες αὐτοῖς) ("In addition, those with excessive good fortune, strength and wealth and friends and other such things, do not wish to be ruled and don't know how (and this applies already when they are children at home, since because of *truphē*, they are unaccustomed to be ruled even in the schools)." Arist., *Pol.* 4.1295b13–18).

[Are not *truphē* and softness censured for the slackening and relaxation of this same part, whenever it produces cowardice in it?] (Plato, *Rep.* 9.590b)

The part of the soul in question is the leonine θυμοειδές, the seat of courage and love of victory and honor. The effect of τρυφή is sometimes to loosen its moral fiber to the point of failure and δειλία. This is something like the process of enervation that modern scholarship regularly associates with τρυφή.[115]

Incompatible with *Rep.* 9.590b, on the other hand, is Plato's representation of the effect of τρυφή on morals—this time in the context of the proper rearing of infants—in the *Laws*:

ἡ μὲν τρυφὴ δύσκολα καὶ ἀκράχολα καὶ σφόδρα ἀπὸ σμικρῶν κινούμενα τὰ τῶν νέων ἤθη ἀπεργάζεται.

[*Truphē* makes the characters of the young presumptuous and quick to anger and excessively moved by small things.] (Plato, *Leg.* 7.791d)

We can see the contradiction clearly if we look at the lines immediately preceding the mention of τρυφὴ καὶ μαλθακία in *Republic* 9.590a–b:

ἡ δ' αὐθάδεια καὶ δυσκολία ψέγεται οὐχ ὅταν τὸ λεοντῶδές τε καὶ ὀφεῶδες αὔξηται καὶ συντείνηται ἀναρμόστως;

[Are not willfulness and presumptuousness censured whenever the lion- and snakelike part is increased and stretched inharmoniously?]

In the *Republic*, τρυφή may cause a relaxation of the proper psychological tautness, while discontent (δυσκολία) may bring on a corresponding hypertension.

115. This view reappears elsewhere in the dialogues. Perhaps the best parallel is from the *Euthyphro,* where Socrates criticizes his interlocutor for being unwilling or unable to continue the argument about piety: ἐπειδὴ δέ μοι δοκεῖς σὺ τρυφᾶν, αὐτός σοι συμπροθυμήσομαι [δεῖξαι] ὅπως ἄν με διδάξῃς περὶ τοῦ ὁσίου. καὶ μὴ προαποκάμῃς . . . τρυφᾷς ὑπὸ πλούτου τῆς σοφίας. ἀλλ᾽, ὦ μακάριε, σύντεινε σαυτόν· καὶ γὰρ οὐδὲ χαλεπὸν κατανοῆσαι ὃ λέγω ("But since you seem to me to be exhibiting *truphē*, I will help you show some enthusiasm so that you can teach me about the Holy. And don't quit on me . . . You're exhibiting *truphē* because of your wealth of wisdom. Just exert yourself, friend. For it is not difficult to understand what I mean." Plato, *Euthphr.* 11e–12a). Note in particular the weakness imputed to Euthyphro by προαποκάμῃς ("quit because of weariness") and the metaphor of tension in σύντεινε σαυτόν, which is the same figure of thought evident in the phrase χαλάσει τε καὶ ἀνέσει at *Rep.* 9.590b. It will be apparent that the same show of feebleness that draws Socrates' rebuke also induces him to do most of Euthyphro's work for him. Even here the idea of τρυφή as presumptuousness and an imposition on others is not absent.

In the *Laws*, by contrast, it is τρυφή that leads to δύσκολα ἤθη. Apparently, then, Plato sees τρυφή as a cause sometimes of indulgence (ἄνεσις), sometimes of exertion (συντονία).[116] The latter view, in which τρυφή entails a kind of force or strength, is more common.[117]

Although Plato's evidence on the effects of τρυφή is inconsistent, the philosopher's relatively frequent use of the term allows us to further illuminate its meaning. Toward the end of the *Laws*, Plato offers an argument to establish the existence of divine providence. Integral to the proof is the drawing of a connection between ἀμέλεια ("negligence") and τρυφή (*Leg.* 10.900e). The line of reasoning is straightforward: it is easy to win the interlocutor's agreement both to the claim that τρυφή is a species of vice and that it is a near synonym to the more innocent ἀμέλεια; in this case, the latter must also be an evil; but the gods are virtuous in all ways; therefore, the gods must exhibit the quality opposite to τρυφή/ἀμέλεια, namely ἐπιμέλεια ("care").

This passage of the *Laws* repeatedly emphasizes that ἐπιμέλεια and τρυφή are contraries or opposites. Nor is this an isolated perspective, since the contrast appears in several other dialogues. In the *Republic*, for example, Socrates illustrates the undesirability of allowing riches in his ideal city by sketching their effects on craftsmen:

πλουτήσας χυτρεὺς δοκεῖ σοι ἔτι θελήσειν ἐπιμελεῖσθαι τῆς τέχνης; . . . Ἀργὸς δὲ καὶ ἀμελὴς γενήσεται μᾶλλον αὐτὸς αὑτοῦ; . . . Πλοῦτός . . . ὡς τοῦ μὲν τρυφὴν καὶ ἀργίαν καὶ νεωτερισμὸν ἐμποιοῦντος, . . .

---

116. A similar contradiction concerns Plato's depiction of the relation of τρυφή to cowardice (δειλία): at *Rep.* 9.590b, τρυφή and μαλθακία produce δειλία, while at *Leg.* 10.901e the implication is that δειλία generates τρυφή: δειλίας γὰρ ἔκγονος ἔν γε ἡμῖν ἀργία, ῥᾳθυμία δὲ ἀργίας καὶ τρυφῆς ("For among us laziness is the offspring of cowardice and loafing the offspring of laziness and *truphē*").

117. At Plato, *Leg.* 3.691a, τρυφή makes certain Greek monarchs turn against each other: . . . βασιλέων τοῦτ᾽ εἶναι νόσημα ὑπερηφάνως ζώντων διὰ τρυφάς. {ΑΘ.} Οὐκοῦν δῆλον ὡς πρῶτον τοῦτο οἱ τότε βασιλῆς ἔσχον, τὸ πλεονεκτεῖν τῶν τεθέντων νόμων ("{Clinias} 'This is a disease of kings living arrogantly because of *truphai*.' {Athenian} 'So it is clear that the kings of that day had this characteristic, to make claims beyond the established laws.'"). In the same way, the rulers of Atlantis were at first "obedient to the laws" (κατήκοοι τῶν νόμων, Plato, *Criti.* 120e) and kind toward each other, and they were not "made drunk by *truphē*" (οὐ μεθύοντες ὑπὸ τρυφῆς, Plato, *Criti.* 121a). Later, however, they became "filled with unjust greed and power" (πλεονεξίας ἀδίκου καὶ δυνάμεως ἐμπιμπλάμενοι, Plato, *Criti.* 121b). At *Gorgias* 492c, Callicles makes τρυφή part of what he sees as the natural moral code: τρυφὴ καὶ ἀκολασία καὶ ἐλευθερία, ἐὰν ἐπικουρίαν ἔχῃ, τοῦτ᾽ ἐστὶν ἀρετή τε καὶ εὐδαιμονία ("*Truphē* and licentiousness and freedom, if they have the support of force, are virtue and happiness."). The strength of will with which Callicles associates τρυφή is plain from his description of the type of man that possesses it: μὴ μόνον φρόνιμοι, ἀλλὰ καὶ ἀνδρεῖοι, ἱκανοὶ ὄντες ἃ ἂν νοήσωσιν ἐπιτελεῖν, καὶ μὴ ἀποκάμνωσι διὰ μαλακίαν τῆς ψυχῆς ("They are not only intelligent, but also brave—they are up to accomplishing whatever they set their minds to, and they don't give up from softness of the soul." Plato, *Gorg.* 491b).

[Do you think that a potter, on becoming rich, will still be willing to pay attention to his art? . . . But he himself will become more lazy and negligent than he was? . . . Wealth [must be kept out of our city] since it causes *truphē* and laziness and innovation.] (Plato, *Rep.* 4.421d–422a)

Wealth turns ἐπιμέλεια into ἀμέλεια, and, as the reformulation in the final sentence of the passage indicates, another way to describe this process is to say that wealth produces τρυφή.

Ἐπιμέλεια may indicate a discrete act or series of acts, but it more commonly refers to the predilection to act. It is usually a disposition or attitude. Moreover, from the way that Plato sets τρυφή against ἐπιμέλεια, we are entitled to assume certain parallels between the terms. The juxtaposition would have little point if what Plato meant by τρυφή was a luxury item or a group of objects or even a more abstract idea such as "a life of luxury." For Plato, τρυφή, like ἐπιμέλεια, is an attitude or psychological disposition, and the rich evidence of his dialogues supports the interpretation we have drawn on the basis of other authors.

We may fix more closely just what kind of attitude τρυφή represents for Plato if we turn from its antonym ἐπιμέλεια to ἀμέλεια, a concept with similar meaning. In order for Plato's argumentation at *Leg.* 10.900e and *Rep.* 4.421d–422a to work, the reader must accept without qualm the substitution of τρυφή for the idea of ἀμέλεια. At the same time, there must be a significant difference between the two, or the change would not be necessary. We suggest the following interpretation: in Plato, as elsewhere, to have τρυφή means to be the object of ἐπιμέλεια, and therefore τρυφή is functionally contrary to ἐπιμέλεια;[118] hence Plato can casually assume the equivalence of τρυφή and ἀμέλεια. But τρυφή is not simply the absence of a quality, the failure to show concern—again, to exhibit τρυφή is to receive ἐπιμέλεια, and to expect to receive it as one's due.[119] Of

---

118. In the *Protagoras* (327c–e), the eponymous character accuses Socrates of displaying τρυφή because he takes for granted the protections of a civilized society. In this context, Socrates exhibits τρυφή in that he enjoys a more comfortable situation owing to the efforts of others. The concern for virtue (ἀρετῆς ἐπιμελεῖσθαι) which civilized people show is itself the product of the constant ἐπιμέλεια of their relatives, friends and fellow citizens; Protagoras's speech on behalf of the teachabilty of ἀρετή contains eleven occurences of ἐπιμέλεια or a cognate, emphasizing the labor, both psychological and physical, involved. By predicating τρυφή of Socrates, the text represents him as the presumptuous beneficiary of other people's toil.

119. As we have already seen, this expectation or presumption is perhaps most clearly visible when the subject is sex or romance. Recall the young girl of Ar., *Eccl.* 900–905 and the courtesan of Xen., *Mem.* 3.11.10. Those who are beloved in Plato's dialogues share this perspective, as is evident from the following exchange between Socrates and the youthful Meno: [ΣΩ.] Κἂν κατακεκαλυμμένος τις γνοίη,

course such an expectation can be offensive, and Plato capitalizes on the pejorative implications of this attitude to propel his arguments.

If this analysis of Plato's usage is correct, the evidence for the meaning of τρυφή in the dialogues supports the view we have developed from other authors: τρυφή does not indicate a luxury item nor the objective fact of possessing luxury. Rather, τρυφή, like ἐπιμέλεια, implies a subjective attitude of mind. Furthermore, this attitude is not characterized, like ἀμέλεια, by the mere lack of a quality; it is not by any means mental passivity. Τρυφή is the presumptuous demand to be the focus of ἐπιμέλεια and should not necessarily be seen as weakness or softness.

In the context of Plato's view of the relationship between τρυφή and ἐπιμέλεια, a passage in *Alcibiades* 1 is worthy of special mention in our study of the historiographical significance of pernicious luxury. In this dialogue, the contrast of τρυφή and ἐπιμέλεια appears not in an argument about divine providence or the economy of the ideal city, but in a discussion of the salient differences between Greek and Persian. Socrates upbraids the young Alcibiades for wishing to set himself up, without proper preparation, as a leader of the Athenians against their traditional enemies, the Persians. He draws Alcibiades' attention to the Persians' material advantages:

εἰ δ᾽ αὖ ἐθέλεις εἰς πλούτους ἀποβλέψαι καὶ τρυφὰς καὶ ἐσθῆτας ἱματίων θ᾽ ἕλξεις καὶ μύρων ἀλοιφὰς καὶ θεραπόντων πλήθους ἀκολουθίας τήν τε ἄλλην ἁβρότητα τὴν Περσῶν, αἰσχυνθείης ἂν ἐπὶ σεαυτῷ, αἰσθόμενος, ὅσον αὐτῶν ἐλλείπεις.

ὦ Μένων, διαλεγομένου σου, ὅτι καλὸς εἶ καὶ ἐρασταί σοι ἔτι εἰσίν. [MEN.] Τί δή; [ΣΩ.] Ὅτι οὐδὲν ἀλλ᾽ ἢ ἐπιτάττεις ἐν τοῖς λόγοις· ὅπερ ποιοῦσιν οἱ τρυφῶντες, ἅτε τυραννεύοντες, ἕως ἂν ἐν ὥρᾳ ὦσιν. καὶ ἅμα ἐμοῦ ἴσως κατέγνωκας, ὅτι εἰμὶ ἥττων τῶν καλῶν. χαριοῦμαι οὖν σοι καὶ ἀποκρινοῦμαι. ("[Socr.] 'Even blindfolded, Meno, a person could tell from the way you act in conversations that you are beautiful and are still pursued by lovers.' [Meno] 'What do you mean?' [Socr.] 'Because your conversation consists of nothing but commands, just as those do who show *truphē*, insomuch as they act the tyrant as long as they are in bloom. And perhaps also you are using against me the knowledge that I am a pushover for beautiful boys. So I'll indulge you and answer.'" Plato, *Meno* 76b–c.) Although the word ἐπιμέλεια does not appear here, the attitude it represents is on display in Socrates' indulgence of Meno's demands. For the word itself in a pertinent context we may compare *Rep.* 5.474d: πάντες οἱ ἐν ὥρᾳ τὸν φιλόπαιδα καὶ ἐρωτικὸν ἀμῇ γέ πῃ δάκνουσί τε καὶ κινοῦσι, δοκοῦντες ἄξιοι εἶναι ἐπιμελείας τε καὶ τοῦ ἀσπάζεσθαι ("All those in their prime in some way sting and stimulate the boy-lover and romantic, appearing to be worthy of care and devotion."). Socrates then goes on to relate how lovers describe their beloved's physical flaws as marks of beauty. In this respect, the ἐπιμέλεια of the lovers resembles the solicitude shown to the *demos* by ambitious politicians eager to keep public favor (cf. Dem. 9.4.2, quoted in n. 112 above). It is reasonable therefore to use the contrast between τρυφή and ἐπιμέλεια that is drawn by Plato to help elucidate occurrences of τρυφή elsewhere.

[If, on the other hand, you are willing to look at the wealth and *truphai* and clothing and draggings of cloaks and slatherings of perfume and ministrations of a number of servants and the rest of the *habrotēs* of the Persians, you would be ashamed for your own situation, perceiving the extent of your inferiority to them.] (Plato, *Alc.* 1.122b–c)

Socrates then contrasts the prosperous resources of the Persians to the locus of Athenian power, a matter known "even to the women of the enemy":

εἴ τις εἴποι τῇ βασιλέως μητρί, Ξέρξου δὲ γυναικί, Ἀμήστριδι, ὅτι ἐν νῷ ἔχει σοῦ τῷ υἱεῖ ἀντιτάττεσθαι ὁ Δεινομάχης υἱός . . . θαυμάσαι ἂν ὅτῳ ποτὲ πιστεύων ἐν νῷ ἔχει οὗτος ὁ Ἀλκιβιάδης τῷ Ἀρτοξέρξῃ διαγωνίζεσθαι, καὶ οἶμαι ἂν αὐτὴν εἰπεῖν, ὅτι οὐκ ἔσθ᾽, ὅτῳ ἄλλῳ πιστεύων οὗτος ἀνὴρ ἐπιχειρεῖ πλὴν ἐπιμελείᾳ τε καὶ σοφίᾳ· ταῦτα γὰρ μόνα ἄξια λόγου ἐν Ἕλλησιν. . . . ἀλλ᾽, ὦ μακάριε, πειθόμενος ἐμοί τε καὶ τῷ ἐν Δελφοῖς γράμματι, γνῶθι σαυτόν, ὅτι οὗτοι ἡμῖν εἰσιν ἀντίπαλοι . . . ὧν ἄλλῳ μὲν οὐδ᾽ ἂν ἑνὶ περιγενοίμεθα, εἰ μή ἐπιμελείᾳ τε ἂν καὶ τέχνῃ.

[If anyone should say to Amestris, the mother of the King and wife of Xerxes, that the son of Dinomache . . . has it in mind to oppose her son, she would wonder what on earth gives this Alcibiades the confidence to plan to contend with Artaxerxes. And I think she would say that the only things that this man could be relying on in this attempt are *epimeleia* and wisdom. For these are the only things worthy of consideration among the Greeks. . . . My friend, listen to me and the saying at Delphi ("know yourself"): these people are our rivals. . . . We won't gain the advantage on them in anything, except *epimeleia* and skill.] (Plato, *Alc.* 1.123c–124b)

Thus then, although τρυφή and ἐπιμέλεια are opposed to each other, both qualities are positive and both are sources of political and military strength. The Delphic motto, γνῶθι σαυτόν, is a leitmotiv for *Alcibiades* 1, and the Great King, it is implied, wisely recognizes that among the bases of power and empire in his case are "wealth and *truphai* . . . and the rest of the *habrotēs* of the Persians."[120]

---

120. This is not to say that ἐπιμέλεια has no place at the Persian court. Rather, as we might expect from the importance of τρυφή, the Great King is remarkable for the ἐπιμέλεια of which he is the object. This fact is evident in Plato's description of the care given to rearing and educating the Persian heir: μετὰ τοῦτο τρέφεται ὁ παῖς οὐχ ὑπὸ γυναικὸς τροφοῦ ὀλίγου ἀξίας, ἀλλ᾽ ὑπ᾽ εὐνούχων οἳ ἂν

Furthermore, it is Plato's view in this dialogue that τρυφή is consonant with personal qualities of the highest level of integrity.[121] Though ἐπιμέλεια may entail the physical and moral betterment of the object, τρυφή does not necessarily mean the decline of its possessor.

The Septuagint

The Septuagint is an extremely valuable document for our discussion because it contains the most extensive extant Greek-language texts from the Hellenistic period. Written principally in the third and second centuries, it encapsulates the Jewish philosophical tradition, as it was translated into Greek, presumably by scholars well learned in both. As a result, the occurrences of τρυφή provide critical insight on the meaning of this term in Hellenistic usage. The Septuagint offers a fitting capstone to the preceding discussion because it confirms the consistent, precise meaning as well as the beneficial moral implications of τρυφή, both of which we have already established in the Classical sources.

In the Septuagint, τρυφή is most regularly a good thing, and God is its usual source. The most striking instance comes from the Creation story, where Eden is described as ὁ παράδεισος τῆς τρυφῆς ("The paradise of *truphē*," Gen. 3:23, 24). The New English Translation of the Septuagint renders this phrase as "the

---

δοκῶσιν τῶν περὶ βασιλέα ἄριστοι εἶναι· οἷς τά τε ἄλλα προστέτακται ἐπιμελεῖσθαι τοῦ γενομένου, καὶ ὅπως ὅτι κάλλιστος ἔσται μηχανᾶσθαι, ἀναπλάττοντας τὰ μέλη τοῦ παιδὸς καὶ κατορθοῦντας ("After this the boy is reared, not by a female nurse of little worth, but by the eunuchs who are considered to be the best at court. They are ordered to take care of (ἐπιμέλεσθαι) the newborn, especially contriving that he be as beautiful as possible by molding and straightening the boy's limbs." Plato, *Alc.* 1.121d). Plato's point in this relatively detailed portrayal of the upbringing of the prince is precisely to emphasize the continual and systematic ἐπιμέλεια which is directed at the future monarch and by this means to illustrate the lack of ἐπιμέλεια given to even the most prominent Athenian youth. It will be left for Alcibiades ἐπιμελεῖσθαι αὑτοῦ ("to take care of himself").

121. In the third stage in the raising of the Persian prince, four elders are selected as his tutors, the wisest, the most just, the most temperate, and the bravest: ὧν ὁ μὲν μαγείαν τε διδάσκει τὴν Ζωροάστρου τοῦ Ὡρομάζου—ἔστι δὲ τοῦτο θεῶν θεραπεία—, διδάσκει δὲ καὶ τὰ βασιλικά, ὁ δὲ δικαιότατος ἀληθεύειν διὰ παντὸς τοῦ βίου· ὁ δὲ σωφρονέστατος μηδ᾿ ὑπὸ μιᾶς ἄρχεσθαι τῶν ἡδονῶν, ἵν᾿ ἐλεύθερος εἶναι ἐθίζηται καὶ ὄντως βασιλεύς, ἄρχων πρῶτον τῶν ἐν αὑτῷ ἀλλὰ μὴ δουλεύων· ὁ δὲ ἀνδρειότατος ἄφοβον καὶ ἀδεᾶ παρασκευάζων, ὡς ὅταν δείσῃ δοῦλον ὄντα. ("The one teaches the lore of the Magi concerning Zoroaster the son of Horomazes—this is the ministry of the gods—and he teaches also the things pertinent to a king. The most just man teaches him to be truthful all his life. The most temperate man teaches him not to be ruled by even one of the pleasures, so that he that he might be accustomed to be a free man and a genuine king, ruling rather than serving the things in himself. The bravest man, training him to be fearless and dauntless, teaches him that whenever he is afraid, he becomes a slave." Plato, *Alc.* 1.122a).

orchard of delights," but this seems to us somewhat imprecise:[122] the essential meaning of τρυφή is the expectation that one's comforts will be seen to; it may also refer by extension to the fulfillment of that expectation. In Eden, Adam and Eve receive everything they need from God without effort: it is simply presented to them, since God nurtures them in every way. It is no surprise then that the idea of τρυφή would be prominent in this context.

Since the translators chose to equate τρυφή with Eden, it is reasonable to try to supplement our understanding of the Greek term with information from the Hebrew. Since as early as the 1880s, a Babylonian etymological source had been posited for "Eden," where God planted the garden. Evidence for this origin has been found in Nineveh in the form of a cuneiform syllabary (Syllabary b) containing a list in three columns. The center column contains Sumerian pictograms, while the left gives a phonetic rendering of the Sumerian. The right column presents the Akkadian equivalent of the first two columns. Two lines of this text are relevant to our discussion.

90) e-di-in : edin : edinu
91) e-di-in : edin : ṣe-e-ru

From these two lines it can be established that Sumerian *edin* is equivalent to Akkadian *ṣēru*. In Akkadian, *ṣēru* is a well attested term meaning "steppe, plain." Thus, the suggestion was made that Akkadian *edinu* "was identical with the Hebrew name" and that Hebrew ʿēden was connected with the Sumero-Akkadian word and not with the other principal etymological candidate, "words for 'delight' from the base ʿdn."[123] This derivation became widely accepted as the predominant explanation for the etymology of Eden for the next 100 years.

However, some Semitic philologists have objected to this derivation for several reasons:

1. The Akkadian *edinu* is attested only in this syllabary and may well be a semitized version of the Sumerian that was created by the syllabary's

---

122. Cf. Ezek. 28:13, 31:9, 16, 18; Joel 2:3. All English translations from the Septuagint are those of the New English Translation of the Septuagint unless otherwise noted. For more on ancient views of paradise, see: Greenfield 1984; Holger 1986; Russon 1988; and the essays in Bockmuehl and Stroumsa 2010.
123. Millard 1984, 103.

scribe. It is unlikely that such a term would have been adopted by the author of Genesis.

2. The phonology of a Sumerian origin presents a difficulty. The initial syllable of the Akkadian *edinu* has no / ʿ /. This absence is significant, since "if the Hebrew term were a Sumerian loanword in West Semitic via Akkadian *edinu*, the expected form would be ʾ*ēden*."[124]

3. Semantically, a meaning "steppe, plain" does not fit the context in Genesis.

Consequently, some have preferred a West Semitic derivation. According to this line of thought, ʿ*ēden* belongs etymologically with words such as ʿ*ădānîm* ("delights": Jer. 51:34, 2 Sam. 1:24, Ps. 36:8). This view is of particular interest for our work, since early evidence for it supports a meaning for ʿ*ēden* that is consistent with the meaning of τρυφή which we have identified. This evidence comes from two texts, the first was found at Ugarit and thus has a *terminus ante quem* of c. 1170 BCE. The second was uncovered at Tell Fekheriyeh and has been assigned to the mid-ninth century BCE.[125] The Ugaritic text is part of the Baal Cycle and reads as follows:

wn ʾp ʿdn mṭrh bʿl yʿdn ʿdn (KTU 1.4:V:6–7)

Cassuto, evidently relying on the emphasis in Genesis upon Eden as a well-watered place, suggests "moisture" as the essential meaning of ʿ*dn* and translates the Ugaritic thus:

and now also the moisture of his rain / Baal shall surely make moist[126]

Eden, then, is so named because of its "exceedingly rich water supply,"[127] but this meaning for ʿ*dn* is difficult to reconcile with the Septuagint's use of τρυφή to translate Eden.

An inscription from Tell Fekheriyeh, published in 1982, has provided new information on the meaning of West Semitic ʿ*dn*. The inscription, containing a

124. Tsumura 1989, 125.
125. Millard 1984, 105.
126. Texts and translations from Tsumura 1989, 127; Tsumura's translation here reflects Cassuto's interpretation of ʿ*dn*.
127. Cassuto 1984, 107.

description of the god Hadad, is bilingual, with its text in Aramaic and Akkadian. The operative expression describes an aspect of Hadad's benefaction:

m'dn mt kln || muṭaḫḫidu kibrāti

The Akkadian *muṭaḫḫidu* is a participial form of the denominative verb corresponding to the adjective *ṭaḫdu* "überreichlich" and the noun *ṭuḫdu* "überreichliche Fülle."[128] The verb therefore means something like "to enrich, make abundant," and the Aramaic *'dn* may be assumed to have the same force. One might translate this part of the Fekheriyeh inscription "who makes all lands abound." Applying this information to the Ugaritic text yields something like the following meaning:

wn 'p 'dn mṭrh b'l y'dn 'dn

[Now moreover Baal will abundantly give an abundance of rain.]

This sense fits well with the Classical meaning of τρυφή that we have identified. The "Paradise of *truphē*" indicates a place where one may assume that one's needs and desires will be met. By choosing to translate ʿēden by τρυφή, the authors of the Septuagint reveal that in their eyes the essential element of ʿdn lay in the *act* of provision rather than in what was provided. This focus has not been made clear in discussions of ʿēden and its cognates.

To move now from the Garden of Eden to a more general discussion of the evidence, the recurring theme in many passages from the Septuagint is that God will provide to the righteous and that that provision is called τρυφή, an unfailingly good possession.[129] At Psalms 36:4, humans are commanded, κατατρύφησον τοῦ κυρίου, καὶ δώσει σοι τὰ αἰτήματα τῆς καρδίας σου. The NETS translation, "Take delight in the Lord, and he will give you the requests of your heart," is a nebulous rendering. A more nuanced translation would be, "Look to the Lord to take care of you, and he will give you the requests of your heart." Likewise, at Ezechiel 34, the Lord is searching for his sheep:

(13) καὶ ἐξάξω αὐτοὺς ἐκ τῶν ἐθνῶν καὶ συνάξω αὐτοὺς ἀπὸ τῶν χωρῶν καὶ εἰσάξω αὐτοὺς εἰς τὴν γῆν αὐτῶν καὶ βοσκήσω αὐτοὺς ἐπὶ τὰ ὄρη Ισραηλ καὶ ἐν ταῖς φάραγξιν καὶ ἐν πάσῃ κατοικίᾳ τῆς γῆς·

---

128. Tsumura 1989, 128.
129. 2 Esd. 19:25; Ps. 35:9, 36:11, 138:11; Prov. 4:9; Wisd. 19:11; Isa. 55:2, 58:13, 66:11; Ezek. 36:35.

(14) ἐν νομῇ ἀγαθῇ βοσκήσω αὐτούς, καὶ ἐν τῷ ὄρει τῷ ὑψηλῷ Ισραηλ ἔσονται αἱ μάνδραι αὐτῶν· ἐκεῖ κοιμηθήσονται καὶ ἐκεῖ ἀναπαύσονται ἐν τρυφῇ ἀγαθῇ καὶ ἐν νομῇ πίονι βοσκηθήσονται ἐπὶ τῶν ὀρέων Ισραηλ.

(15) ἐγὼ βοσκήσω τὰ πρόβατά μου καὶ ἐγὼ ἀναπαύσω αὐτά, καὶ γνώσονται ὅτι ἐγώ εἰμι κύριος. τάδε λέγει κύριος κύριος

[(13) And I will bring them out from the nations and gather them from the countries and will bring them into their land, and I will feed them upon the mountains of Israel and in the ravines and in every habitation of the land.

(14) I will feed them in a good pasture; their folds shall be on the lofty mountain of Israel; there also shall they lie down, and there they shall rest in fine luxury (*en truphē agathē*), and they shall be fed in a rich pasture on the mountains of Israel.

(15) It is I who will feed my sheep, and it is I who will give them rest, and they shall know that I am the Lord.]

God is adamant that food and rest for his people comes from him, and no one else. They need not look elsewhere, nor need they themselves toil.

By way of contrast, at Isaiah 57, when humans do look elsewhere for the fulfillment of their wants, the Lord grows angry:

(3) ὑμεῖς δὲ προσαγάγετε ὧδε, υἱοὶ ἄνομοι, σπέρμα μοιχῶν καὶ πόρνης·

(4) ἐν τίνι ἐνετρυφήσατε; καὶ ἐπὶ τίνα ἠνοίξατε τὸ στόμα ὑμῶν; . . .

(5) οἱ παρακαλοῦντες ἐπὶ τὰ εἴδωλα ὑπὸ δένδρα δασέα . . .

(8) . . . ᾤου ὅτι ἐὰν ἀπ' ἐμοῦ ἀποστῇς, πλεῖόν τι ἕξεις . . .

(10) . . . διὰ τοῦτο οὐ κατεδεήθης μου σύ.

(11) τίνα εὐλαβηθεῖσα ἐφοβήθης καὶ ἐψεύσω με καὶ οὐκ ἐμνήσθης μου οὐδὲ ἔλαβές με εἰς τὴν διάνοιαν οὐδὲ εἰς τὴν καρδίαν σου; κἀγώ σε ἰδὼν παρορῶ, καὶ ἐμὲ οὐκ ἐφοβήθης.

(12) κἀγὼ ἀπαγγελῶ τὴν δικαιοσύνην μου καὶ τὰ κακά σου, ἃ οὐκ ὠφελήσουσίν σε.

[(3) But as for you, draw near here, you lawless sons, you offspring of adulterers and of a whore.

(4) In what have you indulged (*enetruphēsate*)? And against whom have you opened your mouth wide? . . .

(5) You are the ones who call on their idols under thick trees . . .

(8) . . . You supposed that if you should desert me, you would obtain something greater. . . .

(10) . . . Because you have accomplished these things, therefore you did not entreat me.

(11) Of whom were you cautious and afraid, and you lied to me and did not remember me, nor did you take me into your thought or into your heart? And when I see you, I disregard you, and you have not feared me.

(12) And I will declare my righteousness and your evils, and will not help you.]

"Indulged"—containing the sense "In what have you expected to fulfill your desires?"—is better. These people have turned to idols. Verse 8 is particularly telling: "You supposed that if you should desert me, you would obtain something greater." The people are looking for a better deal elsewhere and, as a result, the Lord will not help them now. Thus τρυφή is not in itself something godly here, but rather is something that, in the Septuagint, ought to be sought in God alone.

While τρυφή is often associated with calamity here and elsewhere, in the Septuagint it is never the cause of that misfortune or of a weakening or effeminacy. Instead, just as people who are virtuous receive τρυφή from God, so people who are wicked have their τρυφή taken away from them.[130] For example:

διὰ τοῦτο ἡγούμενοι λαοῦ μου ἀπορριφήσονται ἐκ τῶν οἰκιῶν τρυφῆς αὐτῶν, διὰ τὰ πονηρὰ ἐπιτηδεύματα αὐτῶν ἐξώσθησαν·

[Therefore, leaders of my people shall be cast out of their homes of luxury (truphē). On account of their evil practices, they have been expelled.] (Mic. 2:9)

In the same vein he condemns the virgin daughter of Babylon:

(1) . . . ὅτι οὐκέτι προστεθήσῃ κληθῆναι ἁπαλὴ καὶ τρυφερά.

(2) λαβὲ μύλον, ἄλεσον ἄλευρον, ἀποκάλυψαι τὸ ατακάλυμμά σου, ἀνακάλυψαι τὰς πολιάς, ἀνάσυραι τὰς κνήμας, διάβηθι ποταμούς·

(3) ἀνακαλυφθήσεται ἡ αἰσχύνη σου, φανήσονται οἱ ὀνειδισμοί σου· . . .

---

130. Deut. 28:54, 56; Jer. 27:2, 28:34; Lam. 4:5; Mic. 1:16; Dan. 4:31–32. Even at Bar. 4:26, where God seems to be in sympathy, his people are still suffering for their transgressions: οἱ τρυφεροί μου ἐπορεύθησαν ὁδοὺς τραχείας ("My pampered children have traveled rough roads," NETS). This theme of people losing τρυφή in conquest is also seen, e.g., at Diodorus Siculus 13.58, 89, 17.35.4–5.

[(1) . . . because you shall no longer be called tender and delicate (*truphera*).

(2) Take a millstone; grind meal; uncover your covering; expose your gray hairs; bare your legs; pass through rivers.

(3) Your shame shall be uncovered; your reproaches shall be seen.] (Isa. 47:1–3)

This woman is made to fall from a position in which all her wants are taken care of to one in which she toils for others, grinding meal with shamefully bare legs. Among her offenses are presumption and witchcraft. She presumes when she made the burden of the Israelites heavy, while at the same time boasting, εἰς τὸν αἰῶνα ἔσομαι ἄρχουσα ("I shall be a ruler forever," Isa. 47:7), and then, Ἐγώ εἰμι, καὶ οὐκ ἔστιν ἑτέρα· οὐ καθιῶ χήρα οὐδὲ γνώσομαι ὀρφανείαν ("I am, and there is no other;[131] I shall not sit as a widow or know bereavement," 47:8). She employs witchcraft rather than turning to God for her wants: . . . ἐν τῇ φαρμακείᾳ σου ἐν τῇ ἰσχύι τῶν ἐπαοιδῶν σου σφόδρα (". . . [loss will come] in your witchcraft, exceedingly in the strength of your enchantments," 47:9). God here calls her ἡ τρυφερά ("you delicate woman"). Indeed she enjoys τρυφή so long as she "sits securely" (ἡ καθημένη πεποιθυῖα) in her position of power, with her needs being satisfied. But God is promising her widowhood and the loss of her children in the same day (47:9), and toil and utter destruction for herself (47:11). He then taunts her to find help in her magic (12): στῆθι νῦν ἐν ταῖς ἐπαοιδαῖς σου καὶ τῇ πολλῇ φαρμακείᾳ σου . . . εἰ δυνήσῃ ὠφεληθῆναι ("Stand now in your enchantments and your abundant witchcraft . . . if you will be able to receive benefit."). She is looking to have her needs fulfilled from the wrong source.

Elsewhere in the Septuagint the word τρυφή occurs in a context separate from its close connection with God, but in a way entirely consistent with the definition we have established, indicating the expectation that wants will be fulfilled by others. Thus Esther (5:1–3) can lean on her maid for support, ὡς τρυφερευομένη. This phrase is badly translated as "gently." Instead, the word implies that she is a woman of some position who can expect to be attended by others: "genteelly" would be a better rendering. The second maid who accompanies her holds her dress up out of the dirt (κουφίζουσα τὴν ἔνδυσιν αὐτῆς, "holding her train"). Likewise, the virtuous Susanna is τρυφερά when she arrives to answer the false accusations made against her, and she comes accompanied not only by her father, mother, and four children, but also five hundred servants and maids (Sus. 30–31). At Eccles. 2:8, cupbearers and pitchers are the

---

131. Repeated twice more in the chapter, in verse 10.

ἐντρυφήματα υἱῶν τοῦ ἀνθρώπου, translated as "delights of human beings" rather than the better "privileges," while in Proverbs, it is said: οὐ συμφέρει ἄφρονι τρυφή, καὶ ἐὰν οἰκέτης ἄρξηται μεθ᾽ ὕβρεως δυναστεύειν ("It is not fitting for a fool to have delights, nor if a domestic should begin to rule with hubris." Prov. 19:10). Once more, "delights" is a poor rendering of a word whose meaning is made more apparent in the second half of the sentence: a foolish man should not expect to be taken care of by others, just as a servant should not think to rule, which would be hubris.

Kings demand τρυφή, as we see with Asher: δώσει τρυφὴν ἄρχουσιν (Gen. 49:20), again translated as "shall give delight to rulers." The word must mean that he will attend upon kings and fulfill their desires. Likewise, when the Chaldeans are roused to conquer God's people, seemingly unjustly, Habakkuk complains,

καὶ αὐτὸς ἐν βασιλεῦσιν ἐντρυφήσει, καὶ τύραννοι παίγνια αὐτοῦ, καὶ αὐτὸς εἰς πᾶν ὀχύρωμα ἐμπαίξεται καὶ βαλεῖ χῶμα καὶ κρατήσει αὐτοῦ.

[And at kings he [the Chaldean] will scoff (*entruphēsei*), and tyrants will be his toys. He will jest at every fortress and heap up earth and take it.] (Hab. 1:10)

Here we see the proposed meaning of τρυφή yet again, for the Chaldean will treat men who had been kings as his servants, expecting them to take care of him. We see this interpretation reinforced in the following lines, were the kings will become playthings and fortresses will be laughably-easy to sack, in a reversal of fortune so common to the Septuagint.[132]

Thus, according to the Septuagint, it is perfectly correct to possess τρυφή so long as it comes from God and is fitting to your station. The only warnings against τρυφή come when its source is wrong, like idols or a life away from God. Antiochus was guiding them on the wrong path when he urged the seven Jewish brothers to abandon their heritage: καὶ μεταλαβόντες Ἑλληνικοῦ βίου καὶ μεταδιαιτηθέντες ἐντρυφήσατε ταῖς νεότησιν ὑμῶν· ("Enjoy your youth [*entruphēsate*] by embracing a Greek way of life and changing your mode of living," 4 Macc. 8:8). A man who toils too much in order to make money can enjoy τρυφή badly (Sir. 31:3), but it is not because the τρυφή itself is his downfall, but rather because his love of gold leads him away from God. Likewise, in

---

132. Cf. Sir. 11:27, 14:4, 14:16.

admonishing that "not everything confers benefits to everyone, and every soul is not pleased by everything" (Sir. 37:28–29),[133] Sirach warns against being greedy for τρυφή, because gluttony itself is a kind of sickness. Equally, at Sir. 18:32, τρυφή is a bad thing, only because it leads to poverty, since the admonished is expecting a mode of life that is beyond his financial means. Τρυφή is a symptom of wanton desire, not the cause of that illness.

Thus the unswerving evidence offered by the Septuagint is that τρυφή is a desirable characteristic, ensuring that one's wants will be taken care of and life will be comfortable. It comes most usually as a gift from God, and the act of seeking it elsewhere is punished by its loss. We would stress two points. First, the meaning of τρυφή which may be established from the evidence of the Septuagint is exactly that which we have argued is also established by the Classical material. The authors of the translation were not innovative in this regard. They used a Classical term in its proper sense. Second, these same authors *were* innovative in the almost invariably positive connotations with which they used τρυφή. Although the term can be positive in Classical authors, this use is rather limited.

These two ideas fix our position with respect to recent scholarship which attempts to explain the putatively anomalous use of τρυφή in the Septuagint.[134] These works find the answer in the political vocabulary of the Ptolemaic court, where τρυφή was a watchword. Two Ptolemies (III and VIII) styled themselves *Truphōn* as well as *Euergetēs*, and the appellation *Truphaina* was common for females of the house. It is suggested that the Lagid dynasty recast τρυφή from an original meaning of "prosperity," "delight," and "luxury" to evoke the idea of "the ruler as guarantor of fortune and his rule as a regime providing prosperity and divine goodwill."[135] In this respect, τρυφή was the linguistic equivalent of the cornucopia which appeared on Ptolemaic coinage: it represented the rulers as providers of all their people's wants.

We find half of this argument persuasive. It is not surprising, given this background, if the Septuagint should adopt τρυφή for the name of Eden and the idea of divine largess. On the other hand, the Ptolemies had no need to reformulate the denotation of τρυφή, since the concept they wished this term to

---

133. οὐ γὰρ πάντα πᾶσιν συμφέρει, καὶ οὐ πᾶσα ψυχὴ ἐν παντὶ εὐδοκεῖ. μὴ ἀπληστεύου ἐν πάσῃ τρυφῇ καὶ μὴ ἐκχυθῇς ἐπὶ ἐδεσμάτων.

134. See Heinen 1983 and Husson 1988, with bibliography.

135. Heinen 1983, 122: "den Herrscher als Garanten des Glücks und seine Regierung als ein Segen und Wohlstand spendendes Regiment."

bear was quite close to its Classical sense of expecting one's concerns to be seen to or the fulfillment of that expectation.

Conclusion

This chapter began by asking when the theme that pernicious luxury caused the demise of Sybaris developed in Greek literature. We determined that, setting aside for the moment the fragmentary evidence, there is no directly transmitted testimony for this theme before the Roman era. We then examined the question of whether and to what extent the idea of pernicious luxury was important more generally in Greek thought prior to the Hellenistic period. Before the evidence for the valorization of luxury could be studied, a necessary preliminary was a survey of the relevant terminology. In this section we have argued that modern interpretations of the ancient view are influenced by the vagueness with which the elements of the vocabulary of luxury are often treated. These terms can generally be defined with much more precision. The word ἁπαλός and its compounds refer primarily to the physical softness of skin, while χλιδή has a narrow meaning centered on the concept of ornamentation in the form of gold, fine clothing, beautiful hair, and generally the rich accoutrements of life. The word ἁβρός and its compounds denote an idea of "luxurious," in the sense of "refined," "dignified," or "affected." Τρυφή, the word upon which we concentrate our investigation, refers to the expectation that one will be the object of solicitous concern (μέλημα). It is itself not a general moral or physical weakness or a laziness brought on by partaking in luxury. Rather than a reference to creature comforts per se, it is a strong-minded presumption or a willfulness that assumes one's needs and wants will be fulfilled by others. It is functionally contrary to ἐπιμέλεια.

As for the moral implications of luxury, the evidence that τρυφή—for modern scholarship views this term as key to the concept—was assumed to be a cause of general moral decline is both weaker and more complicated than usually assumed. Thus, where socially appropriate (such as among kings and potentates), τρυφή can be a positive quality, though it may be associated with μαλακία and effeminacy, since it may lead young men to neglect discipline and education, and therefore becomes unwarlike. At the same time and occasionally by the same authors, τρυφή is more often presented as contrasting with, or even antithetical to, μαλακία. In such passages, τρυφή involves the imposition of the subject's will on others. It may sometimes lead to violence and hubris.

In sum, τρυφή may, under certain circumstances, have negative effects on the character of its possessor. Both softness and violence are its occasional corollaries, but neither is a regular associate. The evidence does not support the claim that the idea of pernicious luxury as a natural and general process was part of the Classical Greek worldview. What is more, the evidence positively contradicts the interpretation that there existed at this time the conceptual model that was allegedly of great importance to certain Hellenistic historians: the idea that luxury led to effeminacy, which generated acts of hubris, which provoked retribution and ruin. The linking of τρυφή with effeminacy, on the one hand, and with hubris, on the other, are for the Classical Greeks incompatible views, not to be combined in a single process. The evolutionary chain of wealth, τρυφή, effeminacy, satiety, hubris, and punishment does not exist in any trustworthy evidence from this period.

CHAPTER 2

Luxury as a Historiographical Principle in Herodotus

With the evidence developed in the preceding chapter firmly in mind, we may now move on to an investigation of the moral dimension of luxury in the *Histories* of Herodotus. This work is of central importance to an understanding of the place of the idea of pernicious luxury in Greek thought, since scholars widely believe that Herodotus's acceptance of this concept and his use of it as a theme in his narrative legitimized luxury as a force of historical causation.[1] In fact, the apparent continuity with the Herodotean theory of luxury is a major argument in favor of the importance of the idea in the fragmentary historiography of the fourth to the second centuries BCE. In highlighting the corrosive effects of luxury, it is said, Ephorus, Theopompus, Timaeus, Phylarchus, and others were following the lead given to them by the Father of History. In view of the crucial role assigned to the *Histories* in this regard, we feel that a detailed examination of Herodotus's evidence is in order.

This examination will be prolonged, since the relevant evidence is not at all straightforward. Given the practically unanimous acceptance in Herodotean scholarship of the "fact" of the historiographical significance of pernicious luxury, a student of this idea will be surprised to hear that, in truth, Herodotus never says clearly and in so many words that luxury contributed to the ruin of this or that person or people. The prevailing interpretation relies rather on sub-

---

1. E.g., Hall 1989, 69–70: "The mythologizing of the Persian wars relied heavily on the moral shape with which Aeschylus invested them and which Herodotus developed: a moral shape based on the fundamental Greek law of human existence, which prescribed that excessive prosperity and satiety lead first to hubris and then to destruction."

text. One must read between the lines to find Herodotus referring obliquely to a concept that would, it is claimed, be readily familiar to his audience. Thus Bischoff, explaining the significance of Pausanias's criticism after Plataea of Mardonius's opulent lifestyle, invites his reader to see past the literal meaning, which concerns only a secondary foolishness ("die Torheit zweitens Grades"), to a deeper Persian failing ("die Grundtorheit ersten Grades"). This "fundamental stupidity" is the failure to take into account the loss of vitality that follows from luxury.[2]

Reliance on such indirect evidence does not, of course, entail that the interpretation based upon it is incorrect. Hidden meanings and a preference for implication over explication are certainly possible, but they must be elucidated carefully, through a process that is inherently risky. In a study of Herodotus's political thought, including the idea of pernicious luxury, Raaflaub is laudably aware of how difficult it is to move beyond the explicit and literal meaning of a text to discern the author's intentions and the reader's understanding.[3] He carefully delineates the conditions that must necessarily obtain if an interpretation based on such a subtext is to be persuasive. Most emphatically, the thought imputed to Herodotus should be both clearly topical and familiar to his audience. The suspected Herodotean concept should not be tangential, but should reflect the central concerns of contemporary Greek society; at the same time, it is crucial "to make sure that what we compare is really comparable."[4] In other words, parallels from other authors must be produced.

As we have seen, classical parallels for the working of pernicious luxury as a historical force are not strong. While the appearance on the scene of the term τρυφή does seem to indicate a newly felt concern with the moral implications of opulence, surviving references from the fifth century are too rare for us to be confident that pernicious luxury would have been familiar enough to Herodotus's readership to allow him to avoid spelling out his meaning. If the *Histories* does make the decadence of individuals and communities into an explanation for and cause of historical events, we should recognize this view as an innovation on the part of Herodotus. The concept of pernicious luxury would be a major part of Herodotus's own contribution to Greek thought rather than a

---

2.   Bischoff (1932) 1965, 683–84.
3.   Raaflaub 1987, 235: "as soon as we deal with political concepts that are not explicitly designated as such, with an author's thoughts and intentions, and the audience's perceptions and reactions, the case becomes nearly hopeless."
4.   Raaflaub 1987, 236.

reflection of contemporary *mores*. Our investigation of Herodotus's beliefs on this subject will therefore give primary consideration and the greater weight to what Herodotus says about luxury explicitly and directly. Instances of irony, allusion, and indirection may certainly be relevant to the question at issue, but they must be explained with continuous reference to the more straightforward material.

We will pay particular attention to the pathology of decadence. The preceding chapter has shown that the fully developed concept of pernicious luxury that is attributed to Hellenistic writers—wealth leading to effeminacy and weakness to satiety to acts of contemptuous violence—has no complete analogue in the Classical period. Rather, luxury occurs as a corollary to one of two different paths to decadence: either (1) excessive indulgence in τρυφή may cause one to demand acquiescence and even subordination of others to one's own comforts, an attitude that may eventually manifest itself in acts of ὕβρις, or (2) the pursuit of τρυφή may be associated with the neglect of the proper ἐπιμέλεια for one's own physical and moral condition, leading to indolence and enervation. The two syndromes do not seem to occur in a single subject as part of a single process, and neither is a necessary end of τρυφή. Most people enjoy luxury within reasonable bounds.

This analysis is pertinent to the question of luxury in Herodotus: influential studies of the subject have found one or both types of decadence to be a key force in the *Histories*, while at the same time failing to recognize that pernicious luxury is not simplex and its aspects are in some ways incompatible. For example, Bischoff, in his influential study of the "Warner" in Herodotus, fixes his attention on the effeminizing process of decadence. He considers that theme to be one of overarching importance to the *Histories*. The idea that an opulent lifestyle brings softness and loss of manliness is among the "Lebengesetze" that cannot be set aside, the "Gesetze der Geschichte." It is "the curse of every ruling power."[5] The harmful consequences of soft living are integral to the "geschichtsmetaphysischen Pessimismus," which is the hallmark of Herodotus's thought.[6]

Cobet, often cited as an authority for the theme of pernicious luxury in the *Histories*, resembles Bischoff in the importance he assigns the idea. However, Cobet focuses on the other Classical aspect of demoralizing luxury, finding in

---

5. "Den Fluch jeder Herrschaft," Bischoff (1932) 1965, 683.
6. Bischoff (1932) 1965, 687; in Bischoff's view, Herodotus's reader is meant to understand the *Gesetze*, which inform the historian's pessimism as perhaps universal and certainly not limited to the events of the past related in the *Histories*. These laws should be taken as operative even in Periclean Athens.

it a cause of an imperialistic hubris common in Herodotus. In particular, a key to understanding the workings of Herodotus's notorious κύκλος τῶν ἀνθρωπηίων πρηγμάτων, and therefore to gaining insight into the structure of his work, is recognizing the significance in Herodotean thought of the concept of the "blindness of the ruler" ("Verblendung des Herrschers"), a general failure to observe human limitations and, in particular, a failure to perceive the advantages inherent in "primitiveness" (*Ursprünglichkeit*), a concept embodied by relatively simple peoples like the Massagetae, the Ethiopians, the Scythians, and the Greeks.[7] Primitive people, it seems, enjoy a crucial self-sufficiency, being satisfied with their own lands, powers, and possessions. While other scholars may have noticed the existence of this kind of moral blindness as an instrument of historical causation in Herodotus,[8] Cobet believes that his investigations go farther: he can identify the "*Gründe* für der Verblendung" and the manner in which it works its ill effects. The chief culprit is luxury. Luxury clouds the vision of those who possess it; an "inclination to luxury" overturns self-sufficiency and leads to unjust imperial expansion and the consequent ruin of the invader.[9] The great example of this trajectory in Herodotus is manifested in the Persians, who go from the virtues of the primitive in the days of Cyrus, when they knew no luxuries, to an extreme of moral blindness in Xerxes' desire to possess the whole world. However, Herodotus does not offer the deleterious consequences of luxury merely as an ad hoc explanation for the differences between Greeks and barbarians. Rather, Cobet argues, the historian emphasizes "die Allgemeinheit des Gedankens": moral decay brought on by luxury is a "natural process" that helps set the boundaries of human achievement.[10]

In a more recent study, Lateiner presents us with a Herodotus who combines the two effects of luxury. On the one hand, "Herodotus believed that the Persians lost their freedom-loving and manly qualities and sank into luxury and self-indulgent frivolity." Yet at the same time, this process of degeneration is a characteristic of "oriental expansion and megalomania."[11] The incoherence of this view is apparent: the Persians are from a single cause made to

---

7. Cobet 1971, 113.
8. In particular, Hellmann 1934.
9. Cobet 1971, 113–16; note especially, with reference to Pausanias's comparison after Plataea of Persian and Greek meals: "es wird zugleich die Art der Verblendung des reichen Despoten in seiner Zuneigung zu solchem Luxus . . . charakterisiert" (115–16).
10. Cobet 1971, 174–76. Cobet shares with Bischoff the belief that Herodotus saw the same "natural processes" at work in the Athenian empire and was fearful for the future of the city.
11. Lateiner 1989, 48–50; unlike the Persians, the Greeks are "the agents of an eternal balance" (49) and so apparently immune from the dangers of luxury.

sink into self-indulgence and to expand into empire, to become both frivolous and megalomaniacal.

Thus the aspects of pernicious luxury that we have identified in Chapter 1 are thoroughly implicated in the various theories about historical causation in Herodotus. It is therefore disturbing to note that most discussions show little awareness of distinctions that hold throughout the Classical period. Certainly, there is a tendency in the scholarship to fail to recognize the boundaries between the two principal processes of decadence that are evident in the other material from the fifth and fourth centuries; rather, apparent examples of decadence, which seem to us distinct, are regularly treated as instances of a single concept. Contradictions inherent in a concept in which weakness and softness leads to commission of mutilation, rape, and murder are left unobserved, not to mention unexplained. It is part of the goal of this chapter to present a study of luxury in the *Histories* that gives due consideration to the internal contours of the concept. A particular effort will be made to discover whether Herodotus did indeed combine the two processes of decadence into a single principle of causation that could prove attractive to subsequent historians.

Soft Lands and Soft People

The first stage in our discussion will be an examination of passages in which Herodotus, in his own voice or through that of a character, makes a more or less general statement about the effects of luxury. It is from such evidence that most arguments about pernicious opulence in the *Histories* are constructed. After considering these passages, we will move from the general to the particular, focusing on the role that luxury actually plays in the events of Herodotus's narrative as they unfold. Systematic study of this material is much less apparent in the scholarship. While the danger of hubris is indeed an important theme in the *Histories*, we will see that it is not one particularly associated with luxury or specific aspects of lifestyle. Therefore, our especial attention will be given to passages in which rich and luxurious individuals or groups are depicted as acting weakly or effeminately.

To begin, the most famous statement apparently about the moral consequences of luxury occurs at 9.122, the final chapter of the *Histories*. The passage is a digression and comes as a surprise to readers, since 9.121 had ended the account of the events of 479 as the victorious Greeks sailed home to dedicate the cables of Xerxes' bridges across the Hellespont.[12] Hdt. 9.122 is therefore controversial; opinions differ on whether our text of the *Histories* ends as Herodotus intended or is broken off unfinished. The view now prevailing is that 9.122 successfully rounds off the whole work, providing the reader with thematic information illuminating important aspects of Herodotus's thinking about the war.[13] If this is the case, then any criticism of luxury in the passage is of more than local significance.

The digression is introduced genealogically. Just before the Greeks left Sestos, they had executed a certain Artayctes for egregious impieties. Herodotus is reminded of Artayctes' grandfather, Artembares, who had incited the Persians to ask Cyrus to use his new ascendancy to move them from their homeland to a more prosperous territory.[14] Cyrus ridiculed this proposal on the grounds that it would be the equivalent of giving up their hegemony and accepting the rule of others:

φιλέειν γὰρ ἐκ τῶν μαλακῶν χώρων μαλακοὺς [ἄνδρας][15] γίνεσθαι· οὐ γάρ τι τῆς αὐτῆς γῆς εἶναι καρπόν τε θωμαστὸν φύειν καὶ ἄνδρας ἀγαθοὺς τὰ πολέμια.

[For soft men usually arise from soft lands; the same ground does not produce both a wondrous crop and men good at war.] (Hdt. 9.122.3)

These words are generally read as constituting a criticism of luxury, which Cyrus seemed to connect to weakness and servility.[16] However, one should note that no specific mention of luxury or any particular manner of δίαιτα occurs in this passage: though τρυφή and cognates do not appear in the *Histories*, Herodotus does use ἁβρός occasionally and can refer to a luxurious way of life as enjoyment of

---

12. If the work had ended with the concluding words of 9.121, few readers would find it inappropriate: καὶ κατὰ τὸ ἔτος τοῦτο οὐδὲν ἐπὶ πλέον τούτων ἐγένετο ("And this was all that happened in that year.").

13. The older view, that the work is unfinished, is especially championed by Jacoby in his 1913 commentary (*ad* 9.122); Pohlenz 1937; and van Groningen 1960. In favor of completion are: Immerwahl 1966, 1981; Cobet 1971; Ayo 1984; Boedeker 1988; Herington 1991; Dewald 1997; Flower and Marincola 2002. More bibliography is available in Herington (149–50) and Dewald.

14. γῆν γὰρ ἐκτήμεθα ὀλίγην καὶ ταύτην τρηχέαν, μεταναστάντες ἐκ ταύτης ἄλλην σχῶμεν ἀμείνω ("Since we possess a small land and rough besides, let us migrate from here and take some other, better land." Hdt. 9.122.2).

15. Rosén omits.

16. Few scholars, whatever their views on pernicious luxury as historical cause in Herodotus, are uncertain that Cyrus has luxury in mind. Even the generally cautious Flower and Marincola (2002, 311) note that "there is no reason to doubt" that Herodotus is contrasting the luxury evident among the Persians at Plataea with the hardiness of earlier days.

τὰ ἀγαθά and similar expressions. Here, "soft lands" are identified as the source of the potential enervation of the Persians, but this particular expression would have conveyed no specific connotation to Herodotus's audience.[17]

Μαλακός ("soft") and its synonyms are only rarely attested as attributes of some word for a geographical area, and any obvious meaning that would be appropriate for 9.122 is particularly difficult to find. "Soft meadows" are a feature of Archaic epic (e.g., λειμῶνες μαλακοί, Hom., Od. 5.72 and 9.132–33). A few examples from Xenophon's corpus refer simply to the physical softness of the soil (as a place to find animal tracks at Cyn. 10.5, or as suitable for training horses at Eq. 8.6). The most interesting comparandum comes from the depiction of the Shield of Achilles in Iliad 18. Juxtaposed to the scene of bloody battle with two sides fighting over the corpses is an agricultural vignette:

ἐν δ᾽ ἐτίθει νειὸν μαλακὴν πίειραν ἄρουραν
εὐρεῖαν τρίπολον· πολλοὶ δ᾽ ἀροτῆρες ἐν αὐτῇ
ζεύγεα δινεύοντες ἐλάστρεον ἔνθα καὶ ἔνθα.

[And he put in soft fallow-land, rich, arable, plowed three times. And in it many plowmen were turning their teams, driving them back and forth.] (Hom., Il. 18.541–43)

An echo of this contrast between warlike and peaceful pursuits would not be inappropriate in the Herodotean context. Thus, although commentators are right to identify Hdt. 9.122.3 as an example of the analogical reasoning so congenial to the Greek mind, the force of the analogy remains unclear.

The specific meaning of "soft" in ἐκ τῶν μαλακῶν χώρων can only be derived from the Histories itself,[18] where the context points to the means of pro-

---

17. Redfield (1985, 109–14) argues that the Histories is to some degree organized around "the contrast between 'soft peoples and hard peoples'" (109). The contrast is extensive; for example, "Soft peoples are characterized by luxury, the division of labor, and complexity of nomoi, especially in the sphere of religion" (109). However, whether or not Redfield's analysis of societies on these lines is correct, it is unpersuasive to align it with Cyrus's advice at 9.122 by using the distinguishing terms "soft" and "hard," and Redfield himself admits these are not Herodotean terms. For Cyrus at 9.122, the essential characteristic of softness is lack of martial competence; soft people are weak, cowardly, and unwarlike. Redfield does not demonstrate that his "soft peoples" are so depicted, though he does suggest that this point is made by "patterned repetitions in the narrative," claiming, for example, "There are in the Histories no conquests of hard peoples by soft peoples" (113). We shall discuss below the difficulty in finding peoples which are "soft" in Cyrus's particular sense of the word.

18. Flower and Marincola (2002, 314), following Corcella (1984), note that this type of reasoning by analogy was commonly employed by Herodotus and his contemporaries. But however much the

duction of the Persian livelihood, rather than to its manner of consumption. While Artembares spoke vaguely of improving the Persian situation, Cyrus seemed to focus upon the impending change from traditional Persian practices to agriculture.[19] We can assume, for Herodotus's audience, no association between agriculture and a life of unusual ease.[20] Nor would those familiar with the culture of the hoplite-farmer readily see an antithesis between the cereal agriculture and military strength. In sum, neither Cyrus's general formulation about soft lands and soft men nor his more specific references to the production of wondrously bountiful grain harvests was likely to resonate with Herodotus's readership by recalling widely held beliefs about the causes of decadence.

Hdt. 9.122, then, presents no straightforward and specific warning about the well-known perils of luxury. Rather, it is a combination of the familiar and the paradoxical. Its meaning is a matter for interpretation and must be teased out with the help of clearer evidence from elsewhere in the *Histories*. The prevailing view is that μαλακοὶ χῶροι is used to indicate not a particular way of making a living, but great wealth in general, with its accompanying opulence being the catalyst for moral degeneration.[21] This position is supported by the

---

form of this proposition may have been familiar, the term μαλακοὶ χῶροι remains empty of any particular content: it was clear what Cyrus meant by "soft men" and it was reasonable to associate such men with "soft lands," but this phrase is left to connote tautologically whatever land might produce the weak and unwarlike. We will discuss the other general concept to which Herodotus does refer in this passage, geographical determinism, below.

19. Artembares speaks only of moving from a "small and rough land" (γῆν ὀλίγην καὶ τρηχέαν) to another that is "better" (ἄλλην ἀμείνω) with the result that the Persians will become "more marvelous." (θωμαστότεροι). While the precise point of this term is unclear, it is worth noting that Hartog (1988, 234) finds that in the *Histories "thoma"* is more frequently described in terms of quantity than quality; it is relevant that a salient feature of Herodotus's descriptions of the wealth or prosperity of peoples or nations is the quantity of their populations, a principal source for military power. Artembares, then, may be presenting emigration as a way of increasing the size, and therefore strength, of the Persian people. Cyrus prefers to focus on the quality of individual warriors. In any case, Cyrus, for his part, is slightly less vague than Artembares. Incompatible with ἄνδρας ἀγαθοὺς τὰ πολέμια is "wondrous produce" (καπρὸς θωμαστός). This, Herodotus tells us in the narrator's voice, the Persians might have acquired by "sowing the plain" (πεδιάδα σπείροντες). In contrast, Herodotus describes the Persians' ancient homeland as "distressing" (λυπρή). As the commentators point out, the word is used once here and once in Homer, where its negation as applied to Ithaca is illustrated by, *inter alia*, the island's agricultural productivity: οὐδὲ λίην λυπρή. . . . ἐν μὲν γάρ οἱ σῖτος ἀθέσφατος, ἐν δέ τε οἶνος γίνεται· αἰεὶ δ᾽ ὄμβρος ἔχει τεθαλυῖά τ᾽ ἐέρση ("not utterly distressing. . . . For on it grows grain beyond counting and wine, and there is always rain and the blossoming dew," Hom., *Od.* 13.243–45).

20. So, most prominently, in the *Works and Days*, where Hesiod presented himself as one who "was relatively rich, yet worked incessantly, and recommended nothing but work. Work makes the farmer rich, and riches mean not the leisure to write poetry . . . but rather possession of things" (Desmond 2006, 33).

21. Thus Thomas 2000, 107: "a wealthy, fertile environment, a generous beautiful land, is envisaged as enervating or conducive to luxurious living . . ."; Dewald 1997, 68: "Here Herodotus shows Cyrus

fact that Herodotus characterizes the Persians as relatively poor before their conquest of Lydia.[22] The chief obstacle to this interpretation is the counterfactual quality of Artembares' proposal. The last lines of the *Histories* relate that the Persians chose to listen to Cyrus and "to rule, living in a distressing land, rather than, sowing the plain, to be slaves to others." If μαλακοὶ χῶροι refers to general prosperity, and if we take the work's final sentence at face value, we are left with the implication that the Persians opted for empire, while renouncing its material benefits.[23]

This is not the picture that Herodotus presents to us: the wealth of the Persian empire is one of the principal elements of the Herodotean narrative. We note that great wealth and luxury are not depicted as coming to the Persians only gradually in generations after Cyrus. Rather, these become characteristics of the Persians from the conquest of Lydia, immediately subsequent to the time of Cyrus's conversation with Artembares.[24] In fact, in a well-known passage, Cyrus had set out the attainment of luxuries as a goal of his drive to empire. To persuade the tribes of Persia to join him in revolt against the Medes, Cyrus had arranged for them a day of hard labor followed by a day of feasting and leisure.[25]

---

persuading the Persians that they should continue to live, as they always have done, in rugged poverty" [emphasis in original].

22. Hdt. 1.71.3, where Croesus's adviser Sandanis explains that the Persians lack all "good things," a claim verified by the narrator's voice at 1.71.4. In this connection, it is worth observing that Cyrus's advice to Artembares is set after the fall of Astyages, and thus immediately before the war with the Lydians.

23. Dewald (1997, 72), for example, implies a straightforward dichotomy between poverty and prosperity: "What the Persians choose here . . . seems paradoxical: in order to remain free, they must choose to rule. But in order to rule, they must stay rugged. Thus, it appears, rulers of empires must refuse to enjoy the fruits of their labors, in order to survive as rulers."

24. They were always quick to adopt the "best" features of the conquered (Hdt. 1.135.1). The *Histories* does not allow us to assume that the Persian love of comforts was a quality that developed slowly from an earlier primitivism. Croesus's adviser Sandanis, contemplating war with the poor and primitive Persians, identifies in them already a disposition for the comforts of life (Hdt. 1.71.3), and Sandanis was correct in his assessment. Accordingly, Croesus himself, devising a strategy for Cyrus's invasion of the Massagetae, is able to contrast the comforts of the Persians with the hard life of their enemies: Μασσαγέται εἰσὶ ἀγαθῶν τε Περσικῶν ἄπειροι καὶ καλῶν μεγάλων ἀπαθέες ("The Massagetae have no experience of the good things of the Persians and are unfamiliar with the finest things in life," Hdt. 1.207.6). Among the ἀγαθὰ Περσικά are craters of unmixed wine and "all sorts of food" (σιτία παντοῖα), items specified by Sandanis as beyond Persian experience before the Lydian war.

25. Note that this story contradicts in some measure Sandanis' description of Persian simplicity. Cyrus is able to provide both wine and "the most appropriate foods" (σιτίοισι ὡς ἐπιτηδεοτάτοισι, Hdt. 1.126.2) at this feast. It is a feature of adviser speeches for the councilor to exaggerate the wealth or poverty of the prospective enemy, according to whether he wishes to encourage or discourage the proposed course of action. Although the Persians were thus not completely unfamiliar with "good things" before the establishment of their empire, it remains the case that luxuries that are depicted before Cyrus's rise as rare and demanding significant sacrifice (requiring all of Cambyses' resources) become by the time of Cyrus's death characteristic of the Persian nation in general (ἀγαθὰ Περσικά).

Their expressed preference for πάντα ἀγαθά over the evils of hard work becomes the basis of Cyrus's argument:

Ἄνδρες Πέρσαι, οὕτως ὑμῖν ἔχει· βουλομένοισι μὲν ἐμέο πείθεσθαι ἔστι τάδε τε καὶ ἄλλα μυρία ἀγαθά, οὐδένα πόνον δουλοπρεπέα ἔχουσι· μὴ βουλομένοισι δὲ ἐμέο πείθεσθαι εἰσὶ ὑμῖν πόνοι τῷ χθιζῷ παραπλήσιοι ἀναρίθμητοι. νῦν ὦν ἐμέο πειθόμενοι γίνεσθε ἐλεύθεροι.

[Men of Persia, this is how matters stand for you: if you are willing to accept my leadership, you will have these and ten thousand other good things, but no more toil fit for slaves. If, however, you don't want to follow me, there await you countless labors like those of yesterday. So now take me as your leader and become free men.] (Hdt. 1.126.5–6)

Here, in contrast to the usual interpretation of 9.122, life's hardships are associated with servility. Luxuries are the mark of the free. Nor does Cyrus refer to some moderate level of luxury that may be thought compatible with ἄνδρες ἀγαθοὶ τὰ πολέμια; the kind of freedom he intended to win for the Persians would bring luxuries practically without number (τάδε τε καὶ ἄλλα μυρία ἀγαθά). These comments leave little room for the idea of luxury as sufficient cause of decadence and decline. Rather, it seems that the opposite implication is present in the closing words of Cyrus's speech at 1.126, where he apparently addressed an expectation in his audience that the richer and more powerful Medes would be better fighters than their poorer neighbors. These words are difficult to reconcile with a Herodotus intent on illustrating the moral precept that "wealth corrupts."

Generally speaking, those who see pernicious luxury as a theme of the *Histories* pay too little attention to such passages where Herodotus shows wealth as a sufficient cause of military strength. Another passage offers a brief but illustrative example. Here, as the victorious Persians looted Sardis, Croesus advised his new master not to let the men keep their newly won wealth:

Πέρσαι, φύσιν ἐόντες ὑβρισταί, εἰσὶ ἀχρήματοι. ἢν ὦν σὺ τούτους περιίδης διαρπάσαντας καὶ κατασχόντας χρήματα μεγάλα, τάδε τοι ἐξ αὐτῶν ἐπίδοξα γενέσθαι· ὃς ἂν αὐτῶν πλεῖστα κατάσχῃ, τοῦτον προσδέκεσθαί τοι ἐπαναστησόμενον.

[The Persians, though by nature prone to hubris, are poor. So, if you allow them to continue to plunder and to get possession of great wealth, this is what is likely

to happen: whoever gets the most wealth, expect that he will revolt against you.]
(Hdt. 1.89.2)

The passage is clear in its depiction of wealth as a catalyst of manliness and force (unleashing the Persians' latent hubris), not enervation and decadence. A few pages later, this potential effect of wealth was realized, when Pactyas—not a Persian, but a Lydian, to be sure—used the great riches of Sardis to hire mercenaries and rebel against Cyrus and his governor (Hdt. 1.154.1). In spite of the emphasis on wealth as power, and because 1.89 points to the dangerous effects of wealth, Thomas, for example, associates it with 9.122 and other supposed evidence that a luxurious lifestyle entails weakness.[26] It is difficult to see how 1.89 and 9.122 could be interpreted together as manifestations of a Herodotean concept of decadence. In the earlier passage, wealth is explicitly said to make its possessors intractable and hard to rule; in the latter it is assumed to cause the opposite result (ἄλλοισι δουλεύειν). Proponents of the claim that Herodotus gives the moral dimension of wealth historiographical importance need to offer a more thorough accounting of the complexities of the evidence.[27] Meanwhile, passages such as Hdt. 1.126 and 1.89 prevent us from seeing 9.122 as simply the last in a series of references to the debilitating effects of great prosperity.

On the other hand, it is usual for proponents of the thematic importance of pernicious luxury in the *Histories* to find their strongest support for this view, not in Herodotus's own complex evidence, but in certain principals set forth in a roughly contemporary work, the Hippocratic treatise *On Airs, Waters, and Places*. This essay notoriously draws a distinction between the inhabitants of Europe and those of Asia, in which the latter are said to be necessarily deficient in courage and martial vigor. As a result, some scholars see a relationship of

---

26. Thomas 2000, 107–9. Similarly, Flory (1987, 93) sees 1.89 as sketching part of the "corruption" of the Persians from "noble savages" to "prosperous aggressors." For Flory, these latter are "totally effete and enslaved to a luxurious life" (118). It is not clear why gaining the potential to free oneself from subservience to the King should be understood as either morally corrupt or as a step toward weakness or slavery of any sort, even to luxury.

27. Immerwahr ([1966] 1981, 146 n. 190) claims that the reader "should not be confused by the fact that the meaning of" 1.126 and 9.122 "is nearly contradictory." In the first, he says, "the Persians choose wealth and leisure, while in 9.122 they are being advised against luxury." This distinction is not apparent in the text: the μυρία ἀγαθά at 1.126 must include luxuries and not merely leisure as concomitant with freedom and rule, while, as we have seen, the source of the danger referred to at 9.122 is not clear. Immerwahr's interpretation that the "two anecdotes thus illuminate a single problem from two different points of view" is unhelpful in resolving the contradiction. Better is Flower and Marincola's (2002, 312) suggestion that "it is probably wrong . . . to look for a consistent pattern of development in H.'s comments about the Persians' lifestyle." In this vein, scholars should give due weight to passages in which wealth and luxury are assigned positive value as a historical force. Currently, most attention is focused on apparent negative assessments.

influence—or at the very least, parallelism—between *Airs* and the end of the *Histories*. The supposed similarity of the two texts[28] is taken as evidence that belief in the enervating effects of luxury was well established in Herodotus's day. However, a closer look at the relevant parts of *Airs* shows that they are in no way illuminating with respect either to *Histories* 9.122 or to the idea of pernicious luxury more generally.

The author of *Airs* presents a theory of geographical determinism: the climate, soil, and hydrology of an area necessarily shape the character of its inhabitants. In the terms of this theory, much of Asia is bound to produce weaklings:

τὸ δὲ ἀνδρεῖον καὶ τὸ ταλαίπωρον καὶ τὸ ἔμπονον καὶ τὸ θυμοειδὲς οὐκ ἂν δύναιτο ἐν τοιαύτῃ φύσει ἐγγίγνεσθαι μήτε ὁμοφύλου μήτε ἀλλοφύλου, ἀλλὰ τὴν ἡδονὴν ἀνάγκη κρατεῖν.

[Manliness and endurance and acceptance of toil and high spirits are not able to develop in such a nature, neither in native nor alien, but it is necessary that pleasure prevail.] (Hipp., *De aere* 12.6–7)

Although it may be tempting to see the cause of Asian cowardice in the prosperity of the area, which indeed the author has emphasized a few lines earlier, and to find in this process, therefore, a veiled reference to pernicious luxury, the author of *Airs* has another cause in mind. The primary effects of geography on ethos are direct and unmediated:

. . . ἥ τε χώρη τῆς χώρης ἡμερωτέρη καὶ τὰ ἤθεα τῶν ἀνθρώπων ἠπιώτερα καὶ εὐοργητότερα. τὸ δὲ αἴτιον τούτων ἡ κρῆσις τῶν ὡρέων.

[The land is more gentle than the other land, and the character of the people is gentler and more good-tempered. The reason for these things is the temperateness of the seasons.] (Hipp., *De aere* 12.2–3)

Furthermore, when *Airs* returns a few chapters later to the topic of the weakness of the people of Asia, the author explains just how a climate with little variability has its enervating effect:

---

28. Lateiner (1986, 10) goes so far as to say: "Herodotus could even be a source for (rather than a borrower of) the Hippocratic theory of the effect of climate on health." He lists Hdt. 9.122.3 as one of the passages in which "Herodotus on occasion 'explains' national character by climate or topography" (16).

... αἱ ὧραι αἴτιαι μάλιστα, οὐ μεγάλας τὰς μεταβολὰς ποιεύμεναι οὔτε ἐπὶ τὸ
θερμὸν οὔτε ἐπὶ τὸ ψυχρὸν, ἀλλὰ παραπλησίως. οὐ γὰρ γίγνονται ἐκπλήξιες
τῆς γνώμης οὔτε μετάστασις ἰσχυρὴ τοῦ σώματος, ἀφ᾽ ὅτων εἰκὸς τὴν ὀργὴν
ἀγριοῦσθαί τε καὶ τοῦ ἀγνώμονος καὶ θυμοειδέος μετέχειν. . . .

[The seasons are the primary cause, since they do not produce great changes,
either toward heat or cold, but are about the same. For consternation of the
understanding does not occur, nor a strong change of body; from these things
the temperament may be made wild and become somewhat hard-hearted and
high-spirited.] (Hipp., *De aere* 16.1–2)

Chapter 23 repeats this explanation with additional details, and the wording of
this passage makes it especially interesting:

ἐν μὲν γὰρ τῷ αἰεὶ παραπλησίῳ αἱ ῥᾳθυμίαι ἔνεισιν, ἐν δὲ τῷ μεταβαλλομένῳ αἱ
ταλαιπωρίαι τῷ σώματι καὶ τῇ ψυχῇ. καὶ ἀπὸ μὲν ἡσυχίης καὶ ῥᾳθυμίης ἡ δειλίη
αὔξεται, ἀπὸ δὲ τῆς ταλαιπωρίης καὶ τῶν πόνων αἱ ἀνδρεῖαι. διὰ τοῦτό εἰσι
μαχιμώτεροι οἱ τὴν Εὐρώπην οἰκέοντες. . . .

[Indeed, relaxation exists in the constant similarity [of climate], but in change,
exertion for body and for soul. Then, from rest and relaxation grows cowardice,
but from exertion and toils come manliness. For this reason, those living in
Europe are better fighters.] (Hipp., *De aere* 23.3)

This text sets in opposition ῥᾳθυμίη and πόνος in a way that recalls later discussions of the development of pernicious luxury. However, the parallel is merely
specious, since this passage does not allow for an economic dimension: relaxation arises not as a result of wealth, but rather is the unmediated product of the
restful character of a temperate climate. Exertion does not imply poverty, but
the efforts necessary to deal with climatic change.

In the process here described, there is no room for luxury, or indeed for any
aspect of lifestyle, as a cause of the unwarlike qualities of the Asians.[29] To be
sure, the author of *Airs* does find a relevant cause in certain Asian νόμοι, but
these are a matter of political and utilitarian strategy rather than personal and

---

29. This point is made clear by words immediately following this passage: καὶ διὰ τοὺς νόμους ("and
because of their customs"). The author then discusses the implications of Asian political institutions
on the bellicosity of the inhabitants. This transitional phrase indicates just that: previously the discussion was not concerned with νόμοι such as the luxury or frugality of the people of Asia. Only the
direct effects of their physical environment has been at issue.

hedonistic aspects of lifestyle; we will examine these passages below in association with their Herodotean parallels.

Far from supporting an interpretation that makes pernicious luxury the theme of *Histories* 9.122, as many assume, the Hippocratic *Airs* has no apparent connection with ideas about the ill effects of wealth. Indeed, no reference to opulence of any kind appears in the *Airs*. This observation is true even when, at the very end of the work, the discussion turns from the primary cause of human differences (μέγισται διαλλαγαί)—i.e., the disposition of the seasons—to secondary reasons: "the country in which one grows up and the waters" (ἡ χώρη ἐν ᾗ ἄν τις τρέφηται καὶ τὰ ὕδατα, *De aere* 24.7). In this connection, we read that where "the land is rich and soft and well watered" (ἡ γῆ πίειρα καὶ μαλθακὴ καὶ ἔνυδρος), the people are indolent and unsuitable for hardship. It might be tempting to see in this sequence of adjectives a reference—at second hand—to economic prosperity, which might reasonably be associated with fertile fields. Furthermore, given the author's mention of the weakness of the inhabitants of such an area, the richness and softness of the land might even seem to be a third-hand reference to a luxurious δίαιτα. However, this line of interpretation is precluded by the words immediately following the attributes in question:

καὶ τὰ ὕδατα κάρτα μετέωρα, ὥστε θερμὰ εἶναι τοῦ θέρεος, καὶ τοῦ χειμῶνος ψυχρά, καὶ τῶν ὡρέων καλῶς κεῖται.

[and the precipitation plentiful, so that they are warm in summer and in winter cold, and it is finely situated with respect to the seasons.] (Hipp., *De aere* 24.8)

Once again the author's focus is on purely geographical characteristics, and, in a rather confused line of argument, mention of moderate or harsh climate subsumes the subsidiary causes of differing moral qualities—these causes are the announced topic of this section—to the main causes as discussed in the bulk of the treatise.[30] The processes by which the γῆ πίειρα and the χώρη ψιλή bring

---

30. That emphasis is once again on the idea of the influence of a temperate climate is made clear a few lines later, when the Hippocratic author turns to the other side of his comparison, a land that produces fierce and warlike people: ὅκου δ' ἐστὶν ἡ χώρη ψιλή τε καὶ ἄνυδρος καὶ τρηχείη καὶ ὑπὸ τοῦ χειμῶνος πιεζομένη καὶ ὑπὸ τοῦ ἡλίου κεκαυμένη, ἐνταῦθα δὲ σκληρούς τε καὶ ἰσχνοὺς . . . εὑρήσεις ("And where the land is bare and unwatered and rough, and pressed by the winter and burned by the sun, there you will discover men hard and lean . . . ," *De aere* 24.9). Here the swing between cold winters and hot summers corresponds in explanatory force to the seasons disposed "beautifully" in the earlier passage. The χώρη ψιλή καὶ τρηχείη may indeed indicate a county poor and with few luxuries, but the moral implications of a hard life—if any—are immediately dropped in favor of the direct influence of climate.

about their respective results receive no additional explanation. Rather, the argument's concluding words reiterate the author's belief in the unmediated connection between geographic and moral characteristics: καὶ τἄλλα τὰ ἐν τῇ γῇ φυόμενα πάντα ἀκόλουθα ἐόντα τῇ γῇ ("and the rest of the products of the land, being all of them in conformity with the land," *De aere* 24.9). Interpretations that posit an economic dimension in this causal nexus are not merely speculative, but inconsistent with the author's thinking where we can discern it.

In sum, *On Airs, Waters, and Places* does not corroborate the interpretations of Herodotus 9.122 that rely on the existence of a view which held that wealth was dangerous because it could effeminize its possessor. Certainly, no such view could be reconstructed on the basis of *Airs* alone. Indeed, if this were our only source, we would not even suspect the existence of such an idea. Nor, for that matter, is it clear that *Histories* 9.122 contains a reference to any specific idea presented in *Airs*. The version of geographical determinism offered by Herodotus's Cyrus seems only broadly and superficially similar to that in the Hippocratic work. The two differ in the effective details: Cyrus made no mention of climate, wind, or weather. Rather, to the extent that he was at all specific about the danger of the proposed migration, he seemed to locate it in the fertility of the new land and economic consequences of that fertility. Cyrus identified its wondrous harvest (καρπόν θωμαστόν) as the feature incompatible with good warriors, and, a few lines later, Herodotus in his narrative voice notes that the Persians chose not to "sow the plains" (πεδιάδα σπείροντες) and become slaves. *Airs*, as we have observed, shows not the slightest interest in possible economic ramifications of geographic variables.[31]

Since the supposed parallels of *Airs* offers us no useful evidence on the moral dimension of wealth, we must return to the testimony of the *Histories* itself, which we have seen is much more complicated than is usually thought when it pertains to the role of economic prosperity in the κύκλος of history. It remains possible that 9.122 presents, as one aspect of Herodotus's complex position, a criticism of pernicious luxury. In its essential form, the argument in favor of this interpretation is as follows: the *Histories* offers repeated references to Persian weakness and degeneracy. Such references are particularly elaborated in Book 9: in the anecdote of Pausanias in the tent of Mardonius, for example,

---

31. A theory of pernicious luxury would be like the view expounded, in that ease would lead to cowardice and exertion to manliness. However, one must keep in mind that the root cause of weakness is too much similarity and too little change. According to this reasoning, the lifestyle most productive of courage would be one that alternates the most extravagant luxuries with the most burdensome toils.

Persian opulence is associated with their defeat, and the story of Xerxes and the wife of Masistes seems to present the monarch as "the antithesis of the 'hard' Persian described by Cyrus in the concluding chapter."[32] Given these circumstances, and given the prominence of Cyrus's comments in the coda of the *Histories*, the connection drawn there between mode of life and loss of empire must be relevant to the narrative of Persian defeat. Accordingly, the final sentence of the *Histories*, the declaration that the Persians heeded Cyrus and avoided the dangers that he described, is read as containing an irony revealed by the whole course of the preceding narrative of the Persian Wars. The force of the concluding words applies only to a bygone era of Persian toughness.[33] Readers are meant to see the contrast with matters in Xerxes' day and draw the appropriate conclusion.

This seems like a strong argument. However, when we examine it in detail we find that its premises are seriously undermined. In the first place, the episode in the tent of Mardonius does not necessarily support the interpretation that it usually receives. At Hdt. 9.82, we read how Pausanias, having come into possession of Mardonius's κατασκευή and being amazed by its splendor, ordered the captured servants to produce a dinner Persian-style. He then commanded that a typical Spartan meal be set beside it and explained the object lesson to the Greek generals in this way:

Ἄνδρες Ἕλληνες, τῶνδε εἵνεκα ἐγὼ ὑμέας συνήγαγον, βουλόμενος ὑμῖν τοῦδε τοῦ Μήδων ἡγεμόνος τὴν ἀφροσύνην δεῖξαι, ὃς τοιήνδε δίαιταν ἔχων ἦλθε ἐς ἡμέας οὕτω ὀϊζυρὴν ἔχοντας ἀπαιρησόμενος.

---

32. Flower and Marincola 2002, 292; cf. Erbse 1992, 90–91.

33. Thus Dewald 1997, 72: "The larger implicit meaning of the final anecdote ... is not one borne out by the version of the Greco-Persian confrontation found in the rest of the *Histories*"; Thomas 2000, 107: "Cyrus answered with the advice, which we all know was disregarded, at least by later Persians"; Lateiner 1989, 49: "He advises his fellow Persians to avoid gentle climates and fruitful soils insofar as living there (not ruling such lands) would threaten the Persian martial way of life and national character. The Persians, however, did come to enjoy leisure and luxuries whose fruits included the degeneration of Persian courage"; Masaracchia 1977, 213: "il lettore della *Storie* sa che i persiani delle generazioni successive avevano praticamente abbandonato il punto di vista dei loro antenati"; Desmond 2006, 122–23: "By the time of Xerxes' invasion, the Persians have forgotten Cyrus's wise recommendation to retain voluntarily the poverty that geography had initially forced upon them." Moles (1996, 275), observing that a sharp distinction cannot be maintained between Cyrus himself and his successors vis-à-vis this advice: "the epilogue acquires a sharp irony: the last warner of the *Histories* disregarded his own warnings." Redfield 1985, 114: "This bit of wisdom is in fact an ironic criticism of the Persians: ... if Cyrus himself had been true to it, he would not have attacked Babylon and then the Massagetae."

[Men of Greece, I have assembled you for the following reason: to demonstrate to you the foolishness of this Persian leader. Although he has a lifestyle such as this, he came to rob us of this woeful portion that we possess.] (Hdt. 9.82.3)

Taken at face value, Pausanias's remarks reflect an idea we have already seen in the mouth of Sandanis on the eve of Croesus's campaign against Cyrus. This is the imprudence of attacking a relatively much poorer enemy: there is little to gain and much to lose. It is possible that the passage is meant to make only this simple point. However, given that these words bring a kind of closure to the story of Xerxes' invasion, scholars may be correct in assuming that a reference to a greater and more general ἀφροσύνη lies beneath the surface.[34] Many agree with Bischoff in identifying this more "fundamental stupidity" in the blind pursuit of luxury, which, if attained, leads to decadence and defeat. Masaracchia, for example, is typical when he finds here a "central theme of Herodotus's political philosophy," an "iron relationship of cause and effect," namely, that of "wealth and prosperity as sources of softness and weakness."[35]

Unfortunately for this view, the *Histories*' narration of the Battle of Plataea characterizes neither the Persians in general nor Mardonius in particular as in any way soft or unwarlike. In their recent commentary, Flower and Marincola emphasize correctly that Herodotus does not present evidence that allows us to attribute the Persian defeat to softness or lack of courage.[36] Rather, "Book 9 makes it clear that the Persian warriors fought bravely and to the end."[37] As for

---

34. The commentaries note that this passage picks up Mardonius's words to Xerxes at Hdt. 7.5.3, where he held out, as an enticement for Xerxes to act, the beauty and prosperity of Europe; cf. Flower and Marincola 2002, 252–53.

35. Masaracchia 1977, 194–95.

36. On the other hand, Flower and Marincola (2002, 252) argue that it is significant that Pausanias specifies the luxuries in Mardonius's pavilion as τοῦ Μήδων ἡγεμόνος, "belonging to the Persians' leader" (Hdt. 9.82.3). Thus, apparently, the onus of the Spartan's criticism rests on Mardonius alone, and the passage is not evidence for the belief "that the Persian people collectively had become soft through luxury." Against this view, we may observe that at 9.80 Pausanias had sent the Helots ἀνὰ τὸ στρατόπεδον σκιδνάμενοι ("scattering through the camp") to collect plunder, and they had discovered luxuries comparable to those belonging to Mardonius. If Pausanias's strictures do indeed pertain to the effects of the possession and enjoyment of luxury goods, it seems likely they are meant to apply to Persians collectively as well as to their leader. If, as we argue, the focus of the criticism is aimed at an acquisitiveness that cannot be satisfied by any level of opulence, then Mardonius and Xerxes do bear the chief blame, as the instigators of the invasion.

37. Flower and Marincola 2002, 312; cf. the general discussion at pp. 38–39: "H. portrays the Persians as brave fighters, not cowards, and he explains their defeat at Plataea in terms of their lack of proper armour and their absence of hoplite training (62.3). Similarly at Mycale, the Persians put up a staunch fight for a long time, giving in only when they are overwhelmed. In each case the Persians (unlike their allies) fight to the bitter end: there is no sense here that luxury or 'softness' contributed to their defeat."

Mardonius himself, among the barbarian forces, their leader took the palm for courage, in spite of his "gold and silver couches and tables."[38] Thus, if we understand the Pausanias anecdote as assigning the cause of debilitating luxury to the Persian disaster, we would be introducing an unnecessary inconsistency into the text.

Nor is it reductionist to take Pausanias's words at face value. Underlying the claim that it is foolishness for those enjoying many luxuries to try to rob those who enjoy none, there is indeed a principle of thematic importance to the *Histories*, though it is not the concept of pernicious luxury. Rather, the principle in play is the insatiable, and indeed irrational, envy exhibited by tyrants. The clearest exposition of the idea comes in Book 3, during the famous Constitutional Debate between the conspirators against the false Smerdis:

κῶς δ᾿ ἂν εἴη χρῆμα κατηρτημένον μουναρχίη, τῇ ἔξεστι ἀνευθύνῳ ποιέειν τὰ βούλεται; καὶ γὰρ ἂν τὸν ἄριστον ἀνδρῶν πάντων στάντα ἐς ταύτην [τὴν ἀρχὴν][39] ἐκτὸς τῶν ἐωθότων νοημάτων στήσειε. ἐγγίνεται μὲν γάρ οἱ ὕβρις ὑπὸ τῶν παρεόντων ἀγαθῶν, φθόνος δὲ ἀρχῆθεν ἐμφύεται ἀνθρώπῳ. δύο δ᾿ ἔχων ταῦτα ἔχει πᾶσαν κακότητα· τὰ μὲν γὰρ ὕβρι κεκορημένος ἔρδει πολλὰ καὶ ἀτάσθαλα, τὰ δὲ φθόνῳ. καίτοι ἄνδρα γε τύραννον ἄφθονον ἔδει εἶναι, ἔχοντά γε πάντα τὰ ἀγαθά· τὸ δὲ ὑπεναντίον τούτου ἐς τοὺς πολιήτας πέφυκε, . . .

[How can monarchy be a suitable thing? It can do what it wants without giving an account. Such power would move the best of all men to unaccustomed thoughts. For hubris develops from availability of good things, and envy grows in people from the beginning. If he has both these things, then he has complete evil: he does many rash things because he is filled with hubris, and many others, filled with envy. To be sure, a tyrant ought to be without envy, since he has all good things. But he comes to be the opposite of this toward the citizens.] (Hdt. 3.80.3–4)

---

38. κλίνας τε χρυσέας καὶ ἀργυρέας εὖ ἐστρωμένας καὶ τραπέζας τε χρυσέας καὶ ἀργυρέας (Hdt. 9.82.2). On Mardonius's courage: Ἠρίστευσε δὲ τῶν βαρβάρων πεζὸς μὲν ὁ Περσέων, ἵππος δὲ ἡ Σακέων, ἀνὴρ δὲ λέγεται Μαρδόνιος ("Of the barbarians, the Persian infantry was the bravest, and the cavalry of the Sacae. The bravest man is said to be Mardonius." Hdt. 9.71.1). Herodotus had also emphasized Mardonius's martial prowess in the battle narrative itself, at 9.63.1–2. The disappearance of Mardonius's body is also significant. As Immerwahr ([1966] 1981, 298) explains, "It is as if the gods had made sure no defilement would take place, and the story, paralleling as it does the disappearance of other war heroes, tends to raise our estimation of Mardonius."

39. Rosén omits.

In Pausanias's eyes, it seems, the Persian leadership was displaying just these tyrannical qualities. Its δίαιτα already encompassed such luxuries as could scarcely be enhanced by conquest of the relatively poor Greek lands, yet this fact did not render the Persians ἄφθονοι.⁴⁰ The ἀφροσύνη that Pausanias mocks was thus a corollary, not of excessive luxury, but of absolute power. At the same time, luxury does play a part in the process depicted at 3.80: the monarch possesses all sorts of ἀγαθά, a word that in Herodotus may certainly include reference to luxuries of the sort on display in Mardonius's pavilion. However, it is important to recognize that the easy life enjoyed by an absolute ruler does not lead to enervation or softness, but rather to hubris. The sense of superiority imparted by great prosperity spurs the tyrant to transgress the limits of propriety into acts of violence. The scorn for others' concerns and well-being that is inherent in hubris leads the tyrant to yield to the impulses of his natural φθόνος. Thus, hubris, too, is an item in Pausanias's indictment of Mardonius; the Persian attempted to rob (ἀπαιρησόμενος) the Greeks of their pittance.⁴¹

Whether or not it is correct to see Hdt. 9.82 as the recurrence of the theme spelled out at 3.80, one must nonetheless recognize a reference to Persian hubris in Pausanias's words at 9.82.⁴² This fact has clear consequences for an interpretation that links the Pausanias anecdote with 9.122 as evidence of a theme of pernicious luxury. In brief, the commission of acts of hubris is incompatible with a moral disposition marked by μαλακία. Softness of this kind rather makes one into the passive object of such acts. Thus, the situation portrayed in 9.82 cannot be the result of the process foreseen and alluded to by Cyrus at 9.122. As commonly interpreted, the two passages are incompatible.

---

40. To see Pausanias's words as a reference not to decadence, but to the characterization of tyranny at 3.80, it is only necessary to recall Artabanus's explanation, at the inception of Xerxes' expedition, of why he opposed the invasion: ἐμὲ δὲ ἀκούσαντα πρὸς σέο κακῶς οὐ τοσοῦτο ἔδακε λύπη, ὅσον γνωμέων δύο προκειμένων Πέρσῃσι, τῆς μὲν ὕβριν αὐξανούσης, τῆς δὲ καταπαυούσης καὶ λεγούσης ὡς κακὸν εἴη διδάσκειν τὴν ψυχὴν πλέον τι δίζησθαι αἰεὶ ἔχειν τοῦ παρεόντος, τοιουτέων προκειμένων γνωμέων, ὅτι τὴν σφαλερωτέρην σεωυτῷ τε καὶ Πέρσῃσι ἀναιρέο ("I was not pained so much because you spoke ill of me, as because, with two opinions lying before the Persians, one increasing hubris, and the other putting an end to it and indicating how evil it is to teach the soul continually to seek to possess more than is at hand—with these opinions on the table, you chose the one more dangerous for yourself and the Persians." Hdt. 7.16a.2). Here again, where the impact of material wealth is concerned, the crucial nexus is between hubris and greed (πλέον . . . ἔχειν). What matters is the manner and measure of the attainment of goods, not of their enjoyment. On Herodotus's understanding of imperialism as "nourished by *pleonexia*, an insatiable desire for more," see Raaflaub 2002, 176.

41. On greed and hubris in Herodotus, see Balot 2001, 100–108.

42. In addition to the explicit characterization here of the Persians' actions as an attempted robbery, Herodotus's efforts to depict Xerxes' campaign as an unsurpassed example of hubris are well known.

The Weakness of the Persians

To move now beyond the events of Book 9, we have already observed that an essential premise in the argument that 9.122 refers ironically to the Persians' eventual "softening" through pernicious luxury is the "fact" that the *Histories* unequivocally shows the Persians as weak and decadent. However, in spite of the widespread acceptance of this premise, the evidence supporting it is not strong. In approaching this question, it would be both possible and relevant to detail the many times in which the *Histories* notes or depicts the bravery or martial ability of the Persians in the supposedly degenerate era of Darius and Xerxes. However, such a line of investigation would easily surpass the bounds of a single chapter. Instead, we will concentrate on just those passages that are commonly advanced as positive evidence of Persian μαλακία. This discussion will be briefer than one might suppose, since the position in question is based on a set of texts that is unexpectedly small and contains remarks of surprisingly limited range, given the conviction with which this view is held by so many.

The evidence may be divided into groups for convenient discussion. The first group contains three passages in which it is understood that the manly courage of the Persians is explicitly and harshly denigrated.[43] The first of these passages represents Xerxes' thoughts after the repulse of his forces on the first day of fighting at Thermopylae:

δῆλον δ᾽ ἐποίευν παντί τεῳ καὶ οὐκ ἥκιστα αὐτῷ βασιλέϊ, ὅτι πολλοὶ μὲν ἄνθρωποι εἶεν, ὀλίγοι δὲ ἄνδρες.

[They made it clear to everyone, and not least to the King himself, that he had plenty of people, but few real men.] (Hdt. 7.210.2)

The second passage comes from the council of war before the Battle of Salamis. Of the many captains canvassed for their opinion, only Artemisia of Halicarnassus advised Xerxes to avoid a decisive naval battle:

φείδεο τῶν νηῶν μηδὲ ναυμαχίην ποιέο. οἱ γὰρ ἄνδρες τῶν σῶν ἀνδρῶν κρέσσονες τοσοῦτό εἰσι κατὰ θάλασσαν, ὅσον ἄνδρες γυναικῶν.

---

43. Lateiner (1989, 49), for example, cites these passages as evidence that "Herodotus believed that the Persians lost their freedom-loving and manly qualities."

[Spare your ships and don't fight a sea battle, for, by sea, their men are as much stronger than your men, as men are than women.] (Hdt. 8.68α.1)

The third passage is a counterpart to the second; upon observing this same Artemisia's conduct at Salamis, the King disparaged his forces: οἱ μὲν ἄνδρες γεγόνασί μοι γυναῖκες, αἱ δὲ γυναῖκες ἄνδρες ("My men have become women and my women men!" Hdt. 8.88.3)

Evidence for weakness in Xerxes' forces could hardly be clearer.[44] At the same time, further consideration shows that these passages cannot be instances of the fulfillment of Cyrus's warning at 9.122. In each case, the object of the expression of contempt is not the Persians themselves, but one or more of the conquered peoples who comprise the bulk of the barbarian forces. At Thermopylae, Herodotus is careful to distinguish among the parts of Xerxes' army, and the Medes make up the contingent whose ineffective attack presents the appearance of many combatants, but ὀλίγοι ἄνδρες.[45] The Persians themselves are not implicated in this criticism.

Similarly, the analogy Artemisia drew between the ineffectiveness of Xerxes' fleet and womanly weakness was aimed at the subject-nations that constituted the barbarian navy. Artemisia voiced her opinion at a meeting of the leaders of the fleet that the King called to canvass the views of the sailors (Hdt. 8.67.1). Herodotus sets Artemisia in opposition to all the other leaders summoned to the council. These men, from the rulers of Sidon and Tyre to the taxiarchs of ships, advised Xerxes to attack the Greek navy. In view of the contrast established between the queen and the other members of the council, it is reasonable for the reader to take Artemisia's criticism as a rebuke offered to her opponents in this discussion. This interpretation is in fact supported by the words with which she concluded her argument:

---

44. None of these passages is in the narrative voice; even the first passage, which is not, strictly speaking, voiced by one of the *Histories'* characters, seems to represent the thoughts, if not the words, of the Persian leadership. Nonetheless, we may accept that Herodotus would agree with the evaluations given.

45. πέμπει ἐπ᾽ αὐτοὺς Μήδους τε καὶ Κισσίους θυμωθείς . . . ὡς δ᾽ ἐσέπεσον φερόμενοι ἐς τοὺς Ἕλληνας οἱ Μῆδοι, ἔπιπτον πολλοί, ἄλλοι δ᾽ ἐπεσήσαν. . . . ἐπείτε δὲ οἱ Μῆδοι τρηχέως περιείποντο, ἐνθαῦτα οὗτοι μὲν ὑπεξήσαν, οἱ δὲ Πέρσαι ἐκδεξάμενοι ἐπήσαν, τοὺς Ἀθανάτους ἐκάλεε βασιλεύς, τῶν ἦρχε Ὑδάρνης ("Grown angry, he sends against them the Medes and Cissians. . . . When the Medes rushed forth to attack the Greeks, many fell, and others took their turn. . . . And since the Medes had been roughly handled, they withdrew from the place, and the Persians whom the King called the Immortals, led by Hydarnes, went forward in their place." Hdt. 7.210.1–7.211.1). It is worth pointing out that, although the Immortals are no more successful that the Medes, they are subject to no similarly harsh characterization.

πρὸς δέ, ὦ βασιλεῦ, καὶ τόδε ἐς θυμὸν βαλεῦ, ὡς τοῖσι μὲν χρηστοῖσι τῶν
ἀνθρώπων κακοὶ δοῦλοι φιλέουσι γίνεσθαι, τοῖσι δὲ κακοῖσι χρηστοί. σοὶ δὲ
ἐόντι ἀρίστῳ ἀνδρῶν πάντων κακοὶ δοῦλοι εἰσί, οἳ ἐν συμμάχων λόγῳ λέγονται
εἶναι, ἐόντες Αἰγύπτιοί τε καὶ Κύπριοι καὶ Κίλικες καὶ Πάμφυλοι, τῶν ὄφελός
ἐστι οὐδέν.

[In addition, O King, take this to heart. It is natural that to worthy men belong
bad slaves and to bad men worthy ones. You, being the best of all men, have bad
slaves, these who are reckoned in the number of your allies. I mean the Egyptians and Cyprians and Cilicians and Pamphylians. They are completely useless.] (Hdt. 8.68γ.1)

To take Artemisia's statement as referring to *Persian* effeminacy is therefore to
ignore the unmistakable implications of its context. Hdt. 8.68α.1 is not relevant
to the case for Persian decadence.[46]

Nor can Xerxes' cry of despair at the events unfolding at Salamis (Hdt.
8.88.3) be taken as a proof text for the view that by then the Persians had suc-
cumbed to the process of enervation about which Cyrus cautioned. Once again,
as Xerxes' exclamation was directed toward the fighting qualities of his navy,
the focus of his discontent was likely to be the σύμμαχοι. This view is evident
from the King's words themselves: "my women have become men" refers to the
actions of the Halicarnassians' female taxiarch. This fact implies, at the very
least, that Xerxes' comment pertains to allies as well as Persians. In addition,
that the σύμμαχοι and not the Persians should bear any and all blame for cowardice at Salamis is the point made by Mardonius shortly after the battle:

δέσποτα, μήτε λυπέο μήτε συμφορὴν μηδεμίαν μεγάλην ποιεῦ τοῦδε τοῦ
γεγονότος εἵνεκα πρήγματος. οὐ γὰρ ξύλων ἀγὼν ὁ τὸ πᾶν φέρων ἐστὶ ἡμῖν,
ἀλλ᾽ ἀνδρῶν τε καὶ ἵππων.... σὺ Πέρσας, βασιλεῦ, μὴ ποιήσῃς καταγελάστους
γενέσθαι Ἕλλησι· οὐδὲν γὰρ ἐν τοῖσι Πέρσῃσι δεδήληταί τῶν πρηγμάτων, οὐδὲ
ἐρέεις, ὅκου ἐγενόμεθα ἄνδρες κακοί. εἰ δὲ Φοίνικές τε καὶ Αἰγύπτιοι καὶ
Κύπριοί τε καὶ Κίλικες κακοὶ ἐγένοντο, οὐδὲν πρὸς Πέρσας τοῦτο προσήκει τὸ
πάθος.

---

46. In her discussion of the Artemisia passages, Munson (1988, 92) is careful to indicate that the Queen's
   scorn is directed at the barbarian fleet, not the Persians specifically, as "Artemisia somehow partakes
   of the Greek-Barbarian antithesis cast in terms of a contrast between male and female."

[Master, do not be anguished or count it a great disaster because of this business that has occurred. For us the decisive contest is not a matter of timbers, but of men and horses. . . . My King, for your part, do not make the Persians into laughingstocks to the Greeks. No fault for any harm done to your affairs lies among the Persians, nor will you mention any point where we have been cowards. If indeed the Phoenicians and Egyptians and Cyprians and Cilicians have proven to be cowards, this misfortune has nothing to do with the Persians.] (Hdt. 8.100.2–4)

Apparently persuaded by Mardonius's claim that the Persians were not responsible for the defeat (emphasized again at 8.100.5: οὐ Πέρσαι τοι αἴτιοί εἰσι), Xerxes was ready to accept his general's plan to detach a picked force of infantry and cavalry to overcome the Greeks. To be sure, Herodotus depicts Mardonius's argument as self-serving.[47] However, the care that Herodotus applies to make the speech suitable to its occasion does not give us license to discount the pertinence of Mardonius's words to our understanding of Xerxes' outburst at Hdt. 8.88.3.[48] Rather, we should pay attention to the trouble Herodotus takes to distinguish components of the barbarians' forces and, recognizing that the bravery of the Persians in the remainder of the campaign bears out Mardonius's claims, we should admit that it is uncertain whether Xerxes' ἄνδρες γεγόνασί μοι γυναῖκες refers to the Persians at all. *A fortiori*, the phrase cannot be elevated to the status of evidence of general applicability, establishing the degeneracy of Persian manhood from the days of Cyrus the Great.

As evidence for the possible effects of pernicious luxury as manifested among the Persians, this first set of passages, then, has little value. In each case, context seems to indicate that the statements in question apply to the fighting quality of the King's subject-allies and not to the Persians themselves.

The second group of passages is about the compulsion of the lash required on servile men. These passages are of a similarly weak evidentiary status for similar reasons. Book 7 presents us the famous conversation between Xerxes and the Spartan exile Damaratus on the likelihood of Greek resistance. The King stated that the Persian political system makes them more likely to face unfavorable odds than the Greeks:

---

47. As noted by Asheri 2006, 300.
48. The fact that Mardonius's words echo Artemisia's advice before the battle (cf. Asheri 2006, 300) may serve to emphasize that the Persians themselves were free from the taint of κακία arising from the defeat.

κῶς ἂν δυναίατο χίλιοι . . . , ἐόντες γε ἐλεύθεροι πάντες ὁμοίως καὶ μὴ ὑπ' ἑνὸς ἀρχόμενοι στρατῷ τοσῷδε ἀντιστῆναι, . . . ὑπὸ μὲν γὰρ ἑνὸς ἀρχόμενοι κατὰ τρόπον τὸν ἡμέτερον γενοίατ' ἂν δειμαίνοντες τοῦτον καὶ παρὰ τὴν ἑωυτῶν φύσιν ἀμείνονες καὶ ἴοιεν ἀναγκαζόμενοι μάστιγι ἐς πλέονας ἐλάσσονες ἐόντες·

[How could a thousand, . . . being all alike free and not under the rule of one man, stand up to an army such as this? . . . For if they were ruled by one man according to our custom they might, fearing this man, become better beyond their own nature, and might go under compulsion of the whip against a larger number, even though they are fewer.] (Hdt. 7.103.3–4)

Xerxes' belief that without fear of punishment his men would not face a superior force is taken as an indication of the degeneracy of the Persians from their primitive bellicosity. So Rosalind Thomas:

> Xerxes had insisted that Persians would never fight a far larger force unless they were made to by fear: it was fear that would make them "stronger than their *physis*" . . . quite different, we note, from the Persians under Cyrus. (Thomas 2000, 110)

Men who would fight against odds only through "fear of the whip, fear of their ruler" would certainly deserve to be characterized by Cyrus's μαλακία. However, as was the case in reference to the womanish men of Salamis, the context does not support an interpretation that puts the focus of Xerxes' statement on the Persians per se. In the first place, the debate between Xerxes and Damaratus took place immediately after the King's great review of his army, which gives opportunity for Herodotus to catalog both his land and naval forces. Nowhere in the *Histories* is the size and multinational makeup of Xerxes' expedition so present to the reader's mind. In the subsequent discussion, he keeps the astounding dimensions of his military might in the foreground of his argument (στρατιῇ τοσῇδε, 7.103.1; στρατῷ τοσῷδε, 7.103.3), contrasting their magnitude with the much smaller Greek army. In these circumstances, it is natural to assume that the terms of comparison were still the same when Xerxes made the comments quoted above: the Greeks are free and thus cannot be brought to stand against greater numbers; the barbarian army *as a whole* is ruled by one man and so is made braver than its nature by fear of the King and the punishment he may inflict.

This view receives support from the words directly after Xerxes' mention of the whip, where the King made an *a fortiori* argument by restricting his claims to the "Persians alone" (Πέρσῃσι μούνοισι, 7.103.4). If the Greeks were to contend with this one component of the barbarian army, they would not fight. The tightening of focus in this way is a good indication that the immediately preceding reference to those ὑπὸ ἑνὸς ἀρχόμενοι encompasses the entire barbarian horde. In the light of these words we cannot assume that the mention of monarchy "according to our custom" had narrowed the subject to Xerxes' own compatriots.

Also pertinent to identifying the referent of ἀναγκαζόμενοι μάστιγι is Xerxes' explicit claim that at least some Persians will do as Damaratus said the Spartans would act:

εἰσὶ γὰρ Περσέων τῶν ἐμῶν αἰχμοφόρων, οἳ θελήσουσι Ἑλλήνων ἀνδράσι τρισὶ ὁμοῦ μάχεσθαι·

[For there are those among my Persian spearmen who will be willing to fight three Greeks at the same time.] (Hdt. 7.103.5)

For these Persians, there is no question of compulsion: they fight of their own will (ἐθελήσουσι). Thus, given that the only clear specification in this passage describes the bravery of the Persians, as well as the prominence in the context of the greater barbarian force, we suggest that it is better not to interpret the text at 7.103.3–4 as characterizing *Persian* martial qualities. Rather, it is possible that this passage is drawing a distinction between the bravery of the Persians and that of the subject-allies who must be driven into battle. If those manuscripts that read ἀλλὰ παρ᾽ ἡμῖν μὲν μούνοισι τοῦτό ἐστι τὸ σὺ λέγεις at Hdt. 7.105.3 are correct,[49] Persian eagerness for battle contrasts with the reluctance of those who must be spurred by the lash. Among the King's subjects, *only* the Persians (ἡμῖν μούνοισι) will fight of their own accord if the outcome is in doubt.[50] The earlier words of Artemisia and Mardonius about the combatants at Salamis makes it plausible that Xerxes would make such a distinction.

---

49. Relying on manuscript group a, Hude puts μὲν μούνοισι in square brackets.

50. We prefer to take μούνοισι as distinguishing the Persians (ἡμῖν) from the levies of the other nations. On this interpretation, Xerxes is making a claim about the superiority of the Persians to these other peoples. Less attractive is an interpretation that takes μούνοισι as restricting the focus of the sentence, giving a sense something like: "If we look at the Persians alone, we can find some men with this quality. Let's leave the others out of consideration."

Indeed, if we examine Herodotus's narrative for the application of the whip in the barbarian forces, we find that it is not specifically said to be used on Persians, but with a vague and general reference which may well, at the same time, not include this people at all. At Hdt. 7.22.1, "all the peoples of the army" (παντοδαποὶ τῆς στρατιῆς) dug the canal to bypass Mt. Athos ὑπὸ μαστίγων. The author does not identify the contingents that made up this advance force. At Hdt. 7.55, where Herodotus describes the barbarian army crossing the Hellespont, we may speak with more confidence. The Ten Thousand and other elite units led the expedition across the bridges. Xerxes followed and took up a position to observe.

Ξέρξης δὲ ἐπεὶ διέβη ἐς τὴν Εὐρώπην, ἐθηεῖτο τὸν στρατὸν ὑπὸ μαστίγων διαβαίνοντα.

[When Xerxes had crossed over to Europe, he viewed his army crossing under the whip.] (Hdt. 7.56.1)

The object of the King's attention is described in this passage as ὁ ἄλλος στρατός ("the rest of the army," Hdt. 7.55.3). The barbarian order of march had been given in a more elaborated form at 7.40, and the phrase ὁ ἄλλος στρατός of 7.53 seems to correspond to two components of the army as described leaving Sardis in the earlier passage. In the van, marching in front of the Persian elite, were

στρατὸς παντοίων ἐθνέων ἀναμὶξ οὐ διακεκριμένοι. τῇ δὲ ὑπερημίσεες ἦσαν, ἐνθαῦτα διελέλειπτο, καὶ οὐ συνέμισγον οὗτοι βασιλέϊ.[51]

[an army of all sorts of nations promiscuously, not separated out. These made up over half of the force, then an interval was left and these men did not come near the King.] (Hdt. 7.40.1)

After Xerxes and other select Persian units, a gap of two stades was maintained, "and then the rest of the multitude marched promiscuously" (καὶ ἔπειτα ὁ λοιπὸς ὅμιλος ἤε ἀναμίξ, Hdt. 7.41.2). Thus, comparison between the two passages indicates that ὁ ἄλλος στρατός, which Xerxes watched whipped over the

---

51. MSS d and P put still more emphasis on the disorganization of this part of the army, with the reading σύμμικτος στρατός.

Hellespont, was essentially the bulk of the 1,700,000 man host, minus the most prestigious and prominent Persian divisions.

The last passage in this group is open to similar interpretation. Hdt. 7.223 relates the final day of battle at Thermopylae. Xerxes' men fell in great numbers, driven with whips to meet the advancing Greeks under Leonidas. Unlike his description of the first day of battle at 7.201, where Herodotus identifies the Cissians, the Medes, and the Persians as the barbarian divisions involved and distinguishes the attack of the first two from that of the third, here at 7.223, he speaks only in general terms of "the barbarians around Xerxes" (οἵ τε δὴ βάρβαροι οἱ ἀμφὶ Ξέρξην, 7.223.2) or simply "the barbarians." We cannot therefore conclude that the passage illustrates the cowardice of the Persians in particular.[52]

This set of passages showing the compulsion of the lash used on barbarian forces does not, then, count for much as evidence of the putative effects of Persian decadence manifested in the field of battle. In only one of the three passages, 7.56, can we specify to any degree those to whom the lash is applied, and in this case the fixed *datum* is simply that it is not the Persian elite who were the victims of the whip.[53] But it is precisely among this elite that we would expect to find the most significant damage wrought by pernicious luxury, if the standard interpretation of 9.122 were correct. These men, the "rulers of all Asia," possessing the greatest wealth and luxury, ought to exhibit the greatest degree of softness and cowardice. Even if we accept that the need for the lash is an indication of the presence of μαλακία, the passages in question do not clearly connect this characteristic with those to whom Cyrus addressed his admonition.

If we cannot establish that the Persians themselves were among those driven to battle under the whip, and if the first set of evidence for Persian weakness seems rather to apply to subject-peoples, some scholars will nonetheless hold to the view that these passages support the importance of the idea of pernicious

---

52. Thus to take this passage as evidence that "the Persians were driven into battle with whips" (Hunt 1998, 49) seems to go too far, even though in the first sentence of the next section, the text speaks of "the Persians" rather than "the barbarians": δόρατα μέν νυν τοῖσι πλέοσι αὐτῶν τηνικαῦτα ἤδη ἐτύγχανε κατεηγότα, οἱ δὲ τοῖσι ξίφεσι διεργάζοντο τοὺς Πέρσας ("By this time most of their spears had been shattered, but they continued killing Persians with their swords," Hdt. 7.224.1). The use of οἱ Πέρσαι is unremarkable, since Herodotus has shifted his point of view from Xerxes' battle line (οἵ βάρβαροι οἱ ἀμφὶ Ξέρξην) to the Spartans'.

53. Munson (1988, 93 n. 9 and 95 n. 18) associates these passages with others in which Herodotus mentions "forced participation in war (anank-)" by some under the King's command. Both kinds of passages are in turn connected with the idea of a "society made up of effeminate and enslaved men." The relevant passages, however, all refer to subject peoples and not the Persians: 7.108.1, those met by Xerxes' army on its way from the Hellespont; 7.110.1, Thracian tribes; 7.172.1, the Thessalians. Thus, these passages too do not speak to the idea of degeneracy among the Persians.

luxury as a historical process. Such distinctions as we have found might not invalidate "a generic contrast, of great importance in Herodotus . . . between hard peoples and soft peoples."[54] In response, we note that the texts in question do indeed reflect Herodotus's concern with a historically significant causal nexus, but that this process does not involve pernicious luxury or moral degeneration.

In brief, there is reason to think that the evidence we have examined illustrates the *Histories'* insistence on the rather obvious principle that there may be a strong tension between concerted action and narrow self-interest. With special pertinence to Xerxes' expedition is the link Herodotus finds joining military weakness or apparent cowardice to tyranny, not, we reiterate, to luxury. This connection is clearly stated at Hdt. 5.78, in a well-known passage that explains the growth of Athenian power after the expulsion of the Peisitratids:

> . . . εἰ καὶ Ἀθηναῖοι τυραννευόμενοι μὲν οὐδαμῶν τῶν σφέας περιοικεόντων ἦσαν τὰ πολέμια ἀμείνους, ἀπαλλαχθέντες δὲ τυράννων μακρῷ πρῶτοι ἐγένοντο. δηλοῖ ὦν ταῦτα, ὅτι κατεχόμενοι μὲν ἐθελοκάκεον ὡς δεσπότῃ ἐργαζόμενοι, ἐλευθερωθέντων δὲ αὐτὸς ἕκαστος ἑωυτῷ προεθυμέετο κατεργάζεσθαι.

> [When the Athenians were ruled by tyrants, they were no better at war than their neighbors. Once rid of the tyrants, they became by far the best. These things show that while under someone's control they played the coward on purpose, as doing their master's work, but when they became free, each man strove to accomplish something for himself.] (Hdt. 5.78)

Herodotus and his contemporaries seemed to find the strategy of being cowardly by choice to be a reasonable means for subjects to protect their own interests against those of their masters.

By way of corroboration, the author of the Hippocratic *Airs, Waters, and Places* presents this strategy as a more sympathetic alternative to a strict geographical determinism:

> ὅκου δὲ μὴ αὐτοὶ ἑωυτέων εἰσὶ καρτεροὶ ἄνθρωποι μηδὲ αὐτόνομοι, ἀλλὰ δεσπόζονται, οὐ περὶ τούτου αὐτοῖσιν ὁ λόγος ἐστίν, ὅπως τὰ πολέμια

---

54. Redfield 1985, 109.

ἀσκήσωσιν, ἀλλ᾽ ὅκως μὴ δόξωσι μάχιμοι εἶναι. οἱ γὰρ κίνδυνοι οὐχ ὅμοιοι εἰσίν. τοὺς μὲν γὰρ στρατεύεσθαι εἰκὸς καὶ ταλαιπωρέειν καὶ ἀποθνήσκειν ἐξ ἀνάγκης ὑπὲρ τῶν δεσποτέων, ἄπο τε παιδίων καὶ γυναικὸς ἐόντας καὶ τῶν λοιπῶν φίλων. καὶ ὁκόσα μὲν ἂν χρηστὰ καὶ ἀνδρεῖα ἐργάσωνται, οἱ δεσπόται ἀπ᾽ αὐτῶν αὔξονταί τε καὶ ἐκφύονται, τοὺς δὲ κινδύνους καὶ θανάτους αὐτοὶ καρποῦνται.

[Wherever people are not in control of their own lives and independent, but are under a master, they don't think about how they might train themselves in matters of war, but rather how they might appear unfit for battle. For the dangers are not shared equally: for under compulsion they march and likely suffer and die for their masters' sake, far from their children and wives and friends. And whatever valiant and manly things they perform, by these the masters are increased and flourish. They themselves reap dangers and death.] (Hipp., *De aere* 16.3–4; cf. 23).

From this viewpoint, the martial weakness evident in the two sets of passages examined is seen as a matter of rational calculation (λόγος) in the face of the compulsion of subjects to participate in actions that would bring them only disadvantage, while any profit would go to others. At the same time, it is natural that the *Histories* characterizes this phenomenon harshly and in moral terms when it is seen from the perspective of the ruling elites. At Hdt. 7.103, for example, Xerxes identified this sort of cowardice as a manifestation not of λόγος but of φύσις, an instinct to be overcome by the force of Persian custom.[55] Freedom lacking compulsion, he noted, is incompatible with such amelioration and is therefore militarily inferior.

Although Xerxes' description of the military advantages of despotism seems directly to contradict the reason Herodotus assigns for Athenian military success at Hdt. 5.78.1, the two lines of argument are based on the same premise: men fight better when fighting for self-advantage.[56] This elementary

---

55. We observe that reluctance in battle exhibited by Persian subjects is characterized as effeminacy or cowardice only by barbarian leaders. As far as we are aware, no Greek makes such a claim, nor does Herodotus as narrator.

56. How and Wells (1936, 2.44), for example, point out the apparent contrast: "Xerxes maintains the opposite view," but the context of 7.103 makes clear that the force of nature that Xerxes refers to is the impulse not to act to one's own obvious disadvantage, as would be the case for those "going against a superior force, although they were inferior" (ἴοιεν . . . ἐς πλέονας ἐλάσσονες ἐόντες, 7.103.4). The Athenians displayed the corresponding impulse—αὐτὸς ἕκαστος ἑωυτῷ προεθυμέετο κατεργάζεσθαι ("each man was eager to accomplish something for himself") after gaining their freedom.

principle is on display throughout the *Histories*, and, most significantly for our purposes, affects the fortunes of war for both Greeks and barbarians. On the one hand, we have seen how the very magnitude of Xerxes' horde lessens the military effectiveness of many of its individual members, since only compulsion and fear lead them to see their interests as the same as the King's. For the Greeks, the matter is somewhat different. As free men, they must be persuaded that they fight for their own benefit. When so persuaded, they fight willingly and bravely, but their conviction is fragile: especially when acting as part of an alliance or coalition, they must be often reminded that the common good profits their own interests, while they are frequently suspicious that they are, in fact, being taken advantage of by others.

Thus, in the narrative of events leading to Salamis, Herodotus repeatedly describes the Greek alliance as on the point of dissolution under the pressure of self-interest.[57] Emblematic of the jealous self-regard that continually undermines the Greek effort to preserve their freedom was the competition for leadership of the Greek forces. In Book 7, both Argos and Gelon of Syracuse refused to join forces against the barbarian invaders unless they were accepted in a position of command.[58] *Histories* 8.3 is especially illuminating with respect to Herodotus's thoughts on this vying for precedence. In the early days of the alliance, the possibility was raised that the Athenians should command at sea. But because the allies objected, the Athenians ceded their claims for the common good. However, Herodotus goes on to reveal that self-interest underlay even this apparent altruism:

στάσις γὰρ ἔμφυλος πολέμου ὁμοφρονέοντος τοσούτῳ κάκιόν ἐστι, ὅσῳ πόλεμος εἰρήνης. ἐπιστάμενοι ὦν αὐτὸ τοῦτο οὐκ ἀντέτεινον, ἀλλ᾽ εἶκον, μέχρι ὅσου κάρτα ἐδέοντο αὐτῶν, ὡς διέδεξαν· ὡς γὰρ δὴ ὠσάμενοι τὸν Πέρσην περὶ

---

57. For example, at Hdt. 8.4–5, the majority of the Greeks were on the point of sailing away from Artemisium, refusing to delay even to help the Euboeans save their families. Only a bribe paid by Themistocles to Eurybiades the Spartan and Adimantus the Corinthian induced the Greeks to remain and defend Euboea. Similarly, it took all of Themistocles' wiles to prevent the Peloponnesian component of the Greek fleet from abandoning Salamis to the Persians and withdrawing to the Isthmus, where they thought to defend their own interests more directly.

58. The response of the Argives to the ambassadors of the allies recalls the attitude of the Ionians before Lade: οὕτω δὴ οἱ Ἀργεῖοί φασι οὐκ ἀνασχέσθαι τῶν Σπαρτιητέων τὴν πλεονεξίην, ἀλλ᾽ ἑλέσθαι μᾶλλον ὑπὸ τῶν βαρβάρων ἄρχεσθαι ἤ τι ὑπεῖξαι Λακεδαιμονίοισι ("So the Argives said that they would not put up with Spartan grasping, but would rather choose to be ruled by the barbarians than yield anything to the Lacedaemonians." Hdt. 7.149.3). The Ionians, too, expressed a preference for Persian rule over an improper command by fellow Greeks, as we will discuss below. For "disunity as a salient feature of the Greeks," see Bowie 2007, 91.

τῆς ἐκείνου ἤδη τὸν ἀγῶνα ἐποιεῦντο, πρόφασιν τὴν Παυσανίεω ὕβριν προϊσχόμενοι ἀπείλοντο τὴν ἡγεμονίην τοὺς Λακεδαιμονίους.

[Civil strife is as much worse than war waged with one mind, as war is worse than peace. Aware of this fact, they did not resist, but gave way as long as they had great need of them. This is quite clear: when they had thrown out the Persian and the contest was now for his territory, they took the leadership from the Lacedaemonians, offering Pausanias's arrogance as their excuse.] (Hdt. 8.3.1–2)[59]

As the Athenians looked to their own advantage in preserving the Greek coalition, so the peoples subject to the Persians did the same through the practice of deliberate cowardice. Thus, we may emphasize that the *Histories* does not present the behavior in question—a hesitancy to fight that can be characterized by onlookers as effeminacy and countered with the lash—as due to some process of decadence or degeneracy. Nor does it represent a particularity by which "hard" peoples can be distinguished from "soft." Rather, it is a general human trait that regularly hinders large-scale endeavors, and the *Histories* is in part an illustration of how this quality manifests itself, albeit in different ways, both in empires and among free peoples.[60]

---

59. This attitude of *Realpolitik* has disturbed some scholars, who deny that the Athenians are in fact the subject of the clause μέχρι ὅσου κάρτα ἐδέοντο αὐτῶν. For discussion with references, see Masaracchia 1977, 201; Bowie 2007, 92–93.

60. For Herodotus, power and success come when the selfish impulse is channeled and directed, and the case of the Thracians indicates that the form this direction may take is contingent: Θρηίκων δὲ ἔθνος μέγιστόν ἐστι μετά γε Ἰνδοὺς πάντων ἀνθρώπων. εἰ δὲ ὑπ᾽ ἑνὸς ἄρχοιτο ἢ φρονέοιτο τὠυτό, ἄμαχόν τ᾽ ἂν εἴη καὶ πολλῷ κράτιστον πάντων ἐθνέων κατὰ γνώμην τὴν ἐμήν. ἀλλὰ γὰρ τοῦτο ἄπορόν σφι καὶ ἀμήχανον μή κοτε ἐγγένηται· εἰσὶ δὴ κατὰ τοῦτο ἀσθενέες ("The nation of Thracians is the largest of all peoples after the Indians. If they were ruled by one man or were of the same mind, they would be invincible and by far the mightiest of all nations, in my opinion. But this is impracticable for them and it is impossible for it ever to come about. For this reason they are weak." Hdt. 5.3.1). The idea of self-interest underlies the dichotomy: in the case of despotism, the interests of ruler and common soldier are at odds, but the ruler is in a position to compel action from the soldiers; in a free society, as for the Athenians at Hdt. 5.78, there can be no war unless the common soldiers agree with their leaders (φρονέοιατο κατὰ τὠυτό) that fighting is for the common good. There is no hint in this passage that the appropriateness of either (im)possibility (ὑπ᾽ ἑνὸς ἄρχοιατο ἢ φρονέοιατο κατὰ τὠυτό) is predetermined by geography or lifestyle or any other factor, although the customs that the *Histories* assigns to the Thracians would put them among Redfield's "hard peoples" and Flory's "noble savages." It is of great interest that Herodotus does not express a preference between the two paths to becoming a great power described here. The same distinction is the basis for the debate between Xerxes and Damaratus at Hdt. 7.102–4. Xerxes champions the first alternative, since it is the source of his might. The Spartan defends the second, though his words are less obvious and the point is sometimes missed in discussions of the passage: . . . Λακεδαιμόνιοι κατὰ μὲν ἕνα μαχόμενοι οὐδαμῶν εἰσι κακίονες ἀνδρῶν, ἀλέες δὲ ἄριστοι ἀνδρῶν ἁπάντων (". . . Fighting in-

In this connection, it is important to observe that the Persian elite—exactly those men whose luxury is emphasized in the anecdote about the tent of Mardonius—are depicted, with respect to the workings of self-advantage, as more like the free Greeks than their own subjects. Although even the richest and most powerful Persians are conventionally referred to as the King's slaves, nonetheless Xerxes did not rely on compulsion and violence, which he associated with those who are ὑπ' ἑνὸς ἀρχόμενοι when he led them to war. Instead, he took pains to persuade the leading Persians that his interest in the campaign against the Greeks was also their own.

ὦ Πέρσαι, τῶνδ' ἐγὼ ὑμέων χρῄζων συνέλεξα, ἄνδρας τε γίνεσθαι ἀγαθοὺς καὶ μὴ καταισχύνειν τὰ πρόσθε ἐργασμένα Πέρσῃσι, ἐόντα μεγάλα τε καὶ πολλοῦ ἄξια, ἀλλ' εἷς τε ἕκαστος καὶ οἱ σύμπαντες προθυμίην ἔχωμεν· ξυνὸν γὰρ πᾶσι τοῦτο ἀγαθὸν σπευδέτω. τῶνδε δὲ εἵνεκα προαγορεύω ἀντέχεσθαι τοῦ πολέμου ἐντεταμένως· ὡς γὰρ ἐγὼ πυνθάνομαι, ἐπ' ἄνδρας στρατευόμεθα ἀγαθούς, τῶν ἢν κρατήσωμεν, οὐ μή τις ἡμῖν ἄλλος στρατὸς ἀντιστῇ κοτε ἀνθρώπων.

[Persians, I have gathered you together to make this demand of you: that you be brave men and do not disgrace the previous deeds of the Persians—these were great and noteworthy—but let each each of us individually and all of us together show eagerness. For the good each must strive for is common to all. Thus, I urge you to apply yourselves strenuously to the war. I am informed that the men we march against are brave; if we defeat them, no other army in the world will ever stand against us.] (Hdt. 7.53.1–2)

The Persians, if not their allies, should be motivated by the common good and traditions of honor. And, as has been noted, the Persians heeded Xerxes' exhor-

---

dividually, the Lacedaemonians are second to none, but together they are the best of all men." Hdt. 7.104.4). The adjective ἀλέες can indicate unity of purpose as well as a close ordered military formation. This unanimity is imposed upon the Spartans by their famous δεσπότης νόμος, which "commands the same thing always" (ἀνώγει δὲ τὠυτὸ αἰεί, Hdt. 7.104.5). As the Master Law is always the same and, implicitly, identical for every Spartan, it results in fighters who share the same mind (φρονεοίατο κατὰ τὠυτό). Thus, the *Histories* is, *inter alia*, an exploration of the two roads to power specified at Hdt. 5.3.1. The light that this last passage may shed on the more famous comments at 5.78 and 7.102–4 is too often overlooked. For example, an understanding of Herodotus's observation on the Thracians as parallel to these other statements about the sources of military power makes it more difficult to accept Forsdyke's (2001) argument that these latter passages are marked by Athenian democratic ideology rather than a more generally Greek point of view.

tation. The *Histories* shows them conducting the campaign ἐντεταμένως ("strenuously"), its eventual failure due to other causes than weakness or cowardice.

So much for what is said to be the best of the explicit evidence that Herodotus depicts the Persians as suffering the effects of a luxury-based decadence.[61]

Strength in Poverty

We will now turn more briefly to the most important indirect evidence of the theme of corrupting luxury in Herodotus. It is argued that "the danger and limitations of the wealth of prosperous aggressors [is] most often reflected in the moral superiority that poverty has conferred on Herodotus' noble savages," and that "poverty can propel to conquest" and thus "a praise of poverty is an essential theme of Herodotus."[62] In other words, some scholars point to the presence in the *Histories* of the idea that poverty is an important, or even neces-

---

61. We cannot treat in detail every passage in the *Histories* that may have been advanced in support of the idea of the Persians as victims of pernicious luxury. All such passages of which we are aware are as open to objection as those we have discussed. For example, Thomas (2000, 113) finds in "strikingly rhetorical arguments used by the characters in the narrative" evidence for "clichés and stereotypes about barbarians (or Persians) being effeminate and weak." Her principal evidence is the attempt by Aristagoras to persuade the Spartans to help the Ionians. She paraphrases the relevant part of the Milesian's argument: the barbarians were "easy to defeat since they wore trousers and turbans." Apparently, Thomas takes these words as a reference on the part of Aristagoras to aspects of the Persian lifestyle to explain their relative weakness, as does Pelling (1997),who identifies the Persians' trousers as "a principal signifier of their nambypambiness." This is not the best interpretation of the text: οὔτε γὰρ οἱ βάρβαροι ἄλκιμοί εἰσι, ὑμεῖς τε τὰ ἐς τὸν πόλεμον ἐς τὰ μέγιστα ἀνήκετε ἀρετῆς πέρι. ἥ τε μάχη αὐτῶν ἐστι τοιήδε· τόξα καὶ αἰχμὴ βραχέα, ἀναξυρίδας δὲ ἔχοντες ἔρχονται ἐς τὰς μάχας καὶ κυρβασίας ἐπὶ τῇσι κεφαλῇσι. οὕτω εὐπετέες χειρωθῆναί εἰσι ("For the barbarians are not strong, but you, in matters of war, have reached the highest levels for bravery. And their way of war is this: bows and short spears, and also, they come to battle wearing trousers and turbans on their heads. Thus, they are easy to subdue." Hdt. 5.49.3). The point is not that the barbarians in everyday life wore clothing that connoted, via cliché and stereotype, luxury or effeminacy. Rather, it is that they wore this clothing *into battle* (ἔχοντες ἔρχονται ἐς τὰς μάχας). This interpretation is confirmed when the Milesian tries his pitch on the Athenians: ὁ Ἀρισταγόρης ταὐτὰ ἔλεγε, τὰ καὶ ἐν τῇ Σπάρτῃ περὶ τῶν ἀγαθῶν τῶν ἐν τῇ Ἀσίῃ καὶ τοῦ πολέμου τοῦ Περσικοῦ, ὡς οὔτε ἀσπίδα οὔτε δόρυ νομίζουσι εὐπετέες τε χειρωθῆναι εἴησαν ("Aristagoras said the same things that he had said in Sparta about the good things to be found in Asia and the Persian way of war, how they were accustomed to neither shield nor spear and would be easy to subdue." Hdt. 5.97.1). Here, in closely parallel language, bows, shorts spears, trousers, and turbans have been recast as "neither shield nor spear." If we accept at face value Herodotus's statement of equivalency (ταὐτὰ ἔλεγε), then it is best to understand the mention of in the first passage as a reference to the barbarian armory, not the barbarian lifestyle. The narrative bears this out, for among the causes of Persian defeat is their equipment: λήματι μέν νυν καὶ ῥώμῃ οὐκ ἥσσονες ἦσαν οἱ Πέρσαι, ἄνοπλοι δὲ ἐόντες ("The Persians were not outdone in courage and strength, but being without armor," Hdt. 9.62.3). Cf. the emphatic repetition of this point at 9.63.2 and the discussion in Flower and Marincola 2002, 216–19.

62. Noble savages: Flory 1987, 87. Praise of poverty: Desmond 2006, 106.

sary, factor in the development of military strength.[63] Such a concept, if it could be shown to play a significant role in Herodotus's thinking about historical cause and effect, would certainly provide strong support to the complementary claims about pernicious luxury in the *Histories*. However, the evidence for this "essential theme" of strength through poverty is, if anything, even less persuasive than the direct evidence for weakness from wealth.

Pride of place is given in this argument to Hdt. 7.102, once again from Demaratus's advice to Xerxes. The King had just claimed that all the Greeks and all the other peoples of the west would not be able to field a force large enough to stand against his multitude (οὐκ ἀξιόμαχοί εἰσι, Hdt. 7.101.2).[64] He then asked the Spartan to comment. The reply is notorious:

τῇ Ἑλλάδι πενίη μὲν αἰεί κοτε σύντροφός ἐστι, ἀρετὴ δὲ ἔπακτός ἐστι, ἀπό τε σοφίης κατεργασμένη καὶ νόμου ἰσχυροῦ·τῇ διαχρεωμένη ἡ Ἑλλὰς τήν τε πενίην ἀπαμύνεται καὶ τὴν δεσποσύνην.

[Poverty has always been native to Hellas, but virtue is an import, attained from wisdom and mighty law. Using it, Hellas wards off both poverty and despotism.] (Hdt. 7.102.1)

These words are taken by some to mean that Herodotus saw poverty as an inherent cause of ἀρετή and a natural source of martial strength.[65]

Such an interpretation faces several difficulties. In the first place, we observe that Demaratus's mention of poverty was motivated by the immediately preceding context. The extensive narrative of the great review of the barbarian army and fleet emphasizes that Xerxes' military power was a function of his wealth, here manifested in number of men and quantity of materiel.[66] From this

---

63. Lateiner (1989, 161) for example, understands Demaratus's words to Xerxes as including the idea that "poverty is necessary, but not sufficient" as a basis for military virtue.

64. In Herodotus, the term ἀξιόμαχος is usually, if not always, a reference to quantity, not to quality, a fact obscured by Powell's (1938, *s.v.* ἀξιόμαχος) definition, "a match in battle for." This sense is clear, for example, at Hdt. 8.63.1: ἀπολιπόντων γὰρ Ἀθηναίων οὐκέτι ἐγίνοντο ἀξιόμαχοι οἱ λοιποί ("With the Athenians leaving, the remaining men would not have been enough to fight"). Given that Xerxes had, at 7.53.2, described the Greeks to his chief lieutenants as ἄνδρας ἀγαθούς, a qualitative meaning here is unlikely.

65. Thus Flory 1987, 104: "The king ignores the warnings of a wise adviser that the people he is attacking possess certain moral and physical qualities, inherent in their poverty, that will make them formidable opponents." Similarly, Desmond 2006, 117: "the *arête, sophia* and lawfulness that poverty forces the Greeks to adopt will overcome Xerxes' material superiority."

66. Herodotus's Persians see number as the basis of power (Hdt. 1.136.1). Compare Mardonius's claim at

perspective, when Xerxes spoke of the Greeks' inability to assemble enough men to meet him (οὐκ ἀξιόμαχοι), he was focusing upon their relative poverty. Thus, Demaratus's πενία is anaphoric, serving as both a transition from and a concession to Xerxes' words: "It's true we've always been poor, but . . ." Recognizing this connection removes a degree of obscurity from this passage—why should Demaratus have mentioned Greek poverty in a defense of their military abilities—which some have sought to explain as a reference to a traditional belief that πενία fosters power. Lacking, as we will see, explicit evidence that such a belief exists in Herodotus, this interpretation is questionable; given the prominence in this passage of wealth (i.e., number of fighters) as a weapon of war, understanding πενία as an allusion to such a subtext is unnecessary.

Nor does the passage's metaphorical language support an interpretation of these words as a praise of poverty. In his choice of attributes, Herodotus has focused on the origin or source of poverty and virtue. Πενία is domestic or native, while ἀρετή is brought in from the outside. It is thus reasonable to see the two qualities as having no close or necessary relationship. If Herodotus meant to connote that poverty is a source or cause of Greek virtue, it is difficult to understand the emphasis on their separate lineages as denoted by σύντροφος and ἔπακτος.

In addition, proponents of reading this text as an allusion to traditions in praise of poverty must explain the last sentence of the passage: "using virtue, Greece wards off both poverty and despotism." If πενία, in its first occurrence, may mean "the benefits of poverty," this sense is prohibited in its second occurrence by its conjunction with δεσποσύνη, where the word must have it usual negative meaning.[67] Rather than assume the harsh transition such a move implies, it is better to take both instances of πενία in its common sense. The resultant line of thought would be something like: "Greece is indeed poor in resources, but through virtue we overcome this weakness and the foreign domination it might cause." This sentiment is in harmony with Demaratus's

the beginning of Book 7 that the Persians had nothing to fear from the Greeks: κοίην πλήθεος συστροφήν; κοίην δὲ χρημάτων δύναμιν; ("What sort is the assembly of their multitude? What the power of their riches?" Hdt. 7.9a.1). Powell's suggestion of "wealth" as the pertinent definition of δύναμις here is unnecessary, since Mardonius is concerned with the politico-military uses of Greek resources (Powell 1938, s.v. δύναμις).

67. One might argue that an assertion that the benefits of poverty drive away its ill effects would constitute a paradox of the kind which the Greeks found quite attractive; thus Desmond 2006, 105: "latent in the Greek popular consciousness is the notion that under certain circumstances, powerlessness is power." However, the distinction of origin between poverty and virtue, which Herodotus has emphasized by his use of σύντροφος and ἔπακτος makes it, as far as we can judge, nearly impossible to understand this passage as an example of that "latent notion."

subsequent argument, and this reading has the advantage of giving due consideration to the surface meaning rather than privileging a subtext that runs counter to it. Consequently, Demaratus's reference to the "native poverty" of the wise and manly Greeks is not solid evidence that the *Histories* reflects a belief in a causal relationship between poverty and military ability. This passage might instead represent in more general terms a view that poverty is by nature associated with weakness and servitude but that this natural causal nexus can sometimes be broken by human ingenuity and institutions (σοφία καὶ νόμος).

The principal remaining pieces of evidence for the idea of poverty as a basis for strength are like the Demaratus passage in that they also represent advice given to "prosperous aggressors" about whether to attack "noble savages." The first occurs at Hdt. 1.71, where Croesus's adviser, Sandanis, tried to persuade the king not to invade the lands held by the Persians. The main thrust of Sandanis's argument was the poverty of the Persians: "if you win, you will gain little; if you are defeated, you will lose much." We may accept the Lydian's words at face value and find in Croesus's refusal to listen an iteration of the theme of the insatiable desire of kings for the goods of lesser men, as stated by Otanes during the Constitutional Debate (Hdt. 3.80.4). However, Flory, for example, sees a further significance. In his view, Persian poverty "fosters hardiness and physical and military strength, for Sandanis clearly fears the Persians."[68] It is not clear that this interpretation of the adviser's words is correct. Certainly, Sandanis thanked the gods for not leading the Persians to invade Lydia, since he believed that a Lydian defeat would mean that they would never be rid of the Persians. But Sandanis's focus was as likely to be on the Persians' naïve greed as on their supposed primitive toughness: if a Lydian defeat allowed the Persians to be introduced to the good things of that country, they would become fixated on these things and never leave the Lydians alone (Hdt. 1.71.3). In other words, the Lydian luxuries would become a continual objective of the Persians, whether or not their toughness would allow them ultimately to overcome the Lydians. Thus, as 1.71 makes no explicit connection between the poverty and the military ability of the Persians, so it also presents no necessary implication to this effect.[69]

At Hdt. 1.207, on the eve of battle with the Massagetae, Cyrus consulted his

---

68. Flory (1987, 91) states that it is Persian "frugality" which contributes to their military prowess, but it is surely wrong to see in Sandanis's words the implication that the Persian lifestyle represents a moral choice. Rather, they live without the finer things of life because they must (Hdt. 1.71.2).

69. Flory (1987, 92) infers much from Sandanis's closing words, saying: "The savage Persians are therefore hungry and strong but not intrinsically predatory or prone to overseas conquests." We doubt whether the Lydian's relief at the apparent disinterest of the Persians can bear such weight with regard to the intrinsic nature of the Persians or to their attitude to those "overseas."

council of war. This time Croesus played the role of wise adviser, warning Cyrus, we are usually told, not to attack this primitive people.[70] As reasons for this caution, he stressed "the simple life of the Massagetae, the trivial gain possible from such a poor people, and above all, the great likelihood that such an attack and contact between the two races may give the Massagetae a taste of Persian luxury and lead to a disastrous counterattack."[71] Unfortunately for those who argue for a Herodotean praise of poverty, none of these points is accurate.

In the first place, Croesus's words cannot be construed as a warning not to attack the Massagetae. The campaign against this people was well under way by the time Croesus gave his advice, and the issue before Cyrus's council was whether to join battle on the near or far side of the river Araxes. Secondly, unlike Sandanis earlier, Croesus did not consider whether much or little may be gained by defeating the Massagetae; by this time, Cyrus seemed to be intent on conquest for its own sake, not for the increase in resources it might bring.[72] Third, Croesus mentioned the fact that the Massagetae are unfamiliar with Persian luxuries by way of introducing his suggestion of a stratagem: food and wine should be left for the Massagetae to capture, feast upon, and thus be taken by surprise. Given that the Lydian himself suggested that the enemy be introduced to the "good things of the Persians," it makes no sense to see here a reference to the belief that exposure to Persian wealth would provoke a return invasion. Such an outcome is not raised as a possibility, let alone a "great likelihood." Finally, no reference is made to the toughness or bravery of the Massagetae, or, in this connection, to their primitive nature or poverty. Rather, although Croesus alone recognized the possibility of defeat at the hands of the Massagetae, the danger that he saw in the pending attack was not located in any particular characteristic of the Persians' foe, but in the most general circumstances of human life. This is the context in which Herodotus introduces his famous "wheel of human affairs." Because they are men and not gods, the Persian army and its leader must admit the possibility of disaster: περιφερόμενος δὲ οὐκ ἐᾷ αἰεὶ τοὺς αὐτοὺς εὐτυχέειν ("Spinning around, the wheel does not permit the same men to prosper always." Hdt. 1.207.2). Thus, neither Persian weakness nor Massagetan strength is at issue here. The principal subtext is not the pernicious effects

---

70. Flory (1987, 94) calls the Massagetae "completely noble savages."

71. Flory 1987, 94. Desmond (2006, 120) offers a similar interpretation: "Croesus warns Cyrus that the Massagetae are very valiant, but too poor to enjoy the luxuries of the Persian lifestyle. Victory would gain Cyrus nothing."

72. So at 1.204.2 Herodotus tells us that many things spurred Cyrus on to attack the Massagetae, but he specifically identifies only Cyrus's belief that he would continue to go from success to success.

of luxury or the praise of poverty, but the impermanence of power and success, an indubitable Herodotean idea.[73]

Another text said to illustrate the connection between poverty and strength occurs at Hdt. 3.20–22, where the Persian ruler Cambyses sent an embassy of "Fish Eaters" to spy on the Long-lived Ethiopians. Two aspects of this episode are taken to be especially relevant: the general characterization of the Ethiopians as "poor, and warlike,"[74] and more particularly the reaction of the Ethiopian king to the gifts sent him by Cambyses. Neither line of argument is strong.

In respect to the first point, while it is clear that the Ethiopians may be considered primitive—they eat boiled meat and drink milk (3.23.1), for example—it does not follow directly that they were poor. In fact, they enjoyed a superabundance of gold while bronze was scarce (3.23.4), did not need to toil for their daily sustenance, received all they needed from the Table of the Sun (3.18), and enjoyed the benefits of a fountain of youth (3.23.2–3). Thus, we cannot assume that Herodotus intends a causal connection between any military virtue the Ethiopians may exhibit and their poverty, since this last may be an invention of modern scholarship.[75] In any case, the military excellence of the Ethiopians was somewhat ambiguous. On the one hand, they "are said to be the tallest and most beautiful of all people" (λέγονται εἶναι μέγιστοι καὶ κάλλιστοι ἀνθρώπων πάντων, 3.20.1). Their superlative stature seems to translate into formidable military might: their king—who was chosen for being the tallest and strongest of his people—sent his bow to Cambyses with a warning that the Persians should not march against the Ethiopians until the Persians could draw such a great bow easily (3.21.3). Among the Persians, only Cambyses' brother Smerdis was able to draw the bow even a few inches. In this way Herodotus may symbolize the military superiority of the simple Ethiopians over the civilized Persians.[76] However, this superiority remains notional. Cambyses' expedition

---

73. Cf. the famous programmatic statement at Hdt. 1.5.3–4.
74. Desmond 2006, 120.
75. In evaluating evidence for a Greek praise of poverty, one should establish that a given example fits a definition for poverty that the Greeks would themselves recognize. Desmond (2006, 31–40) carefully distinguishes two concepts of poverty that had currency from the Archaic period: (1) poverty as the need to work for a living; and (2) poverty as the lack of a certain quantity of material possessions. We may observe that, since the Table of the Sun provided them with food, the Ethiopians are apparently wealthy by the first criterion (according to this concept, characterization as rich or poor was essentially dichotomous, with everyone belonging in one of the two categories). The second concept is also doubtful, since the Ethiopians possess much gold and so may not be classified as poor under this criterion either. For his part, Flory (1987, 98) recognizes that the Ethiopians "possess certain amenities associated with 'soft' primitivism."
76. Thus, the martial prowess of the Ethiopians, such as it is, comes from their unusual physical size and

never reached Ethiopia, and the *Histories* never shows us the two peoples meeting in battle. Rather, Cambyses failed because he set out for the ends of the earth without properly provisioning his army (3.25.1). The significance of this passage as evidence for the idea that poverty is a better source of military ability than wealth is also undercut by the fact that the Ethiopians were listed among the other subject-nations serving in Xerxes' expedition (Hdt. 7.69, 9.32).[77]

Cambyses had sent his embassy on the pretext of carrying gifts to the Ethiopian king to win his friendship and alliance. These gifts—a purple cloak, golden jewelry, myrrh, and palm wine—are sometimes assigned special importance in Herodotus's view of wealth and poverty. In particular, they are taken as symbols of luxury and their rejection by the Ethiopian indicates the superiority of the primitive. With respect to the king's refusal of the incense and cloth, Flory declares: "A society based upon the enjoyment of luxury is thus intrinsically corrupt from the point of view of the noble savage."[78] We may respond to this claim by pointing out that, although Herodotus refers often enough to the wealth and luxury of the Persians, he nowhere gives evidence that he thought Persian society was "based upon the enjoyment of luxury." On the contrary, the *Histories'* description of Persian νόμοι (Hdt. 1.131–40) gives luxury barely a passing mention. However, even if we stipulate that the presents offered by the Fish Eaters do represent Persian decadence, the fact remains that the kind of corruption symbolized by the purple and the myrrh is not weakness but dishonesty. The Ethiopian king saw through the gifts of friendship to Cambyses' hostile intentions, but his criticism addressed Persian deceitfulness, with no allusion to any failure of military capability: δολερούς μὲν τοὺς ἀνθρώπους ἔφη εἶναι, δολερὰ δὲ αὐτῶν τὰ εἵματα ("he said that both the men and the clothing were treacherous," Hdt. 3.22.1). The Persian king's deceitful purpose here finds a parallel in Cyrus's approaches to Tomyris, queen of the Massagetae. To her the Persian sent an offer of marriage instead of his favorite luxuries, but like the Ethiopian, Tomyris was not misled (Hdt. 1.205.1). The similarity of the two passages lends support to our skepticism: Cyrus's false offer of marriage does not

---

strength, and not from toughness of any sort brought on by an impoverished regimen. On the contrary, we have seen that Herodotus emphasizes the ease of life which they enjoy. Note as well that Herodotus has related that the Ethiopian king is the largest man of an unusually large people. The *Histories'* readers might well hesitate to infer from the Persians' failure to draw such a man's bow that the Persian army in general would be no match for the Ethiopian forces, although this, of course, is what the Ethiopian king means to imply.

77. See Flory 1987, 99, for a discussion of this contradiction.
78. Flory 1987, 98.

seem plausibly to symbolize some general failing of Persian society, but rather was another of that conqueror's stratagems. Just so for Cambyses' gifts.[79]

The jewelry brought by the Fish Eaters was also rejected by the Ethiopian, who mistook the gold necklace and bracelets for fetters. This element of the story is taken as a sign that "the Persians are enslaved by luxury."[80] This interpretation, too, is open to more than one objection. For example, on the view in question we are presumably meant to read ironically the king's comment that the Ethiopians have stronger fetters than the ones being offered to him (Hdt. 3.22.2).[81] However, a few paragraphs later, Herodotus relates that the Fish Eaters visited a prison where all the inmates wore shackles of gold (Hdt. 3.23.4). Thus, the *Histories* offers its audience a literal and straightforward meaning for the king's words: in Ethiopia, gold, being common, was made into chains not for adornment, but for everyday use, and the king naturally mistook the nature of this gift. The presence of this passage to some extent undermines and blocks the development of the proposed ironic interpretation.

In addition, as the image of golden fetters is offered as evidence for the association among poverty, freedom, and strength only *a contrario*—through an association among wealth, slavery, and weakness—the second grouping must be established independently in the *Histories* if the argument is to have any force. We have already examined the most prominent evidence on the supposed connection between Persian wealth and their failures in battle and have found it unconvincing. On the other hand, δουλοσύνη is clearly identified as an important characteristic of Xerxes' horde, and this servility is connected with barbarian defeats. However, the quality in question seems to be restricted to the Persians' subject-allies. As noted above, it is the allies who were whipped into battle as if they were slaves, and it is the allies who were referred to as the king's δοῦλοι. But the military ineptitude of these subordinate peoples is due to a calculation of self-interest, not to moral degeneration. In contrast, we can find no unequivocal passage in which the Persians in general, and in particular the

---

79. To be sure, both deceptive offers may have deeper significance, but that is likely to be the insatiable desire of the Persian rulers to expand their empire. Apparently, this is the motive attributed to Cyrus and Cambyses by Tomyris and the Ethiopian king at Hdt. 1.206.1–2 and 3.21.2. In neither case does Herodotus give an indication that any immorality possibly underlying these *ruses de guerre* should be applied to the Persians more generally.

80. Flory 1987, 98.

81. Note that there is no irony at the level of the story: Herodotus depicts the king as "believing the things to be fetters" (νομίσας εἶναί σφεα πέδας), rather than as being intentionally cryptic or portentous. The relevant irony would be at the level of the narrator and audience.

Persian nobles, are called slaves of the king.[82] Thus, there is little reason to accept the idea of an enervating enslavement to luxury. If luxury were to have this effect, we might expect to find it to a greater degree in the imperial power than among the conquered, since the prosperity of the victors should be greater than that of the vanquished. But Herodotus does not clearly depict the Persians as slaves of any kind; it is doubtful that the Ethiopian's "golden fetters" alluded to an association between wealth and slavery or poverty and freedom.[83]

The last of the four gifts sent by Cambyses was palm wine. Unlike the other goodwill offerings, the Ethiopian king accepted the wine enthusiastically, seeing in it the cause of whatever physical vigor the Persians might claim. Eating bread, on the other hand, was for the Ethiopian the equivalent of "eating dung" (σιτεόμενοι κόπρον) and was to be blamed for the Persians' relatively short life spans. If Herodotus had meant this passage to convey to his audience a connection between Persian lifestyle and luxuries and their inevitable decline as a military power, it is extremely odd that the passage makes no explicit link between any of the gifts and physical weakness, while drawing just such a link between Persian frailty and cereal agriculture. Rather, the king's comments about the bread and wine make it unlikely that this episode represents the author's serious views about the moral and physical effects of the Persians' lifestyle. It seems to us more reasonable to understand king's reactions to Cambyses' gifts as an example of the paradoxical customs at the far ends of the earth.

---

82. At Hdt. 7.135.3, two prominent Spartans are the ones who depict Hydarnes, a Persian general, as a slave. At 8.102.2, Mardonius is called the king's δοῦλος by Artemisia, who is minimizing the importance to Xerxes of that general's possible defeat. Hunt (1998, 48–49) cites 7.96.2 as evidence that "The Persian defeat too was due in part to the slavish character of their empire. . . . the Persian generals 'were slaves just like the rest of the troops.'" By now we are familiar with the frequent failure to observe when Herodotus is speaking of the Persians and when he is referring to their subjects. Hdt. 7.96.1–2 clearly belongs in the latter category.

83. After a careful review of the evidence, Isaac (2004, 267) observes "it is clear that Herodotus himself never intended to convey the message that the Persian army functioned as an army of slaves." In this connection, we may recall that, at Hdt. 1.126.5, when trying to persuade the Persians to free themselves from the yoke of Median rule, Cyrus contrasted the luxuries they would so attain (μυρία ἀγαθά) with the "servile toil" (πόνον δουλοπρεπέα) they would so avoid. The idea is reiterated at the end of Cyrus's life, when Darius's father Hystaspes praised Cyrus in terms of slavery and freedom: ὃς ἀντὶ μὲν δούλων ἐποίησας ἐλευθέρους Πέρσας εἶναι, ἀντὶ δὲ ἄρχεσθαι ὑπ᾽ ἄλλων ἄρχειν ἁπάντων ("You have made the Persians free instead of slaves, and the rulers of all instead of ruled by others." Hdt. 1.210.2). Since these words are spoken by characters in the narrative, we cannot claim they represent Herodotus's view more closely than those cited in the preceding note, where Artemisia and the Spartans Sperthias and Bulis call Persian nobles slaves. However, taken together they indicate a certain tension in the *Histories* between the way the Persian elite saw itself and the way it was seen by outsiders. Herodotus is aware of this tension, as is clear at 7.135, where the Persian Hydarnes characterizes his relationship with the king as that of a φίλος, whom Xerxes rewards with τιμή and ἀρχή because of his ἀνδραγαθία. To the Spartans, in contrast, Hydarnes is merely Xerxes' δοῦλος.

Thus, the best evidence offered in support of the idea that poverty was a source of martial strength amounts to very little. Nothing would be gained from looking at the evidence of lesser caliber.[84] Accordingly, we feel confident in claiming that, from the text of the *Histories*, one cannot establish either directly or indirectly that the Persian defeat at the hands of the Greeks was to any extent attributable to moral or physical enervation caused by their immoderate wealth. It is not, then, reasonable to read as ironic Herodotus's statement at 9.122 that the Persians heeded Cyrus's advice. The words are meant literally: they remained in their sorry land and thus avoided slavery.

Ἐπιμέλεια

Our conclusion presents a question: if 9.122 makes no reference to a natural process by which prosperity can be expected to bring about eventual decay, of what then is Cyrus afraid? Why should he want his subjects to avoid soft lands so that they would not become soft men? Another line of interpretation is available, and we offer it as a possibility. We have suggested above that, unlike the direct and unmediated geographic determinism of the Hippocratic *Airs*, the proximate cause of the imagined Persian decline includes an economic dimension. However, we differ from the proponents of pernicious luxury in that we think it plausible that Cyrus's words focus on economic production, and not consumption. After all, the only clue the *Histories* provides about why soft lands produce soft men is that there the Persians would become slaves by "sowing the plain" (πεδιάδα σπείροντες) to bring forth the "wondrous harvest" (καρπὸν θωμαστὸν) that is incompatible with "men good at war." Such an emphasis would make sense if Herodotus was trying to imply that Persian military success was integrally intertwined with the manner in which the Persians had traditionally made a living, not with whether they enjoyed a few good things or a myriad. The details of Persian dress, cuisine, hairstyle, and the like are not at issue.

---

84. Desmond (2006, 105), for example, sets Herodotus 8.111 as an epigraph for his discussion of the praise of poverty in connection with war. His intention must be ironic since the passage has nothing to do with the idea of poverty as a matrix in which physical and mental toughness might be expected to develop. Rather, relating how the Andrians relied on their native gods, Poverty and Helplessness (Πενίην τε καὶ Ἀμηχανίην, 8.111.3), to avoid paying tribute to the Athenians, it makes the point that there is no getting blood from a turnip. Although Andrian inability in this regard is stronger than Athenian power (οὐδέκοτε γὰρ τῆς ἑωυτῶν ἀδυναμίης τὴν Ἀθηναίων δύναμιν εἶναι κρέσσω, 8.111.3), such poverty is no basis for more general success.

In other words, a move such as suggested by Artembares would distract the Persians from their constant exercise in archery and horsemanship, the basis of their empire. This result is exactly that usually posited for pernicious luxury, but there is an important distinction: that view supposes a *process* of decadence (prosperity, perhaps inexorably, leads to luxury and thence to an effeminacy, which shuns military exercise); our interpretation puts the locus of Cyrus's concern in a contingent decision that *in and of itself* is sufficient to unmake Persian power. Although expressed as a generality—"soft lands produce soft peoples"—, the *Histories* does not verify this statement as an "iron law of nature versus culture."[85] Cyrus's warning is directed to the Persians, and *for them* the very act of emigrating and becoming a people of the agricultural plain would have this result, regardless of whether they adopted an austere or opulent lifestyle.[86]

The Greeks were well aware that civilized life afforded distractions from the intensive military training that Herodotus attributed to the Persians. For example, some Greeks felt that an intellectual life was a life of cowardice and effeminacy.[87] A notorious instance comes from Pericles' defense of Athenian self-indulgence in the Funeral Speech: φιλοσοφοῦμεν ἄνευ μαλακίας ("we pursue wisdom without softness," Thuc. 2.40.1). We may assume that this claim would have little point unless Thucydides could be confident that his readers were familiar with the opposite belief. As Gomme notes, the view is elaborated—*mutandis mutatis*—by Callicles in Plato's *Gorgias*: philosophy is fine for the young, but when a grown man continues to devote himself to it, he cannot defend himself or his friends among the perils of civic life:[88]

ὑπάρχει τούτῳ τῷ ἀνθρώπῳ, κἂν πάνυ εὐφυὴς ᾖ, ἀνάνδρῳ γενέσθαι φεύγοντι τὰ μέσα τῆς πόλεως καὶ τὰς ἀγοράς . . . τὸν δὲ τοιοῦτον, εἴ τι καὶ ἀγροικότερον εἰρῆσθαι, ἔξεστιν ἐπὶ κόρρης τύπτοντα μὴ διδόναι δίκην.

[This fellow, even if he is naturally quite talented, will become unmanly by shunning the city center and the marketplaces. . . . If I may use a rather rough

---

85. Georges (1994, 184–85) supports this statement with the claim, frequently made by those who believe in pernicious luxury, that "the savage is stronger than civilization and will always defeat it." Generalizations of this sort ignore inconvenient details. For example, it is unlikely Herodotus's audience would have thought of the Ionians as "more civilized" than their Lydian conquerors (from whom the Ionians were said to have learned luxury). Likewise, the civilized Persians defeated the savage Thracians, and accepted earth and water from others such as the Macedonians.

86. If Cyrus's precept was truly of general application, we would expect the Babylonians, producers of the most wondrous harvest, to be militarily quite deficient. This is not the case.

87. For a recent discussion see Sandridge 2012, 101.

88. Gomme 1956, 121.

expression, it is possible to bitch slap such a person and get away with it.] (Plato, *Gorg.* 485d–486c)

Callicles is intent upon philosophy's ill effects on the relationship of citizen with citizen, while Pericles has his eye on the Athenians' fitness for war. Nonetheless, it is reasonable to compare the passages, since in both places intellectual pursuits are linked with a kind of μαλακία. Significantly for our interpretation of Herodotus 9.122, it is not an inherent feature of philosophy which, according to Callicles, makes its practitioners unfit, though it is easy to imagine such a claim. To recall a charge made against modern academics and intellectuals, a critic might say that the habit of looking at the different sides of every question makes one apt to sympathize with the position of one's enemy and leads to a paralyzing loss of nerve. Callicles has no such process in mind. As we have suggested for Herodotus's Cyrus, he is referring not to what philosophers do, but what they refrain from doing: ἀμελεῖς, ὦ Σώκρατες, ὧν δεῖ σε ἐπιμελεῖσθαι ("You are neglecting, Socrates, the things to which you should be devoting yourself." Plato, *Gorg.* 485e).

The terms of Callicles' criticism are familiar. A life of philosophy has, from an outsider's point of view, the same deleterious outcome that we have seen Socrates ascribe to τρυφή in the *Republic:* it diverts the proper focus of ἐπιμέλεια. This surprising overlap between the effects of φιλοσοφία and τρυφή should help us to see that many aspects of civilized life might lead to the μαλακία to which Cyrus and Pericles refer, insofar as these things turn one's ἐπιμέλεια away from the development of martial skills. Referring to the civic sphere of action, Callicles blames philosophers for neglecting work in oratory and politics, making themselves ineffective friends and contemptible enemies. Pericles, directing his comments at least in part to Athens' foreign foes, alludes in a backhanded way to the analogous idea that intellectuals neglect military training for mental gymnastics.

In Chapter 1, we examined the evidence that, while occasionally luxury might induce the μαλακία of military weakness, there was no assumption that this process was general or necessary. Just as it was possible to φιλοσοφεῖν ἄνευ μαλακίας, so luxury without degeneration was also a perfectly reasonable expectation, even when the subject is the Persians: Xenophon has much to say about the ἐπιμέλεια that the Great King and his government lavished on preparing their youth for war:

ὅταν δὲ ἐξίῃ βασιλεὺς ἐπὶ θήραν, ἐξάγει τὴν ἡμίσειαν τῆς φυλακῆς· ποιεῖ δὲ τοῦτο πολλάκις τοῦ μηνός. . . . διὰ τοῦτο δὲ δημοσίᾳ τοῦ θηρᾶν ἐπιμέλονται,

καὶ βασιλεὺς ὥσπερ καὶ ἐν πολέμῳ ἡγεμών ἐστιν αὐτοῖς καὶ αὐτός τε θηρᾷ καὶ
τῶν ἄλλων ἐπιμελεῖται ὅπως ἂν θηρῶσιν, ὅτι ἀληθεστάτη αὐτοῖς δοκεῖ εἶναι
αὕτη ἡ μελέτη τῶν πρὸς τὸν πόλεμον.

[Whenever the king goes out to a hunt, he leads with him half of the garrison.
He does this several times a month. . . . On account of this, the government
oversees hunting and the king is the chief of the hunters, as he is the chief in
war; he both hunts himself and takes care that the others hunt. This is done
because they think this is the most genuine training for the demands of war.]
(Xen., *Cyr.* 1.2.9–10)

The luxurious lifestyle of the Persian elite need not bring about a decline in
their strength, as long as it does not preclude rugged physical exertion.[89] Likewise, the existence of an idea of pernicious luxury is not necessary to make
sense of Cyrus's words at 9.122, and it is plausible to understand Herodotus's
point to be not a warning about the destructive properties of opulence, but a
recognition that the Persians owed their empire to ἡ μελέτη τῶν πρὸς τὸν
πόλεμον, which was inseparably tied to their native land and traditions.

It is not difficult to find evidence in the *Histories* for the view that it was not
luxury in general, but neglect of practice in arms that had the kind of dire consequences Cyrus predicts for the Persians. At Hdt. 1.155, hearing of the Lydian
rebellion under Pactyas, Croesus advised Cyrus to modify their customs to prevent a similar occurrence in the future:

Λυδοῖσι δὲ συγγνώμην ἔχων τάδε αὐτοῖσι ἐπίταξον, ὡς μήτε ἀποστέωσι μήτε
δεινοί τοι ἔωσι· ἄπειπε μέν σφι πέμψας ὅπλα ἀρήια μὴ κεκτῆσθαι, κέλευε δέ
σφεας κιθῶνάς τε ὑποδύνειν τοῖσι εἵμασι καὶ κοθόρνους ὑποδέεσθαι, πρόειπε
δ᾿ αὐτοῖσι κιθαρίζειν τε καὶ ψάλλειν καὶ καπηλεύειν παιδεύειν τοὺς παῖδας. καὶ
ταχέως σφέας, ὦ βασιλεῦ, γυναῖκας ἀντ᾿ ἀνδρῶν ὄψεαι γεγονότας, ὥστε οὐδὲν
δεινοί τοι ἔσονται μὴ ἀποστέωσι.

[Granting pardon to the Lydians, give them these commands, so that they neither rebel nor be dangerous to you: send to them and forbid them to possess
weapons of war, but order them to put on chitons under their cloaks and to

---

89. Xenophon's description of Persian education does not seem to concern only the earliest days of their
hegemony, but to be more general, with a pronounced decline only in recent times.

wear buskins. Tell them to teach their sons to pluck and strum the cithara and to keep shops. Quickly, O King, you will see them become women instead of men, so that they will be no threat to you, that they will rebel.] (Hdt. 1.155.4)

The passage may be familiar since, ironically, it is often cited as the best evidence that Herodotus thought luxuriousness could effeminize and that this process was of historical significance. We maintain that this interpretation is untenable.[90] In the first place, its supporters produce no good proof that κιθῶνες, κοθόρνοι, cithara-playing, and shopkeeping are closely associated with a luxurious life. If Herodotus were trying to convey a sense of luxury, we would expect him rather to speak of fine jewelry, purple clothing, soft cushions, gold and silver place settings, and lavish feasting. Second, the standard interpretation of 1.155 is inconsistent with Herodotus's previous narration of the Lydian λόγος. In view of what Herodotus has already said, it makes no sense to hold that the Lydians became women instead of men because they were forced to a life of luxury after the second capture of Sardis.

Herodotus makes it quite clear that the Lydians were distinguished by prosperity and luxury well before the change in their way of life ordered by Cyrus. This is evident in a passage we have already examined, the Wise Counselor scene between Sandanis and Croesus (Hdt. 1.71.3–4). Here we are told of the many good and fine things that the Lydians enjoy, in contrast to the Persians (ὅσα ἀγαθά . . . τῶν ἡμετέρων ἀγαθῶν . . . οὔτε ἁβρὸν οὔτε ἀγαθόν).[91] If further proof were needed that the Lydians lived a life of luxury before Cyrus ordered a change in their customs, one need look no further than Croesus himself. As every reader of the *Histories* knows, the wealth of the Lydian ruler is painstakingly emphasized; we may without objection take Croesus's own lifestyle as

---

90. Those who claim that 1.155.4 is an instance of feminization through luxury usually do not argue the point in detail, but take it as self-evident. The reason for their confidence seems to be the belief that the idea of luxury causing softness was a commonplace of Greek thought. We have shown above that this is far from the case.

91. It is worth recording the analysis by Asheri, Lloyd, and Corcella (2007, 132; cf. Asheri and Antelami 1988, 313) of the comparison made here between Lydians and Persians: "The Persians are portrayed here as an uncouth but virile people in contrast with the Lydians, who are civilized but effeminate." In spite of this claim, there is no sign that the antithesis in this passage is between virility and effeminacy. On the surface, the contrast is one of wealth versus poverty, and the point is that Croesus has everything to lose and nothing to gain in a war with Persia. An explicit reference to the presumed moral contrast is not to be expected in such a context. It would be an offense against rhetorical appropriateness for Herodotus to introduce a counselor who emphasizes to Croesus the weak and womanly nature of the Lydian people. Thus we must look for an indirect indication of this idea. There is none. If we leave aside the very fact of Lydian luxury, since its relevant aspects are *sub iudice*, we find no morally significant characteristic attributed to the Lydians.

epitomizing the ἁβρά and ἀγαθά of the Lydian empire. Furthermore, the luxury of king and kingdom—apparent again in the Pythia's address to the king as "easy-living Lydian" (Λυδὲ ποδαβρέ, Hdt. 1.55.2)—was not of recent acquisition. At the time of Solon's visit, Croesus had conquered most of Asia west of the Halys, and Lydia was at the peak of its prosperity (Hdt. 1.29.1). However, the policy of expansion, and the wealth and luxury that accompanied it, went back for generations.

Although, in Herodotus's telling, luxury was a Lydian characteristic many years before the arrival of Cyrus on the scene, there is no sign in the narrative of the *Histories* that this lifestyle in any way weakened either the Lydians or their king. Even in the last days of their empire, when one might expect a process of decadence to be at its most pronounced, Herodotus allows it no role in events. In contrast, at the Lydians' last stand in front of Sardis, although he had already beaten Croesus's army at Pteria, Cyrus was not confident that he could overcome his difficult foe and relied upon a stratagem, frightening the Lydian horse with camels so that the Lydians had to give up their preferred method of combat:

(1.79.3) ἦν δὲ τοῦτον τὸν χρόνον ἔθνος οὐδὲν ἐν τῇ Ἀσίῃ οὔτε ἀνδρειότερον οὔτε ἀλκιμώτερον τοῦ Λυδίου. ἡ δὲ μάχη σφέων ἦν ἀφ᾽ ἵππων, δούρατά τε ἐφόρεον μεγάλα καὶ αὐτοὶ ἦσαν ἱππεύεσθαι ἀγαθοί. . . . (1.80.6) οὐ μέντοι οἵ γε Λυδοὶ τὸ ἐνθεῦτεν δειλοὶ ἦσαν, ἀλλ᾽, ὡς ἔμαθον τὸ γινόμενον, ἀποθορόντες ἀπὸ τῶν ἵππων πεζοὶ τοῖσι Πέρσῃσι συνέβαλλον. χρόνῳ δὲ πεσόντων ἀμφοτέρων πολλῶν ἐτράποντο οἱ Λυδοί, κατειληθέντες δὲ ἐς τὸ τεῖχος ἐπολιορκέοντο ὑπὸ τῶν Περσέων.

[(1.79.3) At this time, no nation in Asia was more manly or warlike than the Lydians. They did battle from horseback; they carried large spears and were themselves skilled at riding. . . . (1.80.6) Nor indeed at this moment did the Lydians turn coward, but, when they learned what was happening, they leapt off their horses and attacked the Persians on foot. Many fell on both sides, but after a while the Lydians were beaten, driven within the walls, and besieged by the Persians.] (Hdt. 1.79.3, 80.6)

As far as bravery and skill at battle, there is very little to support the idea, prevalent in the scholarship, of a dichotomy between the Persians, a "popolo rozzo ma virile" and the "citified and effeminate" Lydians.[92]

---

92. Cf. the descriptions of the Battle of Pteria (Hdt. 1.76–77) and the siege of Sardis (Hdt. 1.84).

As for Croesus himself, those who maintain the importance of pernicious luxury as a historical cause in Herodotus are faced with a paradox that demands explanation: the ruin of the king is undoubtedly a paradigmatic instance of the κύκλος τῶν ἀνθρωπηίων πρηγμάτων ("circle of human affairs"), and we may assume that Herodotus details with such attention Croesus's wealth at least in part to make his reversal of fortune the more memorable. If the demoralizing effects of luxury were indeed a factor that gives impetus to the κύκλος, we might reasonably expect to find, in the context of the depiction of Croesus's wealth, some focus on the Lydian's δίαιτα. But this is not the case, as Herodotus's attention remains fixed on the quantification of Croesus's prosperity, while he seems to give no thought to the idea of Croesus in the act of enjoying his riches. The passage at 1.50.1 makes Herodotus's perspective in this regard particularly clear:

μετὰ δὲ ταῦτα θυσίῃσι μεγάλῃσι τὸν ἐν Δελφοῖσι θεὸν ἱλάσκετο· κτήνεά τε γὰρ τὰ θύσιμα πάντα τρισχίλια ἔθυσε, κλίνας τε ἐπιχρύσους καὶ ἐπαργύρους καὶ φιάλας χρυσέας καὶ εἵματα πορφύρεα καὶ κιθῶνας νήσας πυρὴν μεγάλην κατέκαιε.

[After this, he tried to win over the god in Delphi with great sacrifices. He offered, in all, three thousand sacrificial animals, and he piled in a great pyre couches covered with gold and silver and golden vessels and purple cloaks and tunics, and burned them up.] (Hdt. 1.50.1)

We have in this passage evidence that the principal accoutrements of luxury were present in great abundance in the household of Croesus. However, Herodotus seems uninterested in any moral implications of their use. Rather, he moves on immediately to specify the size and number and weight of ingots of precious metals that Croesus dedicated at Delphi. The luxury goods mentioned here are thus merely indications of the wealth of the Lydian king and appear to have no further significance. Nor is Herodotus's failure here to make a moral point about opulence unusual. As we will see, many are the places in the *Histories* where an author interested in τρυφή—an author such as Athenaeus—would find a clear example of luxury contributing to ruin, though Herodotus says nothing about the matter. Though this is an *argumentum ex silentio*, it gains force by the frequency of its applicability.

Thus, Herodotus does not take the opportunity offered by the fall of Croesus to refer directly to the harmful consequences of an opulent δίαιτα. Nor does he portray them more subtly through the narrative, since Croesus showed no signs of the supposedly corrosive effects of a life of luxury. In the first place, he exhibited no weakness or effeminacy. He led his army against the enemy in person and he accepted his defeat at Pteria well, considering it a temporary setback owing to bad odds. He returned to Sardis with the intention of renewing the campaign in the spring (Hdt. 1.76–77). There, Croesus was caught unprepared by Cyrus's surprising advance. Herodotus emphasizes that the Lydian, although in great difficulty, did not fall into despair or passivity:

ἐνθαῦτα Κροῖσος ἐς ἀπορίην πολλὴν ἀπιγμένος, ὥς οἱ παρὰ δόξαν ἔσχε τὰ πρήγματα ἢ ὡς αὐτὸς κατεδόκεε, ὅμως τοὺς Λυδοὺς ἐξῆγε ἐς μάχην.

[Then Croesus, finding himself in dire straits, since events had turned out contrary to his expectation, nevertheless led the Lydians to battle.] (Hdt. 1.79.2)

Nor did Croesus suffer from the other supposed effects of luxuriousness. Though Cobet finds a taste for luxury at the root of the imperialism that is so prominent in the *Histories*,[93] no word of this explanation appears in our text in connection with Croesus's expansionist policy. Instead, Herodotus gives three different causes for the Lydian's move against Cyrus. At 1.46, Croesus was snapped out of his lengthy mourning for his son by the news that the kingdom of the Medes had fallen to the Persians. He set in motion plans to attack the upstarts from a motive that seems to be largely one of self-defense:

ἐνέβησε δὲ ἐς φροντίδα, εἴ κως δύναιτο, πρὶν μεγάλους γενέσθαι τοὺς Πέρσας, καταλαβεῖν αὐτῶν αὐξανομένην τὴν δύναμιν.

[He began to consider if somehow it might be possible to restrain the growing power of the Persians before they became great.] (Hdt. 1.46.1)

Later, at 1.73, we are told, first, that a desire for land (γῆς ἱμέρῳ) and, second, the wish to take revenge on Cyrus for the fall of Astyages were the reasons that Croesus took his army across the Halys into Cappadocia. Luxury does not figure here.

Far from owing his ruin to physical or moral decadence arising from his

---

93. Cobet 1971, 174–76.

lifestyle, Croesus is depicted as a good man brought low by the dictates of fate. According to Lydian sources, Apollo rescued Croesus from his pyre and Cyrus recognized him as "favored by god and a good man" (θεοφιλὴς καὶ ἀνὴρ ἀγαθός, Hdt. 1.87.2). This interpretation is confirmed by the Pythia. Croesus fell from power because of the offence (ἁμαρτάδα) committed by his ancestor, Gyges. In the view of the god himself, Croesus did not deserve to suffer the collapse of his power:

προθυμεομένου δὲ Λοξίεω ὅκως ἂν κατὰ τοὺς παῖδας τοῦ Κροίσου γένοιτο τὸ Σαρδίων πάθος καὶ μὴ κατ᾽ αὐτὸν Κροῖσον, οὐκ οἵός τε ἐγένετο παραγαγεῖνΜοίρας.

[Loxias was eager that the calamity of Sardis take place at the time of Croesus's sons and not during Croesus's own time; but he was not able to divert the Fates.] (Hdt. 1.91.2)

Thus, while it is clear from the text of the *Histories* that luxury is a characteristic of the Lydian king and his subjects, Herodotus does not make his readers aware of any link between the Lydians' way of life and their overthrow by the Persians.[94] Given that Herodotus indisputably emphasizes the prosperity of the Lydians up to the eve of their destruction, we may take the point to be that Croesus fell not because of, but in spite of, his wealth.[95]

How, then, are we to understand the process by which Cyrus is supposed to turn the rebellious Lydians into "women instead of men" if this transformation is not the result of luxury? The answer is simple. The catalyst for the enervation of the Lydians lies in the prohibition against bearing arms (ἄπειπε μέν σφι . . .

---

94. It may seem that there is something to the claim that Herodotus depicts a Croesus whose wealth makes him blind to his own limitations and that this is a character flaw that leads to his defeat. On the contrary, it seems to be Herodotus's view that Croesus's actions vis-à-vis Persia were in an important way immaterial. He would have ended up in the hands of Cyrus, whatever he had done: ὡς ὕστερον . . . ἁλοὺς τῆς πεπρωμένης ("since he was captured later than was fated," Hdt. 1.91.3). Asheri and Antelami (1988, 322; cf. Asheri, Lloyd, and Corcella 2007, 143) note that this passage reflects a "'dogma' of predestination" and constitutes important evidence for Herodotean pessimism. However this may be, a better candidate for an instance of moral blindness occurs at Hdt. 1.34–45, where Croesus's favorite son Atys dies because the king did not recognize the limits of human prosperity: ἔλαβε ἐκ θεοῦ νέμεσις μεγάλη Κροῖσον, ὡς εἰκάσαι, ὅτι ἐνόμισε ἑωυτὸν εἶναι ἀνθρώπων ἁπάντων ὀλβιώτατον ("A great retribution from god overtook Croesus, apparently because he considered himself the most fortunate of all people," Hdt. 1.34.1).

95. One might facetiously suggest that it was through his ἁβρά that Croesus kept his kingdom as long as he did. By sending luxurious gifts to Delphi, Croesus was able to propitiate the god, and Apollo arranged for the Lydian empire to last three years longer than the fates had decreed.

ὅπλα ἀρήια μὴ ἐκτῆσθαι that Cyrus sends them, not in the injunction to change their dress and pastimes (κέλευε δέ σφεας κιθῶνάς τε ὑποδύνειν κτλ.). Giving up the practice of arms is to make the Lydians effeminate and unthreatening.

The story of Croesus's son, Atys, supports this interpretation. Although we may assume that, as Croesus's heir, Atys had access to all the luxuries available to the Lydians, he was no less brave and manly on that account. Then Croesus, dreaming that his son would be killed by an iron spearhead (Hdt. 1.34.2), hid away the weapons that were in his palace and forbade Atys to use them. The effects of this change were apparent in Atys's complaint to his father:

ὦ πάτερ, τὰ κάλλιστα πρότερόν κοτε καὶ γενναιότατα ἡμῖν ἦν ἔς τε πολέμους καὶ ἐς ἄγρας φοιτέοντας εὐδοκιμέειν· νῦν δὲ ἀμφοτέρων με τούτων ἀποκλήσας ἔχεις οὔτε τινὰ δειλίην μοι παριδὼν οὔτε ἀθυμίην. νῦν τε τέοισί με χρὴ ὄμμασι ἔς τε ἀγορὴν καὶ ἐξ ἀγορῆς φοιτέοντα φαίνεσθαι; κοῖος μέν τις τοῖσι πολιήτῃσι δόξω εἶναι, κοῖος δέ τις τῇ νεογάμῳ γυναικί; κοίῳ δὲ ἐκείνη δόξει ἀνδρὶ συνοικέειν;

[Father, once it was the best and noblest pursuit for us to win good reputation by going to wars and on hunts. But now you keep me away from both these things, although you have seen neither cowardice nor lack of spirit in me. What face must I now put on as people watch me going back and forth from the marketplace? What sort of person do I seem to the citizens? What sort do I seem to my new wife? With what kind of man does she think she lives?] (Hdt. 1.37.2–3)

The implicit answer to this last question is of course: no kind of man at all. As far as Herodotus's text is concerned, Atys shows no sign of any decadence or weakness due to luxury (πρότερόν κοτε).[96] It was Croesus's decision, paralleled in his later advice to Cyrus, not to allow Atys the practice of arms that put the son's virility in doubt and threatened to "make him a woman instead of a man." As luxury has no place in the feminization alluded to here at 1.37, so there is no need to see it as an essential part of the same process envisioned at 1.155.

Let us return now to 9.122. If, as is often suggested, we read Cyrus's warning to his people in the light of Croesus's recommendation at 1.155, we find that the example of the Lydians does not induce us to understand Cyrus as referring to

---

96. Herodotus vouches in his narrative voice for Atys's claims of εὐδοξία: ὁ δὲ ἕτερος τῶν ἡλίκων μακρῷ τὰ πάντα πρῶτος· οὔνομα δέ οἱ ἦν Ἄτυς ("The other son was by far the first of all his peers in all things. His names was Atys." Hdt. 1.34.2).

the idea that luxury corrupts and feminizes. On the contrary, the passage in Book 1 supports the interpretation that the *Histories* ends by raising a much less provocative idea: the Persians will become soft and the slaves of other men if they give up the regular exercise of military skills, skills that they have developed while struggling for a living in their rugged homeland.

Pernicious Luxury in History

To this point we have been focusing on the case for pernicious luxury among the Persians. In particular, we have examined the evidence on whether Cyrus's words at Hdt. 9.122 provide a kind of thematic lens through which we are meant to understand the failure of the great eastern empire in its war against the Greek allies. We have found such evidence very weak and unconvincing. Frequently it seems that scholars are absolutely persuaded that the idea of effeminizing luxury was a significant part of the Greek concept of the Persian "other" in the second half of the fifth century;[97] correspondingly, Herodotus's evidence on this matter is often not subjected to close scrutiny.[98] It will be important for those who continue to maintain that the *Histories* paints for us a picture of the "soft" Persian and the "hard" Greek to answer the objections we have raised.

In any case, Cyrus's supposed condemnation of the effects of luxury is not usually assumed to be limited in application to the Persians or their empire,

---

97. A well-nuanced discussion of certain barbarian peoples and Herodotus's "concern with explaining historical phenomena" (232) is found in Lloyd 1990, 232–36.

98. We find additional support for our position in two important reevaluations of the Greek view of the barbarian "other," although neither study pays close attention to the evidence on luxury. Gruen (2011, 39), summarizing his discussion of Herodotus's position, has this to say about the supposed depiction of Greek and Persian as opposed polarities: "The chronicler of the great war between Greece and Persia finds numerous reasons for bitter enmity between the nations. But a cultural divide does not take precedence among them. . . . Value systems overlapped rather than clashed. Customs and practices could be distinguished, but not necessarily to the advantage of one or the other. . . . Herodotus did not compose a manifesto to advocate the superiority of a constitutional system, to celebrate Hellenic values, or to suggest essentialist characteristics that entailed an irremediable separation between the peoples." Isaac (2004, 261), in his magisterial study of racism in antiquity, points out the layers of unexamined assumptions regularly made by those who see in the *Histories* the story of an epochal clash between East and West: "Thus it appears that many modern historians confidently associate Greek civilization with all or many of the most important values which contemporary western culture cherishes for itself, while Persian civilization represents the opposite. They further assume that this was also Herodotus's view of the conflict in his time and—a third assumption—that Herodotus represents fifth-century common thinking in Greece on these matters. I would claim that these assumptions are not self-evident and should be reconsidered." The same criticism could be applied with little change to proponents of the importance of pernicious luxury.

but, from its position at the end of the *Histories,* is thought to take on "wider relevance for human societies and the processes of history."[99] Thus, we will now look beyond the Persians and we will argue that—whatever "soft lands" may mean exactly—the idea of a process of decadence is of little importance to the Herodotean narrative. Indeed, the course of events as presented in the *Histories* nowhere offers an example of pernicious luxury with historical importance, whether it be of an individual or of a group.

This is a categorical statement of broad scope, but it applies even where we might least expect it: in the case of the Lydians themselves. Although Herodotus states that Cyrus was persuaded by Croesus and took the recommended measures, the feminization of the Lydians is an idea that is then dropped. When the Greeks attack Sardis during the Ionian revolt, "the Lydians and as many Persians as were in the city" (οἱ Λυδοί τε καὶ ὅσοι Περσέων ἐνῆσαν ἐν τῇ πόλι, Hdt. 5.101.2) acted together to drive the invaders off. Herodotus does not distinguish between the martial qualities of the Lydians and their Persian overlords. There is no sign of the weak and womanish people that 1.155 would lead us to expect.[100]

In the same way, Herodotus seems to have forgotten that Cyrus compelled the Lydians to give up training in arms. In the catalogue of Xerxes' forces in Book 7, we may be surprised to hear that the Lydians are present: "The Lydians carried arms most like those of the Greeks" (Λυδοὶ δὲ ἀγχοτάτω τῶν Ἑλληνικῶν εἶχον ὅπλα, Hdt. 7.74.1). Thus, the process of feminization depicted at 1.155 is isolated and has no sequel. It is implicated in no events that unfold in the later pages of the *Histories,* and it is inconsistent with the few appearances of the Lydians in the narrative after Cyrus's recapture of Sardis. Notwithstanding 1.155, the Lydians in the Herodotean narrative are not particularly demoralized or decadent.

---

99. Flower and Marincola 2002, 311.

100. DeVries (2000) compares the supposed literary depiction of Lydians as soft and effeminate with their portrayal in Attic vase painting. In this material he finds only two examples that may be relevant. One is "the celebrated depiction of Croesus on the pyre by Myson" (358). DeVries characterizes the image as "dignified." The other, a late sixth-century oinochoe, presents "drunken, overweight men who . . . cavort, collapse, and defecate." DeVries thinks these men are probably Lydian and sees here a graphic representation of the "ethnic decadence" related in the literary sources. He concludes from this single depiction that "in the case of the Lydians, it looks as if, for better or worse, the pejorative judgments Greeks held about them found expression both in literature and art" (363). It is an indication of pervasiveness of the modern belief in a Greek idea of pernicious luxury that DeVries does not generalize from the positive depiction of Croesus to a correspondingly sympathetic and general Greek judgment. This in spite of the likelihood that there are more examples in classical literature of Lydians as brave and good fighters rather than the opposite.

Likewise, an examination of the implications of wealth and prosperity throughout the *Histories* gives similar results: nowhere in the work are riches and luxury said to lead to softness of body or character and ensuing misfortune. Before describing the war between the Greeks and Persians, the *Histories* tells the story of the rise of the Persian empire. As it grew, Persian might overcame many nations that had previously been themselves prosperous and powerful. If the idea of pernicious luxury were important to Herodotus, we would expect to find examples of this process at work in the fall of so many rich lands.

The first people to be brought under the Persians' yoke were their overlords, the Medes. The wealth of Media was, to be sure, an important stimulus behind the Persian revolt. Cyrus, after calling his army together and giving them the finest feast he could afford, promised the Persians "these and ten thousand other fine things" (τάδε τε καὶ ἄλλα μυρία ἀγαθά, Hdt. 1.126.5) if they would follow him into rebellion.[101] However, as Herodotus sees it, the cause of the fall of the Medes was far removed from any kind of softness. Summing up the tale of the defeat of Astyages, Herodotus offers an explanation for the turn of fortune: "the Medes became subjects of the Persians because of his bitterness" (Μῆδοι δὲ ὑπέκυψαν Πέρσῃσι διὰ τὴν τούτου πικρότητα, Hdt. 1.130.1).[102] Πικρότης as applied to a person means something like "implacability." In particular, Herodotus has in mind the Median king's actions when he ordered the exposure of the infant Cyrus and when he tricked Harpagus into making a meal of his own son.[103] Astyages' πικρότης, manifesting itself as such severity, is practically the antonym of the μαλακία of 9.122.

From the point of view of Herodotus's attitude toward luxury, the *Histories'*

---

101. Scholars have noticed that Cyrus's point here at Hdt. 1.126, that empire will bring a beneficial change of lifestyle, with an increase of luxury and a decrease of toil, seems to be inconsistent with his warning at 9.122, that a change in lifestyle will induce μαλακία; see Immerwahr (1966) 1981, 146; and Flower and Marincola 2002, 311–12. According to Herodotus, the Persians first learned luxury from the Lydians (Hdt. 1.71.4), while Xenophon sees Media as the source: τότε μὲν γὰρ ἔτι τῇ ἐκ Περσῶν παιδείᾳ καὶ ἐγκρατείᾳ ἐχρῶντο, τῇ δὲ Μήδων στολῇ καὶ ἁβρότητι ("For at that time they still used Persian training and self-control, but the apparel and luxury of the Medes," Xen., *Cyr.* 8.8.15).

102. Diodorus Siculus's narrative of the end of Median hegemony seems to have been consonant with that of Herodotus in that it makes Astyages a man of harshness and cruelty, qualities that provoked the king's subjects to conspire against him (Diod. Sic. 9.23.1, where the wording is that of the excerptor). We have seen that Aristotle, in contrast, knew a version according to which Astyages' luxuriant lifestyle was implicated in his overthrow (Arist., *Pol.* 5.1312a9–14). Xenophon follows an entirely different tradition in which Cyrus remained loyal to Astyages, his beloved grandfather, until the latter's death (Xen., *Cyr.* 1.5.2).

103. In developing his conspiracy, Harpagus emphasizes the similarity between his own treatment at the hands of Astyages and the sufferings of Cyrus; at the same time, Harpagus enlists others who have experienced Astyages' "bitterness" (Hdt. 1.123.1–2).

narrative of the rise of the Medes is as informative as the tale of their fall. Herodotus relates how a certain Median sage named Deioces used his reputation for wisdom to gain sovereign power (Hdt. 1.96–101). After seeing to the building of Ecbatana as his capital, Deioces proceeded to establish the κόσμος, essentially the rules of the court ceremonial:[104]

μήτε ἐισιέναι παρὰ βασιλέα μηδένα, δι᾽ ἀγγέλων δὲ πάντα χρέεσθαι, ὁρᾶσθαί τε βασιλέα ὑπὸ μηδενός, πρός τε τούτοισι ἔτι γελᾶν τε καὶ ἀντίον πτύειν καὶ ἅπασι εἶναι τοῦτό γε αἰσχρόν. ταῦτα δὲ περὶ ἑωυτὸν ἐσέμνυνε τῶνδε εἵνεκεν, ὅκως ἂν μὴ ὁρῶντες οἱ ὁμήλικες, . . . λυπεοίατο καὶ ἐπιβουλεύοιεν, ἀλλ᾽ ἑτεροῖός σφι δοκέοι εἶναι μὴ ὁρῶσι.

[No one could come into the King's presence, but all business should be done through messengers, and the King seen by no one. In addition to this, it was shameful for all to laugh and spit in front of the King. He established these forms of solemnity around his person for the following reasons: so that his peers would not, seeing him, . . . feel pain and plot against him, but so that he might seem to them different in kind, if they did not see him.] (Hdt. 1.99.1–2)

In this passage we are acquainted with the supposed origins of the notorious inaccessibility of the Asian monarchs. It is significant that Herodotus does not associate this withdrawal from public view with any kind of effeminacy, since it is in just this way that the practice is taken by later historians. Diodorus Siculus (2.21.2) relates that the second king of the Assyrians, Ninyas, son of Ninus, secluded himself in his palace so that he could pursue the pleasures of τρυφή and amusement, and that, by the time of Sardanapalus, the last king of Assyria, royal inaccessibility had become a veil for extremely effeminate behavior, including adorning himself with women's clothing, makeup, voice, and seeking sexual pleasure from men as well as women (Diod. Sic. 2.23).[105] One thread of the tradition, reported by Athenaeus, who was citing "Duris and others," says that he was assassinated as a result.[106] This version, which attributed Sardana-

---

104. On the Assyrian sources for Median court practices, see Asheri, Lloyd, and Corcella 2007, 150–51; cf. Asheri and Antelami 1988, 328; They further note that the Greek historians extrapolated the Median ceremonial from what they knew of the customs of the Persians.

105. It is ironic that a custom that Herodotus says was created to make the king seem more than human was eventually interpreted as allowing him to be less than a man.

106. Athen. 12.529a. But we know from Athenaeus that Ctesias told another version of the end of Assyrian rule: Κτησίας δὲ λέγει εἰς πόλεμον αὐτὸν καταστῆναι καὶ ἀθροίσαντα πολλὴν στρατιὰν καὶ

palus's fall to revulsion at his womanly ways, seems already to have been in common circulation by the time of Aristotle's *Politics*, and certainly in the *Eudemian Ethics* the name Sardanapalus had become a watchword for hedonism.[107] Yet Herodotus himself only mentions Sardanapalus once in passing and without moral implication:

τὰ γὰρ Σαρδαναπάλλου τοῦ Νίνου βασιλέος ἐόντα μεγάλα χρήματα καὶ φυλασσόμενα ἐν θησαυροῖσι καταγαίοισι ἐπενόησαν κλῶπες ἐκφορῆσαι

[Thieves formed a plan to carry off the riches of Sardanapalus, the King of Nineveh, which were great and stored in underground treasuries.] (Hdt. 2.150.3)

When evaluating Herodotus's commitment to the idea of pernicious luxury, we would do well to keep in mind examples such as this and recognize those places where later writers saw the ill effects of luxury working on the historical plane, but Herodotus did not.

Of all the Asian nations conquered by the Persians, the Assyrians, with their capital then at Babylon, were the most prosperous, supplying fully one-third of the annual revenue of the Persian Empire (Hdt. 1.192). The *Histories* strongly emphasizes the richness and fertility of the arable land; it is, Herodotus says, by far the best of all the lands he knows at producing the fruits of Demeter. In fact, the yield is 200- and, sometimes, 300-fold (Hdt. 1.193.2–3). Given the stress that Herodotus lays upon the agricultural productivity of Babylonia, and recalling Cyrus's claim at 9.122 that "the same ground does not produce both a wondrous crop and men good at war," we might expect the inhabitants of this territory to be distinguished by an unusual degree of μαλακία. And among the customs of

---

καταλυθέντα ὑπὸ τοῦ Ἀρβάκου τελευτῆσαι ἑαυτὸν ἐμπρήσαντα ἐν τοῖς βασιλείοις ("But Ctesias says that he went to war and gathering a large army and, being defeated by Arbaces, he died by burning himself on a pyre in his palace." Athen. 12.529b). If Ctesias did not relate the personal attack of Arbaces upon Sardanapalus, it is also possible that he did not detail the effeminacy which was said to have caused it. The words in which Athenaeus cites Ctesias to open his treatment of Sardanapalus do not allow us to conclude anything about the contents of Ctesias, since the phraseology is Athenaeus's own. For a fuller discussion, see Chapter 4, pp. 270–82.

107. αἱ δὲ διὰ καταφρόνησιν, ὥσπερ Σαρδανάπαλλον ἰδών τις ξαίνοντα μετὰ τῶν γυναικῶν, εἰ ἀληθῆ ταῦτα οἱ μυθολογοῦντες λέγουσιν· εἰ δὲ μὴ ἐπ᾿ ἐκείνου, ἀλλ᾿ ἐπ᾿ ἄλλου γε ἂν γένοιτο τοῦτο ἀληθές ("Other [attacks against rulers] took place on account of contempt, as when someone saw Sardanapalus combing among the women, if the things are true that the tellers of tales say. If it is not true of him, it may well be true of someone else." Aris., *Pol.* 5.1312a). Cf. οἱ δὲ Σαρδανάπαλλον μακαρίζοντες ἢ Σμινδυρίδην τὸν Συβαρίτην ἢ τῶν ἄλλων τινὰς τῶν ζώντων τὸν ἀπολαυστικὸν βίον ("And some might praise Sardanapalus or Smindyrides the Sybarite or some of the other men who live a life devoted to enjoyment." Aris., *Eth. Eud.* 1.1216a16).

the Babylonians as related by Herodotus, we do find some things that later writers will associate with decadence: they wear long hair, turbans, and large amounts of perfume (Hdt. 1.195.1).[108]

However, in spite of the καρπός θωμαστός of their land and the luxuries it afforded them, the Babylonians were as stern in war as the Persians themselves. This is made clear in the story of the second capture of Babylon after its revolt from Darius.[109] On the eve of rebellion, after making all preparations for a long siege, the Babylonians took the harshest of measures: to ensure that their provisions would last, many of the women of the city were put to death (Hdt. 3.150). Darius exerted himself fully against the rebels, but his efforts made no impression: although the Persians tried all the stratagems that their skill at war allowed them, nothing worked in the face of keen resistance (Hdt. 3.151–2).[110] Ironically, it was only when a Persian leader was willing to make a sacrifice as extreme as the Babylonian measures that Darius was able to take the city. Zopyrus, one of the Seven, cut off his own nose and ears so that he could make a convincing defection to the enemy, an action that Darius himself frequently regretted after the fact (Hdt. 3.160.1). Yet the mutilation gained Zopyrus admission into the enemy's highest councils, whence he soon ruined the Babylonians. Cyrus's *dictum* that "soft lands produce soft men" is of no application in the context of the Assyrians and Babylonians.

We might look next for signs of historical implications of soft living in Herodotus's account of the downfall and death of Polycrates, tyrant of Samos. By Roman Imperial times, he had come to be blamed for leading his people into disaster, not through mistaken policies, but due to his decadent mode of life. According to this tradition, the Samian was a collector of the finest products of all countries. In addition to his taste for fine foods and *objets d'art*, he was particularly devoted to sexual relationships with men. Because of these interests, we are told, Polycrates was ruined.[111] Yet Herodotus draws no connection be-

---

108. For evidence on the moral connotations of perfume, see Bernhardt 2003, 217–19; for the relevance of hairstyles, see the entries of same author's index, *s.v.* "Haar, Haartracht."

109. The Babylonians had manfully resisted Cyrus at the time of the first fall of the city. They met the Persian army in battle before the walls (Hdt. 1.190), and nowhere in the narrative of the city's capture does Herodotus explicitly indicate any weakness on part of the Babylonians. Of course, one could argue that this point is implicit in the fact that the Babylonians lost the campaign and control of their city. However, as Herodotus presents the course of events, luck, and not the relative martial capabilities of the principals, was the deciding factor (Hdt. 1.191.5).

110. For a review of the evidence from the Behistun inscription relevant to the Babylonian rebellions, see Asheri, Lloyd, and Corcella 2007, 528–537.

111. Athen. 12.540c–f, variously ascribed to Clytus, Alexis, and Clearchus.

tween Polycrates' fate and his lifestyle. He does focus on the Samian's "great good fortune" (αἱ . . . μεγάλαι εὐτυχίαι, Hdt. 3.40.2), but no weakness or feminization is implicit. Rather the opposite: ὅκου γὰρ ἰθύσειε στρατεύεσθαι, πάντα οἱ ἐχώρεε εὐτυχέως ("Wherever he would direct his forces, everything would turn out well for him." Hdt. 3.39.3). Polycrates' success, like Croesus's prosperity, threatened to attract the jealousy of the gods (τὸ θεῖον . . . φθονερόν, Hdt. 3.40.2), and, although it is a commonplace to see divinely induced immorality in those to be brought low by celestial envy,[112] Herodotus does not ascribe the death of Polycrates to any sin on his part. Indeed, the historian characterizes the tyrant's end in a most sympathetic tenor:

> ἀπικόμενος δὲ ἐς τὴν Μαγνησίην ὁ Πολυκράτης διεφθάρη κακῶς οὔτε ἑωυτοῦ ἀξίως οὔτε τῶν ἑωυτοῦ φρονημάτων, ὅτι γὰρ μὴ οἱ Συρηκοσίων γενόμενοι [τύραννοι][113] οὐδὲ εἷς τῶν ἄλλων Ἑλληνικῶν τυράννων ἄξιός ἐστι Πολυκράτεϊ μεγαλοπρεπείην συμβληθῆναι.

> [Coming to Magnesia, Polycrates died horribly, in a way worthy neither of himself nor his designs. For leaving aside the tyrants of the Syracusans, not a single one of the other Greek tyrants was worthy of being compared to Polycrates in magnificence.] (Hdt. 3.125)

In Herodotus's opinion, Polycrates died οὐκ ἀξίως, because his unusual μεγαλοπρεπεία should have earned him a better fate. This statement bears on Herodotus's view of luxury, because, as it happens, μεγαλοπρεπεία most often refers to feasting which, when cast in a pejorative light, is often given the sobriquet of τρυφή (though not by Herodotus).[114] For example, Pausanias's notorious feast after the battle of Plataea—a passage taken as among the best evidence

---

112. Asheri and Medaglia (1990, xlvi–xlvii) consider Polycrates to be guilty of hubris, which presumably— they quote the proverb *quos deus vult perdere dementat prius*—is further exacerbated by the gods until it seals the tyrant's fate. In this analysis, they rely upon a meaning of hubris as an "overweening self-satisfaction," which Fisher's (1992) research has since shown to be untenable. In Asheri, Lloyd, and Corcella (2007, 387–88), hubris is not mentioned, though Polycrates is described as one of the "tragic figures who, at the peak of success, lose their reason" (387). Arguably, hubris in its genuine sense may indeed be present in Polycrates' desire to bring Ionia and the island under his sway (Hdt. 3.122), but the text here gives no indication that its author saw the Samian's plan as immoral.

113. Rosén omits.

114. In addition to 9.82, discussed immediately below, μεγαλοπρεπεία and cognates are used at Hdt. 5.18.1 and 6.128.1 to depict fine dining. Elsewhere it is used in reference to names (1.139), a festival (4.76), and the manner in which Xerxes led his army (7.57). A further use, concerning a gift at 6.122, is generally thought to be an interpolation.

that Herodotus accepts the concept of pernicious luxury[115]—is described in terms of its "magnificence":

... τὸν Παυσανίην ἰδόντα κλίνας τε χρυσέας καὶ ἀργυρέας εὖ ἐστρωμένας καὶ τραπέζας τε χρυσέας καὶ ἀργυρέας καὶ παρασκευὴν μεγαλοπρεπέα τοῦ δείπνου ἐκπλαγέντα τὰ προκείμενα ἀγαθὰ ...

[... Pausanias, seeing the golden and silver couches with their fine coverlets and the golden and silver tables and the magnificent preparations of the feast, was astonished at the good things set before him ...] (Hdt. 9.82.2)

Expensive dinnerware and fine food, elsewhere the epitome of a luxuriant lifestyle,[116] are in this passage signs of greatness.[117] Accordingly, in one of the very few places in the *Histories* where a connection is explicitly drawn between an opulent lifestyle and historical events, the evidence runs contrary to the idea of decadent luxury: far from being a cause of a ruinous fate, a luxuriant existence is inconsistent with that outcome. Polycrates died not because of, but in spite of, his wealth and comforts.[118] Thus, the example of Polycrates is due

115. Masaracchia (1977, 194) maintains that this episode reflects a theme of "wealth as a source of soft-ness and weakness" that is present at crucial points in the *Histories*. As principal evidence for this interpretation he cites Hdt. 1.155, Croesus's advice on the feminization of the Lydians, and 9.122, Cyrus on "soft lands." We have already seen that significance of the passages vis-à-vis pernicious luxury is not clear-cut. Even the more judicious Flower and Marincola (2002, 251) see at Hdt. 9.82 a contrast "of oriental wealth with Greek poverty, and the moral disposition that results from each." Both commentaries do note that by introducing the story of Pausanias's feast with λέγεται, Herodo-tus indicates his doubt about the historicity of the event.

116. We may recall Hdt. 3.123.1, where Polycrates' successor Maeandrius is said to have dedicated the furnishings of the murdered tyrant's dining hall in the temple of Hera; Herodotus calls the offering ἀξιοθέητον ("worthy of seeing"), from which we may infer luxury similar to that of Cleisthenes and Amyntas, if not Mardonius.

117. Flower and Marincola (2002, 251) seem to take παρασκευὴν μεγαλοπρεπέα τοῦ δείπνου as referring primarily to the food served to Pausanias. While this interpretation cannot be ruled out, it seems better to understand the phrase as summative, referring to the impression made by the feast as a whole, including the fantastic couches and tables just mentioned. In support we may note that Pau-sanias's command, κατὰ ταὐτὰ Μαρδονίῳ δεῖπνον παρασκευάζειν ("to prepare a feast in the same way as for Mardonius," Hdt. 9.82.1), is immediately answered by the reference to couches, tables and good things quoted above. By the same token, when Pausanias subsequently orders his own atten-dants παρασκευάσαι Λακωνικὸν δεῖπνον ("to prepare a Spartan feast"), we may assume that it is implicit for the point of the anecdote that the reader imagine that the simple fare was served in the usual Spartan way, and not on Persian gold and silver.

118. We cannot say that Herodotus thinks that, as a general rule, those who live with μεγαλοπρεπεία do not deserve to die badly. In the first place, Polycrates seems to have been killed in a particularly hei-nous manner, which Herodotus refuses to describe (οὐκ ἀξίως ἀπηγήσιος, Hdt. 3.125.3), and it may be that Herodotus means that Polycrates' magnificence is inconsistent not with any harsh fate, but rather with a death as shameful as that inflicted by Oroetes. Secondly, the basis of Polycrates'

more careful consideration when the historical dimensions of luxury are being evaluated.

Certain scholarship on the *Histories* has advanced the claim that "Herodotus's work seems to be pervaded by a systematic bias against Ionians."[119] Examining the whole of this interpretation would take us beyond the bounds of this study. We may, however, look at any evidence for the view that the Ionians were weak and effeminate because of luxury.

Pride of place among passages taken to support this view is given to Hdt. 6.11–12, where Herodotus describes preparations by the Ionian fleet before the battle of Lade. A certain Dionysius, a general of the Phocaeans, convinced the others to place themselves in his hands for a regime of rigorous training in naval maneuvers. Eventually, the Ionians grew weary of this toil and refused to participate. Morale collapsed and defeat by the Persians soon followed. This presentation of events seems to some to allude to the common idea that the Ionians' soft lifestyle led to weakness and loss of political independence.[120] Such a reading overlooks the main thrust of the passage, which an examination of its wording may bring to light. First, from Dionysius's exhortation:

(11.2) νῦν ὦν ὑμεῖς ἢν μὲν βούλησθε ταλαιπωρίας ἐνδέκεσθαι, τὸ παραχρῆμα μὲν πόνος ὑμῖν ἔσται, οἷοί τε δὲ ἔσεσθε ὑπερβαλόμενοι τοὺς ἐναντίους εἶναι ἐλεύθεροι· εἰ δὲ μαλακίη τε καὶ ἀταξίῃ διαχρήσησθε, οὐδεμίαν ὑμέων ἔχω ἐλπίδα μὴ οὐ δώσειν [ὑμᾶς][121] δίκην βασιλέι τῆς ἀποστάσιος. (3) ἀλλ᾽ ἐμοί τε πείθεσθε καὶ ἐμοὶ ὑμέας αὐτοὺς ἐπιτρέψατε. . . . (12.1) ταῦτα ἀκούσαντες οἱ Ἴωνες ἐπιτρέπουσι σφέας αὐτοὺς τῷ Διονυσίῳ.

μεγαλοπρεπεία is compound: it arises both from his person and from his plans. By this latter, Herodotus refers to the Samian's designs for a thalassocracy. It is therefore possible that Herodotus is emphasizing the disjunction between the tyrant's death and his grandiose achievements and intentions, and that he is not indicating a particular interest in Polycrates' lifestyle.

119. Alty 1982, 11. He also speaks of "one of the best documented and apparently most influential aspects of the contrast between Dorian and Ionian, the supposed effeminacy or lack of resolution of the Ionians" (7). While we restrict ourselves to examining the Herodotean evidence for Ionian weakness, we may observe that Alty's evidence for this "best documented" tradition consists of Athenaeus 12.524–26, including several passages in which comic writers "make fun of the Ionians' luxuriousness" (8). We will discuss in Chapter 3 how unreliable a witness Athenaeus is for pernicious luxury.

120. For example, Nenci 1998, 179: "il racconto erodoteo sottintende e rafforza . . . il luogo comune della riluttanza ionica alla fatica e della atavica propensione alla mollezza (τρυφή)." Note that Nenci thinks that the belief that the Ionians displayed a culpable softness is widespread and of long-standing. In our examination, below, of pertinent evidence, it will be clear that both claims are dubious. He also seems to take softness or weakness as the essential meaning of τρυφή. We have already seen that this interpretation is mistaken.

121. Omitted by Hude and Rosén.

["So if you are now willing to accept hardships, there will be toil for you in the short term, but you will be able to overthrow your enemies and be free. If, on the other hand, you indulge in softness and lack of discipline, I have no hope at all for you: you will pay the penalty to the King for your rebellion. Rather, give me your obedience and put yourselves under my orders." When they heard this, the Ionians put themselves under Dionysius's command.] (Hdt. 6.11.2–12.1)

Then, the sailors' reaction to a week of exercise:

μέχρι μέν νυν ἡμερέων ἑπτὰ ἐπείθοντό τε καὶ ἐποίευν τὸ κελευόμενον, τῇ δὲ ἐπὶ ταύτῃσι οἱ Ἴωνες, οἷα ἀπαθέες ἐόντες πόνων τοιούτων, τετρυμένοι τε ταλαιπωρίῃσί τε καὶ ἡλίῳ, ἔλεξαν πρὸς ἑωυτούς, τάδε· τίνα δαιμόνων παραβάντες τάδε ἀναπίμπλαμεν, οἵτινες παραφρονήσαντες καὶ ἐκπλώσαντες ἐκ τοῦ νόου ἀνδρὶ Φωκαιέϊ ἀλαζόνι παρεχομένῳ νέας τρεῖς ἐπιτρέψαντες ἡμέας αὐτοὺς ἔχομεν; ὁ δὲ παραλαβὼν ἡμέας λυμαίνεται λύμῃσι ἀνηκέστοισι, καὶ δὴ πολλοὶ μὲν ἡμέων ἐς νούσους πεπτώκασι, πολλοὶ δὲ ἐπίδοξοι τὠυτὸ τοῦτο πείσεσθαί εἰσι· πρό τε τούτων τῶν κακῶν ἡμῖν γε κρέσσον καὶ ὅ τι ὦν ἄλλο παθεῖν ἐστι, καὶ τὴν μέλλουσαν δουληίην ὑπομεῖναι, ἥτις ἔσται, μᾶλλον ἢ τῇ παρεούσῃ συνέχεσθαι.

[Now for seven days they were obedient and did what they were ordered, but on the next day, the Ionians, being unaccustomed to such toils, and worn out by hardships and the sun, began to say this to each other: "What god have we insulted that our measure is filled in this way? Going out of our senses and drifting out of our wits, we have put ourselves under the command of a Phocaean upstart—he provides three ships! Having got hold of us, he has outraged us with irreparable outrages. In addition, many of us have fallen sick and many are likely to fall sick in the future. From our point of view, it is better to suffer anything else before these evils and to await our future enslavement, whatever it will be, rather than to continue to be oppressed by this one."] (Hdt. 6.12.2–3)

To be sure, from the fact that Dionysius warned his fellows against the dangerous consequences of μαλακία, the passage could seem to refer to a subtext that portrays Ionians as a luxury-loving people who cannot face hard work. However, the presence of such a subtext is certainly not necessary for the reader to grasp fully the point of this description of the Ionians before Lade. The reference to μαλακία is sufficiently explained by the immediate context. Dionysius

had just asked the sailors to undertake a difficult labor, and it is an obvious rhetorical ploy to steer one's listeners to choose a unpleasant course by labeling the
alternative as somehow immoral. And we must emphasize, as Herodotus does,
the harsh character of the training that Dionysius has in mind. His plan involves,
said Dionysus, both πόνος and ταλαιπωρίαι.[122] This last word is rare in the *Histories,* and denotes extremely painful and wearying distress, not, as one reader
has expressed it, "inflamed hands and blistered buttocks."[123] Outside of the present passage, Herodotus uses the word only for the punishing conditions of
the forced march by which Darius's army escaped Scythia (Hdt. 4.134.3). In
Thucydides, ταλαιπωρία and its cognates are used for the travails of the plague
(Thuc. 2.49, 3.3), and for particularly sharp suffering on the field of battle, especially where damage inflicted by the enemy is compounded by privation of supplies or the heat of the day, as, for example, of Nicias's army during the disaster
at Syracuse (Thuc. 7.84) or both sides in the press of fighting at Pylos (Thuc.
4.35.4). It is therefore noteworthy that, after describing the practices instituted by
Dionysius, Herodotus repeats the term, this time in the narrative voice:
τετρυμένοι τε ταλαιπωρίῃσί τε καὶ ἡλίῳ ("worn out by hardships and the sun").

Herodotus's choice of words, then, underlines the severity of the Ionians'
suffering as they made their preparations. Seen from this perspective, the characterization of the Ionians as ἀπαθέες ἐόντες πόνων τοιούτων is no longer "obviously a reference to traditional Ionian softness."[124] Dionysius recreated to a
great degree the distresses of actual battle (ταλαιπωρίαι), and this for seven
straight days. We may imagine that very few Greeks would have been "accustomed to such toils," and thus we may understand πόνων τοιούτων at face
value. The phrase is not an ironic nod toward an idea of Ionian diffidence and
softness of lifestyle (e.g.,: "being unaccustomed to such toils—after all, they
never submit to any at all"); it simply adds to the emphasis that Herodotus gives
to the rigor of Dionysius's arrangements.

Highlighting this rigor and severity is integral to the argument of this passage. Clearly, Hdt. 6.11–13 serves to put at least part of the blame for the defeat
of the Greeks at Lade squarely on their own shoulders.[125] If, as we argue, the

---

122. Nenci (1998, 177) prefers to accept the singular ταλαιπωρίην (the reading of MS D), which would be
     taken as the abstraction "hardship."
123. Evans 1976, 35.
124. Nenci 1998, 179.
125. How and Wells (1936, 2.69) see a pro-Samian impulse in Herodotus's attempt to fix the blame: "His
     primary motive for insisting on the insubordination and effeminacy of the Ionians is to whitewash
     the Samians."

Histories does not offer a special—and widely recognized—penchant for μαλακία as the locus for this blame, where then is it to be found? We suggest that the point of Herodotus's explanation for the Ionian defeat is best discovered on the basis of the second of the two failings against which Dionysius warned his listeners: not μαλακία but ἀταξία.

Ἀταξία ("disorder") may be used, in what we may consider an objective sense, to refer to a literal anarchy caused by, perhaps, the death of a commanding officer;[126] in a similarly objective way, the word may convey chaotic loss of organization on the battlefield.[127] But in our passage, a more subjective meaning is present. In Dionysius's remarks, ἀταξία is parallel to μαλακία, and both should be understood to be psychological or moral failings. And, for Dionysius to make sense, both failings should be specious; "softness" and "disorder" negatively color a course of action that Dionysius recognized as holding a natural attraction for his audience. On this line of interpretation, μαλακία, of course, causes no difficulty, depicting a natural preference for physical comfort as a weak-minded reluctance to take on the hard training necessary in Dionysius's scheme. Moreover, while it is easier to miss exactly what the subjective and moral dimension of ἀταξία may be, close attention to the details of the passage bring it to light: Dionysius sought to forestall what the Ionians might feel was a reasonable preference for independence and a natural reluctance to submit to the will of another by branding this line of thinking as the failing of "disorder."

To understand the force of this passage, one must keep in mind that the Phocaean general was not simply persuading the Ionians to follow a more demanding course of training; he was asking to be installed at their head, as commander-in-chief of the fleet.[128] So much is established by the repetition of the verbs ἐπιτρέπω and πείθομαι. Ἐπιτρέπω (or its Ionic variant ἐπιτράπω) is straightforward, since in Herodotus it frequently refers to the establishment of a person in charge of a group.[129] Interpreting πείθομαι is more complicated. A principal meaning of the middle voice of πείθω is, of course, "obey," but, given

---

126. So Xenophon uses it for the state of the Greek force after Tissaphernes captured and executed many of its officers: λαβόντες δὲ τοὺς ἄρχοντας ἀναρχίᾳ ἂν καὶ ἀταξίᾳ ἐνόμιζον ἡμᾶς ἀπολέσθαι ("Capturing our leaders, they thought we would be destroyed through anarchy and disorder." Xen., *Anab.* 3.2.29). Plato uses ἀταξία in the same sense at *Crito* 53d, speaking of unruly Thessaly, where the laws do not command obedience.

127. Thus Thuc. 2.92.1, 5.10.6, 7.43.7, 7.68.1. Herodotus has the adjective ἄτακτος in this sense at 6.91.3.

128. Nenci (1989, 178), following Cassola, correctly notes that Dionysius was named commander in chief of the Ionians' campaign

129. At Hdt. 3.83.2, 1.64.2, 1.153.3, and 7.52.2. Of particular relevance to our passage is 8.3.1, where command of the fleet is also the topic.

the active meaning of "win over, or "persuade,"[130] the lexica do not make it sufficiently clear that πείθομαι in the sense of "obey" may indicate, not a discrete act of acquiescence, but a continuous state of subservience.[131] Thus, ἡμερέων ἑπτὰ ἐπείθοντό implies not "they went along with Dionysius's suggestion for seven days," but "they served under his command" for that length of time.[132]

With his admonition against ἀταξία, then, Dionysius sought to make the Ionians more amenable to a united command, with himself in the lead. It is therefore easy to understand why certain of the Ionians' subsequent complaints against Dionysius were put in terms of the usurpation and abuse of power. For instance, ἀλαζών, as the men in their discontent labeled their commander, indicates an imposter, one who presumes to advantages he does not possess.[133] On what grounds did the Ionians accuse Dionysius of ἀλαζονεία? To be sure, the charge may indicate that the fleet had lost confidence in Dionysius's plan and did not feel that the continual exercise would bring the intended result.[134] However, the text links the characterization of Dionysius as ἀλαζών with his status rather than his strategic abilities: he had provided only three ships to the assembly. His presumption may thus be seen in the act of a general of a small contingent thinking himself suited to command the navy.[135] He is not a figure of sufficient eminence to subject the Ionians to such hardships.

The phrase λυμαίνεται λύμῃσι also deserves scrutiny. These words elsewhere in the *Histories* describe the violent and insulting abuse of the powerless

130. Because the middle is often "to be convinced" or "persuaded" and Dionysius has just presented an argument to the Ionians, it is natural to take the Phocaean's ἐμοί πείθεσθε as "listen to me" or the like, as do, for example Rawlinson (1942: "be persuaded by me") and Godley (1921: "Believe me"). Such a translation is probably mistaken, although it is conceivable that Herodotus is playing with the ambiguity of the word.

131. A clear example comes from 5.29.2, where, during the story of the Parian arbitration of the Milesian stasis, we are told that control of the government was given to those with the best kept farms: ἀπέδεξαν τούτους μὲν τὴν πόλιν νέμειν . . . τοὺς δὲ ἄλλους Μιλησίους τοὺς πρὶν στασιάζοντας τούτων ἔταξαν πείθεσθαι ("And they appointed these men to manage the city . . . and they ordered the other Milesians who were previously at odds to be obedient to them.").

132. The tenses of the verbs in ἐποίευν τὸ κελευόμενον support this interpretation; the Ionians did whatever Dionysius ordered them throughout the week. If τὸ κελευόμενον meant the original exhortation of Dionysius, we would expect the aorist.

133. So Arist., *Eth. Nic.* 1108a21–22, where a contrast is drawn with self-depreciating irony.

134. A fear that the Phocaean could not pull off what he had promised might certainly justify the epithet ἀλαζών, as Xenophon points out in a discussion of Socrates' efforts against that vice: πολὺ δὲ μέγιστον ὅστις μηδενὸς ἄξιος ὢν ἐξηπατήκοι πείθων ὡς ἱκανὸς εἴη τῆς πόλεως ἡγεῖσθαι ("Much the worst is he who, though worthless, tricks the city into trusting that he is worthy to lead it." Xen., *Mem.* 1.7.5).

135. Xenophon so describes the solemnity with which the Great King was isolated from his subject (Xen. *Ages.* 9.1–2). Herodotus's ἀλαζών may therefore impute the assumption of an irksome air of superiority by Dionysius.

by the powerful. Herodotus uses the verb λυμαίνομαι in three passages concerning the defilement of the body of a slain enemy by a monarch. After the battle near the Araxes River, Tomyris drenched Cyrus's head in a wineskin of blood and mocked her foe (Hdt. 1.214.4). In Egypt, Cambyses had the body of Amasis disinterred and treated with violence (Hdt. 3.16.1). And at Plataea, Pausanias refused to outrage the corpse of Mardonius, when he was urged to cut off the Persian's head and impale it on a stake (Hdt. 9.79.1). In two other occurrences, λυμαίνομαι characterizes torture inflicted on the lowly by a magnate. At Hdt. 5.33.2–3, Megabates, the Persian commander and cousin of Darius, has Scylax, the captain of a Myndian ship, bound and stuffed through a port hole. Most horribly, λυμαίνομαι, intensified with the prefix δια-, is the general term under which fall the vicious acts of mutilation by which Amestris destroyed the innocent wife of Masistes.[136]

As one might expect, the noun λύμη also usually indicates an insulting act of violence by a superior against an inferior. When the Egyptian king Apries cut off the nose and ears of a prominent subject who was trying to look after the king's interests, this outrageous behavior caused the other Egyptians to desert the king's side (Hdt. 2.162.6). Again, upon the capture of Egypt by the Persians, Cambyses forced the country's former king, Psammenitus, to watch his daughter performing the tasks of slaves, his son led out to his execution, and his friends made to beg in the streets. Cambyses imposed these tribulations upon his foe in order to test his spirit ἐπὶ λύμῃ (Hdt. 3.14–15).

Thus the language with which the Ionians characterized their situation was very strong indeed. They depicted themselves as irreparably damaged by the insulting cruelty of their commander, a man whose claims to power are belied by his minor status. The same tone is manifest in the conclusion of their argument: the present arrangement constituted a δουληίη whose evils are beyond bearing. They saw in Dionysius and his strictures something worse than submission to Persian overlords.[137]

---

136. ἡ Ἄμηστρις μεταπεμψαμένη τοὺς δορυφόρους τοὺς Ξέρξεω διαλυμαίνεται τὴν γυναῖκα τὴν Μασίστεω· τούς τε μαζοὺς ἀποταμοῦσα κυσὶ προέβαλε καὶ ῥῖνα καὶ ὦτα καὶ χείλεα καὶ γλῶσσαν ἐκταμοῦσα ἐς οἶκόν μιν ἀποπέμπει διαλελυμασμένην ("Amestris, sending for Xerxes' bodyguards, thoroughly outraged the wife of Masistes: cutting off her breasts, she threw them to the dogs; she cut off her nose and ears and lips and cut out her tongue. Then she sent her home, utterly outraged in this fashion." Hdt. 9.112.1). One might object to our view of the connotations of λυμαίνομαι that the wife of Masistes is hardly a "lowly" person suffering at the hands of power, considering her place in the Persian court. While this may be true, the fact remains that she was delivered to her tormentor by the authority of Xerxes himself.

137. Alty (1982) misconstrues the meaning of these words by taking them to reflect the μαλακία of the

By putting the Ionians' complaints in this exaggerated form, Herodotus dramatizes the quality of ἀταξία.[138] The Ionians are shown as touchy in the extreme about any constraints on their independence, especially when those constraints are imposed by fellow Greeks, and most particularly when imposed by Greeks of a rival city.[139] As the narrative of Lade continues, we see that the centrality of ἀταξία to the explanation that Herodotus offers for the defeat is confirmed when the commanders of the Samian forces—whose desertion during the battle doomed the Greeks—made up their minds to change sides:

ὁρῶντες ἅμα μὲν ἐοῦσαν ἀταξίην πολλὴν ἐκ τῶνἸώνων . . . ἅμα δὲ κατεφαίνετό σφιν εἶναι ἀδύνατα τὰ βασιλέος πρήγματα ὑπερβαλέσθαι,

[Seeing that there was great disorder on the part of the Ionians . . . and since it was obvious to them that it was impossible to overthrow the power of the King,] (Hdt. 6.13.1)

If, as it seems, the independent-mindedness of the Ionians eclipsed any idea of μαλακία as a cause for the failure of their revolt, it is important to remember that what Dionysius called ἀταξία is a hallmark throughout the *Histories* of all the Greeks, not a distinguishing characteristic of the Ionians. We have seen, for example, how Xerxes singled out the Greeks' lack of unitary command as a decisive advantage for himself (Hdt. 7.101). Following an impulse similar to that

Ionians: "even slavery [is] preferable to the agony of training" (12 n. 64). Likewise Hunt (1998, 48): "Herodotus represents the Ionians as preferring 'their coming slavery' to the discomfort of training for battle." Such an interpretation ignores the Ionians' claim that they are suffering not only hardship but also dishonor at Dionysius's hands. It does injustice to the Ionians' position and obscures what the wording of the original makes clear: the sailors at Lade see their decision as a choice between two kinds of slavery (τὴν μέλλουσαν δουληίην . . . μᾶλλον ἤ τῇ παρεούσῃ). They are not represented as finding slavery in general preferable to anything else.

138. *If* the Ionians' complaints are in fact exaggerated. It is quite possible that λυμαίνεται λύμῃσι ἀνηκέστοισι refers not in a general way to the difficulty of the exercises, but to particular instances of corporal punishment inflicted at the command of Dionysius. In this case, the Ionians' characterization of the treatment they had received would be meant to be taken at face value. The run of the Greek permits either reading: after bewailing the "irreparable outrages," the Ionians added further details: καὶ δὴ πολλοὶ μὲν ἡμέων ἐς νούσους πεπτώκασι, πολλοὶ δὲ ἐπίδοξοι τὠυτὸ τοῦτο πείσεσθαί εἰσι ("Many of us have fallen sick and many are likely to fall sick in the future."). The clause-initial sequence καὶ δὴ is ambiguous—indicating either a result ("and so") or a simple addition ("and also"). If the first meaning is apt, the outrages committed by Dionysius led to widespread illness. If καὶ δὴ introduce a new set of grounds for complaint, then hardship *and* dishonorable treatment caused Ionian disaffection. Herodotus would thus be depicting the Ionians with sympathy, since any free Greek could be expected to consider withdrawing from such contemptuous handling.

139. Thus the point of including in the Ionians' discourse the phrase ἀνδρὶ Φωκαιέϊ: "what are we doing obeying this man from Phocaea?"

displayed by the Ionians, the Spartans and Athenians respectively refused to give up their positions of command, even in order to gain the great resources of Gelon of Syracuse; likewise, Argos refused to join the alliance against Persia if it entailed serving under Lacedaemonian leadership (Hdt. 7.148–62).

For the *Histories,* then, ἀταξία, in the sense of reluctance to serve under another, is a concomitant feature of ἐλευθερία and a characteristic common to the free Greeks.[140] Herodotus was concerned with showing the dangers of too much independence.[141] Accordingly, his description of the behavior of the Ionians before Lade does indeed serve as an object lesson to his readers. However, the point at issue is not the peril of μαλακία, whether caused by luxury from some other source. The Ionians were defeated at Lade, in spite of the bravery many showed in the battle, because they could not sufficiently subordinate individual interests.[142] Furthermore, in dwelling on the weakness of ἀταξία on the part of the Ionians, Herodotus is not making a distinction between the Greeks of Asia and those of the motherland. The passage is not evidence for anti-Ionian feeling in the *Histories* and far less for the idea that the Ionians were brought low by luxury.

Other passages referring to the inferiority of the Ionians are similarly ambiguous. For example, at 1.143, Herodotus describes them as the weakest ἔθνος

---

140. The phenomenon of τὸ ἐθελοκακεῖν also reinforces the idea of suspicion of authority by the Ionians and other Greeks. Herodotus characterizes the half-hearted Ionian effort at Lade in terms of τὸ ἐθελοκακεῖν: Hdt. 6.15.1, the Chians are exceptional because they do not join the rest in ἐθελοκακέοντες. Deliberate cowardice in battle is a manifestation of the same process that is at work in the Ionians' withdrawal from training. In both cases, members of the larger community (in the first place, the sailors; in the second, the leaders of the various contingents) came to believe that continuing to work in the common cause was to their own disadvantage: Hdt. 6.12 and 13.2. Τὸ ἐθελοκακεῖν is not a result of decadence due to high living; at Hdt. 5.78.1 it is a quality of the Athenians under the Peisistratids. The Hippocratic *De aere* (16, 23) approvingly identifies it as a calculated strategy adopted by those living under despotism. The behavior of the Ionians—both rank and file and the leadership—is viewed as a natural reaction common among those who see themselves as oppressed or misled. It is not presented as a distinguishing characteristic of a particular ethnic group.

141. As we would expect, Herodotus treats this theme with subtlety. To limit ourselves to two examples discussed above: at Plataea, the Athenians are shown in a positive light when they said they would abide by the Spartans' decision about the order of battle, since it would not be right to press their claim at such a time (Hdt. 9.27.6). On the other hand, at Salamis the Athenians threatened to withdraw from the alliance if their strategy was not adopted (Hdt. 8.62).

142. Neville (1979) gives a thoughtful discussion of the evidence for the connection that Herodotus makes between Ionian disunity and the weakness consequent to it. He notes especially that Herodotus himself clearly approved of the attempts to unite Ionia that the *Histories* records. For example, Hdt. 1.170.1 expresses the author's approval for the proposal that the Ionians emigrate to Sardinia and form a single polity: πυνθάνομαι γνώμην Βίαντα ἄνδρα Πριηνέα ἀποδέξασθαι Ἴωσι χρησιμωτάτην, τῇ εἰ ἐπείθοντο, παρεῖχε ἄν σφι εὐδαιμονέειν Ἑλλήνων μάλιστα ("I have heard that Bias, a citizen of Priene, advanced an opinion most advantageous for the Ionians; if they had followed it, it would be possible for them to be the most prosperous of the Greeks."). Hdt. 6.12, with its emphasis on the ill effects of independence, should be given more prominence in studies on this question.

of the weak Greek γένος (Hdt. 1.143.2). This statement is taken to emphasize "the Ionians' physical and moral softness."[143] If this interpretation is correct, we must recognize that the Greek nation as a whole is open to the same criticism, for the text distinguishes the Ionians and the rest only by degree. But this parallelism makes it absurd to understand the effects of luxury as the cause of Ionian inferiority: what then makes the Greek race in general ἀσθενές? Does it also suffer from pernicious luxury, albeit to a lesser extent?

The difficulties that Hdt. 1.143 entails for those who see decadence at work among the Ionians also apply more widely: whatever may have been Herodotus's attitude toward the Ionians, he nowhere indicates that their prosperity was to blame for subsequent misfortunes or, more specifically, that a luxurious lifestyle made them weak and unwarlike. The *Histories* contains no explicit statements to this effect, nor have scholars been able to produce a convincing argument that such a causal link is implicit in the relevant passages.[144]

We may conclude our search for possible examples of pernicious luxury among the objects of Persian conquest with the case of Egypt. Cambyses began his invasion of Egypt when that country was ruled by Amasis. This was a time of unusual prosperity:

ἐπ' Ἀμάσιος δὲ βασιλέος λέγεται Αἴγυπτος μάλιστα δὴ τότε εὐδαιμονῆσαι καὶ τὰ ἀπὸ τοῦ ποταμοῦ τῇ χώρῃ γινόμενα καὶ τὰ ἀπὸ τῆς χώρης τοῖσι ἀνθρώποισι, καὶ πόλις ἐν αὐτῇ γενέσθαι τὰς ἀπάσας τότε δισμυρίας τὰς οἰκεομένας.

---

143. Hunt 1998, 146.

144. Scholars such as Alty (1982) can, for example, point to passages in Attic comedy in which Ionian luxury is mocked, as well as to others where they are taken to be cowards. It is much harder to produce evidence in which both elements are present. And even where this is the case, we must keep in mind that a reference to cowardly and luxury-loving Ionians is not necessarily proof of a concept of pernicious luxury. Because certain luxuries—fine clothing, perfume, a careful coiffure—are frequently associated with women, such things may be a *symbol* of Ionian weakness rather than its *source*. The perfectly reasonable suggestion has been made that other Greeks saw the Ionians as womanish and cowardly because their cities in Asia Minor had been enslaved first by Lydians and then by Persians. No explanation other than, for example, geographic proximity to these empires or failure to unite against them was necessary for these historical facts. We may infer belief in some such contingent cause from the Hippocratic *De aere* 16.5: ὁκόσοι γὰρ ἐν τῇ Ἀσίῃ Ἕλληνες ἢ βάρβαροι μὴ δεσπόζονται, ἀλλ' αὐτόνομοί εἰσι καὶ ἑωυτοῖσι ταλαιπωρεῦσιν, οὗτοι μαχιμώτατοί εἰσι πάντων ("However many Greeks or barbarians in Asia are not under a monarchy, but are autonomous and suffer hardships on their own behalf, these are the most warlike of all."). The Ionians had not been corrupted; in their nature they were extremely warlike, but circumstances prevented nature from taking its course. And this change came about only after the Ionians fell under the control of δεσπόται. Thus, the idea that Ionians were dedicated to luxury—to the extent that there was such an idea—may have been understood as a consequence or corollary to their apparent decline, not its cause.

[It is said that while Amasis was king Egypt was especially prosperous, both with respect to what the river provided to the land and to what the land provided to the people, and that at that time there were altogether twenty thousand inhabited cities in the land.] (Hdt. 2.177.1)

It is by now no surprise that the Egyptians, in spite of their great wealth, displayed no particular weakness or cowardice before the advancing Persians. More revealing for our purposes is the characterization of Amasis himself. Of all the people appearing in the *Histories,* this man perhaps comes closest to being portrayed in a way that, in later authors, would make him an unmistakable example of τρυφή. At 2.173.1 Herodotus describes the king's daily routine, noting that in the first part of the day Amasis attended conscientiously to business, but after that he gave himself over to drink, jokes, and foolishness (ἔπινέ τε καὶ κατέσκωπτε τοὺς συμπότας καὶ ἦν μάταιός τε καὶ παιγνιήμων).[145] Amasis's lifestyle did not meet with the approval of his friends, who scolded him for behavior unbecoming a "great man" and "not at all kingly." The king, however, was not chastened, and defended his actions with a proverb: a bow kept strung would break, and would not be ready at need; so a man always busy with serious affairs would soon go mad (Hdt. 2.173.3–4).[146]

Here, then, is a rare instance in which Herodotus draws attention to the wider implications of a leader's lifestyle. It reveals no trace of a commitment to the idea of pernicious luxury. Amasis's friends, for example, are not concerned about the effects of loose living on his physical health or moral character. Rather, they feel his daily relaxations are harming his reputation among his subjects (ἄμεινον σὺ ἂν ἤκουες, Hdt. 2.173.2). And it is noteworthy that the king is presented as getting the better of the argument and that his response is practically a contradiction of the ideas of pernicious luxury and strength through poverty. For Amasis, an increase in πόνοι and a decrease in εὐπάθειαι would produce not a harder, more courageous warrior, but a man ineffective in time of crisis. The king's mixed regime of toil and revelry is incompatible with a concept that sees an easy lifestyle as naturally and inevitably followed by weak-

---

145. While indulging in mockery and jocularity is not normally a manifestation of τρυφή in later authors, drunkenness certainly is. At Hdt. 2.174.1, in a description of the king's earlier life, Amasis spends his resources πίνοντά τε καὶ εὐπαθέοντα ("drinking and enjoying himself"). This last word and its cognates are commonly included among Herodotus's terms for "luxury": cf. the notorious claim about the Persians made at Hdt. 1.135.1, καὶ εὐπαθείας τε παντοδαπὰς πυνθανόμενοι ἐπιτηδεύουσι ("And when they learn of any types of luxuries, they make a practice of them.").

146. See Lloyd 1989, 391, for Herodotus's use of apothegms; cf. Asheri, Lloyd, and Corcella 2007, 370.

ness and disaster. Nor should we dismiss Amasis's remarks as self-serving. When Cambyses' invasion reached Egypt, the Persian found that Amasis had escaped him:

ἀλλὰ βασιλεύσας ὁ Ἄμασις τέσσερα καὶ τεσσεράκοντα ἔτεα ἀπέθανε, ἐν τοῖσι οὐδέν οἱ μέγα ἀνάρσιον πρῆγμα συνηνείχθη.

[And Amasis died, having ruled for forty-four years, in which no serious, unfitting matter befell him.] (Hdt. 3.10.2)

Thus, Herodotus confirms in his narrative voice that a man whose actions in his daily life were thought not at all fitting for a king (οὐδαμῶς βασιλικά, Hdt. 2.173.2) met with nothing unfitting (ἀνάρσιον) in his reign. A clearer disjunction between details of lifestyle and the unfolding of historical events is difficult to imagine.

In summary, we contend that nowhere in the *Histories* does Herodotus present an example of destructive luxury as a principle of historical causation. Even though scholars accept this idea as a major theme of the work, whether as text or subtext, Herodotus never explicitly states that luxury brought about the ruin of a people or an individual. Prosperity is never offered as the source of softness or weakness, but rather of military strength and success. The downfall of people enjoying opulence is never the subject of moral approbation. Instead, such a collapse is cast tragically, as a result of the inexorable cycle of historical events where great things become small and small things great.

Given the absence of clear examples of pernicious luxury in the work that is taken as the best evidence for that concept in Classical thought, we should admit that the case for the importance of this idea is unconvincing. Supposed indirect and subtle references to this concept outside of the *Histories* are said to be identifiable because Herodotus makes clear that the belief was widely and firmly held. Such interpretations are, we conclude, untenable: it is not persuasive to maintain the existence of a subtext in, for example, Euripides, by pointing to a subtext in the *Histories*. Rather, the claim that the Greeks thought that certain lifestyles could ruin powerful individuals and nations—and, as a matter of historical fact, had done so—must at some point rest on an explicit text. This does not seem to be the case for the Classical period.

CHAPTER 3

Citation and Cover Text in Athenaeus

The previous chapters have argued that the evidence for the idea of pernicious luxury is unexpectedly weak both in the scanty remains of Archaic literature and in the authors of the Classical period, and that what evidence does exist for decadence arising from luxury is not well understood. Focusing on the concept of τρυφή, we have found that there are indications of incipient belief in two different, morally harmful processes associated with it. The possessor of immoderate τρυφή may give excessive ἐπιμέλεια to his own creature comforts and correspondingly too little ἐπιμέλεια to duties such as military practice. As a result, he becomes weak and womanish and is easily dominated. Alternatively, one endowed with excessive τρυφή may demand that others pay undue attention to his or her comforts. Such demands are readily perceived as disrespectful, and, if they are insisted upon too vigorously, easily shade into hubris. Hubris, according to the well-known tradition, may bring ruinous punishment from the gods or retribution from men. We have seen that scholarship on the idea of decadence pays little or no attention to this distinction, though it is of fundamental significance. As far as we can tell, the two processes we have identified are never comingled in any Classical text. Τρυφή may be attended by the weakening of a subject or by the movement of a subject toward acts of hubris. It does not do both to the same person.

In addition, the connection between luxury and moral decay, of whatever nature, remained a tentative one in the Classical period. Pernicious luxury was not at that time a widely accepted and influential historiographical concept. It is not offered as a serious explanation for significant historical events. We have made Herodotus's *Histories* the principal evidence for this claim, since this work is commonly considered to give pernicious luxury a place of central importance as a force of historical causation. In contrast, our discussion of the *Histories* has shown that no clear and explicit references to the concept in question occur in that text; the evidence that is usually advanced admits of other interpretations. Perhaps of more importance, we find no indication in the course of the Herodotean narrative that luxury decisively contributed to the ruin of any nation or individual. Instead, the concept of pernicious luxury has been imported into the *Histories* by later interpreters.

The results of the investigations in earlier chapters are pertinent to our examination of the theme of pernicious luxury in Hellenistic historiography.[1] In essence, the study of the evidence from the Classical era establishes that the case for the importance of pernicious luxury in historical literature of the later period must stand or fall almost completely on its own merits. It is the modern *communis opinio* that Hellenistic historiography made use of a *topos* in which wealth begat τρυφή (understood as a state of effeminate self-indulgence), τρυφή engendered κόρος (satiety), and κόρος in turn led to hubris and eventual ruin. Since this pattern does not appear in the Classical material, the Hellenistic texts that reflect this *topos* must be scrutinized with added care.

The belief that pernicious luxury is given significant causative force by Hellenistic historians is often espoused by modern scholars. Bernhardt, for example, in his wide-ranging survey of *Luxuskritik,* identifies the historical implications of τρυφή as an important theme in Ephorus, Timaeus, Theopompus, Clearchus, Phylarchus, Polybius, and Posidonius, to name only the most prominent.[2] Studies on individual authors generally agree. Most recently Tsitsiridis considers this chain of destruction an obvious matter in the fragments of Clearchus's *Lives.*[3] However, given our demonstration that pernicious luxury had practically no historiographical importance in the earlier period, such a use of the concept in Hellenistic writers would have to be recognized as an innovation. Its development would have to be explained in terms appropriate to

---

1.   We use "Hellenistic historiography" as a convenient shorthand for the relevant literature after Xenophon and before Diodorus Siculus, although we recognize that it is not *stricto sensu* accurate for authors such as Ephorus, who were active earlier in the fourth century, or for authors in genres not strictly defined as history.
2.   Bernhardt 2003, 226–47, 308.
3.   Tsitsiridis 2008, 70–71. Theopompus: Flower 1994, Shrimpton 1991; Timaeus: Champion (in *BNJ*); Clearchus: Tsitsiridis 2008, Bollansée 2008; Phylarchus: Schepens 2007, 258–60; Stelluto 1995.

the concerns of Hellenistic historians; it can no longer be viewed as the application of an inherited theme.

Thus, our discussion of the moral dimension of luxury as evident in the Classical era has significantly redefined the framework in which later examples must be interpreted. In view of this change, it should not be surprising that in this chapter we will argue that the standard view of the place of τρυφή in Greek historiography from Xenophon to Diodorus is in need of serious modification. In addition, the scope of the revisions in this later material that are entailed by our assessment of the Classical evidence has been compounded by a growing realization of the dangers inherent in using Hellenistic fragment collections. This problem has been receiving particular notice of late,[4] yet no systematic method of approaching those dangers has been generally adopted. That is, while scholars accept that one must take into account both the missing context of the original passage and the issues of authorial intent of the quoting source when attempting the messy task of separating fragment from cover text, this undertaking is often left indeterminate and pushed into the background. Baron sums up the problem: "Although taking into account the preserving author is sometimes breezily dismissed as common sense, scholars continue to demonstrate the various and subtle ways in which distortion can occur."[5] We will explore those dangers in great detail in regards to Athenaeus, and propose a method of addressing them that is both specific and productive. The extent of the resulting modifications we recommend making to the common opinion about Hellenistic historiography may be disconcerting: it is our view that the evidence does not support the use of τρυφή as a historical concept of any importance whatsoever in this period. Rather, this belief is based on consistent misreading of the pertinent evidence.

---

4. Examples of judicious recent work include especially Baron (2013) on Timaeus and Barnes (2005) on the Tarentine War.

5. Baron 2013, 4. It is troubling that a recent conference proceedings devoted to the collecting of fragments (Most 1997) makes little mention of Athenaeus and only vaguely touches on the problems of cover text: Scheppens (1997, 196–99) and Kidd (1997) have short discussions of context. Scheppens (166) rightly notes: "Of course, the context of the latter work [the cover text] must not always entail a distortion of the original meaning of a fragments, but it often does. The student of historical fragments should be aware of the fact that his basic working material—the texts quoted with the author's name—consists for the greater part of references that are made with a special purpose, mostly with a critical or polemical spirit. . . . [T]he reference by name always needs to be examined critically before we can think of using it as evidence for reconstructing the contents of lost works." He goes on to recommend separating the fragment from the context of the cover text without specifying a method by which to do so.

The Parlor Games of Athenaeus

The second-century CE polymath Athenaeus of Naucratis was keenly interested in the demoralizing effects of τρυφή, a subject to which he dedicates the entire twelfth book of his *Deipnosophistae*. Because his work weaves a web of citations of earlier authorities, and because he takes pains to refer to his sources by name, title, and even book, Athenaeus is responsible for preserving the lion's share of material relevant to this chapter. Establishing his reliability as transmitter of these fragments is of first importance to our investigation. We will therefore preface our treatment of the Hellenistic evidence on τρυφή with a methodological investigation that seeks to put on firmer footing our understanding of the *Deipnosophistae* as a cover text for historical fragments.

A careful appraisal of Athenaeus's methods of citation is even more necessary because, unfortunately, scholars publishing studies about individual Hellenistic historians have tended to accept without much scrutiny that Athenaeus's citations of those historians are generally accurate and trustworthy.[6] This confidence often seems to be based on Brunt's influential article, in which he comes to the conclusion that "in general Athenaeus is fairly reliable."[7] While this claim may be correct in broad terms, we will see that it is misleading because it causes readers to underestimate the significance of the exceptions to this rule.

To form an estimation of Athenaeus's accuracy in reporting earlier texts, the fundamental procedure is to examine that author's treatment of material from extant works, comparing citations in the *Deipnosophistae* to their sources as transmitted through their own traditions. Thus, Brunt draws his conclusion from a comparison of Athenaeus's citations of Herodotus and Xenophon with the texts of the originals. But such a comparison is less straightforward than it may seem, and, relying on the same comparative data, scholars can reach strikingly different conclusions. The first extensive study of this kind was done by K. Zepernick, who claimed that his work showed that the *Deipnosophistae* deserved "die größte Glaubwürdigkeit."[8] In contrast, an attitude of extreme mistrust has been called for by A. Tronson: "out of 162 quotations of extant prose

---

6. This confidence in Athenaeus's citations reaches to the level of diction. For example, Shrimpton (1991, 137) feels able to say on the basis on material from Athenaeus that "*akrasia* (as opposed to the alternative ἀκρατεία) is a favorite of Theopompus," and Schütrumpf (2008, 71) argues on the same basis about the possible use of Aristotelian terminology by Heraclides Ponticus.
7. Brunt 1980, 481.
8. Zepernick 1921, 363.

authors by Athenaeus, 90 are found to have been drastically shortened, adapted or deliberately misquoted."[9]

This sharp discrepancy sets in relief the extent to which an interpreter's beliefs about the purpose of the *Deipnosophistae* can affect the way that even the relatively objective data in question are understood. Zepernick, for instance, believes that Athenaeus's chief aim is to accurately report to his readers the statements made by his sources: Athenaeus wished "above all to provide a reservoir of all matters to do with dining, so that his contemporaries and posterity could read without pains the reports of ancient writers."[10] With this goal in mind, Athenaeus makes every effort to reproduce as exactly as possible the words of his sources. Thus, Zepernick supposes that the places where the *Deipnosophistae* diverges from the texts of the originals are not due to any conscious action on the part of Athenaeus. In the first place, Zepernick argues, the majority of the discrepancies at issue are corruptions of the same sort as appear regularly in manuscripts of Greek authors. What had been verbatim quotations made by Athenaeus, then, came to differ from the source text through copyists' mistakes.[11] Secondly, in a good many cases, the exemplars from which Athenaeus draws his materials must have contained variants that, when adopted by Athenaeus, led to the pertinent differences. Thence he assumes the general trustworthiness of citations in the *Deipnosophistae*.[12]

Brunt takes a more sophisticated approach, urging the readers of historical fragments to take into account the "interests and purposes" of the transmitting authors.[13]Although he does not specify these aspects of the *Deipnosophistae*, Brunt seems to understand Athenaeus's intentions in more or less the same way

---

9. Tronson 1984, 125 n. 54. Although Tronson announced his intention to publish an article in support of these claims, it seems never to have appeared.
10. Zepernick 1921, 312: "vor allem aber ein Sammelbecken aller mit dem Mahl zusammenhängenden Dinge geben, damit Zeitgenossen und Nachwelt ohne Mühe die Ausführungen der allen Schriftsteller lesen könnten."
11. Zepernick 1921, 324–50. Pelling (2000, 188–90) discusses this aspect of Zepernick's argument and finds it unconvincing.
12. A third, and perhaps most important, reason that these textual discrepancies do not shake Zepernick's confidence in Athenaeus is his belief that the whole of the *Deipnosophistae* as we now have it is an epitome. On this view, championed by Kaibel, Athenaeus originally composed his work in 30 books; the present 15 book edition constitutes a later abridgement. This interpretation was generally accepted until quite recently, but has begun to wane in popularity. For a discussion of the principal arguments, see: Rodríguez-Noriega 2000; Arnott 2000. Zepernick, understanding our text of the *Deipnosophistae* to represent roughly half of what Athenaeus wrote, was able to explain away many differences between fragment and source as deletions, condensations, and other variations introduced by the epitomator.
13. Brunt 1980, 478.

as does Zepernick. Examining Athenaeus's citations of Herodotus, for example, Brunt classifies the observed deviations as "errors," which he considers "not very serious" and marks down the cause as *lapsus memoriae*.[14] Thus, like Zepernick, Brunt presents Athenaeus as trying to provide his readers with accurate representations of his sources.

In a parallel fashion, Tronson's deep skepticism about Athenaeus's reliability is contingent upon his interpretation of the aims of the *Deipnosophistae*. Since Tronson's focus is on one particular historical fragment, he does not develop a general theory about this matter, but his point of view is easily inferred. For Tronson, Athenaeus's interests and purposes are argumentative: citation of authorities serves to persuade the reader of the validity of claims made by Athenaeus's banqueters.[15] Since he sees Athenaeus as pursuing this end, Tronson may reasonably interpret differences between citation and extant model as deliberate changes made by an author who "even distorts the meaning of his source in order to support his own arguments."[16]

Since the results of an examination of Athenaeus's citations of extant texts are so clearly dependent upon how one understands just what the *Deipnosophistae* is, it is proper that we say a few words about our view before beginning a detailed investigation of the data.

The last dozen years have seen an unprecedented flourishing of Athenaean studies, with many important works being produced.[17] This concentration of effort has led to a sharper insight into the structure and workings of the *Deipnosophistae*. Of particular interest to us here is the light that has been thrown on the playful nature of Athenaeus's composition. Jacob, in his extensive introduction to the monumental Italian translation of and commentary on the *Deipnosophistae*, has discussed this aspect in detail. Jacob calls Athenaeus's work

---

14. Brunt 1980, 480–81. Dalby (1996, 173) claims that the texts quoted by Athenaeus are sacrosanct, within the limits of memory, and then goes on to say, "Athenaeus has been praised for accuracy and has also been criticized for inaccuracy. But he has never been caught adjusting quoted texts to suit an argument." We would disagree, having discovered him doing precisely that, as we will demonstrate in this chapter.

15. In this instance, Tronson (1984, 125) is examining the fragment of the *Lives* of Satyrus the Peripatetic cited at 13.557b–d. Roughly speaking, the line of argument that Athenaeus is following is that "love and politics do not mix"; Satyrus provides Athenaeus with a list of the wives of Philip II of Macedon, along with sufficient additional details to establish Philip as a case in point.

16. Tronson 1984, 125.

17. A valuable addition to our resources for this author is the Italian translation and commentary produced under the direction of Luciano Canfora (2001). Most pertinent to our investigation is Maria Luisa Gambato's treatment of Book 12.

"the story of the playing of a fascinating parlor game."[18] The rules of this "gioco di società" require the players to draw connections, based on relevance to a given topic, among the greatest possible number of pertinent citations, and these taken from the widest range of sources.[19]

Quite unexpectedly for a game that consists of accumulating material from Greek books from Homer's time forward, the rules put a high premium on novelty. For example, at the beginning of Athen. 6, we find the following complaint addressed by the character Athenaeus to his interlocutor Timocrates.

ἐπειδὴ ἀπαιτεῖς συνεχῶς ἀπαντῶν, ἑταῖρε Τιμόκρατες, τὰ παρὰ τοῖς δειπνοσοφισταῖς λεγόμενα, καινά τινα νομίζων ἡμᾶς εὑρίσκειν, ὑπομνήσομέν σε τὰ παρὰ Ἀντιφάνει λεγόμενα ἐν Ποιήσει τόνδε τὸν τρόπον·

μακάριόν ἐστιν ἡ τραγῳδία
ποίημα κατὰ πάντ', εἴ γε πρῶτον οἱ λόγοι
ὑπὸ τῶν θεατῶν εἰσιν ἐγνωρισμένοι,
πρὶν καί τιν' εἰπεῖν· ὥσθ' ὑπομνῆσαι μόνον
δεῖ τὸν ποιητήν.
. . . .
ἡμῖν δὲ ταῦτ' οὐκ ἔστιν, ἀλλὰ πάντα δεῖ
εὑρεῖν, ὀνόματα καινά, . . .

[Since, friend Timocrates, when we meet you continuously demand the words of the deipnosophists, thinking that we discover certain new things, I will remind you of what Antiphanes said in the *Poesis*: "Tragedy is a fortunate creation in all ways. First, since the stories are known by the spectators before anything is said; thus, it is only necessary for the poet to remind them. . . . But this doesn't

---

18. Jacob 2001, cii: "L'opera di Ateneo, in questa prospettiva, sarebbe, più che il resoconto di un banchetto, il racconto di una partita di un affascinante gioco di società." This introduction has since been revised and printed as a stand-alone work, translated into English (Jacob 2013), but it has come out too late to be incorporated into this volume.

19. Jacob (2001, ci) describes Athenaeus's procedure metaphorically, in spatial terms. Each "giocatore," giving his particular collection of citations, maps an itinerary of a mental journey taken through the many areas of "la biblioteca . . . quella che ogni deipnosofista reca impressa nella memoria." According to Jacob, "il solo imperativo" of the game is to create a nexus among the largest number of "elementi testuali," while at the same time traversing "il tragitto più lungo in assoluto, se possibile tra poli estremamente lontani tra loro" (cii). Thus, citations from a wide range of genres would be an indication of skill at this game. Cf. Danielewicz 2006; König 2008, 88–94.

apply for us, but it is necessary to discover all new names. . . ."] (Athen. 6.222c–223a = Antiphanes, frag. 189 KA)

Timocrates is eager to hear of the dinner conversation because he believes it holds something new. Athenaeus reminds him of the difficulty entailed by such innovation, comparing it to the demands of writing comedy. Because coming up with καινά τινα requires such an effort, we may expect the discovery of novelty to be one of the chief ways of scoring points in the contest of wit and memory in which the deipnosophists are engaged.[20] In any case, at the opening of the work's last book, the character "Athenaeus" emphasizes that the search for something new is perhaps the most salient feature of the discussion he is trying to relate.

εἴ μοι τὸ Νεστόρειον εὔγλωσσον μέλος
Ἀντήνορός τε τοῦ Φρυγὸς δοίη θεός,

κατὰ τὸν πάνσοφον Εὐριπίδην, ἑταῖρε Τιμόκρατες, οὐκ ἂν δυναίμην ἀπομνημονεύειν ἔτι σοι τῶν πολλάκις λεχθέντων ἐν τοῖς περισπουδάστοις τούτοις συμποσίοις διά τε τὴν ποικιλίαν καὶ τὴν ὁμοιότητα τῶν ἀεὶ καινῶς προσευρισκομένων.

["If a god gave me the eloquent phrasing of Nestor and Phrygian Antenor," in the words of the all-wise Euripides, I would not be able, Timocrates, my friend, to recall for you more of the many things said in these much-sought-after symposia on account both of the variety and of the similarity of the new discoveries continuously being turned up.] (Athen. 15.665a = Eur., frag. 891 *TrGF*)

Apparently, innovations are constantly being discovered. These new discoveries could be a matter of adducing rarely seen texts, which would presumably be unknown to the reader. Likewise, they could consist in drawing new connections, juxtaposing authorities not usually associated.[21] There is also another

20. Wilkins (2000b, 31) points out that Athenaeus's discussion of καινά τινα at the beginning of Book 6 indicates "that novelty is contained in the internal dialogue and not the finished literary work of Athenaeus. . . . There will then be 'certain novelties' in the work, but they will all be the invention of Ulpian, Cynulcus and their companions at the table of Larensis."

21. So Braund (2000, 18) identifies "an idiosyncratic form of originality, achieved by the rediscovery, citation, quotation and juxtaposition of texts, largely culled from the distant past and deployed under headings or to address specific (and often very minor) issues."

possibility, as Jacob points out. Expert players of the game are expected to avoid relying on obvious authorities,[22] but to produce from their journey through the library of memory "paradoxical routes and unexpected explanations."[23]

The emphasis laid on paradox and surprise in the *gioco di società* of the *Deipnosophistae* has corollaries that are important for any evaluation of Athenaeus's use of Hellenistic historiography. For example, if the processes of pernicious luxury were presented explicitly as an significant theme by Theopompus or Timaeus, the banqueter citing these authors would receive little credit for referring to trite and well-known sources. We might rather expect the virtuoso *giocatore* to cite from works whose authors were not known to be particularly interested in moral decadence, or at least to draw from a source instances of, for example, τρυφή that had not been identified as such in the originals. In this way, familiar passages might be seen in a new light and be given a new significance. The pertinence of the material to the idea of pernicious luxury would then be one of the discoveries for which Athenaeus shows such pride.

Thus recent appreciations of the *Deipnosophistae*, such as that offered by Jacob, have modified the prevailing view of Athenaeus's intentions and methods and have promoted a more sophisticated and nuanced interpretative framework for understanding Athenaeus's relationship to his sources.[24] Relying on this framework, we do not see discrepancies between Athenaean citations and extant sources as due to scribal errors or lapses of memory, for we do not

---

22. Jacob 2001, cii: "i giocatori provetti . . . cercano cose sofisticate, . . . vietandosi a volte il ricorso alle fonti piú ovvie." In support of this claim, Jacob cites Athen. 15.676f, where Myrtilus demands from Ulpian "names of wreathes": σὺ δὲ μὴ τὰ ἐκ τῶν ἐπιγραφομένων Αἰλίου Ἀσκληπιάδου Στεφάνων φέρε ἡμῖν ὡς ἀνηκόοις αὐτῶν, ἀλλ' ἄλλο τι παρ' ἐκεῖνα λέγε ("Don't you give us material from Aelius Asclepiades' *Wreathes*, as if we've never heard of it. Tell us anything other than that stuff."). Ulpian's then turns first to the authority of Semus of Delos's *History* of that island.
23. Jacob 2001, ci: "la regola del gioco è quella di produrre il *kainón*, di fare uscire l'inedito da questo spazio intellettuale e linguistico identitario, e di risvegliare questi giacimenti di parole e di sapere attraverso percorsi paradossali e spiegazioni inattese."
24. A recent, stimulating study of Athenaeus's aims is Paulas 2012. This work argues that the *Deipnosophistae* in part dramatizes the combination of "the pleasure of varied reading and reading for smooth, aesthetic connections among texts, represented by Cynulcus, with the pleasure of recalling or finding difficult connections between texts, which Ulpian represents" (429). Paulas is not closely concerned with the accuracy of Athenaeus's quotations, but we are reinforced in our belief that Athenaeus's use of sources is anything but straightforward by his discussion of how that author is interested in the interplay between reading to attempt to answer particular questions (ζητήσεις) and a type of easy reading enchanted by the variety of material to be found in miscellanies. Similar in its emphasis on the need to recognize the sophistication and complexity of Athenaeus's treatment of his material is the collcetion of essays published in Grandjean, Heller, and Peigney 2013. Here Romeri 2013 and Peigney 2013 are of particular interest to us because they examine the evidence for ambivalence in Athenaeus's valorization of luxury and frugality. Unfortunately, this work has appeared too late for us to incorporate its arguments into our discussion.

assume that our author was composing a compendium of verbatim quotations or true paraphrases from which his readers might draw. On the other hand, neither do we follow Tronson in seeing deliberate distortions meant to be thought genuine by his audience and made by Athenaeus to support his own argument. Such an argumentative strategy would seem to require that those to be persuaded—whether the fictive interlocutors or Athenaeus's intended readership—were unaware that the words of the authorities are being manipulated. Given the fact that significant discrepancies occur in Athenaeus's citation of authors such as Homer and Herodotus, the audience's unfamiliarity with the sources cannot be assumed. Thus, it is preferable to view the differences between citation and source as part of a process of reinterpretation carried out in full view of the audience. Sometimes the new interpretation will be meant seriously: for example, events described by an original author without regard to τρυφή would be accepted by Athenaeus's contemporaries as obvious or plausible or possible examples of that phenomenon. Sometimes it seems that Athenaeus's tongue is firmly in his cheek, and the interpretation presented is patently absurd. In such an instance, the author illustrates—or perhaps satirizes—the excesses that may occur in this citation game. Unfortunately, it is often difficult to tell if a particular distortion of a source's meaning is presented humorously or in earnest. Thus we have all the more reason to be cautious with sources no longer available.

Alteration and Reinterpretation

As we turn to examine Athenaeus's mode of citation in detail, we recognize at once that any attempt to estimate the reliability of Athenaeus's use of his sources must immediately face a difficulty at the most basic level. There is substantial disagreement about the categorization of the objective facts. Most fundamentally, two experts may differ on what constitutes a verbatim quotation. For example, Zecchini, in his extensive examination of Athenaeus's "cultura storica," classifies 2.45a–b as among those citations "fideli 'ad verbum.'" On the other hand, in her recent detailed study of Herodotean fragments, Lenfant considers this citation a paraphrase:[25]

---

25.   Lenfant (2007b, 48 n. 17) herself draws attention to this disagreement.

ὁ Περσῶν βασιλεύς, ὥς φησιν ἐν τῇ α´ Ἡρόδοτος, ὕδωρ ἀπὸ τοῦ Χοάσπεω πιεῖν ἄγεται τοῦ παρὰ Σοῦσα ῥέοντος·τοῦ μόνου πίνει ὁ βασιλεύς. τοῦ δὲ τοιούτου ὕδατος ἀπεψημένου πολλαὶ κάρτα ἅμαξαι τετράκυκλοι ἡμιόνειαι κομίζουσαι ἐν ἀγγείοις ἀργυρέοισιν ἕπονταί οἱ.

[The King of the Persians, as Herodotus says in Book 1, brings water to drink from the Choaspes, which runs past Susa. The King drinks only from this. When the water has been boiled, a great many four-wheeled wagons drawn by mules follow him, carrying it in silver jars.] (Athen. 2.45a–b)

στρατεύεται δὲ δὴ βασιλεὺς ὁ μέγας καὶ σιτίοισι εὖ ἐσκευασμένοισι ἐξ οἴκου καὶ προβάτοισι, καὶ δὴ καὶ ὕδωρ ἀπὸ τοῦ Χοάσπεω ποταμοῦ ἅμα ἄγεται τοῦ παρὰ Σοῦσα ῥέοντος, τοῦ μούνου πίνει βασιλεὺς καὶ ἄλλου οὐδενὸς ποταμοῦ. τούτου δὲ τοῦ Χοάσπεω τοῦ ὕδατος ἀπεψημένου πολλαὶ κάρτα ἅμαξαι τετράκυκλοι ἡμίονεαι κομίζουσαι ἐν ἀγγηίοισι ἀργυρέοισι ἕπονται, ὅκῃ ἂν ἐλαύνῃ ἑκάστοτε.

[Now the Great King goes to war with both food and cattle well-provided from home, and also brings water from the river Choaspes, which runs past Susa. The King drinks only from this and from no other river. When this water of the Choaspes has been boiled, a great many four-wheeled wagons drawn by mules follow wherever he may march at any time, carrying it in silver jars.] (Hdt. 1.188)

Such differences in the basic terms of analysis make a summary of earlier scholarship complicated. In addition, the relatively restricted compass of most previous studies limits the usefulness of their conclusions. Lenfant, for example, identifies categories of citation that may accurately reflect Athenaeus's Herodotean material, but a wider focus would necessitate additional refinements:[26] for example, when citing verse, Athenaeus may quote two lines

---

26. On the basis of Herodotean citations, Lenfant (2007b, 46–50) constructs the following typology: Type 1, the lexical reference of one word (seven examples); Type 2a, literal citation of a phrase (four examples); Type 2b, literal citation of one or more sentences (10 examples); Type 3, paraphrase (twelve examples); Type 4, summary or allusion (five examples); Type 5, mixed fragments (four examples). In the same volume, Maisonneuve (2007, 80–83) presents a somewhat different schema, this time on the basis of citation of Xenophon: mentions (nine examples), verbatim citations (nine examples), literal citations (fifteen examples), quasi-literal citations (four examples), citations with

verbatim while omitting one or more lines between the two; similarly, he may conflate lines to produce a new verse. In sum, given the range of kinds of textual reproductions common in the *Deipnosophistae*, it is no simple matter even to arrive at a scheme for the classification of Athenaeus's citations. We will therefore not attempt to provide a systematic and general evaluation of Athenaeus's reliability, but rather will concentrate on those passages that we find most instructive for anyone using the *Deipnosophistae* to reconstruct lost texts.

As we confront Athenaeus's practice of citation, we may dismiss those that consist of single words or phrases, adduced as lexical data, since they are of little historiographical interest. As for longer citations, Athenaeus's ability to produce even lengthy word-for-word quotations is not in question.[27] However, even a word-for-word citation may be re-purposed by Athenaeus in a way that might have been misleading for an ill-informed or unsuspecting reader. Passages of this sort will be of particular interest for our purposes, while paraphrases and summaries, too, provide a fruitful source of examples of Athenaeus's work of discovery and invention.

We will begin, as is appropriate, with Homer. Unsurprisingly, he is by far the most frequently cited extant author in Athenaeus. A recent study estimates between 400 and 450 references of all kinds.[28] A large number of these are lexical citations of a single word. Of the remaining approximately 200 references (outside the epitomized books), nearly seven-eighths of the examples are exact quotations or near-exact quotations of relatively limited length.[29] The remain-

---

internal cuts (two examples), paraphrases (six examples), allusions (fifteen examples), mixed citations (four examples).

27. For example, in the case of Herodotean citations, Lenfant (2007b, 49) points out that the ratio between verbatim citations and "reformulations au moins partielles" is essentially one-to-one (twenty-one examples to twenty-two). This observation, if we assume it roughly characterizes Athenaeus's general practice in citation, would give us some confidence when interpreting fragments of lost works, since the odds that we were reading the actual words of the original would be even. Unfortunately, Lenfant goes on to explain that when we exclude lexical references and very short literal citations (type 2b), there remain less than half as many "citations littérales" (ten examples) as reformulations (twenty-two). This would represent a much more precarious situation for the interpretation on this basis of lost historians.

28. Bréchet (2007, 328) who adds that this number "fait d'Athénée un des tout premiers citateurs d'Homère de l'Antiquité." In addition, references to Homer make up around 200 of the approximately 500 references to extant sources occurring in the directly transmitted sections of the *Deipnosophistae*. All of the first two books of Athenaeus and part of the third (to 3.74) have been preserved only through a Byzantine epitome. In general, we omit discussion of evidence coming only from the epitome, since trying to decide whether to attribute features to Athenaeus or his excerptor would further complicate an already difficult task. For the manuscripts of Athenaeus, see Arnott 2000.

29. By "near-exact" quotations we mean those with minor morphological changes such as tense, number, or the like. The longest of these passages is *Il.* 11.632–37 at Athen. 11.487f.

ing twenty-eight cases hold our attention for their divergence from the vulgate of the epics.³⁰

As noted above, Athenaeus sometimes omits material within a quotation. These lacunae vary significantly in extent and transparency. At Athen. 8.363f the omission amounts only to a half line from *Od.* 3.395–96.³¹ At Athen. 8.363e, *Od.* 1.22 and 25 are cited contiguously and without indication that lines are omitted, but the alteration seems to have no significance to the argument. The passage in question shows Poseidon at the sacrifices of the Ethiopians; and the omitted lines simply add geographical detail. A gap is filled in the same way, without a visible seam, at Athen. 10.412b–c, where three and a half lines are cited exactly from *Od.* 7.215–18, but the quotation is completed with the second half of line 221. The change was perhaps made for rhetorical effect.³² A more complex example comes from Athen. 11.492e–f, where, in order to prove that the Pleiades were an appropriate decoration for Nestor's cup, the speaker produces a ten line quotation from the *Iliad*. The passage is compiled from three discrete sets of Homeric verses (*Il.* 11.624, 628–32, and 638–41), and neither meter, apparently, nor syntax would readily lead a reader unfamiliar with the original to suspect the lacunae.³³

A similar gap of six lines occurs at Athen. 5.191a–b, where Athenaeus offers a citation consisting of three and a half lines from *Od.* 4.123–26, followed im-

---

30. Bréchet (2007, 327) points out that the Homer of the *Deipnosophistae* is essentially the author of the *Iliad* and the *Odyssey*. He is practically not concerned with the *Hymns* or with minor works in the Epic Cycle.

31. Athen. 8.363f: ἐπεὶ ἔσπεισάν τ᾽ ἔπιόν θ᾽ ὅσον ἤθελε θυμός, ἔβαν οἰκόνδε ἕκαστος ("when they had poured libations and drunk to their hearts' content, each man went home"): Hom., *Od.* 3.396: οἱ μὲν κακκείοντες ἔβαν οἰκόνδε ἕκαστος ("the others each went to his own home to lie down").

32. The thesis is that Homer presents Odysseus as a glutton: Athen. 10.412c, ἀλλ᾽ ἐμὲ μὲν δορπῆσαι ἐάσατε κηδόμενόν περ· / οὐ γάρ τι στυγερῇ ἐπὶ γαστέρι κύντερον ἄλλο / ἔπλετο, ἥ τ᾽ ἐκέλευσεν ἕο μνήσασθαι ἀνάγκῃ / καὶ μάλα τειρόμενον καὶ ἐνιπλησθῆναι ἀνώγει ("But allow me to dine, although I am in distress, for nothing is more shameless than the wretched belly. It commands a man to remember it by necessity and it forces him to take his fill, even though very oppressed."). In Homer, the final line reads καὶ μάλα τειρόμενον καὶ ἐνὶ φρεσὶ πένθος ἔχοντα ("even though very oppressed and having sorrow in his heart," *Od.* 7.218). In the epic, Odysseus's next point is that eating and drinking allows him to forget all his sorrow, a sentiment that the Athenaean speaker declares unworthy even of Sardanapalus. Thus, to serve the climactic arrangement of the argument, the introduction of πένθος is postponed until the first point (that Odysseus makes man the slave of his belly) is dealt with. This passage will be discussed more thoroughly below.

33. The metrical structure is apparently integral: three words are missing from the manuscript of Athenaeus, but are restored on the basis of Homer. Admittedly, *Il.* 11.632–37 had been quoted at the beginning of the discussion of Nestor's cup (Athen. 11.487f–488a), so it was possible for a keenly attentive reader to recognize the existence of the second gap at Athen. 11.492e–f, but not to judge its length. Also, Athenaeus changes the Homeric ἐπ᾽ of line 134 to ἐν.

mediately by three more lines, 133–35. The metrical fault makes the lacuna stand out, but a reader would be left to wonder about its length and the possibly relevance of the omitted material, which in this instance is significant.

τῇ δ᾽ ἄρ᾽ ἅμ᾽ Ἀδρήστη κλισίην εὔτυκτον ἔθηκεν·
Ἀλκίππη δὲ τάπητα φέρεν μαλακοῦ ἐρίοιο,
Φυλὼ δ᾽ ἀργύρεον τάλαρον φέρε, τόν οἱ ἔδωκεν
Ἀλκάνδρη, Πολύβοιο δάμαρ . . . <*lacuna*>
τόν ῥά οἱ ἀμφίπολος Φυλὼ παρέθηκε φέρουσα
νήματος ἀσκητοῖο βεβυσμένον· αὐτὰρ ἐν αὐτῷ
ἠλακάτη τετάνυστο ἰοδνεφὲς εἶρος ἔχουσα.

[And at the same time Adraste set out for her a well-wrought chair, and Alcippe carried a rug of soft wool, and Phylo carried a silver basket, which Alcandre had given her, the wife of Polybius . . . < *lacuna* > This her attendant Phylo brought and put beside her full of practiced yarn. And on it stretched the distaff, holding wool the color of a violet blossom.] (Athen. 5.191a–b)

The passage is cited to illustrate the "love of toil" (τὸ φίλεργον) of Helen of Troy. It is meant to be an explicit example (οὐ παρέργως, "not incidental") of inferring from an illustration a quality that is not explicitly mentioned in the passage (indicated, as commonly, by γοῦν). It is therefore worth noting that the six lines left out by the Deipnosophist emphasize the wealth and luxury that Helen and Menelaus received in Egyptian Thebes. Given the frequent position taken in Athenaeus that luxury and toil are incompatible, this lacuna is not innocent, but would constitute an ingenious move in Jacob's *gioco*.

As we might expect, paraphrases and summaries of Homer are common in Athenaeus. A favorite pattern is a paraphrase/summary introducing a verbatim quotation, such as this:

τί οὖν ἔχομεν λέγειν περὶ τοῦ Νέστορος ποτηρίου, ὃ μόλις ἂν νέος βαστάσαι ἴσχυεν, Νέστωρ δ᾽ ὁ γέρων ἀμογητὶ ἄειρε.[34]

---

34. Underlining marks the shared material: Hom., *Il.* 11.636–37, ἄλλος μὲν μογέων ἀποκινήσασκε τραπέζης / πλεῖον ἐόν, <u>Νέστωρ δ᾽ ὁ γέρων ἀμογητὶ ἄειρεν</u> ("Another man would lift the cup with a struggle from the table when it was full, but Nestor as an old man took it up easily.").

[What then are we able to say about the cup of Nestor, which a young man is scarcely able to hold aloft, but Nestor as an old man took it up easily.] (Athen. 11.461d)

In such examples it is immediately apparent to the reader that the original has been modified, but the result could nonetheless be treacherous if that reader does not have Homer by heart. These passages may serve as a precautionary object lesson vis-à-vis the much more difficult citations from prose sources.

Another good illustration of a potentially misleading citation:

πλεῖστον δὲ ἔπινε τῶν μὲν ἡρώων Νέστωρ ὁ τριγέρων· φανερῶς γὰρ αὐτὸς προσέκειτο τῶν ἄλλων μᾶλλον τῷ οἴνῳ καὶ τοῦ Ἀγαμέμνονος αὐτοῦ, ὃν ὡς πολυπότην ἐπιπλήσσει ὁ Ἀχιλλεύς. ὁ δὲ Νέστωρ καὶ τῆς μεγίστης μάχης ἐνεστηκυίας οὐκ ἀπέχεται [καὶ]³⁵ τοῦ πίνειν. φησὶ γοῦν Ὅμηρος·

Νέστορα δ᾽ οὐκ ἔλαθεν ἰαχὴ πίνοντά περ ἔμπης.

καὶ μόνου δὲ τούτου τῶν ἡρώων τὸ ποτήριον ἡρμήνευκεν, ὡς τὴν Ἀχιλλέως ἀσπίδα.³⁶

[Of the heroes, Nestor, the thrice-old, drank the most, for he was clearly more devoted to wine than the others, even Agamemnon himself, whom Achilles rebuked as a hard drinker. Nestor, even with the greatest battle at hand, did not leave off drinking. Anyway, Homer says, "The shout did not escape Nestor, though he was drinking." And of the heroes, the only cup he described was his, like the shield of Achilles.] (Athen. 10.433b–c = Hom., *Il.* 14.1)

For one familiar with Athenaeus's mode of citation, a clear pattern is illustrated here: a Deipnosophist proposes a thesis (e.g., Nestor is the most bibulous hero), then he produces an interpretative paraphrase (Nestor was drinking even with battle raging), and finally the ancient authority is cited directly (very often introduced by γοῦν). This sequence occurs with great frequency in Athenaeus, and causes confusion in the case of historical fragments, since, when dealing with lost works, particularly those in prose, it is extremely difficult to

---

35. Deleted by Wilamowitz.
36. Olson (2006–12, ad loc.) reads this reference to Achilleus's, and not Nestor's, shield as a "misguided gloss that has intruded into the text," and therefore deletes Ἀχιλλέως.

distinguish thesis from paraphrase from citation. In this Homeric instance, we see an example of a playful paradox, employed along the lines suggested by Jacob: the speaker discovers τὸ καινόν by using Homeric evidence in a way that would be quite unexpected. In this context, Nestor happens to be drinking when he hears a shout from the battlefield. He immediately leaves his companion to continue the repast and himself goes to investigate the excitement. A casual reader of the *Deipnosophistae*, one who was not familiar with Athenaeus's game and its methods, might reasonably assume that some hard evidence underlay the emphatic language of the claim advanced that Nestor was more devoted to drink than the others, a claim that would startle and amuse anyone who knew his *Iliad*.

The problems inherent in the tendentious character of Athenaeus's paraphrases become clearer when no citation is adduced. The case for Nestor as drunkard continues:

ἀλλὰ μὴν καὶ διὰ τὴν φιλοποσίαν ὁ Νέστωρ καὶ παρ' Ἀχιλλέως φιάλην λαμβάνει δῶρον ἐν τῷ ἐπὶ Πατρόκλῳ ἐπιτελουμένῳ ἀγῶνι,[37]. . .

[But again because of his love of drink, Nestor received from Achilles a bowl as a gift at the contest established for Patroclus, . . .] (Athen. 10.433d)

Reading this passage, we should ask ourselves what kind of original we would reconstruct if we did not possess the *Iliad*. Similarly, we should ask what kind of moral stance would we attribute to Homer on the basis of the phrase διὰ τὴν φιλοποσίαν. Categorizing the words of his authorities in moral terms such as this is a favorite move of Athenaeus. Parallel expressions occur in many historical fragments, where they are often accepted automatically as accurately representing the character of the original.

Of special interest to our study are those examples in which Athenaeus attributes a general rule or norm to his authority on the basis of a passage that we would classify as purely descriptive or narrative. Frequent Homeric examples

---

37. Olson (ad loc.): "Something has gone seriously wrong with the text at this point, perhaps via a combination of intrusive notes and the loss of some lines. . . ." His argument is based on the facts in Homer: that Nestor received the bowl not from taking part in the contests, for which he is too old, but as a gift of honor. We would argue that this alteration may well represent a deliberate manipulation intended to reinforce the thesis that Nestor was a drunkard. Our anonymous reader suggests that perhaps the phrase "at the contest established for Patroclus" could be taken as a source citation rather than implying that Nestor took part in a contest.

appear in Book 5, where Athenaeus makes the poet into a teacher of symposia-stic etiquette. A small selection will suffice. The first rule is that one must invite chiefly A list guests:

ἔπειθ᾽ ὁ μὲν Ὅμηρος ἐκδιδάσκει τίνας κλητέον, εἰπὼν ὡς τοὺς ἀρίστους τε καὶ ἐντίμους χρὴ καλεῖν·

κίκλησκεν δὲ γέροντας ἀριστῆας Παναχαιῶν.

[Next Homer teaches who should be invited, saying that one ought to invite the best and the honored: "he called the elders, the excellent in valor among all the Achaeans."] (Athen. 5.186f = Hom., Il. 2.404)

Some need no invitation:

ἐδίδαξεν δ᾽ Ὅμηρος καὶ οὓς οὐ δεῖ καλεῖν, ἀλλ᾽ αὐτομάτους ἰέναι, πρεπόντως ἐξ ἑνὸς τῶν ἀναγκαίων δεικνὺς τὴν τῶν ὁμοίων παρουσίαν·

αὐτόματος δέ οἱ ἦλθε βοὴν ἀγαθὸς Μενέλαος.

[Homer taught also whom one should not invite, but should come of their own accord, fittingly pointing out from one of the kinfolk the presence of others in the same category: "of his own accord there came to him Menelaus, good at the war cry."] (Athen. 5.177c = Hom., Il. 2.408)

And due ceremony must be observed:

καὶ πρὸ τοῦ θοινᾶσθαι δὲ ἃ δεῖ ποιεῖν ἡμᾶς διδάσκει πάλιν Ὅμηρος, ἀπαρχὰς τῶν βρωμάτων νέμειν τοῖς θεοῖς. οἱ γοῦν περὶ τὸν Ὀδυσσέα καίπερ ὄντες ἐν τῷ τοῦ Κύκλωπος σπηλαίῳ·

ἔνθα δὲ πῦρ κείαντες ἐθύσαμεν ἠδὲ καὶ αὐτοὶ
τυρῶν αἰνύμενοι φάγομεν.

[Again Homer teaches us what one must do also before the feast, apportioning the first-fruits of the food to the gods. At all events, Odysseus and his compan-ions did, although they were in the cavern of the Cyclops: "There, having lit a

fire, we made an offering and picked up and ate some of the cheese."] (Athen.
5.179b–c = Hom., *Od.* 9.231–32)

When we see how Athenaeus transforms the *Iliad* and *Odyssey* into didactic
works, and how slender is the basis upon which Homer's teachings are established, we may suspect that the identification from Athenaean citations of a
similarly didactic stance in lost works—such as a criticism of the destructive
force of τρυφή—may be likewise dubious.

If it is clear that Athenaeus's paraphrases are to be used with care, we must
also be aware that the distortion sometimes occurs in the text of the quotation
itself. At Athen. 12.511a–c, a lengthy preamble is followed by a four line quotation from *Od.* 8.329–32:

διόπερ Ὅμηρος ἐπονείδιστον βουλόμενος ποιῆσαι τὴν ἡδονὴν καὶ τῶν θεῶν
φησι τοὺς μεγίστους οὐδὲν ὑπὸ τῆς σφετέρας ὠφελεῖσθαι δυνάμεως, ἀλλὰ τὰ
μέγιστα βλάπτεσθαι παρενεχθέντας ὑπ᾽ αὐτῆς. . . . καὶ ὁ Ἄρης ἀλκιμώτατος ὢν
ὑπὸ τοῦ ἀσθενεστάτου Ἡφαίστου συνεποδίσθη καὶ ὦφλεν αἰσχύνην καὶ ζημίαν
ἐκδοὺς ἑαυτὸν ἔρωσιν ἀλογίστοις. φησὶ γοῦν πρὸς τοὺς θεούς, ὅτ᾽ ἦλθον
αὐτὸν θεασόμενοι δεδεμένον·

> οὐκ ἀρετᾷ κακὰ ἔργα· κιχάνει τοι βραδὺς ὠκύν,
> ὡς καὶ νῦν Ἥφαιστος ἐὼν βραδὺς εἷλεν Ἄρηα
> ὠκύτατόν περ ἐόντα θεῶν οἳ Ὄλυμπον ἔχουσι,
> χωλὸς ἐών, τέχνῃσι τὸ καὶ ζώαγρι᾽ ὀφέλλει.

[Wherefore Homer, wishing to make pleasure a most shameful thing, says that
even the greatest of the gods are not a bit helped by their power, but suffer the
greatest harm when misled by pleasure. . . . And Ares, though the strongest, was
bound hand and foot by Hephaestus, the weakest god. He was forced to pay in
shame and with a fine for giving himself over to unreasonable love affairs. At all
events, someone said to the gods, when they had come to see him in bonds:
"Evil deeds do not prosper. The slow overtake the fast. Thus now Hephaestus,
though slow, has taken Ares, though he is the fastest of the gods who dwell in
Olympus; though a cripple he has taken him through his craft. Ares must pay a
ransom for his life."]

Athenaeus's citation differs from the direct transmission only by a single word. This fact would seem to increase support for those who place great confidence in Athenaeus's reliability. However, a closer look reverses this impression. The change made by Athenaeus is to replace Homer's μοιχάγρι' ("adultery price") with ζωάγρι' ("life price"). Although both words are Homeric (ζωάγρια occurs shortly after this passage, at *Od.* 8.462), Bréchet argues that their rarity precludes the possibility of a simple mistake.[38] Furthermore, ζωάγρια is clearly the most important word in the citation from the point of view of Athenaeus's interpretation. The passage is quoted to establish that Homer maintained an anti-hedonistic position by depicting pleasure inflicting "the greatest harm" (τὰ μέγιστα βλάπτεσθαι) upon the gods. Ζωάγρι'/μοιχάγρι' is the only word in the passage that indicates the requisite βλάβη. Athenaeus bolsters his view by substituting the stronger for the weaker term, since ζωάγρια implies that Ares' life was at Hephaestus's disposal, while μοιχάγρια would indicate a lesser peril. Thus, Athenaeus, though making a minimal alteration, has significantly changed the force of the original. Athenaeus's contemporaries, as familiar with Homer as he was, may have applauded the elegant virtuosity of his move,[39] but for those who must deal with fragments preserved only in the *Deipnosophistae*, the way in which both Athenaeus's thesis and its supporting paraphrase depend on a fabrication will be highly disconcerting.

A similar example—the alteration of a single word bringing a marked change in significance—occurs at Athen. 5.181e–f. The thesis that is supported by Homeric authority is that there were no songs at the symposium celebrated in the house of Menelaus, but only conversation among the guests (Athen. 5.181d). This claim is established by the behavior of Telemachus on that occasion. The young man does not pay attention to any entertainment, but this indifference cannot be due to a lack of manners on his part. Like father, like son: Odysseus noticed such things, even when distracted by weightier concerns:

ὁ γοῦν Ὀδυσσεὺς προσέχει τοῖς τῶν Φαιάκων ἀσματοποιοῖς·

αὐτὰρ Ὀδυσσεὺς
μαρμαρυγὰς θηεῖτο ποδῶν, θαύμαζε δὲ θυμῷ,

---

38. Bréchet 2007, 330–31: "on ne confond pas, dans l'antiquité, un hapax homérique abondamment glosé (μοιχάγρια) avec un autre mot à peine plus fréquent (ζωάγρια)."
39. Bréchet 2007, 330: "il n'est plus question de faute, mais de virtuosité, de jeu."

καίπερ ἔχων πολλὰ τὰ περιέλκοντα καὶ δυνάμενος εἰπεῖν·

κήδεά μοι καὶ μᾶλλον ἐνὶ φρεσὶν ἤπερ ἀοιδαί.

[At all events, Odysseus paid attention to the song-makers of the Phaeacians: "but Odysseus gazed on the flashing of their feet, and he was amazed in spirit," although having many distractions and being able to say "cares have more place in my heart than songs."] (Athen. 5.181e–f = Hom., *Od.* 8.264–65, 154)

Thus, Odysseus's sensitivity to the details of Phaeacian hospitality is established, and it follows that the Deipnosophist's argument *ex silentio* is proven: it was not by accident that Telemachus fails to remark upon songs at Menelaus's festivities. Or so it may seem. Those of Athenaeus's readers who were familiar with the Homeric context would appreciate the ironical subtext. *Od.* 8.154, the source for the second quotation, ends not with ἀοιδαί but with ἄεθλοι.

This change may serve to draw the reader's own attention to the inappropriateness of the evidence. While Athenaeus suggests that ἀοιδαί may make up part of the background to a symposium and therefore escape the inattentive, the contests to which Odysseus refers were by no means a peripheral part of the celebration in the hall of Alcinous. Rather, the Phaeacian king had announced them with great fanfare and with the expressed purpose of offering a display of skill to their guest (*Od.* 8.97, 100–103). The words of the king and the change of location from the hall to the outdoors make it difficult to imagine that the passage could in any way illustrate remarkable powers of observation in Odysseus: this commotion could not escape his notice. And even if Odysseus had been inclined to let his attention drift away from these entertainments, one of the contestants forces Odysseus to confront the situation by challenging him to participate (*Od.* 8.145–48). It is in this context that Odysseus declares that his heart has little place for ἄεθλοι. These words express his intentions rather than his attention; the distractions to which Odysseus refers (Athenaeus's πολλὰ τὰ περιέλκοντα) indicate his lack of interest in the contests, not lack of awareness. Nor, even after declaring his preference for nursing his own κήδεα, is Odysseus allowed to ignore the contests. Instead, the Phaeacians' coaxing turns to insult, and he is spurred to join the games and demonstrate his athletic skill.

Athenaeus's alteration of ἄεθλοι to ἀοιδαί runs parallel to his transformation of the entertainments at the Phaeacian feast from the focus of the narrative to a background phenomenon. Furthermore, the musical components of Alcinous's hospitality, these ἀοιδαί themselves, were far from being of secondary importance. The dancing, which Athenaeus specifically identifies as something a man of little culture (τρόπον ἀγροίκων τινῶν) might overlook, is in fact announced as emphatically as the athletic contests (*Od.* 8.250–53), while the songs intoned by the bard stir Odysseus to sorrow and, eventually, lead to the revelation of his identity and story.

Thus the Phaeacian entertainments—whether ἄεθλοι or ἀοιδαί—comprise an integral part of the narrative of Book 8, and, more particularly, their effects on Odysseus's psyche is a recurrent and significant idea in this part of the epic. Athenaeus's audience would be aware of how strange it was to draw from this material to argue for Odysseus's sensitivity to his cultural surroundings. The rewriting of ἄεθλοι to ἀοιδαί, then, is a flourish accompanying one of the *Deipnosophistae*'s playfully novel "discoveries" (or perhaps "inventions") about which Athenaeus boasts.

Bréchet identifies another such "intervention volontaire sur le texte" at Athen. 10.412d–e, a context that we have already examined. The speaker has advanced the claim that "Homer also presents Odysseus as an over-eater and a glutton" (καὶ τὸν Ὀδυσσέα δὲ Ὅμηρος πολυφάγον καὶ λαίμαργον παραδίδωσιν, Athen. 10.412b). Odysseus's comments among the Phaeacians about the solace one may find in food (*Od.* 7.215–21) are adduced as evidence. The argument is then rounded off with the statement that Odysseus was worse than Sardanapalus, as well as with the following quotation:

ἤσθιεν ἁρπαλέως κρέα τ' ἄσπετα καὶ μέθυ ἡδύ.

[He greedily consumed countless pieces of meat and sweet wine.] (Athen. 10.412d)

This verse occurs nowhere in Homer, but is adapted from another, which appears a half dozen times in the *Odyssey* (9.162, 557; 10.184, 468, 477; 12.30):

ἥμεθα δαινύμενοι κρέα τ' ἄσπετα καὶ μέθυ ἡδύ.

[We sat feasting upon countless pieces of meat and sweet wine.]

Athenaeus's transformation of the original here deserves close attention.[40] The topic under discussion is the inappropriate use and valorization of food among the heroes. Seen from this angle, the original verse in each of its occurrences could hardly be less apt. This verse always reflects the communal dimension of taking a meal and emphasizes Odysseus's well-deserved position of respect and leadership in the community of the Ithacan forces returning from Troy. Thus, in *Od.* 10.184, the line in question comes at the culmination of a scene in which Odysseus bolsters the spirits of his men after the attack of the Laestrygonians by bringing them the body of a great stag he has killed. Any hint of greed or gluttony is far removed from this passage.

Likewise, in the other passages in which it occurs, the verse has similar connotations. At *Od.* 9.162, a hunt and subsequent feast serve to restore the spirits of Odysseus's men after the episode of the Lotus Eaters; his comrades have just recognized his status by awarding him an extra portion of their kill (*Od.* 9.159–60). At *Od.* 9.557, after the adventures in the cave of the Cyclops, Odysseus has found those he left behind "sitting and weeping" (*Od.* 9.545) and he comforts them by sharing the livestock taken from the monster. Again he is awarded a special portion (*Od.* 9.550–51). At *Od.* 10.468, Odysseus and his men celebrate after he forces Circe to restore those whom she has enchanted. Significantly, Odysseus had refused to eat until his men were safe. The passage at *Od.* 10.475 marks Odysseus's agreement to his men's request to leave Aeaea after their year's stay and sail for the Underworld, and *Od.* 12.30 highlights their final departure from Circe, after their journey to Hades and burial of Elpenor. In none of these passages is food used as an example of gluttony.

If we turn now to examine the other component of Athenaeus's hybrid line, we are led to suspect that its use is no more innocent than the rest of the verse. Bréchet notes that a lapse of memory is unlikely, because the adverb ἁρπαλέως occurs only twice in Homer, both times in verse-initial position, both times as an enjambment from the preceding line, and both times referring to the appetite of Odysseus.[41] Thus, we might expect it to be well-known to such Homeric experts as the deipnosophists and not liable to be confused by Athenaeus. Presumably, then, the alteration was deliberate, and it is significant that the context

40. Athenaeus quotes the line correctly at 12.513e, in a passage that argues Odysseus was a devotee of pleasure.
41. Bréchet 2007, 330: "C'est donc un nouvel hexamètre qui est forgé ici."

for each occurrence of ἁρπαλέως is directly contrary to the image of Odysseus as a proto-Sardanapalus. In the first example, Nausicaa offers a storm-tossed Odysseus food after days of deprivation:

ἦ τοι ὁ πῖνε καὶ ἦσθε πολύτλας δῖος Ὀδυσσεὺς
ἁρπαλέως· δηρὸν γὰρ ἐδητύος ἦεν ἄπαστος.

[Indeed, god-like Odysseus, the much-enduring, drank and ate greedily, for he was long without taste of food.] (Hom., *Od.* 6.249–50)

The second passage describes the disguised Odysseus at table in the hut of the swineherd Eumaeus, who has emphasized the plainness of the fare he can offer:

ἔσθιε νῦν, ὦ ξεῖνε, τά τε δμώεσσι πάρεστι,
χοίρε'· ἀτὰρ σιάλους γε σύας μνηστῆρες ἔδουσιν,
οὐκ ὄπιδα φρονέοντες ἐνὶ φρεσὶν οὐδ' ἐλεητύν.
. . . .
ὣς φάθ'· ὁ δ' ἐνδυκέως κρέα τ' ἤσθιε πῖνέ τε οἶνον,
ἁρπαλέως ἀκέων, κακὰ δὲ μνηστῆρσι φύτευεν.

["Stranger, eat now the kind of swine which is available to slaves. The suitors eat the fatted hogs, taking no account, in their hearts, of providence or pity." . . . Thus he spoke, and Odysseus ravenously ate meat and drank wine, greedily in silence, but he was nurturing evils for the suitors.] (Hom., *Od.* 14.80–82, 109–10)

In Book 6, Odysseus's greed is seen to be the result of severe want. The passage from Book 14 presents us with an Odysseus who, although he greedily eats his poor man's food, does so distractedly, with his mind on heroic deeds of destruction and revenge. Thus, the verse presented at Athen. 10.412d is an extraordinary construction: it pulls together a wide range of Homeric passages, all pertinent to the thesis at issue, but in a way that stands the evidentiary value of these references on its head.

Athenaeus's creation here can be considered a tour de force when it is understood as an effort to discover τὸ καινόν in familiar places and to produce the most surprising and paradoxical citation on the given topic. On the other hand, the impression given by this passage is quite different for those who must treat the *Deipnosophistae* as a cover text, transmitting material that is crucially important to our understanding of lost works. Not only does Athenaeus present his composite verse as if it were a verbatim quotation. This example demonstrates that even where the *Deipnosophistae* makes most emphatic claims about the meaning of a source text and the intention of its author, a reader of the original who was not involved in playing Athenaeus's game of citations might reasonably understand the significance of the cited passage as essentially the opposite of the Athenaean interpretation.

From the passages we have examined so far, we can see that the lack of correspondence between the Homeric citation and the thesis and/or paraphrase that introduces it is frequent. Such dissonance is not limited to places where Athenaeus has altered the quoted text but also occurs where the quotation itself agrees with our received text. In addition, when the citation serves to support a deipnosophist's moral point—as opposed to, for example, a lexical or grammatical one—we may consider reinterpretations and distortions of the Homeric context to be the rule and not the exception.

An example of a completely accurate quotation that misconstrues the meaning of the original occurs at Athen. 12.513d–e. Against the background of a discussion of Homer's putative hedonism, the particular claim is made:[42]

εἰσὶ δ᾽ οἵ φασι ταύτης εἶναι τῆς γνώμης τὸν Ὅμηρον, προτάττοντα τοῦ σπουδαίου βίου πολλάκις τὸν καθ᾽ ἡδονήν,

[There are some who say that Homer thinks this way, frequently preferring the life lived according to pleasure over the serious life.] (Athen. 12.513d)

To prove this point three passages are quoted with complete accuracy. None of these can reasonably be interpreted as illustrating Homer's preference for pleasure.

---

42. There is some room to doubt whether this claim and its supporting evidence are Athenaean. Gulick (ad loc.) thinks that the passage is part of a larger quotation from a certain Megacleides. A reference to that author occurs at 12.513b, where we are told that this Megacleides believed that Odysseus's praise of the Phaeacians' luxury was not sincere, but meant to gain their favor and help. Citations follow from Pindar and Sophocles; in these, the life of the sea polyp, which changes its color to suit its environment, is apparently recommended. On Gulick's view, then, the words ταύτης τῆς γνώμης here would refer to the opinion that one should adapt oneself to the prevailing views. It is difficult to see how Megacleides would have made that case from the particular passages of Homer cited. We take ταύτης τῆς γνώμης rather as pointing to a general idea, referred to several times in the near context, of an Epicurean preference for pleasure. Admittedly, the Homeric citations do not support that claim either, but that disjunction is consistent with Athenaean procedure in his *gioco*.

The first citation consists of the first three and a half lines of *Iliad* 4. These describe how the gods were holding an assembly, sitting on Zeus's golden floor and being served nectar in golden cups. Pleasure is hardly the focus, or even an important component, of the *Iliad*'s narrative here. The question before the divine assembly is of utmost seriousness: ἤ ῥ' αὖτις πόλεμόν τε κακὸν καὶ φύλοπιν αἰνὴν / ὄρσομεν, ἢ φιλότητα μετ' ἀμφοτέροισι βάλωμεν ("whether we will again stir up evil war and the dread din of battle, or put friendship between the two sides," *Il.* 4.15–16). The gods are shown, then, as concerned with matters of life and death, and, as they approach this issue, they are characterized not by pleasure, but by strong anger toward each other.[43]

The second citation comes from *Od.* 4.178–79, where Menelaus tells Telemachus how he would have liked to move Odysseus and his family from Ithaca to Argos, so that they could have spent the rest of their days together. Although the image conjured by Menelaus involves pleasure (τερπομένω), the essential point of the passage is his sorrow for the loss of Odysseus: at the end of his speech the entire company breaks down weeping. We may admit that the passage implies a preference for the pleasure of the company of friends over the pain of their absence, but sadness is the keynote and any hint of hedonism is far removed.

The third citation is the single line: ἥμεθα δαινύμενοι κρέα τ' ἄσπετα καὶ μέθυ ἡδύ. In itself, the verse only indicates that the subjects have plenty to eat and drink; there is no explicit indication of devotion to pleasure. As for the wider context, we have noted above that the line occurs several times in the *Odyssey*, where it is regularly used to describe a meal that strengthens the bonds of community between Odysseus and his men in times of unusual danger or despair. Taken together, then, the three citations do not look like a serious attempt to prove that Homer was a precursor to Epicurus, but rather like an example of Athenaeus's taste for the unexpected and paradoxical.

We may close our discussion of Athenaeus's use of Homer with a passage that may offer the most strikingly paradoxical interpretation of that author in the *Deipnosophistae*. The thesis being supported is the penchant for drunkenness among ancient rulers. As evidence, the *Odyssey*'s report on Agamemnon's death scene is cited:[44]

---

43. ἤτοι Ἀθηναίη ἀκέων ἦν οὐδέ τι εἶπε, / σκυζομένη Διὶ πατρί, χόλος δέ μιν ἄγριος ᾕρει· / Ἥρη δ' οὐκ ἔχαδε στῆθος χόλον, ἀλλὰ προσηύδα· . . . τὴν δὲ μέγ' ὀχθήσας προσέφη νεφεληγερέτα Ζεύς ("Indeed, Athena was silent, nor did she say anything, in her anger at Father Zeus, and a wild rage held her. Hera's breast did not contain her rage, but she addressed him. . . . Full of wrath, Zeus, gatherer of clouds, addressed her." Hom., *Il.* 4.22–24, 30).
44. Jacoby (*FGrH* 76) includes the words in question as part of F 15 of Duris. This attribution seems to

καὶ τὸν θάνατον δ᾽ ἀποσημαίνων τοῦ βασιλέως φησίν·

ὡς ἀμφὶ κρητῆρα τραπέζας τε πληθούσας
κείμεθα,

δεικνύων καὶ τὸν θάνατον αὐτοῦ παρ᾽ αὐταῖς ταῖς ἐπιθυμίαις τῆς μέθης
γενόμενον.

[And alluding to the king's death, he says, "We lay around the mixing bowl and heaped-up tables," showing that his death occurred in the midst of his yearning for drunkenness.] (Athen. 12.546d = Hom., *Od*. 11.419–20)

By now it will come as no surprise that there is no sign of any appetite (ἐπιθυμίαι) on the part of Agamemnon. Rather, he attends the fatal banquet at the invitation of Aegisthus, and the function of feasting as a way to strengthen social ties is evoked in the simile, which describes the slaughter of Agamemnon and his men: they were killed like swine "at a wedding or a pot-luck or a sumptuous feast" (ἢ γάμῳ ἢ ἐράνῳ ἢ εἰλαπίνῃ τεθαλυίῃ, *Od*. 11.415). It seems, then, that if the place of Agamemnon's death should suggest anything about his character, it is not drunkenness and appetition, but dutifulness in carrying out his social obligations.[45] Be that as it may, we suggest that no reader of Homer would find Athenaeus's interpretation natural or obvious; once again fidelity to the wording of the original coexists with a tendentious interpretation of its meaning.

Thus, the evidence of Homeric citation in the *Deipnosophistae* indicates that, in the case of lost works, both the quoted text and Athenaeus's interpretation must be treated with more than a little diffidence.

---

us incorrect. Indisputably, the thesis at issue and the first of the two Homeric quotations are assigned by Athenaeus to the authority of the historian. The reference to Agamemnon's death, however, is likely to be an addition by Athenaeus. In the first place, it is not unusual to find Athenaeus moving, without indication, from a citation of a named authority to material from another source. We will discuss this phenomenon later in this chapter. Secondly, while the immediate introduction to the first quotation is in indirect discourse of the infinitival type, the equivalent material for the second quotation is in direct speech. This change reflects an underlying seam. Third, the material that frames the first quotation is merely descriptive ("Achilles insults Agamemnon and says"); the second quotation is accompanied by an interpretive paraphrase ("in the midst of his longing after drunkenness"). Such guidance in finding the paradoxical meaning of a citation is, as we have seen, regular in Athenaeus. Finally, we have the paradoxical character of the quotation itself. In the quotation adduced by Duris, Achilles explicitly accuses Agamemnon of being drunk. For the second quotation, there is no similar indication in the text of the *Odyssey*. This difference in the character of the citations corresponds to a difference in their sources, and paradoxical interpretations are Athenaeus's métier.

45. In contrast, Kebric 1977, 21: "For Duris all monarchs were drunkards, and Agamemnon may have been able to prevent his death had he been sober at the time."

The picture of Athenaeus's handling of his sources is not materially changed by an examination of his citations of extant drama. In the majority of cases, especially when used in a lexical argument, quotations are precise, although there are the familiar types of discrepancies: minor alterations, unmarked ellipses, and conflations. Likewise familiar is the audacious liberty of interpretation taken by Athenaeus to support a moral point. Twice in the *Deipnosophistae*, at 7.280b–c and 12.547c, Sophocles is characterized, as was Homer, as an Epicurean authority.[46] This judgment is based in each instance on the same half dozen lines from the *Antigone*:

τῆς δ' ἡδονῆς πρὸ Ἐπικούρου εἰσηγητὴς ἐγένετο Σοφοκλῆς ὁ ποιητὴς ἐν Ἀντιγόνῃ τοιαῦτα εἰπών·

τὰς γὰρ ἡδονὰς
ὅταν προδῶσιν ἄνδρες, οὐ τίθημ' ἐγὼ
ζῆν τοῦτον, ἀλλ' ἔμψυχον ἡγοῦμαι νεκρόν.
πλούτει τε γὰρ κατ' οἶκον, εἰ βούλει, μέγα
καὶ ζῇ τύραννον σχῆμ' ἔχων· ἐὰν δ' ἀπῇ
τούτων τὸ χαίρειν, τἄλλ' ἐγὼ καπνοῦ σκιᾶς
οὐκ ἂν πριαίμην ἀνδρὶ πρὸς τὴν ἡδονήν.

[Before Epicurus, the poet Sophocles was a proponent of pleasure, saying these things in the *Antigone*: "Whenever men leave aside pleasures, I account that man as no longer alive, but rather I consider him to be an animate corpse. Heap up great wealth in your house, if you want to, and cut the figure of a tyrant. But if joy is missing from these things, then I would not buy the rest from a man for the shadow of smoke, compared with pleasure."] (Athen. 12.547c = Soph., *Ant.* 1165–71)

The quotation is made with near-perfect accuracy,[47] but, once again, the suggested interpretation would be perverse, if seriously intended. Athenaeus advances this passage as parallel to Epicurean sentiments such as "the begin-

---

46. At 7.280b, the introductory thesis statement reads: πρότερος δὲ τοῦ Ἐπικούρου Σοφοκλῆς ὁ τραγῳδιοποιὸς ἐν Ἀντιγόνῃ περὶ τῆς ἡδονῆς τοιαῦτα εἴρηκεν ("But before Epicurus, Sophocles, the tragedian, said the following about pleasure in the *Antigone*").

47. The Sophocles manuscript is corrected by most editors, following Seyffert, to read καὶ γὰρ ἡδοναί. Some editors maintain the ἀνδρός, the most common manuscript reading (one reads ἄνδρας), though some adopt the Athenaean ἄνδρες.

ning and root of all good is the pleasure of the belly" (ἀρχὴ καὶ ῥίζα παντὸς ἀγαθοῦ ἡ τῆς γαστρὸς ἡδονή, Athen. 7.280a) and "I spit upon the Good and those who marvel at it, when it produces no pleasure" (προσπτύω τῷ καλῷ καὶ τοῖς κενῶς αὐτὸ θαυμάζουσιν, ὅταν μηδεμίαν ἡδονὴν ποιῇ, Athen. 12.547a). But any reader who recognizes these lines of the *Antigone* could also be expected to see how inappropriate they are as evidence of hedonism. They come from a messenger speech in which we are told that catastrophe has befallen the house of Creon through the death of Haemon. The messenger laments human weakness before the tides of fortune, noting in particular how Creon, now cast down, was recently envied for his pleasures. These pleasures, we should note, are explicitly contrasted with wealth and the accoutrements of a tyrant; they are thus distinct from the vulgar corporeal pleasures commonly associated with Epicurus. In fact, the messenger had identified these ἡδοναί quite clearly in the immediately preceding lines:

> Κρέων γὰρ ἦν ζηλωτός, ὡς ἐμοί, ποτέ,
> σώσας μὲν ἐχθρῶν τήνδε Καδμείαν χθόνα,
> λαβών τε χώρας παντελῆ μοναρχίαν
> ηὔθυνε, θάλλων εὐγενεῖ τέκνων σπορᾷ·
> καὶ νῦν ἀφεῖται πάντα.

> [Once Creon was, in my opinion, envied: he saved the land of Cadmus from its enemies. He took complete and sole rule over the country and set it on a straight course. He flourished with a noble crop of children. Now all these things are lost.] (Soph., *Ant.* 1161–65)

Omitting this context allows Athenaeus to transform the most un-Epicurean of activities—fighting for one's country, governing justly, and raising children—into a hedonism that rates everything except pleasure as "the shadow of smoke." Again, the *Deipnosophistae* turns the meaning of an authority on its head in the interests of τὸ καινόν.

An examination of Athenaeus's use of extant prose sources confirms the picture already evident. We may concentrate primarily on the works of Herodotus and Xenophon, since Athenaeus's treatment of these authors has recently been the subject of careful reevaluation.[48] As was the case for Homer, we find

---

48. Herodotus: Lenfant 2007b; Xenophon: Maisonneuve 2007 ; both: Ambaglio 1990.

passages in which the text of the citation deviates only slightly from the original, but with a significant change in the sense. For example, Book 14 of the *Deipnosophistae* opens with a presentation of evidence associating wine drinking with madness; among the authorities is Xenophon:

μέθης μὲν ἀπέχεσθαι ὁμοίως ᾤετο χρῆναι καὶ μανίας, σίτων δὲ ὑπερκαίρων ὁμοίως καὶ ἀργίας.

[He thought that he should avoid drunkenness like madness and too much food like laziness.] (Athen. 14.613c)

The quotation comes from Xenophon, *Agesilaus* 5.1, where the text is a bit different:

μέθης μὲν ἀποσχέσθαι ὁμοίως ᾤετο χρῆναι καὶ λαιμαργίας, σίτων δ᾽ ὑπὲρ καιρὸν ὁμοίως [ὡς] καὶ ἁμαρτίας.

[He thought he should avoid drunkenness like gluttony and excessive eating like a failure.]

Without the change of λαιμαργίας for μανίας, the citation would not be pertinent to Athenaeus's argument.[49]

We might attribute these differences to accidental causes if it were not for the fact that something quite similar occurred just a few lines before this passage. At 14.613b, Athenaeus elaborates the *Odyssey*'s claim that the centaur Eurytion, "when he had ruined his heart with wine, running mad, did evil in the house of Perithous."[50] A quotation from Herodotus adds to this story's probability:[51]

κατιόντος γοῦν τοῦ οἴνου ἐς τὸ σῶμα, ὥς φησιν Ἡρόδοτος, ἐπαναπλέει κακὰ ἔπεα καὶ μαινόμενα.

---

49. Kaibel notes: "mutila haec et quae secuntur."
50. ... ὃ δ᾽ ἐπεὶ φρένας ἄασεν οἴνῳ, / μαινόμενος κάκ᾽ ἔρεξε δόμοις ἐνὶ Πειριθόοιο (Athen. 14.613a = Hom., *Od.* 21.297–98).
51. Lenfant (2007b, 49) classifies this passage as a paraphrase rather than a "citation littérale" even though the differences from the original are quite minor: κατιόντος τοῦ οἴνου ἐς τὸ σῶμα ἐπαναπλέειν ὑμῖν ἔπεα κακά (Hdt. 1.212.2). Athenaeus has merely changed the verb to the infinitive, inverted ἔπεα and κακά and omitted ὑμῖν. We might therefore be tempted to categorize this citation as literal, and a consideration of this point highlights the how difficult it is to produce even a basic classification system for citations.

[Evidentially, when the wine goes down into the body, as Herodotus says, evil and crazy words float up in return.] (Athen. 14.613b)

The last two words of the citation are an addition and do not appear in Herodotus 1.212.2. Lenfant is partially correct in pointing out that Athenaeus's modification does not misrepresent Herodotus's meaning, since the *Histories* had just explicitly linked "l'abus de vin à la folie" at Hdt. 1.212.2: ἀμπελίνῳ καρπῷ, τῷ περ αὐτοὶ ἐμπιπλάμενοι μαίνεσθε οὕτως ὥστε κατιόντος τοῦ οἴνου κτλ. ("by means of the fruit of the vine, with which you fill yourselves up and go crazy, so that when the wine goes down . . .").[52] Nonetheless, the passage is a distortion, not of the original's meaning, but of its authority. The cited words are not spoken by Herodotus as narrator, but are attributed to Queen Tomyris. The alteration of μαίνεσθε to μαινόμενα, while it does not materially change the meaning of the original, has the effect of obscuring from the reader the fact that sentiment comes from a reported speech. If we observe that the other principal modification of the original is the omission of ὑμῖν, it seems probable that shifting authority from Tomyris to the historian himself was precisely Athenaeus's intention. Thus, scholars who work with Athenaean fragments must be aware that the *Deipnosophistae* may deliberately elide indications that the words of a citation do not necessarily represent the views of the author to whom it is attributed.

Thus, in both the quotation from the *Histories* and from the *Agesilaus* it seems that the original wording has been adjusted to better fit Athenaeus's literary conceit. In his study of Athenaeus's use of Herodotus, Thucydides, and Xenophon, Ambaglio finds side-by-side distortions of sense and "la riproduzione esatta di un testo."[53] Athenaeus used information attested by a historian to support the argument of the *Deipnosophistae*, without regard for whether such a use was consistent with the meaning of the passage in its original context.[54] For example, at 6.75, Herodotus relates the suicide of Cleomenes of Sparta, who, though physically restrained and under guard, managed to obtain a knife and fatally mutilate himself. Athenaeus cites this passage tendentiously: ὅτι δὲ διὰ μέθην ἑαυτὸν καὶ μαχαίρᾳ κατέτεμεν Ἡρόδοτος ἱστόρησε ("Herodotus reports that he cut himself up with a knife out of drunkenness," Athen. 10.436e–f). Although there is no indication in the Herodotus text that Cleomenes was drunk,

---

52. Lenfant (2007b, 62). She argues (58 n. 62) that this misattribution "résulte plus de l'absence de contextualisation que d'une intention délibérée d'Athénée."
53. Ambaglio 1990, 52.
54. Ambaglio 1990, 53: Athenaeus "in questo caso come altrove, mostra di usare il testo di Erodoto senza riguardo alcuno per il suo significato."

and further, although Athenaeus knew of *Histories* 6.84, where Herodotus rejects the Spartan tradition that Cleomenes' madness was caused by a preference for strong wine that he learned from the Scythians, Athenaeus clearly implies that it was Herodotus's view that Cleomenes acted out of drunkenness.[55]

Elsewhere, the original is subjected to more extensive alteration. A striking examples come from Book 13, where Myrtilus, one of the dinner guests, raises the subject of liaisons between philosophers and prostitutes. After relating a story about how the painter Apelles predicted a career as a hetaera for a certain young girl, Myrtilus adds this surprising parallel:

τὸ δ᾽ αὐτὸ καὶ Σωκράτης ἐμαντεύσατο περὶ Θεοδότης τῆς Ἀθηναίας, ὥς φησι Ξενοφῶν ἐν Ἀπομνημονεύμασιν· ὅτι δὲ καλλίστη εἴη καὶ στέρνα κρείττω λόγου παντὸς ἔχοι λέγοντός <τινος>[56], ἰτέον ἡμῖν, ἔφη, θεασομένοις τὴν γυναῖκα· οὐ γὰρ δὴ ἀκούουσιν ἔστιν κρῖναι τὸ κάλλος.

[Socrates, too, made the same prophecy about Theodote the Athenian, as Xenophon says in the *Memorabilia*: with someone saying that she was most beautiful and that her breasts were better than any words, he said, "We must go and look at this woman, for beauty cannot be judged by hearsay."] (Athen. 13.588d)

A comparison with the text of Xenophon shows that Socrates makes no prophecy concerning the young woman, nor does he say anything that may be construed as a prediction of her "beauty in the service of future pleasure."[57] In addition, the quotation itself sharply twists the tone of the original:

. . . τινὸς καὶ εἰπόντος ὅτι κρεῖττον εἴη λόγου τὸ κάλλος τῆς γυναικός, καὶ ζωγράφους φήσαντος εἰσιέναι πρὸς αὐτὴν ἀπεικασομένους, οἷς ἐκείνην ἐπιδεικνύειν ἑαυτῆς ὅσα καλῶς ἔχοι, ἰτέον ἂν εἴη θεασομένους . . .

[. . . and with someone saying that the woman's beauty was better than words, and relating that painters were coming to her residence to take her likeness, to

55. Herodotus indicates that he prefers the explanation of the majority of Greeks, according to which Cleomenes was driven mad as divine retribution for tampering with the Oracle. Athenaeus quotes from this passage (6.84) at 10.427b, where he is interested in the Scythian connection.
56. Added by Kaibel.
57. Athen. 13.588d: αὐτὴν εἰς μέλλουσαν ἀπόλαυσιν . . . καλὴν. These are Apelles' words, which it is claimed Socrates reiterates (τὸ αὐτό). For a useful discussion of this passage, see Maisonneuve 2007, 92–93.

whom she displayed as much of herself as was fitting, he said, "We must go to look. . . ."] (Xen., *Mem.* 3.11.1)

By changing Theodote's ineffable quality from her "beauty" to her "breasts," Athenaeus has, as Maisonneuve says, transformed Socrates from a "inquisitive philosopher" to a "dirty old man."[58]

We also find examples in which an accurate quotation is given an interpretation at odds with its original meaning. A whimsically comic example comes from Athen. 3.78e, in a discussion of the extraordinarily useful nature of the fig:

ὁ δὲ θαυμασιώτατος καὶ μελίγηρυς Ἡρόδοτος ἐν τῇ πρώτῃ τῶν ἱστοριῶν καὶ μέγα ἀγαθόν φησιν εἶναι τὰ σῦκα οὑτωσὶ λέγων· βασιλεῦ, σὺ δ' ἐπ' ἄνδρας τοιούτους παρασκευάζεαι στρατεύεσθαι, οἳ σκυτίνας μὲν ἀναξυρίδας, σκυτίνην δὲ τὴν ἄλλην ἐσθῆτα φορέουσι . . . οὐ σῦκα ἔχουσι τρώγειν, οὐκ ἄλλο οὐθὲν ἀγαθόν.

[The most wonderful and sweet-voiced Herodotus in the first book of the *Histories* also says that figs are a great good, in the following words: "My King, you are preparing a campaign against the kind of men who wear leather trousers, and the rest of their clothes are leather too. . . . They have no figs to eat, nor any other good thing."]

Lenfant acutely remarks that Athenaeus is not genuinely misleading in his introductory words, since any reader, even one unfamiliar with the *Histories*, would know to mistrust the Athenaean interpretation on the basis of the obvious lack of fit between introduction and quotation. However, this same naïve reader, as Lenfant also notes, might assume that Herodotus addressed himself to a king, indeed the king of the Persians, given Athenaeus's immediately preceding reference to the *Persae* of Pherecrates.[59] The words are actually those of the Lydian Sandanis to his king Croesus on the folly of attacking these same Persians.

More insidious is Athenaeus's citation of Herodotus at 12.541b about Smindyrides:

---

58. Maissonneuve 2007, 93: "De philosophe curieux . . . en personnage égrillard intéressé par les courtisanes."
59. Lenfant 2007b, 60–61 with n. 72.

περὶ δὲ Σμινδυρίδου τοῦ Συβαρίτου καὶ τῆς τούτου τρυφῆς ἱστόρησεν
Ἡρόδοτος ἐν τῇ ἕκτῃ . . . ἀπὸ μὲν Ἰταλίης <ἦλθε>[60] Σμινδυρίδης ὁ Ἱπποκράτεος
Συβαρίτης, ὃς ἐπὶ πλεῖστον δὴ χλιδῆς εἰς ἀνὴρ ἀφίκετο.

[Concerning Smindyrides the Sybarite and his *truphē,* Herodotus in the sixth
book relates. . . . "From Italy <came> Smindyrides, son of Hippocrates, a Sybarite, who had outdistanced all others in his degree of ornamentation."]

Unlike the previous passage, there is no obvious conflict between interpretation
and text. In fact, Athenaeus scarcely seems to offer an interpretation at all, but
merely a setting of the scene. Only a careful comparison with the original reveals that Athenaeus has altered the meaning of the Herodotean text. There,
Smindyrides is listed among a group of men who are vying for recognition as
"the best man of all the Greeks" (Hdt. 6.126.1). Smindyrides' χλιδή seems to be
mentioned as part of his claim to that title.[61] Thus, to characterize the passage
as being about the Sybarite's τρυφή—a term generally pejorative in Athenaeus's
day—is to misconstrue Herodotus, but subtly and in a manner that would be
undetectable if the *Histories* had not survived.

Athen. 4.150f–151e presents a lengthy and literal quotation from *Anabasis*
7.3.21–33. Xenophon's subject is a banquet held to seal an alliance between the
Greek mercenaries and the Thracian leader Seuthes. Generally, Athenaeus re-
produces the passage quite accurately, but he also omits a good deal of material.
Strictly speaking, the material left out was irrelevant to his purpose of describing the customs of the Thracian at table. All the same, these omissions change
the character of the original text.

Xenophon introduces the episode in words that make clear its politico-
military character:

---

60. Kaibel supplies this word from the Herodotean original.
61. Contrary to the supposed connection between luxury and effeminacy, Herodotus apparently means
us to understand Smindyrides as taking part in contests to show his physical excellence: ἐνθαῦτα
Ἑλλήνων ὅσοι σφίσι τε αὐτοῖσι ἦσαν καὶ πάτρῃ ἐξωγκωμένοι, ἐφοίτων μνηστῆρες· τοῖσι Κλεισθένης
καὶ δρόμον καὶ παλαίστρην ποιησάμενος ἐπ᾽ αὐτῷ τούτῳ εἶχε ("Thereupon, those of the Greeks who
were proud of themselves and their country came as suitors. For his purpose, Cleisthenes set up races
and wrestling matches for them." Hdt. 6.126.3). This sentence occurs immediately before mention of
Smindyrides; no incompatibility between χλιδή and manly virtues is implied. Nenci (1998, 306) calls
Smindyrides "un sibarita famoso per la sua mollezza." This may have been true in Athenaeus's day,
but, as we have shown in Chapter 1, there is no good evidence for a fifth-century association between
softness and either Smindyrides in particular or Sybaris in general.

ἐπεὶ δὲ εἰσῆλθον ἐπὶ τὸ δεῖπνον τῶν τε Θρᾳκῶν οἱ κράτιστοι τῶν παρόντων καὶ
οἱ στρατηγοὶ καὶ οἱ λοχαγοὶ τῶν Ἑλλήνων καὶ εἴ τις πρεσβεία παρῆν ἀπὸ
πόλεως, . . .

[When there had arrived for the dinner the mightiest of the Thracians who
were at hand and the generals and the captains of the Greeks and any embassy
from a city that was present. . . .] (Xen., *Anab.* 7.3.21)

In Athenaeus, this becomes: ἐπειδὴ δὲ εἰσῆλθον ἐπὶ τὸ δεῖπνον πάντες ("when
everyone had arrived for the dinner"). Then follows, in an accurate quotation,
descriptions of the seating arrangement of the guests, the manner in which the
food was served, and later, a custom requiring guests to give gifts to Seuthes.
The climax of the story comes when Xenophon, at a loss to give his host a suitable gift, offers the Thracian a pledge. Here is Athenaeus's version:

Ξενοφῶν δὲ ἀνέστη θαρσαλέως καὶ δεξάμενος τὸ κέρας εἶπεν· ἐγώ σοι, ὦ
Σεύθη, δίδωμι ἐμαυτὸν καὶ τοὺς ἐμοὺς τούτους ἑταίρους φίλους εἶναι πιστοὺς
καὶ οὐδένα ἄκοντα. καὶ νῦν πάρεισιν οὐδέν σε προσαιτοῦντες, ἀλλὰ καὶ πονεῖν
ὑπὲρ σοῦ καὶ προκινδυνεύειν βουλόμενοι. καὶ ὁ Σεύθης ἀναστὰς συνέπιε καὶ
συγκατεσκεδάσατο μετ᾽ αὐτοῦ τὸ κέρας. μετὰ δὲ ταῦτα εἰσῆλθον κέρασί τε
οἵοις σημαίνουσιν αὐλοῦντες καὶ σάλπιγξιν ὠμοβοείαις ῥυθμούς τε καὶ οἱονεὶ
μάγαδιν σαλπίζοντες.

[But Xenophon stood boldly and taking the horn said, "Seuthes, I give you myself and these companions of mine to be your faithful friends, and none unwilling. And now they are all here asking nothing of you, but are willing to toil and
face danger on your behalf." Standing up, Seuthes drank with him and joined
him in sprinkling out the horn. After this came in pipers playing on horns such
as those used for signals and trumpets of raw oxhide; they played rhythms and
a *magadis* as it were.] (Athen. 4.151d–e)

Here, the role to which Xenophon commits himself and his companions remains unspecified. Perhaps they will be part of Seuthes' entourage and serve
him as courtiers and companions. The hint of their true purpose implicit in
πονεῖν καὶ προκινδυνεύειν is quickly left behind with the arrival of the musicians. Not so in the original, where, between the offer and its acceptance, the
value to the Thracian of Xenophon and company is made explicit:

μεθ᾽ ὧν, ἂν οἱ θεοὶ θέλωσι, πολλὴν χώραν τὴν μὲν ἀπολήψῃ πατρῴαν οὖσαν, τὴν δὲ κτήσῃ, πολλοὺς δὲ ἵππους, πολλοὺς δὲ ἄνδρας καὶ γυναῖκας καλὰς κτήσῃ, οὓς οὐ λήζεσθαί σε δεήσει, ἀλλ᾽ αὐτοὶ φέροντες παρέσονται πρὸς σὲ δῶρα.

[With them, if the gods are willing, you will get hold of much land; you will get that belonging to your father and you will take possession of other land besides. You will take possession of many horses, many men and beautiful women. These you will not need to carry off as plunder, but my men will come to you bearing them as gifts.] (Xen., *Anab.* 7.3.31)

Thus, by means of a few well chosen cuts, Athenaeus presents his readers with a Xenophon and Seuthes who appear "comme de pacifiques banqueteurs, partageant mets et divertissements à la mode thrace, et non plus comme le prince ambitieux ou le général mercenaire qu'ils étaient en réalité."[62] In a sly and skillful manner, Athenaeus has made the focus of his *Deipnosophistae* and Xenophon's *Anabasis* merge and become one and the same: Θρᾳκίων δὲ δείπνων μνημονεύει Ξενοφῶν ἐν ζ Ἀναβάσεως ("Xenophon calls to mind Thracian dinners in Book 7 of the *Anabasis*," Athen. 4.150f). Once again we may observe that while Athenaeus's ability to present Thracian dinners as the subject of this part of the original may have seemed to a contemporary readership to be a sign of his wit and literary panache, it also exemplifies one more way in which we may be led astray when we must reconstruct lost texts on the basis of the *Deipnosophistae*.

Thus, even with literal quotations, Athenaeus can give a reinterpretation that can be dangerous for the unwary. When the citation is a paraphrase, Athenaeus's imagination is under less restraint, and the result can be wildly at odds with the meaning of the original. The most notorious example is from Book 6 of Athenaeus, in a section that gathers evidence for the lack of precious metals among the ancients: σπάνιος γὰρ ὄντως ἦν τὸ παλαιὸν παρὰ τοῖς Ἕλλησιν ὁ μὲν χρυσός ("In antiquity, gold was really rare among the Greeks," Athen. 6.231b). Athenaeus treats this topic with the lack of seriousness it deserves, offering a series of largely frivolous citations.[63] Among these is an example drawn from Book 2 of Herodotus:

---

62. Maisonneuve 2007, 94.
63. Take, for example, the first item of evidence following immediately after the contention that the ancients had little gold: διὸ καὶ Φίλιππον τὸν τοῦ μεγάλου βασιλέως Ἀλεξάνδρου πατέρα φησὶν Δοῦρις ὁ Σάμιος φιάλιον χρυσοῦν κεκτημένον ἀεὶ τοῦτ᾽ ἔχειν κείμενον ὑπὸ τὸ προσκεφάλαιον ("For that reason Duris of Samos says that Philip, the father of King Alexander the Great, always kept a small golden saucer that he owned stashed under his pillow." Athen. 6.231b–c). Leaving aside other considerations, from our observations of Athenaeus's method of citation it is clear that it was he, and not

Ἡρόδοτός τέ φησι τοὺς Αἰγυπτίων ἱερεῖς χαλκοῖς ποτηρίοις πίνειν, τοῖς τε
βασιλεῦσιν αὐτῶν θύουσί ποτε κοινῇ οὐχ εὑρεθῆναι πᾶσι δοθῆναι φιάλας
ἀργυρᾶς· Ψαμμήτιχον γοῦν νεώτερον ὄντα τῶν ἄλλων βασιλέων χαλκῇ φιάλῃ
σπεῖσαι τῶν ἄλλων ἀργυραῖς σπενδόντων.

[And Herodotus says that the Egyptian priests drink from bronze cups, and
once, when their kings were sacrificing together, silver bowls could not be
found to give to all of them. Psammetichus, at any rate, being younger than the
other kings, made his libation with a bronze bowl, while the others used silver.]
(Athen. 6.231d)

This narrative is a serious distortion of Herodotus 2.151; indeed, Lenfant suggests that, if Herodotus were not explicitly mentioned as the source, modern
scholars would not allow the attribution.[64] To mention only the main difference, in the original passage the chief priest, through an oversight, provided all
the kings except Psammetichus with golden bowls, so that king poured his libation from his bronze helmet. The fact that the bowls were golden in the original
belies Athenaeus's premise, so he transforms them into silver.

This citation has provoked a variety of comments. Pelling, for one, does not
find plausible Brunt's assumption that Athenaeus has simply misremembered
the passage: "Is it not too much of a coincidence that this bizarre lapse of memory happens to provide Athenaeus . . . with exactly what he wants for his
argument?"[65] While Pelling finds evidence for a practice of deliberate manipu-

---

Duris, who saw a causal link (διὸ) between Philip's behavior and the scarcity of gold. From Duris Athenaeus drew, then, the story of the tableware under the pillow, but suppressed any reason his source might
have suggested to explain the phenomenon. Duris's purpose in relating this information is perhaps dis-
cernable in the doublet of this fragment cited at Athen. 4.155d: ἐπιλελησμένοι δ᾽ ἦσαν οὗτοι, ὡς καὶ
Δοῦρις ἱστορεῖ, ὅτι καὶ Φίλιππος ὁ τοῦ Ἀλεξάνδρου πατὴρ ποτήριον χρυσοῦν ὁλκὴν ἄγον πεντήκοντα
δραχμὰς κεκτημένος τοῦτο ἐλάμβανε κοιμώμενος ἀεὶ καὶ πρὸς κεφαλὴν αὐτοῦ κατετίθετο ("But these
men had forgotten, as Duris too recounts, that Philip, the father of Alexander, possessing a golden cup
weighing fifty drachmas, always took along when he went to bed and set it by his head."). The fragment
here contrasts the prodigality of the courtiers of Alexander (the οὗτοι of the opening words) with the
forgotten frugality of Philip. If, as is by no means certain, this point was made by Duris himself, we must
recognize in Athen. 6.231b–c another example of an Athenaean citation standing the meaning of the
original on its head. The forgetfulness of Alexander's friends consisted in wrapping food in gold foil,
which was eventually discarded with the trash. Thus, this passage of Duris may have occurred in connection with an anecdote based on the existence of a superabundance of gold. This interpretation is open to
doubt, particularly since Athenaeus cites not Duris, but Agatharchides, for the story of the gold foil. What
is certain is that Athenaeus cites the same original both in a context which takes for granted the wealth of
τὸ παλαιόν in gold and its lack thereof. Once again, his whimsical virtuosity is startling.
64. Lenfant 2007b, 57.
65. Pelling 2000, 185. Brunt (1980, 480) characterizes this change as "not very serious" based on the
   presumption that Athenaeus "wrote from memory."

lation, Lenfant discounts the implications of this citation; for her, it is a "cas singulier," and its interpretation should not affect our view of the other Herodotean fragments.[66] We find Pelling's position more defensible, for while Lenfant may be correct that there is no close parallel for such a misrepresentation among Athenaeus's citations of Herodotus, we have seen him sharply alter the meaning of passages from Homer, Sophocles, and Xenophon.[67] We view this transformation of Herodotus as an extreme example of Athenaeus's game of novel interpretation.

Thus, we see how Athenaeus's alterations and reinterpretations of many of the texts he cites can be understood in terms of his avowed search for novelty and discovery. Because we may assume that Athenaeus expects his readers to be familiar with Homer and the other original sources, it seems likely that his manipulations were intended to be recognized and his ingenuity admired. For the modern reader, on the other hand, the reaction to Athenaeus's literary sleight-of-hand may be quite different. Deliberately altered texts occur alongside verbatim quotations; among straightforward and uncontroversial interpretations appear willfully perverse misunderstandings of the force of the original. These circumstances reveal just how tentative and provisional we must consider any text that is reconstructed primarily on the basis of the *Deipnosophistae*.

---

66. Lenfant 2007b, 57.
67. Lenfant (2007b, 57 with n. 57) believes that this fragment has "le caractère étrange et corrompu" arising from its "indéniable incohérence interne." The line of thought in the passage is admittedly difficult, but Pelling (2000, 185) points the way toward a plausible solution. First of all, the thesis to be proven is announced: at one time, "those considered very rich drank from bronze cups" (ἐκ ποτηρίων δὲ χαλκῶν ἔπινον οἱ σφόδρα δοκοῦντες πλουτεῖν, Athen. 6.231d). Next, an interpretive paraphrase of the evidence is given: Ἡρόδοτός τέ φησι τοὺς Αἰγυπτίων ἱερεῖς χαλκοῖς ποτηρίοις πίνειν (Athen. 6.231d). Note that the citation is to chosen in order to show that in Herodotus the Egyptian priests used bronze cups. These seem to be the οἱ σφόδρα δοκοῦντες πλουτεῖν just mentioned. The fact that eleven of the Egyptian kings were given silver bowls for the libation does not seem to contribute directly to the argument. Rather, the claim that the priests used bronze is substantiated (the inference is indicated by γοῦν) by the fact that Psammetichus poured his libation from a bronze bowl. As Pelling suggests, this seems to imply that, lacking the ceremonial bowl, the priests provided one of their own cups. Lenfant is incorrect in saying that the passage relates that, in the absence of bronze cups, the kings used silver. The only absence applies to Psammetichus alone, and it was made good with bronze. Nor is the γοῦν-clause "contradictoire" to the point it supports; as frequently in Athenaeus γοῦν (Olson ad loc. prints οὖν here) marks the specific textual basis of a generalization, and the statement Ψαμμήτιχον χαλκῇ φιάλη σπεῖσαι contradicts neither the statement that the priests drank from bronze cups nor that the very wealthy did the same. Thus we cannot follow Lenfant in assuming "un texte mal transmis."

Formulae of Citation

Given, then, that Athenaeus's citations range from extremely precise verbatim quotations to wildly inaccurate paraphrases and summaries, the question arises whether there is any reliable a priori way to distinguish among types of citation based on formal aspects of the text of the *Deipnosophistae*. Drawing on her detailed examination of Athenaeus's use of Herodotus, Lenfant has tried to correlate the type of citation with the words used to introduce it. Focusing on these "formules d'insertion" such as ἱστορεῖ + infinitive, φησὶν ὅτι, ὥς φησιν Ἡρόδοτος, and the like, Lenfant has made the following observations:

(a) The verb ἱστορεῖ logically indicates a reformulation (i.e., a paraphrase or summary/allusion).

(b) Indirect discourse of the accusative+infinitive type is the sign of a paraphrase or, sometimes, a summary.

(c) Direct discourse interrupted or followed by the formula ὥς φησιν corresponds to a paraphrase.

(d) A statement introduced by φησιν ὥς, φησιν ὅτι, or φησί preceded by a simple reference to a source followed by a syntactic break is marked as being a literal quotation. In one case, a few words of paraphrase precede the quotation.

(e) The occurrence of οὕτως before the material indicates a literal citation.

(f) The occurrence of φησίν used parenthetically within a statement indicates a verbatim quotation. If the parenthesis is located in the middle of a passage, it indicates the transition from paraphrase to verbatim quotation.[68]

Lenfant's work marks a significant advance in its clarity and precision. An examination of a more extensive body of Athenaean citations, however, con-

---

68. Lenfant 2007b, 50–53. Her example for this last usage is Athen. 6.261c: Ἡρόδοτος δέ φησιν Ἄμασιν Αἰγυπτίων βασιλέα παιγνιήμονα ἐόντα σκώπτειν τοὺς συμπότας, καὶ ὅτε ἰδιώτης, φησίν, ἦν, φιλοπότης ὑπῆρχε καὶ φιλοσκώμμων καὶ οὐ κατεσπουδασμένος ἀνήρ ("Herodotus says that Amasis, while king of the Egyptians, was a jokester and mocked his drinking companions, and when he was a private citizen was already a drinker and a lover of insults and was not a serious man."). Herodotus says at 2.174: λέγεται δὲ ὁ Ἄμασις, καί ὅτε ἦν ἰδιώτης, ὡς φιλοπότης ἦν καὶ φιλοσκώμμων καὶ οὐδαμῶς κατεσπουδασμένος ἀνήρ ("It is said that Amasis, even when he was a private citizen, acted like a drinker and a lover of insults and was in no way a serious man"). Material from 2.173 is paraphrased in the first half of the sentence.

firms the suspicion that conclusions based on such a limited sample of data can reveal general tendencies, but not rules firm enough to bring much confidence in any situation when we cannot compare a fragment to its original.

Already Maisonneuve, in the same volume of conference proceedings in which Lenfant's study appears, has produced a set of citations from Xenophon that serve as counter-examples to some of Lenfant's points. One passage from Athen. 11.476c will suffice for our purposes.

καὶ Ξενοφῶν δ᾿ ἐν τῇ ζ᾿ τῆς Ἀναβάσεως διηγούμενος τὸ παρὰ τῷ Θρᾳκὶ Σεύθῃ συμπόσιον γράφει οὕτως· ἐπεὶ δὲ Ξενοφῶν σὺν τοῖς μετ᾿ αὐτοῦ εἰσῆλθε πρὸς τὸν Σεύθην, ἠσπάζοντο μὲν πρῶτον ἀλλήλους καὶ κατὰ τὸν Θράκιον νόμον κέρατα οἴνου προύτεινον.

[And Xenophon in the seventh book of the Anabasis, telling about the symposium at the home of the Thracian Seuthes, writes thus: "When Xenophon and those with him entered Seuthes' place, first they greeted each other and held out horns of wine according to the Thracian custom."] (Athen. 11.476b–c)

This is a citation of *Anabasis* 7.2.23, and, while from ἠσπάζοντο to the end it is essentially a verbatim quotation, the preceding clause is a paraphrase rather than a quotation. The *Anabasis* reads:

ἐπεὶ δ᾿ ἐγγὺς ἦσαν, ἐκέλευσεν εἰσελθεῖν Ξενοφῶντα ἔχοντα δύο οὓς βούλοιτο. ἐπειδὴ δ᾿ ἔνδον ἦσαν, ἠσπάζοντο . . .

[When they were close by, he ordered Xenophon to come in and bring any two companions that he might wish. When they were inside, they greeted . . .] (Xen., *Anab.* 7.2.23)

Here, Athenaeus's paraphrase in no way distorts the meaning of the original, but merely simplifies it to fit into his own context. Yet the fact remains that, according to the data from Herodotean citations, we have a right to expect that the citation consists of literal quotation and not a mixture of quotation and paraphrase. In particular, the citation is introduced by the formula γράφει οὕτως followed by a syntactic break. The presence of paraphrase thus violates Lenfant's generalization e) (οὕτως) and, *mutatis mutandis*, d), since

Maisonneuve shows that γράφει is functionally equivalent to φησί as a formula of citation.[69]

If we expand our data to include not only citations of Herodotus and Xenophon, but other extant prose authors as well, we find that the uses of φησί and similar words do usually indicate literal quotation, but exceptions occur. Discoursing on vegetables in Book 9, Athenaeus calls upon the authority of Theophrastus in words that should indicate a close quotation: Θεόφραστος δὲ οὕτως γράφει· τῆς δὲ ῥαφάνου (λέγω δὲ τὴν κράμβην) ἢ μέν ἐστιν οὐλόφυλλος, ἢ δὲ ἀγρία ("Theophrastus writes thus: 'One kind of *rhaphanus* (I mean cabbage) is crinkly-leaved, the other wild.'" Athen. 9.369f). The reference is to *Hist. pl.* 7.4.4, and the citation turns out to be a loose paraphrase: τῆς δὲ ῥαφάνου τριχῇ διαιρουμένης, οὐλοφύλλου τε καὶ λειοφύλλου καὶ τρίτης τῆς ἀγρίας ("with the *rhaphanus* divided into three kinds, crinkly-leaved, smooth-leaved, and wild"). A particularly telling example occurs at Athen. 7.317d–e, where Athenaeus discusses the reproduction of polyps at some length, employing Aristotle as his main source and introducing him thus: ἐν δὲ πέμπτῳ μορίων φησὶν Ἀριστοτέλης· πουλύπους ὀχεύει τοῦ χειμῶνος . . . ("Aristotle in the fifth book of the *Parts [of Animals]* says: 'The polyp copulates in the winter . . .'"). What follows is not the verbatim quotation we would expect, but a mixture of several quotations bound together with some paraphrase. This conglomeration is derived from three different passages in the original (*Hist. An.* 544a6 ff., 549b31 ff., and 550b4 ff.).[70]

Not only φησίν + a syntactic break, but also φησιν ὅτι as a sign of a "citation littérale" admits of counterexample. Book 8 includes a lengthy tirade against the ἀκρίβεια of Aristotle, which includes the following passage:

φησὶν γὰρ ὅτι κήρυκες μὲν καὶ πάντα τὰ ὀστρακόδερμα ἀνόχευτον αὐτῶν ἐστι τὸ γένος καὶ ὅτι ἡ πορφύρα καὶ ὁ κῆρυξ μακρόβια. ζῆν γὰρ τὴν πορφύραν ἔτη ἓξ πόθεν τοῦτο οἶδε;

---

69. Maisonneuve (2007, 83 with n. 24) indicates that it is not just οὕτως that may indicate an exact quotation, but a group of demonstratives, including (for Xenophon citations) τάδε, οὑτωσί, τοιαυτί, ὧδε, and ταῦτα. However, the occurrence of such words does not necessarily guarantee that the citation is "textuellement." Witness Athen. 14.640e: Πλάτων ἐν τῷ Ἀτλαντικῷ μεταδόρπια αὐτὰ καλεῖ ἐν τούτοις ("Plato in his story of Atlantis calls it [dessert] *metadorpia*, using these words . . ."). In spite of ἐν τούτοις, the citation is a paraphrase of Plato, *Criti.* 115a–b), and none too exact. Olson (2006–12, ad loc.) calls it "altered and condensed."

70. It is not uncommon for Athenaeus to confuse references to the *De partibus animalium* and the *Historia animalium*.

[For he says that ceryxes and all the testaceans, the family of them, are asexual, and that the murex and the ceryx are long-lived. Where does he get the information that the murex lives six years?] (Athen. 8.352e)

We might describe this citation as an extremely compressed paraphrase of *Hist. an.* 546b15–26, followed by an unmarked ellipsis of roughly 50 lines, followed by a close paraphrase of *Hist. an.* 547b.[71] Here are the relevant parts of the Aristotle:

περὶ δὲ τῆς γενέσεως καὶ τῶν ὀχευομένων καὶ τῶν ἀνοχεύτων λεκτέον, καὶ πρῶτον περὶ τῶν ὀστρακοδέρμων· τοῦτο γάρ ἐστιν ἀνόχευτον μόνον ὡς εἰπεῖν ὅλον τὸ γένος. αἱ μὲν οὖν πορφύραι τοῦ ἔαρος συναθροιζόμεναι εἰς ταὐτὸ ποιοῦσι τὴν καλουμένην μελίκηραν. . . . οὐδὲ γίνονται ἐκ τούτων αἱ πορφύραι, ἀλλὰ φύονται καὶ αὗται καὶ τὰ ἄλλα τὰ ὀστρακόδερμα ἐξ ἰλύος καὶ σήψεως. . . . κηριάζουσι γὰρ καὶ οἱ κήρυκες. . . . ἔστι δὲ [καὶ] ἡ πορφύρα καὶ ὁ κῆρυξ ἀμφότερα μακρόβια· ζῇ γὰρ ἡ πορφύρα περὶ ἔτη ἕξ,

[It is necessary to discuss the generation of both the sexual and asexual animals, and, first of all, the testaceans. This is the only completely asexual genus, practically speaking. The murexes, for example, gathering in the same place in the spring time, produce the so-called honeycomb. . . . But the murexes are not produced from these, but they and the other testaceans grow from mud and putrefaction. . . . The ceryxes spawn from the honeycomb also. . . . The murex and the cyrex are both long-lived. The murex lives around six years.] (Arist., *Hist. an.* 8.546b15–19, 546b22–24, 546b25–26, 547b8–9)

Such a thorough recasting of the source, while it does not here misrepresent the original's meaning, warns us that even when probability tells us we are reading a quotation, we may be quite far from a literal text.[72]

The parenthetical φησί inserted into direct speech, the other of Lenfant's

---

71. It may be that the repetition of ὅτι serves to alert the reader that Athenaeus is skipping to a new part of the original. This question requires further study.

72. Lenfant might prefer to categorize this passage as an accurate summary rather than a loose paraphrase. This may be correct, since one can argue that Aristotle's statement that the entire genus of testaceans is asexual clearly implies that the ceryx has this property and thus that the discussion of the murex's honeycomb and the association of the ceryx with that phenomenon is not a necessary step in Aristotle's demonstration. Be that as it may, the fact remains that the closest thing to a literal quotation in this passage is the infinitival clause ζῆν γὰρ τὴν πορφύραν ἔτη ἕξ, in spite of Lenfant's point b).

principal categories of marks of literal quotation, must also be recognized as usually, but not necessarily, performing this function. Once more, Aristotle's scientific works provide an example of paraphrase instead of the expected quotation.[73] As we have seen, the dinner-guest Cynulcus expresses his skepticism about the reliability of the details of Aristotle's biology in an extended passage at Athen. 8.353a–b:

γλαῦκες δέ, φησί, καὶ κόρακες ἡμέρας ἀδυνατοῦσι βλέπειν· διὸ νύκτωρ τὴν τροφὴν ἑαυτοῖς θηρεύουσι καὶ οὐ πᾶσαν νύκτα, ἀλλὰ τὴν ἀκρέσπερον.

[Little owls, he says, and ravens are not able to see during the day. For this reason they hunt food for themselves by night, and not all night, but at dusk.]

This is a rendition of *Hist. an.* 619b18–21:

γλαῦκες δὲ καὶ νυκτικόρακες, καὶ τὰ λοιπὰ ὅσα τῆς ἡμέρας ἀδυνατεῖ βλέπειν, τῆς νυκτὸς μὲν θηρεύοντα τὴν τροφὴν αὐτοῖς πορίζεται, οὐ κατὰ πᾶσαν δὲ τὴν νύκτα τοῦτο ποιεῖ, ἀλλ᾽ ἄχρι ἑσπέρας καὶ περὶ ὄρθρον.

[Little owls and long-eared owls and all the others that are unable to see during the day provide food for themselves by hunting at night; they do not do this all through the night, but at the brink of evening and around dawn.]

Thus, we find that the formulae identified by Lenfant as introducing literal or verbatim quotations, while serving that function in the great preponderance of examples, sometimes introduce much looser representations of the original. Nor should we be surprised at this conclusion, if we call to mind our earlier discussion of Athenaeus's Homeric citations. The presence of hexameter verse in association with an attribution to Homer would, we think, be taken by the reader as an unequivocal indication of literal quotation; no φησί/γράφει οὕτως could be clearer in this regard. Yet we have seen how Athenaeus rewrote certain verses to suit his context. The demands of τὰ καινά sometimes trump accuracy,

---

73. Other examples include Athen. 7.323e = Aris., *Hist. an.* 541b + 544a (twenty-five words near literal, then seventeen words of paraphrase, then twenty-seven words near literal, with no seams marked); 8.353a–b = Aris., *Hist. an.* 619b18ff. (paraphrase for twenty words, then proceeds seamlessly into an unknown source); 8.353f = Aris., *Hist. an.* 490a8–11 (a loose paraphrase in long series of paraphrases); 15.681f = Theophrastus, *Hist. pl.* 6.8.3 and 9.7.3 (six words altered from four, then a seven-word paraphrase, with no indication of change in source).

even when Athenaeus lays emphasis upon the reliability of his information. Unfortunately, we are rarely in a position to observe when such a move is being made.

Lenfant's generalizations a), b), and c) are of less interest to our study, since they identify features marking paraphrase or summary; our review of Athenaeus's practice in verse citations had already suggested a prudent *modus operandi* for dealing with fragments of lost works. We must assume that any citation, no matter how clearly Athenaeus marks it as a quotation, may in fact be only an approximation of the avowed source. We will therefore deal more briefly with these remaining points.

The verb ἱστορεῖ occurs only eight times in reference to extant works, too small a number from which to draw the firm conclusion that the word logically indicates a reformulation. It is noteworthy that one of the eight examples introduces a mixture of paraphrase and quotation.[74]

Indirect statements of the infinitive type do, as one would suspect, generally occur as paraphrases or the like, but a few appear to be nearly *ad verbum* except for grammatically required changes. For example, Diod. Sic. 11.25.4–5 reads as follows:

κατεσκεύασαν δὲ οἱ Ἀκραγαντῖνοι καὶ κολυμβήθραν πολυτελῆ, τὴν περίμετρον ἔχουσαν σταδίων ἑπτά, τὸ δὲ βάθος πηχῶν εἴκοσι.

[The Agrigentines built also an extravagant diving pool, one having a perimeter of seven stades and a depth of twenty cubits.]

---

74. Athen. 10.438b [similarities underlined]: Μυκερῖνον δὲ τὸν Αἰγύπτιον ὁ Ἡρόδοτος ἱστορεῖ διὰ τῆς δευτέρας ἀκούσαντα παρὰ τῶν μάντεων ὅτι ὀλιγοχρόνιός ἐστι, λύχνα ποιησάμενον πολλά ὁπότε γένοιτο νὺξ πίνειν καὶ εὐπαθεῖν οὔτε ἡμέρας οὔτε νυκτὸς ἀνιέντα· καὶ εἰς τὰ ἕλεα δὲ καὶ τὰ ἄλση νεμόμενον, ἔτι τε ὅπου πύθοιτο ἡβητήρια εἶναι μεθύσκεσθαι ("Herodotus reports in his second book that Mycerinus the Egyptian, hearing from the seers that he had a short time to live, making many lamps, whenever it was night drank and partied without stopping for a day or night. And he even wandered into swamps and forests, wherever he heard that there were places of amusement, and he got drunk."). The reference is to Hdt. 2.133.4–5: ταῦτα ἀκούσαντα τὸν Μυκερῖνον, ὡς κατακεκριμένων ἤδη οἱ τούτων λύχνα ποιησάμενον πολλά, ὅκως γίνοιτο νύξ, ἀνάψαντα αὐτὰ πίνειν τε καὶ εὐπαθέειν οὔτε ἡμέρης οὔτε νυκτὸς ἀνιέντα ἔς τε τὰ ἕλεα καὶ τὰ ἄλσεα πλανώμενον καὶ ἵνα πυνθάνοιτο εἶναι ἐνηβητήρια ἐπιτηδεότατα ("Hearing these things, Mycerinus, since his fate had been decided, making many lamps, whenever it was night lit them, and drank and partied without stopping for day or night. And he wandered into swamps and forests, wherever he heard were the likeliest places of amusement."). Lenfant, with her strict criteria for the classification "quotation," categorizes this citation as a "fragment mixte," consisting of a conglomeration of summary and paraphrase. However this passage may be labeled, it contains more than a negligible amount of verbatim material.

Athenaeus cites the text in Book 12.541e–f:

Διόδωρος δ᾽ ὁ Σικελιώτης ἐν τοῖς περὶ Βιβλιοθήκης Ἀκραγαντίνους φησὶ κατασκευάσαι Γέλωνι κολυμβήθραν πολυτελῆ τὸ περίμετρον ἔχουσαν σταδίων ζ΄, βάθος δὲ πηχῶν κ΄ . . .

[Diodorus Siculus in the work *On the Library* says that the Agrigentines built for Gelon an extravagant diving pool, having a perimeter of seven stades and a depth of twenty cubits . . .]

Thus, while infinitival clauses of this type probably indicate reformulation in a large majority of cases, we cannot, based on formal considerations alone, be certain of this in any given instance.[75]

In like manner, when occurring after or parenthetically within a citation, ὥς φησί does usually introduce a paraphrase. However, in several places, the text is close enough to the original that we might consider it a quotation.[76]

In sum, our examination of a wide range of citations of extant sources confirms that Lenfant's observations on introductory formulae are normally correct. There are, on the other hand, at least a small number of exceptions to every rule, and this fact must be kept in mind when we are trying to derive an author's views on a particular subject, or even features of the text of lost work, from citations in the *Deipnosophistae*.

Compositional Drift

In his penetrating study of transitions in Athenaeus, Christopher Pelling has further complicated the lives of those who work with historical fragments in the *Deipnosophistae*. Most important from our perspective is Pelling's demonstration of how Athenaeus can move from his principal authority for a given

---

75. Other examples include: Athen. 10.452c–d = Plato, *Rep.* 5.479b; 7.303c–d = Aris., *Hist. an.* 543a12–13; 7.308d = Aris., *Hist. an.* 543a29–b1; 7.315a = Aris., *Hist. an.* 543a30–31; 7.321b = Aris., *Hist. an.* 543a7–8; 9.371a = Theophr., *Hist. pl.* 7.4.4.

76. Athen. 7.312e–f = Aris., *Hist. an.* 543a24–27, where the differences are not greater than we might expect as variants between MSS; 7.320e = Aris., *Hist. an.* 543a7–8; 10.423a–b = Plato, *Phlb.* 61b–c (51 words nearly exact, with interlocutor's responses omitted); 14.613b = Hdt. 1.212 (with two words added at end by Athenaeus; see above, note 51). Altogether, of the twenty-two examples of this usage outside the epitome referring to extant works, four (18 percent) may be considered exceptions to the generalization in question.

topic to other sources and then back again, all without any indication. Thus material that Athenaeus apparently associated with a specified source is not necessarily from that author:

> Athenaeus can often use a dominant, named figure only as a framework and can hang independent material on that frame: he can quote Posidonius or Theopompus, drift away and drift back again. . . . All too often we fall into the trap of assuming that the independent material belongs to the dominant framework-figure as well. (Pelling 2000, 175)

To illustrate the allure of the "dominant framework-figure" Pelling gives the example of Wilamowitz.[77] That scholar, relying on Athenaeus's mention of Satyrus at the beginning of his discussion of the luxury of Alcibiades, attributes to that author a long section (Athen. 12.534b–535b), including citations of several other named sources. Pelling is surely correct when he says that these citations are all "presumably Athenaeus's own insertion into a Satyrus framework," since at least two of the four citations are introduced with devices clearly identifiable as among Athenaeus's own techniques.[78] Indeed, we would argue that the citation of Satyrus ends with the initial anecdote, since the pattern apparent here is also found elsewhere in Athenaeus.[79] This pattern consists of a relatively innocuous statement attached to a named authority—here, that Alcibiades could outdo the Ionians in τρυφή, the Spartans in endurance, etc., on the authority of Satyrus— followed by a series of often rather random, but seriously derogatory details.[80]

---

77. Pelling 2000, 176.

78. Pelling 2000, 176. The evidence of Antisthenes on Alcibiades' physical attractiveness is introduced in these words: διὸ καὶ Ἀντισθένης ὁ Σωκρατικὸς . . . φησίν ("And for that reason Antisthenes the Socratic . . . says . . . ," Athen. 12.534c). The collocation διὸ καὶ is fairly frequent as a way of setting up a citation in the *Deipnosophistae,* occurring twenty or more times. From Book 12, for example, 12.530d: διὸ καὶ Ἀριστοτέλης . .ʼ. ἔλεγεν ("And for that reason Aristotle . . . used to say"); and 12.544d: διὸ καὶ ὁ Ξενοφῶν ἐν τοῖς Ἀπομνημονεύμασί φησιν ("And for that reason Xenophon in the *Memorabilia* says"). At 12.534f, a citation of Lysias attests to Alcibiades' participation in a scandalous *ménage à trois*: Λυσίας δὲ ὁ ῥήτωρ περὶ τῆς τρυφῆς αὐτοῦ λέγων φησίν ("Lysias the orator, speaking about that man's τρυφή, says"). Here the phrase περὶ τῆς τρυφῆς is a common tic of Athenaeus, as we will discuss below. Admittedly, such a simple expression could have been used by Satyrus to introduce his evidence, but nonetheless its occurrence makes these citations, in Pelling's words vis-à-vis another passage, "very much in Athenaeus's own manner" (176).

79. For example, Timaeus on the Sybarites (12.519b–520c = *FGrH* 566 F 50), discussed in Chapter 4, below; also Theopompus on the sexual customs of the Etruscans (12.517d–518b = *FGrH* 115 F 204). In this passage, as Pelling notes (2000, 180), there is a seam in the material indicated by a shift from indirect to direct speech. Before the break we find ethnographical characteristics of a type often predicated of barbarians (holding wives in common, etc.). After the break come more scurrilous details.

80. Pelling (2000, 176) speaks of a "catch-all medley from general knowledge."

Another illustration Pelling gives for this procedure is the case of Smindyrides of Sybaris, whom Athenaeus advances at 12.541b–c as an example of τρυφή.[81]

περὶ δὲ Σμινδυρίδου τοῦ Συβαρίτου καὶ τῆς τούτου τρυφῆς ἱστόρησεν Ἡρόδοτος ἐν τῇ ἕκτῃ, ὡς ἀποπλέων ἐπὶ τὴν μνηστείαν τῆς Κλεισθένους τοῦ Σικυωνίων τυράννου θυγατρὸς Ἀγαρίστης, φησίν, ἀπὸ μὲν Ἰταλίης <ἦλθε> Σμινδυρίδης ὁ Ἱπποκράτεος Συβαρίτης, ὃς ἐπὶ πλεῖστον δὴ χλιδῆς εἷς ἀνὴρ ἀφίκετο. εἵποντο γοῦν αὐτῷ χίλιοι μάγειροι καὶ ὀρνιθευταί. ἱστορεῖ περὶ αὐτοῦ καὶ Τίμαιος ἐν τῇ ἑβδόμῃ.

[About Smindyrides of Sybaris and his *truphē*, Herodotus tells the story in his seventh book of how he sailed to the wooing of Agariste, the daughter of Cleisthenes the tyrant of Sikyon. He says "the Sybarite Smindyrides the son of Hippocrates came from Italy; he was the one man who had reached the furthest extent of luxury [*chlidē*]." At any rate one thousand cooks and fowlers accompanied him. Timaeus too wrote about him in his seventh book.]

As Pelling points out, "if we did not have Herodotus, the sentence about cooks and fowlers would surely have been taken as a Herodotus fragment."[82] Nor should we take the "fowler sentence" as coming from Timaeus, as is generally done (*FGrH* 566 F 9). Athenaeus has the same material in Book 6. Here again he does not indicate that he is directly quoting from a source.[83] The fowler sentence "is an extra fact hung on the framework of quotation, either just before or

---

81. Discussed above, for the significance of the word *chlidē*.
82. Pelling (2000, 176) remarks that the words "perhaps . . . would even have been taken as part of the direct speech, with the γῶν Atticised to γοῦν." We think Pelling's "perhaps" is too generous. Baron (2113, 261–62) doubts its Timaean authenticity.
83. ἀλλ᾽ οὐ Σμινδυρίδης ὁ Συβαρίτης τοιοῦτος, ὦ Ἕλληνες, ὃς ἐπὶ τὸν Ἀγαρίστης τῆς Κλεισθένους θυγατρὸς ἐξορμῶν γάμον ὑπὸ χλιδῆς καὶ τρυφῆς χιλίους συνεπήγετο οἰκέτας, ἁλιεῖς καὶ ὀρνιθευτὰς καὶ μαγείρους· οὗτος δ᾽ ὁ ἀνὴρ καὶ ἐνδείξασθαι βουλόμενος ὡς εὐδαιμόνως ἔζη, ὡς ἱστορεῖ Χαμαιλέων ὁ Ποντικὸς ἐν τῷ περὶ ἡδονῆς (τὸ δ᾽ αὐτὸ βιβλίον καὶ ὡς Θεοφράστου φέρεται) οὐκ ἔφη τὸν ἥλιον ἐτῶν εἴκοσιν οὔτ᾽ ἀνατέλλοντα οὔτε δυόμενον ἑωρακέναι. καὶ τοῦτ᾽ ἦν αὐτῷ μέγα καὶ θαυμαστὸν πρὸς εὐδαιμονίαν. οὗτος, ὡς ἔοικεν, πρωὶ μὲν ἐκάθευδεν, ὀψὲ δ᾽ ἠγείρετο, κατ᾽ ἀμφότερα δυστυχῶν ("But Smindyrides of Sybaris was not such a man, O Greeks, who going off to the wedding of Agariste the daughter of Cleisthenes took a thousand slaves with him out of *chlidē* and *truphē*— fishers and fowlers and cooks. This is the man who wanted to demonstrate how happily he lived, as Chamaeleon of Pontus says in his *On Pleasure* (this same book is also ascribed to Theophrastus); he said that he had not seen the sun rise or set in twenty years. He considered this a great and wonderful mark of happiness. It seems he went to bed early and got up late, unfortunate on both counts." Athen. 6.273b–c). Note that Athenaeus cites Chamaeleon as authority for Smindyrides' sleeping habits, but not for the fowler sentence.

just after quotations, and it can simply be a fact drawn from his general knowledge."[84]

With the whimsy that we have seen so often, Athenaeus seems here to make a small but masterly move in his citation game. The reader unfamiliar with the text of Herodotus would assume that the sentiments, if not the words, were his, and this suppositional addition to the Father of History would generate the novelty Athenaeus is seeking. For those who know the original, what Athenaeus is creating is a nexus of authority, crafting not a new text, but new lines of support. The juxtaposition of the fowler-sentence with the Herodotus passage provides the reader license to give credence to the more outlandish—and probably authorless—stories about Smindyrides' extravagance. By the invocation of the historian's name, the hint is made that Herodotus, too, saw the Sybarite as the later traditions depict him.

Further cases of compositional drift involving extant material can be identified. As we have already noted, at 8.353a–b, Athenaeus paraphrases Aristotle, *Hist. an.* 619b18, on birds that hunt in the night. To this is appended a statement about the color of their eyes.[85] Although this material appears in a series of Aristotle citations, and the context includes repeated indications that citations—and even quotations—are being given, this ophthalmic information cannot be identified as Aristotelian.[86]

Of special interest is Athenaeus's use of Herodotus's testimony on the martial use of music among the Lydians. At Athen. 12.517a, the reference serves as evidence for Lydian decadence:

καὶ εἰς τοὺς πολέμους δὲ ἐξιόντες οἱ Λυδοὶ παρατάττονται μετὰ συρίγγων καὶ αὐλῶν, ὥς φησιν Ἡρόδοτος, καὶ Λακεδαιμόνιοι δὲ μετ᾽ αὐλῶν ἐξορμῶσιν ἐπὶ τοὺς πολέμους, καθάπερ Κρῆτες μετὰ λύρας.

[And when they are going to war, the Lydians assemble to the music of pipes and flutes, as Herodotus says, and the Lacedaemonians also set out for battle to the music of flutes, as the Cretans do to the music of lyres.]

---

84. Pelling 2000, 177.
85. καὶ τὰς ἰδέας δὲ τῶν ὀφθαλμῶν αὐτῶν οὐκ ἐμφερεῖς εἶναι; τοῖς μὲν γὰρ γλαυκαί, τοῖς δὲ μέλαιναι, τοῖς δὲ χαροποί ("And that the appearance of their eyes is not similar, for some have grey, others black, and still others blue-grey." Athen. 8.353b).
86. The preceding sentence contains a parenthetical φησί, the following is introduced by ὅτι (short for φησί ὅτι), and the statement in question is in an infinitival construction. Although this last is more frequently found in paraphrases than quotations, it clearly marks the material as part of the sequence of citations.

The citation reappears at Athen. 14.627d to support the incompatible claim that "in olden days music was an inducement to bravery" (τὸ δ᾽ ἀρχαῖον ἡ μουσικὴ ἐπ᾽ ἀνδρείαν προτροπὴ ἦν, Athen. 14.626f):

διόπερ καὶ οἱ ἀνδρειότατοι Λακεδαιμόνιοι μετ᾽ αὐλῶν στρατεύονται, Κρῆτες δὲ μετὰ λύρας, μετὰ δὲ συρίγγων καὶ αὐλῶν Λυδοί, ὡς Ἡρόδοτος ἱστορεῖ. πολλοὶ δὲ καὶ τῶν βαρβάρων τὰς ἐπικηρυκείας ποιοῦνται μετ᾽ αὐλῶν καὶ κιθάρας, καταπραΰνοντες τῶν ἐναντίων τὰς ψυχάς.

[For this reason the most virile Lacedaemonians march to war accompanied by flutes, the Cretans to lyres, and the Lydians to pipes and flutes, as Herodotus reports. And many of the barbarians too make peace negotiations to flutes and cithers, soothing the souls of the other side.] (Athen. 14.627d)

A reader unfamiliar with the *Histories* would be surprised to learn that the original mentions only the Lydians:[87]

ἐστρατεύετο δὲ ὑπὸ συρίγγων τε καὶ πηκτίδων καὶ αὐλοῦ γυναικηίου τε καὶ ἀνδρηίου,

[[Alyattes] marched his army accompanied by pipes and Lydian lyres and both the treble and bass flute.] (Hdt. 1.17.1)

Several things are noteworthy here. First, neither citation is an accurate reproduction of Herodotus's words about the Lydians, but both give a shortened and altered version. Second, because the non-Herodotean material is essentially the same in both citations, an unsuspecting reader, taking confidence from this apparent double-confirmation, would not hesitate to attribute this entire passage to that original. Finally, we may observe that in the Book 12 passage, the extraneous material follows the attribution, while the Herodotean material precedes. In Book 14, the information before the ὡς Ἡρόδοτος ἱστορεῖ is once again genuine, but only in part. Foreign matter (drawn from common knowledge?) precedes the Herodotean data with no indication of a change in source. Other such extra material immediately follows the attribution, likewise

---

87. A careful reader of either passage would smell a rat. In Book 12, Athenaeus includes the Lacedaemonians with the Lydians as an example of τρυφή, while, in Book 14, he groups the Lydians with the Lacedaemonians as an example of ἀνδρεία. This switch is evidence that the original has been repurposed by Athenaeus.

with no clear hint of a different origin. Without the preservation of the *Histories*, such citations would naturally lead to a misinformed view of what Herodotus had said.

Thus, the emphasis that Pelling gives to the cautionary force of compositional drift is justified. The cases involving citations of extant texts show how insidious this phenomenon may be, since it is for all practical purposes invisible. It can occur between sentences and also within a single sentence. It can occur before or after the mention of the dominant framework-figure, or in both places. When we turn to examine Athenaeus's evidence for τρυφή in fragmentary authors, we must remember that, in any series of facts presented under the aegis of a named authority, it is possible that only a single item may derive from the source mentioned, a sobering thought indeed.

Athen. 12.519b–520b presents us with an example of a citation of a fragmentary author that shows strong signs of drift. The passage begins with the claim that ἐφόρουν δ᾽ οἱ Συβαρῖται καὶ ἱμάτια Μιλησίων ἐρίων πεποιημένα ("the Sybarites wore cloaks made of Milesian wool," Athen. 12.519b) and that this circumstance was the source of friendship between the two cities. These remarks are placed under the authority of Timaeus (*FGrH* 566 F 50)—and perhaps revealed as a paraphrase—through the common formula ὡς ὁ Τίμαιος ἱστορεῖ. After this rather innocuous statement of affinity there follows what can fairly be described as a hodge-podge of unrelated facts: Sybarite horsemen wore saffron cloaks; their young men visited the caverns of the Nymphs in summer; their wealthy took three days to complete a one-day journey; some of their country roads were roofed over; they piped their wine from their vineyards to their wine cellars; and so forth. Although Athenaeus gives no indication that Timaeus was responsible for only part of this material, the lack of internal coherence arouses that suspicion. The variety of details have no unifying thread except the idea of excessive τρυφή itself. Strengthening the doubt about the origin of this mélange is our difficulty in imagining its function in its original context; the passage as it stands can have had no apparent purpose in the *Histories* other than the use to which Athenaeus puts it: to illustrate Sybarite decadence. It is most prudent to mark the end of the citation immediately after the statement about the φιλίαι of Sybaris and Miletus.

Thus, Pelling's observation about unmarked transitions in the *Deipnosophistae* allows the formulation of a principle of great importance for the interpretation of prose fragments: inconsistencies within an apparent citation, and especially a lack of clear connection with the material nearest the naming of Athenaeus's authority, should be taken as signs of a possible change in source.

Framing Language

The previous sections have shown that, while formal considerations reveal tendencies and probabilities, they do not allow us a priori to tell close and accurate representations of an original from those that are loose or misleading. Furthermore, Athenaeus can end a citation and move on to material from another source in a manner that leaves this process completely undetectable by the modern reader. In such circumstances, anyone developing an argument involving Athenaean fragments must search for all means to ensure that this evidence is most reliable. Our research has led us to believe that it is indeed often possible to distinguish, to a degree not yet recognized, between the phrasing purportedly derived from an original source and that which is added by Athenaeus as a framework for the citation. Failure to differentiate the two elements is a trap into which fall many who work with prose fragments from the *Deipnosophistae*. Such missteps are frequently avoidable.

We will generally limit our examination of Athenaean framing language to passages involving τρυφή, and we will start with citations of extant works. Before beginning, we may observe that in the 185 uses of the word and its cognates in Athenaeus only six are associated with citations of extant sources. Such a distribution is surprising and suggests that Athenaeus was indeed adding novel interpretations to citations that had no such meaning in their originals. Otherwise, we would expect to find more citations from extant Classical works with which we know Athenaeus was familiar.[88] Nevertheless, a closer examination of these passages can provide us with important insights about Athenaeus's τρυφή citations. Of these citations, in only two is the word τρυφή found in the original. In the other four, τρυφή is added to the citation. This ratio is significant in itself. Although the control group of six extant references is admittedly small,

---

88. Another possible way to account for this small proportion is to postulate that Athenaeus may have used an intermediate source for much of his evidence on τρυφή. A work such as Aristippus's Περὶ παλαιᾶς τρυφῆς has often been proposed. The matter is very complicated and probably insoluble. At any rate, a proper examination would not fit in the confines of this book. In general, we will postulate that Athenaeus took his τρυφή citations directly from the sources named.

we cannot rule out the possibility that it is representative of Athenaeus's practice in general. If so, then we may assume that the majority of the passages in question are misrepresented to some degree.

An accurate citation of an extant original occurs in Book 10, in the midst of an extended discussion of customs relating to drink and drunkenness. The relevant citation is from Plato's *Laws* 1.637d–e; Athenaeus quotes fairly closely for 68 words.[89] The passage ends with this sentence:

Πέρσαι δὲ καὶ σφόδρα μὲν χρῶνται καὶ ταῖς ἄλλαις τρυφαῖς, ἃς ὑμεῖς ἀποβάλλετε, ἐν τάξει δὲ μᾶλλον τούτων.

[The Persians, too, employ to a great extent also the other *truphai*, which you [Spartans] reject, but in a more orderly way than these peoples.] (Athen. 10.432a)

The sentence exhibits several features that are characteristic of those τρυφή-citations that we judge likely to be accurate.

(1) The reference to τρυφή occurs in what we may term the body of the citation. It is not part of the introduction. It does not form a transition between identifiable components of the citation. Although it occurs at end of this quotation, the sentence does not function as a summary or culmination of what proceeds it.

(2) Τρυφή is an integral part of the sentence structure. In this example, the dative complement of χρῶνται.

(3) The word is not causal. As we shall see, firm examples of τρυφή as a cause of some event or process are very rare before the Roman period, but common in passages that can be persuasively attributed to Athenaeus himself.

(4) Τρυφή is morally nuanced, in that it is not merely negative in tone. The Persians practice it ἐν τάξει. In our discussion of Athenaeus's treatment of Homer, we have established that Athenaeus, to suit his argument, frequently gives a passage a moral implication absent in the

---

89. The only substantial alteration is the substitution of Lydians for Scythians in the first line, but there are many minors modifications that might lead some to call this a paraphrase. The meaning is not changed and the final line, containing ταῖς ἄλλαις τρυφαῖς is unaltered.

original, and there is no doubt that he presents himself as a most harsh critic of τρυφή.

(5) The sentence does not contain any of the diction clearly identifiable as Athenaeus's own.[90]

These features constitute a set of criteria for estimating the likelihood that a τρυφή-citation is accurate. As more of these characteristics are present, the likelihood increases that the citation is correct. The converse also seems true: the more of these criteria that a citation fails to fulfill, the greater the skepticism it should receive.

Another citation, probably accurate at least with respect to the occurrence of τρυφή, is Polyb. 4.20.5–21.9, quoted at Athen. 14.626a–f. Because of Polybius's Roman context—we argue that the idea of pernicious luxury undergoes a transformation under Roman influence—discussion of this passage will be postponed to Chapter 5.[91]

Examples of other apparently genuine non-extant references to τρυφή are in order. First, Athen. 6.258d cites from the comic poet Antiphanes' *Lemnian Women* (frag. 142 KA) to emphasize a flatterer's praise of his own life. After reference to the hardships met by painters and farmers and soldiers come the following lines:

πρόσεστι πᾶσιν ἐπιμέλεια καὶ πόνος.
ἡμῖν δὲ μετὰ γέλωτος ὁ βίος καὶ τρυφῆς.

[All face care and toil, but for us is a life with laughter and τρυφή.]

To rehearse the criteria set out above: (1) the occurrence of τρυφή comes in the middle of the passage and neither forms the introduction nor summarizes the meaning of the citation, nor forms a bridge between identifiable segments; (2)

---

90. We will discuss Athenaean diction later in this chapter. We might add as a sixth criterion that the citation be marked by its formula of introduction as a quotation; admittedly, we have argued above that such formulae indicate only probabilities, but these certainly need to be taken into account when deciding whether evidence about pernicious luxury goes back to the original of an Athenaean citation.

91. On the other hand, we examine Diod. Sic. 11.25.4–5 in spite of his Roman date because Athenaeus adds τρυφή to an original in which it does not occur. For such a case, the meaning of τρυφή for Diodorus and the way the term was used both in the *Bibliotheca* and in contemporary sources is irrelevant.

τρυφή is, along with γέλως, the attribute predicated of the subject of its clause; (3) τρυφή does not cause any event; (4) τρυφή expresses the approbation of the speaker quoted; (5) the lines contain none of Athenaeus's favorite turns of phrase. Thus, we can find no reason to doubt the accuracy of this citation, at least vis-à-vis Antiphanes' use of τρυφή. It is likely genuine.

A good number of the most plausible occurrences of τρυφή, like the passage from Antiphanes, are in citations of verse.[92] Similarly unobjectionable cases of τρυφή in prose citation are extremely rare. Once such is given in evidence of the obesity (πάχος) of Ptolemy X Alexander:

> φησὶ γοῦν περὶ αὐτοῦ Ποσειδώνιος ἐν τῇ ἑβδόμῃ καὶ τεσσαρακοστῇ τῶν Ἱστοριῶν οὕτως· ὁ δὲ τῆς Αἰγύπτου δυνάστης μισούμενος μὲν ὑπὸ τῶν ὄχλων, κολακευόμενος δ᾽ ὑπὸ τῶν περὶ αὐτόν, ἐν πολλῇ δὲ τρυφῇ ζῶν, οὐδὲ περιπατεῖν οἷός τε ἦν, εἰ μὴ δυσὶν ἐπαπερειδόμενος [ἐπορεύετο]. εἰς δὲ τὰς ἐν τοῖς συμποσίοις ὀρχήσεις ἀπὸ μετεώρων κλινῶν καθαλλόμενος ἀνυπόδητος συντονωτέρας αὐτὰς τῶν ἠσκηκότων ἐποιεῖτο.

[Posidonius [frag. 77 EK], at all events, in the forty-seventh book of his *Histories* speaks about him as follows: "The ruler of Egypt, hated by the crowds, flattered by his entourage, living in abundant τρυφή, was not able to walk about unless supported by two men. But at symposia, jumping barefoot from his high couch into the dances, he would do them more strenuously than the trained dancers."] (Athen. 12.550b)

We need only dwell on criteria 3 and 4. With respect to the causal force of pernicious luxury, Posidonius does not seem to have made the fact that Ptolemy lived in τρυφή into a cause of historiographical significance; τρυφή is not given as the reason, for instance, that the king was hated by the mass of his subjects. On the other hand, it may be correct to see τρυφή as the cause of Ptolemy's inability to walk without support. This interpretation is not certain because the relation between τρυφή and this inability may be one of general characteristic and particular instantiation rather than cause and effect. After all, a core meaning of τρυφή is the expectation or the act of being taken care of by others, and Ptolemy's ambulatory customs are an extreme example of such care.

---

92. In verse citations the meter makes it clear that Athenaeus meant the references to be taken as quotations rather than paraphrases, regardless of the formula of citation.

Nor is τρυφή explicitly marked here as morally negative. The passage *may* be morally charged and Posidonius may have used the Egyptian to exemplify the disability resulting from a certain lifestyle. But the point may also have been simply the paradox of a man who was sometimes apparently so enervated as not to be able to walk without support and who at other times showed unusual physical vigor.[93] A good decision among these and other possible interpretations can only be made on the basis of a thorough investigation of the moral tenor of Posidonius's *Histories* in which any dubious evidence from the *Deipnosophistae* itself must be set aside. In sum, this passage meets most of our criteria fairly well. We would therefore tend to interpret this occurrence of τρυφή as an accurate representation of the original.[94]

In contrast, in the remaining four citations from extant works in which a concern with τρυφή is attributed to the source, the term does not appear in the original. Nonetheless, the manner in which Athenaeus adds this element to each passage provides us with valuable insights into the way he handles evidence about pernicious luxury. At Athen. 4.144b, Athenaeus cites fifty-seven words accurately from Xen., *Ages.* 9.3, but not before framing the citation with the following introduction: περὶ δὲ τῆς τρυφῆς τῶν ἐν Πέρσαις βασιλέων Ξενοφῶν ἐν Ἀγησιλάῳ οὕτω γράφει ("Concerning the τρυφή of the Persian kings, Xenophon in the *Agesilaus* writes thus . . ."). Even if we did not possess the passage from Xenophon, it would be self-evident that the identification of the topic as περὶ τρυφῆς is a interpretation by Athenaeus, just as he provides the bibliographical information. Claiming that a source was writing περὶ τρυφῆς is a favorite move of Athenaeus.[95] We will see below that skepticism is called for

---

93. We must point out that this passage is not evidence that Posidonius described Ptolemy Alexander as obese. That claim is made by Athenaeus: εἰς πάχος δ᾽ ἐπεδεδώκει καὶ ὁ υἱὸς αὐτοῦ Ἀλέξανδρος ("His son, Alexander, too, also grew fat," Athen. 12.550a). While Posidonius evidently did report about the girth of the father (Athen. 12.549e = Posidonius, frag. 58 EK), it is Athenaeus who draws the inference (indicated by γοῦν) from the father's obesity to the son's. This assumption is based on Ptolemy Alexander's inability to walk unassisted, but Posidonius may have attributed this characteristic to other causes besides the king's weight.

94. The issue is not definitively settled, however, since data exist that lend weight to the opposite conclusion. In particular, the expression ἐν τρυφῇ ζῶν (vel sim.) is not evidenced before the Roman period. We will discuss the implications of such diachronic analyses of diction later in this chapter.

95. To cite only one passage where the phrase is obviously Athenaeus's rather than part of the original: Ἀντιφάνης δ᾽ ὁ κωμῳδιοποιὸς ἐν Στρατιώτῃ τὰ ὅμοια λέγει περὶ τῆς τῶν ἐν Κύπρῳ βασιλέων τρυφῆς. ποιεῖ δέ τινα ἀναπυνθανόμενον στρατιώτου τάδε ("Antiphanes the comic poet in his *Soldier* says similar things about the τρυφή of the kings on Cyprus. He depicts someone asking a soldier the following: . . ." Athen. 6.257d = Antiphanes, frag. 200 KA). This framing passage is followed by more than a dozen lines of verse quotation. It is worth noting that here, even though Antiphanes' lines do exhibit τρυφή as it would have been understood by his contemporaries (the king was kept cool by being fanned by trained pigeons), Athenaeus apparently misrepresents the original to some degree.

when this phrase seems to be part of a fragmentary passage. For the present, it is sufficient to note that τρυφή is not Xenophon's concern. That author focuses on various points of distinction between his Spartan hero and the Persian monarchs. These differences include that the Great King held himself apart from his subjects and that he transacted business with a dignified slowness. Agesilaus and the Persian also are contrasted in the matter of εὐπάθεια; Agesilaus's simplicity is contrasted to exotic eastern tastes, and this is the passage cited by Athenaeus. Thus, the description of the passage as περὶ τρυφῆς only reflects, at most, one part of Xenophon's thinking. In addition, the context of the *Agesilaus* does not indicate that Persian luxury is morally, or politically, corrosive.[96] For Athenaeus, this effect is a principal characteristic of τρυφή, and it is inaccurate for him to impute this sense to the original.

The next τρυφή citation from an extant source shows a similar pattern, but this time Athenaeus's framework presents the passage as having a meaning contrary to its original force. The citation is the now-familiar reference to Herodotus 6.127.1 on Smindyrides of Sybaris:

> περὶ δὲ Σμινδυρίδου τοῦ Συβαρίτου καὶ τῆς τούτου τρυφῆς ἱστόρησεν Ἡρόδοτος ἐν τῇ ἕκτῃ, ὡς ἀποπλέων ἐπὶ τὴν μνηστείαν τῆς Κλεισθένους τοῦ Σικυωνίων τυράννου θυγατρὸς Ἀγαρίστης, φησίν, ἀπὸ μὲν Ἰταλίης <ἦλθε>[97] Σμινδυρίδης . . .

> [Concerning Smindyrides the Sybarite and his *truphē*, Herodotus wrote in his sixth book that sailing to pay court to Agariste, the daughter of Cleisthenes, the tyrant of Sicyon, he says, from Italy came Smindyrides . . .] (Athen. 12.541b)

As in the passage from Xenophon, the ascription of topic would be obvious as Athenaeus's handiwork, even absent the text of the *Histories*. Since the parenthetical φησίν frequently indicates the beginning of a quotation, the preceding material, beginning with ὡς, is marked as a paraphrase. The phrase περὶ . . . τῆς τούτου τρυφῆς, then, is clearly one step further removed from being a representation of Herodotus's words. On the other hand, a reader without knowl-

---

The Antiphanes passage refers only to a single king of Paphos. This case is generalized to implicate Cypriote kings as a group.

96. It is true that Xenophon says that in his lifestyle the Persian king was "imitating the life of the weakest beasts" (θηρίων τῶν ἀσθενεστάτων βίον μιμούμενον, Xen., *Ages.* 9.5), but the author does not indicate in any way that τρυφή is a cause of this bestial state. As elsewhere in Xenophon, excessive attention to the demands of τρυφή may rather be a symptom of Persian decadence.

97. Added by Kaibel from the text of Herodotus.

edge of the *Histories* would not be able to tell that Athenaeus's characterization of the topic of this citation is seriously misleading. Herodotus says that Smindyrides displayed extreme χλιδή, and the contemporary audience of the *Deipnosophistae* might assume that χλιδή meant τρυφή. However, we have seen in Chapter 1 that these terms were not synonymous in the fifth century: χλιδή refers to physical ornamentation and might be well translated with the today's slang term "bling." This word did not have the behavioral implications associated with τρυφή. Athenaeus, it seems, was aware of the difference, and apparently sought to efface it by adding the extraneous material about Smindyrides' entourage: εἵποντο γοῦν αὐτῷ χίλιοι μάγειροι καὶ ὀρνιθευταί ("At any rate, one thousand cooks and bird-catchers followed him"); the γοῦν implies that this "fact" is an example of the Sybarite's χλιδή. Such a crowd of servants would be an indisputable instance of τρυφή and would justify the way Athenaeus classifies the topic of this citation. In fact, Herodotus includes Smindyrides in a group of men competing to be recognized as "the best man in Greece" (Ἑλλήνων ἁπάντων . . . τὸν ἄριστον, Hdt. 6.126.1). We may therefore suggest that both the material foisted on Herodotus and the identification of the original as περὶ Σμινδυρίδου τοῦ Συβαρίτου καὶ τῆς τούτου τρυφῆς are calculated ploys in Athenaeus's literary legerdemain.

While it is easy to ascertain that Athenaeus provides the topic of this citation, just as he provides author and book, and parallels from fragmentary citations are therefore unlikely to cause confusion, other elements of Athenaeus's framing language are more insidious. In the next of the extant τρυφή citations, at 12.541a, Athenaeus refers to the remarkable cloak of Alcisthenes of Sybaris, for which he calls upon the authority of Aristotle:[98]

Ἀλκισθένην δὲ τὸν Συβαρίτην φησὶν Ἀριστοτέλης ἐν τοῖς Θαυμασίοις ὑπὸ τρυφῆς ἱμάτιον τοιοῦτον κατασκευάσασθαι τῇ πολυτελείᾳ ὡς . . .

[Aristotle says in the *Wonders* that Alcisthenes the Sybarite, because of *truphē*, had a cloak made of such extravagance that . . .] (Athen. 12.541a = Ps.-Arist., *Mir.* 96.838a)

---

98. The *De mirabilibus auscultationibis*, or *Mirabilia*, is not a work of Aristotle, and its loosely organized composite structure make it difficult for scholars to agree upon a date of composition. The individual *paradoxa* that make up the work come from a wide range of sources. About the provenance of the Alcisthenes passage, Flashar (1972, 115), following Geffcken (1892, 96), says "Timaios hier sicher zu greifen ist." This attribution is based on the reprise of the story of the mantel by Athenaeus, who adds that Alcisthenes had procured the garment ὑπὸ τρυφῆς. Timaeus's interest in Sybarite τρυφή is taken as unquestionable, and thus his authority for this story seems "sicher."

What follows is close enough to the original that we would consider it a quotation, totaling about 40 words.[99] Athenaeus has faithfully reproduced his source, adding as a frame only the author's name, the title of the work, and the single phrase ὑπὸ τρυφῆς.

This addition, however, is not minor or insignificant. It constitutes an act of interpretation, since the author of the *Mirabilia* had nothing to say about the Sybarite's motives in ordering his marvelous ἱμάτιον. In fact, inserting a causal expression into a citation is one of Athenaeus's favorite moves. Once more the anecdote of Smindyrides may serve as demonstration. Besides the citation in Book 12, where Herodotus is named as the source, Athenaeus alludes to this incident in Book 6, this time with no attribution:

ἀλλ᾽ οὐ Σμινδυρίδης ὁ Συβαρίτης τοιοῦτος, ὦ Ἕλληνες, ὃς ἐπὶ τὸν Ἀγαρίστης τῆς Κλεισθένους θυγατρὸς ἐξορμῶν γάμον ὑπὸ χλιδῆς καὶ τρυφῆς χιλίους συνεπήγετο οἰκέτας, ἁλιεῖς καὶ ὀρνιθευτὰς καὶ μαγείρους.

[Smindyrides of Sybaris was not such a man, O Greeks, who, setting out for the marriage of Agariste, the daughter of Cleisthenes, from ostentation and τρυφή took with him a thousand slaves, fishers and fowlers and cooks.] (Athen. 6.273b–c)

Because of the occurrence of χλιδή, we conclude that Athenaeus has the Herodotus passage in mind as a partial model. From a characteristic of Smindyrides, χλιδή has become a cause of action; τρυφή, rather than being an element in an editorial mise-en-scène, has entered the narrative itself. This passage and the citation from the *Mirabilia* reveal a pattern. We must bear it in mind and be extremely cautious when we find τρυφή reported as a cause in fragmentary evidence.[100]

---

99. According to Lenfant's analysis, the accusative + infinitive form of this citation would led us to consider it a paraphrase, if the original were lost. However, the *Mirabilia* passage itself is cast in this mode of indirect discourse, with φασί occurring where Athenaeus has φησίν. In addition, names always being subject to confusion in the MSS, the original has Alcimenes, while Athenaeus has Alcisthenes. Also manuscripts ACE have the phrase περὶ τρυφῆς before Θαυμασίοις: Casaubon deleted it.

100. The phrase ὑπὸ τρυφῆς is rarely obvious as being part of the language of citation. A good example is Athen. 12.518b: ὑπὸ δὲ τῆς τρυφῆς οἱ Τυρρηνοί, ὡς Ἄλκιμος ἱστορεῖ, πρὸς αὐλὸν καὶ μάττουσιν καὶ πυκτεύουσι καὶ μαστιγοῦσιν ("From *truphē* the Etruscans, as Alcimus reports [*FGrH* 560 F 3], knead and box and flog to the flute."). Associating these three activities with decadence makes little sense, but if we consider that a few pages earlier the *Deipnosophistae* had listed marching to war to the sound of music as one of the examples of Lydian τρυφή (Athen. 12.517a), it seems likely that ὑπὸ τῆς τρυφῆς gives Athenaeus's view rather than Alcimus's. A useful comparison occurs at Athen. 9.381f: ὁ καλὸς ἡμῶν ἐστιάτωρ Λαρήνσιος, καὶ πόσῳ κάλλιον, ἔφη, τὰ τοιαῦτα ἐκμανθάνειν τοὺς μαγείρους ἢ

The last in this set of passages is a long citation from Diodorus Siculus about a pool (κολυμβήθρα) built at Agrigentum that became both a fishpond and a roosting place for swans (Athen. 12.541f; Diod. Sic. 11.25.4–5). Though in indirect speech, the passage is close enough to the original for 47 words that we are comfortable calling it a quote, followed by a five-word summary of the 34 words that in the original expressed in much greater detail the destruction of the pond over time. We must note that the reader has no way of determining from the text of Athenaeus where the literal citation ends and the summary begins. More to the point here, Athenaeus makes significant but unusually subtle changes to the original. In Diodorus, the context is the rewards that Gelon of Syracuse showered upon the Sicilian Greeks after the Battle of Himera. More specifically, Diodorus is discussing some of the wonders that were built by enslaved Carthaginian captives. The Agrigentine pool is one such example, a public benefit from the king to the people. It served, Diodorus says, to provide fish εἰς τροφὴν καὶ ἀπόλαυσιν ("for nourishment and pleasure").

Athenaeus changes the purpose of the pool with the simplest of alterations: εἰς τὴν τρυφὴν καὶ ἀπόλαυσιν τῷ Γέλωνι ("for the *truphē* and pleasure of Gelon"). In doing so, he completely reverses the facts, indicating that this impressive work was constructed as a gift to Gelon and transforming it into an item of self-indulgence. In this case, it might seem that the simplest explanation is to assume that Athenaeus's copy of Diodorus read εἰς τὴν τρυφὴν instead of εἰς τροφὴν, but the dative of interest τῷ Γέλωνι suggests otherwise. For the name has been inserted into the original, not only after εἰς τὴν τρυφὴν καὶ ἀπόλαυσιν, precisely at the juncture of the quotation and the summary paraphrase—a transitional location where we may expect Athenaean intervention in his source—but also in the introduction to this citation:

Διόδωρος δ' ὁ Σικελιώτης ἐν τοῖς περὶ Βιβλιοθήκης Ἀκραγαντίνους φησὶ κατασκευάσαι Γέλωνι κολυμβήθραν πολυτελῆ . . .

[Diodorus of Sicily says in the *Bibliotheca* that the Agrigentines built for Gelon an expensive pool . . .] (Athen. 12.541e)

ἅπερ παρά τινι τῶν πολιτῶν ἡμῶν, ὃς ὑπὸ πλούτου καὶ τρυφῆς τοὺς τοῦ θαυμασιωτάτου Πλάτωνος διαλόγους ἠνάγκαζεν ἐκμανθάνοντας τοὺς μαγείρους . . . ("Our noble host Larensis said, 'How much better that the cooks learn such things than the things at one of our countrymen's, who from wealth and *truphē* compels his cooks to learn the dialogues of the most wondrous Plato . . .'"). Here is a close parallel, from the framing conversation, of the function of ὑπὸ τρυφῆς in the three citations we have examined.

We have just seen with περὶ τρυφῆς and ὑπὸ τρυφῆς that the introductory framing sentence is an obvious locus for such interpretive alterations. Thus, we judge that the change from τροφὴν to τρυφὴν, like the insertions of Γέλωνι, is a deliberate recasting of the passage by Athenaeus.[101]

This conclusion has particularly disturbing implications. With a few small changes to an otherwise a very accurate text, what had been both beneficial and aesthetically pleasing to the citizens of Agrigentum is transformed by Athenaeus into a private pleasure for Gelon, and this transformation results in evidence for τρυφή that would be accepted as genuine under the criteria outlined above. The reference to τρυφή, for example, occurs in the body of the fragment, in a phrase that seems integral to the sentence structure, and in wording that is not identifiable as an Athenaean stock phrase. If we did not possess this section of Diodorus, Athenaeus's rather elegant innovation would have been undetectable. In other words, the criteria that we have suggested, although they lead us to treat the fragmentary evidence on τρυφή quite skeptically, do not go far enough in this direction. They are not adequate for the job of detecting questionable testimony by Athenaeus on the subject of τρυφή. At least some of the evidence that we consider as genuine will not be so. We may only hope that the proportion of undetectable "false positives" will not be as large as the occurrence of one such among the six extant τρυφή-citations might suggest.

Thus, we know from an examination of existing originals that Athenaeus uses the framing language around his citations to interject his own moral schema, such as τρυφή (or gluttony, sycophancy, drunkenness, and the like) into otherwise unlikely passages. Athenaeus frames the introductions to his citations especially in a very consistent pattern, and that is where we find the clearest examples of alterations, but he also adds interpretive summaries at the

---

101. Zecchini (1989, 116) maintains that the route by which this passage came to Athenaeus is "certo indiretta." This view is based on the fact that this is the only reference to Diodorus in the *Deipnosophistae* and on the occurrence of the rare word for "pool," κολυμβήθρα. Zecchini thus reasons that Athenaeus found the passage in a lexicon. This interpretation is plausible, as far as it goes, but it does not explain the citation's mistaken insistence that the construction at Agrigentum was carried out for the sake of Gelon of Syracuse. It is difficult to see why a lexicographer would have emphasized this point. A better intermediate source for Athenaeus might be a collection of famous examples of τρυφή with its material organized, like Athenaeus's own Book 12, at least partially περὶ τῶν κατ᾽ ἄνδρα τρυφῶν ("about instances of τρυφή committed by individuals"; cf. 12.528e). The author of such a work might well exceed the evidence of his sources to identify individual beneficiaries of apparent instances of excessive luxury. The existence of a compendium of examples of ancient decadence is, however, speculative and controversial. Lacking a consensus on such an intermediary, we assume, *argumenti causa*, that the alterations in the citation are Athenaeus's own. Cf. Zecchini 1987.

end of a quotation. At other times he paraphrases a long passage in a misleading fashion. Given this situation, it is imperative for the reader to learn to distinguish between Athenaean language and that which at least possibly comes from his sources. If Athenaeus has framed the few sources that we have extant in a manner which would have led to misunderstanding if we did not possess the originals, we must assume that he does the same thing in at least some portion of the places where he cites authors who are now lost to us.

When we look for familiar framing patterns among citations of lost authors, we see that they recur repeatedly in the passages that involve τρυφή. The matter is, of course, clearest when dealing with citations from lost works of verse. Here there is little danger of confusing the poetic diction of the original with Athenaeus's prose additions, though some readers may see the framing language as a paraphrase of lost lines. However, we may be led astray if we assume that Athenaeus is correctly identifying the focus of the original. A good example of the word τρυφή inserted by Athenaeus before a verse citation occurs at 12.553e: Κρατῖνός τ' ἐν Χείρωσι τὴν τρυφὴν ἐμφανίζων τὴν τῶν παλαιτέρων φησίν ("Cratinus [frag. 257 KA] demonstrates the *truphē* of the olden days in *The Cheirons* when he says . . ."). What follows is two verses about someone sitting in the assembly with a flower tucked behind his ear and dallying in the agora with an apple in hand. The verses are hardly the stuff of scandal, and they do not constitute evidence that Cratinus was interested in the idea of decadence or in the self-indulgent entitlement that is integral to Classical τρυφή. One may fairly assume that it was Athenaeus who identified the topic as such.

Likewise, in another passage at Athen. 12.525e, the format is all-too familiar:

περὶ δὲ τῆς Σαμίων τρυφῆς Δοῦρις ἱστορῶν παρατίθεται Ἀσίου ποιήματα, ὅτι ἐφόρουν χλιδῶνας περὶ τοῖς βραχίοσιν καὶ τὴν ἑορτὴν ἄγοντες τῶν Ἡραίων ἐβάδιζον κατεκτενισμένοι τὰς κόμας ἐπὶ τὸ μετάφρενον καὶ τοὺς ὤμους.

[Concerning the *truphē* of the Samians, Duris [FGrH 76 F 60] records the verses of Asius [frag. 13 Bernabé] showing that they wore bracelets [*chlidōnes*] around their arms and, when they celebrated the festival of Hera, they marched with their hair combed down over their chests and shoulders.]

He follows with a quotation of six verses. Clearly the mention of τρυφή is part of Athenaeus's thesis about this citation. He begins his interpretive or argumentative paraphrase with ὅτι; a few lines later follow the verses from Asius, which include a reference to χλιδή, but not τρυφή.[102] The relevance of this term to the Asius passage is an inference made by Athenaeus; there is no sign in the quoted verses of any disapproval of the luxury described. The fragment is not evidence for a concern with decadence in the Archaic period.[103] Incidentally, we would argue that this passage is likewise not good evidence that Duris was interested in decadence:[104] the τρυφή is part of the introductory frame of the section and expresses Athenaeus's opinion about the topic of the citation. As a result, from this fragment we can assume that Athenaeus found the quotation from Asius in the historian, but we cannot assume that Duris, like Athenaeus, presented the verses as evidence περὶ δὲ τῆς Σαμίων τρυφῆς.

Two additional passages feature verse references that are introduced with a prose framework containing the word τρυφή. At Athen. 12.527c, we find:

διαβόητοι δ᾽ εἰσὶ περὶ τρυφὴν Σικελιῶταί τε καὶ Συρακόσιοι, ὡς καὶ Ἀριστοφάνης φησὶν ἐν Δαιταλεῦσιν

[Famous for their *truphē* are the Sicilians and Syracusans, as Aristophanes says in the *Banqueters*.]

Three verses follow [Aristophanes, frag. 225.1–3 KA] about feasting, drinking, and dirty songs, without explicit mention of τρυφή. In a parallel instance, Anacreon is cited as the source for more τρυφή, this time concerning a man named Artemon: καὶ γὰρ Ἀνακρέων αὐτὸν ἐκ πενίας εἰς τρυφὴν ὁρμῆσαί φησιν ἐν τούτοις ("And Anacreon [frag. 388 *PMG*] says that he set off from poverty into *truphē* in these words . . . ," Athen. 12.533f). Nine verses follow with no mention of τρυφή itself, but rather containing a rags-to-riches story about a thoroughly unpleasant man, "a knave who keeps company with bread-selling catamites"

---

102. A reference at Athen. 12.528c to Phylarchus (*FGrH* 81 F 23) citing Aeschylus (frag. 306 *TrGF*) is similar to the reference to Herodotus (6.127.1) and to this one (Athen. 12.525e), in that all are introduced with the word τρυφή and yet all the originals contain the word χλιδή instead.

103. Thus, Bowra (1957, 393) points out, "We have no right to assume that we must interpret Asius as Duris did." Bowra finds the source of Duris's interpretation in the occurrence of χλιδῶνες in the poem: "not only did it suggest χλιδή, but in his time bracelets were hardly ever worn by men, and the mere suggestion of them would be enough to excite his disapproval." Bowra does not notice any influence by Athenaeus on the passage and he therefore overlooks the possibility that Duris may be as innocent of an "ethical preoccupation" with τρυφή as is Asius. For problems with determining the length of citations to Duris in Athenaeus, see Baron 2011.

104. Cf. Kebric 1977, 20: "Duris' fragments constantly mirror his cognizance of extravagance and luxury."

(ἀρτοπώλισιν κἀθελοπόρνοισιν ὁμιλέων ὁ πονηρὸς) and uses deceit to obtain a success that is manifested in golden necklaces, an ivory parasol, and the use of a chariot. Again, one could argue that Anacreon was describing τρυφή, especially in characterizing Artemon's newfound habits as effeminate (σκιαδίσκην ἐλεφαντίνην φορεῖ γυναιξὶν αὔτως, "he carries his ivory parasol like a woman"), but the characterization is not explicit in the lines cited. Certainly, the term itself is added.

The twenty-two examples of a τρυφή word within verse citations themselves, which we may generally assume to be genuine, are noticeably different from the uses of τρυφή in the framing language.[105] In brief, most τρυφή words are used descriptively, usually with reference to the expectation of receiving good food or drink, and with no particular negative moral connotation. One passage may serve to give the general tone. The poet Alexis (frag. 223 KA) expounds on the eating habits of certain philosophers:

τρυφῶσιν οὗτοι πρὸς ἑτέρους. ἆρ᾽ οἶσθ᾽ ὅτι
Μελανιππίδης ἑταῖρός ἐστι καὶ Φάων
καὶ Φυρόμαχος καὶ Φᾶνος, οἳ δι᾽ ἡμέρας
δειπνοῦσι πέμπτης ἀλφίτων κοτύλην μίαν.

[These men enjoy *truphē* compared with others. Don't you know that Melanippides is his friend, and Phaon and Phyromachus and Phanus, who dine on half a pint of barley every fourth day?] (Athen. 4.161c)

Sometimes, τρυφή is part of an unspecified description of the good life, as we read in Athen. 13.558e–f, once again from Alexis (frag. 150 KA):

ὦ δυστυχεῖς ἡμεῖς < . . . οἱ> πεπρακότες
τὴν τοῦ βίου παρρησίαν καὶ τὴν τρυφήν·
γυναιξὶ δοῦλοι ζῶμεν ἀντ᾽ ἐλευθέρων.

[We are unfortunate . . . , having sold life's freedom of speech and its *truphē*. We live as slaves to women instead of free men.]

---

105. Athen. 4.158e, 160a, 161c; 6.228f (Olson [ad loc.] prints σύντροφα), 258d, 268f; 7.281a; 10.414d, 437e, 449c; 11.471c, 472d; 12.511a, 524f, 526d, 528d, 549c bis, 553a; 13.558e, 581e, 608d.

We may note that there is no sign here of the idea that τρυφή is a vice. Furthermore, while Athenaeus is especially interested in τρυφή functioning as a cause of decadence, the only clear causal use among the verse examples occurs at Athen. 4.158e, citing Euripides (frag. 884 *TrGF*):

ἐπεὶ τί δεῖ βροτοῖσι κατὰ τὸν σὸν Εὐριπίδην, γραμματικώτατε, πλὴν δυοῖν μόνον,

Δήμητρος ἀκτῆς πώματός θ᾽ ὑδρηχόου;
ἅπερ πάρεστι καὶ πέφυχ᾽ ἡμᾶς τρέφειν.
ὧν οὐκ ἀπαρκεῖ πλησμονή· τρυφῇ γέ τοι
ἄλλων ἐδεστῶν μηχανὰς θηρεύομεν.

[What, according to your Euripides, O most critical of scholars, do mortals need except two things only? "A *terra firma* of grain and a river of poured water? These things are readily at hand and by their nature nourish us. An excess of these things is not enough for us; from *truphē* we hunt mechanisms for other victuals."]

Here we may understand τρυφῇ as a rare dative of cause, but what it causes is dissatisfaction. This expression is essentially tautological, since we have seen in Chapter 1 that part of τρυφή's basic meaning is an expectation that others will satisfy the subject, which implies at least a potential state of dissatisfaction. In any case, this causal τρυφή is far from the picture Athenaeus paints in Book 12, where τρυφή is identified as leading to the ruination of individuals and the destruction of cities.

If the meaning of τρυφή terms within most verse citations is innocuous and out of harmony with Athenaeus's claims elsewhere, the same can be said about its formal characteristics. The passages do not contain any language that can be classified as formulaic and among Athenaeus's regular turns of phrase, as we will examine shortly.

Certain instances of formulaic framing language we have already identified above, and these can often be easily found introducing fragmentary prose authors. A clear-cut illustration in the pattern of Athen. 4.144b (Xenophon) and Athen. 12.541b (Herodotus) is the passage at Athen. 12.534f: Λυσίας δὲ ὁ ῥήτωρ περὶ τῆς τρυφῆς αὐτοῦ λέγων φησίν ("Lysias the orator, speaking concerning the *truphē* of [Alcibiades], says . . ."). The story follows in direct speech (Lysias, frag. 8 Carey) that Alcibiades and Axiochus went to Abydus where they shared a wife and, when she had a daughter, they later slept with her as well. Such activities, though indecent, are not readily categorized as instances of τρυφή in its classical sense: someone with τρυφή would demand extra bed-mates for himself, not share the one he had. It is unlikely that the word occurred in the original.

At the other end of the spectrum of complexity, Athen. 12.514d illustrates how difficult it can be to decide on the accuracy of Athenaeus's topical language. The citation begins: Κλέαρχος δὲ ὁ Σολεὺς ἐν τετάρτῳ Βίων προειπὼν περὶ τῆς Μήδων τρυφῆς καὶ ὅτι . . . ("Clearchus of Soli in the fourth book of his *Lives*, having said already about the *truphē* of the Medes also that . . .").[106] The phrasing contains the usual bibliographic reference, while the topic tells the reader how to interpret the content of the ὅτι clause.[107] And at first glance, it seems as though the classification of the citation as περὶ τρυφῆς is justified, since the word τρυφή follows again twice more in what may seem the body of the fragment. However, the first of these instances occurs in material that shows indications of being a paraphrase.[108] The second example sounds distinctly like an Athenaean editorial comment:

δύναται γάρ, ὡς ἔοικεν, ἡ παράκαιρος ἅμα καὶ μάταιος αὐτῶν περὶ τὸν βίον τρυφὴ καὶ τοὺς ταῖς λόγχαις καθωπλισμένους ἀγύρτας ἀποφαίνειν. καὶ προελθὼν δὲ γράφει·

[For it is possible, as it seems, for ill-timed and at the same time thoughtless *truphē* in life to render even men armed with spears into beggars. For continuing, he [Clearchus] also writes: . . .] (Athen. 12.514d)[109]

The δύναται sentence is clearly an inference about the Persian custom that had just been related about "apple-bearing" (μηλοφορία), but it is a matter of interpretation whether the inference was made by Athenaeus or his source. It is

---

106. Introducing Clearchus, frag. 49 Wehrli.
107. Although Lenfant's schema would support the assumption that the ὅτι clause is a quotation, we will see below that the diction of the clause is more consistent with a paraphrase.
108. The word occurs within an indirect statement clause of the acc. + infinitive type; the indirect statement also contains an expression—εἰς ὅσον ἦλθον ἀνανδρίας ("how far into cowardice they had gone")—which follows a pattern frequent in Athenaean framing language dealing with evidence on moral questions.
109. Introducing Clearchus, frag. 51a Wehrli.

relevant to observe that the sentence in question is located immediately before the announcement of a seam in the citation: προελθών indicates that Athenaeus is about to cite from a different portion of the *Lives*, and it is not unusual to find likely Athenaean comments near such a suture. In addition, the phrase ὡς ἔοικεν, admittedly a common Greek expression, is used elsewhere to make clear that Athenaeus is providing his own slant on material cited.[110] Finally, there are the implications of the part of the fragment that seems likely to come most closely from Clearchus: following immediately upon γράφει and in direct speech comes a description of the rewards allotted for bringing to the king delectable culinary inventions; this matter is related without obvious disapproval.[111] The approach to this particular Persian custom seems ethnographical rather than moralizing. This attitude is out of harmony with the concerns on view in the earlier parts of the fragment. For these reasons, we conclude that the section of the citation before γράφει is not reliably Clearchan and that we are not justified in accepting Athenaeus's claim that the original was περὶ τῆς Μήδων τρυφῆς.[112]

In addition to framing language setting the topic for fragmentary citation,

---

110. For example, at Athen. 14.628c–d, in the context of a discussion of the idea that music reveals the soul of the performer, Athenaeus relates an anecdote told by Herodotus (6.129) about the reaction of Cleisthenes of Sicyon to the behavior of one Agariste's wooers: ἰδὼν γάρ, ὥς φασι, φορτικῶς ὀρχησάμενον ἕνα τῶν τῆς θυγατρὸς μνηστήρων (Ἱπποκλείδης δ᾽ ἦν ὁ Ἀθηναῖος) ἀπωρχῆσθαι τὸν γάμον αὐτὸν ἔφησεν ("Seeing, as they say, one of his daughter's suitors dancing in a vulgar manner [he was Hippocleides the Athenian], he said that the fellow had danced away his marriage."). Athenaeus then adds an interpretation that links this anecdote to his immediate concerns: νομίζων ὡς ἔοικεν καὶ τὴν ψυχὴν τἀνδρὸς εἶναι τοιαύτην. καὶ γὰρ ἐν ὀρχήσει καὶ πορείᾳ καλὸν μὲν εὐσχημοσύνη καὶ κόσμος, αἰσχρὸν δὲ ἀταξία καὶ τὸ φορτικόν ("thinking, as it seems, that the man's soul was also such. For both in dancing and walking gracefulness and orderliness are noble, but disorder and vulgarity are dishonorable."). Here the principal function of ὡς ἔοικεν seems to be to alert the reader to the fact that the νομίζων participial clause is part of the interpretation that follows rather than the source material that precedes.

111. τοῖς γοῦν πορίσασί τι αὐτῷ ἡδὺ βρῶμα διδοὺς ἆθλα τοῦ πορισθέντος οὐχ ἑτέραις ἡδύνων ταῦτα τιμαῖς παρετίθει, πολὺ δὲ μᾶλλον αὐτὸς ἀπολαύειν αὐτῶν, νοῦν <οὐκ> ἔχων· τοῦτο μὲν γάρ ἐστιν ὁ λεγόμενος, οἶμαι, [καὶ] Διὸς ἅμα καὶ βασιλέως ἐγκέφαλος ("While to those, at any rate, who bring to him some tasty food he gives prizes for procurement, he does not sweeten these things with other rewards and share them, but rather prefers to enjoy them by himself—senselessly. This, I think, is the 'a morsel for Zeus and for the king.'" Athen. 12.514e). Note that some editors emend the text based on 12.529d in order to make Clearchus's comment on the custom disapproving (νοῦν <οὐκ> ἔχων; e.g., Kaibel), while others accept the MSS and assume irony while ignoring the contradiction between the two passages (e.g., Olson). Both moves are apparently based on Athenaeus's tendentious presentation of Clearchus's moral stance. It is quite possible that the transmitted text is to be understood literally and that Clearchus supported his view that such exotic fare was appropriate for kings alone by quoting the proverb.

112. We do assume that Clearchus discussed the Persian practice of castration and the adoption of the "Apple-bearers" from the Medes. On the other hand, the fragment does not provide trustworthy evidence that Clearchus treated these customs as moral *exempla*.

we also observe in such passages Athenaeus's penchant to insert τρυφή as a cause. Like περὶ τῆς τρυφῆς, διὰ τὴν τρυφὴν is frequent. For example, before breaking off into a lacuna, Athen. 12.526d begins with the following framework: Θεόφραστος δ' ἐν τῷ περὶ Ἡδονῆς καὶ δὴ καὶ τοὺς Ἴωνάς φησι διὰ τὴν ὑπερβολὴν τῆς τρυφῆς ("Theophrastus also in his work *On Pleasure* says that the Ionians, because of their excess of *truphē* . . .").[113] At 12.550d, Athenaeus frames a transition to a different book of Agatharchides (*FGrH* 86 F 11) by saying that the Spartans summoned before the assembly Naucleides, who was very fat διὰ τρυφὴν, and Lysander reviled him as such.[114] Two more examples occur at 12.552f and 12.518e, both in the opening frame of a paraphrased story. Finally at Athen. 12.536b, the phrase διὰ τρυφὴν occurs in a long citation from Nymphis of Heracleia (*FGrH* 432 F 9) about Pausanias, the victor at Plataea. At first glance, it seems to belong to Nymphis, but then we see that it is being used to introduce the text of an inscription: . . . ὃν ἔτι καὶ νῦν εἶναι συμβαίνει, ἐτόλμησεν ἐπιγράψαι ὡς αὐτὸς ἀναθείη, ὑποθεὶς τόδε τὸ ἐπίγραμμα, διὰ τὴν τρυφὴν καὶ ὑπερηφανίαν ἐπιλαθόμενος αὑτοῦ ("He dared to write that he had dedicated it [a bronze mixing bowl], engraving this inscription, which still survives, forgetting his place because of his *truphē* and arrogance."). It is possible that Nymphis wrote this line, but it is more likely that he merely recorded the text of the epigram upon which Athenaeus himself then comments within his moral schema.

We have concentrated so far on citations in which a paraphrase preceding a quotation can be identified. There are also many cases where the fragment consists of a paraphrase alone. In these passages we cannot compare framing language to probable source material, and therefore our ability to judge the reliability of the citations is even more limited. Anyone attempting to use the evidence of these citations should be on the lookout for typically Athenaean phrasing. For example, we cannot be sure that in the following fragment that Satyrus was interested in the moral dimension of Dionysius's dining arrangements:

περὶ δὲ τῆς Διονυσίου τοῦ νεωτέρου Σικελίας τυράννου τρυφῆς Σάτυρος ὁ περιπατητικὸς ἱστορῶν ἐν τοῖς Βίοις πληροῦσθαί φησιν παρ' αὐτῷ τριακοντακλίνους οἴκους ὑπὸ τῶν εὐωχουμένων.

---

113. Introducing Theophrastus, frag. 549 Fortenbaugh.
114. Since the word repeats in Lysander's insult, it may derive from the original.

[Concerning the *truphē* of Dionysius the Younger, tyrant of Sicily, Satyrus the Peripatetic writing in his *Lives* says that rooms in his palace, which held thirty couches, were filled with revelers.] (Athen. 12.541c = Satyrus, frag. 21 Schorn)

Nor can we trust that, in the original of this passage at Athen. 12.540c–d (= Clytus, *FGrH* 490 F 2), τρυφή was identified as the motive force for Polycrates' imports:

Κλύτος δ᾽ ὁ Ἀριστοτελικὸς ἐν τοῖς περὶ Μιλήτου Πολυκράτην φησὶ τὸν Σαμίων τύραννον ὑπὸ τρυφῆς τὰ πανταχόθεν συνάγειν, κύνας μὲν ἐξ Ἠπείρου, αἶγας δὲ ἐκ Σκύρου, ἐκ δὲ Μιλήτου πρόβατα, ὗς δ᾽ ἐκ Σικελίας.

[Clytus the Aristotelian in his books *About Miletus* says that Polycrates, the tyrant of Samos, because of *truphē*, brought in things from everywhere: dogs from Epeirus, goats from Skyros, sheep from Miletus, and pigs from Sicily.]

By analogy with the references to extant sources, the cautious conclusion is that the details about the imported goods and the furniture of the banquet hall were probably in the originals, but, without any further evidence, one cannot say that Satyrus or Clytus made any mention of τρυφή or that either was presenting the information reported in these citations in order to make a moral point. To judge by the extant sources, that idea was more likely than not added by Athenaeus.

Formulae with Τρυφή

In the preceding discussion we have several times made the claim that certain turns of phrase can be identified as Athenaean diction and that the presence of such material is an indication that at least the wording of a citation comes from the author of the *Deipnosophistae* rather than the original source. We will now examine the evidence for some of the most prominent of the Athenaean stock expressions that pertain to the idea of pernicious luxury.

To identify suspicious phraseology we have considered the diction of Athenaeus's citations along two axes of analysis. The first step consists of examining the material horizontally, or synchronically: the pattern of occurrence of diction within the *Deipnosophistae* is mapped. Material that recurs in citations from several sources is marked for further investigation. For phrases so identified we develop a profile of usage considered vertically, or diachronically: was each usage rare or common through the course of extant Greek literature from Homer to Athenaeus's own day? When Athenaean diction is considered from these two perspectives, a strong case can often be made that the wording under consideration does not come from Athenaeus's original source.

A clear example of a horizontal analysis occurs with phrase (ἐξ)οκέλλειν εἰς τρυφήν. Properly speaking, ἐξοκέλλειν is a navigational term meaning "to run aground" or "to shipwreck." In the extant part of the *Deipnosophistae*, the phrase ἐξοκέλλειν εἰς τρυφήν or into some other vice occurs in connection with six different quotations and three (or four) different authors:

4.141f: . . . οἱ Λάκωνες ἐξώκειλαν εἰς τρυφήν. Φύλαρχος γοῦν . . . ("The Laconians ran aground on *truphē*. At least Phylarchus [says] . . .") (Phylarchus, *FGrH* 81 F 44)

12.521c: Συβαρῖται, φησίν [sc. Φύλαρχος], ἐξοκείλαντες εἰς τρυφὴν ἔγραψαν νόμον ("The Sybarites, he [Phylarchus] says, running aground on *truphē*, wrote a law") (Phylarchus, *FGrH* 81 F 45)

12.521d: [sc. Συβαρῖται] ἐξοκείλαντες εἰς ὕβριν (probably again from Phylarchus) ("[The Sybarites] ran aground on hubris") (Phylarchus, *FGrH* 81 F 45)

12.522a: Κροτωνιᾶται δ᾽, ὥς φησι Τίμαιος, . . . ἐξώκειλαν εἰς τρυφήν ("The Crotoniates, as Timaeus says, . . . ran aground on *truphē*") (Timaeus, *FGrH* 566 F 44)

12.523c: οἱ τὴν Σῖριν δὲ κατοικοῦντες . . . , ὥς φησι Τίμαιος καὶ Ἀριστοτέλης, εἰς τρυφὴν ἐξώκειλαν ("Those who inhabit Siris . . . , as Timaeus and Aristotle say, ran aground on *truphē*") (Timaeus, *FGrH* 566 F 51 and Arist., frag. 601)

12.526a: Κολοφώνιοι δ᾽, ὥς φησι Φύλαρχος, . . . ἐπεὶ εἰς τρυφὴν ἐξώκειλαν ("The Colophonians, as Phylarchus says, . . . when they ran aground on *truphē*") (Phylarchus, *FGrH* 81 F 66)

12.528a–b: Πολύβιος δ᾽ . . . Καπυησίους τοὺς ἐν Καμπανίᾳ . . . ἐξοκεῖλαι εἰς τρυφὴν καὶ πολυτέλειαν ("And Polybius [says] . . . the Capuans in Campania ran aground on *truphē* and extravagance") (Polyb. 7.1.1–3)

12.543b: Νικόλαος δ' ὁ περιπατητικὸς . . . Λεύκολλόν φησιν . . . ἐξοκεῖλαι εἰς πολυτελῆ δίαιταν ("Nicolaus the Peripathetic . . . says the Lucullus ran aground on an extravagant lifestyle") (Nicolaus, *FGrH* 90 F 77a)[115]

Thus, Athenaeus attributes the construction in question (ἐξοκέλλειν completed by a preposition whose object is τρυφή or a similar moral term) perhaps to Aristotle and without doubt to Timaeus, Phylarchus, Polybius, and Nicolaus. This synchronic pattern of use arouses suspicion and warrants a study of the diachronic evidence.

A brief examination of the history of this idiom is instructive. Leaving aside for the moment the examples cited in Athenaeus, there is no securely attested instance of the phrase ἐξοκέλλειν εἰς τρυφήν before the Common Era. The verb ἐξοκέλλειν is used most often in early literature in its proper literal sense, to refer to actual groundings by ships and also animals such as dolphins and snakes.[116]

The remaining—metaphorical—uses from before the Common Era are worth examining in detail, for there are only six of them. Aesch., *Supp.* 438 uses the phrase intransitively to describe a predicament: δεῦρο δ' ἐξοκέλλεται, meaning "It has come to this moment of crisis." He goes on to explain that he must choose between waging war against one side or the other. Euripides' Hecube also uses the phrase ἐς τάνδ' ἐξώκειλ' ἄταν ("I have shipwrecked in this ruin," Eur., *Tro.* 137), but she does so in the context of an apostrophe to the very ships that brought the Greeks to Troy. Thus her usage is set in a strictly nautical framework. Isocrates uses the verb three times, to characterize the results of bad government as a shipwreck (Isoc. 7.18), to advise young men not to get bogged down on the arguments of the sophists (μηδ' ἐξοκείλασαν εἰς τοὺς λόγους τοὺς τῶν παλαιῶν σοφιστῶν, Isoc. 15.268), and to promise to end a discussion too lengthy for a letter instead of shipwrecking in lengthy discourse

---

115. Cf. Athen. 6.274f, where again according to Nicolaus (*FGrH* 90 F 77), Lucullus runs his life aground on extravagance (ὤκειλεν εἰς πολυτελῆ δίαιταν). For the implications of this doublet on the question of attribution, see Gorman and Gorman (2007).

116. Aesch., *Ag.* 666; Hdt. 6.16.1, 7.182.1 *bis*, 8.84.1; Thuc. 2.91.4, 4.11.4, 4.12.1, 4.26.7, 8.102.3; Eur., *IT* 1379; Xen., *Anab.* 7.5.12; Arist., *Hist. an.* 533b and 631b, *Mir.* 844a; Nicander, *Ther.* 295 and 321; Polyb. 1.20.15, 1.51.9, 4.41.2; Diod. Sic. 1.31.4, 12.62.3, 13.13.6, 20.87.2; Dion. Hal., *Ant. Rom.* 20.9; Strabo 9.5, 16.3. Wilkins (2008, 149) argues that the sources of the *Deipnosophistae* are sometimes "reshaped for 'navigational purposes,'" and that "[t]he shipwreck of a city or people through its wealth and extravagance is the most striking application of the navigational metaphor" in Athenaeus. These comments give us further reason for confidence that the "run aground on" metaphor was not original to the various fragments in which it occurs.

(ἀλλ᾿ εἰς λόγου μῆκος ἐξοκείλας, Isoc., *Ep.* 2.13). These instances differ significantly from those quoted in Athenaeus, because they are a matter of running aground on something external to the subject (bad luck or the like), not on the subject's own proclivity for vice.

Finally, Polybius 4.48.11, transforms the early metaphorical uses. The context describes Achaeus, viceroy in command of Asia west of Mt. Taurus. He avenged the assassination of King Seleucus and usurped the throne from the Seleucid heir in 220 BCE, but did not maintain his position long. He was captured and executed as a traitor in 213. Achaeus, it seems, ran aground not on vice, but on good fortune: ἐπαρθεὶς τοῖς εὐτυχήμασι παρὰ πόδας ἐξώκειλε ("elated by his good fortune, he immediately ran aground"). It is possible to see in this second-century BCE passage a step toward the usage evident in Athenaeus, since in the latter author good fortune, riches, and the like are often precursors to shipwrecking on some moral failing. However, this example seems to us a closer parallel to the earlier metaphorical uses than to the later ones: not only is the verb used absolutely, but the implied idea of running aground on good fortune is simply a witty inversion of the more straightforward use that we have seen in Euripides and Isocrates. No serious moral culpability in Achaeus is necessarily entailed, but merely an inability to manage affairs in his new position.

By contrast, moral blame on the part of the subject is regularly part of the usage in the Common Era. The first clear parallel to our examples from Athenaeus occurs in Philo during the first century CE. In contrast to Classical writers, he *never* uses the word for a literal shipwreck, but it is one of his favorite turns of phrase for moral failings, since he uses it this way nine times, in particular for the indulgence of appetites that are better kept in check: general vice (*LA* 2.60; *Praem.* 170); things eyes should not be looking at (*Agr.* 34); love of unattainable things (*Conf.* 7); lust for a kinswoman (*Somn.* 1.246); intemperate language, gluttony, and licentiousness (*Somn.* 2.211); general incontinence (*Spec. leg.* 2.135); and passions (*Mut.* 38.215). In this last passage, it may be significant that Philo elaborates the metaphor:

μικρᾶς πρὸς εὐτυχίαν αὔρας λαβόμενοι, πάντα κάλων ἀνασείσαντες, λαμπρὰ φυσῶμεν καὶ πνεύσαντες μέγα καὶ σύντονον πλησίστιοι πρὸς τὰς ἀπολαύσεις τῶν παθῶν φερόμεθα καὶ οὐ πρότερον στέλλομεν τὰς ἀνειμένας καὶ κεχαλασμένας ἀκρατῶς ἐπιθυμίας, ἕως ἂν ἐξοκείλαντες ὅλῳ τῷ ψυχῆς ναυαγήσωμεν σκάφει.

[Catching the smallest breezes blowing toward good fortune, shaking out every reef, we puff a keen breeze and blowing to our utmost we move with full sails toward the enjoyment of our passions; we don't stop our slack and uncontrollably loose desires until, running aground, we shipwreck the whole vessel of our soul.] (Philo, *Mut.* 38.215)

After Philo, the expression occurs with frequency in a wide range of authors of the first and second centuries CE. The idiom is adopted by Josephus, who uses it almost entirely in a moral sense,[117] and it becomes a preferred expression for Plutarch,[118] Cassius Dio, [119] and Clement of Alexandria[120] especially, the latter of whom is the first outside of Athenaeus to relate the term to τρυφή (at *Paed.* 3.8.44.1 and 3.11.53.2).

Given these facts, it seems best to identify the phrase ἐξοκέλλειν εἰς τρυφήν in Athenaeus as that writer's own contribution. Such an interpretation is supported by a further consideration: it is imprudent to assume that Athenaeus, in selecting examples of τρυφή from Timaeus, Phylarchus, and the rest, would by some coincidence quote so many instances of what was unlikely to have been anything but a rare phrase. Thus we conclude that ἐξοκέλλειν εἰς τρυφήν represents a moral embellishment applied to the evidence cited by Athenaeus, and we should be careful not to attribute these words to the authorities named.[121]

While in the case of ἐξοκέλλειν both synchronic and diachronic patterns of use provide strong reasons to consider the phrase a later addition, in other cases the relative importance of the two avenues of investigation may vary greatly. For example, throughout the *Deipnosophistae* we find sentences with the following elements: a verb of motion (e.g. ἔρχομαι) with a dependent directional preposition (e.g., εἰς); a neuter singular pronoun as the object of εἰς; dependent on the pronoun, a genitive noun denoting the name of a vice; a result clause indicating the extent of the vice ("He went so far into vice that . . ."). Here is a representative sample of Athenaean passages:

---

117. The one exception is *AJ* 1.95, concerning the landing of the ark, in which he is citing from Nicolaus of Damascus. Otherwise: *Vit.* 123; *AJ* 17.113; *BJ* 4.261, 4.381, 2.251.2.

118. Plut., *Tim.* 36.8; *Luc.* 38.4; *Brut.* 1.2; *Mar.* 2, 45; *Mor.* 5b, 160f, 161a, 347b, 654e, 940f, 981b, 985c.

119. Cassius Dio 19.62.1; 24.83.2; 25.85.1; 54.21; 55.16.3; 57.13; 58.23; 67.14.2; 75.16; 79.3.3; 141; 286; S223.

120. Clement Alex., *Paed.* 2.1.4.1, 2.2.28.3, 2.8.61.1, 3.2.10.3, 3.8.44.1, 3.11.53.2; *Strom.* 3.5.41.2; *QDS* 40.3. Also Herodian 5.7.6, 6.1.5, 7.10.2; Aelius Aristides, *Pros Platona* 149; Paus. 8.24.9; and Ael., *NA* 14.20; at *VH* 12.24 and 12.30 it is used with τρυφή.

121. Flower (1994, 166), for example, suggests that Timaeus "coined the evocative phrase 'to run aground into luxury.'" However, it would be difficult to explain why Polybius would have imitated in his use of this expression a writer whom he notoriously despised.

2.37b: Τίμαιος δὲ ὁ Ταυρομενίτης . . . φησι . . . νεανίσκους τινὰς . . . ἐς τοσοῦτον ἐλθεῖν μανίας . . . ὡς . . . ("Timaeus of Tauromenium . . . says . . . that certain young men . . . went to such an extent of madness . . . that . . .") (Timaeus, *FGrH* 566 F 149)

4.165e: καὶ Κτήσιππος δ᾽ ὁ Χαβρίου υἱὸς εἰς τοσοῦτον ἦλθεν ἀσωτίας ὡς . . . ("Ctesippus the son of Chabrias, too, went to such an extent of prodigality that . . .")

4.167d–e: εἰς τοσοῦτον δ᾽ ἀσωτίας ἐληλύθει καὶ Δημήτριος ὁ Δημητρίου τοῦ Φαληρέως ἀπόγονος, ὥς φησιν Ἡγήσανδρος, ὥστε . . . ("Demetrius, the descendent of Demetrius of Phalerum, as Hegesander says, had also gone to such an extent of prodigality that . . .") (Hegesander, frag. 8, *FHG* iv.415)

8.341a: καὶ Ἀνδροκύδης δ᾽ ὁ Κυζικηνὸς ζωγράφος φίλιχθυς ὤν, ὡς ἱστορεῖ Πολέμων, ἐπὶ τοσοῦτον ἦλθεν ἡδυπαθείας ὡς . . . ("Androcydes, too, the painter from Cyzicus, being a lover of fish, as Polemon relates, went to such an extent of pleasant living that . . .") (Polemon, frag. 66 Preller)

12.514e: Χάρης δ᾽ ὁ Μιτυληναῖος . . . εἰς τοῦτο, φησίν, ἦκον τρυφῆς οἱ τῶν Περσῶν βασιλεῖς ὥστε . . . ("Chares of Mytilene . . . says that the kings of the Persians reached such an extent of *truphē* that . . .") (Chares, *FGrH* 125 F 2)

12.515d: Λυδοὶ δὲ εἰς τοσοῦτον ἦλθον τρυφῆς ὡς . . . , ὡς ἱστορεῖ Ξάνθος ὁ Λυδός ("The Lydians went to such an extent of *truphē* that . . . , as Xanthus the Lydian relates") (Xanthus, *FGrH* 765 T 5)

12.522d: Ταραντίνους δέ φησι Κλέαρχος . . . εἰς τοσοῦτο τρυφῆς προελθεῖν ὥστε . . . ("Clearchus says that the Tarentines . . . advanced to such an extent of *truphē* that . . .") (Clearchus, frag. 48 Wehrli)

This sentence pattern is unremarkable in earlier Greek literature. It is, however, unusually common in Athenaeus, and, more significantly, the list above shows that it often occurs as part of the introduction of a citation, a location in which some degree of paraphrase is certain. In addition, at Athen. 4.165e, the claim about the prodigality of Ctesippus appears in what is unmistakably an interpretive paraphrase before quotations from the verses of Diphilus, Timocles, and Menander.[122] Thus, the pattern of use within the *Deipnosophistae* itself, though

---

122. Immediately after the sentence quoted above, the poetic evidence is brought in at Athen. 4.165e:

not supported by strong diachronic data, indicates that Athenaeus favors this form of expression. Thus, even when such phraseology occurs in the body of a fragment rather than its introduction, it should be treated with caution. The historical facts that are couched in such wording and any implied moral overtones should likewise be considered dubious unless other evidence in the same vein can be brought to bear.[123]

Keeping in mind the usefulness of mapping Athenaeus's use of diction both synchronically and diachronically, we may now identify other phrases that constitute part of the *Deipnosophistae*'s stock of formulae for discussions of τρυφή and related moral terms.

An unmistakable example of language typical to Athenaeus, and which therefore should not be blithely attributed to his sources, can be found in the word διαβόητος ("famous"), often used in conjunction with the preposition ἐπί, as in διαβόητος ἐπὶ τρυφῇ ("famous for *truphē*").[124] We have already seen it in the framing language before the verses of Aristophanes at Athen. 12.527c. The adjective does not occur anywhere in extant Classical literature.[125] Its first secure appearances are in grammarians from the second century BCE. Apollodorus (10.63 Müller) refers to the famous River Styx, and Ptolemy writes to

---

Δίφιλος γοῦν ἐν τοῖς Ἐναγίζουσί φησι ("Diphilus, at all events, in his *Sacrificers to the Dead* says . . . ," frag. 37 KA). As frequently, γοῦν indicates evidence cited to prove the previous claim.

123. While the construction is common enough, the specific expression, with the genitive τρυφῆς limiting the prepositional phrase, is extremely rare. Before the seven uses in Athenaeus, it can be found only at Xen., *Hell.* 6.2.6. It is worth noting the sharp differences between the significance of τρυφή in the Xenophon and that which Athenaeus gives it. In the *Hellenica*, the soldiers of the Spartan general Mnasippus sack many rich Corcyraean farms with their associated wine cellars: ὥστ᾿ ἔφασαν τοὺς στρατιώτας εἰς τοῦτο τρυφῆς ἐλθεῖν ὥστ᾿ οὐκ ἐθέλειν πίνειν, εἰ μὴ ἀνθοσμίας εἴη ("People say that as a result the soldiers reached such an extent of *truphē* that they were unwilling to drink wine unless it had a fine bouquet."). In the first place, Xenophon shows a degree of diffidence (ἔφασαν) toward what is an exaggeration or merely a *bon mot*. As we have seen, Athenaeus does not distance himself from even the most extravagant claims about pernicious luxury. Secondly, while Athenaeus regularly uses τρυφή to indicate general moral decay, no such phenomenon is present in the *Hellenica* passage. In fact, Xenophon mentions no symptom of the soldiers' τρυφή, no indulgence in luxury, beside their taste for good wine. Pownall (2004, 86–87) may be correct in her assertion that Xenophon intends the reader to see the soldiers' τρυφή as a moral failure on the part of Mnasippus, but that is not relevant to the effects of luxury per se. Finally, Xenophon's reference to τρυφή has no narrative sequelae: when Mnasippus and his men were defeated by the Corcyraeans, the author suggests that the cause lay in the general's overconfidence, which led him to dismiss some soldiers and leave the others unpaid (Xen., *Hell.* 6.2.16). Thus, the common phraseology may highlight the distance between Xenophon and Athenaeus with respect to the historical importance of τρυφή.

124. Occasionally περί is used.

125. The related word περιβόητος occurs infrequently before the first century BCE: Thuc. 6.31.6; Soph., *OT* 192; Plato, *Phlb.* 45e; Lysias 3.30 (*bis*); Dem. 17.5, 18.297, 34.29, 40.11; Aeschines, *Tim.* 70 and 113; Dinarchus, *Aris.* 15; Lycurgus, *Leoc.* 69; Polybius 2.57.3, 10.35.3, 31.28.4, 32.6.6. Afterwards it is used abundantly by Philo, Diodorus Siculus, Dionysius of Halicarnassus, Plutarch, and, of course, Athenaeus.

distinguish the antonyms διαβόητος and ἐπιβόητος, saying that the former is "used everywhere for something good," while the latter "has a bad reputation,"[126] a distinction that is not honored by many subsequent authors, including Athenaeus. After these two writers, we must wait until the late 1st century CE to find other examples of the word used only occasionally, in Plutarch, Josephus, Dio Chrysostom, and others.[127] In the second century CE, there are more than fifty uses, about half of which occur in Athenaeus, and the word goes on to become a favorite of Christian authors such as Eusebius and especially Cyril, who alone employs the word 90 times.

Athenaeus uses διαβόητος on more than 20 different occasions outside of the epitomes. In the *Deipnosophistae*, one can be famous for profligacy (ἐπὶ ἀσωτίᾳ, 4.168e; cf. 4.165d), for gourmandism (ἐπὶ ὀψοφαγίᾳ, 8.338b, cf. 3.100c; and ἐπὶ πολυφαγίᾳ, 9.401c), for prostitution (ἐπὶ ἑταιρείᾳ, 13.588b), for soft living (ἐπὶ ἡδυπαθείᾳ, 15.690b; ἐπὶ μαλακίᾳ, 11.496d and 12.543a–b), for flattery (ἐπὶ κολακείᾳ, 6.252f), or for nothing in particular (4.165d, 11.462b), but Athenaeus's favorite object of fame, occurring eight times, is τρυφή.[128]

Fully twelve of the occurrences of διαβόητος are indisputably placed in the voice of the narrating deipnosophist, and seven of these occur in language that can only be viewed as part of a frame.[129] The clearest possible examples of this practice fall at the very end of Book 11 and the very beginning of Book 12. Athenaeus concludes Book 11 with the words, ἑξῆς δὲ ἐροῦμεν περὶ τῶν ἐπὶ τρυφῇ διαβοήτων γενομένων ("Next we will talk about the people who became famous for *truphē*." 11.509e). He starts Book 12 with a short anecdote and then the line, ἀλλ' ἐπεὶ πάνυ λιπαρῶς ἡμᾶς ἀπαιτεῖς καὶ τὸν περὶ τῶν ἐπὶ τρυφῇ διαβοήτων γενομένων λόγον καὶ τῆς τούτων ἡδυπαθείας ("Since you are demanding very persistently the discussion about the people who are famous for their *truphē* and their enjoyment of life . . ." 12.510b). Likewise, after a discussion about the nature of enjoyment and pleasure, he progresses into a long catalog of

---

126. διαβόητος μὲν γάρ ἐστιν ὁ ἐπ᾽ ἀγαθῷ παρὰ πᾶσιν ἐγνωσμένος· ἐπιβόητος δὲ ὁ μοχθηρὰν ἔχων τὴν φήμην, Ptol. gram., *De diff. voc.* 396.12–14. The word ἐπιβόητος is much rarer, although it does have early occurrences at Thuc. 6.16 and in a one-word fragment of Sophocles (*TrGF* 1048). After these come Ptolemy, other grammarians citing Ptolemy, and Cassius Dio, who employs the word six times (*Hist. Rom.* 43.47.5, 45.47.4, 58.21.5, 60.28.5, 153, 180).

127. Plut., *Lyc.* 5.3, *Luc.* 6.2; *De prov. Alex.* 29; Josephus, *AJ* 7.309, 8.284, 9.182; Dio Chrys., *Or.* 3.73, 31.39, 33.48; Ps.-Ammonius, *De adfin.* 135, 136 (paraphrasing Ptolemy); Herennius Philo, *De div. verb.* delta.44, delta.50, *De prop. dict.* 16 (all paraphrasing Ptolemy); Ignatius *Ep.* 1.8.1.

128. Athen. 11.496d, 11.509e, 12.510b, 12.513e–f, 12.518c, 12.527c, 12.543b–c (*bis*).

129. Frame: Athen. 4.165d, 4.168e, 6.252f, 11.509e, 12.510b, 12.513e–f, 13.594b. Non-frame: Athen. 6.231c, 9.401c, 13.594b, 15.690b. Athen. 13.588b may be interpreted either way.

peoples and individuals, a directory that begins: διαβόητοι δὲ ἐπὶ τρυφῇ ἐγένοντο πρῶτοι πάντων ἀνθρώπων Πέρσαι ("Famous first of all men for their *truphē* are the Persians . . ." 12.513e). By placing διαβόητος in first position, he awards it pride of place, a situation that occurs again at 6.252f, 12.518c, 12.527c, 12.543b, 13.594b, and 13.602c, conspicuously marking the opening of a transitional frame voiced by the narrator.

In a number of instances, διαβόητος is employed near a source citation, but in a way that makes it clear that the phrasing belongs rather to Athenaeus, as we have seen above. The familiar pattern of framing language is repeated: "Famous for his τρυφή (or another attribute) is X, as is reported in the work of Author Y, who says. . . ." Athenaeus then continues into a source quote or paraphrase intended to illustrate the fame. For example:

Διαβόητος δὲ ἐγένετο ἐπὶ κολακείᾳ καὶ ὁ τῶν Ἀθηναίων δῆμος. Δημοχάρης γοῦν, ὁ Δημοσθένους τοῦ ῥήτορος ἀνεψιός, ἐν τῇ εἰκοστῇ τῶν Ἱστοριῶν διηγούμενος περὶ ἧς ἐποιοῦντο οἱ Ἀθηναῖοι κολακείας πρὸς τὸν Πολιορκητὴν Δημήτριον, καὶ ὅτι τοῦτ᾽ οὐκ ἦν ἐκείνῳ βουλομένῳ, γράφει οὕτως·

[Famous for their flattery are the Athenian people too. At least Demochares, a kinsman of the orator Demosthenes, in the twentieth book of his *Histories*, reporting about the flattery which the Athenians demonstrated toward Demetrius Poliorcetes, that it was not something he approved of, writes thus: . . .] (Athen. 6.252f–253a = Demochares, *FGrH* 75 F 1)

The following ten lines appear to be a quote from Demochares. Thus the pattern is repeated: topic, source citation, optional paraphrased context, and quote. No one should read this passage and assume that the phrase διαβόητος ἐπὶ κολακείᾳ is cited verbatim from Demochares rather than added by Athenaeus, nor that it reflects the ethical judgment of the original.

The same motif reoccurs elsewhere. At Athen. 13.574c, the "notorious courtesan" (τῆς διαβοήτου ἑταίρας) of the framing language is merely "the courtesan" (τῆς ἑταίρας) within the citation from Polemon. The fact that at 12.543b "just about everybody (σχεδὸν πάντες) records that Pausanias and Lysander were famous for *truphē*" suggests that the phrasing belongs to Athenaeus.[130] Mnesimachus does not tell us that Dorion was famous as a gourmand: his verses (frag. 10 KA) merely say that he was still hanging about the host's home

---

130. Παυσανίαν δὲ καὶ Λύσανδρον ἐπὶ τρυφῇ διαβοήτους γενέσθαι σχεδὸν πάντες ἱστοροῦσι.

at nighttime (Athen. 8.338b). Neanthes of Cyzicus (*FGrH* 84 F 16) does not use the word διαβόητος in first position as a transitional line to describe the events surrounding Cratinus, as Athenaeus does at 13.602c, and Hippias the Sophist (*FGrH* 6 F 3) does not describe women as notorious for their beauty at Athen. 13.608f, but merely tells a story about Thargelia of Miletus. Finally, Phylarchus does not say that many people know the place in Illyria as famously called The Cups, but rather that this site was near the tomb of Cadmus and Harmonia (Athen. 11.462b = Phylarchus, *FGrH* 81 F 39).[131]

Thus, in such a context where the same pattern is followed but without an ensuing quote, it would be perilous to assume that Athenaeus derived his language from the source. For example:

Προυσίας. ὅτι τὸ ποτήριον τοῦτο ἔξορθόν ἐστι προείρηται. καὶ ὅτι τὴν προσηγορίαν ἔσχεν ἀπὸ Προυσίου τοῦ Βιθυνίας βασιλεύσαντος καὶ ἐπὶ τρυφῇ καὶ μαλακίᾳ διαβοήτου γενομένου ἱστορεῖ Νίκανδρος ὁ Καλχηδόνιος ἐν τετάρτῳ Προυσίου Συμπτωμάτων.

[Prusias. It has already been said that this is the cup that stands upright. That it is named after Prusias, the King of Bithynia, who was famous for *truphē* and softness, is recorded by Nicander of Calchedon in the fourth book of the *Adventures of Prusias*.] (Athen. 11.496d–e = Nicander, *FGrH* 700 F 1)

Nicander may have said nothing more than that the cup derived its name from the king or even just the mere fact that there was such a king. The phrase ἐπὶ τρυφῇ καὶ μαλακίᾳ διαβοήτου cannot be ascribed to him with any confidence.

What appears to be a paraphrase from Clearchus is best identified as the narrator's phraseology:

διαβόητοι δ᾽ εἰσὶν ἐπὶ τρυφῇ καὶ αἱ τῶν Σικελῶν τράπεζαι, οἵτινες καὶ τὴν παρ᾽ αὐτοῖς θάλατταν λέγουσιν εἶναι γλυκεῖαν, χαίροντες τοῖς ἐξ αὐτῆς γινομένοις ἐδέσμασιν, ὥς φησι Κλέαρχος ἐν πέμπτῳ Βίων.

[Famous for their *truphē* were the tables of the Sicilians, who say that even the sea along their coast is sweet, since they enjoy eating the food that comes out of

---

131. πολλοῖς δὲ καὶ ὁ ἐν Ἰλλυριοῖς τόπος διαβόητός ἐστιν ὁ καλούμενος Κύλικες, παρ᾽ ᾧ ἐστι τὸ Κάδμου καὶ Ἁρμονίας μνημεῖον, ὡς ἱστορεῖ Φύλαρχος ἐν τῇ δευτέρᾳ καὶ εἰκοστῇ τῶν Ἱστοριῶν ("Famous to many people is the place in Illyria called The Cups, near which is the tomb of Cadmus and Harmonia, as Phylarchus reports in the twenty-second book of his *Histories*.").

it so much, as Clearchus writes in the fifth book of his *Lives*.] (Athen. 12.518c = Clearchus, frag. 59 Wehrli)

Clearchus probably commented on the propensity of Sicilians to eat fish or offered a local gnomic saying about the sweetness of the sea. At Athen. 13.594b, the section that begins διαβόητος δ᾽ ἑταίρα γέγονε καὶ ἡ Μιλησία Πλαγγών ("A famous courtesan was Plangon of Miletus") is clearly phrased by Athenaeus, so one is not stretching credulity to assume the second mention of διαβόητος in this long passage—this time used to describe a necklace—is possibly also Athenaeus's own (13.594c), even though the entire story is attributed to Menetor (*FHG* iv.452). Then, at Athen. 12.543a–b, Rutilius Rufus (*FGrH* 815 F 5) may have written about Sittius. He lived late enough (*cos.* 105 BCE) to make such a usage plausible. However the phrasing is typical Athenaean framing language: διαβόητος δ᾽ ἦν παρὰ Ῥωμαίοις καὶ Σίττιος ἐπὶ τρυφῇ καὶ μαλακίᾳ, ὥς φησι Ῥουτίλιος ("Famous for *truphē* and softness among the Romans was Sittius, according to Rutilius."). Thus, without additional evidence, one cannot argue that the word τρυφῇ derived from Rutilius.

At this point, the question may arise whether the word διαβόητος *ever* occurs in the language of quoted authors. The necklace from Menetor is the best possible candidate. Every other passage in which someone is famous for *truphē* has been discussed above.[132] The only one remaining upon which one might base such a claim is:

Ἀναξιμένης δ᾽ ὁ Λαμψακηνὸς ἐν ταῖς πρώταις ἐπιγραφομέναις ἱστορίαις τὸν Ἐριφύλης ὅρμον διαβόητον γενέσθαι διὰ τὸ σπάνιον εἶναι τότε <τὸ> χρυσίον παρὰ τοῖς Ἕλλησι· καὶ γὰρ ἀργυροῦν ποτήριον ἦν ἰδεῖν τότε παράδοξον. μετὰ δὲ τὴν Δελφῶν ὑπὸ Φωκέων κατάληψιν πάντα τὰ τοιαῦτα δαψίλειαν εἴληφεν. ἐκ ποτηρίων δὲ χαλκῶν ἔπινον οἱ σφόδρα δοκοῦντες πλουτεῖν καὶ τὰς θήκας τούτων ὠνόμαζον χαλκοθήκας.

[Anaximenes of Lampsacus writing in his work *First Inquiries* says that the necklace of Eriphyle was famous because of the rarity of gold among the Greeks at that time. Even silver drinking cups were rare occurrences in those days. But after Delphi was taken by the Phocians, all these sorts of things became commonplace. Even those who seemed to be very rich men drank from bronze cups

---

132. Athen. 11.496d, 11.509e, 12.510b, 12.513e–f, 12.518c, 12.527c, 12.543b–c (*bis*).

and called the boxes that held them "bronze boxes."] (Athen. 6.231c = Anaximenes, *FGrH* 72 F 3[133])

It is just possible that Anaximenes used the word διαβόητος here, but the facts
weigh against him. First, the indirect statement suggests that Anaximenes is not
being cited verbatim, but rather paraphrased. Second, we have already seen that
no one within several centuries of his lifetime in the sixth century BCE can be
seen with any certainty to employ the word. Third, both of the strongest con-
tenders for an original attribution are necklaces, suggesting an idiom peculiar
to Athenaeus, not repeated in extant Greek. Finally, its position, at the beginning of a new section, is what would be expected for framing material added by
Athenaeus. The conclusion drawn from this evidence is that διαβόητος ἐπὶ
τρυφῇ represents a definite formulaic expression in Athenaeus, just as
ἐξοκέλλειν εἰς τρυφήν does. The presence of either is an indication of paraphrase, at the very least.

While διαβοήτος and the metaphorical use of ἐξοκέλλω are nearly unparalleled in material contemporaneous to cited authors, additional expressions
cannot as unambiguously be assigned to Athenaeus. There are many other
phrases that are Athenaean favorites, but for which the diachronic data are less
clear-cut. Many of these turns of phrase consist of common vocabulary but
employ those words in an unusual or metaphorical way, as we saw with
ἐξοκέλλω. Such phrases are particularly noteworthy if they occur in the framing language or in conjunction with other diction of the same type. Once identified, any one of these expressions should provoke suspicion, even deep within
an apparent quotation.

We may illustrate this point with selected examples. One such phrase contains a form of ὁρμάω ("set out"), usually combined with ἐπί, πρός, or εἰς, and
an object that represents vice: e.g., ἐπὶ τὴν τρυφήν ὁρμᾶν ("to set out into
truphē" or "to be eager for *truphē*"). The verb originates as a concrete action
word used extremely frequently in Greek literature from all eras for physical
movement, especially in a martial context. Examples easily number in the
thousands, but a very few will suffice: ἐπολέμεον γὰρ ἔκ τε Ἀχιλληίου πόλιος
ὁρμώμενοι ("setting out from Achillion, they fought," Hdt. 5.94.2); ἐς φυγὴν
ὁρμώμενοι ("setting out into flight," Eur., *Rhes.* 143); οἵ μοι ἐφώρμησαν πόλεμον
("[The gods] who set this war upon me," Hom., *Il.* 3.165). It is easy to see how

---

133. Where the citation is taken to end at παράδοξον.

such a word can then be used for military metaphors, which in turn expand in scope. In Classical times, one can set out to form or destroy a government,[134] or to do good or evil deeds.[135] It is a short step from actual traveling to the metaphorical journey into friendship or love,[136] or into education and philosophy,[137] thence into reasoning (ἐπὶ τοὺς λόγους), investigation or analysis (ἐπὶ κρίσιν or ἐπὶ σκέψιν), or even truth (ἐπ' ἀλήθειαν), imagery that is employed frequently by Plato.[138]

Uses of ὁρμάω with terms of virtue and vice are much rarer in Greek literature. In the Classical Era, Sophocles uses a blatant military metaphor when he says: ἐχθρῶν δ' ὕβρις ὧδ' ἀταρβήτως / ὁρμᾶτ' ἐν εὐανέμοις βάσσαις ("The dauntless hubris of your enemies sets off into the windy glades," Ajax 196–97). Notably, the hubris is the subject of ὁρμάω, not its goal. Other moral uses are confined to a few passages in Plato, Aristotle, and Isocrates: in Plato, there is one passage each in which one can set out into ἡδονή (Gorg. 502c), hubris (Res. 9.572c), or an impious life (Leg. 10.886b), while ἡδονή is the goal once in Isocrates (15.221) and three times in Aristotle.[139] While continuing its frequency of occurrence in the literal sense during the Common Era, some authors from that time also pick up this moral usage, but only to a small degree. Most notably Philo, Aelius Aristides, Sextus Empiricus, Cassius Dio, Clement of Alexandria, John Chrysostom, Eusebius, and a few others compose a handful of passages each in which one sets off into or out of virtue (ἀρετή),[140] pleasure (ἡδονή),[141] hubris,[142] or other good or bad behaviors.[143]

Diodorus Siculus is an example of an author with the propensity to employ ὁρμάω with a moral source or destination. Like so many others, he uses the verb in hundreds of instances to denote physical motion or in its expanded

---

134. Thuc. 8.47.2; Isoc. 12.114; Dem., Ep. 3.10; Diod. Sic. 9.4.1. Again, a few examples should be sufficient for each of these uses; many more are available.

135. Dem. 7.21, 15.28; Plato, Res. 391d; Arist., Mor. 2.13.2, 2.3.13.

136. Dem. 23.194; Xen., Mem. 2.6.28; Plato, Symp. 181d.

137. Isoc. 15.10, 12.27; Plat., Res. 587c. The early Christian writers as well as rhetoricians and philosophers of the Common Era take up this idiom frequently.

138. Plato, Phaedo 100a, Theat. 184a, Soph. 228c and 242c, Parm. 130b and 135d, Symp. 185e, Leg. 1.641d, Tim. 80d, Res. 510d.

139. In Isocrates, one can also set out for private enrichment (8.126) or for public distinction (5.106). Arist., Pol. 5.1312b; VV 1250a11; paired with ἀπολαύσις, "enjoyment," at VV 1250b13.

140. Philo, LA 3.18, 245; Plut., Mor. 341e; Ael. Arist., Pan. 134.21 Jebb; Cass. Dio 71.35; 37.57; Clem. Al., Strom. 6.2.241; John Chrys., In Gen. 53.159.

141. Plut., Mor. 151d; Ael. Arist., Pros Plat. 236.9 Jebb; Sex. Emp., Pyr. 3.194; MAthen. 11.96.

142. John Chrys., De virg. 75.23; Clem. Al., Paed. 2.10.99.

143. ἐπ' αὐτὸν μάτην (Cass. Dio. 42.47); ἐπὶ μοιχείας (Clem. Al., Paed. 2.10.83); ἐπὶ πορνείαν (Clem. Al., Ecl. Proph. 39.1); ἐπὶ τὴν εὐσέβειαν (Euseb., Praep. Evan. 9.17.3); πρὸς ἀσέβειαν (Philo, Mos. 2.161); ἐπὶ τὴν ἀπόλαυσιν (Euseb., Praep. Evan. 8.14.69); εἰς τὰ ἀφροδίσια ἐρεθιζούσης (Euseb., Praep. Evan. 3.11.16); πρὸς εὐωχίαν (Jos., AJ 11.156).

meaning slightly removed from actual motion: setting off into rebellion, danger, plunder, freedom, tyranny, education, and the like. But he also has passages in the extant books in which that meaning has been extended into ethical ground: πρὸς ἀρετήν ("into virtue," 17.26); πρὸς εὐεργεσίαν ("into gratitude," 1.90); πρὸς τὴν ἡδίστην ἀπόλαυσιν ("into sweet enjoyment," 3.17); εἰς τὸ πίνειν ("into drinking," 19.24). Interestingly, he is also the only author outside of Athenaeus to pair ὁρμάω with τρυφή: when Alexander's army first went to Babylon, the populace welcomed them and ὥρμησαν πρὸς ἄνεσιν καὶ τρυφήν ("they set off into relaxation and *truphē*," 17.112).

In contrast to the other Greek writers, Athenaeus has a predilection for phrases involving ὁρμάω paired with ethical terms. He is far less likely than most writers to use the verb for physical motion: he has only 13 instances, with two additional military metaphors. Ten of these may occur in the cited author, while the remaining five are in the narrator's words.[144] Six additional passages with metaphorical uses may also derive from original authors.[145] The most compelling of these is in verse and so has a high probability of accurately representing the poet's own words, in this case Antiphanes (frag. 91 = Athen. 12.526d):

πόθεν οἰκήτωρ, ἤ τις Ἰώνων
τρυφεραμπεχόνων ἁβρὸς ἡδυπαθὴς
ὄχλος ὥρμηται.

[Where do they come from? Where do they live? Or is it a crowd of Ionians in luxurious clothes, dainty and living a soft life, being stirred up?]

The quote features a number of notable words, including the *hapax legomenon* τρυφεραμπεχόνων ("in luxurious clothes"). Note that his Ionians are being stirred up in the passive voice, without a destination: τρυφεραμπεχόνων is

---

144. Original author: 4.160b (against a city; Sopater, frag. 3), 6.259a (for Delphi; Hippias of Erythrae, *FGrH* 421 F 1), 6.265d (into the mountains; Nymphodorus of Syracuse, *FGrH* 572 F 4), 7.323d (intransitive; of cuttlefish; Aristotle, frag. 239), 8.354b (into the army; Epicurus, frag. 171 Usener), 9.377c (intransitive; Poseidippus, frag. 29), 10.448a (into matters; Amphis, frag. 33), 11.781d (for the Cattle of Geryones; Stesichorus, frag. 185 *PMG*), 12.550e (against opponents; Agatharchides, *FGrH* 86 F 11), 14.639e (water rushed out through a gap; Bato of Sinope, *FGrH* 268 F 5). Narrator: 5.221c and 5.221d (against the Gorgon), 7.302b (intransitive), 12.516b (by oppression), 13.575d (in his chariot). He uses compounds of the verb only five times outside the epitomes, and each represents physical action: 5.214f, 6.262e, 12.517a, 13.607d, 15.676b.

145. One's soul sets out in a direction (4.164c; Alexis, frag. 140); one sets out to read tragedy (4.164d; Alexis, frag. 140); one sets out in desire for a sexual partner (8.339b; Antiphanes, frag. 27); and one sets out into sophistry (8.354d; Epicurus, frag. 172 Usener) or philosophy (13.588b; Epicurus, frag. 117 Usener).

merely an adjective modifying them. Another eight passages are plainly written in the voice of the deipnosophist, with phrasing reminiscent of other writers setting out for education and the like,[146] but he also has people setting out for such things as eating and drinking (11.461b; 14.627e) and enjoyment (ἐπὶ τὰς ἀπολαύσεις, 8.363d).[147]

Athenaeus incorporates ὁρμάω into his framing language on several occasions, such that the unwary reader often attributes this word to his source rather than recognizing it for the addendum that it is. These frames typically introduce the concept of τρυφή thus:

Ἐρατοσθένης γοῦν ὁ Κυρηναῖος . . . ἐν τῷ ἐπιγραφομένῳ Ἀρίστωνι παρεμφαίνει τὸν διδάσκαλον ὡς ὕστερον ὁρμήσαντα ἐπὶ τρυφήν, λέγων ὧδε· ἤδη δέ ποτε καὶ τοῦτον πεφώρακα τὸν τῆς ἡδονῆς καὶ ἀρετῆς μεσότοιχον διορύττοντα καὶ ἀναφαινόμενον παρὰ τῇ ἡδονῇ.

[At least Eratosthenes of Cyrene . . . demonstrates in the work called *Ariston* that his teacher later set off into *truphē*, saying these things: "Occasionally already, like a thief, digging through the wall between pleasure and virtue, and appearing beside pleasure."] (Athen. 7.281c = Eratosthenes, *FGrH* 241 F 17)

This typical framing language adds the topic τρυφή, which does not occur in the citation that follows, where it is also unclear that Athenaeus is justified in interpreting Eratosthenes' description of Ariston (ποτε . . . διορύττοντα) as imputing a purposeful change (ὁρμήσαντα) of lifestyle to his teacher. Likewise at 12.533f (= Anacreon, frag. 388 *PMG*), we read: καὶ γὰρ Ἀνακρέων αὐτὸν ἐκ πενίας εἰς τρυφὴν ὁρμῆσαί φησιν ἐν τούτοις ("For even Anacreon says that he set out from poverty into *truphē* in these words . . ."). What ensues is a long verse description of a man who rose literally from wearing from rags to donning gold jewelry and using a chariot and a parasol (cited above). Again, τρυφή is nowhere in the quote.[148]

A further instance of the word ὁρμάω is set in the context of τρυφή without the two words being grammatically related. Again, they occur in what we would

---

146. One sets out for sophistry/education (5.211f; 6.274e); for paths to excellence (5.187b); driven by financial need (12.547f) or by a fact (13.555d). Cf. 3.83b.

147. Based on what we have seen already, it is likely that the phrase πρὸς αὐτὰς τὰς ἐν ἀλλήλοις παρατριβὰς καὶ φιλοτιμίας ὁρμήσαντες ("setting off into friction and rivalry among themselves," 14.626e is also Athenaeaus's phrasing, and not part of what is usually considered to be an extremely long quote from Polybius (14.626a–f = Polyb. 4.20.5–21.9).

148. A long frame at 10.418b includes the topic ὁρμήσαντες ἐπ᾽ εὐωχίας ("setting off into feasting").

designate as framing language, in this instance a closing editorial comment. Following a quotation from Philonides about people applying perfumed oils to their heads at parties in order that the wine have less effect on them, Athenaeus summarizes:

προστιθεὶς δ' ὁ βίος ἀεὶ τοῖς χρειώδεσιν καὶ τῶν εἰς ἀπόλαυσιν καὶ τρυφὴν ἀγόντων ἐπὶ τὴν τῶν μύρων χρῆσιν ὥρμησεν. χρηστέον οὖν, ὦ Κύνουλκε Θεόδωρε, μύροις παρὰ πότον . . .

[Because human life has always added to what is useful something of what is conducive to enjoyment and *truphē*, it has set out to use perfumes. Therefore, Theodorus Cynulcus, it is necessary for us to use those perfumes at our drinking party . . .] (Athen. 15.692b)[149]

We are left with three passages from Athenaeus that feature the verb ὁρμάω, two of which combine it with τρυφή. None are in clear framing material, but all are suspect because of the frequency with which he uses this idiom.

At 12.531e, Athenaeus begins a shift to a new subject with the following framing language: ἐν δὲ τῇ πρώτῃ τῶν Φιλιππικῶν Θεόπομπος περὶ Φιλίππου λέγων φησίν ("Speaking about Philip in the first book of the *History of Philip*, Theopompus says:"). An apparent quotation follows (*FGrH* 115 F 31), specifying how Philip went to a particularly lovely estate. Next comes this statement:

ἦν γὰρ καὶ τῶν ὑπὸ Κότυος προκριθέντων, ὃς ἁπάντων τῶν βασιλέων τῶν ἐν τῇ Θρᾴκῃ γεγενημένων μάλιστα πρὸς ἡδυπαθείας καὶ τρυφὰς ὥρμησε, . . .

[[The estate] was one of those preferred by Cotys, who, more than any other of the kings of Thrace set out especially for pleasant living and *truphē*, . . .] (Athen. 12.531e)

The phrase "set out for pleasant living and *truphē*" catches one's eye and immediately provokes suspicion that this passage may not belong to Theopompus. A second clue occurs in the phrase "more than any other of the kings of Thrace,"

---

149. Gulick's edition (1927–41, ad loc.) includes the first sentence of this passage as the last sentence of the longer quotation of Philonides, when it clearly belongs with what follows, as part of the narrator's words. Similar language, including the phrase οὔτε πρὸς τὰς ἀφροδισίους ἡδονὰς ὁρμήσας ("nor did he set out for sexual pleasures"), occurs at Athen. 12.543c. We would also designate it as a closing frame by the narrator, but Gulick, for example, extends the preceding quote from Theopompus to include it.

a superlative that represents another favorite Athenaean idiom (see the discussion below). A final indication is that one may very naturally read this line as a transition back to the voice of the narrator, a transition that must take place somewhere in the next few lines, since, slightly lower, we have the resumptive, διηγεῖταί τε ἑξῆς ὁ συγγραφεὺς ὅτι ("Later the writer set down that . . . ," 12.531f). It is certainly possible that section 531e and most of 531f represent one long quote from Theopompus (as both Jacoby and Gulick have chosen to punctuate it) and that this statement, "Later the writer set down that . . ." is the bare transition. But these three suspect elements factored together tell against attributing the material to Theopompus rather than Athenaeus. In prudence, the quotation from Theopompus should be taken to extend for just one sentence, ending before the statement that shifts our attention to Cotys.

Likewise the passage at 12.524d has phrasing that raises many red flags:

καὶ περὶ Σκυθῶν δ' ἑξῆς ὁ Κλέαρχος τάδε ἱστορεῖ· . . . ἐτρύφησαν μὲν γὰρ ὡς οὐδένες ἕτεροι . . . τρυφήσαντες δὲ καὶ μάλιστα δὴ καὶ πρῶτοι πάντων τῶν ἀνθρώπων ἐπὶ τὸ τρυφᾶν ὁρμήσαντες εἰς τοῦτο προῆλθον ὕβρεως ὥστε πάντων τῶν ἀνθρώπων εἰς οὓς ἀφίκοιντο ἠκρωτηρίαζον τὰς ῥῖνας·

[And concerning the Scythians, Clearchus next writes these things: . . . They indulged in *truphē* as no other people did. . . . For indulging in *truphē* and especially also being first of all men to set off into *truphē*, they advanced to such a point of hubris that they cropped the noses of all the people they could reach.] (Athen. 12.524d = Clearchus, frag. 46 Wehrli)

The passage continues with a catalog of brutal crimes. Most editors assume that this passage and, indeed, its extension through the next page (down to 12.524f) represents a more-or-less accurate quote from Clearchus. Yet there are lexicographical reasons to doubt this view, including the phrase "set off into *truphē*," which raises suspicions immediately. The word τρυφή occurs twice in one sentence and a third time in the immediate context in this short passage. The Pelling Principle states that we should assume that a quote is shorter and simpler rather than longer. Finally, there are other phrases in this passage that raise questions, which we will deal with shortly.

Thus, ὁρμάω combined with a preposition whose object is τρυφή occurs four times in Athenaeus and the verb itself is connected with other vices eight more times, with τρυφή appearing in the larger context three times.[150] In each instance, the diction is far better attributed to Athenaeus than to some original source. Thus ὁρμάω should join ἐξοκέλλω and διαβόητος in the catalog of Athenaean idioms.

Another suspicious choice of words concerns the practice of excessive τρυφή, using some form of the verb ὑπερβάλλω ("excel") or the noun ὑπερβολή ("excess"). The combination is unusual in earlier literature.[151] The two words occur in proximity, though not grammatically related, one time in Demosthenes, while Aristotle's *Politics* contrasts τρυφή with γλισχρότητα ("stinginess") in a passage about the two extremes of life.[152] Beyond these examples, we have to wait until the first century before the Common Era for Diodorus to employ the two words in the same phrase, but even then infrequently.[153]

Athenaeus far surpasses his predecessors, using the combination in twelve different passages from the *Deipnosophistae*.[154] In eight of those, the two words occur in the same phrase. While it is possible that he derives the diction from his sources, we consider this less likely in view of the frequency with which Athenaeus uses the combination in conspicuous framing language or one-sentence summations:

Θεόπομπος δ᾽ ἐν πεντεκαιδεκάτῃ Φιλιππικῶν Ἱστοριῶν Στράτωνά φησι τὸν Σιδώνιον βασιλέα ὑπερβάλλειν ἡδυπαθείᾳ καὶ τρυφῇ πάντας ἀνθρώπους.

---

150. With τρυφή: Athen. 7.281c, 12.524d, 12.531e, 12.533f. With other vices: 8.363d, 10.418b, 10.442f, 11.461b, 12.543c, 14.626e, 14.627e, 15.692b. With τρυφή in the context: 12.524d, 12.547f, 15.692b.

151. We do see ὑπερβάλλω used with other virtues or vices from an early time. The best examples are: Eur., *Hipp.* 924; Plato, *Tim.* 86b, *Crit.* 110e, *Gorg.* 475a–e; *Rep.* 2.358e, 402e; Xen., *Cyr.* 5.3.32; Dem. 8.16; Isoc. 9.6, 12.36, 121, 198; Isaeus 6.13.

152. Dem. 8.34: νῦν δὲ δημαγωγοῦντες ὑμᾶς καὶ χαριζόμενοι καθ᾽ ὑπερβολὴν οὕτω διατεθήκασιν, ὥστ᾽ ἐν μὲν ταῖς ἐκκλησίαις τρυφᾶν καὶ κολακεύεσθαι πάντα πρὸς ἡδονὴν ἀκούοντας ("Now leading you and rejoicing in excess, they have arranged it thus, so that in the assemblies you act with *truphē* and are flattered by hearing everything that you want to hear . . ."). Aris., *Pol.* 7.1326b37–9: διὰ τοὺς ἕλκοντας ἐφ᾽ ἑκατέραν τοῦ βίου τὴν ὑπερβολήν, τοὺς μὲν ἐπὶ τὴν γλισχρότητα τοὺς δὲ ἐπὶ τὴν τρυφήν (". . . because of those that drag us toward either extreme of life, some toward stinginess and others toward *truphē*").

153. Same phrase: Diod. Sic. 3.42.2, 17.35.4, 17.108.6; Plut., *Agis* 7.3. Same sentence: Diod. Sic. 1.45.2, 5.40.3, 13.82.8; Plut., *Mor.* 668b; cf. Josephus, *AJ* 11.47.

154. He uses ὑπερβάλλω/ὑπερβολή fifty-four times outside the epitomes (two other examples involve textual problems).

230 CORRUPTING LUXURY IN ANCIENT GREEK LITERATURE

[Theopompus says in the fifteenth book of his *History of Philip* that Straton, the King of Sidon, excelled all men in soft-living and *truphē*.] (Athen. 12.531a = Theopompus, *FGrH* 115 F 114) [155]

Ἡρακλείδης δ᾽ ὁ Ποντικὸς ἐν τῷ περὶ Ἡδονῆς Σαμίους φησὶ καθ᾽ ὑπερβολὴν τρυφήσαντας διὰ τὴν πρὸς ἀλλήλους μικρολογίαν ὥσπερ Συβαρίτας τὴν πόλιν ἀπολέσαι.

[Heraclides Ponticus in his work *On Pleasure* says that the Samians, since they lived in excessive *truphē*, because of their small-mindedness toward each other, lost their city, just as the Sybarites did.] (Athen. 12.525f–526a = Heraclides, frag. 57 Wehrli [frag. 41 Schütrumpf])

Θεόφραστος δ᾽ ἐν τῷ περὶ Ἡδονῆς καὶ δὴ καὶ τοὺς Ἴωνάς φησι διὰ τὴν ὑπερβολὴν τῆς τρυφῆς . . . [*lacuna*]

[Theophrastus in his work *On Pleasure* says that also the Ionians, because of their excessive *truphē*, . . .] (Athen. 12.526d = Theophrastus, frag. 549 Fortenbaugh)

Φύλαρχος δὲ ἐν τῇ δεκάτῃ τῶν Ἱστοριῶν Θρᾳκῶν φησι τῶν καλουμένων Κροβύζων βασιλέα γενέσθαι Ἰσάνθην, τρυφῇ πάντας τοὺς καθ᾽ ἑαυτὸν ὑπερβαλλόμενον.

[Phylarchus in the tenth book of his *Histories* says that Isanthes, who became King of the Thracians who are called Crobyzi, exceeded all men of his time in *truphē*.] (Athen. 12.536d = Phylarchus, *FGrH* 81 F 20)

Another clear frame uses both words closely, though not in the same phrase, and with the equally dubious ἐξοκεῖλαι ("ran aground on"):

---

155. Shortly after he also says, in another suspect phrase, καὶ τοσούτῳ μᾶλλον ἐκείνων παρεκεκινήκει πρὸς τὰς ἡδονάς ("by so much more was he out of his senses for pleasure . . . ," Athen. 12.531b).

Πολύβιος δ᾽ ἐν τῇ ἑβδόμῃ Καπυησίους τοὺς ἐν Καμπανίᾳ διὰ τὴν ἀρετὴν τῆς γῆς πλοῦτον περιβαλομένους ἐξοκεῖλαι εἰς τρυφὴν καὶ πολυτέλειαν, ὑπερβαλλομένους τὴν περὶ Κρότωνα καὶ Σύβαριν παραδεδομένην φήμην.

[Polybius in the seventh book says that the Capuans in Campania, because of the excellence of their land, embracing wealth ran aground on *truphē* and extravagance, exceeding the fame bestowed on Croton and Sybaris.] (Athen. 12.528b = Polyb. 7.1.1–3)

In another passage, he places the expression in the narrator's mouth when he defines an obscure term: καὶ τὸ τρυφᾶν καθ᾽ ὑπερβολὴν ὑπερμαζᾶν ("to have *truphē* in excess is to be *hypermazān*," Athen. 14.663b).[156]

Thus we must suspect the few remaining combinations of ὑπερβαλεῖν and τρυφή. It is, for example, unlikely that Phylarchus and Agatharchides used the exact same phrasing to describe the companions of Alexander enjoying "excessive *truphē*,"[157] though Athenaeus attributes the phrase to both of them. When Clearchus is supposed to have said that a Paphian prince lay on soft carpets δι᾽ ὑπερβάλλουσιν τρυφήν ("because of excessive *truphē*," Athen. 6.255e = Clearchus, frag. 19 Wehrli), we cannot help suspecting that τρυφή was nowhere in the original, as we likewise distrust the summarizing sentence that opens Heraclides' long quote about the judicial practices of the Persian King: οὗτος δ᾽ ὑπερβάλλει τῇ τρυφῇ καὶ ῥαθυμίᾳ ("That one practices excessive *truphē* and relaxation," Athen. 12.517b = Heraclides, *FGrH* 689 F 4).[158] Thus the combination of ὑπερβάλλω or ὑπερβολή with τρυφή is yet another element of Athenaean diction.

A phrase that is rarer in Athenaeus but which provokes some suspicion is ζῆλος or ζηλόω with τρυφή, meaning to "envy" or "emulate" τρυφή. The classical orators rarely employed ζηλ- with ἀρετή,[159] but the combination with τρυφή

---

156. ὑπερβαλεῖν and ὑπερβολή appear with other objects in framing language at: 4.146e (expense); 7.290e (boasting); 8.342d and 10.412c (gluttony); 10.421b (excess partying); cf. 9.402c (strength).

157. Φύλαρχος δ᾽ ἐν τῇ τρίτῃ καὶ εἰκοστῇ τῶν Ἱστοριῶν καὶ Ἀγαθαρχίδης ὁ Κνίδιος ἐν τῷ δεκάτῳ περὶ Ἀσίας καὶ τοὺς ἑταίρους φησὶ τοὺς Ἀλεξάνδρου ὑπερβαλλούσῃ τρυφῇ χρήσασθαι ("Phylarchus in the twenty-third book of his *Histories* and Agatharchides of Cnidus in the tenth book of his work *On Asia* both say that the companions of Alexander also enjoyed excessive *truphē*." Athen. 12.539b–c = Phylarchus, *FGrH* 81 F 41 = Agatharchides, *FGrH* 86 F 3).

158. Three more passages have the two words only loosely connected, and none of them refer to vice: 6.275a (price); 12.519f (weather); 12.521d (culinary competitions). They may well reflect original phrasing.

159. Isoc. 1.11, 4.159; Lys. 2.26; Dem. 20.141, 61.31; Aeschines 1.146, 151, 191; Lycur. 1.104. Other earlier authors do not use ζηλ- in combination with ἀρετή, τρυφή, or ἡδονή.

does not occur until Dionysius of Halicarnassus in the Augustan Age.[160] Then it appears occasionally in Philo, Diodorus Siculus, Plutarch, and Athenaeus, before trailing off again in popularity.[161] Athenaeus himself only uses the combination three times, and all three are in summarizing paraphrases:

Κλέαρχος δὲ ἐν τετάρτῳ Βίων ζηλώσαντάς φησι τοὺς Μιλησίους τὴν Κολοφωνίων τρυφὴν διαδοῦναι καὶ τοῖς πλησιοχώροις.

[Clearchus in the fourth book of his *Lives* says that the Milesians envied the *truphē* of the people of Colophon, and handed it over to their neighbors.] (Athen. 12.524b = Clearchus, frag. 45 Wehrli)

ὡμολόγηνται δ᾽ οἱ Θετταλοί, ὡς καὶ Κριτίας φησί, πάντων Ἑλλήνων πολυτελέστατοι γεγενῆσθαι περί τε τὴν δίαιταν καὶ τὴν ἐσθῆτα· ὅπερ αὐτοῖς αἴτιον ἐγένετο κατὰ τῆς Ἑλλάδος ἐπαγαγεῖν τοὺς Πέρσας, ζηλώσαντας τὴν τούτων τρυφὴν καὶ πολυτέλειαν.

[It is agreed—and Critias says this too—that the Thessalians of all the Greeks were the most extravagant in their dining and clothes. This is the reason why they brought Persians into Greece, because they envied the *truphē* and extravagance of them.] (Athen. 12.527b = Critias 88 B 31 DK)

This last sentiment is repeated almost verbatim at 14.663a, but without the reference to Critias. All of these passages are doubtful representations of the original wording.

We have already noticed Athenaeus's predilection for calling someone "famous for τρυφή" or "excelling in τρυφή." It is a closely related idea to say that someone was the first in τρυφή or that one displayed it in a superlative degree.[162] While attributions of primacy are commonplace in Greek, Athenaeus is obsessed with the concept of discovery and innovation in vice. We have seen several examples of this predilection in other contexts: the Sybarites were the

---

160. Dion. Hal. 19.17: πλούτου καὶ τρυφῆς καὶ πολυτελείας βασιλικῆς ζῆλον εἰς τοὺς βίους εἰσάγων ("bringing a zeal for wealth and *truphē* and kingly extravagance into their lives").

161. Philo, *Somn.* 1.121; Jos. 44.4; *Spec. leg.* 2.240; Diod. Sic. 2.21.2, 8.18, 11.44, 17.77, 33.18, 37.2; Plut., *Sull.* 1.3, *Agis* 10.3, *Mor.* 226d.

162. Roller (2009, 225–27) for "firsts" in Roman history writing.

first people to shackle their water-carriers and they were the first people to forbid loud professions to practice in town (Athen. 12.518c). Athenaeus reflects the idea dozens of times in his work, and at least nine times indisputably in the context of τρυφή. Five of them occur in framing language and four occur in coincidence with other suspect diction.[163] Let us return to Athen. 12.524c–d (= Clearchus, frag. 46 Wehrli), a passage we have examined above for its use of τρυφή, but which bears repeating here at length in order to view its superlatives (*underlines mark suspect language*):

καὶ περὶ Σκυθῶν δ᾽ ἑξῆς ὁ Κλέαρχος τάδε ἱστορεῖ· <u>μόνον</u> δὲ νόμοις κοινοῖς <u>πρῶτον</u> ἔθνος ἐχρήσατο τὸ Σκυθῶν· εἶτα πάλιν ἐγένοντο <u>πάντων ἀθλιώτατοι</u> <u>βροτῶν</u> <u>διὰ τὴν ὕβριν.</u> ἐτρύφησαν μὲν γὰρ <u>ὡς οὐδένες ἕτεροι, τῶν πάντων</u> εὐροίας καὶ πλούτου καὶ τῆς λοιπῆς αὐτοὺς χορηγίας κατασχούσης. τοῦτο δὲ δῆλον ἐκ τῆς ἔτι καὶ νῦν ὑπολειπούσης περὶ τοὺς ἡγεμόνας αὐτῶν ἐσθῆτός τε καὶ διαίτης. <u>τρυφήσαντες</u> δὲ καὶ μάλιστα δὴ καὶ πρῶτοι πάντων τῶν ἀνθρώπων <u>ἐπὶ τὸ τρυφᾶν ὁρμήσαντες εἰς τοῦτο προῆλθον ὕβρεως ὥστε</u> πάντων τῶν ἀνθρώπων εἰς οὓς ἀφίκοιντο ἠκρωτηρίαζον τὰς ῥῖνας·

[And concerning the Scythians, Clearchus next writes these things: The Scythian nation <u>alone was the first</u> to use common laws. Then they again became the <u>most wretched of all humans</u> <u>because of their hubris.</u> They <u>indulged in *truphē*</u> <u>as no other people did</u>, and <u>of all people</u> prosperity and wealth and abundance gained mastery over them. This is clear from the manner of dress and mode of life that still exist today among the leading men. For <u>indulging in *truphē*</u> and especially also <u>being first of all men</u> <u>to set off into *truphē*, they advanced to such</u> <u>a point of hubris that</u> they cropped the noses of all the people they could reach.]

It is difficult to see how the author could have emphasized the τρυφή of the Scythians in stronger language. The collocation of superlatives and firsts is remarkable: (1) alone was the first to use common laws; (2) most wretched of all humans; (3) practiced τρυφή as no other people did; (4) of all people; (5) being first of all men to set off into τρυφή. He uses ὕβρις twice and τρυφή three times in a short span, as well as ὁρμάω and that other suspect phrase, "they went so far into x that . . ."

---

163. Frame: 12.513e, 515d, 523a, 531e, 543a. In the context of suspect diction: 12.543a (ἐξοκεῖλαι); 12.524d and 531e (ὁρμάω); 12.515d, 523a, 524d ("went so far into x that").

Further expressions that are doubtful also occur in framing language or summaries, though they cannot be cast into suspicion as Athenaean by frequency alone. People are destroyed by τρυφή or in their τρυφή (διαφθαρῆναι ὑπὸ τῆς τρυφῆς, *vel sim.*) at 12.536e and 12.526f.[164] When a similar phrase begins what is supposed to be a quotation at 12.549e, we must suspect that the causal quality is added by the excerptor. Other untrustworthy phrases are ὑπήχθησαν ἡδονῇ καὶ τρυφῇ ("subsumed by pleasure and *truphē*," 12.523f) and περὶ τρυφὴν σπουδάσαι ("to be eager concerning *truphē*," 12.528e).

So far we have looked at expressions that occur with some frequency in Athenaeus's citations on τρυφή. For many of these phrases, we have then been able to show that, when their use is examined diachronically, the resultant patterns make it unlikely that the expressions originated in the Classical period. That fact, along with Athenaeus's predilection for these turns of phrase, reveal that they in all probability represent, at closest, paraphrases by that author. Unfortunately, these expressions may occur not in paraphrases reproducing with some degree of accuracy the sense of the originals, but rather in interpretative passages in which Athenaeus demonstrates that he is able to use old evidence in new ways.

In spite of the difficulty we face in judging the relationship that exists between Athenaeus's original source and the phraseology in which he transmits his citations, the expressions that we have discussed thus far, by virtue of their patterns of occurrence in the *Deipnosophistae*, are liable to come to light during a careful reading of Athenaeus's evidence on τρυφή. Another type of Athenaean modification, however, is much more difficult to discover. To refer once more to our two axes of analysis, there remains one more category of diction to be examined. These are expressions that are not interesting synchronically—they are not among Athenaeus's favorite formulae of introduction or the like—but their diachronic distribution means that they are unlikely to have been in the original.

For the purposes of illustration, we may examine a few passages in which Athenaeus cites the *Lives* of Clearchus.[165] At Athen. 12.522d, in a citation from Clearchus (frag. 48 Wehrli) on the decadence of the Tarentines, we find the following:

ὕστερον δ᾽ ὑπὸ τῆς τρυφῆς εἰς ὕβριν ποδηγηθέντες ἀνάστατον μίαν πόλιν Ἰαπύγων ἐποίησαν Κάρβιναν . . .

---

164. Isocrates uses this phrase once, at 5.124.4–5.
165. For a detailed discussion, see Gorman and Gorman 2010.

[Later, led by *truphē* into *hubris,* they made one city of the Iapygians, Carbina, a ruin . . .]

Leaving aside other grounds for suspicion, the presence of the verb ποδηγέω is evidence supporting the view that this statement is not a verbatim quotation. Ποδηγέω ("to lead the foot," "guide"), along with its cognates and compounds is quite rare before the Current Era, occurring three times in Plato and four times in Lycophron, while, beginning with Philo Judaeus in the first century CE, the word becomes common in all its forms. It is relevant to observe that there is an important distinction to be drawn between the Classical examples and its use in this passage of Athenaeus. The former are all literal, in the sense that the agent is, essentially, a person and the "guiding" that the verb indicates is deliberate. The three Plato passages all refer to the intelligence that steers the motion of the heavenly bodies.[166] The figurative ποδηγηθέντες in the Clearchus fragment apparently indicates a process rather than a deliberate action, a use typical for Athenaeus's contemporary, Galen, who employs the word more than eighty times.[167] It is therefore reasonable to suggest that ποδηγηθέντες is an item of Athenaean rather than Clearchan diction.

From his discussion of the Tarentines, Athenaeus turns to the moral failings of the Iapygians, and it is likely that Clearchus is his source here too.[168] The Iapygian, it seems, underwent a steep moral decline after emigrating from their original Cretan homeland:

οἱ μετὰ τούτους λήθην λαβόντες τῆς Κρητῶν περὶ τὸν βίον εὐκοσμίας εἰς τοῦτο τρυφῆς, εἶθ᾽ ὕστερον ὕβρεως ἦλθον ὥστε πρῶτοι τὸ πρόσωπον ἐντριψάμενοι καὶ προκόμια περιθετὰ [τε] λαβόντες στολὰς μὲν ἀνθινὰς φορῆσαι, τὸ δὲ ἐργάζεσθαι καὶ πονεῖν αἰσχρὸν νομίσαι.

[Their descendents, choosing to forget the decent Cretan way of life, went to such an extent of *truphē*, then later of hubris, that they were the first to rub cosmetics into their face and to put on false forelocks; they wore flowered robes and considered it a shameful thing to work and toil.] (Athen. 12.523a)

---

166. "God" at *Pol.* 269c5 and 270a3, "soul" at *Leg.* *10*.899a4. In Lycophron, *Alex.* 965, the referent is Acestus, who welcomed Aeneas to Sicily

167. E.g., *De sectis* 1.74, τὰ δ᾽ αὐτὰ φάρμακα καὶ οἱ ἐμπειρικοὶ προσφέρουσιν οὐχ ὑπὸ τῆς φύσεως αὐτοῦ τοῦ πράγματος ποδηγούμενοι πρὸς τὴν εὕρεσιν αὐτῶν . . . ("the Empiricists too apply the same drugs, not guided toward their discovery by the nature of the matter . . ").

168. Nenci (1989) gives the arguments for this identification.

The occurrence here of the odd expression λήθην λαβόντες ("taking hold of forgetfulness") is probably not Clearchan diction. Aside from one occurrence in Pseudo-Hippocrates, the phrase does not appear in a directly transmitted author before the 1st century CE. Thereafter, Josephus and Aelian, for example, each use it a handful of times.[169] The mention here of στολὰς ἀνθινὰς has the same effect, since there is no directly attested example of the adjective ἀνθινός "flowery" used to describe the color or pattern of cloth before Strabo: e.g., 3.3.7, ἐν . . . ἀνθίναις ἐσθήσεσι ("in . . . flowery garments").[170] In contrast, Athenaeus has the usage at least eight times in addition to the passage under discussion.[171] Thus, if this passage is taken to be a verbatim quotation of Clearchus, then a single sentence of that author becomes the source of the first ever appearance of two unrelated expressions. It is preferable to assign both expressions to Athenaeus, in whose period they are unexceptional. In consequence, these elements of diction, too, emerge as evidence that this sentence on Iapygian τρυφή should be understood as a paraphrase.

The next example concerns the demoralizing influence of τρυφή upon the Scythians from Athen. 12.524d, a passage that we have already discussed above several times:

τρυφήσαντες δὲ καὶ μάλιστα δὴ καὶ πρῶτοι πάντων τῶν ἀνθρώπων ἐπὶ τὸ τρυφᾶν ὁρμήσαντες εἰς τοῦτο προῆλθον ὕβρεως ὥστε πάντων τῶν ἀνθρώπων εἰς οὓς ἀφίκοιντο ἠκρωτηρίαζον τὰς ῥῖνας·

[For indulging in *truphē* and especially also being first of all men to set off into *truphē,* they advanced to such a point of hubris that they cropped the noses of all the people they could reach.]

This time it is the word ἀκρωτηριάζειν in the sense of "cut off" or "mutilate" that deserves a closer look. Herodotus (3.59) and Xenophon (*Hell.* 6.2.36) each use the word once of cutting off *akroteria* of ships. Demosthenes is the first to

---

169. Hippocrates, *Herm.* 28.2; 2 Peter 1:9:2; Josephus, *AJ* 2.163, 2.202, 4.304, 5.107, 10.242; Ael. *NA* 4.35, 5.39, 8.1, 8.27; *VH* 3.18; Paus. 4.23.5.

170. *IG* 11.1300, cited by *LSJ* (*s.v.* ἀνθινός) as a reference to the color or pattern of women's dress, is not a clear counter-example: ἀπ᾽ οἴνου μὴ προσιέναι μηδὲ ἐν ἀνθινοῖς ("Approach neither from wine nor in florals"). Given the mention of wine, a meaning of "wreaths of flowers" for ἐν ἀνθινοῖς is possible.

171. Athen. 4.153c (authority of Posidonius, frag. 53 EK), 12.521b (Phylarchus, *FGrH* 81 F 45), 12.523d (Timaeus, *FGrH* 566 F 51 and Aristotle, frag. 601), 12.528d–e (Hyperochus, *FGrH* 576 F 1n), 12.530c (Mnaseas, frag. 14 *FHG* iii.152), 12.542c (Duris, *FGrH* 76 F 10), 14.622b (Semus, *FGrH* 396 F 24); at 7.281d it appears not as part of a citation, but in the comments of an unnamed deipnosophist.

extend the word: ἠκρωτηριασμένοι τὰς . . . πατρίδας ("cutting the extremities from their fatherlands," 18.296); it is unclear in this case whether the author intends to personify the nations or if he is invoking the ship-of-state metaphor. The first example in a direct transmission of ἀκρωτηριάζειν with an animate object is in Polybius: ἐπειδὴ δὲ τὰς χεῖρας ἀπέκοψαν, ἠκρωτηρίαζον τοὺς ταλαιπώρους ("when they had cut off their hands, they mutilated the wretches," 1.80.13). The relevant sense is well established in Philo, where it occurs more than a dozen times.[172] Once again, if this word is genuinely Clearchan, the *Lives* would be the first attestation of ἀκρωτηριάζειν with the meaning "mutilate."

The same diachronic distribution of an unusual word occurs in the context of a citation of Clearchus on the customs of the Medes, and thus raises red flags:

Κλέαρχος δὲ ὁ Σολεὺς ἐν τετάρτῳ Βίων προειπὼν περὶ τῆς Μήδων τρυφῆς καὶ ὅτι διὰ ταύτην πολλοὺς εὐνουχίσαιεν τῶν περικτιόνων . . .

[Clearchus of Soli in the fourth book of the *Lives* first talking about the *truphē* of the Medes and that because of this they made eunuchs of many of their neighbors . . .] (Athen. 12.514d = Clearchus, frag. 49 Wehrli)

The verb εὐνουχίζειν is first attested in a direct transmission from the last decades of the first century CE.[173] It is relatively common in works of Athenaeus's contemporaries.[174] Admittedly, it may make very little difference to the sense of the citation if Athenaeus changed whatever word Clearchus used for "castrate." However, the occurrence here of εὐνουχίζειν reveals just how insidious Athenaeus's method of citation can be for those who wish to reconstruct the words of fragmentary authors. For, while the sentence as far as ὅτι is clearly a formula

---

172. Philo, *Cher.* 96; *Sacr.*110, 116; *Deus* 66; *Agr.* 86; *Somn.* 2.84, 95, 168; *Abr.* 44; *Spec. leg.* 1.3, 9, 47, 80; 2.245, 3.179; *Cont.* 44; *Aet.* 49. It appears also at: Diodorus 13.57.3; Strabo 15.1.54, 16.2.31, 17.1.27; Plut., *Alc.* 18.6, *Nic.* 13.3, *Mor.* 479d; and elsewhere.

173. Josephus *AJ* 10.33; Plut., *Mor.* 692c (ἐξευνουχίζειν).

174. Galen has it fifteen times and Athenaeus's compatriot Clement of Alexandria seven. Athenaeus himself uses the verb in the introduction to a fragment of Xanthus. It is worth quoting the first few words: Λυδοὶ δὲ εἰς τοσοῦτον ἦλθον τρυφῆς ὡς καὶ πρῶτοι γυναῖκας εὐνουχίσαι, ὡς ἱστορεῖ Ξάνθος ὁ Λυδός ("The Lydians went to such an extent of *truphē* that they first made eunuchs out of women, as Xanthus the Lydian says." Athen. 12.515d = Xanthus, *FGrH* 765 T 5). It would be rare for a sentence to show Athenaeus's fingerprints so clearly: the formulaic εἰς τοσοῦτον ἦλθον τρυφῆς ὡς . . . , and the indication that the subjects were the first to perform some outrageous act (cf. Clearchus's Tarentines, who were first to shave their bodies and his Scythians, who were first to "throw themselves upon *truphē*"). In this context, it would be unreasonable not to recognize εὐνουχίσαι also as Athenaeus's own contribution.

of citation with author, work, and topic, and therefore is equally clearly phrased by Athenaeus, we would like to feel confident that ὅτι begins the quoted material. This is apparently not the case, but unlike the first part of the sentence, Athenaean origin is far from obvious.

In sum, the diction of citations in the *Deipnosophistae* can be completely devoid of relevant implications when viewed from the perspective of Athenaean usage, but an examination of the history of individual items of diction may reveal valuable evidence about the reliability of these citations. But because this material is relatively uninteresting synchronically, there is no a priori indication about which items may most profitably be studied diachronically. It therefore seems to us to be incumbent on scholars who wish to publish collections of prose fragments to attempt to map the chronological distribution of every significant feature of diction. This task would be Herculean and perhaps it would be beyond the powers of any scholar to do this even for a single fragmentary author.[175] On the other hand, the results of such lexical profiles would be an invaluable contribution to our understanding of the relationship between the original source of prose fragments and their intermediate cover texts.

Conclusion

This chapter has examined a number of factors that must be considered when evaluating Athenaeus's testimony about pernicious luxury. It may be helpful to recapitulate:

- Athenaeus's purpose is uncertain. Though recent scholarship has made progress in understanding the *Deipnosophistae* as a work of literature, much is still opaque. Since the purposes of the quoting author are key to the interpretation of any fragment, our uncertainty about Athenaeus in this regard is a significant hindrance.
- Athenaeus's reliability runs the gamut. With respect to accuracy of text reuse, the *Deipnosophistae* ranges from exact quotation to rough paraphrase to wild misrepresentation. In addition, even where reuse is most accurate, Athenaeus may offer an interpretation that completely belies the original.

---

175. The task would not be mechanical, as exemplified by the case of ἀνθινός described above. It is not the mere occurrence of the adjective, but its use in the meaning "flower-colored," "multi-hued," or the like which is telling.

- There is no reliable a priori method to establish the type of text reuse. Although certain formulae of citation are associated with particular types of reuse, such associations are only tendencies. The presence of introductory wording which, for example, generally is followed by verbatim material, does not carry great weight in the face of counter-indications of paraphrase.
- Athenaean framing material must be distinguished from the source matter. Scholars have been too quick to assume that language that occurs side-by-side with Athenaeus's attribution of a source's title and book number originates in the quoted author. This is very unlikely. Moreover, with careful examination, Athenaean framing language can often be identified. Such material must be separated before plausible evaluation of the content of a fragment is possible.
- Aspects of diction are often crucial. Decisive evidence can regularly be presented on the likelihood that elements of diction within a fragment are original or Athenaean. Lack of awareness in this area contributes to frequent misunderstanding of the relationship between original source and cover text. A thorough study of the relevant features of diction is a fundamental step in the interpretation of fragmentary evidence.

Considerations such as these clearly make investigation of the idea of luxury in the *Deipnosophistae* difficult and laborious. At the same time, they allow us to place on firmer footing our understanding of the strengths and weaknesses of Athenaeus's evidence.

CHAPTER 4

The Fragmentary Writers

In the previous chapter, we demonstrated the complexity involved in evaluating the evidence drawn from Athenaeus, who can be an untrustworthy purveyor even of accurately quoted material. In particular, when the theme turns to moral issues, he often doctors, or at least misrepresents, his quoted sources in order to use them in ways at odds with their original intent and meaning, sometimes for a kind of comic effect. Having cast doubt upon the reliability of the *Deipnosophistae* as a cover text that transmits more or less transparently the sense and even the wording of the original, we will now review what is taken as the best evidence for the historiographical theme of pernicious luxury in lost writers of the late Classical and Hellenistic periods. We will, as previously, focus on evidence for morally corrosive τρυφή, since scholars widely recognize this concept as a key element in the theme of decadence as a historical cause, and more generally in the moralizing tendency of the historiography of this period.[1]

While the principal goal of our discussion is to evaluate the relevant evidence on τρυφή, this chapter will also provide a case study of the methodology that, in the previous chapter, we argued can contribute significantly to a more precise appraisal of the accuracy of prose fragments. We hope that this method will be useful to many scholars who are dealing with fragmentary authors preserved in later texts. To generalize, when confronting a prose fragment, one must ask the following questions: Is the language used in the supposed quote common in the time of the original or the quoting author? Is it cast in vocabulary favored by the quoting author? Special attention must be paid to patterns

---

1. The classic statement is Passerini 1934. Cf. Bollansée 2008, 408, with pertinent bibliography at n. 33.

in the development of individual words or phrases: when their uses are figurative or metaphorical, one must investigate whether such uses are common in the time of the original or the quoting author. If a concrete term takes up a figurative meaning that then becomes commonplace, the temporal dimension of that transition needs to be noted and considered. In addition, at a wider scope, one should examine the narrative features of a fragment in view of what we may surmise about the practices of the source. How does the pattern in the fragments of one author compare to the data from other writers? Comparison with surviving works may allow us to ask whether, for example, the length of the fragment is appropriate to the original genre. Do our extant historical writers make it plausible that a lost author may have written in the short, quotable snippets that we find over and over again in Athenaeus? Or rather, is such a brief treatment far more likely to be an abridgement whose original language and intended meaning may have been considerably altered? Finally, the fragments of an author or the fragmentary evidence on a given topic such as τρυφή must be examined in the aggregate: are all the passages in which an author takes a particular moral stance preserved in one cover text? Do they resemble the other fragments by the same author in form and content? Though we do not discuss this issue at length, in each case we have examined all of the surviving fragments of the original authors discussed below and have discovered an absence of evidence for pernicious luxury—and indeed of morally significant material—outside of the fragments preserved chiefly by Athenaeus. Perhaps this distribution is the result of an accident of selection, because Athenaeus was the only one interested in such matters. But given what the arguments of the previous chapter have revealed about Athenaeus's parlor games, the pattern of the aggregate data is, in and of itself, reason to suspect that Athenaeus is transforming the substance of his sources.

Clearly the implementation of our method of evaluating fragmentary writers is laborious, and the answers to the questions we ask are seldom clear-cut. Many judgments will have to be made. Are two or three Classical examples enough to establish a pattern of usage?[2] When does a concrete image shade into the metaphorical? What constitutes clear examples of framing material in the cover text? Scholars will disagree with some of our individual conclusions,

---

2. We deliberately speak rather imprecisely when we ask whether a particular usage is common at a certain period. For some scholars, a single example from a fifth- or fourth-century text will make a parallel occurrence in a fragment unobjectionable. Others, like ourselves, will find this situation implausible if the usage is better attested nearer in time to the cover text.

which cannot, in any case, all be correct. But the conversation must take place. It is not enough to accept, as is frequently done, that a cover text such as Athenaeus is generally accurate. We hope to open a discussion in which the argument about accuracy will proceed fragment by fragment, sentence by sentence, and even word by word.

In this investigation, a great many fragments from various authors might be considered pertinent to an investigation of τρυφή. In order to avoid too much repetition, we will restrict our examination to a selection of authors who are among the most frequently cited, by Athenaeus and by modern scholars, as proponents of this theme, namely Clearchus, Ctesias, Ephorus, Theopompus, and Heraclides Ponticus. We will also look at a collection of evidence for Sybaris in particular, even where the word τρυφή is itself absent. In preparing this chapter, we have examined all the relevant evidence of which we are aware and are confident that the same methods and arguments presented here can be applied to the fragments of other writers, such as Phylarchus, Timaeus, Poseidonius, and Agatharchides, with results that would make no material difference to our conclusions.

Clearchus

Living in the late fourth century BCE, Clearchus of Soli was a peripatetic philosopher who produced a number of works with titles such as Περὶ γρίφων (*On Riddles*), Περὶ φιλίας (*On Friendship*), Ἐρωτικά (*Love Stories*), Περὶ σκελετῶν (*About Dried Bodies*), and Περὶ παιδείας (*On Education*). Although not strictly speaking a historian, Clearchus is, according to Athenaeus at least, an important witness in arguments about the theme of pernicious luxury in Greek writing. For Clearchus, it is claimed, makes an especially clear connection between τρυφή, understood as a weak and effeminate characteristic, and hubris, as displayed in acts of violent domination. The fragments in question come almost entirely from Athenaeus, and thus offer an excellent point of departure for our discussion: in spite of the weight that scholars have given Clearchus's evidence in this matter,[3] we believe that a better understanding of Athenaeus's methods

---

3.   Bollansée 2008, 405: "The single recurring theme in the fragments is the concept of τρυφή, which we encounter either by itself, or in close combination with its seemingly inevitable corollary, ὕβρις, in no less than 22 of the 26 surviving fragments." Cf. Tsitsiridis 2008; Nenci 1989. By way of contrast see Gorman and Gorman 2010.

of citation casts Clearchus's presumed interest in the relationship between τρυφή and hubris into serious doubt.

Athen. 12.524c–f = Clearchus, frag. 46 Wehrli

(1) καὶ περὶ Σκυθῶν δ᾽ ἑξῆς ὁ Κλέαρχος τάδε ἱστορεῖ· (2) μόνον δὲ νόμοις κοινοῖς πρῶτον ἔθνος ἐχρήσατο τὸ Σκυθῶν· (3) εἶτα πάλιν ἐγένοντο πάντων ἀθλιώτατοι βροτῶν διὰ τὴν ὕβριν. (4) ἐτρύφησαν μὲν γὰρ ὡς οὐδένες ἕτεροι, τῶν πάντων εὐροίας καὶ πλούτου καὶ τῆς λοιπῆς αὐτοὺς χορηγίας κατασχούσης. (5) τοῦτο δὲ δῆλον ἐκ τῆς ἔτι καὶ νῦν ὑπολειπούσης περὶ τοὺς ἡγεμόνας αὐτῶν ἐσθῆτός τε καὶ διαίτης. (6) τρυφήσαντες δὲ καὶ μάλιστα δὴ καὶ πρῶτοι πάντων τῶν ἀνθρώπων ἐπὶ τὸ τρυφᾶν ὁρμήσαντες εἰς τοῦτο προῆλθον ὕβρεως ὥστε πάντων τῶν ἀνθρώπων εἰς οὓς ἀφίκοιντο ἠκρωτηρίαζον τὰς ῥῖνας· (7) [ἀφ᾽] ὧν οἱ ἀπόγονοι μεταστάντες ἔτι καὶ νῦν ἀπὸ τοῦ πάθους ἔχουσι τὴν ἐπωνυμίαν. . . .

(1) About the Scythians also, Clearchus next relates these things: (2) the nation of the Scythians was at first the only one to use common laws. (3) Later, in contrast, they became the most miserable of mortals because of hubris. (4) For they possessed *truphē* as no others, while a prosperous flow of all things and wealth and other provisions gripped them. (5) This is clear from the dress and way of life even now left behind among their leaders. (6) Possessing *truphē*, and most especially first of all people having set out for its possession, they advanced to such an extent of hubris that they sheared off the noses of all people whom they could reach. (7) The descendants of these people moved away, but even now have a name taken from this misfortune.

The fragment continues with an account of how the Scythian women tattooed certain Thracian women who came into their power and how those Thracians sought to pass off the marks of their humiliation as ornamentation. Finally, we are baldly told, διὰ τὸ πένθος ἅμα τόν τε τῶν βίων ὄλβον καὶ τὰς κόμας περιεσπάσθησαν ("on account of grief, they were stripped of their prosperity in life and of their hair at the same time," 12.524e–f).

The sentence marked (1),[4] with its τάδε ἱστορεῖ, leads us to expect a verbatim quotation. However, sentence (2) is evidence we are dealing with a para-

---

4. We follow a practice of numbering each sentence or small group of sentences in order to make the subsequent discussion clear.

phrase: the Scythians' "common laws" are not explained and have no function in the fragment's narrative.[5] Sentence (3) gives what is for Athenaeus the moral of the story. We may observe that the claim that moral decline led to political disaster reminds us of an Athenaean "interpretive paraphrase" as we have identified them in Chapter 3. Certainly, the causal expression διὰ (τὴν) ὕβριν, like διὰ (τὴν) τρυφήν, is found frequently in introductions to citations, and the fragment as transmitted does not explain how or why Scythian hubris caused them to become miserable. We read only that they met with many disasters. No details in the events narrated in this fragment indicate that Clearchus was trying to illustrate this particular relationship of cause and effect; absent the phrase διὰ τὴν ὕβριν, it is unlikely that a reader would have identified as a chief concern of Clearchus the connection between the Scythians' mistreatment of those in their power and their eventual loss of prosperity.

Sentence (4) introduces τρυφή as the basis of the decline that the Scythians experienced. It, too, bears several signs of being a later paraphrase rather than a quotation of Clearchus, since the absolute clause that forms the bulk of the sentence contains several expressions that are unlikely to come from the original. In the first place, the somewhat odd phrase τῶν πάντων εὐροίας ("a prosperous flow of all things") has no good parallel in the Classical period.[6] Beginning with Polybius—for extant literature, at any rate—a meaning of "success" or "prosperity" is attested for εὔροια, though the expression never becomes common. For example, Polybius can use εὔροια absolutely, as at 5.71.1, of Antiochus on campaign: τοιαύτης δὲ γενομένης τῆς εὐροίας ("with the flow having been so favorable"); more commonly, Polybius qualifies the term with the subjective genitive τῶν πραγμάτων, as at 3.10.6: λέγω δὲ τὴν εὔροιαν τῶν κατ᾽ Ἰβηρίαν πραγμάτων Καρχηδονίοις ("I mean the favorable tide of events in Spain for the Carthaginians").[7] The occurrence in sentence (4) seems a stylistic variant of this use.

The second element in sentence (4) that would be anachronistic for

---

5.   Thus Wehrli (1969, 62) makes the observation: "der Text ist durch Verkürzungen z. T. entstellt: stecken hinter κοινοὶ νόμοι Gesetze, welche Privateigentum verbieten?"

6.   We are told (by, e.g., Sext. Emp., *Math.* 11.30) that the members of the Old Stoa defined happiness as εὔροια βίου (" a favorable flow of life"). We doubt that this esoteric expression is pertinent to the more general use of εὔροια from Polybius onward. Besides the Stoics, Plato has two metaphorical uses: *Phdr.* 238c, where εὔροια describes Socrates' fluency of argument, and *Leg.* 6.784b, where εὔροια τῆς γενέσεως indicates the engendering of a satisfactory number of children. The two other Classical occurrences are literal: Plato, *Leg.* 6.779c refers to the proper flow of rain water; Arist., *Somn.* 457a25 speaks of the ample flow of blood within those with "good veins."

7.   Examples of the phrase εὔροια τῶν πραγμάτων occur in Plutarch (*Per.* 20.4, *Mor.* 323e) and Diodorus Siculus (2.2.1). Other parallels for the meaning "success" or the like can be found at Plut., *Cim.* 10.1; Diod. Sic. 20.33.3 and 31.11.2; and Josephus, *BJ* 4.510.

Clearchus is the noun χορηγία in the meaning "resources" or "supplies." The Classical sense of χορηγία is "the act of leading a chorus," that is, sponsoring a dramatic production as an act of public service. In the Classical period, a metaphorical use of χορηγία is for practical purposes restricted to Aristotle. This fact may at first seem to favor Clearchus as the source of this expression, since he is said to have been a student of Aristotle. However, the meaning of metaphorical χορηγία in Aristotle differs significantly from that evident in sentence (4). In Aristotle, it occurs in connection with the ideal life for a human being or the ideal constitution for a state. More specifically, χορηγία refers to the presence (or, in the case of the adjective ἀχορήγητον, the absence) of the external goods that contribute to individual happiness or communal prosperity. These goods are "external" because they are beyond the control of the subject benefiting from them. Seen from another perspective, these goods depend on an external agency, whether we consider this to be fortune or the gods.[8]

By the second century BCE, χορηγία has become a dead metaphor, having lost the idea of "endowment" by an external benefactor. The word, now extremely common, is simply another synonym for παρασκευή and the like, with the meaning "supplies." It occurs most often in military contexts, and, not surprisingly, the first extant witness for this sense is Polybius, whose *Histories* contain nearly a hundred examples. Typical is 1.18.9: παρείλετο τὰς ἀγορὰς καὶ τὴν τῶν ἀναγκαίων χορηγίαν τοῖς τῶν ὑπεναντίων στρατοπέδοις ("he took away the provisions and the supply of necessities for the enemies' camps"). The use of χορηγία seems to imply nothing particular about the source of the supplies— whether, for instance, they were gathered by the soldiers or given by others. The same indifference to the source of χορηγία seems true in (4), and so it is prudent to assume a date of origin later than the first securely attested occurrence with this meaning.

Finally, the predicate of the absolute clause in (4) is grounds for suspicion.

---

8.   At *Eth. Nic.* 1099a31–33, Aristotle considers some of the requisites of human happiness: φαίνεται δ' ὅμως καὶ τῶν ἐκτὸς ἀγαθῶν προσδεομένη, καθάπερ εἴπομεν· ἀδύνατον γὰρ ἢ οὐ ῥάδιον τὰ καλὰ πράττειν ἀχορήγητον ὄντα ("Still, it seems to need the external goods as well, just as we said, for it is impossible or else not easy to perform excellent actions if one is unendowed."). Because of this dependency, it is a question whether happiness κατά τινα θείαν μοῖραν ἢ καὶ διὰ τύχην παραγίνεται ("comes about through a some kind of divine apportionment or even through fortune," *Eth. Nic.* 1099b10–11). In the *Politics* the city is similarly dependent for success on χορηγία τυχηρά. Thus, when, at *Pol.* 6.1325b37–38, Aristotle states, οὐ γὰρ οἷόν τε πολιτείαν γενέσθαι τὴν ἀρίστην ἄνευ συμμέτρου χορηγίας ("the best constitution is not possible without commensurate endowments"), we are not surprised to find in the subsequent discussion of πολιτικὴ χορηγία (*Pol.* 7.1326a5) items such as size of population, extant and fertility of the countryside, and communication of a city's territory with the sea. Such χορηγία are beyond the control of politicians. These advantages, too, can only reasonably be said to be provided by god or fortune.

Wealth, the favorable flow of all things and the other provisions "gripped" or "took possession of" the Scythians (αὐτοὺς κατασχούσης). This again is a strange expression, and the pattern of its profile of occurrence is similar to the other items in this sentence. For κατέχει to have an abstract noun as its semantic agent and one or more persons as its patient is a rarity in the Classical period. Especially infrequent are cases where it is fortune or misfortune that "grips" a person, but such an expression is better attested in the Roman period. In particular, we find the συμφορά as the subject of κατέχει in Dionysius of Halicarnassus.[9] Furthermore, we may be confident that the phrase συμφορὰ τὸν δεῖνα κατέχει is the model for εὐροίας καὶ πλούτου καὶ . . . αὐτοὺς χορηγίας κατασχούσης in (4) because this very phrase appears in the final sentence of this fragment, relating the eventual comeuppance of the Scythians: διὰ τὸ πλῆθος οὖν τῶν κατασχουσῶν αὐτοὺς συμφορῶν ("On account of the number of misfortunes gripping them . . . ," Athen. 12.524e–f). It is clear that the two clauses are balanced to highlight the story of Scythian decline. The question is whether this stylistic turn is due to Clearchus or Athenaeus. In our opinion, the presence of τῶν πάντων εὐροίας and τῆς λοιπῆς χορηγίας in this sentence make Athenaeus by far the more reasonable choice. It should be an axiom of prudent scholarship to discount any interpretation that results in attributing the first occurrence of lexical or stylistic usage to a prose fragment in Athenaeus.

All these considerations lead us to judge that the description of the Scythians as a people who ἐτρύφησαν ὡς οὐδένες ἕτεροι is cast in Athenaeus's words and represents Athenaeus's views. We may imagine that the original presented the Scythians enjoying the fruits of unusual prosperity. We cannot tell from this sentence if Clearchus wrote about the moral consequences of this life of ease.

Sentence (5) may likewise be counted evidence for an alteration of the original; its references to the clothing and δίαιτα of the Scythian leaders would have required further explanation in order to be as clear to the reader as it is claimed to be.[10] We are entitled to speculate that Clearchus discussed particularly striking features of the elite's dress and lifestyle, but the details are not recoverable.[11]

---

9. Dion. Hal., *Antiq. Rom.* 3.53.3, 6.87.7, 9.18.5, *Lys.* 1.10.
10. The words ἐκ τῆς ἔτι καὶ νῦν ὑπολειπούσης ("even now left behind") need not indicate that the sentence is a verbatim quotation, but only that Athenaeus included in his reworking a reference by Clearchus to Scythian customs in his own time.
11. Wehrli (1969, 62) compares this passage to the Hippocratic *De aere* 22, where Scythian dress, specifically, wearing trousers, contributes to impotence, especially among the rich. Apparently, Wehrli bases this note on the assumption that those who ἐτρύφησαν are subject to emasculation caused by

The sentence therefore at least marks an abridgement. As we will see, it comes between two sentences that are almost certainly paraphrases. We may plausibly assume the same status for this sentence.

In sentence (6), the connection between τρυφή and hubris, a putative characteristic of Clearchus's moralizing, is explicitly made for the only time in this fragment. Once again, the sentence must be no more than a paraphrase, leaving us without reliable evidence on Clearchus's view about τρυφή and hubris. In the previous chapter we have argued that three elements in this sentence are Athenaean turns of phrase. To "set out into *truphē*" (ἐπὶ τὸ τρυφᾶν ὁρμήσαντες) reflects one of that author's ways of expressing moral causation. The clause "they advanced to such an extent of hubris that" (εἰς τοῦτο προῆλθον ὕβρεως ὥστε . . .) exhibits a pattern we have identified in the introductions to many citations. Finally, the strongly emphasized superlative, repeated twice, is an Athenaean favorite. In addition, we have already pointed out that ἠκρωτηρίαζον, if actually in the Clearchan original, would be the first example of that verb with the meaning "mutilate."[12] Thus, the diction of (6) is compelling evidence that its wording is not from Athenaeus's source.

As for the thought behind the words, nothing we know about τρυφή from its well-attested uses in Classical authors allow us to make sense of this alleged connection between Scythian indulgence in certain types of luxury and their mutilation of the faces of their neighbors.[13] On the other hand, we are familiar with Athenaeus's misinterpretation of texts in order to demonstrate his skill in his citation game. The goal in Book 12 is producing evidence from the ancients on the corruptive force of τρυφή. The only words in this fragment which support that view are manifestly Athenaeus's own. We may suggest that if Clearchus had actually depicted Scythian dress and δίαιτα as the cause of their brutal behavior, Athenaeus may have been expected to report some of Clearchus's reasoning along these lines. Instead, we have extremely vague Athenaean formulations. Accordingly, we find it likely that Clearchus made no such causal connection in the original of this citation.

---

overindulgence. We have seen in Chapters 1 and 2 that there is, in texts with direct transmission, no solid evidence for this process. Certainly, the Hippocratic *De aere* envisions no such process among the Scythians, but blames their feminization on constant horseback riding, a practice far removed from any association with τρυφή. It is best to admit that we do not know what aspects of Scythian dress Clearchus discussed.

12. See above (pp. 236–37).

13. Nor do we find elucidating parallels in the more elaborate treatments of the theme of τρυφή and hubris, which can be found in authors of the Roman period. We will discuss this material in the next chapter.

With this in mind, we may look at sentence (7): the savage actions of the Scythians gave certain people their name "even to this day." This fact is not pertinent to τρυφή or its connection with hubris. It is therefore not pertinent to Athenaeus's argument in this section. In addition, similar etymologizing occurs twice more in the part of the fragment that we have not quoted: the origins of "the phrase 'Scythian'" (τὴν ἀπὸ Σκυθῶν ῥῆσιν) and the verb ἀπεσκυθίσθαι are explained. It is possible that Clearchus related the stories of mutilation and humiliation in order to provide these explanations rather than to illustrate a theory of decadence. Etymology and etiology, not pernicious luxury, seem to have been the focus of the original.

Athen. 12.522d–e = Clearchus, frag. 48 Wehrli

(1) Ταραντίνους δέ φησι Κλέαρχος ἐν τετάρτῳ βίων ἀλκὴν καὶ δύναμιν κτησαμένους εἰς τοσοῦτο τρυφῆς προελθεῖν ὥστε τὸν ὅλον χρῶτα παραλεαίνεσθαι καὶ τῆς ψιλώσεως ταύτης τοῖς λοιποῖς κατάρξαι. (2) ἐφόρουν δέ, φησίν, καὶ παρυφίδα διαφανῆ πάντες, οἷς νῦν ὁ τῶν γυναικῶν ἁβρύνεται βίος. (3) ὕστερον δ᾽ ὑπὸ τῆς τρυφῆς εἰς ὕβριν ποδηγηθέντες ἀνάστατον μίαν πόλιν Ἰαπύγων ἐποίησαν Κάρβιναν, ἐξ ἧς παῖδας καὶ παρθένους καὶ τὰς ἐν ἀκμῇ γυναῖκας ἀθροίσαντες εἰς τὰ τῶν Καρβινατῶν ἱερὰ σκηνοποιησάμενοι γυμνὰ πᾶσι τῆς ἡμέρας τὰ σώματα παρεῖχον θεωρεῖν. . . .

[(1) Clearchus says in the fourth book of his *Lives* that the Tarentines, having gained possession of strength and power, advanced to such an extent of *truphē* that they would shave their whole skins and they initiated depilation for other men. (2) And, he says, they all wore transparent robes with borders, with which the life of women today is made decorous. (3) And later, guided by *truphē* into hubris, they made Carbina, one city of the Iapygians, into a ruin. From it they herded into the temples of Carbina the boys and the girls and the women in their prime and, building an enclosure, provided their naked bodies all day for viewing by all. . . .]

The fragment continues by relating the consequences of this mass rape: the gods killed all the perpetrators with thunderbolts; "even today" commemorative stelae stand in front of the houses of the descendants of the rapists; every year the Tarentines perform no rituals of mourning for these men, but sacrifice to Zeus instead.

Sentence (1) is an introductory paraphrase, bearing many indications that it does not closely reproduce Clearchus's words. The pairing ἀλκὴν καὶ δύναμιν is a phenomenon of the Roman period.[14] The expression εἰς τοσοῦτο τρυφῆς προελθεῖν, as we have noted several times, is a favorite introductory formula of Athenaeus. Therefore, the apparent causal relationship between Tarentine power and lifestyle may not have been a concern of the original: ἀλκὴν καὶ δύναμιν κτησαμένους could be Athenaeus's assumption based on the capture of Carbina; their advance into τρυφή would seem to him self-evident from the details of Tarentine dress and hygiene in this sentence and the next. With or without a prefix, the verb λεαίνω ("make smooth") in the sense of "remove hair" or "shave" is quite rare and relatively late. In non-fragmentary texts, the earliest comes from Diodorus Siculus in the first century BCE, followed by Lucian and Pseudo-Lucian.[15] The related noun ψίλωσις is for practical purposes a coinage of the first century CE, unattested before Plutarch (*Mor.* 646d) and Josephus (*AJ* 17.308).[16] The use of ψίλωσις in the sense of "depilation" apparently occurs first in Galen.[17] Thus, we may accept that Clearchus reported on the Tarentine custom of hair removal, but not that he called it τρυφή or made it a consequence of their prosperity.

Sentence (2), with its parenthetical φησίν, is perhaps closer to a quotation than a paraphrase. In any case, it holds little of interest for the moral value of luxury, since the association of the diaphanous clothing of the Tarentines with ἁβροσύνη need not be negative. We have seen in Chapter 1 that ἁβρός and its cognates often indicate a positive valuation. Even if ἁβρύνεται does indicate Clearchus's disapproval, it does not follow that the customs so described were presented as a cause of moral degeneration.

Sentence (3) is at least partially a paraphrase. It marks a transition between Tarentine customs and their outrageous actions, and so may represent a move by Athenaeus from one part of the *Lives* to another. Certainly, we must be alert for Athenaean diction in a sentence that may be transitional, and we do not have far to seek: the expression εἰς ὕβριν ποδηγηθέντες is a variety of the metaphor, common in Athenaeus, of physical motion into a vice. The phrase ὑπὸ τῆς

---

14. Earliest at Polybius 6.5.9. Otherwise: Diod. Sic. 3.35.8, 5.82.4; Strabo 11.2.19; Philo, *Opif.* 85, *Praem.* 89.2; Plut., *Pomp.* 76.2, *Alex.* 5.3, *Ant.* 84.7, *Mor.* 362b.

15. Diod. Sic. 5.28.3; Plut., *Mor.* 352d10, 410d5; Lucian, *Adv. indoct. et lib. em.* 23.17; Ps.-Lucian, *Cyn.* 19.16.

16. The term ἀποψίλωσις occurs once in Theophrastus (*Caus. Pl.* 5.9.11).

17. For example, Galen, *De simp. med.* 12.212.8, εἰς τὰς ψιλώσεις τῶν τριχῶν ("for the stripping of the hair"). Thereafter, the meaning is not unusual in the medical writers.

τρυφῆς is also to be found among Athenaeus's inventory of introductory formulae; its occurrence in a transition is therefore suspect. In Chapter 3, we have discussed the diachronic distribution of ποδηγεῖ and its derivatives and cognates.[18] It is much more at home in Athenaeus's milieu than in Clearchus's. Thus, it seems clear that the form of (3) is not original to Clearchus, but is an adaptation by Athenaeus.[19]

As for the content that Athenaeus reformulated, Clearchus must have related the capture of Carbina and the subsequent degradation and rape of the captives, but he need not have presented τρυφή as a cause of these atrocities. Indeed, once again it is difficult to see a plausible process of development between the effeminizing customs of the Tarentines—depilation and see-through clothing—and the hyper-masculine sexual predation they are said to produce. Given that the words that make this unlikely connection are Athenaeus's, we are justified in wondering if the causal nexus is also his interpretation, rather than Clearchus's. In addition, as in the previous fragment, the passage ends with the explanation of a contemporary custom (the stelae and the sacrifice to Zeus). Again, this explanation, and not the processes of decadence, may have been the original author's main concern.

Athen. 12.522f–523a

(1) Ἰαπύγων τε αὖ τὸ γένος ἐκ Κρήτης ὄντων κατὰ Γλαύκου ζήτησιν ἀφικομένων καὶ κατοικησάντων, οἱ μετὰ τούτους λήθην λαβόντες τῆς Κρητῶν περὶ τὸν βίον εὐκοσμίας εἰς τοῦτο τρυφῆς, εἶθ᾽ ὕστερον ὕβρεως ἦλθον ὥστε πρῶτοι τὸ πρόσωπον ἐντριψάμενοι καὶ προκόμια περιθετὰ [τε] λαβόντες στολὰς μὲν ἀνθινὰς φορῆσαι, τὸ δὲ ἐργάζεσθαι καὶ πονεῖν αἰσχρὸν νομίσαι. (2) καὶ τοὺς μὲν πολλοὺς αὐτῶν καλλίονας τὰς οἰκίας ποιῆσαι τῶν ἱερῶν, τοὺς δ᾽ ἡγεμόνας τῶν Ἰαπύγων ἐφυβρίζοντας τὸ θεῖον πορθεῖν ἐκ τῶν ἱερῶν τὰ τῶν θεῶν ἀγάλματα . . .

[(1) And, again, the nation of Iapygians, being from Crete, came in search of Glaucus and settled down; succeeding generations, choosing to forget the Cretan decency of life, went to such an extent of *truphē*, then later of hubris, that they were the first to rub cosmetics onto their face and adopt false forelocks

---

18. See above (pp. 234–35).
19. Note that ἐν ἀκμῇ, while occasionally attested in Classical material, is much more frequent in the Roman period. Not just the connection between τρυφή and hubris, but also the narration of events after the fall of Carbina may well be an Athenaean reworking.

around their heads and to wear flowery garments, and so that they considered it shameful to work and toil. (2) The majority of them made their houses more beautiful than the temples, but the leaders of the Iapygians, committing hubris against heaven, looted the statues of the gods from the temples . . .]

The passage continues by relating that, as a result of their impiety, the Iapygians were struck by "fire and copper from heaven." Some of these missiles survived much later to serve as evidence of this case of divine vengeance. In addition, all the descendants of those so punished wore their hair short and took up a "mourning garment" (πένθιμον στολὴν) instead of their earlier finery.

Although Athenaeus does not attribute this passage to Clearchus, it follows in the *Deipnosophistae* immediately after frag. 48 Wehrli, and scholars have argued that the similarities between this passage and the fragment of the *Lives* about the Tarentines indicate that this discussion of the τρυφή of the Iapygians is from the same source.[20] This interpretation may be correct, if the key similarities are not in fact due to Athenaeus. However this may be, it is convenient to examine this purported citation here.

It should be immediately apparent that sentence (1) is not a verbatim quotation. In Chapter 3 we identified several elements of diction that are unlikely to have been Classical. Thus, the expression λήθην λαβόντες ("taking hold of forgetfulness") is an idiom of the Roman period and, with the possible exception of Pseudo-Hippocrates, does not appear in a directly transmitted author before the first century CE. Thereafter, Josephus and Aelian, for example, each use it a handful of times.[21] The connection between τρυφή and hubris is made in one of the most recognizably Athenaean turns of phrase: εἰς τοῦτο τρυφῆς, εἶθ' ὕστερον ὕβρεως ἦλθον ὥστε. The mention of στολὰς ἀνθινὰς is also significant vis-à-vis authorship; there is no securely attested example of the adjective ἀνθινός "flowery" used to describe the color or pattern of cloth before Strabo: e.g., 3.3.7, ἐν ἀνθίναις ἐσθήσεσι ("in flowery garments"). In contrast, Athenaeus himself has the usage at least eight times in addition to the passage under discussion.[22] The original source—whether Clearchan or not—has clearly been recast by Athenaeus.

---

20. See the discussion in Nenci 1989.
21. Ps.-Hipp., *Herm.* 28.2. Otherwise: 2 Peter 1:9:2; Josephus, *AJ* 2.163, 2.202, 4.304, 5.107, 10.242; Ael., *NA* 4.35, 5.39, 8.1, 8.27; *VH* 3.18; Paus. 4.23.5.
22. Athen. 4.153c (authority of Posidonius, frag. 53 EK), 12.521b (Phylarchus, *FGrH* 81 F 45), 12.523d (Timaeus, *FGrH* 566 F 51), 12.528d–e (Hyperochus, *FGrH* 576 F 1), 12.530c (Mnaseas, frag. 14 = frag. 5 Cappeletto), 12.542c (Duris, *FGrH* 76 F 10), 14.622b (Semus, *FGrH* 396 F 24); at 7.281d, it appears not as part of a citation but in the comments of an unnamed deipnosophist.

Unlike the first two passages that we have examined, a possible run of thought linking Iapygian τρυφή to hubris is not obscure. The Iapygians were interested in beauty, their own and that of their houses, and in pursuit of this interest they robbed the temples. Of course, we cannot be confident that any such relationship of cause and effect was actually depicted in the original, since the language that reports the movement from effeminate self-indulgence to violence is so clearly a later creation. But even if we stipulate that the original contents were as we have suggested, the resultant interpretation holds little relevance. A picture of decadence in which τρυφή begets hubris through an obsession with beauty would be of extremely limited use as an explanation of historical events.[23]

Significantly, this passage also ends with an etiological explanation of contemporary customs, this time the somber dress and short hair of some Iapygians. Again we suspect this aspect of the passage may reflect its original focus.[24]

Athen. 12.515e–516c = Clearchus, frag. 43 Wehrli

(1) Κλέαρχος δ᾽ ἐν τῇ τετάρτῃ περὶ Βίων Λυδοί, φησί, διὰ τρυφὴν παραδείσους κατασκευασάμενοι καὶ ἀνηλίους αὐτοὺς ποιήσαντες ἐσκιατροφοῦντο, τρυφερώτερον ἡγησάμενοι τὸ μηδ᾽ ὅλως αὐτοῖς ἐπιπίπτειν τὰς τοῦ ἡλίου αὐγάς. (2) καὶ [τέλος] πόρρω προάγοντες ὕβρεως τὰς τῶν ἄλλων γυναῖκας καὶ παρθένους εἰς τὸν τόπον τὸν διὰ τὴν πρᾶξιν Ἀγνεῶνα κληθέντα συνάγοντες ὕβριζον. (3) καὶ τέλος τὰς ψυχὰς ἀποθηλυνθέντες ἠλλάξαντο τὸν τῶν γυναικῶν βίον, διόπερ καὶ γυναῖκα τύραννον ὁ βίος εὕρετο αὐτοῖς μίαν τῶν ὑβρισθεισῶν Ὀμφάλην· ἥτις πρώτη κατῆρξε μὲν τῆς εἰς Λυδοὺς πρεπούσης τιμωρίας. . . . (4) πρὸς ἣν εἷς τῶν Λυδῶν εὐγενὴς ἀνὴρ ὁρμήσας καὶ τῇ παρ᾽ αὐτοῖς Μίδου βασιλείᾳ βαρυνθείς, τοῦ μὲν Μίδου ὑπ᾽ ἀνανδρίας καὶ τρυφῆς [καὶ] ἐν πορφύρᾳ κειμένου καὶ ταῖς γυναιξὶν ἐν τοῖς ἱστοῖς συνταλασιουργοῦντος, Ὀμφάλης δὲ πάντας τοὺς συγκατακλιθέντας αὐτῇ ξενοκτονούσης, ἀμφοτέρους ἐκόλασε, τὸν μὲν ὑπὸ ἀπαιδευσίας κεκωφημένον τῶν ὤτων ἐξελκύσας, ὃς διὰ τὴν τοῦ φρονεῖν ἔνδειαν τοῦ πάντων ἀναισθητοτάτου ζῴου τὴν ἐπωνυμίαν ἔσχε.

---

23. It may be argued that a transformation from τρυφή to hubris with beauty as its pivot point is a peculiar instantiation of a more general concept of decadence through pernicious luxury. Given that such a speculation would be based on the presumption that Athenaeus accurately presented the thought of his source, such an interpretation would have little value.

24. We may observe that the adjective πένθιμον, when used to qualify an article of clothing, is primarily a phenomenon of the Roman period. Thus, πένθιμον στολήν, whose presence in the last sentence of the passage, seems to ironically respond to the στολὰς ἀνθινὰς of its first sentence, may indicate that Athenaeus reworded this part of the fragment as well.

[(1) The Lydians, says Clearchus in the fourth book of his *Lives,* having built parks on account of *truphē* and having made them sun-proof, kept to the shade; they considered it more in accord with *truphē* that the sun's rays should not fall on them at all. (2) And [finally] advancing far into hubris, they gathered together the women and girls of the other men into the place called, because of this action, the "Holy Place" and raped them. (3) And finally, becoming effeminate in their souls, they changed to the life of women, and for this reason life also found for them a woman tyrant, Omphale, one of the raped women; she first initiated a fitting revenge against the Lydians. . . . (4) Setting out for this [i.e., revenge], one wellborn man of the Lydians, weighed down by the monarchy of Midas among them—Midas, because of lack of manhood and *truphē,* used to lie around in purple and work wool with the women at the loom; Omphale used to kill all the strangers who had had sex with her—this man punished them both. Midas, who was struck deaf because of his ignorance, he dragged away by the ears; Midas received the name of the most senseless animal of all because of his lack of wits. . . .]

Between (3) and (4) we have omitted the details of Omphale's revenge: she gave the daughters of the men who had raped her to the slaves of their households. The slaves raped the girls in the same place in which Omphale had been raped (i.e., the place called Hagneon). The Lydians then renamed the place euphemistically "Sweet Embrace" (Γλυκὺς Ἀγκών). Then comes a digression in which we are informed that others besides the Lydians offered their women to chance strangers, particularly those who consecrate their daughters to prostitution: this seems to be a reminder of some ancient outrage and revenge (παλαιᾶς τινος ὕβρεως ἔοικεν εἶναι πρὸς ἀλήθειαν ὑπόμνημα καὶ τιμωρίας, Athen. 12.516b).

This passage contains some real difficulties. We will limit our discussion to those aspects that are most directly relevant to Clearchus's views on τρυφή. First, we may consider significant items of diction, since these are relatively straightforward. The parenthetical φησί in sentence (1) is often the sign of a verbatim quotation. However, the phrase διὰ τρυφὴν is an Athenaean favorite in a citation's introduction. It should be noted also that (2) constitutes a transition from the theme of the pursuit of luxury as embodied in building of shady enclosures to the theme of rape and revenge. At just such a juncture we might expect signs of Athenaean adaptation and in fact the familiar metaphor of advancing into a vice occurs: πόρρω προάγοντες ὕβρεως ("advancing far into hubris"). An assumption of paraphrase rather than quotation is the prudent course for these sentences.

Sentence (3) contains the expression τὰς ψυχὰς ἀποθηλυνθέντες ("becoming women in their souls"). This occurrence is suspicious. A Clearchan origin might seem secure, since Clearchus, frag 41 Wehrli, has the related form συνεκθηλύνειν. But the latter passage also derives from Athenaeus (15.687a), and the usage in both passages is probably anachronistic: θηλύνειν and its compounds become a regular part of the vocabulary of decadence in the Roman era, and in works of this period, their primary function is describing a moral process.[25] Earlier, the lexical group is rare and the moral dimension secondary.[26] This pattern of distribution must be taken into consideration.

Sentence (4) likewise presents material that is probably due to Athenaeus rather than Clearchus. The sentence is another transition, this time from the details of Omphale's vengeance and the digression on sacred prostitution to the punishment inflicted upon Midas and Omphale herself. Thus, we find significance in the expression "setting out for [revenge]" (πρὸς ἣν ὁρμήσας), which begins this transition. The turn of phrase (ὁρμάω + a vice) is another that we have previously argued is an Athenaean formula. Next, when we read that Midas's offensive behavior was ὑπ᾽ ἀνανδρίας καὶ τρυφῆς ("because of lack of manhood and *truphē*"), we recognize Athenaeus's technique of attributing causation in order to support his interpretation of a citation. Later in (4), the men who raped Omphale are referred to with the participial phrase πάντας τοὺς συγκατακλιθέντας. The verb is very rare in the Classical period, but common enough after the first century BCE. In addition, the use of the word here in (4) for Omphale's attackers corresponds to an earlier occurrence in the material we have omitted from our citation. Specifically, Omphale "would lay the mistresses down with their slaves" (συγκατέκλινε τοῖς δούλοις τὰς δεσποίνας). No Classical parallels for the active use of συγκατακλίνω in the sense of "give [the accusative] to [the dative] for sex" can be found, though it occurs in, for example,

---

25. Philo, for example, has ἐκθηλύειν ten times, all referring to the idea of moral decay. *Som.* 2.9 is especially instructive for its cluster of terms that are frequently found in Roman-era discussions of moral decline: εἰσὶ δὲ οὗτοι μὲν τῆς μαλακωτέρας καὶ τρυφερᾶς διαίτης, τὸν πλείω χρόνον ἐν γυναικωνίτιδι καὶ τοῖς γυναικωνίτιδος ἐκτεθηλυμμένοις ἔθεσιν ἀπ᾽ αὐτῶν σπαργάνων ἀνατραφέντες ("These are people of a way of life softer and marked by *truphē*, raised continuously from the crib in the woman's chamber and in its effeminized customs.").

26. At Xen., *Oec.* 4.2, the bodies of certain craftsmen are "effeminized" (τῶν σωμάτων θηλυνομένων) due to being kept indoors by their jobs. It is noteworthy that Xenophon spells out the moral corollary: καὶ αἱ ψυχαὶ πολὺ ἀρρωστότεραι γίγνονται ("and their souls become much weaker"); from Philo's time, this addition would have been unnecessary. Perhaps the only solid example before Philo of -θηλύνειν with a primarily moral sense is at Euripides, frag. 360.28–29, τὰ μητέρων δὲ δάκρυ᾽ ὅταν πέμπῃ τέκνα, / πολλοὺς ἐθήλυν᾽ εἰς μάχην ὁρμωμένους ("Whenever mothers' tears escort their children, they effeminize many men setting off to battle.").

Plutarch and Parthenius.[27] Finally, the Lydian insurgent grabs Midas's ears, since he is "struck deaf because of his ignorance" (ὑπὸ ἀπαιδευσίας κεκωφημένον): while the adjective κωφός ("deaf") is Classical, the denominative verb κωφάω meaning "be/become deaf" is extremely scarce before Philo.

Thus, the diction in this citation gives several indications that it is not a verbatim quotation from Clearchus. The content of the passage points to the same conclusion. In the first place, it gives the impression of being a rather confused amalgam. Most obviously, it contains a peculiar doublet: two different euphemistic names are given to the same place as the result of two mass rapes. Another version of the fragment seems to cloud the issue even more. The lexicographer Hesychius reports:

Κλέαρχος δέ φησιν <τοὺς Λυδοὺς> ἐξυβρίζειν εἰς τὰς τῶν καταδεεστέρων γυναῖκας καὶ παρθένους, καὶ τὸ χωρίον, ἐν ᾧ ταῦτα ἔδρων, ὀνομάσαι Γλυκὺν ἀγκῶνα.

[Clearchus says that <the Lydians> raped the wives and daughters of their inferiors, and that they named the place in which they did these things "Sweet Embrace."] (Hesych., gamma 685)

If the editor has, as it seems, correctly restored τοὺς Λυδοὺς (instead of τὴν Ὀμφάλην) as the subject of ἐξυβρίζειν, the result is evidence that it was the first rape reported in the Athenaean passage that resulted in the euphemism there said to be the result of the second act of violence. Note that there is no place in this version for Omphale, and the confusion that her presence brings to the *Deipnosophistae* passage may well be due to Athenaeus. We have seen in Chapter 3 how recent work has demonstrated that Athenaeus sometimes attaches extraneous material to the authority of his named source. This citation shows signs of such exaggeration: Athenaeus, whose concern in Book 12 is to show the malignant consequences of τρυφή, by adding the Omphale story doubles, so to speak, the hubris of which the Lydians are guilty; we may recall that the Lydians' advance into such behavior is evidently introduced in Athenaeus's own words (πόρρω προάγοντες ὕβρεως). At the same time, this addition reaffirms the Lydian effeminacy implicit in the mention of their "life in the shade" (ἐσκιατροφοῦντο); they become "women" duly ruled by a woman. Thus, the

27. Plut., *Mor.* 618d, 655a; Parth., *Amat. nar.* 1.3, 5.3, 8.5, 16.3.

muddled character of the rape narratives should make us aware of the possibility of a pastiche.

This impression is strengthened when, in the last quarter of the fragment, we suddenly come upon King Midas and the unnamed Lydian noble who seeks to punish him. Midas, not a Lydian but a Phrygian in most traditions, is here apparently Omphale's husband and co-ruler. The transition to this theme is comically abrupt: the custom of sacred prostitution on Crete and elsewhere is actually a vestige of an ancient crime and its revenge, "and it was revenge the fellow who punished Midas was after" (πρὸς ἣν εἷς τῶν Λυδῶν εὐγενὴς ἀνὴρ ὁρμήσας . . .). That this shift marks a suture in the material would be an obvious interpretation even if πρὸς ἣν ὁρμήσας were not identifiable as an Athenaean expression. Since we know that Athenaeus can be quite skillful in his transitions, the ham-handed segue may indicate that the author wished to draw attention to the novelty of the connection he was making.

For these reasons, it seems to us likely that this fragment does not closely represent the narrative structure of an original in the *Lives*, but is a composite of several sources. On the other hand, it is certainly possible that the fragment is a combination of several different passages drawn from Clearchus. Working with that assumption, we will look again at the citation to see what it may tell us about τρυφή.

First, we may accept that the original characterized the Lydian paradises in terms of τρυφή, since, although we can disregard the διὰ τρυφὴν in sentence (1) as Athenaean, it remains that the Lydians considered it τρυφερώτερον to spend their days in the shade. This reference to τρυφή is unobjectionable in terms of the meanings well attested in Classical authors: the parks, presumably built and maintained by the labor of others, had as their main purpose the enhancement of the comfort of the elite. Τρυφή is, in its essence, the attitude of mind that presumes that others will put a high value on fulfilling the subject's needs or desires. Thus, the creation, by the many, of shady parks for the benefit of the few is an example of τρυφή in the Classical sense.

The move from τρυφή to hubris, however, is not paralleled in good Classical evidence and is, in fact, unmotivated. It is not self-evident that the possession of places in which one could avoid the sun is sufficient reason to use one of the parks as the scene for a mass rape. Nor, again, is it clear how τρυφή, which is associated with the effeminate behavior of staying out of the sun, could develop into a cause for aggressive sexual violence. Thus, at the very least, the words πόρρω προάγοντες ὕβρεως obscure a process that would need to be explained to Clearchus's intended readers just as much as to us.[28] Unless we can find evidence for that explanation in contemporary sources, it is prudent to assume that the causal relationship between luxury and violence represents Athenaeus's interpretation.[29]

The next step in the narrative is similarly difficult. The acts of rape are depicted as part of a process (καὶ τέλος) that causes the guilty men to lose their masculinity "in their souls" and become subject to a woman tyrant. Once again the reasoning is opaque: why, for a Greek, would committing rape be a step toward emasculation? The connection is so tenuous that we doubt that it occurred in the original. Rather, the existence of a tradition that the Lydians came to be ruled by Omphale, one of the women they raped, would have been sufficient evidence that Lydian society, including gender roles, had been turned topsy-turvy. So, while τέλος in the Athenaean text hints at a process of degeneration, it could equally have indicated, in the original, the result of a sequence of historical events that made Omphale ruler. However this may be, there is no sign that this second round of feminization (ἐσκιατροφοῦντο constituting the first) was attributed to τρυφή.

Finally, there is the case of Midas and his punishment.[30] The king is portrayed as "reclining in purple" and working wool with the women. As we will discuss in the case of Ctesias and the story of Sardanapalus, the view that the seclusion of eastern monarchs hid contemptible practices has Classical roots, although early examples seem to have derived from moralizers and not historians. Here it is sufficient to point out an inconsistency. Outside of fragmentary texts, τρυφή seems never to mean "effeminacy" or the like in the Classical period.[31] Rather, it indicates the act of being taken care of, or the assumption that one deserves such attention. Thus, it is in line with Classical usage to character-

---

28. The MSS read καὶ τέλος πόρρω προάγοντες ὕβρεως. Kaibel omits τέλος, which indeed may be due to dittography, as it recurs in (3). On the other hand, it may be a remnant of the original, indicating, perhaps the culmination of a sequence of hubristic acts. In this case, Athenaeus has apparently chosen the most heinous to make his point.

29. It is true that in this passage the causal connection between τρυφή and hubris is not made explicit. Rather, Athenaeus first says that the Lydians had τρυφή and then that they became rapists. The reader is left to fill in the gaps. Given the general argument of Book 12, there is no doubt what assumption the reader was intended to make.

30. We may omit the discussion of Omphale's revenge and the origins of sacred prostitution, since pernicious luxury is not mentioned or implied.

31. The pairing ἀνανδρίας καὶ τρυφῆς is noteworthy for its extreme rarity: we never find this conjunction in Classical literature. If the two words were synonyms, we might expect otherwise. Plutarch (Mor. 20a3) has the words in the same sentence, but not conjoined; likewise Athen. 12.514d. Otherwise, they are paired in Clement of Alexandria, citing Diogenes (Clem. Al., Strom. 2.20.119.6).

ize ἐν πορφύρᾳ κειμένου as an action ὑπὸ τρυφῆς, but the same is not true for συνταλασιουργοῦντος. Working wool is in direct opposition to being taken care of, and the application of τρυφή to that action is anachronistic, unless we interpret it as a reference to Midas's willful avoidance of the toil involved in the duties of a ruler and of public life more generally. There is all the more reason to consider the causal phrase ὑπ᾽ ἀνανδρίας καὶ τρυφῆς to be Athenaean.

Like other Clearchan material, the anecdote about Midas ends with an etiological rationalization: the tradition that Apollo punished the king by giving him donkey's ears is explained as a reflection of the attack upon Midas by the Lydian avenger. The fragments that we have examined so far share this interest in the phenomenon of the ὑπόμνημα ὕβρεως καὶ τιμωρίας. As one might expect, acts of violence play a far more central role in the explanations of this hubris than do acts of τρυφή. We suggest that illustrating the links between ancient violence and contemporary customs was Clearchus's preoccupation. If this is so, the prominence of minor displays of τρυφή in these fragments is presumably the result of Athenaeus's efforts at reinterpretation. That author seized upon ethnological details that his readers might recognize as marks of τρυφή— Scythian dress, for example, and Tarentine depilation—and gave them causal force.

Athen. 12.541c–e = Clearchus, frag. 47 Wehrli, as compared to Aelian, VH 9.8

We have quoted frag. 47 Wehrli in full because in this case we have a rare opportunity to compare Athenaeus's version of a fragmentary passage to a text transmitted by another author.[32] Here Aelian has recourse to the same source, and his complete version is also given.

The first observation we can make is that at least one of these citations must be a paraphrase. In spite of the γράφει οὕτως in sentence (1), it will be no surprise that in our view Athenaeus's text shows the greater evidence of departure from its source: note only the narration of Dionysius's rape of the Locrian girls. Aelian writes συνῆν αὐταῖς ἀκολαστότατα ("have intercourse with them most licentiously"), while Athenaeus has the more exuberant γυμνὸς μετὰ γυμνῶν οὐδὲν αἰσχύνης παρέλιπεν ἐπὶ τοῦ στρώματος κυλινδούμενος ("naked, with the girls naked, he omitted no bit of shamefulness while rolling around on the

---

32. Wehrli (1969, 63) without explanation prints Athenaeus's version as the fragment of Clearchus. He has nothing to say about the differences between the two texts, except that Aelian is "teils ausführlicher, teils knapper als Athenaeus."

TABLE 2

Athenaeus	Aelian
(1) καὶ Κλέαρχος δὲ ἐν τῷ τετάρτῳ τῶν Βίων γράφει οὕτως (2) Διονύσιος δ᾽ ὁ Διονυσίου ἁπάσης γενόμενος Σικελίας ἀλάστωρ εἰς τὴν Λοκρῶν πόλιν παρελθὼν οὖσαν αὐτῷ μητρόπολιν (Δωρὶς γὰρ ἡ μήτηρ αὐτοῦ τὸ γένος ἦν Λοκρίς) στρώσας οἶκον τῶν ἐν τῇ πόλει τὸν μέγιστον ἐρπύλλοις καὶ ῥόδοις μετεπέμπετο μὲν ἐν μέρει τὰς Λοκρῶν παρθένους· (3) καὶ γυμνὸς μετὰ γυμνῶν οὐδὲν αἰσχύνης παρέλιπεν ἐπὶ τοῦ στρώματος κυλινδούμενος. (4) τοιγαροῦν μετ᾽ οὐ πολὺν χρόνον οἱ ὑβρισθέντες γυναῖκα καὶ τέκνα ἐκείνου λαβόντες ὑποχείρια ἐπὶ τῆς ὁδοῦ στήσαντες μεθ᾽ ὕβρεως ἐνηκολάσταινον αὐτοῖς· (5) καὶ ἐπεὶ τῆς ὕβρεως πλήρεις ἐγένοντο, κεντοῦντες ὑπὸ τοὺς τῶν χειρῶν ὄνυχας βελόναις ἀνεῖλον αὐτούς. (6) καὶ τελευτησάντων τὰ μὲν ὀστᾶ κατέκοψαν ἐν ὅλμοις, τὰ δὲ λοιπὰ κρεανομησάμενοι ἐπηράσαντο [πάντες] τοῖς μὴ γευσαμένοις αὐτῶν· (7) ὅθεν πρὸς τὴν ἀνόσιον ἀρὰν κατήλεσαν αὐτῶν τὰς σάρκας, ἵν᾽ ἡ τροφὴ σιτοποιουμένων κατεδεσθῇ· τὰ δὲ λείψανα κατεπόντωσαν. (8) αὐτὸς δὲ Διονύσιος τέλος μητραγυρτῶν καὶ τυμπανοφορούμενος οἰκτρῶς τὸν βίον κατέστρεψεν. (9) εὐλαβητέον οὖν τὴν καλουμένην τρυφὴν οὖσαν τῶν βίων ἀνατροπὴν ἁπάντων τε ὀλέθριον ἡγεῖσθαι τὴν ὕβριν	(1) ὁ νέος Διονύσιος ἐς τὴν τῶν Λοκρῶν πόλιν παριὼν (εἴ γε Δωρὶς ἡ μήτηρ αὐτοῦ Λοκρὶς ἦν) τοὺς οἴκους τῶν μεγίστων τῶν ἐν τῇ πόλει, ῥόδοις καὶ ἑρπύλλοις καὶ ἄλλοις ἄνθεσι καταστρωννὺς τὰς τῶν Λοκρῶν θυγατέρας μετεπέμπετο, καὶ συνῆν αὐταῖς ἀκολαστότατα. (2) ὑπὲρ δὴ τούτου ἔτισε δίκην· ἐπειδὴ γὰρ αὐτοῦ ἡ τυραννὶς κατελύθη ὑπὸ Δίωνος, ἐνταῦθα οἱ Λοκροὶ τὴν γυναῖκα τοῦ Διονυσίου καὶ τὰς θυγατέρας κατεπόρνευσαν, καὶ ἀνέδην αὐταῖς ἐνύβριζον πάντες, μάλιστα οἱ προσήκοντες ταῖς παρθένοις ταῖς ὑπὸ Διονυσίου διεφθαρμέναις. (3) ἡνίκα δὲ διακορεῖς ἐγένοντο ὑβρίζοντες, κεντοῦντες αὐτὰς ὑπὸ τοῖς ὄνυξί τοῖς τῶν χειρῶν βελόναις ἀπέκτειναν. (4) τὰ δὲ ὀστᾶ κατέκοψαν ἐν ὅλμοις, καὶ τὰ κρέα τῶν ὀστῶν ἀφελόντες ἐπηράσαντο τοῖς μὴ γευσαμένοις αὐτῶν· (5) εἰ δέ τι περιελείφθη ἐξ αὐτῶν, κατεπόντωσαν. (6) ὁ δὲ ἐν Κορίνθῳ πολλαῖς καὶ ποικίλαις χρησάμενος βίου μεταβολαῖς διὰ τὴν ὑπερβάλλουσαν ἀπορίαν, τελευταῖον δὲ μητραγυρτῶν καὶ κρούων τύμπανα καὶ καταυλούμενος τὸν βίον κατέστρεψεν.
(1) Clearchus in the fourth book of his *Lives* writes as follows: (2) Dionysius, the son of Dionysius, having become the scourge of all Sicily, arrived at the city of the Locrians, his mother city (Doris, his mother, was a Locrian by race). He strewed the largest house in the city with roses and thyme, then sent for the Locrians' girls in turn. (3) Naked, with the girls naked, he omitted no bit of shamefulness while rolling around on the petals. (4) Accordingly, not much later, the men who had been outraged took captive his wife and children, and making them stand on the street, they had their way with them violently. (5) And when they had their fill of raping, they killed them by sticking them with needles under their fingernails. (6) And when they were dead, they smashed up the bones in mortars and, dividing the rest of the flesh between them, they put a curse on those who would not taste them. (7) They ground up their bodies for the unholy curse, so that the food would be done away with as they had their bread, and they sank the remainder in the sea. (8) Dionysius himself became a mendicant of Cybele and carried the tympanum; he ended his life pitifully. (9) One must beware of the thing called *truphē*, since it is the ruination of lives, and hubris should be considered destructive to all things.	(1) Dionysius the Younger, coming to the city of the Locrians (his mother Doris was a Locrian), seizing the houses of the greatest men in the city and strewing them with roses and thyme and other flowers, would send for the daughters of the Locrians and have intercourse with them most licentiously. (2) For this he paid the penalty, since when his tyranny was overthrown by Dion, the Locrians made Dionysius's wife and daughters into prostitutes and they all raped them without restraint, especially those belonging to the girls ruined by Dionysius. (3) And when they were sated with raping, they killed the women by sticking them with needles under their fingernails. (4) They smashed up their bones in mortars and, taking the flesh off the bones, they cursed those who would not taste it. (5) If anything remained, they sank it in the sea. (6) Dionysius underwent in Corinth many and various changes of life because of extreme poverty, and, finally, becoming a mendicant of Cybele and beating the tympanum and accompanied by the flute, he ended his life.

petals"). The verb used by Aelian for the sexual activity, σύνειμι, is well attested in this meaning from the fifth century BCE. In contrast, there seem to be no good parallels for κυλίνδω/κυλινδέω (or its compounds or derivatives) with a sexual meaning before the Roman period, when the use occurs in Plutarch.[33] The same pattern holds with respect to diction in the description of the rape of Dionysius's wife and daughters. Aelian's καταπορνεύω (and the simplex πορνεύω) occurs in this sense from Herodotus onward. Athenaeus's ἐνακολασταίνω (and ἀκολασταίνω) are not clearly used to refer to sex before the Common Era.[34]

In any case, explicit mention of τρυφή and its connection with hubris occurs only in sentence (9) of Athenaeus's version. It is possible that Aelian cut off his citation before the story had ended in his source. However, there is better evidence that Athenaeus recast the ending. Whatever words in the original are reflected in the beginning of Aelian (6)—ὃ δὲ ἐν Κορίνθῳ πολλαῖς καὶ ποικίλαις χρησάμενος βίου μεταβολαῖς διὰ τὴν ὑπερβάλλουσαν ἀπορίαν ("Dionysius underwent in Corinth many and various changes of life because of extreme poverty")—are missing in Athenaeus. It is easy to see why. Athenaeus presents this citation as an example of the calamitous results of a life of τρυφή and hubris. But Aelian's βίου μεταβολαῖς is a mild expression that need not imply catastrophe. Likewise, Aelian attributes Dionysius's new life not to τρυφή, but to ἀπορία, "lack or resources" or "poverty." Admittedly, the phrase διὰ τὴν ὑπερβάλλουσαν ἀπορίαν supplies only the cause of Dionysius's surprising occupation in Corinth, not the woes that befell him in general. Still, the presence of the causal expression might confuse Athenaeus's readers and distract from the effectiveness of the citation, since the miserable consequences of luxury rather than of want make up Athenaeus's point.

---

33. At Plut., *Otho* 2.2, among the mental punishments suffered by the hated Praetorian Prefect Tigellinus is the loss of αὐτάς τε τὰς ἀνοσίους καὶ ἀρρήτους ἐν γυναιξὶ πόρναις καὶ ἀκαθάρτοις ἐγκυλινδήσεις ("the unholy and unspeakable acts themselves of rolling around amid impure and whoring women"). At *Mor.* 766b, the subject is the man who, after death, comes to know the true form of Love and does not come running back to the physical world where ἐν θύραις νεογάμων καὶ δωματίοις κυλινδοῦνται ("he rolls about in the Newlywed Suite"). In connection with this last expression, we may refer to the lexicon of Athenaeus's contemporary Julius Pollux. In a list of expressions (6.188), which may be applied to ὁ δ' ἐπ' ἀφροδισίοις μαινόμενος ("the sex-crazed man"), appears the following: περὶ τὰς τῶν ἑταιρῶν θύρας κεκυλινδημένος ("one who has rolled around at prostitutes' doors").

34. Clearest is at Plut., *Mor.* 997b: ἐν γυναιξὶν κόρον ἡδονῆς οὐκ ἐχούσαις ἀποπειρώμενος πάντα καὶ πλανώμενος <ὁ> ἀκολασταίνων ἐξέπεσεν εἰς τὰ ἄρρητα ("having his way with women who can't get enough pleasure, trying everything and losing his way, the man would fall into unspeakable things"). Again, in Julius Pollux's list of terms for men obsessed with sex, the participle ἀκολασταίνων comes immediately before πορνοκοπῶν ("whore-knocker").

While Athenaeus's concluding text lacks material present in Aelian, it also contains a significant addition. As the citation closes in Aelian, Dionysius simply "ended his life." In Athenaeus, the ex-tyrant's death is qualified: he ended his life οἰκτρῶς, "piteously." No such value judgment is made in Aelian, nor is such necessarily implied.[35] For Athenaeus, on the other hand, this valorization of Dionysius's final role in life is integral to his interpretation of the passage. Thus, we can identify a clear motive for the insertion of οἰκτρῶς by Athenaeus, but not its omission in Aelian.

In view of these factors, it is reasonable to allow the possibility that sentence (9) is essentially an addition by Athenaeus, summarizing what he sees as the moral of the citation. Perhaps his words here represent his understanding of whatever original was reflected in Aelian's "changes of life." If, in Athenaeus's view, Dionysius's position as a begging priest of Cybele truly rendered his dying οἰκτρῶς, then Athenaeus's τῶν βίων ἀνατροπὴν ("the overthrow of lives") might be a more illuminating turn of phrase than Aelian's βίου μεταβολαῖς. Certainly, Athenaeus would have had no problem seeing τρυφή as the genuine cause of upheaval in the tyrant's life. Supporting our view that τρυφή as τῶν βίων ἀνατροπὴν is an Athenaean expression rather than Clearchan is the usage profile of the noun ἀνατροπή. The basic meaning of the word is "an overturning," and in the Classical period it occurs only rarely and with a meaning close to the literal sense. Thus, for example, the chorus at Aeschylus, *Eum.* 355 says δωμάτων εἱλόμαν ἀνατροπάς ("I have chosen the overturning of houses"), and the connection between the physical toppling of buildings and the ruin of the families who live within is an easy metaphor.[36] In contrast, during the Roman period a more abstract meaning is very common. Plutarch writes of the overturning of "the important matters," and Philo Judaeus and Dionysius of Hali-

35. While Plutarch's Cleomenes certainly uses μητραγύρτης as an epithet of reproach for Ptolemy Philopater (*Agis* 57.7), Dionysius of Halicarnassus presents the occupation in a more neutral way: ὥσπερ τὰ τῆς Ἰδαίας θεᾶς ἱερά. θυσίας μὲν γὰρ αὐτῇ καὶ ἀγῶνας ἄγουσιν ἀνὰ πᾶν ἔτος οἱ στρατηγοὶ κατὰ τοὺς Ῥωμαίων νόμους, ἱερᾶται δὲ αὐτῆς ἀνὴρ Φρὺξ καὶ γυνὴ Φρυγία καὶ περιάγουσιν ἀνὰ τὴν πόλιν οὗτοι μητραγυρτοῦντες, ὥσπερ αὐτοῖς ἔθος, . . . καταυλούμενοι πρὸς τῶν ἑπομένων τὰ μητρῷα μέλη καὶ τύμπανα κροτοῦντες (". . . as, for example, the rites of the Idaean Goddess: for the Praetors carry out the sacrifices and games to her every year according to Roman customs, but a Phrygian man and a Phrygian woman act as her priests and it is they who wander through the city acting as holy beggars, as is their custom, accompanied by their followers on flutes and beating the Mother's measures upon their tympanums." Dion. Hal., *Antiq. Rom.* 2.19.3–4). The role of μητραγύρτης, then, need not be *inherently* "piteous," and we cannot be confident whether Athenaeus's characterization of it as such is more accurate to Clearchus than Aelian's silence in this regard.

36. The same image occurs at Antiphon, *Tetr.* 2.2 and Plato, *Prot.* 325c. A simple literal use occurs at Arist., *Met.* 1013b10 of the capsizing of a ship. These are apparently the only Classical uses of ἀνατροπή.

carnassus of the overturning of "the customs and traditions."[37] Whatever an examination of the diction of Athenaeus sentence (9) may tell us, the lack of a reflection of it in Aelian means we cannot presume a Clearchan original unless we can plausibly explain why Aelian omitted the moral to this story.

Athen. 15.687a–c = Clearchus, frag. 41 Wehrli

(1) νῦν δὲ τῶν ἀνθρώπων οὐχ αἱ ὀσμαὶ μόνον, ὥς φησιν Κλέαρχος ἐν γ' περὶ Βίων, ἀλλὰ καὶ αἱ χροιαὶ τρυφερὸν ἔχουσαί τι συνεκθηλύνουσι τοὺς μεταχειριζομένους. (2) ὑμεῖς δὲ οἴεσθε τὴν ἁβρότητα χωρὶς ἀρετῆς ἔχειν τι τρυφερόν; (3) καίτοι Σαπφώ, γυνὴ μὲν πρὸς ἀλήθειαν οὖσα καὶ ποιήτρια, ὅμως ἠδέσθη τὸ καλὸν τῆς ἁβρότητος ἀφελεῖν λέγουσα ὧδε·

ἐγὼ δὲ φίλημ' ἁβροσύναν,
καί μοι τὸ λαμπρὸν ἔρος ἀελίω καὶ τὸ καλὸν λέλογχε,[38]

φανερὸν ποιοῦσα πᾶσιν ὡς ἡ τοῦ ζῆν ἐπιθυμία τὸ λαμπρὸν καὶ τὸ καλὸν εἶχεν αὐτῇ· ταῦτα δ' ἐστὶν οἰκεῖα τῆς ἀρετῆς. (4) Παρράσιος δὲ ὁ ζωγράφος, καίπερ παρὰ μέλος ὑπὲρ τὴν ἑαυτοῦ τέχνην τρυφήσας καὶ τὸ λεγόμενον ἐλευθέριον ἐκ ῥαβδίων [ἔκ τινων ποτηρίων] ἑλκύσας, λόγῳ γοῦν ἀντελάβετο τῆς ἀρετῆς, ἐπιγραψάμενος τοῖς ἐν Λίνδῳ πᾶσιν αὐτοῦ ἔργοις· (5)

ἁβροδίαιτος ἀνὴρ ἀρετήν τε σέβων τάδ' ἔγραψεν
Παρράσιος.

(6) ᾧ κομψός τις, ὡς ἐμοὶ δοκεῖ, ὑπεραλγήσας ῥυπαίνοντι τὸ τῆς ἀρετῆς ἁβρὸν καὶ καλόν, ἅτε φορτικῶς μετακαλεσαμένῳ εἰς τρυφὴν τὴν δοθεῖσαν ὑπὸ τῆς τύχης χορηγίαν, παρέγραψε τὸ "ῥαβδοδίαιτος ἀνήρ." (7) ἀλλ' ὅμως διὰ τὸ τὴν ἀρετὴν φῆσαι τιμᾶν ἀνεκτέον. ταῦτα μὲν ὁ Κλέαρχος.

[(1) Now, it is not only people's smells, as Clearchus says in Book 3 of his *Lives*, but also their colors, which, possessing some aspect of *truphē*, contribute to

---

37. Plut., *Mor.* 158e; Philo, *Leg.* 134; Dion. Hal., *Antiq. Rom.* 4.80.1.
38. This fragment of Sappho has received intense scrutiny of late with the announcement in Gronewald and Daniel (1994) of the discovery of the "New Sappho" papyrus (*PColon.* 21351) containing this same text, augmenting the original *POxy* 1787. The collected papers in Greene and Skinner (2009, with bibliographies) offer a thorough examination of the issues involved with this new text. For Athenaeus's role in quoting Sappho, see Hammerstaedt 2009, 23–24 and Lardinois 2009, 43–44.

making those who take them up into women. (2) But do you think that elegance without virtue has "an aspect of *truphē*"? (3) Even Sappho, though truly a woman and a poetess, nonetheless was ashamed to separate elegance from excellence when she said, "But I love an elegant life, and love of the sun has gained for me splendor and excellence" [frag 58]. She makes it clear to all that her appetite for living provided her with splendor and excellence; these are properties of virtue. (4) And Parrhasius the painter, although inharmoniously exhibiting *truphē* beyond his craft and drawing the so-called liberal life from his brushes, at least in word preferred virtue, since he signed all his works in Lindus thus: (5) "Parrhasius, a man of elegant lifestyle and revering virtue, drew these." (6) Some clever fellow—in my opinion because he was upset at a man contaminating the elegance and excellence of virtue by vulgarly summoning toward *truphē* the abundance he had been given by fortune—changed the wording to "a man of stile."[39] (7) But still, because he said he honored virtue, he must be accepted. So much for Clearchus.]

The interpretation of this passage is quite complicated. Perhaps the first thing to notice is the internal inconsistency. Clearchus is cited for the view that αἱ χροιαί (and/or αἱ ὀσμαί; the text is ambiguous) are associated with τρυφή and effeminize men. There is, however, in the remainder of the citation, no discernible reference to scents or coloring. It seems that Cynulcus, Athenaeus's speaker here, has lost the tread of his thought. Cynulcus, as so often, is in a rage; while he dozed, a servant anointed his face with perfume, which the Cynic then considers "polluted" (μεμολυσμένον). In his agitated state, Cynulcus breaks off in the middle of his citation to give his fellow banqueters a lesson in philosophy.

The presence of the digression receives support in Book 12, where the same passage of Clearchus is referred to:

(A) οὕτω δὲ παρὰ τοῖς ἀρχαίοις τὰ τῆς τρυφῆς καὶ τῆς πολυτελείας ἠσκεῖτο ὡς καὶ Παρράσιον τὸν ζωγράφον πορφύραν ἀμπέχεσθαι, χρυσοῦν στέφανον ἐπὶ τῆς κεφαλῆς ἔχοντα, ὡς ἱστορεῖ Κλέαρχος ἐν τοῖς Βίοις. (B) οὗτος γὰρ παρὰ μέλος ὑπὲρ τὴν γραφικὴν τρυφήσας λόγῳ τῆς ἀρετῆς ἀντελαμβάνετο καὶ ἐπέγραφεν τοῖς ὑπ᾽ αὐτοῦ ἐπιτελουμένοις ἔργοις·

---

39. We have adopted the witticism of Gulick's translation here, with "stile" meaning the painter's brush or wand.

(C) ἁβροδίαιτος ἀνὴρ ἀρετήν τε σέβων τάδ᾽ ἔγραψεν.

(D) καί τις ὑπεραλγήσας ἐπὶ τούτῳ παρέγραψεν ῥαβδοδίαιτος ἀνήρ.[40]

[(A) Among the ancients matters of *truphē* and extravagance were practiced to such an extent that even Parrhasius the painter covered himself with purple, wearing a golden crown on his head, as Clearchus relates in his *Lives*. (B) This man, although inharmoniously exhibiting *truphē* beyond the level of a painter, at least in word preferred virtue and he signed the works completed by him thus: (C) "A man of elegant lifestyle and revering virtue, drew these." (D) Someone, upset at him, changed the wording to "a man of stile."] (Athen. 12.543c–d = Clearchus, frag. 42 Wehrli)

Presumably, the purple and gold attire mentioned in Book 12 correspond to the luxurious colors of sentence (1), although they were left out when the focus in the Book 15 passage shifted to τι τρυφερόν ("an aspect of *truphē*") and the lapse was not made good.

More than one explanation is possible for the difference between the two citations. For example, the substance beneath sentences (2) and (3) could have been omitted from the Book 12 citation rather than inserted in Book 15. However, (2) and (3) represent an addition that would be very much in character for the interlocutor Cynulcus; the material constitutes an argument of a type familiar from philosophical literature of the Hellenistic and Roman periods, the paradox which ascribes all of life's good things to the virtuous and wise person alone. Thus, "only the sage is happy," "only the sage is healthy," "only the sage is wealthy," or even "only the sage is eloquent." In this passage the paradox is of the form "only the sage possesses τρυφή."

The argumentation of the paradox is relatively straightforward. First, the thesis is established: there is no τρυφή without virtue (i.e., only the sage is τρυφερός). In formulating this proposition, the speaker substitutes for τρυφή the related term, ἁβρότης. This move prepares the way for the introduction of the authority of Sappho, which will be decisive, since what is so obvious that even a woman and a poetess can see it must be true. The replacement of τρυφή by ἁβρότης makes the Sappho passage relevant, since the equivalence of

---

40. Wehrli ends the fragment here, although more material on Parrhasius follows. He is probably correct in setting these limits, since Athenaeus seems to be drawing from other sources; Theophrastus is mentioned explicitly (Athen. 12.543f).

ἁβρότης and her ἁβροσύνα is unobjectionable. Next comes the exegesis of the authority: Sappho "loves an elegant life" (ἁβροσύνα). This statement is said to be nominalized in the next verse through the words ἔρος ἀελίω ("love of the sun"), which the speaker glosses as ἡ τοῦ ζῆν ἐπιθυμία ("appetite for life"). According to this same verse, ἔρος ἀελίω has provided the poet with τὸ καλὸν ("beauty"). Of course, any reader with the rudiments of philosophy would realize that τὸ καλὸν is another word for ἀρετή. But ἀρετή belongs to the wise person only. Therefore, only the sage has τρυφή.[41]

The argument presented here is, in our view, more likely to be a creation of Athenaeus than of Clearchus. There are several reasons for this conclusion. First, the willful alteration of a poetic quotation to support a novel interpretation is a common enough practice in the *Deipnosophistae*, as discussed in the previous chapter. In this case, we can assume that the quotation has been shortened to make Cynculus's exegesis easier to sustain.[42] Second, the analysis of Sappho that is offered is a humorous misinterpretation.[43] In the original, ἀελίω specifies the meaning of τὸ λαμπρὸν and τὸ καλὸν ("the splendor and beauty of the sun"), rather than ἔρος. Once again, this is standard operating procedure in Athenaeus's literary game.[44] Third, it is part of Athenaeus's characterization of Cynulcus to depict him as applying serious philosophical doctrines to the immediate circumstances of the dinner party. Here, in Book 15, he connects τρυφή with virtue because he has unwillingly been made τρυφερός by being smeared in perfume. In a similar fashion, at Athen. 8.354d, to urge that food be served

41. See the discussion at Lardinois 2009, 44.
42. The papyri indicate that more than one word is missing after ἁβροσύναν (Hammerstaedt 2009, 23–24). Interestingly, Hammerstaedt agrees that Clearchus is not the author, saying (23 n.19): "I plan to prove in a further article that the Sappho quotation does not derive from the third book of Clearchus *On Ways of Life* (fr. 41 Wehrli)." He gives there no hint as to his reasoning and that article has, apparently, not yet appeared.
43. Different translations of this passage are discussed at Boedeker 2009, 72–73. Lardinois (2009, 44) also suggests that ἁβροσύναν refers to Sappho's speaker's practice of singing and playing the lyre. We might suggest another possibility: ἁβροσύναν perhaps indicates sexual attractiveness, particularly the expectation it may bring of solicitous attention given by the lover to the beloved. We have observed above that τρυφή and its cognates sometimes have this meaning. See, for example, Plato, *Meno* 76b.
44. Wehrli (1969, 61) points out that Sappho's text is treated "nach der gewaltsam Methode sophistischer Dichterinterpretation," with the implication that Clearchus followed in sophistic footsteps in his violent interpretation. Wehrli may be correct in noting that an exegesis that pays little regard to original meaning has a long history in Greek philosophy, and that Clearchus's *Lives* could certainly have presented such a reading of Sappho. The difficulty for the view that this exegesis comes from Clearchus lies in explaining why the Peripatetic would have elaborated the connection between using perfumes and virtue. The other fragments of the *Lives* do not reveal similar displays of wit and humor, while such qualities are rife in the *Deipnosophistae*.

even if it is not the perfect temperature, Cynulcus refers to the idea that τὸ ἀγαθόν is good everywhere and always. He then uses in his argument the epistemological concepts of the cataleptic perception and the probable—διαφέρειν δὲ τὴν καταληπτικὴν φαντασίαν τοῦ εὐλόγου ("the cataleptic appearance differs from the probable")—to prove that he should be fed immediately. Fourth, the paradox drawn from the evidence of Sappho is a Cynic one.[45] Thus, the substance of the poetic interpretation make Athenaeus's the more likely source for this bit of literary fun.

Other considerations point in the same direction. For extant texts, formulae such as ὥς φησιν Κλέαρχος correlate strongly with paraphrase. We have argued that θηλύνω ("effeminize") and its compounds are more appropriate for moralizing of the Roman period than the third century BCE. The second person plurals ὑμεῖς οἴεσθε pick up Cynulcus's earlier (Athen. 15.686d) οὐκ οἴδατε καὶ τὸν καλὸν Ξενοφῶντα ("don't you know that the noble Xenophon . . .").[46] The preposition phrase πρὸς ἀλήθειαν ("with respect to truth," i.e., "truly") used as an attribute of a noun is practically unexampled in the Classical period but common in Philo, for example. The noun ποιήτρια ("poetess") seems not to occur before Strabo; Athenaeus has it three times besides this passage. Taken together, these aspects of diction and content make a strong case against a Clearchan origin for the interpretation of Sappho.

A comparison of the two citations indicates that sentence (4) once again reflects material from the *Lives*. Its essence is the anecdote about the artist Parrhasius, who, although living with more τρυφή than one would expect for one

---

45. The concept underlies the anecdote, told by Plutarch about a Cynic encounter experienced by Dionysius the Younger, who was living among the taverns and brothels after his fall from power: Πλάτων μὲν οὖν οὐκ ἐπεῖδεν ἐν Κορίνθῳ Διονύσιον, ἀλλ᾽ ἔτυχεν ἤδη τεθνηκώς, ὁ δὲ Σινωπεὺς Διογένης ἀπαντήσας αὐτῷ πρῶτον, "ὡς ἀναξίως" ἔφη "Διονύσιε ζῇς." ἐπιστάντος δ᾽ ἐκείνου καὶ εἰπόντος· "εὖ ποιεῖς ὦ Διόγενες συναχθόμενος ἡμῖν ἠτυχηκόσι," "τί γάρ;" εἶπεν ὁ Διογένης "οἴει μέ σοι συναλγεῖν, οὐ διαγανακτεῖν, ὅτι τοιοῦτον ἀνδράποδον ὤν, καὶ τοῖς τυραννείοις ὥσπερ ὁ πατὴρ ἐπιτήδειος ἐγγηράσας ἀποθανεῖν, ἐνταῦθα παίζων καὶ τρυφῶν διάγεις μεθ᾽ ἡμῶν;" ("Plato did not see Dionysius in Corinth, for it happened he was already dead. But Diogenes of Sinope, upon meeting him, first said to him: 'How undeservingly you live such a life, Dionysius.' Dionysius stopped and said in return, 'Kind of you, Diogenes, to feel bad at my misfortune.' 'What!' said Diogenes, 'Do you think that I am sympathizing with you and I am not enraged that you, although such a slave and a fit person to grow old and die with the trappings of tyranny, as your father did, are spending your life here, playing and indulging in *truphē* with us?'" Plut., *Tim.* 15.8). In other words, a fool, who is a slave to impulse and appetite, should, if life were fair, be punished through the lifelong possession of power; τρυφή, in contrast, is appropriate for the Wise. For a discussion of this passage as a summing up of many Cynic dichotomies, see Desmond 2006, 70–71.

46. Wehrli (1969, 60), observing that "der Text verkürzt und sonst enstellt zu sein scheint," cannot feel confident that ὑμεῖς etc. comes from Clearchus, and that the *Lives* therefore contained dialogue.

in his profession, could still claim to "revere virtue" in his autographs.[47] This claim was seen as risible to one of his contemporaries, who mutilated his dedicatory verses.

The point of the anecdote in the dramatic context of the *Deipnosphistae* is clear. If a mere painter, and a rather profligate one at that, could maintain a claim to virtue, then, *a fortiori*, Cynulcus implies, the virtue of a philosopher such as himself cannot be tarnished by a smear of perfumed oil. In addition, the explicitly moralizing elements in this section are apparently Athenaean and not Clearchan. The words ῥυπαίνοντι τὸ τῆς ἀρετῆς ἁβρὸν καὶ καλόν, ἅτε φορτικῶς μετακαλεσαμένῳ εἰς τρυφὴν τὴν δοθεῖσαν ὑπὸ τῆς τύχης χορηγίαν are the only explicit reference to the vicious effects of τρυφή. We may observe that they are absent in (D), where we are told only that someone was "upset" with Parrhasius for an unspecified reason. Further, the idea of "befouling the elegance and beauty of virtue" makes sense only in connection with the paradoxical exegesis of Sappho that precedes. In fact, the conjunction of καὶ καλόν with τὸ τῆς ἀρετῆς ἁβρὸν seems to have no other purpose than to form a link with the earlier argument, since "beauty" does not occur in Parrhasius's verses. Given the evidence that the interpretation of Sappho is not Clearchan, the same conclusion follows for the moralizing interpretation of the action of Parrhasius's enemy.

Thus, Clearchus evidently told the anecdote about Parrhasius with minimal moral implications, perhaps only the observation that the artist was unusually given to τρυφή. This seems to us the best solution to the many difficulties that the double citation offers. If we are wrong, and the exegesis of Sappho accurately reflects the argument of the original, the result would be difficult to reconcile with the traditional view of the *Lives*. That view makes the *Lives* hostile to τρυφή, which ruins individuals and communities. The interpretation of Sappho, in contrast, presents luxury positively, as associated with virtue. While it is possible to imagine that Clearchus was presenting here a view other than his

---

47. Note that, while some parts of sentences (4) and (B) are very close, there are also significant discrepancies. One might argue that the shorter version (B) is an abbreviation of a fuller original (containing καὶ τὸ λεγόμενον ἐλευθέριον ἐκ ῥαβδίων [ἔκ τινων ποτηρίων] ἑλκύσας). In our opinion, the rather scornful tone marks this as an addition by Athenaeus in the querulous voice of Cynulcus. It should be emphasized as well that even where the prose text matches very closely between the passages, this proximity *does not ensure* that this text presents the wording of the original source. It is possible that excerptors such as Athenaeus worked from a notebook containing material from their reading. If Athenaeus was relying on a notebook in a case such as this, both items in a double citation could be verbatim matches, but this fact would enable us only to reconstruct the wording of the notebook entry, which may itself have been a loose paraphrase. For the use of notebooks by Plutarch, see Pelling 1979 and 1985; Van der Stockt 1999. For Athenaeus, see Jacob (2001) lxxiv–lxxxiii.

own, this conjecture is superfluous, given the framing context and Cynulcus's motive for justifying τι τρυφερόν.

By now the problems with Athenaeus's testimony about Clearchus should be evident. Thus, while there are a few more fragments that may appear relevant to the idea of pernicious luxury, we will deal with them much more briefly.

At Athen. 12.540f–541a (= Clearchus, frag. 44 Wehrli), Clearchus seems to have related that Polycrates of Samos "was destroyed" because of decadence. However, the causal connection occurs in the first, introductory, sentence and is expressed in a typically Athenaean manner: διὰ τὴν ἀκολασίαν ("because of lack of self-control"). The sentence contains other diction likely to be Athenaean (e.g., ζηλώσας τὰ Λυδῶν μαλακά, "emulating the softness of the Lydians").[48] Language probably not Clearchan also occurs within the body of the fragment. Thus, we are told that Polycrates built a district in Samos that provided all kinds of pleasures: καὶ τῶν πρὸς ἀπόλαυσιν καὶ ἀκρασίαν πάντων βρωμάτων ὄντως ἐνέπλησε τὴν Ἑλλάδα ("and it supplied Greece with all foods for enjoyment and licentiousness"). Here, we may argue that it is anachronistic to take πρὸς ἀπόλαυσιν καὶ ἀκρασίαν as Clearchus's words. The noun ἀπόλαυσις used absolutely with the meaning of "enjoyment" or "pleasure" is rare before the Roman period, but then becomes unremarkable.[49] The presence of signs of paraphrase within the fragment as well as in its introduction keeps us from feeling confident that Clearchus was interested in luxury as a factor contributing to the fall of Samos.[50]

---

48. On the distribution of ζηλόω used in this way, see above (pp. 231–32).

49. A relevant use of ἀπόλαυσις does appear in a handful of passages from Aristotle (e.g., *Eth. Eud.* 7.1245b5, *Rhet.* 1361b5) and so one might see πρὸς ἀπόλαυσιν καὶ ἀκρασίαν as a bit of Peripatetic technical terminology originating with Clearchus. On the other hand, the term was in common parlance by the 1st century BCE. Cf. Diod. Sic. 1.57.2, 4.84.1; Strabo 11.8.5; Philo, *Op.* 77. It is worth observing that Athenaeus follows the citation of Clearchus with an observation about his own time: οἶδα δὲ κἀγὼ παρὰ τοῖς ἐμοῖς Ἀλεξανδρεῦσιν λαύραν τινὰ καλουμένην μέχρι καὶ νῦν Εὐδαιμόνων, ἐν ᾗ πάντα τὰ πρὸς τρυφὴν ἐπωλεῖτο ("I myself know a district among my own Alexandrians called even to this day 'Rich Men's Street,' in which all the things for *truphē* were for sale." Athen. 12.541a). Here the πάντα τὰ πρὸς τρυφὴν is parallel to the allegedly Clearchan τῶν πρὸς ἀπόλαυσιν πάντων; we have argued above (pp. 188–89) that at 12.541f Athenaeus altered the text of Diodorus 11.25 to join τρυφή to ἀπόλαυσις: εἰς τὴν τρυφὴν καὶ ἀπόλαυσιν τῷ Γέλωνι ("for the *truphē* and enjoyment of Gelon").

50. The citation ends with a lacuna in the text: ἔτι δὲ τῆς συμπάσης πόλεως ἐν ἑορταῖς τε καὶ μέθαις [*lacuna*] καὶ ταῦτα μὲν ὁ Κλέαρχος ("And then, with the whole city in feasts and carousals [*lacuna*] So much for Clearchus." Athen. 541a). This sentence may have given the circumstances for the Persian capture of Samos, but that remains speculation.

Athen. 12.539b (= Clearchus, frag. 50 Wehrli) states that the "King of the Persians" gave prizes to those who procured pleasures for him, not realizing that by doing this he was "defeating himself" and effecting the loss of his kingdom. This seems a straightforward connection between luxury and political catastrophe, although there is no sign here of the supposedly usual role played by hubris in Clearchus's descriptions of decadence. However this may be, the fragment is not secure evidence even for Clearchus's belief in the simpler idea that luxury-induced weakness or effeminacy caused the Persian defeat: the body of the citation consists of a single sentence, and this sentence can be no better than a paraphrase. It contains two participles, ἀθλοθετῶν ("acting as prize giver"), and καταγωνιζόμενος ("defeating"), for which this passage would be the earliest attestation, if the language is genuinely Clearchan.[51] The interpretation of this material as a paraphrase receives at least partial confirmation from the unusual circumstance that Athenaeus cites this same source twice more: at Athen. 12.514e, the awarding of prizes is διδοὺς ἆθλα ("giving prizes"), and at 12.529d, ἆθλα ἐτίθει ("he would establish prizes").[52] Moreover, neither at 12.514e nor at 12.529d is any clear mention made of the search for new pleasures bearing responsibility for the collapse of the Persian empire.[53] Rather, the Great King's custom serves as an etymology for a proverb: Διὸς ἅμα καὶ βασιλέως ἐγκέφαλος ("a morsel for Zeus and at the same time for the King").[54] Thus, given that 12.539b on luxury and the fall of Darius shows the marks of Athenaean manipulation of its language, and given that the other citations of the original do not confirm an interest in the ramifications of decadence, we conclude that the connection between Darius's pleasures and his ruin was quite possibly made by Athenaeus rather that Clearchus.

---

51. The denominative ἀθλοθετέω occurs first in Philo (or at 4 Macc 17:12, if this is earlier). It remains rare at any period, but the compound καταγωνίζομαι, which is first recorded in Polybius, is common enough from the first century BCE. It is, therefore, reasonable to assume that the choice of wording stems from Athenaeus.

52. Both Athen. 12.514e and 12.529d present significant textual problems, so the matter is clouded in uncertainty, but it is possible that all three citations are paraphrases.

53. Apparently with this difference in mind, Wehrli separates the passages into two "fragments." Athen. 12.539b is his frag. 50, while 12.514e is frag. 51a and 12.529d is frag. 51d.

54. The paroemiographer Zenobius also refers to the same original: ἐπὶ τῶν ἡδυπαθούντων ἡ παροιμία τέτακται. Κλέαρχος δὲ ἐν τῷ πέμπτῳ περὶ βίων φησὶ, τὰ πολυτελῆ βρώματα παρὰ τοῖς Πέρσαις Διὸς καὶ βασιλέως ἐγκέφαλον καλεῖσθαι ("A proverb applied to those enjoying pleasure. Clearchus in the fifth book of his *Lives* says that the costly foods among the Persians were called 'Zeus' morsel and the king's.'" Zen. 3.41).

Ctesias

The fragments of Ctesias of Cnidus have had a disproportionate place in the history of the idea of pernicious luxury. Although only a very few citations of this historian are at all relevant to this question, Ctesias has been assigned a large measure of responsibility for popularizing among his contemporaries and later generations the concept of Eastern decadence. Ctesias, who served as physician to Artaxerxes II (404–358 BCE), wrote a history of the Persian empire and its predecessors in twenty-three books. His relatively early date and his claims of unusual access to the Persian court perhaps explain the influence that Ctesias is believed to have had on later Greek thinking about the East. The most important expression of the interpretation that sees Ctesias's *Persica* as a foundational text for the idea of eastern decadence is perhaps that of Sancisi-Weerdenburg:

> Ctesias might in another respect be credited with something really new, something to be found in his work, in my opinion, for the first time in European historiography: the concept *Orient*. The term Orient provokes associations of harems, eunuchs, luxury and intrigues. It has connotations of softness, closedness, indulgence and lack of rigour. To sum this up: it means effeminacy. (Sancisi-Weerdenburg 1987, 43–44)[55]

In spite of the prevalence of this view, an examination of the Ctesian evidence does not find a historiographically important role for decadence and pernicious luxury. The most important citation comes, not surprisingly, from Athenaeus.

Athen. 12.528e–29d = Ctesias, FGrH 688 F 1n, F 1pα, F 1q[56]

(1) Κτησίας ἐν τρίτῃ Περσικῶν καὶ πάντας μέν φησι τοὺς βασιλεύσαντας τῆς Ἀσίας περὶ τρυφὴν σπουδάσαι, μάλιστα δὲ Νινύαν τὸν Νίνου καὶ Σεμιράμιδος

---

55. The view is still firmly entrenched in the relevant scholarship. For example, Bichler (2011, 22) insists that while Ctesias may not have been the first to impute decadence to the East, "so is doch die Wirkungsgeschichte, die Ktesias mit seinen literarisch eindrucksvoll gestatlten Bildern und Szenen eines Orient *avant la lettre* entfalten, kaum zu überschätzen." Similarly, Briant (2011, 513) rejects arguments that Ctesias did not offer "un regard de type 'orientaliste.'"

56. Jacoby's fragments divide the text of Athenaeus in this way: F 1n = Κτησίας ἐν τρίτῃ . . . τῶν ἰδίων γυναικῶν. F 1pα = τοιοῦτος δ᾽ ἦν . . . συγκεντηθέντα ἀποθανεῖν. F 1q = Κτησίας δὲ λέγε . . . γενναίως ἐτελεύτησεν.

υἱόν. (2) καὶ οὗτος οὖν ἔνδον μένων καὶ τρυφῶν ὑπ᾽ οὐδενὸς ἑωρᾶτο εἰ μὴ ὑπὸ τῶν εὐνούχων καὶ τῶν ἰδίων γυναικῶν. (3) τοιοῦτος δ᾽ ἦν καὶ Σαρδανάπαλλος, ὃν οἳ μὲν Ἀνακυνδαράξεω λέγουσιν υἱόν, οἳ δὲ Ἀναβαραξάρου. (4) ὅτε δὴ οὖν Ἀρβάκης, εἷς τῶν ὑπ᾽ αὐτὸν στρατηγῶν Μῆδος γένος, διεπράξατο διά τινος τῶν εὐνούχων Σπαραμείζου θεάσασθαι Σαρδανάπαλλον καὶ μόλις αὐτῷ ἐπετράπη ἐκείνου ἐθελήσαντος, ὡς εἰσελθὼν εἶδεν αὐτὸν ὁ Μῆδος ἐψιμυθιωμένον καὶ κεκοσμημένον γυναικιστὶ καὶ μετὰ τῶν παλλακίδων ξαίνοντα πορφύραν ἀναβάδην τε μετ᾽ αὐτῶν καθήμενον, τὰς ὀφρῦς <ὑπογεγραμμένον>, γυναικείαν δὲ στολὴν ἔχοντα καὶ κατεξυρημένον τὸν πώγωνα καὶ κατακεκισηρισμένον—ἦν δὲ καὶ γάλακτος λευκότερος καὶ ὑπεγέγραπτο τοὺς ὀφθαλμούς—ἐπεὶ δὲ καὶ προσεῖδεν τὸν Ἀρβάκην τὰ λευκὰ ἐπαναβαλὼν τοῖν ὀφθαλμοῖν, οἱ μὲν πολλοί, ὧν ἐστι καὶ Δοῦρις, ἱστοροῦσιν ὑπὸ τούτου ἀγανακτήσαντος εἰ τοιοῦτος αὐτῶν βασιλεύει συγκεντηθέντα ἀποθανεῖν. (5) Κτησίας δὲ λέγε εἰς πόλεμον αὐτὸν καταστῆναι καὶ ἀθροίσαντα πολλὴν στρατιὰν καὶ καταλυθέντα ὑπὸ τοῦ Ἀρβάκου τελευτῆσαι ἑαυτὸν ἐμπρήσαντα ἐν τοῖς βασιλείοις . . . (6) ὁ μὲν οὖν Σαρδανάπαλλος ἐκτόπως ἡδυπαθήσας ὡς ἐνῆν γενναίως ἐτελεύτησεν.

[(1) Ctesias, in the third book of the *Persica,* says that all the other kings of Asia were eager for *truphē,* but especially Ninyas the son of Ninus and Semiramis. (2) He, too, remaining inside and enjoying *truphē,* was seen by no one except the eunuchs and his own women. (3) Such a one also was Sardanapalus, who some say was the son of Anacyndaraxes, others the son of Anabaraxarus. (4) When Arbaces, one of his generals, a Mede by race, arranged through Sparameizes, one of the eunuchs, to observe Sardanapalus, and the opportunity was reluctantly granted to him with the King's consent, the Mede entered and saw him painted and bejeweled like a woman; he was carding purple wool with his concubines, and sitting among them with his feet up; he had colored his eyebrows and wore a woman's gown and had shaved his beard and smoothed it with pumice. He was whiter than milk and had put on eyeliner. Well, when Sardanapalus looked at Arbaces, rolling the whites of his eyes at him, most people, including Duris, [*FGrH* 76 F 42] record that he was stabbed and killed by Arbaces, who was angry that such a man was their king. (5) Ctesias, on the other hand, says that Sardanapalus went to war; he gathered a great army and, when defeated by Arbaces, killed himself by immolation in the palace. . . . (6) So Sardanapalus, having enjoyed himself extraordinarily, died as nobly as possibly.]

The first relevant point is the extreme enthusiasm for τρυφή displayed by King Ninyas. While this characterization of the Assyrian monarch is explicitly ascribed to the third book of Ctesias's history, this datum is of little significance. It occurs in the introductory sentence of the citation alongside of the bibliographical information; for this reason alone, we could reasonably assume that the characterization of Ninyas is at most a paraphrase of the original. However, more than merely its position indicates that the claim about Ninyas's pursuits is dubious. In the previous chapter, we have discussed the place of σπουδάω and its cognates in Athenaeus's repertoire. In brief, saying that such and such a person was "eager for" some object or activity is a common method by which Athenaeus effects a transition in topic or source. For example, at 13.602a, Athenaeus shifts from giving specific instances of man-boy love affairs, to theorizing about their cause:

Ἱερώνυμος δ᾽ ὁ περιπατητικὸς περισπουδάστους φησὶν γενέσθαι τοὺς τῶν παίδων ἔρωτας, ὅτι . . .

[Hieronymus the Peripatetic says that love for boys became very popular because . . .]

At 13.607f, the focus moves from philosophers lusting for flute-girls to the same phenomenon among royalty:

ἐσπουδάκεσαν δὲ καὶ οἱ βασιλεῖς περὶ τὰς μουσουργούς, ὡς δῆλον ποιεῖ Παρμενίων ἐν τῇ πρὸς Ἀλέξανδρον Ἐπιστολῇ . . .

[Kings, too, were enthusiastic about female musicians, as Parmenion makes clear in his *Letter to Alexander* . . .]

Further illustrations are easy to accumulate, but it is unnecessary to examine them in detail. It will be sufficient to recall that common introductory expressions such as σπουδάζειν περί and the like must be treated with caution not only because they represent Athenaean paraphrases of the original. Frequently, they also serve as statements of inference or argument: Athenaeus's introductory statement often presents a more or less tendentious hypothesis that he intends to prove. In accordance with this pattern, we interpret sentence (2) as offering the evidence that Athenaeus was drawing from Ctesias to support the claim made in (1). Thus, it seems safe to assume that Ctesias wrote of the adoption by Ninyas of the custom of royal seclusion. At the same time, sentences (1) and (2) do not provide a sound basis from which to assert that Ctesias considered Ninyas's action morally deficient or even that he expressed any negative view of this custom.[57]

In contrast, the moral implications are clear when we come to the description of the behavior in his seclusion of the last king of the Assyrians, Sardanapalus. In this case, seclusion is associated with effeminacy and leads directly to the collapse of Assyrian rule. Far less certain is which, if any, of the details contained in (3) were reported by Ctesias.[58] There is an obvious seam between sentences (2) and (3): the words with which sentence (3) begins, τοιοῦτος δ᾽ ἦν, are easily identifiable as one of Athenaeus's formulae of introduction or transition.[59] The formula occurs several times, for example, in Book 6 alone:

6.230d: τοιοῦτός ἐστι καὶ ὁ παρὰ Νικοστράτῳ ["Such also is the man in Nicostratus's work . . ."]

6.252a: τοιοῦτος ἦν καὶ Ἡρακλείδης ὁ Μαρωνείτης ["Such also was Heraclides of Maroneia . . ."]

6.254b: τοιοῦτοι τότ᾽ ἐγένοντο οἱ Ἀθηναῖοι ["Such had the Athenians become at that time . . ."]

6.257c: ἀλλ᾽ οὐ Λεύκων τοιοῦτος ἦν ὁ Ποντικὸς τύραννος ["But such was not Leukon, the Pontic tyrant . . ."]

6.273b: ἀλλ᾽ οὐ Σμινδυρίδης ὁ Συβαρίτης τοιοῦτος ["But such was not Smindyrides the Sybarite . . ."]

---

57. This is the case even if the description of Ninyas as τρυφῶν is in Ctesias's own words. As shown in Chapter 1, Classical authors might treat τρυφή as a positive quality, especially when it was the characteristic of royalty. If we assume the τρυφῶν is original, then Athenaeus may be changing the connotations of the text, since the latter author certainly means to imply that Ctesias wrote pejoratively here.

58. Jacoby prints (3) and (4)—his F 1pα—in a reduced font size to indicate that he considered the material dubiously Ctesian.

59. The seam between the two sentences is obvious, even without recourse to an examination of Athenaeus's language of citation. It is very unlikely that Ctesias, who treats Assyrian history in some detail, jumps directly from Ninyas to Sardanapalus in this way, even if we assume that his focus in the relevant part of the source was on the dedication to τρυφή among Asian rulers. Thus, editors apportion the first three sentences of this passage among two fragments of Ctesias; e.g., Jacoby as *FGrH* 688 F 1n and F 1pα; Lenfant 2004, using the same numeration.

The use of this formula has implications for the origin of sentence (3). In all parallel uses of τοιοῦτός ἐστι, etc. the introduction of the new subject is accompanied by a change in the authority being cited.[60] In this passage, new sources are mentioned, but left vague (οἳ μὲν ... λέγουσιν ... οἳ δὲ), which suggests that Athenaeus is presenting the material as general knowledge that he has picked up from his reading. This impression is strengthened by sentence (5), where Ctesias's authority is reintroduced. Again, there is an unmistakable suture in the story, with material in sentence (4) coming from "the many" (οἱ μὲν πολλοί ... ἱστοροῦσιν) and not from the Persica. Thus, because the τοιοῦτος δ᾽ ἦν of (3) implies a change of source from what precedes, because other authorities are indeed alluded to, and because the re-establishment of Ctesias's as source in (5) refers only to the material that follows, any interpretation of this "fragment" must accept as a basic datum that Athenaeus does not attribute (3) and (4) to Ctesias.

Yet we do have evidence that Ctesias probably told the story of the confrontation of Sardanapalus and Arbaces. The lexicographer Julius Pollux makes the following statement:

Κτησίας δέ πού φησιν ἀναβάλλειν τὰ λευκὰ τῶν ὀφθαλμῶν τὸν Σαρδανάπαλλον

[I suppose Ctesias says that Sardanapalus rolled up the whites of his eyes.] (Pollux, Onom. 2.60 = Ctesias, FGrH 688 F 1ργ)

We also know, from Athenaeus, that some writers seem to have presented this gesture by Sardanapalus as the last straw, provoking his murder, but that Ctesias did not. However, this information does not get us very far. Beyond the distinction explicitly made, it is not possible for us to tell with any confidence just how extensive this disagreement was between Ctesias and the anonymous "many." We may infer that, because Arbaces' anger at Sardanapalus's unfitness to rule serves to explain his murder of the king, these words are best understood as reflecting the unnamed sources rather than Ctesias.[61] And we should

---

60. By "parallel" we mean all singular uses of τοιοῦτός ἐστι. Thus, at Athen. 3.98e, the authority of Heraclides Lembus replaces Athanis; at 4.159a, Chrysippus for Euripides; at 4.167d, Demetrius of Scepsis for Duris; at 6.230d, personal knowledge for Nocostratus; at 6.252a, Xenophon for Agatharchides; at 6.257c, personal knowledge for Clearchus; at 6.273b, personal knowledge for Cotta; at 10.415c, Pherecrates for Sositheus; at 12.513c, Pindar for Megaclides; and at 12.549d, Posidonius for Nymphis or Menander. The plural τοιοῦτοί εἰσιν is usually not strictly parallel, since it frequently summarizes a series of examples; yet it too is generally accompanied by a change in the source used.
61. Thus Jacoby (FGrH, ad loc.); Stronk 2010, 163.

not assume that the behavior indicated by τοιοῦτος is limited to the king rolling his eyes;[62] the rage that "such a man is their king" is best understood with reference to Sardanapalus's effeminate behavior in the bulk of sentence (4). It follows that Athenaeus's anonymous sources contained the portrayal of a womanish king. Whether Ctesias contained a similar depiction cannot be established from the evidence presented so far.

Other evidence is also pertinent, but it does not bring much clarity to the question. The description of Sardanapalus's mode of life in (4) is very close to Diodorus Siculus's account of the same topic.[63] The similarity is such that a common source is probable. Since we know that Diodorus used Ctesias in his presentation of Assyrian history, the simplest conclusion would make Ctesias the model for both Diodorus and Athenaeus.

There are, however, contraindications. Scholarship has established that Diodorus may combine multiple sources in creating his narrative.[64] In addition, as we will discuss below in our focused treatment of this author, patterns of diction in Diodorus indicate that he supplemented his main sources to add examples of τρυφή. And as is indicated by Athenaeus's οἱ πολλοί . . . ἱστοροῦσιν, other treatments of Sardanapalus were available for Diodorus to choose from. The Assyrian king had caught the public imagination already in the fifth century, when one of Aristophanes' characters exclaims of another, "Who is this Sardanapalus?"[65] By the middle of the fourth century, the story of Sardanapalus's decadent behavior—elaborated with some, at least, of the details repeated by Diodorus and Athenaeus—was circulating outside the pages of any history book. This much is clear from Aristotle:

αἱ δὲ διὰ καταφρόνησιν, ὥσπερ Σαρδανάπαλλον ἰδών τις ξαίνοντα μετὰ τῶν γυναικῶν (εἰ ἀληθῆ ταῦτα οἱ μυθολογοῦντες λέγουσιν· . . .).

---

62. Ctesias's attribution of this gesture to Sardanapalus sheds little light on whether the historian characterized the Assyrian ruler as extremely effeminate. The expression is very rare and its occurrences in the Sardanapalus story do not make clear the connotations. Pollux gives the above citation at the end of a list of attributes, which may qualify a βλέμμα ("glance"). These include γυναικεῖον, θηλυπρεπές, ἀχρεῖον ("womanish, befitting a female, useless"), so Pollux assumes a similar meaning for Sardanapalus's action. Lenfant (2004, 250) suggests "un regard lubrique," as both Clement of Alexandria (*Paed.* 3.11.70.3) and Justin (1.3.2) characterize the gesture as sexually suggestive. On the other hand, Dio Chrysostom describes the look as a pained one: τοὺς δὲ ὀφθαλμοὺς ἀναστρέφων, ὥσπερ ἐξ ἀγχόνης ("turning up his eyes, as if from strangling," Dio Chrys., *Or.* 62.6). None of these authors indicate that Sardanapalus directed this gesture, whatever that meant, at Arbaces.

63. See our discussion , below (pp. 362–64).

64. Sacks 1990.

65. Ar., *Av.* 1021.

[Other revolutions happen because of contempt, as when someone saw Sardanapalus combing with the women—if these things which the myth-tellers say are true.] (Arist., *Pol.* 5.1311b40–1312a2)

Here, reference to οἱ μυθολογοῦντες seems to point to a source other than Ctesias.[66] Nor did Aristotle know the story of Sardanapalus only thorough "the myth-tellers," whoever they may have been. In his *Eudemian Ethics*, Aristotle presents Sardanapalus, alongside Smindyrides of Sybaris, as a model for the hedonists:

οἱ δὲ Σαρδανάπαλλον μακαρίζοντες ἢ Σμινδυρίδην τὸν Συβαρίτην ἢ τῶν ἄλλων τινὰς τῶν ζώντων τὸν ἀπολαυστικὸν βίον, οὗτοι δὲ πάντες ἐν τῷ χαίρειν φαίνονται τάττειν τὴν εὐδαιμονίαν·

[Those considering happy Sardanapalus or Smindyrides the Sybarite or some of the others living the life of enjoyment, all these seem to place happiness in feeling delight.] (Arist., *Eth. Eud.* 1.1216a16–19)[67]

The same pairing was also made by Theophrastus:

οὐδεὶς δὲ λέγει τὸν Ἀριστείδου βίον ἡδύν, ἀλλὰ τὸν Σμινδυρίδου τοῦ Συβαρίτου καὶ τὸν Σαρδαναπάλλου. καίτοι κατά γε τὴν δόξαν, φησὶν ἐν τῷ περὶ Ἡδονῆς Θεόφραστος, οὐχ ὁμοίως λαμπρός ἐστιν· ἀλλ᾽ οὐκ ἐτρύφησεν ὥσπερ ἐκεῖνοι.

[Nobody calls the life of Aristides sweet, but that of Smindyrides the Sybarite and Sardanapalus. And yet, with respect to reputation, Theophrastus says in his *On Pleasure*, he is more splendid. But he does not enjoy *truphē* as they do.] (Athen. 12.511c = frag. 551 Fortenbaugh)

Each passage seems to reflect the ideas of the adherents of those who made pleasure the aim of life. The connection between the pursuit of pleasure and Sardanapalus and Smindyrides is not drawn by Aristotle or Theophrastus, but

---

66. Lenfant (2004, 250) notes that the attribution is open to doubt, "étant donné que la connaissance des *Persica* par Aristote n'est pas assurée et que Ctésias n'avait pas le monopole des descriptions de Sardanapale." Stronk (2010, 164), on the other hand, thinks that the reference to Ctesias's tale of Sardanapalus is "so striking that its inclusion is . . . completely justified."

67. Discussed above (p. 20).

by those to whom these two philosophers respond. Thus, οἱ Σαρδανάπαλλον μακαρίζοντες ἢ Σμινδυρίδην seems to presuppose a line of argument that took the Assyrian and the Sybarite as exemplars. In the same way, Theophrastus apparently countered with the example of Aristides to those who pressed the claims of Sardanapalus and Smindyrides to a happy life.

We may infer that, in the fourth century, the story of Sardanapalus's way of life was part of the ethical and moralizing literature then in circulation. The debates about which way of life was preferable were subject to an embellishment and exaggeration that need not preserve historical truth.[68] In this respect, the association of Sardanapalus with Smindyrides may have further significance. Like Sardanapalus, Smindyrides first appears in Greek literature in a single sentence in Herodotus, but for Smindyrides no *historical* source for the elaborated presentation of his lifestyle can be persuasively established. Timaeus of Tauromenium is often proposed as the authority for later reports about his entourage of a thousand cooks, but Pelling has characterized the attempt to fix Timaeus as the source as "a hopeless mess of uncertain speculation" and attributes Athenaeus's familiarity with the example of the Smindyrides to "general knowledge."[69] In any case, Timaeus is too late for Aristotle, and if there is reason to believe that the exaggerated details in the Smindyrides tradition may be due to a process that detached the Sybarite from the historical narrative to make him an ethical exemplar, the same may be true of Sardanapalus.[70]

However this may be, the evidence of Aristotle and Theophrastus establishes at least that, in the Classical period, the story of Sardanapalus in the harem—whatever its origin—passed through the hands of those engaged in ethical debate. Because sentence (4), besides being blatantly moralizing in nature, is unattributed and practically devoid of genuine historical detail, the possibility exists that some elements in this sentence are elaborations produced by this debate rather than parts of a historical narrative. Thus, we must be careful not to give too much weight to sentences (3) and (4) in elucidating Ctesias's views.[71]

---

68. Consider, for example, Xenophon's retelling of the moralistic story from Prodicus about Heracles meeting personified Virtue and Vice (*Mem.* 2.1.21–34), repeated with variation at Dio Chry., *Or.* 1.66ff, and discussed at length in Chapter 5 (below, pp. 408–10).

69. Pelling 2000, 177.

70. Examining the changes undergone by the Sardanapalus story in the Classical period, Lenfant (2001, 50) explains that the Assyrian became "avant tout l'incarnation d'un mode de vie . . . la vie de jouissance." In this process, Sardanapalus *qua* moral paradigm was "freed from time and space"; details that linked him to a specific historical context were effaced.

71. Two fragments of Nicolaus of Damascus (*FGrH* 90 F 2, F 3) on the revolt against Sardanapalus are

Athenaeus once more cites Ctesias explicitly in sentence (5). There follows a more complete description of Sardanapalus's self-immolation, and the treatment of the last Assyrian king is ended with the summary given by sentence (6). This sentence requires a closer examination, since it expresses an evaluation of the life of pleasure. The sentence implies a conflict between the behavior expressed in the participial clause ἐκτόπως ἡδυπαθήσας ("having enjoyed himself extraordinarily") and the fortitude Sardanapalus showed in dying "as nobly as possible" (ὡς ἐνῆν γενναίως). Underlying this statement is the assumption that indulgence in pleasure is incompatible with nobility of action.

It is important to our purposes to consider whether this assumption can be reliably attributed to Ctesias. If so, this conclusion would support the view that Ctesias laid some emphasis on "Oriental decadence," since it would be evidence for a general interest in Ctesias about the moral effects of certain lifestyles.

Once more, a close consideration of the sentence's diction will provide useful information in the effort to distinguish between the influence of source and cover text. Thus, Lenfant argues, based on the rarity of the term γενναίως in Athenaeus, that "le jugement de valeur" probably comes from Ctesias.[72] This assessment that the historian praised Sardanapalus for the manner of his end may be correct, as far as it goes, but it does not follow that it was Ctesias who drew the contrast between lifestyle and death. Instead, analysis of the diction of the rest of the sentence points in a different direction. First, in the Classical period, the works of Xenophon supply the only direct evidence for ἡδυπάθεια ("pleasant living") and its verbal derivative.[73] In contrast, Plutarch uses them more than two dozen times, and they are common in Athenaeus. More significantly, almost all the examples in the *Deipnosophistae* come from material that is clearly attributable to Athenaeus rather than his sources.[74] Next, the occur-

---

now generally thought to reflect Ctesias as their source. Details of Sardanapalus's effeminacy are given in F 2 (= *Exc. de Virtutibus* p.329.16 Büttner-Wobst): ἐγχριόμενος δὲ τὸ πρόσωπον καὶ τοὺς ὀφθαλμοὺς ὑπογραφόμενος, πρός τε τὰς παλλακίδας ἁμιλλώμενος περὶ κάλλους καὶ ἐμπλοκῆς, τό τε σύμπαν γυναικείῳ ἤθει χρώμενος ("Anointing his face and penciling his eyes and competing against his concubines in beauty and hairstyle, and altogether adopting a female manner"). The wording of this section is not particularly close to Athenaeus's and presents nothing that, given the notoriety of the *topos* of Sardanapalus in the harem, could not have come from the imagination of Nicolaus or his Byzantine excerptor.

72. Lenfant (2004, 250) notes the contrast between this passage's γενναίως and the judgment offered by Diodorus: τοιοῦτος δ᾽ ὢν τὸν τρόπον . . . αἰσχρῶς κατέστρεψε τὸν βίον ("Being such a man in his customs, he ended his life shamefully," Diod. Sic. 2.23.4). For Lenfant, the difference is explained by assuming that Athenaeus reflects the sources' opinion and Diodorus his own.

73. The verb ἡδυπαθέω appears at Xen., *Cyr.* 1.5.1; *Mem.* 2.6.24; *Oec.* 5.1; *Symp.* 4.9, 4.41; *Anab.* 1.3.4 (καθηδυπαθέω). The noun ἡδυπάθεια is at *Cyr.* 7.5.74 and *Oec.* 5.1.

74. More precisely, most occurrences of ἡδυπαθ- are in passages framing verse quotations or in the in-

rence here of ἐκτόπως has similar implications. Adjectives and adverbs from the stem ἐκτόπ- are rare at all periods, but the pattern of use favors Athenaeus as the source in this sentence. The sense of "to an extraordinary degree," which the word bears here, has only three examples directly attested from the Classical period, two in Theophrastus and one in Menander.[75] The stem ἐκτόπ- becomes relatively more common from Diodorus Siculus on. Athenaeus himself has the adverb ἐκτόπως in two other places besides the passage under consideration. Both are introductory sentences to prose citations and therefore very likely Athenaean in diction. Finally, data on the use of the phrase ὡς ἔνεστι / ἔνι / ἐνῆν, ("[as x] as possible") likewise show a profile that make it improbable that the wording is Ctesian. The phrase is found only a handful of times in Classical texts, but is much more common in the Roman period. From before the first century CE, seven examples (in five authors) may be compared to several times that many in Plutarch alone.[76]

In view of this evidence, we should admit that sentence (6) offers little firm information about Ctesias's presentation of pernicious luxury. Indeed, the only part of this sentence for which a Ctesian origin is indicated is the positive characterization of Sardanapalus's death as "noble." As a result, we must conclude that, as a whole, Athenaeus's citation of Ctesias on Assyrian τρυφή is of little or no evidentiary value for the subject of decadence as a historiographical force.

---

troductory sentence of a prose citation. An example of the first type comes from Athen. 4.165e: καὶ Κτήσιππος δ᾽ ὁ Χαβρίου υἱὸς εἰς τοσοῦτον ἦλθεν ἀσωτίας ὡς καὶ τοῦ μνήματος τοῦ πατρός, εἰς ὃ Ἀθηναῖοι χιλίας ἀνάλωσαν δραχμάς, τοὺς λίθους πωλῆσαι εἰς τὰς ἡδυπαθείας. Δίφιλος γοῦν ἐν τοῖς Ἐναγίζουσί φησι . . . ("Also Ctesippus, the son of Chabrias, went to such an extent of wastefulness that he sold for pleasant living even the stones of his father's memorial, for which the Athenians had paid a thousand drachmas. At least Diphlus says in *Worshipers* [frag. 37] . . ."). As usual, the moral terms with which Athenaeus characterizes his subjects (here ἀσωτία and ἡδυπαθεία) do not appear in the verses quoted in support of his interpretation. A good illustration of ἡδυπαθεία in the first sentence of a prose "fragment" is Athen. 12.531a (= Theopompus, *FGrH* 115 F 114): Θεόπομπος δ᾽ ἐν πεντεκαιδεκάτῃ Φιλιππικῶν Ἱστοριῶν Στράτωνά φησι τὸν Σιδώνιον βασιλέα ὑπερβάλλειν ἡδυπαθείᾳ καὶ τρυφῇ πάντας ἀνθρώπους ("Theopompus, in the fifteenth book of his *Philippic Histories*, says that Straton, the king of Sidon, excelled all people in pleasant living and *truphē*."). Significantly, these two terms, τρυφή and ἡδυπαθεία, are similarly conjoined at the beginning of Book 12, where Athenaeus announces its theme: 12.510b, ἐπεὶ πάνυ λιπαρῶς ἡμᾶς ἀπαιτεῖς καὶ τὸν περὶ τῶν ἐπὶ τρυφῇ διαβοήτων γενομένων λόγον καὶ τῆς τούτων ἡδυπαθείας ("since you very importunately require the story of those who became famous for *truphē* and of their pleasant living . . .").

75. The stem ἔκτοπ- also appears a handful of times in Classical material with the meaning "foreign" or in expressions such as ἔκτοπος ἔστω "get him out of the way" (Eur., *Bacch.* 70).

76. The Classical examples are Hyp., *Athen.* 1.7; Xen., *Mem.* 3.8.4, 4.5.9; Men., *Dys.* 669, *Sam.* 274; Demosthenes 21.19; of dubious date and authorship is Plato, *Ep.* 359d2. The expression almost always occurs modifying a superlative, most often μάλιστα. Examples of ὡς ἔνεστι / ἔνι / ἐνῆν with a positive are very difficult to find. Perhaps Athenaeus's ὡς ἐνῆν γενναίως is the result of a combination of paraphrase (ὡς ἐνῆν) with verbatim quotation (γενναίως)?

Nor does it shed any light on the more specific thesis that "Orientalism" had its origin as a feature of Greek thought about the Eastern "other." Rather, an argument can be made that the pejorative evaluations of Assyrian behavior found in this passage are not merely cast in Athenaeus's words, but that they represent the interpretation of a later age and not that of Ctesias.

If we read between the lines in the relevant sections of Athenaeus and Diodorus, we do not receive the impression that Ctesias was particularly interested in the concept of decadence. On the authority of Ctesias, Athenaeus reports that "all the kings of Asia" were characterized by τρυφή, and that this was especially true of Ninyas.[77] Neither Ninyas's particular dedication to self-indulgence, nor its general pursuit by Asian monarchs—including presumably the Assyrians—seems to have had seriously negative consequences.[78] Ctesias himself emphasized the durability of the Assyrian empire, which, in spite of the lifestyle of its rulers, lasted well over a thousand years (Diod. Sic. 2.21.8).

Even Sardanapalus himself does not seem to act as one enfeebled by decadence if we focus on the narrative of events in his story and not the description of his manner of life behind closed doors—and we have seen that this description may not come from Ctesias. Although his supposed effeminacy is said to have led Arbaces to revolt against the Assyrian as unfit, once the rebellion is

---

77. Athen. 12.528e. Note that in Athenaeus's citation Sardanapalus is not singled out as especially given to τρυφή or effeminacy; he is apparently a further example of the seclusion practiced by Ninyas. On the other hand, Diodorus does make Sardanapalus a singular libertine: Σαρδανάπαλλος . . . ὑπερῆρεν ἅπαντας τοὺς πρὸ αὐτοῦ τρυφῇ καὶ ῥαθυμίᾳ ("Sardanapalus . . . excelled all those before him in truphē and laziness," Diod. Sic. 2.23.1). This discrepancy may reflect Diodorus's use of sources additional to Ctesias in his discussion of the end of Assyrian hegemony.

78. Diodorus makes a connection between the practice of royal seclusion, which Ninyas instituted, and his pursuit of pleasure (2.21.2). Later, at the conclusion of his presentation of aspects of Assyrian court and government, Diodorus states explicitly that seclusion served to hide the monarch's lifestyle from his subjects: τὸ δὲ μηδ' ὑφ' ἑνὸς τῶν ἔξωθεν θεωρεῖσθαι τῆς μὲν περὶ αὐτὸν τρυφῆς ἄγνοιαν παρείχετο πᾶσι ("not to be observed by anyone from outside provided for all a veil of ignorance concerning his truphē," Diod. Sic. 2.21.7). It is important to keep this connection in mind when, a few sentences further on, Diodorus emphasizes the continuity of customs throughout the history of the Assyrian monarchy: παραπλησίως δὲ τούτῳ καὶ οἱ λοιποὶ βασιλεῖς, παῖς παρὰ πατρὸς διαδεχόμενος τὴν ἀρχήν, . . . ἐβασίλευσαν ("The remaining kings too, son receiving the kingdom from father, . . . ruled in the same way as this one." Diod. Sic. 2.21.8). We cannot be sure that Diodorus's source here is Ctesias, but it is apparent that certain behavior, which could later be construed as τρυφή, was imputed to both Ninyas and all his successors. From Diodorus's point of view, τρυφή was a characteristic of the Assyrian rule for as long as it lasted. In this context, the contrast between Diodorus and Nicolaus may be significant, since the latter sharply distinguishes Sardanapalus from his predecessors: ὅπλων μὲν οὐχ ἁπτόμενος, οὐδ' ἐπὶ θήραν ἐξιών, ὥσπερ οἱ πάλαι βασιλεῖς ("not touching weapons, nor going out for a hunt, as the old kings," FGrH 90 F 2). Once again there seem to be multiple sources in play.

under way, Sardanapalus reacted, according to Diodorus, with vigor and effectiveness. Sardanapalus immediately (εὐθὺς) led his army against Arbaces and defeated the upstart and his confederates in several battles. Eventually, the tide turned and Sardanapalus was besieged in Nineveh. Even so, the Assyrians held out for several years, until nature itself conspired to cast down the city walls. It was only then that Sardanapalus gave himself to the notorious pyre.[79] If Sardanapalus was meant to exemplify the political consequences of personal immorality, the story was not given a very fine point.[80]

The same indifference that Ctesias seems to show toward any political consequences of Sardanapalus's effeminate behavior is also in evidence for the *Persica* more broadly. In Photius's extensive summary of the Median and Persian portions of Ctesias's history, there is almost no trace of the idea of pernicious luxury or of decadence, more broadly, as a historical force.[81] In general, we agree with Lenfant in objecting to the tendency for *ex silentio* arguments to creep into analyses of Ctesias based on Photius's résumé.[82] There is no doubt that Photius's criteria of selection have skewed his epitome to give an inaccurate outline of Ctesias's interests. However, on the subject of the historiographical significance of decadence in the *Persica*, we think that Photius's testimony is unusually strong: political power—its acquisition, maintenance, expansion, and loss—seems to have been a topic of particular interest to Photius. In his précis of Ctesias, he reports more than two dozen instances of royal successions, conquests, revolts, and the like, and neither pernicious luxury nor any other clearly defined form of decadence can be seen in any role.[83]

Based on these various considerations, it seems necessary to reject the traditional view of Ctesias's place in the development of the idea of a decadent

---

79. Diod. Sic. 2.25.1–27.3.
80. Thus Lenfant (2001, 49) remarks, "la dépravation morale n'y est pas à elle seule source de faiblesse politique . . . l'Empire est loin de s'effondrer à la première attaque, puisque le siège de Ninive dure trois ans."
81. Unless one counts the bare fact of women influencing affairs of state as per se evidence of decadence. Thus, for example, Sancisi-Weerdenburg (1987, 38) characterizes most harshly Ctesias's descriptions of women involved in court politics: "Women, in the conception with which he as a Greek was brought up, should stay out of politics: female interference was equal to corruption and decadence." In our opinion, Llewellyn-Jones (2010, 84–87) effectively rebuts this line of argument.
82. Lenfant (2004) clxxxvi.
83. Equally no such topics are addressed in any form in the extensive fragments of the *Indica* or Ctesias's other works. For a recent English translation and commentary, see Nichols 2011.

East, enervated by luxury and self-indulgence.[84] The available evidence does not support this interpretation.

Ephorus

"The fragments of his [i.e., Ephorus's] work indicate decadence was for him an important theme."[85] This statement represents the standard evaluation of the universal history of Ephorus of Cyme. This work in twenty-nine books covered material from the mythological period to 340 BCE and remained influential for centuries. It is this authority that leads us to examine in detail the evidence for pernicious luxury and decadence in Ephorus, since, in spite of the view that these ideas were thematic for the historian, the relevant material is extremely limited, its interpretation is uncertain, and the historiographical importance of themes such as τρυφή is unpersuasive.

Athen. 12.523e–f = Ephorus, FGrH 70 F 183

(1) Μιλήσιοι δ᾽ ἕως μὲν οὐκ ἐτρύφων, ἐνίκων Σκύθας, ὥς φησιν Ἔφορος, καὶ τάς τε ἐφ᾽ Ἑλλησπόντῳ πόλεις ἔκτισαν καὶ τὸν Εὔξεινον Πόντον κατῴκισαν πόλεσι λαμπραῖς, καὶ πάντες ὑπὸ τὴν Μίλητον ἔθεον. (2) ὡς δὲ ὑπήχθησαν ἡδονῇ καὶ τρυφῇ, κατερρύη τὸ τῆς πόλεως ἀνδρεῖον, φησὶν ὁ Ἀριστοτέλης, καὶ παροιμία τις ἐγεννήθη ἐπ᾽ αὐτῶν "πάλαι ποτ᾽ ἦσαν ἄλκιμοι Μιλήσιοι."

[(1) As long as the Milesians did not have *truphē*, they defeated the Scythians, as Ephorus says, and founded the cities on the Hellespont and colonized the Black Sea with splendid communities and all came under the control of Miletus. (2) But when they became subject to pleasure and *truphē*, the manhood of the city went down the drain, says Aristotle, and a proverb for them came into being: "Once long ago the Milesians were mighty."]

---

84. Interestingly, Lanfranchi (2011, 214) adopts another approach to exonerate Ctesias from the charge of being an "Orientalist" *avant la lettre*. He links various characteristics allegedly ascribed to Sardanapalus by Ctesias (e.g., "lavori femminili di tessitura," "vesti femminili," "ricerca di voce femminile," and "estrema libertà sessuale") with aspects of the cult of Ishtar that have been revealed by recent scholarship.
85. Sacks 1990, 48.

From our earlier discussions it will be apparent that this passage is a flimsy foundation on which to rest a claim about an Ephoran theme. In the first place, we may be confident that the entire fragment is a paraphrase rather than a set of quotations. Both sentences are introductory or transitional—in fact, each sentence in and of itself presents a complete citation—and thus it is wise to assume that Athenaeus adapted his sources to fit the run of his argument. We have seen that one such adaptation that seems to occur frequently is the addition of a topic. In sentence (1) that function is served by the clause ἕως μὲν οὐκ ἐτρύφων, while in (2), ὡς δὲ ὑπήχθησαν ἡδονῇ καὶ τρυφῇ is the equivalent. It has also been established that Athenaeus's identification of topic can sometimes be tendentious, argumentative, or even contrary to the meaning of the original. This is reason enough not to assume that Ephorus is responsible for drawing a connection between the Milesians' successes and their lifestyle. Athenaeus was capable of producing the restriction "as long as they did not have *truphē*" from the bare report in his source of Milesian prowess in battle and colonization: for the narrator of Book 12 of the *Deipnosophistae*, victory over the Scythians or the foundation of "splendid cities" guaranteed per se the absence of τρυφή.

Second, sentence (1) does not allow us to conclude that Ephorus presented any process of decadence at Miletus. Ephorus is only given as the authority for Miletus's rise to power. The report of fall is explicitly referred to Aristotle, and, lacking other evidence, we should not assume that Athenaeus cites that author here because the philosopher's explanation for events at Miletus was similar to the historian's.[86] In addition, just what Aristotle may have said in explanation of the παροιμία about the "mighty Milesians" is itself unclear. In sentence (2), the expression κατερρύη τὸ τῆς πόλεως ἀνδρεῖον is quite singular: it is very difficult to find a parallel for καταρρέω ("flow down") used in this figurative way. Nothing like it appears in the extant corpus of Aristotle. In fact, the closest analogue occurs in the *Deipnosophistae* itself. In Book 10, the dinner guest Dem-

---

86. Parmeggiani (2007, 120) makes precisely this assumption: "La particella δέ, infatti, viene ad opporre non i testimoni nelle rispettive opinioni, bensì l'oggetto comune alle loro considerazioni, ossia Mileto, nei suoi due stati nel tempo—la gloria del passato arcaico . . . e la decadenza del presente. . . . In F 183 le osservazioni di Eforo sfumano in quelle di Aristotele. Questo è forse indicativo. Ateneo parrebbe rilevare una continuità di pensiero, un'analogia di fondo, una complicità tra il giudizio dello storico e quello del filosofo." It may be plausible to say that "the observations of Ephorus blend into those of Aristotle," since the change of authority is not evident until a dozen words into sentence (2); however, since we know that Athenaeus sometimes melded sources without regard for their lack of compatibility (e.g., Herodotus and later traditions on Smindyrides the Sybarite), Parmeggiani's argument is not strong.

0

ocritus, discussing the drinking habits of the ancients, speaks of the custom of sitting rather than reclining to imbibe:

ἔτι δὲ καὶ νῦν τοῦτο παραμένει παρ' ἐνίοις τῶν Ἑλλήνων. ἐπεὶ δὲ τρυφᾶν ἤρξαντο καὶ χλιδῶσι, κατερρύησαν ἀπὸ τῶν δίφρων ἐπὶ τὰς κλίνας.

[Yet even now this practice remains among a few of the Greeks. But when they began to exhibit *truphē* and enjoy fine things, they sloshed down from seats to couches.] (Athen. 10.428b)

The metaphor is not quite the same, but the parallel is striking: an introductory clause announcing the onset of τρυφή, then the use of καταρρέω to convey vividly the image of moral collapse—of the city's manliness in Book 12, of the men themselves in Book 10. The passage in the earlier book is clearly Athenaeus's own composition since it is part of the symposiastic dialogue. It therefore seems best to conjecture the same source for κατερρύη τὸ ἀνδρεῖον. Thus, sentence (2) gives us little secure information about Aristotle's exegesis of the proverb.[87]

The same observation applies to the views of Ephorus: from this fragment we can only be confident that the historian mentioned certain achievements of Archaic Miletus. No such confidence can be granted to the belief that Ephorus associated Miletus's prosperity with a moral cause such as the lack of τρυφή. Nor can we establish that Ephorus saw the downfall of Miletus as an example of decadence. Not every decline is a symptom of degeneration; not every defeat need be preceded by decay. Ephorus may as easily have told the story of a prosperous community that fell victim to the power of a great empire. In sum, F183 does not support any positive conclusions about ideas of historical causation in Ephorus.

Strabo 10.4.16 = Ephorus, FGrH 70 F 149

(1) τῆς δὲ πολιτείας ἧς Ἔφορος ἀνέγραψε τὰ κυριώτατα ἐπιδραμεῖν ἀποχρώντως ἂν ἔχοι. (2) δοκεῖ δέ, φησίν, ὁ νομοθέτης μέγιστον ὑποθέσθαι ταῖς πόλεσιν ἀγαθὸν τὴν ἐλευθερίαν. . . . (3) τοῖς δ' ἔχουσι ταύτην φυλακῆς δεῖν· τὴν μὲν οὖν ὁμόνοιαν διχοστασίας αἰρομένης ἀπαντᾶν, ἢ γίνεται διὰ πλεονεξίαν καὶ

τρυφήν· (4) σωφρόνως γὰρ καὶ λιτῶς ζῶσιν ἅπασιν οὔτε φθόνον οὔθ᾽ ὕβριν
οὔτε μῖσος ἀπαντᾶν πρὸς τοὺς ὁμοίους·

[(1) As for the constitution, it would be enough to run through the chief points
that Ephorus wrote down. (2) The Lawgiver seemed, he said, to have assumed
freedom was the greatest good for cities. . . . (3) Those who have it must protect
it. Harmony arises when dissension, which come about through avarice and
truphē, is done away with. (4) For to all those living moderately and frugally
there arise neither envy nor hubris not hatred toward those who are like them.]

The text, from Strabo's discussion of ancient Crete, goes on to describe the custom of eating in public messes, which the Lawgiver enjoined so that obvious
distinctions of wealth might be avoided.

Unfortunately for the traditional hypothesis, this passage tells us little about
Ephorus's view of pernicious luxury. In the first place, the conjunction πλεονεξία
καὶ τρυφή is very much a phenomenon of the Roman period. Avarice and luxury are frequently associated in the Latin writers of the first centuries BCE/CE.
In Greek, Strabo himself seems to be the first author for whom the collocation
is directly attested (Strabo 7.3.7). We suspect that Strabo may have added the
relative clause in (3) in order to clarify to his readers how the Cretan regulations
might eliminate διχοστασία.[88]

Even if we assume Strabo is accurately reporting Ephorus on πλεονεξία καὶ
τρυφή, the context makes it difficult to extrapolate from this fact to a theme of
decadence in the historian. The reference to τρυφή serves to explain the thinking of the Cretan nomothete when he established the custom of common meals.
The fragment does not allow us to determine whether Ephorus agreed with the
Lawgiver's analysis, or whether the historian recognized cases in which
πλεονεξία καὶ τρυφή actually did harm to communities with constitutions less
prudent than the Cretan.[89]

---

88. It may be significant in this regard that the verb of the relative clause is indicative and not an infinitive, as more often in this citation from Ephorus.
89. As a relevant example, Sacks (1990, 49) points to Diodorus Siculus 7.12.8 on Spartan decadence:
μετὰ δὲ ταῦτα . . . καὶ πρὸς τρυφὴν καὶ ῥᾳθυμίαν ἀποκλίνοντες . . . ἀπέβαλον τὴν ἡγεμονίαν ("but
after this . . . turning toward *truphē* and laziness . . . they threw away their empire"). Sacks identifies
this material as Ephoran. However, as Sacks (1990, Chapter 2) himself explains, it is now accepted
that Diodorus did not hesitate to add his own moral interpretation to the narrative of his sources.
The diction of this passage suggest that this is an instance of that phenomenon: Diod. Sic. 11.87.4 has
εἰς τρυφὴν ἀπέκλινον ("they turned to *truphē*"), while the conjunction τρυφη και ῥᾳθυμία occurs at
2.21.2 and 2.23.1.

Other evidence for the idea of pernicious luxury in Ephorus is no better than the two passages we have examined here.[90] Accordingly, any claim that he portrayed τρυφή and consequent decadence as a process of historical causation is distinctly overstated.

Theopompus

Theopompus of Chios was one of the most important historians of the fourth century BCE. His principal works were the *Hellenica* in twelve books covering Greek history from 411 to 394; and, in fifty-eight books, the *Philippica*, which covered events during the reign of Philip II of Macedon (359–336). It is thought that the *Hellenica* was written in the 350s and 340s, while the *Philippica* was probably first undertaken in the 340s and published between Philip's death in 336 and Alexander's in 323.[91]

According to prevailing opinion, Theopompus was a staunch believer in the role played by pernicious luxury in the course of historical events. Passerini, whose work is still regularly cited as the fundamental study of the idea of luxury

90. In support of the importance of pernicious luxury for Ephorus, Sacks (1990, 49) refers to the censure in Diodorus of Pausanias, the victor of Plataea. In what is assumed to be Ephoran material, Diodorus denounces Pausanias because he forsook the traditional Spartan way of life: τὴν δὲ τῶν Περσῶν ἀκολασίαν καὶ τρυφὴν ἐμιμήσατο, ὃν ἥκιστα ἐχρῆν ζηλῶσαι τὰ τῶν βαρβάρων ἐπιτηδεύματα ("the man who least ought to have emulated barbarian customs imitated the intemperance and *truphē* of the Persians," Diod. Sic. 11.46.3). Sacks draws particular attention to "Ephorus' use of decadence to explain the Spartan loss of power" at sea: ἀλλὰ γὰρ αὐτὸς μὲν διὰ τὴν ἰδίαν κακίαν οὐ μόνον τῆς ἀξίας ἔτυχε τιμωρίας, ἀλλὰ καὶ τοῖς πολίταις αἴτιος κατέστη τοῦ τὴν κατὰ θάλατταν ἡγεμονίαν ἀποβαλεῖν ("but, because of his individual wickedness, not only did he himself meet with a fitting punishment, but he was the reason his fellow citizens threw away their supremacy at sea," Diod. Sic. 11.46.4). However, the whole cast of this thought is entirely Diodoran; this one sentence contains two turns of phrase that each occur dozens of times in Diodorus: the expression "to throw away power" (ἀποβάλλειν with τὴν ἡγεμονίαν / τὴν ἀρχήν, or the like) and the attribution of individual responsibility through the preposition διά + the adjective ἴδιος + an abstract noun such as κακία. Two examples will suffice to make this point. At Diod. Sic. 11.68.7, the governance of Syracuse is lost: Θρασύβουλος . . . διὰ τὴν ἰδίαν κακίαν αἰσχρῶς ἀπέβαλε τὴν ἀρχήν ("Thrasybulus . . . because of his individual wickedness shamefully threw away his rule"). In the introduction to Book 14, and therefore in a context generally accepted as of Diodorus's own composition, we find an even closer parallel to 11.46.4, since individual vice harms both those responsible and their country: παρὰ μὲν γὰρ Ἀθηναίοις τριάκοντα τύραννοι γενόμενοι διὰ τὴν ἰδίαν πλεονεξίαν τήν τε πατρίδα μεγάλοις ἀτυχήμασι περιέβαλον καὶ αὐτοὶ ταχὺ τὴν δύναμιν ἀποβαλόντες ἀθάνατον ἑαυτῶν ὄνειδος καταλελοίπασι ("For among the Athenians thirty men became tyrants because of their individual avarice, and they both encompassed their fatherland in great misfortunes and, quickly throwing away their power, themselves left as a legacy their deathless disgrace." Diod. Sic. 14.2.1). Because this pattern of thought and diction is frequent in Diodorus, we cannot agree that the criticisms of Pausanias at 11.46 can be safely identified as Ephoran.

91. For discussion of the dates and contents of these works, see Flower 1994, 26–41.

in historians between Xenophon and Diodorus, claims that Theopompus "ricercò avidamente e . . . qualche volta inventò i tratti di τρυφή dei suoi personaggi."[92] These *tratti di* τρυφή have clear political consequences: "e costantemente si può vedere che la τρυφή precede la rovina dello Stato."[93] Likewise, Connor characterizes Theopompus as "primarily a moralist . . . not . . . uninterested in politics"; the Chian's attention was chiefly drawn to the fact

> . . . that the way to domination and power began in his age in flattery and progressed through successive corruptions to consummate depravity. . . . This pattern recurs time and time again in the fragments, so often, in fact, that the *Philippica* sometimes seems to be a series of inverted Horatio Alger stories, where bad young men succeed in their ambitions and rivalries by flattery and extravagance. . . . In this depraved world . . . virtue has no reward except the occasional glum satisfaction that can be gleaned from the realization that success won by such methods is only temporary, that it leads to soft living (τρυφή), and in turn to destruction (διαφθείρεσθαι). (Connor 1968, 14–15)

More recently, Flower, in a more focused examination of this theme, comes to the conclusion that "Theopompus saw luxury and moral incontinence as a fundamental cause of the social and political turmoil of the fourth century."[94]

The evidence used to support the view represented by these scholars is quite extensive. Passerini, for example, cites nearly thirty fragments that he believes establish the importance of decadence and pernicious luxury in Theopompus.[95] We cannot discuss all of these fragments here. Moreover, we feel such a large scale examination is unnecessary. Almost without exception, the fragments that pertain to the questions at issue are transmitted by Athenaeus—a fact that is significant in itself, since Jacoby recognizes over 400 Theopompan fragments; if decadence and τρυφή were in fact so central to this author, we might expect some traces in citations from other transmitters. In any case, since the relevant material comes from Athenaeus, it is all subject to the same qualifications and need for caution.

For example, Flower supports his interpretation that Theopompus's work

---

92. Passerini 1934, 45.
93. Passerini 1934, 46.
94. Flower 1994, 69.
95. *FGrH* 115 FF 27, 31, 36, 39, 40, 49, 62, 81, 114, 117, 121, 132, 135, 139, 162, 163, 168, 187, 188, 204, 224, 225, 227, 233, 236, 282, and 283.

expressed his "disapproval of luxurious, extravagant, and licentious living" with a passage he describes as the best illustration of this phenomenon. At Athen. 12.527a (= Theopompus, *FGrH* 115 F 49), Athenaeus cites Theopompus for the lifestyle of the Thessalians, who were, it seems, given to consorting with musicians, gambling and feasting. The last sentence of this fragment is the crucial one for Flower's view: Φαρσάλιοι δὲ πάντων, φησίν, ἀνθρώπων εἰσὶν ἀργότατοι καὶ πολυτελέστατοι ("Of all people, he says, the Pharsalians are the laziest and most extravagant."). These words represent a connection between a description of a lifestyle and its criticism on moral grounds, and therefore seem to make Flower's point, but the passage immediately following casts doubts on whether the key connection was made by Theopompus or Athenaeus.

In that passage we are told that the fifth-century Athenian politician and author Critias had already objected to Thessalian behavior:

ὡμολόγηνται δ᾽ οἱ Θετταλοί, ὡς καὶ Κριτίας φησί, πάντων Ἑλλήνων πολυτελέστατοι γεγενῆσθαι περί τε τὴν δίαιταν καὶ τὴν ἐσθῆτα.

[It is agreed that the Thessalians, as Critias too says, of all Greeks were the most extravagant in respect to lifestyle and clothing.] (Athen. 12.527a–b = Critias 88 B 31 DK)

While Athenaeus may assert that Ctesias too, like Theopompus, described his subject as πάντων πολυτελέστατοι, the citation from the Athenian bears the clear marks of being a paraphrase. This construction of πολυτελής—governing περί + an accusative indicating the object of the lavish spending—seems to be directly attested for the first time in Josephus (*BJ* 7.140). In the *Deipnosophistae*, the use occurs, in addition to the present passage, at 13.592f, and, if we trust the epitomator, at 1.18e. Both of these examples are in framing material rather than citations, indicating that the turn of phrase belongs to Athenaeus's idiom. The best explanation, then, for πολυτελέστατοι περί τε τὴν δίαιταν καὶ τὴν ἐσθῆτα in the Critias fragment is that the sentence containing these words is Athenaeus's reformulation.

And, as we have seen, Athenaean statements of this type—those that offer summarizing generalizations with little detail—are often tendentious or argumentative; they identify the point for which Athenaeus has cited the authority in question and may not reproduce the view of that authority. Now, if the opening of the Critias fragment appears to be an Athenaean interpretation, this observation raises the strong suspicion that the concluding sentence of the Theopompus fragment, with its closely parallel diction, serves the same function. It is certainly not safe to use this sentence as evidence for Theopompus's strong disapproval of luxury on moral grounds.

This brief examination of F 49 is intended to show that a thorough reexamination of all Athenaean evidence on morality as historical cause in Theopompus would be profitable. Such a study would demand a book of its own. We will restrict our investigation to those citations that make explicit reference to τρυφή. Since, in the view of modern scholarship, the idea of decadence is most closely associated with the use of this term by authors such as Theopompus, study of these fragments should give us a sense for the quality of the evidence more generally.

Athenaeus 12.531e–532a = Theopompus, FGrH 115 F 31

(1) ἐν δὲ τῇ α′ τῶν Φιλιππικῶν Θεόπομπος περὶ Φιλίππου λέγων φησίν· καὶ τριταῖος εἰς Ὀνόκαρσιν ἀφικνεῖται, χωρίον τι τῆς Θρᾴκης ἄλσος ἔχον πολὺ κατεσκευασμένον καλῶς καὶ πρὸς τὸ ἐνδιαιτηθῆναι κεχαρισμένον ἄλλως τε καὶ τὴν θερινὴν ὥραν. (2) ἦν γὰρ καὶ τῶν ὑπὸ Κότυος προκριθέντων, ὃς ἁπάντων τῶν βασιλέων τῶν ἐν τῇ Θρᾴκῃ γεγενημένων μάλιστα πρὸς ἡδυπαθείας καὶ τρυφὰς ὥρμησε, καὶ περιιὼν τὴν χώραν ὅπου κατίδοι τόπους δένδρεσι συσκίους καὶ καταρρύτους ὕδασι, τούτους κατεσκεύασεν ἑστιατόρια· (3) καὶ φοιτῶν εἰς ἑκάστους ὁπότε τύχοι θυσίας τε τοῖς θεοῖς ἐποιεῖτο καὶ συνῆν μετὰ τῶν ὑπάρχων, εὐδαίμων καὶ μακαριστὸς ὢν ἕως εἰς τὴν Ἀθηνᾶν βλασφημεῖν καὶ πλημμελεῖν ἐπεχείρησεν. (4) διηγεῖταί τε ἑξῆς ὁ συγγραφεὺς ὅτι ... (5) ὁ δὲ βασιλεὺς οὗτός ποτε καὶ ζηλοτυπήσας τὴν αὑτοῦ γυναῖκα ταῖς αὑτοῦ χερσὶν ἀνέτεμε τὴν ἄνθρωπον ἀπὸ τῶν αἰδοίων ἀρξάμενος.

[(1) In the first book of the *History of Philip*, Theopompus, speaking about Philip, says: On the third day he arrived at Onocarsis, a place in Thrace that contained a grove, arranged very beautifully and agreeable for living in anytime, but especially in the summer season. (2) For it was one of the places preferred by Cotys who, of all the kings who arose in Thrace, was especially eager for pleasant living and *truphē*, and whenever he, while traveling about the area, saw locations densely shaded with trees and irrigated with waters, these locations especially he turned into banqueting places. (3) And visiting each of these in turn, whenever he happened to be nearby, he made sacrifices to the gods and he had dealings with his subordinates, being prosperous and living an enviable life until the time when he presumed to commit blasphemy against Athena and sin against her. (4) For the writer thereafter describes how . . . [There follows the story whereby Cotys boasted that he was going to wed the virgin goddess and then murdered certain of his companions who did not play along with his conceit.] (5) This king once being jealously angry at his own wife, cut up this woman with his own hands, beginning with her genitals.]

The most important material for our purposes is given in the relative clause in sentence (2). This clause establishes Cotys as a paradigm for a life of self-indulgence and pleasure. However, the evidence that it is a paraphrase is strong. First, the description of Cotys as one superlatively given to τρυφή (ἁπάντων μάλιστα) is probably Athenaean.[96] Next, ὁρμάω with a complement such as πρὸς τρυφὰς is a favorite expression of Athenaeus, as shown in the previous chapter. Third, the pattern of occurrence of the noun ἡδυπάθεια weighs against a Theopompan origin: in the Classical period, the word is attested in a direct transmission only for Xenophon, while it is common in Athenaeus and among writers of the Roman period. Fourth, σύσκιος ("closely shaded") is secure once in Xenophon and once in Plato; from the first century BCE, we find the expression σύσκιος + dative (e.g., δένδρεσι, "close shaded with trees") several times in geographical descriptions.[97] The phrase καταρρύτους ὕδασι / ποταμοῖς ("irrigated with waters / rivers") shows a similar pattern.[98] Finally, the occurrence of ἱστιατόριον ("banqueting hall") is also suggestive of a date later than the fourth century: although the word is attested scarcely a dozen times in all, only one of these literary texts dates from earlier than Strabo and Dionysius of Halicarnassus.[99]

---

96. Compare Athen. 12.524d (about the Scythians, on the authority of Clearchus), τρυφήσαντες δὲ καὶ μάλιστα δὴ καὶ πρῶτοι πάντων τῶν ἀνθρώπων ἐπὶ τὸ τρυφᾶν ὁρμήσαντες ("displaying *truphē* and especially first of all people setting out toward practicing *truphē*"); also 12.528f (Assyrians *à la* Ctesias), πάντας . . . τοὺς βασιλεύσαντας τῆς Ἀσίας περὶ τρυφὴν σπουδάσαι, μάλιστα δὲ Νινύαν ("all the rulers of Asia were serious about *truphē*, but Ninyas especially").

97. Diod. Sic. 3.68.6, 17.50.4; Arr., *Ind.* 22.8; Pausanias 9.19.2; Clem. Alex., *Protr.* 12.119.1; Dio Chrys., *Or.*, 2.41.5.

98. κατάρρυτος with ὕδασι *vel sim.* at Plut., *Cam.* 16.3; Diod. Sic. 5.19.3, 18.6.2; Strabo 4.1.2, 15.1.13, 15.2.14; the adjective occurs as early as Eur., *Andr.* 215. In addition to the present passage, Athenaeus has the expression at 12.542a: Δοῦρις δὲ ἐν τῇ δ' τῶν περὶ Ἀγαθοκλέα καὶ πλησίον Ἱππωνίου πόλεως ἄλσος τι δείκνυσθαι κάλλει διάφορον καὶ κατάρρυτον ὕδασιν ("Duris in the fourth book of the *Affairs of Agathocles* says that near the city of Hipponium a certain grove is on display, distinguished in beauty and irrigated with waters."). Because these words make up an introductory sentence and the content is given in the accusative + infinitive construction, most students of citation in the *Deipnosophistae* would agree that the phraseology is likely to be Athenaeus's own.

99. Hdt. 4.35 has ἑστιητόριον. Several instances are in evidence from Hellenistic inscriptions.

The diction of sentence (3) contains, as far as we can see, nothing that could not be ascribed to Theopompus without hesitation. On the other hand, the content of the sentence does seem to suggest paraphrase, since it offers a moral exegesis of the story of Cotys's marriage to the goddess: "the king enjoyed good fortune until he blasphemed against Athena." However, sentence (4) indicates that the details of the divine wedding came later in the *Philippica*. It is possible that Theopompus for some reason made such an allusion and offered such an interpretation of the story before he told it, and that he did these things in the context of describing Cotys's sylvan banqueting halls—perhaps the blasphemy took place in one—but, because of the clear seam in the citation (διηγεῖταί τε ἑξῆς), serious consideration must be given to an interpretation that sees (3) as a transition composed by Athenaeus.

A similar flaw in the narrative structure suggests that sentence (5) is also Athenaean in form. After briefly relating how Cotys shot and killed two of his men who did not humor his delusion of marriage, the events of (5) seem to be related almost as an aside, as if to say: "and on one occasion, by the way (ποτε καὶ), this fellow mutilated and killed his wife." We feel that it is unlikely that Theopompus told the story of this murder in so offhand a manner, or that he introduced the second crime as a digression from, or supplement to, the first. In contrast, such an addition is at home in the context of Athenaeus's argument, where narrative coherence is not needed. Thus, Athenaean reformulation is likely, an interpretation supported by the occurrence of ζηλοτυπέω ("be struck by jealousy"). This word appears in only a handful of passages in the fifth and fourth centuries BCE, but later becomes extremely common, beginning with Polybius and Diodorus.[100]

A good case can be made that a significant portion of the form of F 31—both in regard to diction and structure—stems from Athenaeus. What, then, can be made of the content? In spite of his characterization as "most given to *truphē*," Cotys's only material extravagance seems to be the construction of ἱστατόρια in beautiful woodland areas. He used these places, as far as we hear, for sacrificing to the gods and meeting his officers, hardly examples of sumptu-

---

100. The root ζηλοτυπ- (ζηλοτυπέω, ζηλοτυπία, "a stroke of jealousy," and ζηλότυπος "jealous") shows the following distribution. Early uses: Plato, *Symp.* 213d; Isoc. 15.245; Ar,. *Plut.* 1016; Aeschines, *In Tim.* 58, *Ctes.* 81 and 211; Men., *Pk.* 987 and 3 fragments. Second and first century BCE: Polyb. 4.87.4 and three times in the fragmentary books; Diodorus Siculus, eight times in extant works; Dion. Hal., *Pomp.* 1.13; Strabo 14.1.20; as well as a few uses in minor authors. It becomes very common in the first century CE (Josephus sixteen times; Philo twenty times; Chariton sixteen times) and later, especially in Lucian (thirty-five times) and Plutarch (sixty-three times outside the fragments). Athenaeus uses it on three further occasions: 11.504e (in framing language); 12.542f; and 13.588e.

ous living or hedonistic behavior. He was blessed by fortune (εὐδαίμων). Later, he committed blasphemy and murder, even killing his own wife.

This pattern is familiar from our earlier examination of the fragments of Clearchus. An apparently harmless, though perhaps pleasant, behavior is connected—here implicitly—with outrageous action. The passage gives no information that might explain a process of decadence: how pleasurable sojourns in the woods might lead to madness and murder. Set beside this fact is the observation that there is no directly attested source for such a causal link before the Roman period. From these circumstances, we conclude that Theopompus made, in the case of Cotys, no such link and envisioned no such process.[101] This citation has little positive value in support of the idea of pernicious luxury.[102]

Athenaeus 12.532a–b = Theopompus, FGrH 115 F 105

The next sentence after the end of F 31 begins a new citation from Theopompus. In the pertinent section, the general Chabrias was not able to live in Athens, τὰ μὲν διὰ τὴν ἀσέλγειαν καὶ διὰ τὴν πολυτέλειαν τὴν αὑτοῦ τὴν περὶ τὸν βίον, τὰ δὲ διὰ τοὺς Ἀθηναίους· ἅπασι γάρ εἰσι χαλεποί ("both because of his licentiousness and his extravagance of life and also because of the Athenians: they are harsh to all." Athen. 12.532b). There follows a list of other prominent men who have chosen to leave the city. Although this passage does not contain the word τρυφή, it forms for Athenaeus a unit with the subsequent citation (F 213), which does; both are on the subject of the morality of the Athenians and their generals. The words διὰ τὴν πολυτέλειαν τὴν περὶ τὸν βίον, at least, are probably not Theopompan. The prepositional phrase περὶ τὸν βίον seems not to occur as an attribute of a moral quality until Philo and Dionysius of Halicarnassus.[103] It is

---

101. Athenaeus's near contemporary Harpocration, in his *Lexicon* (*s.v.* Κότυς), also relates many of the same details about Cotys that appear in the fragment of Theopompus. No source is named and the passage is of little value to our investigation, since it may derive from Athenaeus.

102. With regard to Cotys's murder of his men at his pseudo-wedding, it is possible to see this action as behavior that the Greeks may have understood to be rooted in τρυφή. The king killed his servants because they naively reported that Athena was not waiting for Cotys in the wedding chamber. In other words, they frustrated his will. As we have seen, Plato ascribed Cambyses' murder of his brother to the fact that he stood between Cambyses and the fulfillment of his desires. Cambyses had been raised to expect to receive what he wished (i.e., in τρυφή); it was the frustration of that expectation which led to aggression and violence. It is very difficult to see how such a link between τρυφή and ὕβρις could be generalized into a principle of historical causation.

103. Philo, *Flac.* 91; Dion. Hal., *Antiq. Rom.* 5.17.6, 8.30.3.

relatively common in the *Deipnosophistae*.[104] Because of Athenaeus's peculiar methods of argumentation and proof, we must be aware that this sentence may be not merely a paraphrase, but Athenaeus's own interpretation of events narrated by Theopompus. The historian may not have meant these to indicate a general condemnation of Chabrias's character.

Athenaeus 12.532c–d = Theopompus, FGrH 115 F 213

(1) καὶ περὶ τοῦ Χάρητος ἐν τῇ πέμπτῃ καὶ τεσσαρακοστῇ φησιν· (2) Χάρητός τε νωθροῦ τε ὄντος καὶ βραδέος, καίτοι γε καὶ πρὸς τρυφὴν ἤδη ζῶντος· ὅς γε περιήγετο στρατευόμενος αὐλητρίδας καὶ ψαλτρίας καὶ πεζὰς ἑταίρας, καὶ τῶν χρημάτων τῶν εἰσφερομένων εἰς τὸν πόλεμον τὰ μὲν εἰς ταύτην τὴν ὕβριν ἀνήλισκε . . .[105] (3) καὶ γὰρ αὐτοὶ τοῦτον τὸν τρόπον ἔζων, ὥστε τοὺς μὲν νέους ἐν τοῖς αὐλητριδίοις καὶ παρὰ ταῖς ἑταίραις διατρίβειν, τοὺς δὲ μικρὸν ἐκείνων πρεσβυτέρους ἐν πότοις <καὶ> κύβοις καὶ ταῖς τοιαύταις ἀσωτίαις, τὸν δὲ δῆμον ἅπαντα πλείω καταναλίσκειν εἰς τὰς κοινὰς ἑστιάσεις καὶ κρεανομίας ἤπερ εἰς τὴν τῆς πόλεως διοίκησιν.

[(1) And concerning Chares he says in the forty-fifth book: (2) Chares, being sluggish and slow, and moreover living a life aimed at *truphē*, went around campaigning with flute-girls and harp-girls and ordinary prostitutes, and of the funds coming in for the war, he spent some on this hubris . . . (3) For they themselves too lived in this way: the young men passed their time among little flute-girls and with whores, those a little older, in drinks and dice and such profligacy; the demos as a whole spent more for communal feasts and meat distributions than for the management of the city.]

The genitive absolute in sentence (2) indicates that Chares is an example of a man dedicated to τρυφή. As elsewhere, this sentence in particular arouses suspicion by its diction. The pattern is familiar: the adjective νωθρός ("sluggish"),

104. Athen. 10.436b, modifying ἀσελγής ("wanton"; citation of Nicolaus of Damascus); 12.514d, τρυφή (Clearchus); 12.523a, εὐκοσμία ("good order"; perhaps Clearchus); 12.528a, ἀσωτία καὶ πολυτέλεια ("wastefulness and extravagance"; Agatharchides); 12.540f, ἀκολασία ("intemperance"; Clearchus). At 6.260b, the phrase is again attributed to Theopompus, modifying ἀσελγής.
105. In the omitted section, Chares is said to have given money to his political partisans among the Athenians; next, that the Athenians in general were not upset by Chares' actions, but rather supported him the more.

when describing the moral or psychological qualities of a human being, is extremely rare in Theopompus's time, while more common in Athenaeus's.[106] The odd expression πρὸς τρυφὴν ζῶντος ("living toward *truphē*") shows a form—ζάω governing πρὸς + an object indicating some moral quality—which seems extremely rare, if not unexampled in the extant corpus of Greek literature. However, there are slim traces of a nominal analogue, βίος πρὸς x, in the Roman period.[107] More significance may perhaps be attached to material in sentence (3), the report of the vices that the Athenians in general shared with Chares. Specifically, the diminutive αὐλητρίδιον ("little flute-player") seems to occur elsewhere only in Diogenes Laertius and Athenaeus himself.[108] The evidence of the term κρεανομία ("distribution of meat") is somewhat more robust: the word occurs fewer than a dozen times in a direct transmission, none being earlier than Josephus, while Athenaeus has it twice in addition to the current passage.[109] More telling is the evidence that κρεανομία may have been part of the language of moralizing rhetoric in Athenaeus's day, an aspect that we will discuss below.

The content of the citation also reveals signs of reformulation. Most obviously, Chares is said to have diverted funds from the war εἰς ταύτην τὴν ὕβριν. In spite of ταύτην, there is no clear indication of what this hubris may have been. Thus, the original evidently has undergone compression and some periphrasis.

Although we judge that the characterization of Chares' behavior—and therefore the behavior of the Athenian demos—under the rubric of τρυφή looks like a modification on the part of Athenaeus, this passage is important because the original may have presented an example of the working of pernicious luxury in a historically plausible way. In particular, Theopompus seems to have criticized the diversion of funds from management of the city and prosecution of the war to entertainment and hedonistic pursuits. Similar concerns appear in other fragments, two of which refer to the conduct of the Athenian politician Eubulus. The first comes from Harpocration's lexicon to the Attic orators:

---

106. Plato, *Tht.* 144b2, Arist., *Rhet.* 1390b30. There are no other good parallels in direct transmission until Polybius, who uses it to characterize the martial abilities of, among others, the Carthaginian general Hanno (1.74.2, 1.74.13) and the Roman Fabius Maximus (3.90.6).

107. τὸν πρὸς ἀρετὴν βίον ("the life of virtue," Philo, *Post.* 45); ὁ πρὸς ἡδονὴν βίος ("the life of pleasure," Ael., *VH* 4.23).

108. Diog. Laert. 7.13, Athen. 13.607e. Both these passages concern the same anecdote about Zeno of Citeum.

109. Josephus, *AJ* 19.130; Athen. 12.534d, 10.425c.

ὅτι δὴ δημαγωγὸς ἦν ἐπιφανέστατος, ἐπιμελής τε καὶ φιλόπονος, ἀργύριόν τε συχνὸν πορίζων τοῖς Ἀθηναίοις διένειμε, διὸ καὶ τὴν πόλιν ἐπὶ τῆς τούτου πολιτείας ἀνανδροτάτην καὶ ῥαθυμοτάτην συνέβη γενέσθαι, Θεόπομπος ἐν τῇ ι΄ τῶν Φιλιππικῶν.

[Theopompus in Book 10 of the *Philippica:* that he [Eubulus] was a most distinguished popular leader, and was attentive and industrious; he also supplied abundant silver and distributed it to the Athenians. For this reason, the city became under his tenure in office most unmanly and most frivolous.] (Harp., s.v. Εὔβουλος = Theopompus, *FGrH* 115 F 99)

The second is from Book 4 of Athenaeus:

Θεόπομπος δ' ἐν τῇ δεκάτῃ τῶν Φιλιππικῶν . . . Εὔβουλόν φησι τὸν δημαγωγὸν ἄσωτον γενέσθαι. τῇ λέξει δὲ ταύτῃ ἐχρήσατο· καὶ τοσοῦτον ἀσωτίᾳ καὶ πλεονεξίᾳ διενήνοχε τοῦ δήμου τοῦ Ταραντίνων ὅσον ὃ μὲν περὶ τὰς ἑστιάσεις εἶχε μόνον ἀκράτως, ὃ δὲ τῶν Ἀθηναίων καὶ τὰς προσόδους καταμισθοφορῶν διατετέλεκε.

[Theopompus in the tenth of the *Philippica* . . . says that Eubulus the popular leader was profligate. He used this expression: in profligacy and greed he surpassed the demos of the Tarentines to the extent that it was intemperate with respect to feasts, but that of the Athenians continued to spend its revenues also on hiring mercenaries.] (Athen. 4.166d–e = Theopompus, *FGrH* 115 F 100)

There are obvious difficulties in developing a coherent interpretation of the two citations. F 99 characterizes Eubulus in terms that are antithetical to understanding him as a man of τρυφή: we have seen in Chapter 1 that ἐπιμέλεια was in an important sense the opposite of τρυφή. The same can be said of φιλοπονία. Thus, F 99 presents Eubulus as a leader free from the taint of pernicious luxury who nonetheless unmanned the Athenians through his handling of the revenues. In contrast, F 100 declares that Eubulus exhibited the vices of ἀσωτία and πλεονεξία to a pronounced degree.[110] The two passages cannot be reconciled in

---

110. It is not certain that Eubulus was, in the original, the subject of διενήνοχε. It is odd to compare the profligacy of a single individual to that of an entire people. In addition, in the sequence ὃ μὲν . . . ὃ δὲ, it seems more natural to take τῶν Ἀθηναίων as specifying the nominative ὃ that precedes it rather than the following τὰς προσόδους. We may suspect that the Athenian demos was the subject of both διατετέλεκε and διενήνοχε, and that Athenaeus has obscured this detail to shore up his claim that Eubulus was ἄσωτος. Such a move is not foreign to Athenaeus's method. We may nonetheless assume

this regard: in the context of F 99, ἐπιμελής apparently refers to the care Eubulus took in exercising control of state funds; in F 100, ἀσωτία implies that Eubulus's disbursements were unreasonable.[111] The pairing of ἀσωτία and πλεονεξία is also noteworthy. While not logically incompatible, the two qualities, profligacy and greed, make an odd couple. Indeed, this passage seems to be the only place in Greek literature where these two nouns are conjoined. In this connection, we should not overlook the fact that rhetorical amplification by means of linking, for example, the names of loosely connected vices is much more a technique of the Roman period than of an earlier time.[112] So, we must be circumspect with regard to a possible paraphrase, in spite of Athenaeus's insistence that the citation is verbatim (τῇ λέξει ταύτῃ).

Solutions to these and other problems presented by the two fragments must probably remain outside our grasp, but we will assume that F 99 and F 100, combined with F 213, indicate that Theopompus saw the diversion of public resources from military use as an important cause for the Macedonian victory over the democracy.[113]

Theopompus's criticism here is important to our study, since, unlike many of the texts that we have examined so far, his apparent account of the effects of pernicious luxury has psychological and historical plausibility. Athenian interest in hedonistic activities, on this view, led the demos to spend on pleasure money that would have been better used in the struggle against Philip. In its reasonableness this process contrasts strongly from the picture of pernicious luxury regularly derived from, for example, the fragments of Clearchus, where a τρυφή marked by extreme effeminacy becomes violent aggression without explanation.

At the same time, it is necessary to recognize the limitations of the evidence of Fragments 99, 100, and 213. In the first place, the process described—dedication to a life of ease causing a diversion of state monies leading to enervation and defeat—is in fact a modern construction within the text of the *Philip-*

---

that Theopompus related the spending on mercenaries as something that happened ἐπὶ τῆς πολιτείας of Eubulus.

111. One could perhaps argue that the assertion of Eubulus's admirable qualities in F 99 was meant ironically, but that Harpocration missed this dimension in his reading of Theopompus. It would be difficult to establish this interpretation.

112. Examples of ἀσωτία καὶ x before the Roman period are Plato, *Rep.* 8.560e (in a series of vices to which oligarchic youth may be tempted); Arist., *Eth. Eud.* 3.1231b37, *Eth. Nic.* 1107b10, 1119b27, 1121a11 (all of which link it with ἀνελευθερία ["illiberality"]).

113. It is generally accepted that the reference is at least partly to the outlay for the Theoric Fund.

pica. No single citation contains all these elements, and we have already remarked upon the difficulty of harmonizing the information offered by these fragments. Second, the very quality that makes it plausible to ascribe this view to Theopompus—its relatively straightforward and simple nature—means that the fragments do not offer strong support for the existence of an overarching concept of decadence or of pernicious luxury in fourth-century thought. That the Athenians diverted resources from war to enjoyment is a phenomenon that requires no explanatory matrix. Furthermore, the only connection with τρυφή, supposedly the key term of reference for this underlying theory of decadence, was probably made by Athenaeus and not Theopompus.

The evidence of these fragments differs in another important way from the prevailing modern view about pernicious luxury. This view holds that great prosperity naturally and inevitably leads to τρυφή and then to disastrous results. Theopompus's explanation for Athenian weakness, on the other hand, seems relatively ad hoc. Even if we leave aside the history of fifth-century Athens, where Thucydides describes the coexistence of prosperity, pleasure, and power, Theopompus's own testimony seems to present a process of luxury-induced decadence as only sometimes operative at in fourth-century Athens. In F 105, Chabrias left the city "because of his licentiousness and extravagance" and the fact that the citizens were "harsh." Apparently they disapproved of his behavior. In F 213, Chares' life of luxury was shared by the Athenians. This evident difference begs the question of what triggered the spread of the debilitating effects of luxury to the general population. Although we may lack the evidence to answer this question with respect to Theopompus's narrative, a proper understanding of pernicious luxury must take into account the aspect of contingency that he seems to have given it.

Nor can we be confident that a luxurious life was, as Theopompus understood it, the cause of personal cowardice and individual effeminacy. It is true that F 99 says that Eubulus's allocation of Athenian silver caused the city to become "most unmanly and most frivolous," but in evaluating this statement we must be aware of how terms such as ἀνανδρία and ῥᾳθυμία were used in the relevant fourth-century context. In brief, lack of masculinity and a lax attitude toward serious affairs were among the characteristics attributed to the opponents of a more active military policy against Philip of Macedon. Most instructive are the arguments of Demosthenes in pursuit of a more vigorous policy. For example, in the *First Philippic* he tries to shame his listeners into supporting his proposals:

δοκεῖ δέ μοι θεῶν τις, ὦ ἄνδρες Ἀθηναῖοι, τοῖς γιγνομένοις ὑπὲρ τῆς πόλεως αἰσχυνόμενος τὴν φιλοπραγμοσύνην ταύτην ἐμβαλεῖν Φιλίππῳ. εἰ γὰρ ἔχων ἃ κατέστραπται καὶ προείληφεν ἡσυχίαν ἔχειν ἤθελε καὶ μηδὲν ἔπραττεν ἔτι, ἀποχρῆν ἐνίοις ὑμῶν ἄν μοι δοκεῖ, ἐξ ὧν αἰσχύνην καὶ ἀνανδρίαν καὶ πάντα τὰ αἴσχιστα ὠφληκότες ἂν ἦμεν δημοσίᾳ·

[Men of Athens, I think that it was one of the gods who, ashamed on the city's behalf about what has happened, has endowed Philip with his meddlesome nature. If he were willing to take what he has won and stolen, and keep quiet and do nothing further, it seems to me that some of you would be content with a situation from which we receive, as a consolation prize for the public resources we have used, dishonor and unmanliness and everything that is most shameful.] (Dem. 4.42)

This passage is of particular interest because it occurs in conjunction with other themes that reappear in FF 99, 100 and 213. At 4.24, Demosthenes has argued against excessive dependence on mercenary forces, while a few pages later a sharp contrast is drawn between conduct of military affairs and

. . . τὴν μὲν τῶν Παναθηναίων ἑορτὴν καὶ τὴν τῶν Διονυσίων . . . εἰς ἃ τοσαῦτα ἀναλίσκεται χρήματα, ὅσα οὐδ᾽ εἰς ἕνα τῶν ἀποστόλων, καὶ τοσοῦτον ὄχλον καὶ παρασκευὴν ὅσην οὐκ οἶδ᾽ εἴ τι τῶν ἁπάντων ἔχει.

[. . . the festival of the Panathenaea and the Dionysia . . . on which more money is spent than on any one of our expeditions, and which get such attendance and such preparation as nothing else I know.] (Dem. 4.35)

A similar connection is made in the *Third Olynthiac*:

ὑμεῖς δ᾽ ὁ δῆμος, . . . ἐν ὑπηρέτου καὶ προσθήκης μέρει γεγένησθε, ἀγαπῶντες ἐὰν μεταδιδῶσι θεωρικῶν ὑμῖν ἢ Βοηδρόμια πέμψωσιν οὗτοι, καὶ τὸ πάντων ἀνδρειότατον, τῶν ὑμετέρων αὐτῶν χάριν προσοφείλετε.

[But you, the Demos, have taken on the role of an underling and second-ranker, well contented if these men give you a share of the Theoric Fund or put on a procession for the Boedromia. And—the most manly thing of all—you owe them gratitude for receiving your own property.] (Dem. 3.31)

Such timidity in the face of those who control the purse strings for the festivals and entertainments increases the "frivolity of each one of you" (τὴν ἑκάστου ῥαθυμίαν ὑμῶν, Dem. 3.33) in foreign policy.

In view of material such as this, it would be wrong to insist that the τὴν πόλιν ἀνανδροτάτην καὶ ῥαθυμοτάτην of F 99 implies that Theopompus saw among the Athenians a significant element who, like Sardanapalus, lived in a distinctly effeminate or luxurious way. In the rhetoric of the anti-Macedonian faction, to support the use of public funds for "trifles" instead of serious business simply *was* effeminacy. In addition, we need not assume the existence of an elaborated concept of decadence or pernicious luxury to understand references in this context to softness or the like. In deliberative rhetoric, the usual strategy is to make the opponent's position seem disadvantageous and dishonorable. Given that the purpose of speaking was to gain support for war, cowardice and womanishness were the obvious aspersions to cast. Given the military achievements of the fifth-century Athenians, pointing out the inferiority of their fourth-century descendants was the obvious move to make. The observation, "you are not the men your fathers were," implies no more or less articulated theory of decadence.

While Demosthenes decries the disproportionate allocation of money to festivals over expeditions, he treats these festivals themselves with a certain care. For example, at 3.19, he suggests that the Theoric Fund should be allotted πρὸς ἃ δεῖ ("toward the things that are necessary") rather than πρὸς ἃ μὴ δεῖ ("toward the things that are not necessary"). The phrase ἃ μὴ δεῖ is a delicate way of referring to the practices that Theopompus seems to describe as hedonistic and morally deleterious. Perhaps this difference represents the historian's own contribution in the search for the explanation of Philip's success. Perhaps he exaggerated the immorality of the activities on which the Demos preferred to spend its money.

Unfortunately, other evidence raises some doubt about whether it was Theopompus who was responsible for the ἀσωτία of the Athenians as reported in F 100 and F 213. In particular, it is possible that the view in question—that at the time of Macedonian expansion, Athens was unmanned by its self-centered concern for festivals and related pleasures—had by Athenaeus's day become something of a rhetorical theme, subject to amplification with only a tenuous connection to historical fact. An illustration may be found in the *Encomium of Demosthenes*, which tradition has attributed to Lucian. A section of this work purports to give an evaluation of the Athenian orator by Philip himself, who said that without Demosthenes the city would have been no obstacle for him:

τί δ᾽ ἂν ἄνθρωποι πράξαιεν διονυσιάζοντες, ἐν κρεανομίαις καταζῶντες καὶ
χοροῖς; εἰ δὲ μὴ Δημοσθένης εἷς ἐν Ἀθηναίοις ἐγένετο . . . . ἀλλ᾽ ἀνίστησι μὲν
ἄκοντας οἷον ἐκ μανδραγόρου καθεύδοντας τοὺς αὐτοῦ πολίτας, ὥσπερ τομῇ
τινι καὶ καύσει τῆς ῥαθυμίας τῇ παρρησίᾳ χρώμενος, ὀλίγον τοῦ πρὸς ἡδονὴν
φροντίσας. μετατίθησιν δὲ τῶν χρημάτων τοὺς πόρους ἀπὸ τῶν θεάτρων ἐπὶ τὰ
στρατόπεδα.

[What would the people, devotees of Dionysus, have done, living among meat
distributions and choruses? If one man, Demosthenes, had not been among the
Athenians . . . . But he raised up his fellow citizens from a slumber as if from
mandrake, using frank talk like it was a lancet and hot iron against frivolity and
giving little consideration to pleasure. Rather, he transferred financial resources
from the theaters to the army camps.] (Ps.-Lucian, *Encom. Dem.* 35–36)

In this version, the festivals, meat distribution, and choruses act as a drug in-
ducing ῥαθυμία. The stupor is dependent on public funding of the these entertainments; Demosthenes cures the demos by shifted the flow of money from
ἡδονή to war.

The possibility that such a treatment of the topic of Athenian decadence
may have influenced Athenaeus in the pertinent citations of Theopompus is
made stronger by the presence in F 213 of the noun κρεανομία. This word is
used in authors of the Roman period in criticisms of public largess.[114] Therefore, since the descriptions of Athenian hedonism in F 100 and F 213 may have
been contaminated by language associated with a later concern with luxury and
the moral ramifications of a policy of bread and circuses, a prudent interpretation of the Theopompan evidence will not put too much weight on the wording
of the citations by Athenaeus. We may assume with some confidence that Theopompus did offer excessive spending on public entertainment as a cause of
Athenian defeat. The same degree of confidence cannot be given to the characterization of the resultant behavior of the demos as distinctly immoral.[115]

---

114. Ps.-Demetrius, *Eloc.* 285, has κρεανομία in context closely related to Theopompus, F 213. After quoting from the Athenian orator Demades, who said the city had, from a "sea fighter" (τὴν ναύμαχον)
become "an old woman . . . slurping down barley gruel" (γραῦν . . . πτισάνην ῥοφοῦσαν), the stylist
gives this explanation: these words are an allegory, ἐπὶ <τοῦ> ἐν κρεανομίαις τότε καὶ πανδαισίαις
διάγουσαν ἀπολλύειν τὰ στρατιωτικὰ χρήματα ("for wasting the army's money by spending its time
then in meat distributions and full-course meals"). According to Josephus, the Emperor Gaius won
the support of the mob, θεωρίαις τε καὶ μονομαχιῶν δόσεσιν καί τινων κρεανομιῶν ἡδοναῖς
("through spectacles and the giving of gladiatorial shows and the pleasures of certain meat distributions," Josephus, *AJ* 19.130).

115. Another factor to be considered is the rather obvious possibility that Athenaeus has attributed senti-

The final point against counting the evidence of F 213 and its companion fragments as supporting the traditional concept of pernicious luxury is its isolation. There seem to be very few parallels for a scenario in which τρυφή is said to lead to the ruin of a community by causing a misallocation of funds. Thus, we view Theopompus's concept of decadence as showing no necessary connection with the idea of destructive τρυφή as generally understood in modern scholarship.

Athenaeus 12.517d–518b = Theopompus, FGrH 115 F 204

(1) Θεόπομπος δὲ ἐν τῇ τεσσαρακοστῇ τρίτῃ τῶν Ἱστοριῶν καὶ νόμον εἶναί φησιν παρὰ τοῖς Τυρρηνοῖς κοινὰς ὑπάρχειν τὰς γυναῖκας· (2) ταύτας δ᾽ ἐπιμελεῖσθαι σφόδρα τῶν σωμάτων καὶ γυμνάζεσθαι πολλάκις καὶ μετ᾽ ἀνδρῶν, ἐνίοτε δὲ καὶ πρὸς ἑαυτάς· (3) οὐ γὰρ αἰσχρὸν εἶναι αὐταῖς φαίνεσθαι γυμναῖς. . . . (4) τρέφειν δὲ τοὺς Τυρρηνοὺς πάντα τὰ γινόμενα παιδία, οὐκ εἰδότας ὅτου πατρός ἐστιν ἕκαστον. (5) ζῶσι δὲ καὶ οὗτοι τὸν αὐτὸν τρόπον τοῖς θρεψαμένοις, πότους τὰ πολλὰ ποιούμενοι καὶ πλησιάζοντες ταῖς γυναιξὶν ἁπάσαις. . . . (6) καὶ γὰρ γίνονται παρ᾽ αὐτοῖς πάνυ καλοὶ τὰς ὄψεις, ἅτε τρυφερῶς διαιτώμενοι καὶ λεαινόμενοι τὰ σώματα. . . .

[(1) Theopompus in the forty-third book of his *Histories* says that it is the custom among the Etruscans that wives are communal. (2) These women take great care of their bodies and often exercise with men, though sometimes with each other. (3) It is not shameful for them to be seen naked. . . . [He goes on to say that Etruscan women dine with other men besides their husbands and that they are capable drinkers.] . . . (4) The Etruscans raise all the children that are born, not knowing who the father is of each. (5) The children, too, live in the same way as those who have raised them, frequently throwing drinking bouts and having sex with all the women. . . . [There follows an account of shameless and promiscuous sexual customs.] (6) [The boys] among them are beautiful in appearance, since they live with *truphē* and smooth their bodies. . . .]

The first thing to note about this unusually long fragment—a discussion of the Etruscans as an example of the outrageous customs found among "all the bar-

---

ments to Theopompus, which were expressed, not by the writer, but by historical figures depicted in the *Philippica*. We have seen, in Demosthenes and the fragment of Demades, that, in the debates about how to respond to the rise of Macedonian power, positions on policy were cast in moral terms. Thus, the claim that Eubulus and Chares were practitioners of ἀσωτία may have been advanced by anti-Macedonian speakers rather than the historian himself. True to his method, Athenaeus would not have scrupled to elide this distinction.

barians of the west" and "many of the Greeks living in Italy"—is that it exhibits an obvious seam. At the end of sentence (4), the structure of the citation shifts from indirect speech of the accusative + infinitive type (φησιν . . . τρέφειν δὲ τοὺς Τυρρηνοὺς) to direct discourse (ζῶσι δὲ). There is a corresponding shift in content: beginning with (5), the material is relatively more detailed and more sensational. If an Etruscan man, for example, is at home having sex when a visitor arrives, he will call out to his guest describing exactly what he is doing at that moment. In comparison, the contents of the earlier sentences are bland and general. Thus Pelling reasonably suggests that here Athenaeus changes from quotation to paraphrase, perhaps deriving the material in part from Theopompus, but probably also obtaining it from elsewhere. Pelling concludes his discussion with the well-justified admonition: "But at least one should not print the present passage without a heavy health warning; and we certainly should not print it with Jacoby's willful quotation marks to indicate verbatim citation."[116]

We may now turn to sentence (6), where the beauty of Etruscan boys is said to be due to a δίαιτα imbued with τρυφή. The manifestation of this τρυφή is the boys' custom of depilating their bodies. We have observed above that, in this sense, λεαίνω and its compounds do not seem to occur in a directly transmitted text until Diodorus Siculus. This evidence tends to confirm Pelling's view that at least some of the material in this fragment is not from Theopompus, and it is thus uncertain that the historian presented the Etruscan lifestyle as an example of τρυφή.

Moreover, even if we assume, for the sake of argument, that much of the material in sentences (5) and following is from Theopompus, it remains doubtful that the passage is pertinent to the concept of pernicious luxury. The fragment may be strictly ethnographic in intent. Describing the outlandish customs of foreign peoples, regardless of whether these customs had historical significance, is a familiar part of Greek historiography from Herodotus onward. No causative force is attributed in this citation to the Etruscan way of life. We should not simply assume that Theopompus meant Etruscan sexual habits to serve as an explanation of their political decline.[117]

---

116. Pelling 2000 177–80, quoted at 180.
117. Flower (1994, 191) claims that "Theopompus advanced a moral explanation" for the erosion of Etruscan power. It is, however, far from certain that, as Flower says, "many Greek writers commented on the extravagance and luxury of the Etruscans." The evidence cited is all fragmentary and subject to many of the same criticisms as the other citations we have examined. For a recent and extensive discussion of this passage and for a consideration of τρυφή in Theopompus, see Liébert 2006, 51–126.

Athenaeus 12.536b–c = Theopompus, FGrH 115 F 192

(1) ἐτρύφησεν δὲ καὶ Φάραξ ὁ Λακεδαιμόνιος, ὡς Θεόπομπος ἐν τῇ τεσσαρακοστῇ ἱστορεῖ· (2) καὶ ταῖς ἡδοναῖς οὕτως ἀσελγῶς ἐχρήσατο καὶ χύδην ὥστε πολὺ μᾶλλον διὰ τὴν αἰτίαν ταύτην αὐτὸν ὑπολαμβάνεσθαι Σικελιώτην ἢ διὰ τὴν πατρίδα Σπαρτιάτην.

[(1) In *truphē* lived Pharax the Lacedaemonian, as Theopompus reports in the fortieth book. (2) He used pleasures so wantonly and abundantly that, for this reason, that man was much more often taken to be a Sicilian than a Spartan, for his homeland.]

This fragment can tell us very little about Theopompus's views on pernicious luxury. Studies of Athenaean techniques of citation have found that expressions of the form ὡς Θεόπομπος ἱστορεῖ often introduce a paraphrase.[118] The verb ἐτρύφησεν, announcing the topic through its initial position, belongs to the introductory frame and can be ascribed with confidence to Athenaeus. As for sentence (2), the implications of the use of ἀσελγ- have already been discussed.[119] The expression ταῖς ἡδοναῖς ἐχρήσατο ("he used pleasures") is unlikely to be Theopompan. The only good parallel in a directly transmitted Classical author seems to be Plato, *Leges* 7.792e.[120] In contrast, it is an unremarkable turn of phrase in the Roman period.[121]

Whoever may be responsible for the wording of the passage, it is practically devoid of historically significant content. We do not know that Theopompus connected Pharax's un-Spartan lifestyle to any historical consequences.

Athenaeus 12.526d–f = Theopompus, FGrH 115 F 62

(1) καὶ τῶν Παρωκεανιτῶν δέ τινάς φησι Θεόπομπος ἐν ὀγδόῃ Φιλιππικῶν ἁβροδιαίτους γενέσθαι. (2) περὶ δὲ Βυζαντίων καὶ Καλχηδονίων ὁ αὐτός φησι Θεόπομπος τάδε· (3) ἦσαν δὲ οἱ Βυζάντιοι καὶ διὰ τὸ δημοκρατεῖσθαι πολὺν ἤδη χρόνον καὶ τὴν πόλιν ἐπ᾽ ἐμπορίου κειμένην ἔχειν καὶ τὸν δῆμον ἅπαντα περὶ τὴν ἀγορὰν καὶ τὸν λιμένα διατρίβειν ἀκόλαστοι καὶ συνουσιάζειν καὶ

---

118. Lenfant 2007b, 50–53.
119. See above (pp. 292–93).
120. Hdt. 7.101 (κότερα ἀληθείῃ χρήσωμαι πρὸς σὲ ἢ ἡδονῇ; ["should I use truth or pleasure toward you"]) is not apt, since the relevant words mean something like "provide pleasure," rather than "enjoy" it.
121. In Philo, for example, at *LA* 1.104, 2.17, 3.139, 3.236; *Det.* 113, 157; *Prob.* 72.

πίνειν εἰθισμένοι ἐπὶ τῶν καπηλείων. (4) Καλχηδόνιοι... ἐπεὶ δὲ τῆς δημοκρατίας τῶν Βυζαντίων ἐγεύσαντο, διεφθάρησαν εἰς τρυφὴν [lacuna] καὶ τὸν καθ' ἡμέραν βίον ἐκ σωφρονεστάτων καὶ μετριωτάτων φιλοπόται καὶ πολυτελεῖς γενόμενοι.

[(1) And Theopompus says in the eighth book of his *History of Philip* that also some people who live near the Ocean enjoy an easy life.[122] (2) Concerning the Byzantines and the Calchedonians he says these things: (3) The Byzantines, both because they already had had a democracy for a long time and because they had a city located at a trading center and because the whole populace spent its time around the marketplace and the shore, were licentious and accustomed to keep company and drink in the taverns. (4) When the Calchedonians had tasted the democracy of the Byzantines, they were destroyed [lacuna] into *truphē* and from the most moderate and reasonable in their daily lives, they became wine-loving and extravagant.]

Sentence (1) is an introductory frame and its language is Athenaean. As we have seen, the accusative + infinitive construction is frequently associated with para-phrase. Words formed on the base παρωκεαν- ("along the Ocean") are not se-curely attested before Polybius. While the term ἁβροδίαιτος appears once in Thucydides (1.6.3) and once in Aeschylus (*Persae* 41), the great preponderance of its direct attestations is in works from the first century BCE and later.

Sentence (3) is important for evaluations of Theopompus's political outlook because it posits democratic government as a cause of an immoral way of life among the Byzantines. Unfortunately, the description of this immorality pres-ents a problem of interpretation: the Byzantines were "accustomed to keep company in taverns." The verb συνουσιάζω is the sticking point.[123] On the one hand, it occurs in three fragments of Theopompus. This fact would seem to

---

122. Gulick habitually translates ἁβροδίαιτος as "effeminacy," but without justification, we feel. See the discussion in Chapter 1. The framing language is echoed immediately after this passage in a one-sentence paraphrase: κἂν τῇ πρώτῃ δὲ πρὸς ταῖς εἴκοσι τῶν Φιλιππικῶν τὸ τῶν Ὀμβρικῶν φησὶν ἔθνος—ἐστὶν δὲ περὶ τὸν Ἀδρίαν—ἐπιεικῶς εἶναι ἁβροδίαιτον παραπλησίως τε βιοτεύειν τοῖς Λυδοῖς χώραν τε ἔχειν ἀγαθήν, ὅθεν προελθεῖν εἰς εὐδαιμονίαν ("And in the twenty-first book of the *History of Philip*, he [Theopompus] says that the tribe of Umbrians—they are on the Adriatic—appropriately occupy an equally easy way of life to the Lydians and have good land, whence they enter into prosperity." Athen. 12.526f).

123. In practically all of its occurrences, συνουσιάζω ("be together") is a euphemism meaning "have sex." We have rendered it "keep company" to try to match the bland tone of the Greek. Of course, this expression may seem quaintly archaic to the modern reader. Perhaps "hook up" would be better.

indicate that the word was in the original. On the other hand, it does not appear in a direct transmission before Plutarch, and it is difficult to overlook a gap in the evidence of roughly four hundred years. In addition, the three Theopompan citations in question all come from Athenaeus, who also uses the word elsewhere.[124] It is therefore imprudent to insist on categorizing (3) as clearly a verbatim quotation rather than a paraphrase.

In sentence (4), the demoralizing effects of democracy prove contagious, but the case that the present text is a reformulation of Theopompus's original is very strong for this sentence. The first point concerns the expression τῆς δημοκρατίας ἐγεύσαντο ("they tasted democracy"). Analogous metaphorical uses of γεύω ("taste") are not entirely lacking in Classical authors.[125] However, such figurative turns become extremely common in the Roman era.[126] The next datum to be considered is the sequence διεφθάρησαν εἰς τρυφήν. The *prima facie* evidence that Theopompus connects the degeneration of the Calchedonians to a concept of pernicious luxury disappears on closer examination. The transmitted text, meaning roughly "they were ruined into *truphē*," is not possible Greek; whatever εἰς τρυφὴν depended on is missing, and a lacuna has been universally accepted. If we look for a model in order to restore the syntactic integrity of the sentence, there are no good parallels in securely dated Classical texts.[127] Athenaeus himself, on the other hand, uses a single possible analogue ἐξοκέλλειν εἰς τρυφὴν ("run aground on *truphē*") a half-dozen times.[128] It is thus probable that the corruption in (4) obscures Athenaean rather than Theo-

---

124. Athen. 12.518f, 12.531c, 13.567d; Plut., *Alex.*22.6. The noun, συνουσία, occurs a very few times in earlier writing: Plato, *Tht.* 168a2, *Phdr.* 239b1; *Leg.* 1.640d10; Isoc. 15.97.3; Diod. Sic. 1.84.6; Dion. Hal., *Thuc.* 6.

125. Hdt. 4.147.3 has ἐγεύσατο ἀρχῆς ("he tasted command"); Hdt. 6.5.1, ἐλευθερίης γευσάμενοι ("having tasted freedom").

126. In Plutarch, for example, metaphorical uses outpace literal by more than three to one. In that author, the things one can "taste" include φρονήματος οὐκ ἀγεννοῦς ("a spirit not ignoble," *Lyc.* 14.4), σεμνοτέρας ὁμιλίας ("an august association," *Num.* 4.2), τῶν ἐν πόλει διατριβῶν ("the pastimes of city life," *Mar.* 3.1), τοῦ τιμᾶσθαι ("being treated with honor," *Sul.* 3.4), ἀδείας καὶ σχολῆς καὶ πρὸς ξένους καὶ οἰκείους ἐπιμειξίας ("freedom from fear and leisure and the ability to associate with strangers and locals," *Nic.* 9.7.2), and χρυσοῦ καὶ ἀργύρου καὶ γυναικῶν καὶ διαίτης βαρβαρικῆς ("gold, and silver and women and a barbarian lifestyle," *Alex.* 24.3).

127. Plato, *Alc.*1.122b–c (εἰ . . . ἐθέλεις εἰς πλούτους ἀποβλέψαι καὶ τρυφὰς . . . τήν τε ἄλλην ἁβρότητα τὴν Περσῶν ["if . . . you will look to the riches and *truphai* . . . and the other opulence of the Persians"]) is not apt since ἀποβλέψαι εἰς τρυφὰς here means "consider the *truphai*" rather than "emulate the *truphai*." At Arist., *Pol.* 4.1291a, the prepositional phrase is attributive: τούτων δὲ τῶν τεχνῶν τὰς μὲν ἐξ ἀνάγκης ὑπάρχειν δεῖ, τὰς δὲ εἰς τρυφὴν ἢ τὸ καλῶς ζῆν ("but of these arts, some must be necessary, others for *truphē* and living nobly").

128. We have given our arguments that this is an Athenaean expression in Chapter 3.

pompan diction.[129] Finally, any interpretation of this passage must take into consideration the presence of the adjective φιλοπότης in this sentence. The word occurs in five fragments of Theopompus, all of which derive from the *Deipnosophistae*.[130] However, it is rare in non-fragmentary Classical texts: once in Herodotus, once in Aristophanes, and once in Aristotle.[131] After this, the next securely dated attestations are in Plutarch. Athenaeus is fond of the word. Leaving aside the Theopompan fragments, φιλοπότης frequently occurs in a context which makes it likely that it should be ascribed to Athenaeus rather than the original.[132]

In view of these considerations, it will be best to interpret F 62 on the basis of the assumption that the original has been reworked by Athenaeus and that the present form of expression in the passage owes much to the cover text. Within this limit, what does the content of the fragment tell us about pernicious luxury as a historical cause?

As regards both the Byzantines and the Calchedonians, demoralization of lifestyle is presented not as a cause, but as a result. For the Byzantines, political, commercial, and geographic circumstances conspire to led them to drink and debauch. In Calchedon, it is democracy by itself that plays this role (if ἐπεὶ δὲ τῆς δημοκρατίας τῶν Βυζαντίων ἐγεύσαντο does not represent a *post hoc ergo propter hoc* inference by Athenaeus). We have no information about how this process may have worked in either community. In any case, the immoral behavior is given no consequences. The drunkenness and loose-living in the two cities apparently did not give rise to great misfortune.[133] Thus, F 62 seems to

---

129. It is certainly possible that the lacuna is larger than usually thought and that εἰς and τρυφὴν did not form a constituent before the corruption. In this case, the role played by τρυφή in the original is probably irretrievable.

130. In addition to this passage, the references are *FGrH* 115 FF 163, 185, 236, 283.

131. Hdt. 2.174, Ar., *Vesp.*79, Arist., *Hist. an.* 559b. The Aristotelian *Problemata* has three more instances, but its date is uncertain. The abstract noun φιλοποσία ("love of drink") appears Classically at Xen., *Mem.* 1.2.22, 2.6.1 and Plato, *Phd.* 81e.

132. Thus we find φιλοπότης in transitional and introductory sentences: καὶ Ἀλκαῖος δ᾽ ὁ ποιητὴς φιλοπότης ἦν, ὡς προεῖπον. Βάτων δ᾽ ὁ Σινωπεὺς ἐν τοῖς περὶ Ἴωνος τοῦ ποιητοῦ φιλοπότην φησὶ γενέσθαι . . . τὸν Ἴωνα ("Alcaeus the poet, too, was a drink-lover, as I said before. And Baton of Sinope says in his *Ion the Poet* that Ion became a drink-lover," Athen. 10.436f); Ἑρμείας δ᾽ ὁ Μηθυμναῖος ἐν τρίτῃ Σικελικῶν φιλοπότην φησὶ γενέσθαι Νικοτέλη τὸν Κορίνθιον ("Hermeias of Methemna in the third book of his *Sicelica* says that Nicoteles the Corinthian became a drink-lover," Athen. 10.438c). It also occurs in exegesis of poetic evidence. At Athen. 10.433d, Athenaeus explains that the gift of a cup, which Nestor received from Achilles at Patrocles' funeral games, is a reference to the old man's φιλοποσία; the award was made even though Nestor had not won a contest: τοῖς γὰρ φιλοπόταις οὐ παρέπεται τὸ νικᾶν διὰ τὸ ῥάθυμον ("victory does not associate with drink-lovers because of their sluggishness").

133. Although the Calchedonians are said to have been ruined (διεφθάρησαν) after tasting democracy,

offer little that is pertinent to a view which makes Theopompus a proponent of decadence as an explanatory force in history. The passage is even less interesting from the point of view of τρυφή as historiographically significant.

Athenaeus 12.531a–d = Theopompus, FGrH 115 F 114

Θεόπομπος δ᾽ ἐν πεντεκαιδεκάτῃ Φιλιππικῶν Ἱστοριῶν Στράτωνά φησι τὸν Σιδώνιον βασιλέα ὑπερβάλλειν ἡδυπαθείᾳ καὶ τρυφῇ πάντας ἀνθρώπους.

[Theopompus in the fifteenth book of his *Histories of Philip* says that Straton, the king of Sidon, exceeded all men in pleasant living and *truphē*.]

So begins the final citation from Theopompus that is explicitly on the subject of τρυφή. The fragment is long and full of difficulties. Of particular concern is the fact that Athenaeus seems to have drawn his material on Straton from two sources; at the conclusion of the discussion of the king's ἡδυπάθεια and τρυφή, Athenaeus adds:

Ἀναξιμένης δ᾽ ἐν τῷ ἐπιγραφομένῳ Βασιλέων Μεταλλαγαὶ περὶ τοῦ Στράτωνος τὰ αὐτὰ ἱστορήσας . . . φησιν . . .

[Anaximenes, in the work entitled *Royal Reversals*, having related the same things about Straton, . . . says . . .] (Athen. 12.531d)

Thus, we cannot be at all confident about which details come from Theopompus and which from Anaximenes.[134] Uncertainty is increased because the citation is an amalgam of possible verbatim elements and likely Athenaean reformulations. As an example of this last, we may take the introductory sentence quoted above. We have already noticed Athenaeus's common trope of saying that his next subject was the most extreme instance of some characteristic

this expression does not imply any disaster greater than becoming "drink-loving and extravagant." Flower (1994, 124–25) discusses Theopompus's ideas about moral causation in light of the fact that Byzantium did not fall to Philip.

134. The same material is also cited, under the authority of Theopompus, at Ael., *VH* 7.2. This evidence does not help in the interpretation of the fragment, since Athenaeus seems to have been among Aelian's sources and there is no material at *VH* 7.2 which would establish that Aelian had independent access to the historian.

(ὑπερβάλλειν ἡδυπαθείᾳ καὶ τρυφῇ πάντας ἀνθρώπους),[135] and we have also examined the implications of the chronological distribution of the noun ἡδυπάθεια.[136]

This introductory sentence is followed by a comparison between Straton's behavior and that of Homer's Phaeacians. While this material could stem from Theopompus, Athenaeus elsewhere often associates the Phaeacians with τρυφή.[137] The ensuing description contains diction emphasizing Straton's involvement in an intense rivalry for pleasure (φιλοτιμούμενος, ὑπερφιλοτίμως, σπουδάζων, ἄμιλλαν, ἐφιλονίκουν ὑπερβάλλεσθαι, ἐσπούδαζον). Again, the presence of this vocabulary cuts two ways. The passage explicitly relates that Straton was engaged in a contest of hedonism with the Cypriote king Nicocles. At the same time, we have seen in Chapter 3 that expressions of this sort (e.g., "he emulated *truphē*," "he was eager for pleasure") are extremely frequent in the *Deipnosophistae* and seem to be among Athenaeus's favorite ways of presenting examples of immorality.

To do full justice to the complexity of this citation would take more space and effort than the passage would repay. For if we stipulate that, although Athenaeus may have reformulated his original, all the information presented here derives from Theopompus, we are nonetheless left with little support for the importance of pernicious luxury. The important details of the passage are these: Straton held frequent parties with female musicians and prostitutes in attendance. He sent for such women from far and wide. In matters conducive to a life of ease, he was eager to outdo King Nicocles, his rival in pleasure. Each king sought to learn about the other what adornments he had made to his buildings and what extravagances he had committed in sacrificing to the gods. Both made every effort to seem prosperous and happy. In spite of these intentions, Straton and Nicocles both died violently.

If we evaluate this material in terms of traditional views about τρυφή, it becomes apparent that the passage is not particularly apropos. Straton provided a supply of drink, music, and sex for himself and his friends; he spent freely on his buildings and on religious displays. Theopompus's contemporaries would have found such behavior egregious only in its degree. More to the point, there is no indication that the king's lifestyle engendered either effeminacy or hubris,

---

135. See above (pp. 232–33).
136. See above (p. 290).
137. Athenaeus 1.9a, 1.16c, 5.192d. Also at 1.9d, 1.14c, 1.15c, 1.16e, 5.177b, 5.178e, 5.180b, 5.181e, 5.193b, 8.336b, 12.513b, 15.669a.

nor is it clear that the self-indulgence described here had the dire consequences that a theory of pernicious luxury would imply. To be sure, we are told that the happiness of the two kings did not last and that they died badly. Although Athenaeus no doubt wanted his readers to draw the connection, the text does not favor the inference that Straton and Nicocles perished *because of* their moral failings:

> ἐσπούδαζον δὲ δοκεῖν εὐδαίμονες εἶναι καὶ μακαριστοί. οὐ μὴν περί γε τὴν τοῦ βίου τελευτὴν διηυτύχησαν, ἀλλ᾽ ἀμφότεροι βιαίῳ θανάτῳ διεφθάρησαν

> [They were eager to appear fortunate and happy. As for the end of their lives, at any rate, they did not continue prosperous, but both were destroyed by a violent death.] (Athen. 12.531d)

The author—be it Theopompus or Athenaeus—concedes (γε) that the kings' efforts at happiness may have been successful until the end. Thus, there is discontinuity between earlier life and ultimate ruin. This break implies that the story originally made the point that Straton suffered a violent death in spite of his dedication to a life of pleasure.

There is no need to deny that Theopompus looked with distaste at Straton's lifestyle, but we should not, on the basis of this flimsy evidence, promote disapproval to a principle of historical causation.

Heraclides Ponticus

Heraclides Ponticus (c. 388–c. 315 BCE) was born in Heraclea, but spent much time at the Academy in Athens, studying under Plato and Speusippus, and possibly under the Pythagoreans as well.[138] From Diogenes Laertes, we know the titles of forty-six works with subjects as diverse as ethics, physics, music, grammar, rhetoric, and history. Close to 150 fragments survive in a wide variety of later sources, dating as early as the third century BCE.[139]

Heraclides has twelve passages preserved in Athenaeus, five of which particularly interest us here as they mention τρυφή. Four are from *On Pleasure*

---

138. Diog. Laert. 5.89–94. See the excellent text and translation by Schütrumpf (2008) for fragments and all related scholarship.
139. Schütrumpf (2008, 284–87) indexes the sources chronologically.

(Περὶ ἡδονῆς), a work whose only six surviving fragments all derive from book 12 of the *Deipnosophistae*.[140] According to Diogenes Laertes, Περὶ ἡδονῆς was composed in the comic fashion (κωμικῶς, Diog. Laer. 5.88), a remark that has been all but forgotten by editors who employ the fragments to make sweeping moral generalizations. One should bear in mind that Heraclides wrote this work to amuse, not only to castigate.

Athen. 12.554e–f = Heraclides Ponticus, frag. 56 Werhli (frag. 40 Schütrumpf)

ἐν μανίᾳ δὲ τρυφὴν ἡδίστην γενομένην οὐκ ἀηδῶς ὁ Ποντικὸς Ἡρακλείδης διηγεῖται ἐν τῷ περὶ Ἡδονῆς οὕτως γράφων· ὁ Αἰξωνεὺς Θράσυλλος ὁ Πυθοδώρου διετέθη ποτὲ ὑπὸ μανίας τοιαύτης ὡς πάντα τὰ πλοῖα τὰ εἰς τὸν Πειραιᾶ καταγόμενα ὑπολαμβάνειν ἑαυτοῦ εἶναι.

[Not unpleasantly does Heraclides Ponticus narrate in his work *On Pleasure* about a *truphē* that became most sweet within madness, writing thus: Thrasyllus, the son of Pythodorus, from the deme Aixone, once suffered from a certain madness, so that he thought that all the ships coming into the Peiraeus belonged to him. . . .]

There ensues a charming story of how Thrasyllus managed the ships in great happiness until his brother had him cured. This passage follows the familiar pattern of framing language, added by Athenaeus and attributing some behavior to τρυφή. In this instance the word makes little sense in the context—unless the assumption that the ships belong to him may be thought of as a kind of τρυφή—and is not repeated in the quote,[141] nor is there any suspicious wording until the very last sentence, when Thrasyllus told the story of his madness later in life: λύπην μὲν γὰρ οὐδ᾽ ἡντινοῦν αὐτῷ παραγίνεσθαι, τὸ δὲ τῶν ἡδονῶν

---

140. The remaining two passages from *On Pleasure* are Athen. 12.533c = frag. 59 Werhli (frag. 43 Schütrumpf), on Pericles living with Aspasia instead of his wife, and Athen. 12.536f–537c = frag. 58 Werhli (frag. 42 Schütrumpf) about Callias, some of which, from the wording, appears to be derived from common knowledge rather than just Heraclides (ἀλλ᾽ ἐπεὶ καινῶς Ἡρακλείδης ὁ Ποντικὸς ἐν τῷ περὶ Ἡδονῆς ἱστορεῖ περὶ αὐτοῦ, ἄνωθεν ἀναλαβὼν <u>διηγήσομαι</u>. ὅτε τὸ πρῶτον εἰς Εὔβοιαν ἐστράτευσαν οἱ Πέρσαι, τότε, <u>ὥς φασιν</u>, Ἐρετριεὺς ἀνὴρ Διόμνηστος κύριος ἐγένετο τῶν τοῦ στρατηγοῦ χρημάτων . . . , "But since Heraclides Ponticus in his work *On Pleasure* reported new things about him, taking it up again from the beginning, <u>I will describe</u> him: when the Persians first marched out to Euboea, then, <u>as they say</u>, Diomnestus, a man from Eretria, got control over the money of the general . . ." [emphasis added]).

141. Although Gulick (1927–41, ad loc.) inserts it gratuitously into his translation: "Thrasyllus . . . was so afflicted by madness resulting from luxurious living that . . ."

πλῆθος ὑπερβάλλειν ("For [during his madness] no other pain afflicted him, while the magnitude of his pleasure was excessive."). This sentence reads like an Athenaean addition, in that it closes the frame of the story and is also the last sentence in Book 12, but even it may be authentic: ἡδονή is associated with ὑπερβάλλω in the Classical era a handful of times, principally in philosophy,[142] which is consistent with Heraclides' own training, chiefly under Plato (Diog. Laer. 5.86). Lacking anything else suspicious about it, it is better to attribute the passage following the framing language—in other words the entire anecdote about the ships and his cure—to Heraclides, while noting that there is nothing in any way harmful or destructive in this entire episode. On the contrary, Thrasyllus was quite happy in his madness.

Athen. 12.552f–553a = Heraclides Ponticus, frag. 57 Werhli (frag. 41 Schütrumpf)

Ἡρακλείδης δὲ ὁ Ποντικὸς ἐν τῷ περὶ Ἡδονῆς Δεινίαν φησὶ τὸν μυροπώλην διὰ τρυφὴν εἰς ἔρωτας ἐμπεσόντα καὶ πολλὰ χρήματα ἀναλώσαντα, ὡς ἔξω τῶν ἐπιθυμιῶν ἐγένετο, ὑπὸ λύπης ἐκταραχθέντα ἐκτεμεῖν αὐτοῦ τὰ αἰδοῖα, ταῦτα πάντα ποιούσης τῆς ἀκολάστου τρυφῆς.

[Heraclides Ponticus in his work *On Pleasure* says that Deinias the perfume-seller, falling in love because of *truphē* and wasting a great deal of money, when he got to the point where he was beside himself with desires, stirred up by his grief, he castrated himself; unbridled *truphē* caused all these things.]

This "fragment" is a one-sentence paraphrase expressed in an infinitive clause after the verb φησὶ. The story it depicts is not very lucid, and it is made more difficult by ἔξω τῶν ἐπιθυμιῶν, a phrase that is unique in Greek literature and so difficult to render; presumably it is similar to ἔξω τοῦ φρονεῖν ("out of one's wits"), itself a rare idiom.[143] The phrase διὰ τρυφὴν is suspect: two occurrences in Aristotle (*Phys.* 230b2 and *Pol.* 4.1295b17) represent the entirety of the Classical evidence, whereas it becomes a fairly ordinary phrase in the Common Era and Athenaeus himself uses it eleven times.[144]

---

142. Plato, *Gorg.* 475a; *Rep.* 3.402e; *Tim.* 86b; *Leg.* 5.733c, 734a, 734c; *Phlb.* 45b; Arist., *Eth. Nic.* 1118b, 1150b, 1154a; *Eth. Eud.* 2.1222b. Also Isoc. 5.71.

143. Eur., *Bacch.* 853; Dem., *Ex.* 42.2.4; Polyb. 1.15.3, 30.4.5; Dion. Hal., *Antiq. Rom.* 4.70.2, 5.29.3; and a few later uses.

144. Besides here, Athen. 12.515e, 518f, 522b, 523c, 523f, 528c, 536b, 549a, 549e, and 550d.

The core of this narrative is the story that Deinias fell in love, spent a lot of money to obtain that love, failed, and, in his distraught state, castrated himself. Yet the causal comments are disjointed and confusing. How is love and then self-castration to be blamed on τρυφή? The final genitive absolute phrase especially is an editorial addition, summing up a flailing narrative that needs something to tie it back to the greater theme in Athenaeus.

This passage stands as a transition within the *Deipnosophistae* from a long section about fat and thin people, in which this story of castration clearly does not belong, to a new section beginning in the next sentence about perfumes as a symptom of τρυφή. The fact that Deinias was a perfume-seller is all the link that exists between his story and those that follow it, unless τρυφή is introduced. We argue that τρυφή is added gratuitously twice by Athenaeus to the story about Deinias in order to fit this story into his narrative, however tendentiously.

Athen. 12.525f–526a = Heraclides Ponticus, frag. 61 Werhli (frag. 4 Schütrumpf)

Ἡρακλείδης δ᾽ ὁ Ποντικὸς ἐν τῷ περὶ Ἡδονῆς Σαμίους φησὶ καθ᾽ ὑπερβολὴν τρυφήσαντας διὰ τὴν πρὸς ἀλλήλους μικρολογίαν ὥσπερ Συβαρίτας τὴν πόλιν ἀπολέσαι.

[Heraclides Ponticus in his work On Pleasure says that the Samians, practicing truphē to excess, on account of stinginess toward each other, destroyed their city, just as the Sybarites had done.]

This is another example of a one-sentence paraphrase in the form φησὶ + indirect speech. We are instantly skeptical of τρυφήσαντας, occurring as it does in the clause immediately after the verb of saying and paired with the suspect word, ὑπερβολή.[145] The word μικρολογία is equally curious: it is common enough in Greek literature, generally meaning "petty-mindedness," "obsessed with triviality," or, in financial terms, "extreme stinginess," the meaning that occurs to the exclusion of all others in Athenaeus.[146] It is not presented as the

---

145. Schütrumpf (2009, 71 n. 13) presumes that the phrase καθ᾽ ὑπερβολὴν τρυφήσαντας comes verbatim from Heraclides, and only questions whether he is here using Aristotelian diction.
146. Athen. 1.3d, 2.44b, 5.177f, 6.246e, 8.359b. Plutarch uses the word more than 50 times, the vast majority of which mean "stinginess" and the remaining few "pettiness."

cause of anything more than minor arguments, or bickering,[147] and it is difficult to understand how we are to interpret mutual stinginess as the cause of a great city's destruction. Nor are μικρολογία and καθ᾽ ὑπερβολὴν τρυφήσαντας internally consistent: the one represents a failure to spend money while the other is associated with spending money to great excess. Thus this disjointed summary could not have been penned by Heraclides: he probably told stories about the Samians enjoyment of pleasure, but his account is too far condensed and distorted here to enable a meaningful reconstruction.

Athen. 12.512a–c = Heraclides Ponticus, frag. 55 Werhli (frag. 39 Schütrumpf)

(1) Ἡρακλείδης δ᾽ ὁ Ποντικὸς ἐν τῷ περὶ Ἡδονῆς τάδε λέγει· (2) οἱ τύραννοι καὶ οἱ βασιλεῖς πάντων ἀγαθῶν ὄντες κύριοι καὶ πάντων εἰληφότες πεῖραν τὴν ἡδονὴν προκρίνουσιν, μεγαλοψυχοτέρας ποιούσης τῆς ἡδονῆς τὰς τῶν ἀνθρώπων φύσεις. ἅπαντες γοῦν οἱ τὴν ἡδονὴν τιμῶντες καὶ τρυφᾶν προῃρημένοι μεγαλόψυχοι καὶ μεγαλοπρεπεῖς εἰσιν, ὡς Πέρσαι καὶ Μῆδοι. [b] μάλιστα γὰρ τῶν ἄλλων ἀνθρώπων τὴν ἡδονὴν οὗτοι καὶ τὸ τρυφᾶν τιμῶσιν, ἀνδρειότατοι καὶ μεγαλοψυχότατοι τῶν βαρβάρων ὄντες. ἐστὶ γὰρ τὸ μὲν ἥδεσθαι καὶ τὸ τρυφᾶν ἐλευθέρων· ἀνίησι γὰρ τὰς ψυχὰς καὶ αὔξει· τὸ δὲ πονεῖν δούλων καὶ ταπεινῶν· διὸ καὶ συστέλλονται οὗτοι καὶ τὰς φύσεις. (3) καὶ ἡ Ἀθηναίων πόλις, ἕως ἐτρύφα, μεγίστη τε ἦν καὶ μεγαλοψυχοτάτους ἔτρεφεν ἄνδρας. [c] ἁλουργῆ μὲν γὰρ ἡμίσχοντο ἱμάτια, ποικίλους δ᾽ ὑπέδυνον χιτῶνας, κορύμβους δ᾽ ἀναδούμενοι τῶν τριχῶν χρυσοῦς τέττιγας περὶ τὸ μέτωπον καὶ τὰς κόρρας ἐφόρουν· (4) ὀκλαδίας τε αὐτοῖς δίφρους ἔφερον οἱ παῖδες, ἵνα μὴ καθίζοιεν ὡς ἔτυχεν. (5) καὶ οὗτοι ἦσαν οἱ τοιοῦτοι οἱ τὴν ἐν Μαραθῶνι νικήσαντες μάχην καὶ μόνοι τὴν τῆς Ἀσίας ἁπάσης δύναμιν χειρωσάμενοι. (6) καὶ οἱ φρονιμώτατοι δέ, φησίν, καὶ μεγίστην δόξαν ἐπὶ σοφίᾳ ἔχοντες μέγιστον ἀγαθὸν τὴν ἡδονὴν εἶναι νομίζουσιν, Σιμωνίδης μὲν οὑτωσὶ λέγων.

[(1) Heraclides Ponticus in his work *On Pleasure* says the following: (2) tyrants and kings who are masters of all good things and have had experience of every-

---

147. The first time that it has more serious undertones occurs in the fragments of Diodorus Siculus (30.21.3) preserved in a the tenth century collection compiled for Constantine VII Porphryogenitus (*Const. Exc.* 2 (1), pp. 279–80), where the μικρολογία of Perseus alienated the Celts and κατέλυσε πολυχρόνιον καὶ μεγάλην βασιλείαν ("destroyed a very old and very strong kingdom."). The meaning of the statement is not further elucidated, though perhaps his stinginess with gifts caused an affront.

thing, prefer pleasure above all, since pleasure makes the souls of men more exalted. For all who esteem pleasure and choose to live in *truphē* are exalted and magnanimous, like the Persians and Medes. [b] For especially of all men they esteem pleasure and *truphē*, and are the most virile and exalted of all the barbarians. To enjoy pleasure and exhibit *truphē* is the characteristic of free men, for it raises up souls and exalts them. In contrast, to labor is the characteristic of slaves and low-born men, whereby they enfeeble their souls. (3) And the city of the Athenians, as long as it enjoyed *truphē*, was the greatest and engendered the most exalted men. [c] For they wore cloaks dyed purple and they put on embroidered tunics. And binding up the tops of their hair, they liked to wear golden cicadas around their foreheads and temples. (4) Slaves carried folding stools for them, so that they did not have to sit wherever they happened to be. (5) And such were the ones who were victorious in the battle at Marathon and alone bested the power of all Asia. (6) Even the most prudent men, he says, and the ones who are most highly regarded for their wisdom think that pleasure is the greatest good, as Simonides, says here.]

Sentence (1) is typical Athenaean framing language, mentioning author and work, but with no paraphrase or topic added. The words introducing the citation, τάδε λέγει are likely to introduce a literal or near literal quotation.[148] Section (2) begins an unstinting praise of τρυφή and pleasure expressed in direct speech. There is little in the language of this passage to raise suspicions, other than the proliferation of superlatives, which is a red flag, but is in itself insufficient to argue for Athenaean authorship.

This passage is the most likely candidate to be a genuine reflection of Heraclides' own language. However, it is difficult to determine with any certainty where a quotation from Heraclides should end. The standard editions continue the "fragment" down through Athen. 512d, while there are a number of reasons to think it ends earlier. First, all of 512d and some of 512c consist of direct references to other authors: besides Simonides, there is mention of both Pindar and Homer. While it is possible that Athenaeus cites Heraclides who in turn cites these three others, the simpler explanation is that Athenaeus shifts sources as

---

148. The phrase occurs only twice with extant quotations: Athen. 5.188e = Hom., *Od.* 4.60–61; Athen. 13.594a = Dem. 59.50. But compare the following, also literal or very nearly so: 1) λέγειν οὕτως: Athen. 4.155f = Plato, *Leg.* 1.637a; Athen. 5.171a = Xen., *Mem.* 1.5.2; Athen. 5.178a = Plato, *Symp.* 174b; Athen. 5.217b–c = Plato, *Symp.* 172c; Athen. 5.219e–f = Plato, *Prot.* 309a; Athen. 7.311c–d = Ar., *Eq.* 361; Athen. 14.614c–d = Xen., *Symp.* 1.11; 2) τοιαυτὶ λέγοντα: Athen. 15.686d = Xen., *Symp.* 2.204. Contrast λέγει ὡς: Athen. 11.504f is a paraphrase of Xen., *Cyr.* 1.3.1.

they are named. A second problem is that the subject changes entirely in the selection quoted above, from the Persians and Medes to the city of Athens, and the language used there (ἕως + τρυφάω) has only one parallel in extant Greek, at Athen. 12.523e, in clearly expressed framing language before a reference to Ephorus. The Athenian material (3) is most likely derived by paraphrasing Thuc. 1.6.3, augmented by the detail of the folding stools (4), probably obtained from general knowledge. (5) is a closing frame, summarizing the Athenian subsection, while (6) contains a resumptive φησίν, indicating according to Lenfant a transition from paraphrase to direct quote,[149] or, perhaps better, from a different source (Thucydides and general knowledge) back to Heraclides.

It is likely that only a very minimal amount of material is actually derived from Heraclides: the information in (2) and the beginning of (6). Even if it all comes from him, the word τρυφή is used four times in it, and, unlike the typical Athenaean passage on the subject, at no time is it denigrated or blamed for hubris or destruction. On the contrary, τρυφή and pleasure are associated with freedom and manliness.

Athen. 12.523f–524b = Heraclides Ponticus, frag. 50 Werhli (frag. 23 Schütrumpf)

Ἡρακλείδης δ᾽ ὁ Ποντικὸς ἐν δευτέρῳ περὶ Δικαιοσύνης φησίν· ἡ Μιλησίων πόλις περιπέπτωκεν ἀτυχίαις διὰ τρυφὴν βίου καὶ πολιτικὰς ἔχθρας· οἳ τὸ ἐπιεικὲς οὐκ ἀγαπῶντες ἐκ ῥιζῶν ἀνεῖλον τοὺς ἐχθρούς. στασιαζόντων γὰρ τῶν τὰς οὐσίας ἐχόντων καὶ τῶν δημοτῶν . . .

[Heraclides Ponticus in the second book of *On Justice* says: The city of the Milesians encountered ill-fortunes because of the *truphē* of their lifestyle and because of political enmities. For, not content with a reasonable stance, they annihilated their enemies down to the roots. Since the wealthy and the people were fighting each other . . .]

His ensuing story of brutal civil strife is probably derived entirely as the exegesis of what is in itself an extremely dubious oracle involving a people known as the Gergithes. The story, containing grotesque atrocities attributed to the poor in conflict with the wealthy, probably does derive from Heraclides. Whether it is true is a different matter: it is extremely difficult to locate civil war plausibly

---

149. Cf. Lenfant 2007b, 50–53.

in the timeline of Milesian history.[150] It is difficult to understand the role of τρυφή in this episode. One could imagine it described as a cause if the conflict was rooted in the treatment of the poor by the overbearing presumptiveness of the rich: such an argument is in contrast to the story as told, in which the poor were the first to start the carnage, exiling the rich and crushing their children under the hooves of oxen. On the other hand, in view of his belief in Milesian τρυφή and given his view of luxury as the root of many violent evils, it is easy to imagine that Athenaeus took the brutalities of the story and generally categorized them as acts of τρυφή. It is likely that the first sentence of the presumed quotation is actually inserted by Athenaeus, despite its position in direct discourse, just as we have seen elsewhere (e.g., Ps.-Arist., *Mir.* 838a).

Outside of these passages, Heraclides does not mention τρυφή again in the fragments. In fact, he rarely offers any moral generalizations or exempla in the remainder of his works (for Sybaris, see below). Thus, despite titles like Περὶ σωφροσύνης (*On Moderation*), Περὶ ἀρετῆς (*On Virtue*), Περὶ τἀγαθοῦ (*On the Good*) Περὶ εὐσεβείας (*On Piety*), Heraclides is far more likely to be quoted for wars, the movement of the stars, and even the origin of sacred mice (Strabo 13.1.48). One is hard pressed to find any remnants of a moral theme outside of the few pieces in Athenaeus and we have seen that they are dubious.

The Fragmentary Evidence for Sybaris

We have examined some of the strongest evidence put forward by modern scholars who argue that the lost authors of the Hellenistic era proposed a historiographical model in which τρυφή leads to ruin and destruction, through either softness or violent hubris, or both. In almost every instance, we find that the evidence for pernicious luxury as a historical force is suspect: attention to probable distinctions between framing material and source material, as well as consideration of patterns of diction and linguistic usage, reveal that, almost always, statements that make luxury the cause of important historical consequences are more reasonably to be attributed to the cover text than the original author. In the few places where this is not apparent, the role of luxury seems ad hoc and no basis from which to postulate a widespread characteristic for Hel-

---

150. For a detailed argument, see Gorman 2001, 102–7.

lenistic historiography. Thus we conclude that the state of the fragmentary evidence does not support the view that τρυφή was a significant theme in these lost writers.

We would like to conclude this chapter by returning to the specific case of Sybaris. Our study of the fragmentary evidence for τρυφή in general has put us in a position to claim that the theme that Sybaris was destroyed because of its luxury was not certainly present in any source before the early years of the first century BCE. Much of the relevant material has been dealt with already, and we will not repeat it; rather we will briefly discuss the remaining evidence

Athenaeus cites Heraclides Ponticus two times on the subject of Sybaris. We have already discussed the first (Athen. 12.525f–526a = frag. 57 Werhli [frag. 41 Schütrumpf]). In the second, recorded at 12.521e–f = frag. 49 Wehrli (frag. 22 Schütrumpf), we are informed that immorality indeed led to the fall of that city: after the overthrow of the tyrant Telys, the members of his faction were slain on the altars. After this, the statue of Hera turned her back on the city, and a fountain of blood issued from her temple. For this reason, and for trying to undercut the Olympic games by setting up a rival contest with richer prizes (ἄθλων ὑπερβολῇ), the Sybarites were destroyed. This evidence, which comes from Heraclides' Περὶ Δικαιοσύνης, shows no explicit sign of τρυφή. To be sure, both the murders and the attempt to suborn the Olympics are acts that might fall under the heading of hubris. However, we have no warrant to assume a causal relationship between hubris and τρυφή without a clear indication that this is the author's intent.

At 6.273c = frag. 8 Wehrli, Athenaeus cites Chamaeleon of Heraclea Pontica, noting that the work Περὶ Ἡδονῆς to which he refers is sometimes attributed to Theophrastus. The subject is once more Smindyrides, in a passage we have discussed above. Athenaeus has reported that Smindyrides, motivated ὑπὸ χλιδῆς καὶ τρυφῆς, took a thousand servants when he went to compete for the hand of Agariste of Sikyon. Pelling astutely observes that this anecdote is unattributed, while Chamaeleon (or Theophrastus) is given responsibility only for the information that for twenty years Smindyrides saw neither sunrise nor sunset: οὗτος δ᾽ ὁ ἀνὴρ καὶ ἐνδείξασθαι βουλόμενος ὡς εὐδαιμόνως ἔζη . . . οὐκ ἔφη τὸν ἥλιον ("This man, wishing to demonstrate how happily he lived, denied that he had seen the sun . . ."). Thus, for Chamaeleon, Smindyrides was a self-professed proponent of hedonism, and Smindyrides' original claim (wherever Chamaeleon may have found it recorded) was no admission of immoral behavior. Nor do we have any reason, beyond its presence in Athenaeus, to assume that Chamaeleon characterized it as an example of τρυφή.[151] In any case, this passage is not evidence for the existence in the fourth century of a tradition of general Sybarite decadence or for a connection between luxury and the city's destruction.

Timaeus of Tauromenium is Athenaeus's favorite source on Sybaris, with at least seven fragments.[152] The first occurs in the epitome at 1.34c (Timaeus *FGrH* 566 F 47), where we are told that the presence of cabbage weakens the effects of wine: διὸ καὶ Συβαρῖται, φησὶ Τίμαιος, πρὸ τοῦ πίνειν κράμβας ἤσθιον ("It is for this reason, Timaeus says, that the Sybarites ate cabbages before drinking"). Some have seen here an allusion to τρυφή, of which drunkenness is certainly a part. We merely note that it is precisely in reporting the motivation explaining such historical "facts" (i.e., διὸ) that Athenaeus's own concerns override those of this sources. The relationship between the Sybarites fondness for cabbage and their putative love of wine may be an observation of Athenaeus, not Timaeus.

The next passage is more pertinent, since it relates a joke from Timaeus about Sybarite laziness:[153]

ἱστορεῖ δὲ περὶ αὐτῶν Τίμαιος ὅτι ἀνὴρ Συβαρίτης εἰς ἀγρόν ποτε πορευόμενος ἔφη ἰδὼν τοὺς ἐργάτας σκάπτοντας αὐτὸς ῥῆγμα λαβεῖν· πρὸς ὃν ἀποκρίνασθαί τινα τῶν ἀκουσάντων, αὐτὸς δὲ σοῦ διηγουμένου ἀκούων πεπονηκέναι τὴν πλευράν.

---

151. The words that close the discussion of Smindyrides—οὗτος, ὡς ἔοικεν, πρωὶ μὲν ἐκάθευδεν, ὀψὲ δ᾽ ἠγείρετο, κατ᾽ ἀμφότερα δυστυχῶν ("This man, it seems, went to bed early and got up late, unfortunate on both counts.")—are to be taken as Athenaeus's rather than Chamaeleon's, since their point seems to be a contrast with the next example, Hestiaeus Ponticus, who "properly boasted" (καλῶς ἐκαυχᾶτο) that he had not seen the sun come up or go down because of his constant dedication to his studies.

152. For an excellent new treatment of Timaeus, see Baron 2013. Older general treatments: Brown 1958 and Pearson 1987.

153. The discussion of Sybarite τρυφή begins a few lines before Timaeus is named. In this section Athenaeus relates that the Sybarites shackled their bath slaves to keep them from bringing the hot water too quickly and scalding their masters; that smiths and carpenters were forbidden by law from working in the city, since they were too noisy; that it was not even permitted to raise roosters in Sybaris. We have seen that Pelling urges caution in such cases: just because Timaeus is the first authority mentioned in this context, we may not assume that Athenaeus is attributing all the material to that author. Cf. Baron 2013, 243–44. By contrast, Zecchini (1989, 176), in his discussion of this passage, does not even seem to be aware of complications such as those laid out by Pelling: "per l'esattezza il testo di Timeo comincia con la formula introduttiva Περὶ δὲ Συβαριτῶν τί δεῖ καὶ λέγειν." In other words, Zecchini accept the anecdotes preceding citation of Timaeus as the historian's own. Unfortunately, Zecchini offers no arguments to explain his confidence.

[Concerning these people Timaeus relates that a man of Sybaris said that when on the way to the country and spying some workmen digging, he ruptured himself. To which one of his audience responded: I myself hurt a rib just listening to you.] (Athen. 12.518d)

Extreme indolence may be one of the manifestations of τρυφή, yet this story is simply a joke, and we need assume neither a historiographically motivated origin nor that it is part of a systematic argument for τρυφή as a leading factor in the destruction of Sybaris.

However, to complicate matters, the passage just quoted is immediately followed by two more anecdotes. Both concern visits by Sybarites to cities that symbolized a more moderate lifestyle. In the first, some Sybarites at Croton see an athlete softening his own ground in the palaestra and the visitors wonder aloud that the Crotoniates have no slaves to do such a task. In the second story, the location is Sparta, where a Sybarite is invited to a common mess to eat the food of the locals. It is no strange thing, he exclaims, that the Spartans act with such courage: the worst coward would prefer to die rather than to live such a life.

These stories may be seen as evidence of historigraphical dimensions of τρυφή, since the contrast between Sybarite luxury and simpler life at Croton and Sparta may point to a theory of historical causation: τρυφή brought Sybaris to ruin, while moderation made the Crotoniates and Spartans powerful. Of course, for such an interpretation to be persuasive, one must establish that these examples appeared in the text of some historian. Unfortunately, we cannot be confident that they come from Timaeus. In addition to Pelling's general caution that Athenaeus sometimes brings foreign material under the aegis of a named authority, there are more particular reasons for skepticism. One such reason is the repetition at 4.138d of the story of the Sybarite at Sparta. Here Athenaeus gives the tale a nonspecific attribution (φασὶ δέ τινες) that we are perhaps justified in taking as a reference to general knowledge.[154] If the Sparta anecdote may be Athenaeus's own contribution, it is economical to posit the same source for the Croton story. The two make the same point, putting Sybarite sloth in the context of more traditional Greek *mores*.[155] The story of the ruptured Sybarite is not parallel. Thus, in order to put Timaeus's evidence on

---

154. As Pelling does in connection with the Smindyrides passage.
155. The placement of the Croton story immediately after the rupture story may have been suggested to Athenaeus by the occurrence in both of the verb σκάπτω.

Sybaris on the most secure footing, we should mark the end of this fragment at the close of the rupture joke.

Another fragment occurs in close succession. Athenaeus reports that, ὥς φησιν ὁ Τίμαιος, the Sybarites were accustomed to keep dwarfs and small Maltese dogs (Athen. 12.518e–f).[156] As usual, the data are characterized in words (διὰ τὴν τρυφὴν) that may belong to Athenaeus. In any event, no historiographical connection to hubris or to the ruin of the city is evident.

Some interpreters maintain that Athen. 12.522a (= Timaeus FGrH 566 F 44) proves that Timaeus understood τρυφή as a morally corrosive contagion that passed by contact from one city to another:

καὶ Κροτωνιᾶται δ᾽, ὥς φησι Τίμαιος, μετὰ τὸ ἐξελεῖν Συβαρίτας ἐξώκειλαν εἰς τρυφήν· ὥστε καὶ τὸν ἄρχοντα αὐτῶν περιιέναι κατὰ τὴν πόλιν ἁλουργίδα ἠμφιεσμένον . . .

[The Crotoniates too, as Timaeus relates, after the capture of the Sybarites, ran aground upon *truphē*, so that their ruler went around through the city wearing purple . . .]

By now it would be belaboring the point unduly if we were to do more than indicate that the words introducing this passage cannot with certainty be assigned to Timaeus. We are left with information on the dress of the Crotoniate leader that may have been merely ethnographical in import.[157]

Timaeus's testimony at 12.523c has been dealt with in connection to Aristotle. Likewise we have seen that Pelling's arguments make short work of the assumption that Timaeus is responsible for the information at 12.541b–c that Smindyrides went courting "with a thousand cooks and fowlers."

---

156. = Timaeus FGrH 566 F 49. The material attributed to Timaeus is preceded by a sentence in which we are told about the extravagant dress of the Sybarite youth. Once again, the source may be general knowledge.

157. The details of this passage, applying as they do to Croton, do not concern us. However, we note that recognition that ἐξώκειλαν εἰς τρυφήν is not of Timaean origin renders otiose Jacoby's suggestion that the alternate explanation offered here for the Crotoniate custom also goes back to Timaeus, who presented it for polemical reasons. The introductory and concluding words of that alternative are germane to our discussion: οἱ δὲ οὐ διὰ τρυφήν φασι τοῦτο γεγονέναι, ἀλλὰ διὰ Δημοκήδη τὸν ἰατρόν. . . . οὐ τρυφῆς χάριν οὐδὲ ὕβρεως, ἀλλ᾽ ἐπηρείας τῆς εἰς τοὺς Πέρσας ("Others say that this occurred not because of *truphē*, but because of Democedes the physician. . . . not for the sake of *truphē* nor of hubris [do they do this] but out of contempt for the Persians."). Just as the insinuation of motive (οὐ διὰ τρυφήν) in the first part of the quotation is typical of Athenaeus's method, so also the parallel part of the summation (οὐ τρυφῆς χάριν οὐδὲ ὕβρεως) stems from Athenaeus or his proximate source. Thus, one cannot assume that the close connection made here between τρυφή and ὕβρις goes back to an early date.

The final fragment of Timaeus that pertains to Sybaris has been taken up somewhat out of its order in the text of Athenaeus, because it has been the most important source on Sybarite τρυφή in the scholarship. The passage begins with Athenaeus noting that the Sybarites wore clothing made from Milesian wool. The wool trade, it seems, was the basis for the close relationship between the two cities:

ἀφ᾽ ὧν δὴ καὶ αἱ φιλίαι ταῖς πόλεσιν ἐγένοντο, ὡς ὁ Τίμαιος ἱστορεῖ· ἠγάπων γὰρ τῶν μὲν ἐξ Ἰταλίας Τυρρηνούς, τῶν δ᾽ ἔξωθεν τοὺς Ἴωνας, ὅτι τρυφῇ προσεῖχον.

[From this the cities became friends, as Timaeus relates, for of the people of Italy they became close to the Etruscans, and of outsiders to the Ionians, because they were devoted to *truphē*.] (Athen. 12.519b–c = Timaeus, *FGrH* 566 F 50)

Attention to Athenaeus's habit of massaging all evidence to fit his argument must make us aware that it is not unlikely that the reference to τρυφή was not in Timaeus. We are left with a fact about Sybarite dress and the observation that friendship follows trade. So far, there is nothing that would make plausible a tradition in which τρυφή might justify the fall of Sybaris.[158]

On the other hand, the words just quoted are followed by a long series of examples that without doubt illustrate a serious decadence. To give just a few: wealthy Sybarites took three days for a one day journey into the country; roads leading to the countryside were roofed over; they publicly crowned cooks who developed fine dishes. The sequence culminates with an oracle that they will prosper until they hold a man in greater honor than the gods. This prophecy is fulfilled, and the city is soon destroyed due to rivalry both among the Sybarites themselves and between Sybaris as a community and all the other cities—rivalry in pursuit of τρυφή.

No case of τρυφή as principle of historical causation could be clearer. However, Pelling's work has taught us that we cannot assume without further argument that all the examples collected here come from Timaeus. The content of the Timaean fragments on Sybaris already examined tells against his author-

---

158. Cf. Baron 2013, 262–63. We recognize that Milesian wool was well known for its softness. Diodorus Siculus knows of a tradition according to which the law of Zaleukos forbade men to wear a ἱμάτιον ἰσομιλήσιον, thus saving the city from τῆς βλαβερᾶς τρυφῆς (12.21.2). Scholars have noticed that the law is not Archaic, and is probably not older than the fourth century BCE; cf. Bernhardt 2003, 31–32, with notes.

ship of the material at 12.519b–e. The facts that can be securely ascribed to Timaeus are these: the Sybarites kept dwarfs and Maltese dogs, and they wore
Milesian wool clothing and traded with Ionia and Etruria. Timaeus also relates
the joke about the ruptured Sybarite. Such tame material is hardly consonant
with the exaggerated and even fantastic data given here (e.g., that the Sybarites
piped wine from vineyard to warehouse or that they were the first to invent the
chamber pot). Nor can we find in Jacoby's collection of Timaeus's fragments
(*FGrH* 566) any parallel for this kind of uncritical credulity, if we assume that
Timaeus seriously presented these items as facts about Sybaris.[159] Furthermore,
in spite of the scholarly orthodoxy, the evidence that Timaeus was in any way
interested in τρυφή is extremely thin.[160] In view of these considerations, we
conclude, as Pelling does in a similar case at 12.534b–535b, that the instances of
τρυφή in this passage are "a catch-all medley from general knowledge."[161]

Setting aside these factors, even if we were to stipulate that this entire passage was indeed drawn from Timaeus, the text would not support, but would
rather undermine, the position that Timaeus reflects material dating back to
the early fifth century. According to the view in question, details of Sybarite
decadence were meant to justify the city's obliteration by the Crotoniates. The
penultimate sentence of the so-called Timaean citation does in fact propose an
explanation for the fall of Sybaris.

ἐξαναλώθησαν δὲ φιλοτιμούμενοι πρὸς ἑαυτοὺς τρυφαῖς, καὶ ἡ πόλις δὲ πρὸς
ἁπάσας τὰς ἄλλας ἡμιλλᾶτο περὶ τρυφῆς.[162]

[They became exhausted rivaling each other in *truphai*, and as a city, too, they
competed in *truphē* with all in other cities.] (Athen. 12.520c)

The difficulty presented by this statement is apparent. Sybaris was not alone in
its τρυφή, but shared its questionable behavior with a number of other cities.
Thus, it is possible to read these words as implying that the war that destroyed

---

159. It is impossible to rule out that Timaeus relates them as funny stories about the Sybarites. After all,
he does tell the rupture joke. But in this case, the passage would not be evidence that Timaeus recognizes as a historical force the evolution from τρυφή to hubris to destruction.

160. Outside of Athenaeus, the best evidence comes from Diodorus. But here the matter is no clearer than
in the *Deipnosophistae*. To be sure, certain information ascribed by name to Timaeus is characterized
as τρυφή, but the characterization could belong to Diodorus, who was unquestionably interested in
the subject of τρυφή. See below (pp. 350–69) for a full discussion.

161. Pelling 2000, 176.

162. This sentence is bracketed by Jacoby.

Sybaris was fought as the result of a "rivalry in decadence." At the same time, it is hard to see how a reader would not naturally assume that a reference to Croton was included in the words "all the other cities" (ἀπάσας τὰς ἄλλας). An archaic or early classical, pro-Crotoniate, origin for this interpretation of Sybarite ruin is implausible. We prefer to see this statement, and the details of life at Sybaris that attend it, as the product of a later tradition, informed by the imagination of moralists.

At 12.521c (= FGrH 81 F 45), Athenaeus quotes Phylarchus (d. after 220/219) on a Sybarite law that women should be invited to festivals and, further, that invitations to these events should be made a year in advance, so that the people attending might prepare the proper clothing and adornments.[163] While the text of Athenaeus's report of this law contains corruptions, we can nonetheless observe that the fragment has little value as evidence for an immoderate and immoral lifestyle at Sybaris. The quotation begins with the now familiar formula: Συβαρῖται, φησίν, ἐξοκείλαντες εἰς τρυφὴν ἔγραψαν νόμον . . . ("The Sybarites, he says, running aground on *truphē*, wrote a law. . . ."). This is the only explicit reference to the moral dimension of this Sybarite practice. The description of the law itself is morally bland: a year's notice should be given so that those invited might prepare, ἀξίως ποιούμενοι τοῦ χρόνου ("acting in a manner fitting for the time").[164] Thus, it is not clear that Phylarchus cited this law in a context critical of Sybarite behavior.[165] Phylarchus apparently, if we can infer from their juxtaposition in Athenaeus, had set the Sybarite law against a strange statute enacted at Syracuse. On the one hand, the Syracusan law contains severe sumptuary regulations on women's clothing and jewelry. If the Sybarite law was meant to form a contrast with this prohibition, then it might be correct to see it as a kind of reverse sumptuary law, promoting luxury by allowing time for the Sybarites to prepare extravagant costumes. On the other hand, the Syracusan law also sharply restricts women's freedom of movement: for a free woman to

---

163. Scholars identify a concern with τρυφή as a salient characteristic of Phylarchus's work. For example, Schepens (2007, 258), relying on a consensus among earlier experts, calls τρυφή a key theme of the author.

164. Plutarch (*Mor.* 147e) has a reference to the Sybarite custom of giving women a year's notice of their invitation to "dinner" (δεῖπνον) rather than to a law inviting them to "feasts" (ἑορταί). This evidence adds further complexity to a difficult exegesis.

165. The sentence in question is immediately followed by a list of measures taken by the Sybarites for the economic benefit of those who provided for them. If this material is genuinely Phylarchan, it would confirm that the historian was indeed interested in decadence at Sybaris, and Athenaeus's paraphrase might be taken as fairly accurate (cf. Stelluto 1995, 66–71). Unfortunately, we are in no position to make such a claim. The passage may be another example of Athenaeus supplementing a named authority with material from elsewhere.

go out after sundown was tantamount to confessing adultery; even during day-light she must be accompanied by a maid and have the permission of the γυναικονόμοι. If Phylarchus meant this stricture to be the point of his com-parison with Sybaris—and it comes immediately before the introduction of the Sybarite law—then perhaps the focus was upon the contrasting treatment of women in the two cities. Phylarchus's intentions for this reference thus remain too obscure for the fragment to be used to support an interpretation that made τρυφή an important factor in the fall of Sybaris.

On the other hand, events leading to the city's destruction are related a few lines later, when we read that the Sybarites eventually turned to hubris. They slaughtered ambassadors from Croton on the altars, provoking the anger of Hera and their own destruction (Athen. 12.521d). Interpretation is not easy. We cannot be confident that this passage comes from Phylarchus, since he is not named in the immediate context. In addition, transition to this passage is ef-fected by the ἐξοκέλλειν-formula: πάνυ οὖν ἐξοκείλαντες εἰς ὕβριν ("running entirely aground on hubris"). We have seen that this phrase usually occurs at the beginning of a citation and may therefore indicate a change of source. On the other hand, since when introductory, the authority's name is normally men-tioned, ἐξοκέλλειν κτλ. may well be resumptive in this instance.[166] In sum, per-haps Phylarchus knew of a tradition in which Sybaris, through acts of hubris, incited divine anger and mortal retribution. It is at the same time uncertain whether he associated Sybaris with an excessively opulent lifestyle. A fortiori, we cannot assert that Phylarchus saw a causal relationship between τρυφή and the capture of Sybaris by the Crotoniates.

A later fragment, from the Roman era (Athen. 12.528a–b = Polyb. 7.1), will be treated in the section on Polybius in Chapter 5.

Thus we may observe that the Hellenistic evidence for the tradition that an ex-travagant lifestyle contributed to the destruction of Sybaris is no less dubious than the Classical material. More generally, the arguments presented in this chapter lead us to the firm, if unexpected, conclusion that fragmentary evi-dence before the first century BCE for a historiographical theme of pernicious luxury causing the ruin of individuals and the devastation of cities is thor-oughly unreliable. Insisting on a method that investigates both synchronically

---

166. If it is resumptive, we may assume that the intervening material (on certain patent laws and tax ex-emptions) is not from Phylarchus.

and diachronically the language of historical quotations preserved in later authors, we have determined that there is no clear and explicit evidence on the effects of pernicious luxury whose origin is not suspected to belong to the cover text rather than the putative source. We have presented arguments based on the consideration of a great many points of linguistic usage and the like, and we realize that some will be more persuasive than others. However, even if one disagrees on aspects of individual arguments, the sheer preponderance of dubious material revealed by our study should be enough to prompt a thorough reinvestigation of historical fragments. Special attention must be given to fragments with morally charged content, since we have found that assuming accuracy in these cases is particularly risky. We strongly suspect that the view that the Hellenistic historians were preoccupied with ethics and correct behavior is no more secure than their supposed preoccupation with τρυφή.

If, then, τρυφή is not a historiographical theme in Classical or even in Hellenistic writers, when and where did this idea of corrupting luxury arise? We see it as an essentially Roman phenomenon motivated by the social and political ramifications of the Romans' burgeoning prosperity and power in the late Republic. The theme is evident from the earliest extant Roman prose: as their empire grew, the formally stern and frugal Romans were corrupted by the ensuing influx of wealth into their simple and virtuous agrarian community. Thus we now turn to the relevant evidence in Latin writers and the Greek literature produced under Roman rule.

CHAPTER 5

The Theme of Corrupting Luxury at Rome

In previous chapters we have established that current beliefs about pernicious luxury in Greek thought are seriously misguided. In the first place, throughout the Classical and Hellenistic periods the key concept of τρυφή does not mean "luxury" in the sense of unnecessary pleasures or comforts or of extravagant objects. Rather, the term primarily denotes an attitude: the willful assumption that one's own wants—usually, but not necessarily, physical—should be provided for by others. Not surprisingly, it can also indicate an action that brings about the realization of such an attitude, or, more generally, a life in which the attitude is central. This aspect of the meaning of τρυφή is made clear by its frequent contrast with the term ἐπιμέλεια "showing concern" or "taking care." Τρυφή is functionally opposed to ἐπιμέλεια: to exhibit τρυφή is to show a heightened expectation for ἐπιμέλεια from others without reciprocation.

Second, there is no compelling reason to accept that the idea of luxury as a corrupting or destructive force was influential in Greek literature in general or in Greek historiography in particular. On close examination we find that very little weight should be given to what is considered the best evidence for the widely held opinion that the Greeks of the Classical and Hellenistic period explained important historical events at least in part through reference to some natural process of decadence and demoralization initiated by the enjoyment of wealth. While τρυφή can sometimes be inappropriate and detrimental, the evidence does not reveal a necessary, or even usual, process whereby a luxurious lifestyle leads to weakness or depravity and thence to catastrophe. To be sure, some writers at times associate excessive τρυφή either with the softness that arises from relaxing discipline or with the hubris and even violence that come from being accustomed to having one's own way. However, neither of these associations can be shown to have been of causal, historiographical significance in Classical or Hellenistic evidence.

Third, our investigation of the fragments that purportedly demonstrate the prevalence of the idea of pernicious luxury in the Greek writers from Xenophon to Diodorus has revealed instead a sharp distinction, which has not to our knowledge been noticed before. Although the contents of the fragments themselves do not allow us to conclude that τρυφή and related concepts constituted a principle of historical causation in the original authors, there is no doubt that they did so in the works through which the fragments are transmitted. Clearly, by the time of Athenaeus, from whom most of the relevant citations come, the idea in question was an unremarkable commonplace.

It is the purpose of this chapter to examine and explain this distinction. We suggest that the existence among Greek writers of τρυφή as a force of historical causation did not long predate its first secure attestation in the years around the beginning of the first century BCE. Furthermore, we argue that the reason for the development of the belief that pernicious luxury played a leading role in the lives of individuals and nations is to be found in the increasing importance of Rome in the intellectual world of the Greeks. Rome provided an eager audience for history writing that described the rise and fall of states and empires. At the same time, the Romans were the source of distinct views about the causes of such changes of fortune. Thus, we propose that the most familiar aspects of the process of decadence usually identified with τρυφή developed in this context; τρυφή as commonly described in the scholarship is the result of the association of a relatively minor Greek moral concept with a the central Roman concern about the implications of the possession and enjoyment of great wealth.

In support of these hypotheses, this chapter presents a detailed study of the most salient evidence on pernicious luxury in Greek literature from Polybius to Athenaeus (c. 200 BCE–c. 200 CE). In addition to historians, we incorporate several prose authors with a moralistic bent. Hence we include the Jewish philosopher, Philo, and that exemplar of the Second Sophistic, Dio Chrysostom, in order to demonstrate the expanding pervasiveness of the theme of pernicious luxury in Greek prose writing of the empire.[1] Before turning to that topic, how-

---

1. For the sake of space, we have omitted the medical writers and writers in other, far-removed genres such as Lucian. We have also reluctantly excluded both Appian and Plutarch from detailed examination, because neither contributes a novel step to the progression of the idea. Plutarch especially is

ever, we will briefly examine a small sample of the evidence for this idea in the works of Latin authors of the same period.

It was a major and common theme of late Republican Latin literature, especially but not exclusively in works of historical narrative, that Rome had suffered a significant moral decline from the older, simpler days of virtuous men to a contemporary morality whose selfish and indulgent attitude toward its material possessions was a significant cause of social decline. This idea is so widespread as to demand no general substantiation here.[2] Yet it will be instructive to review very selectively the specific evidence that, by the first century BCE, the major extant Latin prose authors shared the conventional opinion that degeneracy was rooted in luxury. Even this limited examination will establish that aspects of the idea of pernicious luxury, which modern scholarship portrays as characteristic of Greek thought, but which are only adumbrated in the Greek evidence, are indisputably attested features of the Roman view.

In particular, for the Roman mind, corruption *inevitably* follows upon luxury, with the process developing along twin paths either to a softness that causes one to be easily conquered or else to offensive violence, which provokes retaliation. When the emphasis is on luxury as a life free from toil and self-discipline, the result is softness or feminization, which leaves the subject militarily inept and defenseless. If, on the other hand, the focus is on the luxurious person's obsessive self-indulgence and arrogant selfishness, opulence is coupled with avarice, and enmity is provoked when the man of luxury forcefully and lawlessly takes goods that belong to others and squanders them in loose-living and wickedness. This second pathology is the more dominant interpretation in Roman writers. When it is applied to the affairs of Rome itself, the result is often perilous civil strife; alternatively, when considering examples from the non-Roman past, this path leads to destruction.

---

extremely lengthy and uses the word τρυφή more than 175 times in his extant works, usually as a vice pure and simple, whose precise meaning is no longer as important as the moral implications that it carries. Recent studies on Plutarchan ethics include van Hoof 2010, Swain 1990, Duff 1999, and the essays in Roskam and van der Stockt 2011, but none of these focuses on the theme of luxury.

2.   An excellent discussion of Roman immorality and its relationship to politics especially is Edwards 1993. For example (2): "Conceptions of immorality were central to the way elite Romans (the only ones whose views survive) thought about themselves, both as a people in relation to those who were not Romans and as individuals in relation to the state and to one another. The criticism of immorality was constructed by Romans themselves as a characteristically Roman activity." We argue that this "characteristically Roman activity" is applied to the concept of τρυφή to create a uniquely Roman version of the morality it implies. Cf. Wheeldon 1989; Fornara 1983, esp. 111–20; Connolly 2009. For Roman sumptuary laws, see Zanda 2011.

The Latin Evidence

There is no exact equivalent of τρυφή in the Latin language, a fact that is not surprising given the complexity of its meaning. A study of the corresponding concept in Roman authors is therefore somewhat problematic. The closest equivalent is represented by the word *luxuria/luxuries* that, tellingly, has no Greek equivalent of its own.[3] Thus, a review of pernicious luxury in Latin literature must look at passages containing a range of terms in addition to *luxuria* and its cognates. These terms include *avaritia*, *otium*, and *licentia*.[4] Of particular interest are passages in which these terms appear in clusters. By scrutinizing these, we may identify the moral implications of that expectation which the Romans attributed to a life of ease and the enjoyment of material plenty.

The first point to emphasize is that the paradigmatic relationship between lifestyle and morality is established by the time of our earliest extant prose authors. We will restrict the discussion here to Cicero, Sallust, and Livy, writers who reflect a theme that is already well-formed and mature.[5] Some of the first expressions of this theme occur early in Cicero's career, in his defense of Sextus Roscius of Ameria, from 80 BCE or shortly thereafter.[6] In this speech, the orator argues that Roscius's devotion to a simple life in the country was not, as the prosecution maintained, a sign of an antisocial character, but an indication of probity:

> de luxuria purgavit Erucius, cum dixit hunc ne in convivio quidem ullo fere interfuisse . . . cupiditates porro quae possunt esse in eo qui . . . ruri semper habitarit et in agro colendo vixerit? quae vita maxime disiuncta <a> cupiditate et cum officio coniuncta est.

---

3. Isager (1993) equates the two, but is using an unsophisticated dictionary definition on his way to argue a thesis that Roman attitudes toward *luxuria* reflected the Romans' ambivalence to their Greek heritage.

4. For *luxuria* as material culture and *otium* as luxury time in the writings of the early empire, especially Pliny, see Leach 2003.

5. Lintott 1972, 638: "In my view the tradition which ascribed the political failure of the Republic to moral corruption derived from wealth and foreign conquest, developed from the propaganda of the Gracchan period." For reviews of the ancient ideas on the sources of Roman greatness, see Spawforth 2012; Lind 1972; Walsh 1963 (for Livy); Webster 1936. Lind (235–40) examines the influence of Ennius on the moral views of extant authors. We are not discussing Ennius here because of the fragmentary nature of the evidence and because we believe that the idea that his works set a moral tone embraced by subsequent, surviving authors is uncontroversial.

6. Arguments about the date are contained in Berry 2004. For Cicero's views on history and the writing of history, see Hengst 2010, ch. 1.

[Erucius cleared him from the charge of luxury when he said that Roscius was almost never even present at a banquet. . . . As for feelings of greed, can they exist in one who has always lived in the country and spent his life farming the land? This life is furthest removed from greed and most closely connected with duty.] (Cic., *Rosc. Am.* 39)

The unquestionable virtue of this kind of life is driven home through references to the *maiores*, who were often called from the plow *qui consules fierent* ("to become consuls," 50). These great men were content with their private means: *suos enim agros studiose colebant, non alienos cupide appetebant* ("For they zealously farmed their own fields, and did not longingly desire those of other men." 50). Their simple and restrained natures brought the richest of rewards to the community: *quibus rebus et agris et urbibus et nationibus rem publicam atque hoc imperium et populi Romani nomen auxerunt* ("In this way, they increased the republic and this empire and the name of the Roman people with fields and cities and nations." 50).

Contentment with a life of hard work on one's own modest portion was a quintessential aspect of the old Roman traditional virtue. The famous exemplar of this quality was Cincinnatus. Livy's telling of this story is evocative of conventional Roman values:

operae pretium est audire qui omnia prae divitiis humana spernunt neque honori magno locum neque virtuti putant esse, nisi ubi effuse afluant opes. spes unica imperii populi Romani, L. Quinctius trans Tiberim . . . quattuor iugerum colebat agrum, . . . seu fossam fodiens palae innixus, seu cum araret, operi certe, id quod constat, agresti intentus . . .

[It is worth the effort of listening for those who spurn all aspects of human life in favor of riches and think that there is no place for great honor or virtue except where wealth pours out abundantly. The only hope for the dominance of the Roman people, L. Quinctius, was farming four *iugera* of land across the Tiber . . . perhaps bending over a spade, digging a ditch, perhaps when he was plowing, certainly, it is agreed, when he was busy at some rustic task . . .] (Livy 3.26.7–9)

Wiping off the dust and sweat of his unassuming labors, he came to the rescue of the Roman people.

Sallust, too, in the early chapters of the *Catiline*, describes an idyllic, honorable past at Rome, when a simple lifestyle prioritized patriotic military exploits over material possessions. It was a time without greed: *etiam tum vita hominum sine cupiditate agitabatur, sua quoique satis placebant* ("even then the life of men was pursued without desire, and his own possessions were satisfactory for each," Sall., *Cat.* 2.1). Although Romans did not seek to possess the goods of others, their city prospered through a combination of physical growth and good morals. Rome therefore became a target for its neighbors: *sicuti pleraque mortalium habentur, invidia ex opulentia orta est* ("As often happens in human affairs, envy was born out of prosperity." Sall., *Cat.* 6.3). However, the Romans prevailed against their covetous enemies, since their young men found their luxuries in the implements of war: *magisque in decoris armis et militaribus equis quam in scortis atque conviviis lubidinem habebant* ("They were more eager for beautiful arms and military horses than for prostitutes and banquets," Sall., *Cat.* 7.4). They rivaled each other for glory on the battlefield, in being the first to wound an enemy or climb a wall. Sallust sententiously sums up the relationship between the Old Romans and material possessions: *gloriam ingentem, divitias honestas volebant* ("They wanted enormous fame, but honest wealth." Sall., *Cat.* 7.6). Too great a concern with affluence and comfort is incompatible with the public good: *concordia maxuma, minuma avaritia erat* ("There was the greatest possible harmony and the least possible avarice." Sall., *Cat.* 9.1).

Just as the theme of the simple and triumphant days of old was commonplace, so too the tale of the decline from virtuous parsimony into the corrupting luxury of the current age.[7] In his agrarian speeches, Cicero points to the two possible consequences of abundance: arrogance and weakness.

> Campani semper superbi bonitate agrorum et fructuum magnitudine, urbis salubritate, descriptione, pulchritudine. ex hac copia atque omnium rerum adfluentia primum illa nata est adrogantia qua a maioribus nostris alterum Capua consulem postularunt, deinde ea luxuries quae ipsum Hannibalem armis etiam tum invictum voluptate vicit.

> [The Campanians were always haughty because of the fertility of their fields, the size of their harvests, the healthfulness, arrangement, and beauty of their city.[8]

---

7.   Lind (1972, 243) describes the word in Sallust's time thus: "*luxuria*, a sinister word even to modern Latin peoples, with overtones of gloomy debauchery." For Sallust on the decline of *virtus* and *concordia* at Rome, see Earl 1961.

8.   The phrase *bonitate agrorum et fructuum magnitudine* is very similar to the phrase used by Diodorus

From this abundance and profusion of all things arrogance was born first, because of which they demanded from our ancestors that one of the consuls be
from Capua, then that luxury that conquered Hannibal himself with pleasure,
who up until then had been unconquered by arms.] (Cic., *Leg. agr.* 2.95)

It is significant that, in Cicero's scheme, having more than one needs for a plain
and virtuous life introduces two paths to decadence, one leading to arrogance
and the other to the softness that comes from abandoning military discipline.
Although Cicero does not specify the details of the process (or processes) of
degeneration, it is noteworthy that the *adrogantia* of the Campanians was no
less a result of abundance than was the *luxuria* that overcame Hannibal and his
army with *voluptas*. Thus, Cicero lays blame for *adrogantia* on Campania's *copia
atque omnium rerum adfluentia* because of the effect it has on the inhabitants'
vitae consuetudo. In particular, Cicero locates the source of both *adrogantia* and
luxuria in the easy lifestyle made possible by this abundance, a sentiment emphasized by the contrast he draws with the Ligurians, whose own moral qualities were a product of their laborious way of life.[9]

It should be apparent that, in this passage, Cicero's argument has reference
to the Greek concept of τρυφή, since he is mirroring those two aspects of τρυφή
that we have identified as being widespread in Greek literature. Τρυφή as the
belief that one's needs and desires should be seen to by others may indeed be
rendered into Latin by *adrogantia*.[10] The expectation of an exaggerated
ἐπιμέλεια on the part of others sometimes implies in turn the negligence of
one's proper duties.[11] Thus, during their winter in Capua, *luxuria* turned the

---

Siculus in different variations to describe fertile land, δαψιλῶς τῆς χώρας χορηγούσης τὰ πρὸς τὴν
ἀπόλαυσιν καὶ τρυφήν ("the land provided abundantly the things needed for enjoyment and *truphē*"):
Diod. Sic. 5.19.2. Cf. 2.16.4, 3.42.2, 4.20.1, 5.10.3, 5.19.4.

9. *Ligures duri atque agrestes; docuit ager ipse nihil ferendo nisi multa cultura et magno labore quaesitum*
    ("The Ligurians are tough and wild. The land itself has taught them; it bears nothing unless it is
    sought with much cultivation and great toil." Cic., *Leg. agr.* 2.95).

10. This attitude of entitlement, such an important aspect of τρυφή, is likewise evident in Livy's descrip-
    tion of these same Capuans: *inde Capuam flectit iter, luxuriantem longa felicitate atque indulgentia
    fortunae, maxime tamen inter corrupta omnia licentia plebis sine modo libertatem exercentis* ("From
    there Hannibal turned toward Capua, a city luxuriating in its long good luck and the kindness of
    fortune; mainly, however, among all its corruptions, [it luxuriated] in the license of the common
    people exercising freedom without measure." Livy 23.2). More specifically, the Capuan plebian pop-
    ulation had subordinated the city's senate to its every whim and wish. This behavior is similar to that
    mentioned by Cicero, and it seems fair to say that Cicero's *adrogantia* and Livy's *licentia* indicate the
    same moral characteristic viewed from slightly different perspectives. The attitude in question is an
    integral part of a life of *luxuria* (*luxuriantem* = τρυφῶσαν).

11. Thus the contrast between *luxuria* and *diligentia* in Cicero: *nihil ceterorum simile Graecorum, nulla
    desidia, nulla luxuries, contra summus labor in publicis privatisque rebus, summa parsimonia, summa*

Carthaginian army from military matters to pleasure, with debilitating results. However, while Cicero clearly had τρυφή in mind when he composed this passage, the use that he makes of this concept is sharply different from the way we have usually seen τρυφή used in Greek sources from before the Roman period: he indicates that pernicious luxury was directly responsible for significant, and quite specific, historical events.

Another point of distinction between the Roman view of decadence and the earlier Greek concept of τρυφή lies in the emphasis that Roman sources lay upon the inevitability of moral decay as a consequence of luxury. This necessity can, for Cicero at any rate, be understood as a species of a larger and more generally deterministic world view. Thus, Cicero claims that behavior is based less on inherited qualities than on environmental factors.

> non ingenerantur hominibus mores tam a stirpe generis ac seminis quam ex eis rebus quae ab ipsa natura nobis ad vitae consuetudinem suppeditantur, quibus alimur et vivimus. Carthaginienses fraudulenti et mendaces non genere, sed natura loci . . .

> [Morals are not so much implanted into people from the origin of their race or parentage as from those things that nature itself supplies us for our habit of life, by which we live and are nourished. The Carthaginians are untrustworthy and deceitful, not by race, but from the nature of the place. . . .] (Cic., *Leg. agr.* 2.95)

Because, then, of the richness of Campania, the colonists at Capua were doomed:

> singularis homo privatus, nisi magna sapientia praeditus, vix cancellis et regionibus offici magnis in fortunis et copiis continetur. nedum isti . . . coloni Capuae in domicilio superbiae atque in sedibus luxuriosis conlocati non statim conquisituri sint aliquid sceleris et flagiti, immo vero etiam hoc magis quam illi veteres germanique Campani, quod in vetere fortuna illos natos et educatos nimiae tamen rerum omnium copiae depravabant, hi ex summa egestate in

---

diligentia ("There is nothing similar among the rest of the Greeks: no laziness, no luxury, but rather the utmost toil in public and private business, the utmost parsimony, the utmost diligence." Cic., *Verr.* 2.2.7). Cf. *ex contrario ducitur sic, ut si quis hominem prodigum et luxuriosum inludens parcum et diligentem appell<et>* ("an *ex contrario* move is made if someone mockingly calls an extravagant and luxurious person thrifty and diligent." Ps.-Cic., *Rhet. ad Her.* 4.46).

eandem rerum abundantiam traducti non solum copia verum etiam insolentia commovebuntur.

[A single private citizen, unless he is endowed with great wisdom, scarcely is able to be contained within the bars and bounds of duty when he is exposed to great fortunes and abundance. Still less could those . . . colonists settled at Capua, in the home of haughtiness and in the seat of luxury, avoid immediately seeking out some kind of crime or shameful act, in truth even more so than those older, native inhabitants of Campania, since these were born and raised in an accustomed fortune and nevertheless were corrupted by an excessive abundance of all things. The others, being transferred from the greatest poverty into such an abundance of things, will be swayed not only by the abundance, but also by the fact that it is unaccustomed.] (Cic., *Leg. agr.* 2.97)

The progression is familiar. *Luxuria* is coupled with *superbia*, just as τρυφή is often paired with hubris, and the result is *scelus* and *flagitium*. New wealth is harder to bear than inherited riches, but both corrupt the possessor unless he is an extraordinarily wise man. The vast majority of people simply cannot endure abundance without it turning them to depravity.

The same view of moral decay associated with luxury occurs elsewhere in Cicero. At *De oratore* 2.171 he says, *ex causis autem rerum sic: avaritiam si tollere vultis, mater eius est tollenda, luxuries* ("From the causes of things, you should conclude, if you wish to abolish avarice, you must abolish its mother, luxury."). This passage gains significance from the fact that Cicero presents it as a quotation from a speech given by Crassus the Orator in his youth. If Cicero is correct, the idea that *luxuria* was a sufficient cause of immorality (here *avaritia*) was familiar enough to be used as an argument in a public context already before 100 BCE.

In the *Pro Roscio Amerino*, where Cicero's purpose is to contrast the virtuous agrarian life with the malignant urban setting, we find the clearest evidence that, for Cicero, *luxuria* means primarily to "consume resources immoderately" or the like. Thus Cicero can report, *sperat se posse quod adeptus est per scelus, id per luxuriam effundere atque consumere* ("he hopes that he is able to squander and use up through luxury that which he has acquired through crime." Cic., *Rosc. Am.* 6). Later Cicero contrasts *luxuria* with *parsimonia*, when he laments that cities have destroyed morals:

in urbe luxuries creatur, ex luxuria exsistat avaritia necesse est, ex avaritia erumpat audacia, inde omnia scelera ac maleficia gignuntur; vita autem haec rustica, quam tu agrestem vocas, parsimoniae, diligentiae, iustitiae magistra est

[In the city, luxury comes into being, and from luxury it is necessary that avarice springs forth, and from avarice boldness erupts, and thence all crimes and evils deeds are born. In contrast, the country life, which you call boorish, is the teacher of parsimony, diligence, justice.] (Cic., *Rosc. Am.* 75).[12]

If *luxuria* here can be seen to correspond to τρυφή, then *audacia* may suggest ὕβρις, *avaritia* κόρος, and *diligentia* ἐπιμέλεια. Thus, by Cicero's way of thinking, the progression from luxury to avarice, and then to rashness and crime is inescapable (*necesse est*), and stands in sharp contrast to the lives of those frugal farmers of the past who did not covet things that were not their own.[13] The theme of corrupting luxury is complete.

For Livy, as indeed for Cicero, luxury is often used as a term for private consumption. Working at her wool, Lucretia is contrasted with the other officers' wives, who are feasting (*in convivio luxuque*, Livy 1.57.9).[14] In the programmatic statement at Livy 1.pr.11, *avaritia* and *luxuria* are contrasted with *paupertas* and *parsimonia*, while at 7.25.9 the senators are worried about trying to raise a large army in a situation where *adeo in quae laboramus sola crevimus, divitias luxuriamque* ("Truly we have resolved on the only things toward which we strive, riches and luxury."). Public expenditure is thus contrasted with private opulence. Especially telling is the citation at 34.4.1–2, where Livy has Cato speak in the debate over the Oppian Sumptuary Law:

saepe me querentem de feminarum, saepe de virorum nec de privatorum modo sed etiam magistratuum sumptibus audistis, diversisque duobus vitiis, avaritia et luxuria, civitatem laborare, quae pestes omnia magna imperia everterunt.

---

12. Cf. *Off.* 1.123: *luxuria vero cum omni aetati turpis, tum senectuti foedissima est* ("For in truth luxury, a wicked thing at any age, is most foul in old age"). At *Rhet. ad Her.* 2.34, the author chides those who oversimplify complex ideas by saying, *duae res sunt, iudices, quae omnes ad maleficium inpellant, luxuries et avaritia* ("There are two things, jurors, which push all men to evil deeds, luxury and avarice."). But in doing so he reflects a truism that is current among at least some people of his time.

13. The generally ineluctable link between lifestyle and moral character carries the main force of persuasion at *Rosc. Am.* 75. Cf. *Verr.* 2.2.7.

14. For luxury characterized by feasting, cf. Cic., *Rosc. Am.* 39, *Verr.* 2.3.169, by the seduction of women, cf. *Verr.* 2.2.134.

[Often you have heard me complaining about the expenses of women, but also about those of men, of both private individuals and public officials, and that the state is suffering from two diverse vices, avarice and luxury, the plagues that have overturned all the great empires.]

By distinguishing avarice from luxury (*diversis vitiis*), he is demonstrating for us two sides of the same coin: the first is the unbridled acquisition of wealth and the second is the intemperate spending of wealth on private purchases.

However, another aspect of Livian luxury is reminiscent of Greek τρυφή. In a number of passages, the context is not about money and material possessions at all. Rather, the word *luxuria* denotes an attitude of entitlement, particularly the assumption of political power beyond what is appropriate. For example, after the death of Tarquin is announced:

> sed patribus nimis luxuriosa ea fuit laetitia; plebi, cui ad eam diem summa ope inservitum erat, iniuriae a primoribus fieri coepere.

> [But for the Fathers, their joy was too presumptuous, while the plebs, who up until then had been attended to with utmost consideration, began to be treated unjustly by the leading men.] (Livy 2.21.6)

Luxuriosa laetitia describes a change in relationship between the plebs and patricians in which the previous polarity between expectations and their fulfillment (cf. τρυφή and ἐπιμέλεια) has been essentially reversed. Instead of serving the interests of the plebs (*inservitum erat* ≈ ἐπεμελήσαντο), the patricians were insisting on the primacy of their own concerns (hence *luxuriosa*) and in the process transgressing the bounds of proper behavior (*iniuriae*) toward the common people. A similar passage contains the first instance where the tribunes take over the Senate's power to declare a triumph. As a result, *haec victoria tribunorum plebisque prope in haud salubrem luxuriam vertit* ("This victory of the tribunes and plebs turned them near to an altogether unhealthy luxury." Livy 3.64.1). Livy goes on to explain the nature of that luxury: a conspiracy formed in which the tribunes planned to be reelected to their office, justifying their attempt by complaining that the patricians were attempting to abridge the privileges of the masses. Again, the *luxuria* takes the form of assuming political powers beyond what was right in a context of class factionalization.

This *luxuria* could easily do damage to its possessor. When the decemvirs were created, Livy immediately announces that their reign was to be very short:

minus insignis, quia non diuturna, mutatio fuit. laeta enim principia magistratus eius nimis luxuriavere ("The change in government was less important because it was not long-lasting. For the happy beginning of the office luxuriated too much." Livy 3.33.2). The decemvirs dramatically abused their position and were deposed as a result. In the same way, at Livy 2.48.3, when the consul Caeso Fabius proposed a land distribution law that would benefit the plebs, the patricians scorned it and him: *questi quoque quidam nimia gloria luxuriare et eva-nescere vividum quondam illud Caesonis ingenium* ("And some even complained that the once vigorous good sense of Caeso was luxuriating and vanishing because he had too much glory."). Livy goes on to say that no civil strife resulted (*nullae deinde urbanae factiones fuere*, 2.48.3), implying that one would naturally assume it in these circumstances. Instead, Caeso was sent off to fight the celebrated war between his Fabian clan and the city of Veii, and this was the last we hear of the land bill for the time being.[15]

Thus, for Livy the meaning of the word *luxuria* goes far beyond private spending to include an attitude that one will get one's own way, that others will give one influence and power, especially in the political realm, and that that attitude can be harmful to its bearer.

In his famous proemium, Livy identifies the chief aim of his work as the illumination of the importance of morality in the course of history.

ad illa mihi pro se quisque acriter intendat animum, quae vita, qui mores fuerint, per quos viros quibusque artibus domi militiaeque et partum et auctum imperium sit; labente deinde paulatim disciplina velut desidentes primo mores sequatur animo, deinde ut magis magisque lapsi sint, tum ire coeperint praecipites, donec ad haec tempora quibus nec vitia nostra nec remedia pati possumus perventum est.

[In my opinion, each reader should pay sharp attention to these questions: what was the lifestyle, what were their morals, through what sort of men and by what techniques at home and at war was power gained and increased? Then, let him trace how, with discipline slipping little by little, morals first declined, as it were, then slid more and more, then began to fall headlong, until we arrived at the present situation, in which we are able to endure neither our vices nor their remedies.] (Livy 1.pr.9)

---

15. Other instances of harmful luxury include Livy 7.29.5 and 23.45.2.

The process by which this headlong decline is effected is further specified:

> ceterum aut me amor negotii suscepti fallit, aut nulla umquam res publica nec maior nec sanctior nec bonis exemplis ditior fuit, nec in quam [civitatem] tam serae avaritia luxuriaque immigraverint, nec ubi tantus ac tam diu paupertati ac parsimoniae honos fuerit. adeo quanto rerum minus, tanto minus cupiditatis erat: nuper divitiae avaritiam et abundantes voluptates desiderium per luxum atque libidinem pereundi perdendique omnia invexere.

> [Either love of the task I have undertaken deceives me or no other state was ever greater or more blessed or richer in good examples, nor in any other society did avarice and luxury enter so late, nor was there a place where such great esteem of poverty and frugality existed for so long. For truly the less they possessed, the less they desired. Recently riches have brought in avarice, and abundant pleasures have brought in the desire for ruin and the destruction of all things through luxury and lust.] (Livy 1.pr.11–12)

Again, *avaritia* and *luxuria* are paired, and with them comes a destructive *libido*.[16] They originate in the wealth and pleasure that come from prosperity, and result in individual ruin and widespread destruction.[17] The familiarity of the pattern should not lead us to overlook an important feature of the process of decadence as Livy understands it: his expressed pride in Roman resistance to moral decline implies that that decline is a usual consequence of power and prosperity. Rome was exceptional because avarice and luxury arrived *tam serae* and because frugality was valued *tam diu*. If Livy saw the working of pernicious luxury as merely a possible and contingent result of imperial success, then his

---

16. Feldherr (1997, esp. 269) makes the point that both *avaritia* and *luxuria* are "fundamentally foreign" and threaten great damage to the republic. He goes on to say that, in Livy, greed does not cause the import of riches, but rather the presence of riches spawns greed and luxuriousness. Cf. Evans 2011. Earl (1961, 111–21, esp. 112) believes that Sallust has avarice give rise to luxury, and not the other way around. But Sallust's moral scheme is not entirely consistent from one passage to the next, so Lind (1972, 246) is able to say, "It is soon apparent to even a casual reader that Sallust really has no particular system of ethical values as a foundation for his criticism beyond an unshakable conviction that human nature is totally depraved." Levick (1982) notes Sallust's inconsistencies and dwells at length on the theme of *ambitio*. Cf. Lintott 1972, 627–28.

17. Miles (1995, 80) says that Livy is expressing an original interpretation of history: "where Livy's narrative can be compared with others', the emphasis on *luxuria* appears repeatedly as the result of his own modification of received tradition." Yet Livy is certainly in agreement with the passages from Cicero that we have examined. Forsythe (1999, 43) points out that Livy is more interested in establishing larger moral themes than in critically evaluating the historicity of individual events. For a detailed discussion of process of Latin historical writing, see Cornell 1986a, 1986b.

words would make little sense. Thus, Rome was uniquely worthy of Livy's *nego-tium* due to its unparalleled ability to resist for so long the natural allure of *luxuria* and its inevitable ill effects.

Because moral decline associated with luxury was a necessary process, the Romans, ironically, were ethically far better off before they subjugated Italy, much less the Mediterranean. Conquest brought with it riches, whence came avarice and corruption.[18] In addition, according to Sallust's interpretation of history, moral depravity came not just from the wealth flowing to the Romans as military success expanded their empire; decadence was also inherent in the absence of a worthy foe.[19] Once Carthage was removed, the Romans did not know how to manage their own prosperity:

> . . . iis otium divitiaeque, optanda alias, oneri miseriaeque fuere. igitur primo pecuniae, deinde imperi cupido crevit: ea quasi materies omnium malorum fuere. namque avaritia fidem probitatem ceterasque artis bonas subvortit.

> [. . . to these men leisure and riches, sought after by other men, became a bur-den and a source of misery. Therefore, first desire for money and then for em-pire grew, and these things became as it were the source of all evils. For avarice perverted trust, integrity, and all other good traits.] (Sall., *Cat.* 10.2–4)

This passage introduces another aspect of the theme of decadence through prosperity that is absent in earlier Greek literature: peace is, from the point of view of morality, more perilous than war. Livy, too, establishes this idea in any number of passages scattered throughout his work. For example, at Livy 2.52.2, he says, *ex copia deinde otioque lascivire rursus animi et pristina mala, postquam*

---

18. Evans 2011, 3: "Thus Roman poets and moralists write a narrative of military strength that autode-structs, as Rome's failure springs from its own fantastic success." Evans discussed the further devel-opment of the theme, beginning with Livy and proceeding through Horace, Juvenal, Lucan, and other imperial writers. "Moreover, *every* complaint of foreign contamination is also a celebration of Rome's triumph and its rapidly burgeoning empire" (5).

19. Of course, Sallust's view of early Roman history is distorted, to say the least: Earl (1961, 41) rightly calls it highly idealized and exaggerated. Besides converting early Republican wars of conquest in Italy into righteous self-defensive campaigns, to say that Rome lacked an external enemy after the fall of Carthage in 146 BCE is a gross misrepresentation of events, when Rome was at war more or less constantly for much of the late Republic. His idea that the removal of Carthage was the turning point for Roman morality is followed by Velleius Paterculus 2.1; Florus 1.33.1; Augustine, *De civ. D.* 1.30; Orosius 5.8.2. Livy (39.6.7) places the crisis at 187 BCE, Polybius (31.25.3) at 168 BCE, and Piso (cited in Pliny, *NH* 17.244) at 154 BCE. See the discussion in Earl 1961, esp. ch. 4; Lintott 1972; Ro-mano 2003.

foris deerant, domi quaerere ("From plenty and leisure, their spirits again lost restraint and, since they were absent abroad, they sought the old evils at home.").[20] To be fighting an external enemy is to be serving one's country and competing in patriotism, while peace and prosperity bring with them idleness, luxury, avarice, and a personal ambition that is contrary to the good of Rome.

In earlier Greek sources, greed is not particularly associated with τρυφή, but matters are quite different in these Roman sources, where we have seen *avaritia* closely joined to the depiction of pernicious luxury. For Sallust, at least, the two ideas are so intertwined that avarice may play the role usually reserved for *luxuria*:

> avaritia pecuniae studium habet, quam nemo sapiens concupivit: ea quasi venenis malis inbuta corpus animumque virilem effeminat, semper infinita <et> insatiabilis est, neque copia neque inopia minuitur.

> [Avarice contains the zeal for money, for which no wise man longs. Just as if it is soaked in evil poisons, it feminizes the male body and soul, always unending and insatiable, never diminished by abundance or by lack.] (Sall., *Cat.* 11.3)

Here it is *avaritia*, which strips men of their masculinity, an effect which implies that the *pecuniae studium* does not aim at the possession of money for its own sake, but as a means of the pleasures and luxuries that cause softness.

More usually, however, the combination of greed and luxury—as we have seen above in Cicero's pairing of *adrogantia* and *luxuria*—produce aggressively antisocial behavior:

> igitur ex divitiis iuventutem luxuria atque avaritia cum superbia invasere; rapere consumere, sua parvi pendere aliena cupere, pudorem pudicitiam, divina atque humana promiscua, nihil pensi neque moderati habere.

> [Therefore, out of riches, luxury and avarice came upon the youth along with haughtiness; they stole and they consumed, they accounted their own possessions as little and desired the possessions of others; they thought that shame

---

20. Sniezewski 2001, 342: "According to Livy internal strife tended to erupt whenever peace was established, while foreign wars restored internal concord." But Sniezewski attributes much of the content of Livy's work to the Hellenistic historians in what he calls "a narrative incrusted with the ethical principles" (343), a view that we would dispute. He does not discuss *luxuria* specifically, but concentrates on *felicitas, fortuna,* and *fatum*.

and modesty were the same, as were divine things and human ones, and they had no thought or moderation.] (Sall., *Cat.* 12.2)

Luxury, avarice, and haughtiness join forces, with horrible results for Roman society. *Cat.* 13 details the consequences of excess license, public debauchery, and physical desires satisfied in anticipation of the actual need:

> sed lubido stupri ganeae ceterique cultus non minor incesserat: viri muliebria pati, mulieres pudicitiam in propatulo habere; vescendi causa terra marique omnia exquirere; dormire prius quam somni cupido esset; non famem aut sitim, neque frigus neque lassitudinem opperiri, sed ea omnia luxu antecapere.

> [But eagerness for sexual disgrace and gluttony and other cultivated tastes spread no less; men endured things fit for women, and women exposed their modesty openly. For the sake of feeding their appetite, they sought everything by land and sea; they slept before there was desire for sleep; they did not wait for hunger or thirst or cold or weariness, but anticipated all with luxury.] (Sall., *Cat.* 13.3)

Men act like women, and women abandon all modesty. Youth, he goes on to say, turn to crime to sustain their expensive passions.[21]

As we have noted, there are two processes through which *luxuria* may corrupt the morals of an individual, and, correspondingly, there are two ways in which pernicious luxury may bring disaster upon the community. In the first, avarice and luxury lead to a softening of the manly element. Armies are corrupted as discipline is abandoned and soldiers become indulgent (Sall., *Cat.* 11; Livy 39.6). Coupled with the lack of a worthy foe, the result is devastating: the enervated parties cannot defend themselves and so are ripe for conquest. Sallust justifies in moral terms the downfall of the Persians and the Greeks, who had obtained empire but were corrupted by its possession.

> verum ubi pro labore desidia, pro continentia et aequitate lubido atque superbia invasere, fortuna simul cum moribus inmutatur. ita imperium semper ad optumum quemque a minus bono transfertur.

---

21. Sall., *Cat.* 13.5: *ad facinora incendebant: animus inbutus malis artibus haud facile lubidinibus carebat; eo profusius omnibus modis quaestui atque sumptui deditus erat* ("They burned for crimes: the soul saturated with evil cunning was not at all easily able to leave off from longing and was given to acquisition and spending all the more extremely and in every way.").

[Truly when laziness enters in place of industry, and desire and haughtiness in place of moderation and fairness, fortune changes at the same time as morals. Thus empire is always transferred to the best from the less good.] (Sall., *Cat.* 2.5–6)

On the other hand, the combination of *luxuria* and *avaritia* snaps the bonds of social cohesion. It entails a high degree of self-indulgence and disregard for the rights, status, and concerns of others. Thus, the second direction in which pernicious luxury can lead is to civil strife and internecine violence. Of the two paths to degeneracy, it is this second that primarily concerns historians of the Roman state, for obvious reasons. Rome was not living under the threat of defeat and ruin at the hands of an external enemy. In spite of its growing wealth and luxury, its armies remained generally victorious. They could not plausibly be charged with effeminacy.

In contrast, the breakdown in social harmony, which culminated in the civil wars of the first century BCE, was the most salient datum of recent Roman history and could indeed be blamed on the process of decadence set in motion by an overabundance of resources and an unhealthy desire for luxuries. Thus Catiline was depicted as a man eager for sedition:[22]

huic ab adulescentia bella intestina caedes rapinae discordia civilis grata fuere, . . . alieni adpetens sui profusus, ardens in cupiditatibus; . . . vastus animus inmoderata incredibilia nimis alta semper cupiebat.

[Internal slaughters, plundering, and civil discord were delightful to this man from his youth, . . . seeking the possessions of others, he poured out his own, eager in his covetousness; . . . his huge spirit was always desiring immoderate things, incredible and unattainable.] (Sall., *Cat.* 5.2–5)

In the same context of the Catilinarian Conspiracy, Cicero picks up the dual themes, that peace is a bad thing for Romans because they then turn against each other and that the cause of civil strife is luxury:

omnia sunt externa unius virtute terra marique pacata: domesticum bellum manet, intus insidiae sunt, intus inclusum periculum est, intus est hostis. cum

---

22. Edwards 1993, 178: "The aristocrat Catiline's luxurious habits have undermined his finances to such an extent that revolution is the only remedy." Shaw 1975, for Catiline as the paradigm for the destructive results of luxurious behavior. Cf. Venturini 1979; Vasaly 2009, 251–55.

luxuria nobis, cum amentia, cum scelere certandum est. huic ego me bello du-
cem profiteor, Quirites;

[All foreign wars have been brought to peaceful conclusions, on land and sea,
by the virtue of one man. Domestic war remains, the plots are within, danger is
shut up within, the enemy is within. We must battle against luxury, against
madness, against crime. I offer myself as the general for this war, Romans.]
(Cic., *Cat.* 2.11)

Livy reaffirms the association between luxury and civil strife in a passage
from Book 34, again using Cato the Elder as a mouthpiece speaking in opposition to the repeal of the *lex Oppia*, a sumptuary law limiting the dress and
ornamentation of women.[23] He employs remarkable language to label the
women protesting the law as seditious, exercising unbridled license, and
threatening secession. At one point they cry out, Cato says, *ne ullus modus
sumptibus, ne luxuriae sit* ("Let there be no limit to our extravagance, none to
our luxury!" Livy 34.3.9). The destructive power of luxury is clearly noted:
*diversisque duobus vitiis, avaritia et luxuria, civitatem laborare, quae pestes
omnia magna imperia everterunt* ("The state is laboring under two distinct
evils, avarice and luxury, the plagues that have destroyed all great empires."
Livy 34.4.2).

Thus the earliest extant Latin prose, exemplified by Cicero, Sallust, and
Livy, is permeated with a theme already well-developed in Roman historiography by the first century BCE: the Roman state has suffered a cataclysmic moral
decline, and that decline is rooted in the prosperity and luxury that came with
Rome's expansion in Italy and the Eastern Mediterranean.[24] Luxury is almost
inevitably accompanied by avarice, and leads either to softness and subjugation
or else to haughtiness and crime. Because of this process, peace itself is a misfortune for the Romans; it necessarily entails wealth and leisure, dangerous ele-

---

23. Mastrorosa 2006. According to Astin (1978, 174), no other existing source associates Cato's attitude
toward the Greeks with luxury: "Nevertheless various forms of luxury and extravagance were particularly associated with the Greeks, and therefore, despite the lack of evidence, it is a reasonable
conjecture that such associations fortified Cato's dislike of contemporary Greeks; but it would be rash
to infer that he saw Greece as the principal or fundamental source of the extravagance of which he
complained." Gruen (1992, 70) views the speech as pure invention by Livy, and does not see anti-
Hellenism as the root of Cato's opposition to extravagance.

24. Augustus played a major role in reviving supposedly traditional Roman moral values. Spawforth
(2012) writes about Augustus's efforts to achieve "a process of Greek acculturation to Roman values"
(1), with the argument that "in the Augustan 'restoration' of the Roman state the moral and the political were inextricably intertwined" (4). See Spawforth for a full bibliography on the topic.

ments in a society whose moral fiber was dependent upon patriotic militarism and simple agrarian values.

Greek Literature of the Roman World

We have already seen that the τρυφή of Greek authors before the Roman period simply does not behave like the pernicious *luxuria* of Roman thought. That distinction disappears abruptly from the beginning of the first century BCE, when Ps.-Scymnus ascribes the ruin of the Sybarites to their lax lifestyle:

> τρυφὴν δὲ καὶ ῥάθυμον ἑλομένους βίον
> χρόνῳ προελθεῖν εἰς ὕβριν τε καὶ κόρον,
> ....
> Κροτωνιᾶται πλησίον δὲ κείμενοι
> κατὰ κράτος αὐτοὺς ἦραν ἐν βραχεῖ χρόνῳ

[The Sybarites] choosing *truphē* and the easy life, in time advanced to hubris and satiety. . . . The Crotoniates, their neighbors, did away with them by force in a short time.] (Ps.-Scym. 348–49, 357–58)

Although the passage offers few details about the process of decadence undergone by the Sybarites, we may observe that τρυφή apparently has the effect so clearly delineated in the Latin sources, which we have examined. With κόρος acting as a practical equivalent of *avaritia*, a life of self-indulgence and relaxation leads to a desire to gain possession of the prerogatives of others, as the Sybarites attempted to break up the Olympic games by setting up a rival celebrations (Ps.-Scym. 348–536). This sequence can hardly be paralleled from earlier Greek evidence: for the first time, τρυφή takes on a unquestionable significance as a force of history.

Thus, beginning in the early years of the first century BCE, a strong similarity can be identified between pernicious luxury as the Romans conceptualized it and the way τρυφή comes to play a leading role in Greek historiography of the Roman period. If we review the works of the later Greek writers, we will discover that the development of this theme becomes gradually more pronounced. Finally, depiction of τρυφή as a pernicious historical cause reaches an apex with

Athenaeus, who uses τρυφή in an unnuanced, stereotypical fashion for all manner of vice, including cartoonish feminization and extraordinary acts of hubris.

Polybius

Writing in the mid-second century BCE, Polybius is heir to the traditions of Hellenistic historiography at their most developed. At the same time, he focuses his work on the remarkable expansion of Roman power and seeks to explain the Roman character to his Greek audience. Thus, it is doubly noteworthy that the idea of pernicious luxury has no place in his *Histories*. More generally, Polybius shows little interest in morals and lifestyle as a principle of historical causation, an idea that is supposed to be prominent in the Hellenistic period. Surprisingly, he does not even show awareness of pernicious luxury as a significant theme for many of his predecessors. This omission may not be trivial, since Polybius is notorious for the way he engages with the work of earlier historians.[25]

Polybius does not recognize or respond to a traditional Greek concept of decadence in the explication of the events that he relates, nor does he reflect the Roman view of the destructive power of *luxuria*, *avaritia*, *otium*, and related terms. This fact may be of no importance. On the other hand, by Cicero's time, the complex of ideas in question undoubtedly provided a perspective through which the Romans viewed both their own history and that of others. Its absence in Polybius may suggest that the idea of pernicious luxury had not yet become influential before the last quarter of the second century BCE.

The evidence of the *Histories* on τρυφή can stand as indicative of Polybius's lack of concern for luxury and decadence as historical agents. Polybius only rarely uses the word τρυφή: the single instance in the extant books occurs at 4.21.1, where Arcadian boys train in music, οὐ τρυφῆς καὶ περιουσίας χάριν ("not thanks to

---

25. For discussion and bibliography, see most recently McGing 2012, Rood 2012, Longley 2012. Polybius is particularly interested in showing the importance of τύχη ("chance" or "fortune") in history: Walbank 1957–79,1.16–25; McGing 2010, 195–202; Longley 2012, esp. 73–74. Accordingly, Polybius emphasizes the frequent impact of τὸ παράδοξον ("the unexpected") on the actors in his *Histories*. Thus, even if the concept of pernicious luxury were popular among earlier writers, it might not be odd for Polybius to avoid such an explanation of events: the idea, as generally presented in the scholarship, is deterministic, since τρυφή leads regularly to political decline. The operation of this process would leave less room for the working of τύχη. Nonetheless, precisely because a theory of pernicious luxury would have been in opposition to his own view of historical causation, we might expect Polybius to recognize the historiographical importance of decadence and to explain his objections it.

truphē and excess"), but in order to soften their stubborn and harsh nature.[26] All other examples occur in fragmentary texts. In 7.8.7 (from *Exc. Peir.* p. 13) τρυφή is a benefit: καὶ μὴν ἐν περιουσίᾳ καὶ τρυφῇ καὶ δαψιλείᾳ πλείστῃ διαγενόμενος ἔτη μὲν ἐβίωσε πλείω τῶν ἐνενήκοντα . . . ("And in fact continuing in abundance and *truphē* and plenty, he lived more than ninety years . . .").[27]

Two other occurrences are from paraphrases by Athenaeus. The first, from the epitomized first book, is neutral in content, describing the distance between two rivers in Celtiberia (Athen. 1.16c = Polyb. 34.9.15). The other Athenaean passage is the one usually cited by scholars as the best evidence for Polybius's understanding of corrupting luxury,[28] but our examination in Chapters 3 and 4 of Athenaean fragments has made it clear that this material is of little value for establishing Polybius's views. Scholars of Polybius often fail to distinguish passages from the extant books of the *Histories* and those of less trustworthy transmission, and in the case of Polyb. 7.1.1, it is usually assumed that both the wording and the moral implication of the passage are accurately represented by Athenaeus.[29]

Πολύβιος δ' ἐν τῇ ἑβδόμῃ Καπυησίους τοὺς ἐν Καμπανίᾳ διὰ τὴν ἀρετὴν τῆς γῆς πλοῦτον περιβαλομένους ἐξοκεῖλαι εἰς τρυφὴν καὶ πολυτέλειαν, ὑπερβαλομένους τὴν περὶ Κρότωνα καὶ Σύβαριν παραδεδομένην φήμην. οὐ δυνάμενοι οὖν, φησί, φέρειν τὴν παροῦσαν εὐδαιμονίαν ἐκάλουν τὸν Ἀννίβαν. διόπερ ὑπὸ Ῥωμαίων ἀνήκεστα δεινὰ ἔπαθον.

[Polybius says in the seventh book that the Capuans in Campania, having come into possession of wealth because of the excellence of the land, ran aground on

---

26. See the discussion at Longley 2012, 81–83, on how climate on the one hand and state institutions on the other could shape human nature.

27. In the Loeb, Paton translates the μήν concessively, indicating that he lived to an old age despite these traits, but it is normally a strengthening particle.

28. For example, Clarke (1999, 87) uses this passage without any skepticism to claim the influence of geography on history. Davidson (2009, 126) notes the textual problems, but seems to use the different books of Polybius, whether directly transmitted or epitomized, with equal credulity.

29. For the textual tradition, see Moore 1965. Eckstein (1995, 70–82) makes no distinction, discussing Polybius's "heavily moralizing comments on wealth" (70), but drawing virtually all of his evidence from the non-extant books. Likewise, McGing 2010, 156, shows no hesitation about the transmission of the text, including the passage at 7.1.1: "The people of Capua, for instance, developed such luxurious and extravagant ways . . ." that led to calling in Hannibal and eventual "punishment from Rome that ruined them (7.1). Wealth also corrupted Tarentum. . . ." Even Walbank (1957–79, *ad* 7.1) refers here to the topos of the τρυφή of the cities of Magna Graecia, and cites Timaeus from Athen. 12.523c as his evidence. For an excellent essay on the dangers of relying on later excerptors for an accurate view of Polybius, see Thompson 1985.

truphē and extravagance, outdoing the reputation that has been handed down about Croton and Sybaris. For, he said, being unable to endure their present happiness, they called in Hannibal. Wherefore they suffered ruinous atrocities at the hands of the Romans.] (Athen. 12.528a = Polyb. 7.1.1–2)

Few passages show so clearly the fingerprints of Athenaeus. In addition to the ἐξοκέλλειν formula, we find here the commonplace, from Diodorus especially, that τρυφή comes διὰ τὴν ἀρετὴν τῆς γῆς. The phrase οὐ δυνάμενοι . . . φέρειν τὴν παροῦσαν εὐδαιμονίαν recalls Ps.-Scymnus 345 and Diodorus 10.23. The ὑπερβαλλομένους raises a red flag, suggesting Athenaean authorship. Even the subsequent contrast with the virtue of the Petelians has a now-familiar appearance: Πετηλῖνοι δὲ . . . εἰς τοσοῦτον καρτερίας ἦλθον . . . ὥστε . . . ("the Petelians . . . reached such a state of endurance . . . that . . ."). Without a clear statement of Polybius's concern for morality in the extant books, this passage must be dismissed as an Athenaean reworking; it is likely that the original told the story of Capua's defection from Rome, but the attribution of cause is dubious.

Though it does not contain explicit reference to τρυφή, Polybius's presentation of the theory of the *anacyclosis* of constitutions in his sixth book is often cited as evidence for the importance of decadence resulting from luxury. In his discussion of the decay of monarchy into tyranny, Polybius says:

τότε δὴ ταῖς ἐπιθυμίαις ἑπόμενοι διὰ τὴν περιουσίαν ἐξάλλους μὲν ἐσθῆτας ὑπέλαβον δεῖν ἔχειν τοὺς ἡγουμένους τῶν ὑποταττομένων, ἐξάλλους δὲ καὶ ποικίλας τὰς περὶ τὴν τροφὴν ἀπολαύσεις καὶ παρασκευάς, ἀναντιρρήτους δὲ καὶ παρὰ τῶν μὴ προσηκόντων τὰς τῶν ἀφροδισίων χρείας καὶ συνουσίας. ἐφ᾽ οἷς μὲν φθόνου γενομένου καὶ προσκοπῆς, ἐφ᾽ οἷς δὲ μίσους ἐκκαιομένου καὶ δυσμενικῆς ὀργῆς,

[Following their desires because of their abundance, they thought that the rulers ought to wear special clothes to distinguish them from their underlings, and that the enjoyment and presentation of their food should be special and varied, and that they not be denied their needs and demands for sex, even if it was not appropriate. The former behavior led to envy and diffidence, through the latter hatred and hostility were enflamed.] (Polyb. 6.7.7–8)

Indulgence in fine clothing, culinary delicacies, and inappropriate demands for sex could certainly have been characterized as τρυφή, according to Classical usage.

The same is true of description of the collapse of aristocratic government:

ὅτε δὲ διαδέξαιντο πάλιν παῖδες παρὰ πατέρων τὴν τοιαύτην ἐξουσίαν,
. . . ὁρμήσαντες οἱ μὲν ἐπὶ πλεονεξίαν καὶ φιλαργυρίαν ἄδικον, οἱ δ᾽ ἐπὶ μέθας
καὶ τὰς ἅμα ταύταις ἀπλήστους εὐωχίας, οἱ δ᾽ ἐπὶ τὰς τῶν γυναικῶν ὕβρεις καὶ
παίδων ἁρπαγάς, μετέστησαν μὲν τὴν ἀριστοκρατίαν εἰς ὀλιγαρχίαν

[But again, when the children have inherited the same power from their fathers,
. . . some set out into greed and unjust avarice, others into bouts of drinking and
the insatiate feasts associated with such bouts, others into the assaulting of
women and the raping of boys. Thus they change aristocracy into oligarchy.]
(Polyb. 6.8.4–5)

Drinking and feasting are regular manifestations of τρυφή, which is here linked
to intolerable acts of ὕβρις.[30]

The degeneration from democracy to the law of the jungle is also relevant.
In democratic states, there eventually arise demagogues, whose efforts to gain
preeminence destroy the health of popular government:

διαφθείρουσι τὰς οὐσίας, δελεάζοντες καὶ λυμαινόμενοι τὰ πλήθη κατὰ πάντα
τρόπον. ἐξ ὧν ὅταν ἅπαξ δωροδόκους καὶ δωροφάγους κατασκευάσωσι τοὺς
πολλοὺς διὰ τὴν ἄφρονα δοξοφαγίαν . . .

[They destroy their own resources, luring and corrupting the masses in every
way. Thus, when once, because of their hunger for fame, they have made the
populous accepting of bribes and hungry for bribes . . .] (Polyb. 6.9.6–7)

The ruination of the democracy consists in teaching the people to enjoy and
expect bribes. This view recalls the charges leveled by Demosthenes against
those who opposed his anti-Macedonian policy: it was a sign of τρυφή in the
demos to favor those who promised to use state revenues on public festivals
rather than spend it on the war.[31]

Thus we can find in book 6 of the *Histories* a set of possible references to

---

30. Note that the passage does not make drunkenness and feasting the cause of either avarice or ὕβρις.
Each of the three kinds of degeneracy is presented as parallel; all result from inexperience of the evils
of tyranny.
31. See our discussion of Theopompus and Demosthenes, above (pp. 297–99).

pernicious luxury as a significant historical force. However, a closer look at these passages indicates that they are not consistent with the way in which this concept is usually understood. In particular, none of the three instances of constitutional change shows any trace of weakness or enervation, though feminization is taken to be a distinctive characteristic of decadence induced by τρυφή. First, those responsible for the destruction of monarchy are not depicted as lacking the moral fiber to resist choice cuisine, clothing, and sex. They adopt the relevant behaviors as a matter of policy, to act as a sign of their superior social status. In the second example, no similar motive is reported, but the penchant of the young aristocrats for drunken feasting is no more plausibly to be attributed to softness and womanish character, for such can hardly be reconciled with the avarice and acts of sexual violence that this group displayed. Finally, the treatment afforded the people by ambitious demagogues does not render the masses passive and supine. Rather, they share with the budding tyrants and oligarchs an interest in demonstrating their superiority and imposing their will:

συνειθισμένον γὰρ τὸ πλῆθος ἐσθίειν τὰ ἀλλότρια . . . τότε δὴ χειροκρατίαν ἀποτελεῖ, καὶ τότε συναθροιζόμενον ποιεῖ σφαγάς, φυγάς, γῆς ἀναδασμούς, ἕως ἂν ἀποτεθηριωμένον πάλιν. . . .

[The people grow accustomed to consuming other men's goods; . . . they then begin to rule by force, and then, gathering together, they carry out murder, exile, redistribution of land, until once again they are made into a wild beast. . . .] (Polyb. 6.9.8–9)

The result of all three stages of degeneration is not the contempt to be expected at an unmanly display,[32] but envy and anger. Thus, whatever Book 6 may tell us about second-century BCE ideas of constitutional change, it is not evidence for a putative Hellenistic theory connecting a luxurious lifestyle with moral and political weakness and passivity.

In addition, the processes that Polybius outlines in this book are of no wider importance to the structure of his work. For example, Walbank, who argues that "the theme of excessive prosperity leading to softness and luxury (τρυφή) and the calling in of a master was by this time commonplace," himself admits

---

32. As happens in Plato's description of the transition from oligarchy to democracy, where the young oligarchs are scorned for their fat and feeble bodies by the sons of the poor (Plato, *Rep.* 8.556c–d).

that the political theory of book 6 is in no way related to the view of history in the remainder of Polybius.[33]

From this examination, we can conclude that Polybius may have known of a theme of pernicious luxury, but reflects it only as a subject of political philosophy rather than a principle guiding historical narrative. Because his expressed purpose is to explain the rise of the Romans to world power "in just fifty-three years" (Polyb. 1.1.5), it is striking to find, in the narrative sections of the *Histories,* no emphasis on rural simplicity, frugality, and parsimony as the source of Roman military virtue. Because he is also interested in the seeds of decline contained in the Roman state,[34] it is noteworthy that the vocabulary generally associated with the idea of pernicious luxury is lacking, even when it would have been appropriate. These facts suggest that the complex of ideas encompassing *luxuria* and its opposite, so prominent in Cicero, Sallust, and Livy, was not yet an important enough feature of Roman historiography to influence Polybius.

Diodorus Siculus

Diodorus wrote his universal history in the middle decades of the first century BCE, before Octavian had resolved the civil wars into the Principate. As a contemporary of Cicero and Sallust, we might expect him to demonstrate a thoroughly Romanized conception of pernicious luxury, yet we are disappointed in this expectation. Perhaps Diodorus was not interested in the Roman views on the connections between morality and historical events. Sacks argues that, though probably living in Rome from at least 46 or 45 BCE until the publication of the *Bibliotheca* in about 30 BCE, Diodorus "does not claim a close association with Romans."[35] Diodorus's knowledge of Latin may not have been strong, and

---

33. Walbank 2002, 208, citing as his authority Hoffmann 1942, 54ff. Walbank draws a contrast between the moral lessons of the Hellenistic historians, which we dispute, and the practical utility inherent in Polybius (231–41), with which we agree. See Barnes (2005) for a different interpretation.

34. εἰ γάρ τινα καὶ ἑτέραν πολιτείαν, ὡς ἀρτίως εἶπα, καὶ ταύτην συμβαίνει, κατὰ φύσιν ἀπ᾽ ἀρχῆς ἔχουσαν τὴν σύστασιν καὶ τὴν αὔξησιν, κατὰ φύσιν ἕξειν καὶ τὴν εἰς τἀναντία μεταβολήν. σκοπεῖν δ᾽ ἐξέσται διὰ τῶν μετὰ ταῦτα ῥηθησομένων ("If it is true of any other constitution, it is, as I just said, especially true of this one: from the beginning, its composition and growth were natural; its change to the opposite will also be natural. It will be possible to observe this from the descriptions that follow." Polyb. 6.9.13–14).

35. Sacks 1990, 164. See Sacks, chapter 6, for the relationship between Diodorus and the Romans. For the dating of the work, see Rubincam 1987, 1998.

there is no evidence that he intermingled with the city's intelligentsia or enjoyed the patronage of influential men. On the other hand, Diodorus's general
interest in morality is pervasive throughout his work.[36] Encomia of the great
deeds of the past will lead to similar actions in the future, while illuminating
wicked behavior will be likewise beneficial:

τοὺς δὲ πονηροὺς τῶν ἀνθρώπων ταῖς αἰωνίοις βλασφημίαις ἀποτρέπει τῆς ἐπὶ
τὴν κακίαν ὁρμῆς.

[[History] uses everlasting abuse to turn malicious men away from the impulse
to evil.] (Diod. Sic. 1.1.5)

Among the particular moral interests of Diodorus, Sacks has identified one in
which pernicious luxury might be expected to have some importance. Diodorus
emphasizes the moral dimension of the decline of empires, blaming this phenomenon on the abandonment of moderation and the adoption of excessively
arrogant and violent behavior toward allies.[37] Yet despite this fascination with the
ethical value of his work and the particular attention paid to political decadence,
Diodorus does not elaborate a schema whereby the effects of luxury or an easy
lifestyle lead necessarily or even regularly to moral corruption and ruin.

To turn to τρυφή more specifically, although Diodorus uses the word quite
often in his text—over fifty times in the extant books alone—he does not use it
consistently.[38] At times, Diodorus seems to be sitting squarely in the camp of
traditional Greek writers in using the word to mean an expectation of having
one's wants satisfied by others. Provided that such an expectation is appropriate
to the subject's social circumstances, no moral criticism need be implied; rather,
in these contexts, τρυφή can be a good thing. In a few other places where it is
unquestionably pernicious, it is not explicitly given responsibility for corruption and destruction.

36. We will not go into the whole issue of whether Diodorus was a composer or a plagiarist, but we
    strongly argue that his choice of wording, at least, is quite original. Cf. Palm 1955; Drews 1962; Sacks
    1994; Rubincam 1998; Sulimani 2008. Against Diodorus's originality: Sinclair 1963; Hornblower
    1981, ch. 2; Fornara 1992; Walbank 1992; Stylianou 1992. Generally approving: Carter 1992.
37. Sacks 1990, ch. 2. For moral benefit in general, 23–36; the role of chance, 36–42; and the decline of
    empires, 42–52. The first and third are directly relevant to our argument here. For Diodorus's interest
    in morality, Sacks 1994, esp. 214.
38. At least another twenty-five occurrences fall in the non-preserved books. We have chosen to leave
    those passages to one side when trying to determine Diodorus's own intentions, since we cannot be
    certain that the later excerptors faithfully reproduce either Diodorus's wording or his themes.

Diodorus's application of τρυφή to the Agrigentines provides a splendid example of the positive connotations of the word. Diodorus takes several pages to detail the amazing wealth of the city and its citizens. More precisely, he presents examples of this wealth used both for μεγαλοπρέπεια ("magnificence") and τρυφή. On the one hand, the great public buildings are an indication of the first:

ἥ τε γὰρ τῶν ἱερῶν κατασκευὴ καὶ μάλιστα ὁ τοῦ Διὸς νεὼς ἐμφαίνει τὴν μεγαλοπρέπειαν τῶν τότε ἀνθρώπων.

[The construction of the sanctuaries, and most particularly the temple of Zeus, illustrates the magnificence of the people of that time.] (Diod. Sic. 13.82.1)

Similarly, for more private structures:

δηλοῖ δὲ τὴν τρυφὴν αὐτῶν καὶ ἡ πολυτέλεια τῶν μνημείων

[The extravagance of the monuments also makes clear their *truphē*.][39] (Diod. Sic. 13.82.6)

Next, after reporting the opulent public reception given upon the homecoming of an Olympic victor, Diodorus characterizes the lifestyle of the people in general terms:

καθόλου δὲ καὶ τὰς ἀγωγὰς εὐθὺς ἐκ παίδων ἐποιοῦντο τρυφεράς, τήν τ᾽ ἐσθῆτα μαλακὴν φοροῦντες καθ᾽ ὑπερβολὴν καὶ χρυσοφοροῦντες, ἔτι δὲ στλεγγίσι καὶ ληκύθοις ἀργυραῖς τε καὶ χρυσαῖς χρώμενοι.

[As a whole, they made their manner of life *trupheros* straightaway even from their youth, wearing soft clothing to great excess and gold jewelry, and also using strigils and oil-flasks made of silver and gold.] (Diod. Sic. 13.82.8)

---

39. We should not overlook the force of καί in the phrase καὶ ἡ πολυτέλεια. The immediately preceding context describes an artificial lake built by the Agrigentines that produces a variety of fish "for public festivals" (εἰς τὰς δημοσίας ἑστιάσεις, Diod. Sic. 13.82.5) and, because of the birds which gathered there, "great delight for the spectators" (μεγάλην τέρψιν παρασκευάζειν τοῖς θεωμένοις), a passage specifically adapted by Athenaeus as an example of corrupting τρυφή (see above, pp. 203–4). As the καί indicates, Diodorus evidentially felt that such examples of public munificence were essentially similar to the cases of τρυφή, which he goes on to relate.

Immediately after this statement, the reader is introduced to Tellias, the city's richest man. Though affluent, Tellias was morally irreproachable, generous, and unassuming: γεγονέναι δέ φασι τὸν Τελλίαν τὸ μὲν εἶδος εὐτελῆ παντελῶς, τὸ δὲ ἦθος θαυμαστόν ("They say that Tellias was entirely modest in appearance, but extraordinary in character," Diod. Sic. 13.83.4). He was most remarkable for his hospitality, both private and on behalf of the city. Finally, following several examples of "magnificent uses of wealth" (τοῦ πλούτου μεγαλοπρέπειαν, 13.84.1), the discussion culminates in a remarkable demonstration of Agrigentine τρυφή:

διὰ δὲ τὸ μέγεθος τῆς κατὰ τὴν πόλιν εὐπορίας τοσαύτην συνέβαινε τρυφὴν εἶναι παρὰ τοῖς Ἀκραγαντίνοις, ὥστε μετ᾽ ὀλίγον τῆς πολιορκίας γινομένης ποιῆσαι ψήφισμα περὶ τῶν ἐν τοῖς φυλακείοις διανυκτερευόντων, ὅπως μή τις ἔχῃ πλεῖον τύλης καὶ περιστρώματος καὶ κωδίου καὶ δυεῖν προσκεφαλαίων. τοιαύτης δὲ τῆς σκληροτάτης στρωμνῆς ὑπαρχούσης, ἔξεστι λογίζεσθαι τὴν κατὰ τὸν λοιπὸν βίον τρυφήν.

[Because of the extent of the city's resources, there developed such great *truphē* among the Agrigentines that in the siege, which took place a little later, they passed a law about those who had night guard duty: no one should have more than a mattress and a quilt and a sheepskin and two pillows. With this as their allowance for hard lying, it is possible to estimate the *truphē* in the rest of their life.] (Diod. Sic. 13.84.5–6)

In this discussion, Diodorus makes no apparent moral distinction between εὐπορία and τρύφη. Perhaps the former refers to wealth used for public enjoyment, while the latter indicates more private and personal comforts, but both are treated as similarly praiseworthy. Even in the anecdote about the sleeping arrangements of the night watch, there is no evidence of an imputation of effeminacy nor any hint that the Agrigentine lifestyle contributed to the subsequent ruin of the city.

Agrigentum was besieged by the Carthaginians in 406 BCE, but Diodorus does not attribute its eventual fall to any kind of moral decadence. The Agrigentines prevailed at first, fighting with their allies as far as Hamilcar's own tents. But eventually the food ran out and the order was given for everyone who was able to travel to abandon Agrigentum. Relating the capture of the city, Diodorus singles out the behavior of Tellias, "the first man of the citizens in wealth and virtue" (τὸν πρωτεύοντα τῶν πολιτῶν πλούτῳ καὶ καλοκἀγαθίᾳ, Diod. Sic. 13.90.1). He refused to leave the city, instead taking refuge in the Temple of Athena. When he realized that it was going to be sacked, he opted to burn the temple and himself with it, in order to deny plunder to the Carthaginians. By way of moral contrast, Hamilcar slaughtered the sick and old who were left behind, and both looted and burned the temples.

Diodorus's emphasis on the τρυφή of the Agrigentines—referred to explicitly five times in this account—serves not to provide a moral lesson about the reason for their defeat. Rather, it heightens the pathos of the story. Chapter 89 describes the pitiful scene of the chaotic evacuation, highly reminiscent of Thucydides' own account of the Athenian army fleeing from Syracuse a few years earlier or of an archetypal Herodotean reversal of fortune. Diodorus particularly stresses the transformation from opulence to utter poverty by elucidating the hardships of the women:

αἳ τὴν συνήθη τρυφὴν εἰς ὁδοιπορίαν σύντονον καὶ κακοπάθειαν ὑπεράγουσαν μεταβαλλόμεναι διεκαρτέρουν, τοῦ φόβου τὰς ψυχὰς ἐντείνοντος.

[Those who, having experienced a change of fortune from their accustomed *truphē* into strenuous walking and extended misery, endured because of the fear straining their souls.] (Diod. Sic. 13.89.3)

Thus, in the context of Diodorus's Agrigentine narrative, τρυφή is clearly an enviable quality.

Likewise, in general, Diodorus's portrayal of women with τρυφή is sympathetic. Thus Themistocles' Persian wife was a noble woman:

. . . εὐγενείᾳ τε καὶ κάλλει διαφέρουσαν, ἔτι δὲ κατ᾽ ἀρετὴν ἐπαινουμένην, οἰκετῶν τε πλῆθος πρὸς διακονίαν καὶ παντοδαπῶν ἐκπωμάτων καὶ τὴν ἄλλην χορηγίαν πρὸς ἀπόλαυσιν καὶ τρυφὴν ἁρμόζουσαν.⁴⁰

[. . . excelling in both good birth and beauty, and also praised for her virtue, and furnishing a multitude of household slaves to minister to her and cups of all kinds and other furnishings for their enjoyment and *truphē*.] (Diod. Sic. 11.57.6)

---

40. There may be a lacuna in this text. Capps suggests the addition of a participle such as ἐπιφερομένην after the πλῆθος, and so Oldfather adds to his Loeb translation: "[she brought as her dowry]". Such an emendation seems fitting. For the τρυφή of royal women, cf. Diod. Sic. 19.49.9.

Far from being corrupting, her τρυφή is of a kind with virtue, nobility, and beauty. Compare the pathetic description of the Persian royal women captured by Alexander's army:

ἑκάστη δὲ τούτων διὰ τὴν ὑπερβολὴν τοῦ πλούτου καὶ τῆς τρυφῆς περιήγετο πλῆθος πολυδαπάνου κατασκευῆς καὶ γυναικείου κόσμου. πάθος δ᾽ ἦν δεινότατον περὶ τὰς αἰχμαλωτιζομένας γυναῖκας. αἱ γὰρ πρότερον διὰ τρυφὴν ἐπ᾽ ἀπήναις πολυτελέσι μόγις κατακομιζόμεναι καὶ γυμνὸν μέρος τοῦ σώματος οὐδὲν φαίνουσαι, τότε μονοχίτωνες καὶ τὰς ἐσθῆτας περιρρήττουσαι μετ᾽ ὀδυρμῶν ἐκ τῶν σκηνῶν ἐξεπήδων, ἐπιβοώμεναι θεοὺς καὶ προσπίπτουσαι τοῖς τῶν κρατούντων γόνασι.

[Each of them, because of her extreme wealth and *truphē*, brought with her a multitude of extravagant equipment and womanly ornamentation. And the misfortune of those who were taken prisoner was most terrible. Those women who previously, on account of their *truphē*, would scarcely even be carried around on an expensive wagon and would not bare any part of their bodies, now leapt out from their tents wearing only a chiton, tearing their clothes while wailing, invoking the gods and embracing the knees of their captors.] (Diod. Sic. 17.35.4–5)

Diodorus continues describing their ordeal at length (6–7). The women threw away their jewelry and fled for their lives. Begging for help from anyone who would pity them, they were dragged away by the hair or prodded with spear butts. Their captors stripped, beat, and assaulted them, καὶ τὰ τιμιώτατα καὶ περιβόητα τῶν βαρβάρων ταῖς τῆς τύχης δωρεαῖς ὑβρίζοντες ("raping the most valued and famous possessions of the barbarians, given to them by fortune," Diod. Sic. 17.36.7). Decent men pitied them and their reversal of fortune, and especially were moved by the spectacle of Darius's own family, who were unable to help their people. Although τρυφή was a defining characteristic of these women, there is no indication that they were in any way immoral or indecent. Quite the contrary, the indecency was all inflicted upon them in their misfortune.

Likewise the captured Selinuntians were pitied by the Greek allies of Carthage:

αἱ μὲν γυναῖκες ἐστερημέναι τῆς συνήθους τρυφῆς ἐν πολεμίων ὕβρει διενυκτέρευον, ὑπομένουσαι δεινὰς ταλαιπωρίας· ὧν ἔνιαι θυγατέρας ἐπιγάμους ὁρᾶν ἠναγκάζοντο πασχούσας οὐκ οἰκεῖα τῆς ἡλικίας.

[Some of the women, being deprived of their accustomed *truphē*, passed the night being raped by their enemies, enduring terrible miseries, and of them some were forced to watch their nubile daughters suffering things not suitable for their age.] (Diod. Sic. 13.58.1)

The description continues for some time (13.58.1–2), until it is contrasted with the openhanded generosity of the Agrigentines, who received the small number of fugitives from Selinus into their own doomed city.

Thus, the τρυφή of the women in Diodorus is a virtuous attribute, contrasted here and at Diod. Sic. 17.35 with the outrageous hubris of their captors, and employed as the most effective illustration of the catastrophic change of fortune from prosperity and happiness to wretched enslavement and abuse. It is unmistakably a desirable and noble trait. By emphasizing the luxurious lifestyle of these people, Diodorus is by no means offering moral criticism. Rather, he writes compassionately about these victims of war and shows his sensitivity precisely by highlighting the treatment of these women, once accustomed to living in τρυφή, being attended and adorned with dignity and virtue, and now reduced to wretched captives of brutal men, mere possessions to be beaten and raped.

Moving now to other passages where Diodorus clearly presents τρυφή in a positive light, the word is often used as an attribute of fertile lands whose inhabitants either benefit from the excellence of their soil and resources or suffer from the lack. Thus he describes India as an extremely beautiful and well-watered land, rich in precious metals and exceptional for its elephants. It offers its inhabitants ἄφθονον ἀπόλαυσιν ("unstinting enjoyment," Diod. Sic. 2.16.3) and πλῆθος ἔτι δὲ τῶν ἄλλων ἁπάντων σχεδὸν τῶν πρὸς τρυφὴν καὶ πλοῦτον διατεινόντων ("an abundance also of nearly all the other things fostering *truphē* and wealth," 2.16.4). Coveting their prosperity, the Assyrian queen Semiramis attacked fiercely, but the Indians defeated her armies and forced her to retreat. The τρυφή of the people did not corrupt, feminize, or make them unwarlike in any way.

Similarly, Diodorus describes other lands in terms of the τρυφή they provide. He depicts a palm grove in Arabia thus: ἔχει δὲ πλῆθος τούτου τοῦ φυτοῦ πολύκαρπον καθ᾽ ὑπερβολὴν καὶ πρὸς ἀπόλαυσιν καὶ τρυφὴν διαφέρον ("It has an exceedingly fruitful abundance of this plant that contributes to enjoyment and *truphē*." Diod. Sic. 3.42.2).[41] Lipara is a small but very fruitful

---

41. For πρὸς ἀπόλαυσιν καὶ τρυφὴν and other related phrases, see Meyer 2009, 54ff.

island, furnishing the things useful for the τρυφή of men, and especially able to offer τὴν ἐκ τῆς ἀπολαύσεως ἡδονήν ("the pleasure of enjoyment," 5.10). An unidentified Atlantic island provides the means πρὸς τὴν ἀπόλαυσιν καὶ τρυφήν ("for enjoyment and *truphē*," 5.19.2), and lacks nothing πρὸς τρυφὴν καὶ πολυτέλειαν ("for *truphē* and extravagance," 5.19.4). By way of contrast, the Ligurians have a hard life, far removed from τρυφή (4.20.1) and their cold climate also leaves the Britons τῆς ἐκ τοῦ πλούτου γεννωμένης τρυφῆς πολὺ διαλλάττοντας ("far removed from the *truphē* that comes from wealth," 5.21.6). The city of Alexandria is given pride of place as the leading city of the world:

> καθόλου δ᾽ ἡ πόλις τοσαύτην ἐπίδοσιν ἔλαβεν ἐν τοῖς ὕστερον χρόνοις ὥστε παρὰ πολλοῖς αὐτὴν πρώτην ἀριθμεῖσθαι τῶν κατὰ τὴν οἰκουμένην· καὶ γὰρ κάλλει καὶ μεγέθει καὶ προσόδων πλήθει καὶ τῶν πρὸς τρυφὴν ἀνηκόντων πολὺ διαφέρει τῶν ἄλλων.

> [In general the city has made such progress in recent times that, according to many people, it is numbered as the first city in the inhabited world. For it far exceeds others in beauty and size and the amount of its income and the other things pertaining to *truphē*.] (Diod. Sic. 17.52.5)

In these descriptions, opulence is a laudable quality, and in none of them does Diodorus connect τρυφή with the moral decay, hubris, civil strife, or the destruction that we see in contemporary Latin sources.

The ethnography of the Etruscans in book 5 presents a more complex case. Diodorus begins with a depiction of the former greatness of the Etruscans (5.40.1–2), mentioning their vast territory, naval supremacy, and excellent army organization as well as the trappings of royalty, later adopted by the Romans, and writings on nature and religion. Then, he describes the land:

> χώραν δὲ νεμόμενοι πάμφορον, καὶ ταύτην ἐξεργαζόμενοι, καρπῶν ἀφθονίαν ἔχουσιν οὐ μόνον πρὸς τὴν ἀρκοῦσαν διατροφήν, ἀλλὰ καὶ πρὸς ἀπόλαυσιν δαψιλῆ καὶ τρυφὴν ἀνήκουσαν. παρατίθενται γὰρ δὶς τῆς ἡμέρας τραπέζας πολυτελεῖς καὶ τἄλλα τὰ πρὸς τὴν ὑπερβάλλουσαν τρυφὴν οἰκεῖα, . . .

> [They inhabit a land that is very productive, and, by working this, they have an abundance of fruit, not only sufficient to ward off need, but also enough for

plentiful enjoyment and *truphē*. Twice each day they lay expensive tables and all of the possessions appropriate to excessive *truphē*. . . .] (Diod. Sic. 5.40.3)

He enumerates those possessions: colorful couches, all kinds of silver drinking cups, and beautiful slaves dressed far beyond their station. The Etruscans inhabit magnificent houses of many different descriptions.

So far, this emphasis on τρυφή seems to highlight the prosperity of Etruria, as we have seen done for Agrigentum. However, unlike that case, the lifestyle of the Etruscans does have negative moral implications. They had once been a dominant people:

οὗτοι γὰρ τὸ μὲν παλαιὸν ἀνδρείᾳ διενεγκόντες χώραν πολλὴν κατεκτήσαντο καὶ πόλεις ἀξιολόγους καὶ πολλὰς ἔκτισαν.

[These men, in olden days distinguished in manliness, took possession of much land and founded numerous and noteworthy cities.] (Diod. Sic. 5.40.1)

In Diodorus's own day, the situation had changed:

καθόλου δὲ τὴν μὲν ἐκ παλαιῶν χρόνων παρ᾽ αὐτοῖς ζηλουμένην ἀλκὴν ἀποβεβλήκασιν, ἐν πότοις δὲ καὶ ῥαθυμίαις ἀνάνδροις βιοῦντες οὐκ ἀλόγως τὴν τῶν πατέρων δόξαν ἐν τοῖς πολέμοις ἀποβεβλήκασι.

[In general they have abandoned the fighting spirit prized by them from ancient times, but, living in bouts of drinking and unmanly entertainments, they not unexpectedly have thrown away their fathers' military glory.] (Diod. Sic. 5.40.4)

Such an explanation for the decline of Etruscan power would not be out of place in Sallust or Livy. The text may even imply that luxury is inevitably, or at least regularly, pernicious (οὐκ ἀλόγως). Yet, oddly, the moral dimension of τρυφή is dropped as quickly as it is raised. The sentence immediately following strikes a positive note once again: συνεβάλετο δ᾽ αὐτοῖς πρὸς τὴν τρυφὴν οὐκ ἐλάχιστον καὶ ἡ τῆς χώρας ἀρετή ("The excellence of the land is not the least thing that provided their *truphē*," 5.40.5). Perhaps this swerving from τρυφή as virtue to moral weakness and back again to virtue is an indication of the mixing of geographical or demographical material with a historical tradition. In any case, the passage does not make pernicious luxury the cause of any specific historical event, nor does Diodorus elsewhere in the extant books use τρυφή to explain particular Etruscan defeats.[42]

The lack of military skills associated with τρυφή is a theme picked up in book 20, when Agathocles, the tyrant of Syracuse, decided to attack the Carthaginians in 310 BCE:

τοῦτο γὰρ πράξας ἤλπιζε τοὺς μὲν ἐν τῇ Καρχηδόνι τετρυφηκότας ἐν εἰρήνῃ πολυχρονίῳ καὶ διὰ τοῦτ᾽ ἀπείρους ὄντας τῶν ἐν ταῖς μάχαις κινδύνων ὑπὸ τῶν ἐνηθληκότων τοῖς δεινοῖς ῥᾳδίως ἡττηθήσεσθαι,

[Doing this [invading Libya], he hoped that, since those in Carthage had been for a long time enjoying *truphē* in peace and, because of this, they were inexperienced of the dangers in battle, they would be easily beaten by men who had contended in hard fighting.] (Diod. Sic. 20.3.3)

The idea that peace is conducive to luxury and that the combination of the two corrodes the martial vigor of a nation is familiar from the Latin sources that we have examined. Here, however, expectations are not met. Despite their τρυφή, the Carthaginians successfully fought off Agathocles' attack.

Similarly ad hoc seems Diodorus's exposition of the social reforms of Zaleucus at Italian Locris. At 12.20–21, we are told that, in pursuit of piety, civic harmony, and justice, the mythical lawgiver opposed licentiousness among his people by trying to alter public perceptions in order to shame citizens so they would not approach even an appearance of immorality. Thus, a woman could not wear gold or purple, unless she wanted people to assume that she was a prostitute, and she could not be accompanied by more than one female slave, unless she wished them to think that she was drunk. She could not leave the city at night, without admitting she was planning to commit adultery. Likewise, a man could not wear a gold ring or a Milesian-style cloak without confessing by it that he was a prostitute or adulterer. Diodorus sums up:

---

42. A similar passage, but from one of the books excerpted in Byzantium (Diod. Sic. 26.11.1), pertains to the weakening of Hannibal's army in Capua through a change of lifestyle to one based on "continual *truphē*" and many other good things in life, such as perfumes, soft beds, and rich food. One cannot be certain that the language belongs to Diodorus and not the excerptor. The passage is quoted in full and discussed in the Conclusion (pp. 440–41).

διὸ καὶ ῥᾳδίως ταῖς τῶν προστίμων αἰσχραῖς ὑπεξαιρέσεσιν ἀπέτρεψε τῆς βλαβερᾶς τρυφῆς καὶ ἀκολασίας τῶν ἐπιτηδευμάτων· οὐδεὶς γὰρ ἐβούλετο τὴν αἰσχρὰν ἀκολασίαν ὁμολογήσας καταγέλαστος ἐν τοῖς πολίταις εἶναι.

[Wherefore by the shameful removal of fines, he easily turned them away from the harmful *truphē* and licentiousness of their customs. For no one, going along with shameful licentiousness, wanted to be a laughingstock among the citizens.] (Diod. Sic. 12.21.2)

It would seem that here τρυφή is pernicious (βλαβερᾶς), leading to licentiousness, and certainly Diodorus refers to all these laws as well enacted (καλῶς). Yet the τρυφή of the Locrians has no historical implications. Neither the presence of an immoderate lifestyle nor it later remedy is associated with significant events. Zaleucus's laws are related as an appendage to a discussion of the laws of Charondas at Sybaris/Thurii.

An interesting twist is given to the social function of τρυφή when Diodorus discusses a peculiar law at Syracuse. The Syracusans practiced petalism, a kind of ostracism, whose unintended results were to drive the most excellent and capable men out of politics, for fear of being exiled: ἐπιμελόμενοι δὲ τῆς ἰδίας οὐσίας εἰς τρυφὴν ἀπέκλινον ("turning their attention to their own private matters, they turned aside into *truphē*," Diod. Sic. 11.87.4). The effect was catastrophic for the state: it led to factional quarrels, demagogues, and sycophants, as lesser, rasher men ran public affairs. Finally the law of petalism was revoked, and government returned to the hands of able citizens. Elsewhere in writers of the Roman period (particularly, as we will see, in Dionysius of Halicarnassus), τρυφή is usually the characteristic of the lesser men who are taking the republic in a dangerous direction, not excellent men who have retired to live a strictly private existence. So this passage is a kind of inverted interpretation of pernicious luxury: the civil strife is not caused by τρυφή, but rather τρυφή is seen as an alternative to risks of patriotic involvement in civic life.

Thus, taken as a whole, the association by Diodorus of groups of people with τρυφή is favorable and even flattering. The word can on occasion imply weakness and immorality, but such a connection carries no serious historical ramifications, at least as far as the narrative allows us to judge.

When we look at the portrayals throughout his account of individuals who possess τρυφή, we see much the same pattern. When applied to the god Dionysus, τρυφή represents one of his two forms: he appeared either old and bearded or young and full of τρυφή (Diod. Sic. 4.5.2). He demonstrated the former when he fought in battle, which he did extremely well, and the latter at festivals, when he wore garments that were τρυφερός and extremely soft (4.4.4; cf. 3.64.6 and 4.4.2). Thus his τρυφή in peacetime was contrasted with his warrior persona, but it did not make him less of a fighter. Similarly Darius is offered a choice by Alexander: scorn reputation and yield, and be given as his reward τὴν λυσιτέλειαν καὶ τὴν ἐκ τῆς ῥᾳστώνης τρυφήν ("the advantage and the *truphē* that comes with leisure," 17.54.6). It was not a bad offer and Alexander did not mean it as an insult: Darius could still be the second most powerful man on earth, accepting only Alexander as his ruler.

Τρυφή is almost a defining attribute of the earliest kings of Egypt and Assyria. The Egyptian kings introduced τρυφή and an extravagant way of life (πολυτελῆ βίον, 1.45.1) and, after Ramses III died, ἐπὶ γενεὰς ἑπτὰ διεδέξαντο τὴν ἀρχὴν βασιλεῖς ἀργοὶ παντελῶς καὶ πρὸς ἄνεσιν καὶ τρυφὴν ἅπαντα πράττοντες ("for seven generations, kings took over the rule, being altogether lazy and doing everything with an eye toward indulgence and *truphē*," 1.63.1). No particular harm befell them as a result.[43]

The Assyrian rulers also employed τρυφή, but, again, damning consequences are absent. Semiramis, a fierce warrior queen, built a retreat in Media πρὸς τρυφήν where she spent a great deal of time, πάντων τῶν εἰς τρυφὴν ἀνηκόντων ἀπολαύσασα ("enjoying all of the things pertaining to *truphē*," Diod. Sic. 2.13.4).[44] And yet for all that, she continued her career of conquest unabated. There is no indication that the τρυφή affected either her moral integrity or her martial prowess. Her son Ninyas, avoided wars and devoted his whole life to τρυφή.[45] He hid himself away in the palace in order to keep everyone ignorant of his τρυφή. But he was not a careless ruler as a result: he took the necessary precautions of maintaining a strong army close at hand to frighten his subjects, and of appointing able ministers and generals, financial officials, and judges to run the empire for him (2.21.1–7). The fact that Ninyas concealed his τρυφή only makes sense in a context in which that trait was viewed as a weakness. However, Diodorus does not maintain this perspective. The successors of Ninyas followed both his administrative arrangements and his lifestyle

---

43. According to a story, one king, called Tnephachthus, was forced by circumstances to fast one day and then eat peasant food. As a result of his experience, he adopted this simpler way of life and denounced τρυφή (Diod. Sic. 1.45.2). Clearly he was the exception.
44. Cf. the pleasure park of Tissaphernes at Diod. Sic. 14.80.2.
45. For the phrase, ἐζήλου δὲ τρυφὴν καί ῥᾳθυμίαν, see Meyer 2009, 61–67. Cf. our discussion about Athenaeus and ζηλόω in Chapter 3.

and yet were able to preserve Assyrian rule for thirty generations (2.21.8). Possession of τρυφή does not have the influence on the course of historical events that we might expect from the emphasis that Diodorus gives it.

This misalignment between cause and effect, as contrasted to the working of *luxuria* in Latin writers of the first century, is clearly evident in Diodorus's treatment of the last and most famous of the Assyrian rulers, the man who serves even today as the paradigm of pernicious luxury, Sardanapalus (Diod. Sic. 2.23–27).[46] He is described as ὑπερῆρεν ἅπαντας τοὺς πρὸ αὐτοῦ τρυφῇ καὶ ῥαθυμίᾳ ("excelling all the kings before him in *truphē* and relaxation," 2.23.1). He spent his entire life in the company of women, dressing like them, making up his face, and weaving wool. He composed his own epitaph, an ancient rendition of "eat, drink, and be merry," which Diodorus records in the Greek translation, including in one phrase an association with hubris: ταῦτ' ἔχω ὅσσ' ἔφαγον καὶ ἐφύβρισα καὶ μετ' ἔρωτος ("I have these things: what I ate and what I did insolently and in love," 2.23.3). Diodorus sums up what is to follow with these words:

τοιοῦτος δ' ὢν τὸν τρόπον οὐ μόνον αὐτὸς αἰσχρῶς κατέστρεψε τὸν βίον, ἀλλὰ καὶ τὴν Ἀσσυρίων ἡγεμονίαν ἄρδην ἀνέτρεψε, πολυχρονιωτάτην γενομένην τῶν μνημονευομένων.

[Being a man of such a character, not only did he upset his own life shamefully, but he also utterly overturned the Assyrian empire, being the longest rule of any power remembered.] (Diod. Sic. 2.23.4)

Diodorus seems to be claiming that τρυφή was the cause of his ruin. And yet the subsequent lengthy narration belies that assertion. Arbaces, a Median general, was incited to rebellion by a Babylonian priest who foretold that Arbaces would be ruler, in exchange for which the priest was promised the satrapy of his native city. They allied with other commanders and then, after the groundwork was laid, Arbaces secreted himself into the king's chambers so that he could see Sardanapalus's way of life for himself:

διόπερ δούς τινι τῶν εὐνούχων χρυσῆν φιάλην εἰσήχθη πρὸς τὸν Σαρδανάπαλλον, καὶ τήν τε τρυφὴν αὐτοῦ καὶ τὸν γυναικώδη τῶν

---

46. An extensive discussion of Sardanapalus can be found in the section on Ctesias in Chapter 4.

ἐπιτηδευμάτων ζῆλον ἀκριβῶς κατανοήσας κατεφρόνησε μὲν τοῦ βασιλέως ὡς
οὐδενὸς ἀξίου, προήχθη δὲ πολὺ μᾶλλον ἀντέχεσθαι τῶν δοθεισῶν ἐλπίδων
ὑπὸ τοῦ Χαλδαίου.

[Wherefore, giving one of the eunuchs a gold saucer, he was led into the private
chamber of Sardanapalus, and when he had thoroughly observed his *truphē*
and the eagerness for womanly pursuits, he despised the king as worth nothing,
and he was induced all the more to cling to the hopes offered by the Chaldean.]
(Diod. Sic. 2.24.4)

The narrative indicates that the conspiracy was hatched before Arbaces saw the
effeminacy of Sardanapalus's τρυφή; on the other hand, it was his observation
of the king that hardened his resolve. He launched his rebellion. Thus, the fall
of the Assyrian empire was the result of a double instigation, one general and
political, another personal and moral. Such over-determination perhaps would
not be worth dwelling on if it were not for the fact that the subsequent narration ignores the picture of a king enervated by his lifestyle. In contrast to the
expected association between τρυφή and a general lack of military prepared-
ness, Sardanapalus responded by leading his armies into battle personally and
defeating the rebelling forces in three different engagements. He was only overcome by a combination of treachery and bad luck. The Bactrians secretly de-
fected, and the rebels attacked his men while they were celebrating a festival.
Even then, the king's forces fought valiantly, losing two battles and then holding
off a siege of Nineveh for three years (2.28.1) until the Euphrates flooded and
broke down a section of the city walls, thus allowing the attackers in. To avoid
surrender, Sardanapalus immolated himself and his harem. Thus it would be
difficult to conclude from the details of this narrative that τρυφή caused the
downfall of either Sardanapalus or his kingdom.

This lack of internal coherence suggests that Diodorus's account is the
melding of two different and contradictory traditions together into one story.
We have seen in the previous chapter how Sardanapalus served as a moral *exemplum* from at least the 4th century BCE. At least some sources attributed the
king's death directly to the revulsion felt by his subjects for his dissipated behavior. Thus, at Athen. 12.528e–529d in an account attributed to οἱ μὲν πολλοί,
ὧν ἐστι καὶ Δοῦρις ("most people, including Duris"), Arbaces was so disgusted
when he saw Sardanapalus all made up and effeminate that he stabbed him to
death on the spot. At the same time, Athenaeus reports another tradition, with

Ctesias as his source, according to which the king went to war and, being defeated, set himself on fire, thus dying "as nobly as possible" (ὡς ἐνῆν γενναίως). Apparently, when confronted with these incongruities, Diodorus blended the two accounts.

In this connection, it is important to observe the function of the word τοιοῦτος, as at Athen. 12.528f: τοιοῦτος δ᾽ ἦν καί Σαρδανάπαλλος . . . ("Such a man also was Sardanapalus . . ."). We have seen that Athenaeus regularly uses the word to indicate both a change of subject and a change of source. We would argue that precisely such a switch occurs here as well. At this point, the story changes from an anecdotal account of the king's τρυφή to a narration of the actual events of the rebellion, with the episode of Arbaces' secret visit to the king's chambers inserted in the appropriate place. The stabbing itself had to be omitted, since the two threads cannot be reconciled with that incident left intact. But without it, Diodorus can report both traditions simultaneously without leaving himself open to a charge of excessive inconsistency.

The resulting narrative is instructive for anyone interested in the idea of pernicious luxury. Certainly, Diodorus is aware of the possibility of τρυφή acting as a destructive force with historical consequences.[47] Nonetheless, in a story in which we might expect decadence to be a dominant theme, we instead find it narrowly limited to a brief episode. The tale of the downfall of Sardanapalus therefore reveals a surprising disinterest in τρυφή as historical cause

As conqueror of the East, Alexander the Great was famous for embracing a measure of τρυφή. When he returned from India, ἤρξατο ζηλοῦν τὴν Περσικὴν τρυφὴν καὶ τὴν πολυτέλειαν τῶν Ἀσιανῶν βασιλέων ("he began to imitate the *truphē* of the Persians and the extravagance of the Asian kings," Diod. Sic. 17.77.4). This statement is explained to mean that he not only dressed himself and

---

47. Even the story told by Duris, in which τρυφή is the foremost cause of the end of Assyrian hegemony, does not support the pattern usually ascribed to pernicious luxury in the modern literature. Sardanapalus is an extreme case of the ill results of a life of self-indulgence. Yet, he is not said to have lost his kingdom through a resulting incompetence, either administrative or martial. Rather, his behavior simply aroused the contempt of an underling, and the ruler was consequently murdered. To be sure, the king's exaggerated effeminacy would have made Arbaces' reaction credible to a Greek audience. However, this same exaggeration makes this story of little value as a historical paradigm: few, if any, other figures in Greek historiography matched the Assyrian in the extent of his decadence. Certainly, such blatant effeminacy could scarcely be generalized as a characteristic of any city or nation with which the Greeks were actually familiar. Thus, Sardanapalus's end is better suited to provide moralists with a parable of warning than to give historians a line of explanation for particular events. The Assyrian's prominence in our sources is probably due to his function as a bête noire among popular moralizers, not the importance of a concept of pernicious luxury as the cause of actual historical catastrophes.

his companions in the outfits of Persian royalty and attached a harem to his retinue, but also that he ordered the most prominent men (ἐπιφανεστάτους) to serve as his guard. Diodorus does not mention some of the more extreme details we hear from other sources, such as demanding proskynesis of his Macedonian followers (Arr., *Anab.* 4.10–12), yet apparently the king still recognized that his behavior was offensive. Diodorus says that Alexander in fact adopted these customs sparingly so as not to insult, and he bribed anyone who objected (Diod. Sic. 17.77.7–78.1). The idea of τρυφή is distasteful here because the Macedonian king was *primus inter pares*. In adopting Persian customs, Alexander was, in effect, treating his companions as servants. Thus, Alexander's τρυφή may have been pernicious as the kind of attitude that is associated with hubris, a connection familiar from both Latin and Classical Greek sources. There is no question of τρυφή having feminized the Macedonian or reduced his prowess in war.

Also within the Alexander narrative, Diodorus offers the story of Harpalus, the man left by Alexander in charge of the treasury at Babylon (Diod. Sic. 17.104). Since he did not expect his king to survive his eastern campaigns, Harpalus abused his position, squandering the treasury on prostitutes and fine living. His behavior is described (17.108.4): δοὺς δ᾽ ἑαυτὸν εἰς τρυφήν ("giving himself up into truphē"), εἰς ὕβρεις γυναικῶν καὶ παρανόμους ἔρωτας βαρβάρων ἐξετράπη ("he turned away into the rape of women and illegal liaisons with the natives"), and seeking out ἀκρατεστάταις ἡδοναῖς ("purest pleasures") and δίαιταν πολυδάπανον ("an extravagant way of life"). When Alexander did return, Harpalus fled with a large sum of money and was eventually murdered. Certainly his behavior was extreme, but we must note that Diodorus does not make his τρυφή itself the cause of his undoing. His fault was in stealing from Alexander: he was living in τρυφή beyond his means. If Diodorus had wanted to impress his readers with a model of historical causation in which τρυφή leads through hubris to destruction, this story provided the perfect opportunity. The fact that Diodorus chose not to express it in that light tells us that such a model was clearly not universally applied by the time he was writing.

Likewise he tells the stories of various Spartans who devoted themselves to τρυφή. Cleonymus led a force into Metapontum in 303 BCE, but behaved badly in victory (Diod. Sic. 20.104.4–5). He exacted a high financial tribute and took hostages, not for a guarantee of the city's good behavior, but

. . . ὡς τῆς ἰδίας ἕνεκεν λαγνείας. ἀποθέμενος γὰρ τὴν Λακωνικὴν ἐσθῆτα διετέλει τρυφῶν καὶ τοὺς πιστεύσαντας αὐτῷ καταδουλούμενος·

[. . . for his own private sexual use. And putting aside his Spartan clothing, he spent his time living in *truphē*, and he enslaved those who trusted him.] (Diod. Sic. 20.104.4)

Again, Cleonymus's τρυφή is linked to hubristic behavior, making slaves of people who did not deserve to be treated as slaves (although Diodorus does not use the word "hubris" here). Notably, this conduct has no reported ill effects for Cleonymus.

Less lucky was Acrotatus, who went to help the Sicilians in 314 BCE, but behaved abominably:

τοῦ δὲ χρόνου προϊόντος πρᾶξιν μὲν οὐδεμίαν οὔτε τῆς πατρίδος οὔτε τῆς περὶ τὸ γένος ἐπιφανείας ἀξίαν διεπράξατο, τοὐναντίον δὲ φονικὸς ὢν καὶ τῶν τυράννων ὠμότερος προσέκοπτε τοῖς πλήθεσι. πρὸς δὲ τούτοις τὴν πάτριον δίαιταν μετέβαλεν καὶ ταῖς ἡδοναῖς ἐνετρύφησεν οὕτως ἀσελγῶς ὥστε Πέρσην εἶναι δοκεῖν καὶ οὐ Σπαρτιάτην.

[As time passed, he did nothing worthy either of his fatherland or of his nobility, but rather the opposite. Being a murderer more savage than the tyrants, he offended the people. In addition to these things, he changed his native way of life and enjoyed *truphē* in pleasures so wantonly that he seemed to be a Persian, not a Spartiate.] (Diod. Sic. 19.71.2–3)

He spent the public treasury, and the last straw came when he murdered a local hero. The people removed him from office and attempted to stone him to death, though he escaped back to Laconia. Again, the τρυφή may have been part of his undoing, but Diodorus focuses on his tyrannical conduct, especially murder, rather than on his lifestyle.

The story of Pausanias, the victor of Plataea, completes our section on Diodorus's use of τρυφή. Four times Diodorus says that Pausanias hated the Spartan austerity and preferred the τρυφή of the Persians, even though he of all people should have known how much superior was his own ancestral way of life.[48] In addition, he acted tyrannically toward his Greek subordinates:

ἐγένετο δὲ καταφανὴς καὶ τιμωρίας ἔτυχε τοιῷδέ τινι τρόπῳ. ζηλώσαντος

---

48. Diod. Sic. 11.44.5, 11.46.2, 11.46.3 *bis*.

αὐτοῦ τὴν Περσικὴν τρυφὴν καὶ τυραννικῶς προσφερομένου τοῖς
ὑποτεταγμένοις, χαλεπῶς ἔφερον ἅπαντες, μάλιστα δὲ οἱ τεταγμένοι τῶν
Ἑλλήνων ἐπί τινος ἡγεμονίας.

[He was found out and received his punishment in the following way. Emulating the *truphē* of the Persians and acting tyrannically toward his underlings,
everyone bore his behavior with difficulty, most especially those of the Greeks
who were stationed in some position of command.] (Diod. Sic. 11.44.4–5)

The first sentence in this passage is crucial for understanding the role of τρυφή.
It was through his display of τρυφή that the secret Pausanias became apparent
(καταφανὴς) to the world. For the Spartan had been covertly plotting:

συνετέθειτο γὰρ δι᾿ ἀπορρήτων φιλίαν πρὸς τὸν βασιλέα, καὶ τὴν θυγατέρα
τοῦ Ξέρξου γαμεῖν ἔμελλεν, ἵνα προδῷ τοὺς Ἕλληνας.

[He was arranging in secret an alliance with the King and was going to marry
Xerxes' daughter, in order to betray the Greeks.] (Diod. Sic. 11.44.3)

As in the story of Sardanapalus, preparations for revolution had been going on
for some time. And, as in that case, it was a reaction to τρυφή which set in motion the dénouement. Pausanias's zeal for τρυφή provoked anger in his followers, and complaints were brought to the Ephors in Sparta.[49] Eventually, investigation of the king by Lacedaemonian authorities established his guilt and led to
his death.

It is important to note that in his narrative of the events comprising the fall
of Pausanias, Diodorus does not make τρυφή the cause of the Spartan's treacherous behavior. Instead, it is a manifestation of his inner mind and a cause of its
revelation. Furthermore, no details of lifestyle are associated with the claim that
Pausanias was devoted to τρυφή. We do not hear about the clothing he wore or
the food he ate. As far as we can tell, his τρυφή was coextensive with his rough
treatment of his allies and subordinates. In sum, Pausanias's τρυφή mutated
into a kind of hubris, a quality certainly implicit in Diodorus's τυραννικῶς.

In contrast to this relationship established in the narrative, Diodorus also

---

49. Green (2006, ad loc.; 2010, ad loc.) stresses that Pausanias's Medism was probably a frame-up to
avoid discussing his favoring of the helots. But for our purposes the historical reality is less important
than the historical perception laid down by Dionysius.

presents the moral lesson to be drawn from these facts. In this passage, τρυφή is indeed the cause of Pausanias's transformation from a benefactor of Greece to a model of folly:

ἀγαπήσας τῶν Περσῶν τὸν πλοῦτον καὶ τὴν τρυφήν, ἅπασαν τὴν προϋπάρχουσαν εὐδοξίαν κατῄσχυνεν; ἐπαρθεὶς γὰρ ταῖς εὐτυχίαις τὴν μὲν Λακωνικὴν ἀγωγὴν ἐστύγησε, τὴν δὲ τῶν Περσῶν ἀκολασίαν καὶ τρυφὴν ἐμιμήσατο

[Falling in love with the wealth and *truphē* of the Persians, he turned all his former glory into shame. With his ego over-inflated by his successes, he grew to hate the Laconian way of life, but began to imitate Persian intemperance and *truphē*.] (Diod. Sic. 11.46.2–3)

As we have seen in our discussion of Sardanapalus, Diodorus's portrait of Pausanias's decadence is composed of two images, which do not quite align. It is our view that, in the historical narrative, the king's τρυφή is but one element in an involved story. Its secondary importance can be seen, for example, in the fact that the reports to Sparta about Pausanias's τρυφή did not have immediate repercussions for him. Rather, there follows a complicated story about how Pausanias was betrayed in several ways by one of those carrying his secret communications to the Persians. In addition, the τρυφή shown by the Spartan does not seem to have any ill effects on Pausanias's character. He does not become an incompetent general or adopt an effeminate lifestyle. In the moralizing summary, on the other hand, lifestyle (ἀγωγή) is central, and τρυφή is associated with a more general intemperance (ἀκολασία).

Thus, the pattern is quite similar to that which appears in Diodorus's treatment of Sardanapalus. Both combine narrative and moral explanation, but in a manner which makes it clear that the two threads do not fit together perfectly. It seems to us not accidental that in both passages the narrative element, presumably drawn from the historical tradition, minimizes the impact of lifestyle on history.

To sum up, unlike Polybius, Diodorus uses the word τρυφή quite often, but his practice is to treat τρυφή most commonly as a good, something highly sought after and most pleasant to possess. On rare occasions, τρυφή is clearly a moral failing and seems to influence the course of history. However, in these instances, even Diodorus himself does not seem to accept the causal force of a decadent lifestyle. More generally, if we look at the extant parts of Polybius and Diodorus, the evidence they provide does not allow us to extrapolate a principle that makes a luxurious way of life responsible for historical catastrophe. Polybius has nothing to say on the subject, while, in the two most prominent examples of pernicious τρυφή in Diodorus, its associations are incompatible: Sardanapalus is too effeminate to be tolerated while Pausanias is offensively dominant. Thus, these authors neither confirm the supposed existence of destructive luxury as a theme in Hellenistic histories, nor do they reflect the model of decadence evident in the Latin sources that we have examined.

Dionysius of Halicarnassus

Dionysius of Halicarnassus wrote at the time of Augustus, seeking to prove a Greek origin for Rome in order to justify Roman rule over the Hellenic world (*Ant. Rom.* 1.5.2). In doing so, he attributes Rome's world supremacy to the emulation of Greek virtues as modeled by Isocrates especially.[50] Yet, just as he promotes a fantasy of a Greek ethnic origin for the Romans that cannot stand up to historical scrutiny, he also adapts from Latin authors some distinctly Roman virtues and mores that are at odds with those of his Hellenic models. Certainly he does cite the expected qualities of justice, moderation, and the like, but meanwhile he embraces peculiarly Roman ideals concerning the destructive power of τρυφή and the dangers of peace. By setting these principles in the context of the increasing classicism at Rome, and thus implying that they are Greek to begin with, he attempts to legitimize inherent Roman values to the Greek world.[51]

Much of Dionysius's writing pertains to oratory, and six of his uses of τρυφή

---

50. Dion. Hal., *Ant. Rom.* 1.5.3, 1.6.4, 2.3.2–5, 2.18.1–2, etc. Gabba 1991, 33–35, 75–80. "The faith placed in political and moral Isocratean ideals carried with it a projection of these same ideals onto a wider historical framework" (75). "In fact, Dionysius describes a society structured after the lofty model of Isocratean morality" (77). Fox (1993, 45) claims that Dionysius used myth "to prove that the Romans were in origin Greek, and from the earliest times behaved better than the Greeks themselves"; for the influence of Isocrates, see 41–42. Schultze 1986, 133: "the Romans are not only Greeks but are better than actual Hellenes, more truly Greek in their customs and behavior generally, and above all in their *politeia.*"

51. For the moral aims of Dionysius's history, see Fox 1993, Schultze 1986. Gowing (2009) makes a strong case for a change in the Roman *exempla* tradition, from the concentration on Great Men, in authors such as Livy, to a focus on the collective morality in Dionysius, Appian, and Cassius Dio. For the Classical influence on Dionysius as a social-cultural phenomenon, Wiater 2011.

fall into a rhetorical context.[52] The adjective τρυφερός has come to mean "pleasing," especially as it implies the giving of attention, words that will be pleasing to the listener, who in turn is a person of τρυφή. It can easily become flattery, an extreme form of this sort of speech.[53] A good example occurs at *De compositione verborum* 23.37:

σχήμασί τε οὐ τοῖς ἀρχαιοπρεπεστέροις οὐδ᾽ ὅσοις σεμνότης τις ἢ βάρος ἢ τόνος πρόσεστιν, ἀλλὰ τοῖς τρυφεροῖς τε καὶ κολακικοῖς ὡς τὰ πολλὰ χρῆσθαι φιλεῖ, ἐν οἷς πολὺ τὸ ἀπατηλόν ἐστι καὶ θεατρικόν.

[For they do not love to use the more time-honored figures nor the sort to which a certain dignity or weight or pitch belongs, but on the whole *trupheros* and flattering forms, in which there is much that is deceptive and theatrical.]

In his historical account, the *Antiquitates Romanae*, Dionysius uses the word τρυφή six times.[54] The first three instances occur in Book 6, in the context of the First Secession of the Plebs in 491 BCE. All three are in speeches and all are completely consistent with the Classical meaning as an attitude of entitlement. At the same time, the word occurs without any accompanying implication of softness or effeminacy. Rather, τρυφή is consistently associated with the suggestion that indulgence will lead to tyranny or civil strife.[55]

When Appius Claudius Sabinus urged the Senate to adopt a rigid stance against the plebs, opposing any offer of conciliation and instead exacting rigid punishments according to the inflexible enforcement of the laws, he began his speech with these words:

καὶ γὰρ νῦν, ἔφη, πέρα τοῦ μετρίου τρυφῶσι τελῶν ἀφειμένοι, ὧν ἐτέλουν τοῖς βασιλεῦσι πρότερον, καὶ τῶν εἰς τὸ σῶμα τιμωριῶν, αἷς ἐκολάζοντο ὑπ᾽ αὐτῶν, ὁπότε μὴ ταχέως ὑπηρετήσειάν τι τῶν ἐπιταττομένων, ἐλεύθεροι γεγονότες.

---

52. Dion. Hal., *De ant. orat.* 1.16, 2.11; *Dem.* 26.18, 48.49, 55.15; *Comp.* 23.37. One other use, *Thuc.* 19.27, is a paraphrase of Thuc. 1.6.3, where the Athenians in their τρυφή wore cicadas in their hair.

53. We may compare those passages in which Demosthenes attributes τρυφή to the demos when certain orators tell the people what they wants to hear instead of what he sees as hard truths: e.g., Dem. 8.34 and 9.4.

54. There are another four examples in the excerpts. One should note in caution that all four fragmentary uses come from the same collection of miscellaneous excerpts in a fifteenth-century manuscript (Ambrosianus Q 13).

55. Schultze (1986, 128) identifies one of Dionysius's key themes as "the remarkable avoidance of *stasis*, attributed chiefly to the virtues of the constitution and, to an extent, to the Roman character." Cf. 131–33.

[And even now, he said, they [the seceding plebeians] live in *truphē* beyond measure, since they have been set free from the taxes that they paid to the kings previously, and from corporal punishment with which they were penalized by them whenever they did not obey quickly any time they were ordered to do something, even though they were free men.] (Dion. Hal., *Ant. Rom.* 6.24.2)

This ironic use of τρυφάω is a confirmation of its Classical meaning: the plebs are being taken care of beyond what is due and moderate in that they do not suffer taxation and beatings. By yielding to their demands, Sabinus continued, Rome runs the risk of tyranny originating among the plebs, and notably this tyranny arises through demagogy; this connection of flattery and tyranny is itself a rebuke aimed at the τρυφή of the people:[56]

ἔπειτα δ᾽ εἰς κίνδυνον οὐ τὸν ἐλάχιστον ἥξομεν, εἴ τις ἐκθεραπεύσας αὐτὸν ἐξουσίαν κρείττονα τῶν νόμων κατασκευάσαιτο τυραννικὸς ἀνήρ, τὴν ἐλευθερίαν αὖθις ἀφαιρεθῆναι.

[And also we risk a danger not slight in itself, that if someone, a tyrannical man, by catering to them [the masses], should acquire power that is greater than the laws, we will lose our freedom a second time.] (Dion. Hal., *Ant. Rom.* 6.24.3)

So τρυφή here is associated with a kind of indulgence, but it is not the one linked to effeminacy and weakness, but rather it indicates the softness of wheedling words that a tyrant uses to seduce the masses and, at the same time, the people's expectation of such flattery.

Later, in the same senatorial discussion, Menenius Agrippa counseled reconciliation. He mocked his opponents who thought that they could disown, as it were, the existing body of rebellious plebs and instead import from elsewhere a new, more respectable and more docile underclass. Where, he asked, while under immediate attack, were the Romans to find this new subservient group of men willing to fight for a city to which they have no attachments of blood, tradition, or commerce? οὐ γὰρ εἰρήνης καὶ τρυφῆς μεταληψόμενοι δεῦρο ἥξουσιν, ἀλλὰ κινδύνων καὶ πολέμου ("For they will come here, not in order to share in peace and *truphē*, but rather dangers and war," Dion. Hal., *Ant. Rom.*

---

56. Cf. 6.60.2, 61.3. Livy's account (2.23ff.) makes no mention of the threat of tyranny from the people, but does say that the Senate appointed a dictator to deal with the masses (2.30). Their main problems, according to the sympathetic Livy, were debt and debt slavery, but Claudius Sabinus accused the plebs of license rather than anger over their plight (Livy 2.29.9–10).

6.52.2). Menenius emphasized that Rome needed a respectable lower class, with good ancestry, personal merit, households and trades, not men who were indebted criminals and vagabonds, and therefore willing to accept whatever fortune brought (Dion. Hal., *Ant. Rom.* 6.52.2–3). The former group might presume a share of τρυφή, in the form of jobs and households, but they would also fight for the city in which they were invested, whereas a desperate rabble would be an ill defense for the city.

Thus through Menenius, Dionysius portrays τρυφή as a very positive trait, a natural enticement for immigrants. In addition, τρυφή for Menenius does not entail decadence: the τρυφή of peacetime is compatible with willingness to face dangers during war. Self-indulgent pleasures are apparently normal components of civic life, at least when the city is at peace. And, contrary to Sabinus, Menenius found peace and τρυφή preferable to dangers and war. Thus, in this episode Dionysius is able to present τρυφή as a positive characteristic, as we have seen it in earlier Greek writers, but he also offers a negative view, similar to the one prevalent in Latin texts. And, as we will see, the Roman perspective will dominate elsewhere in his writings.

When eventually the senators agreed to appoint a commission entrusted with plenipotentiary powers to negotiate a compromise,[57] the leader, Manius Valerius, appealed to the plebs to come to an agreement, explaining the Senate's extraordinary goodwill and urging the plebs to be reasonable and open: ἐπὶ δὴ τοσαύτης βεβηκότες εὐτυχίας μὴ μέλλετε λέγειν, ὦ δημόται, τίνων χρῄζετε μηδ᾽ ἐντρυφᾶτε ἡμῖν ("Since you have come into such good fortune, do not hesitate to say, O People, what it is you want, but do not act with *truphē* toward us," 6.71.4).[58] His chiding tone throughout the speech is that of a father reprimanding disobedient and silly children, a comparison made overtly at 6.71.3, ὥσπερ ἂν παίδων ἀφρόνων χρηστοὶ πατέρες ("just as kindly parents of foolish children").[59] The term ἐντρυφάω is quite apt: Valerius is implying that the plebs

---

57. In Livy, the Senate appoints Manius Valerius as dictator (Livy 2.30.1–4), not one of the "envoys" (τοὺς πρεσβευτάς), as Dionysius labels them (*Ant. Rom.* 6.69.4). He is not given any speeches, but merely issues an edict similar to the one previously promulgated by Servilius, which gave certain guarantees against debt slavery for soldiers (Livy 2.24.6–8).

58. The verb form, ἐντρυφάω, is intensive; the prefix ἐν- does one of two things. Either, as here, it directs someone's τρυφή against someone else, insisting that the other person should attend to the original person's wants (e.g.,: Habakkuk 1:10:2; Jos., *AJ* 15.219.2; Plut., *Eum.* 15.4) Elsewhere it focuses on the object of those wants (e.g.: Diod. Sic. 19.71.3 [pleasures]; Isaiah 55:2 [good things]; Philo, *Spec. leg.* 1.304 [justice and equality]).

59. By way of comparison, in a fragmentary excerpt of book 19, King Pyrrhus said to the Roman representatives: ἀλλὰ κωλύσω τοῖς ὅπλοις, ἵνα παύσησθε ἤδη ποτὲ ἄγοντες καὶ φέροντες ὅλην Ἰταλίαν καὶ πᾶσιν ἀνθρώποις ὡς δούλοις ἐντρυφῶντες ("But I will prevent you with my weapons so that you stop

need to avoid extreme behavior and behave sensibly, asking for concessions within reason and not assuming that they are due a higher level of entitlement or demanding that the patricians attend to their needs, as servants take care of masters.[60] Just as a child cannot expect to be treated like an adult, if the plebs behave with τρυφή and disrespect their betters, the situation will become dangerous, resulting in civil war.[61]

This idea of immorality among the masses is reinforced subsequently, when the plebeian leader, Titus Larcius, pleaded with his fellow plebs to accept the Senate's offer of compromise. He agreed that some plebs were driven to their demand of debt remission honestly, by their extreme poverty, but he also reproached many others because:

τὸ δὲ πλεῖον ἀκολασίᾳ καὶ ὕβρει καὶ τῷ καθ᾽ ἡδονὰς ζῆν ἐφεικὸς καὶ δι᾽ ἁρπαγῆς ἐκ τῶν ἀλλοτρίων ὑπηρετεῖν ταῖς ἐπιθυμίαις παρεσκευασμένον, . . .

[Most are longing to give themselves up to licentiousness and hubris and a life of pleasure and are prepared to serve their desires by stealing from other people.] (Dion. Hal., *Ant. Rom.* 6.81.4)

With this passage we see an association between the masses enjoying τρυφή and advancing into ἀκολασία, ὕβρις, ἡδονή, and ἁρπαγή. None of these terms implies the softness of effeminacy or an aversion to fighting, but rather a hubristic avarice that leads to crime.[62] The contrast is made between a life of mod-

---

going wherever you want and taking the whole of Italy and treating all men with *truphē*, as if they were slaves." Dion. Hal., *Ant. Rom.* 19.9.4). The essence of the τρυφή here is exaggerated and bordering on hubris, because it involves treating free men as slaves.

60. Valerius advised the plebs to choose a middle course. The two elements of his demand—μὴ μέλλετε λέγειν . . . τίνων χρῄζετε ("don't hesitate to say what you need") and μηδ᾽ ἐντρυφᾶτε ἡμῖν ("don't act with *truphē* toward us")—are contrary behaviors: in the first, the plebs err by not making their desires clear, in the second, by asking for too much or asking presumptuously.

61. According to Schultze (1986, 140), one of the chief themes of the *Antiquitates* is that of compromise. The Romans were superior in part because they had a constitution that stressed the equilibrium between the rights of masses and those of the elite. The willfulness implicit in the word τρυφή, we would argue, nicely complements this interpretation of Dionysius's text. For the theme of *concordia ordinum* in Livy, see Lind 1986, 67–73.

62. Likewise, in a fragmentary section from the Pyrrhic War, when Fabricius, one of the poorer ambassadors to the king, was offered a bribe, he recounted the accusations that would be leveled against him at home were he to accept it. Even, he said, if he doesn't betray the city and set up a tyranny (μηδ᾽ ἐπὶ προδοσίᾳ καὶ τυραννίδι τῶν σεαυτοῦ πολιτῶν ἐδωροδόκεις), taking the money would still be an act worthy of great punishment: ὅτι διαφθείρεις μὲν τοὺς νέους πλούτου καὶ τρυφῆς καὶ πολυτελείας βασιλικῆς ζῆλον εἰς τοὺς βίους εἰσάγων, οἷς πολλῆς δεῖ σωφροσύνης, εἰ μέλλει σωθήσεσθαι τὰ κοινά ("Because you [Fabricius] would be corrupting the young men by introducing to their lives the ea-

eration and honest poverty on the one hand, and a life of desire, whether for wealth, τρυφή, hubris, or any of the other vices.[63] It is the same contrast that has been laid down in Latin by Cicero, Sallust, and Livy between the rustic, virtuous Romans of the past and the corrupt and iniquitous citizens of the present. Also unambiguous here is the implication that τρυφή is perilous to the common good. It is worth noting that, besides the association with tyranny that we have witnessed in other Dionysian passages, in this instance we see some of the terms that will come to be associated so frequently with destructive τρυφή in authors like Athenaeus: διαφθείρω, πολυτέλεια, and ζῆλος.

So Valerius, Larcius, and Fabricius all expressed the sentiment that Romans need to live in moderation. The plebs especially cannot expect to live as a leisure class when they are the workers of Rome, standing as children in relation to the patricians. They must retain simple Roman traditional values of industry, hard work, and fidelity to family, city, and gods. In the context of the Plebeian Secession, they should accept the debt relief that is being offered them as a favor, and not demand it through violence (ὡς οὐ δικαίως ἀξιούντων βίᾳ μᾶλλον ἀφεῖσθαι τῶν ὀφειλημάτων ἢ χάριτι, Dion. Hal., Ant. Rom. 6.81.3). They are to preserve humble expectations, befitting their social status, because the alternative is moral corruption and civil strife.

We see comparable uses of τρυφή twice in the debate over Coriolanus, a man accused by the plebs of desiring tyranny and fomenting civil war (Dion. Hal., Ant. Rom. 7.21.3, 25.3).[64] Again, the conservative senators accused the plebeians of acting tyrannically, and Manius Valerius responded by reminding his fellow patricians that the best constitution was a mixed one, since a tendency toward tyranny was not a danger exclusive to the lower classes, but any of the three—monarchy, aristocracy, or democracy—could become tyrannical if it

---

gerness for wealth and *truphē* and kingly expenses, when they have need of great moderation, if the community is going to be preserved." Dion. Hal., *Ant. Rom.* 19.17.3). Thus are conjoined the threat of tyranny, corruption of the youth through desire for τρυφή, and the potential destruction of the republic. He goes on to say that he would also bring great shame on his ancestors, not one of whom ever "took up shameful money in place of honest poverty" (ἠλλάξατο πλοῦτον αἰσχρὸν ἀντὶ πενίας καλῆς, Dion. Hal., *Ant. Rom.* 19.17.4).

63. Another occurrence of τρυφή in Dionysius occurs in a brief fragment at *Ant. Rom.* 19.8.1, when a certain Meton wanted to demonstrate with feigned drunken behavior what privileges would be lost with the coming of Pyrrhus to Tarentum, πόλιν ἐλευθέραν καὶ τρυφῶσαν ("a free city and one practicing *truphē*"). Apparently he did not fear destruction or even effeminacy, but only the loss of banqueting and flute-girls.

64. In Livy's account of Coriolanus (2.34ff.), the senators are trying to use a grain shortage as leverage to repeal the privileges that the plebs had won through secession, namely the office of Plebeian Tribune (Livy 2.34.8). The plebs are worried, not about tyranny, but about having to make a choice between death and slavery (*aut mori aut servire*, Livy 2.35.1).

were allowed to proceed unchecked by the others. Thus, he claimed, even the Senate required oversight:

καὶ περὶ μὲν ὑμῶν οὔπω ἔδεισα, μὴ διαφθαρῆτε τὰς διανοίας ὑπό τε μεγέθους καὶ πλήθους ἀγαθῶν, οἳ τυραννίδος τε πολυχρονίου ἠλευθερώκατε τὴν πόλιν ἔναγχος καὶ οὔπω σχολὴν ἐσχήκατε ὑβρίζειν καὶ τρυφᾶν διὰ τοὺς συνεχεῖς καὶ μακροὺς πολέμους· περὶ δὲ τῶν μεθ᾽ ὑμᾶς ἐσομένων ἐνθυμούμενος ὅσας ὁ μακρὸς αἰὼν φέρει μεταβολὰς δέδοικα, μή τι παρακινήσαντες οἱ δυνατοὶ <οἱ> ἐκ τοῦ συνεδρίου λάθωσιν εἰς μοναρχίαν τὸ πολίτευμα περιστήσαντες τυραννικήν.

[And concerning you, I am not afraid that you will corrupt your minds with the greatness and number of good things, you who only recently have freed the city from a long-lived tyranny and who have not had leisure to practice hubris and *truphē* because of your continuous, long warfare. But pondering those who will come after you, I have been afraid of the changes that the great span of time may bring, lest powerful men from this Senate, fomenting revolution somehow, should go unobserved while they return the state to the monarchy of a tyrant.] (Dion. Hal., *Ant. Rom.* 7.55.6; cf. 56.1)

Here the danger is that the senators may become tyrannical. As at 6.52.2, τρυφή is connected with times of peace and is absent when war is being waged.[65] But in this passage such an association has become a corrupting force: peace and leisure lead to hubris and τρυφή, and thence to tyranny. It is morally better even for senators to remain busy in their warfare than to enjoy the profits of those hostilities.[66] Peace was not a healthy state for Rome.

This attitude stands in contrast to that of Dionysius's Greek models, particularly Isocrates, who consistently praises peace and disparages war. The orator makes the unambiguous point that peace is good for the democracy when he says:

---

65. Cf. the excerpted passage at Dion. Hal., *Ant. Rom.* 12.6.2: οὐκ ἐδόκει τοῖς προεστηκόσι τοῦ συνεδρίου βαθεῖαν εἰρήνην καὶ πολυχρόνιον ἄγειν σχολὴν ἐνθυμουμένοις, ὅτι ῥαθυμία καὶ τρυφὴ συνεισπορεύεται ταῖς πόλεσι μετὰ τῆς εἰρήνης, καὶ ἅμα τὰς πολιτικὰς ὀρρωδοῦσι ταραχάς ("For it did not seem fitting to the leaders of the senate to think about having abundant peace and long-lasting leisure, since ease and *truphē* enter into the city together with peace, and at the same time frequent civil disorders full of terrors.").

66. We have already established this same theme in Latin authors, esp. Cic., *Cat.* 2.11 and Sall., *Cat.* 10.

σπουδάζοντες δὲ περὶ τὴν πολιτείαν οὐχ ἧττον ἢ περὶ τὴν σωτηρίαν ὅλης τῆς
πόλεως καὶ τὴν δημοκρατίαν εἰδότες ἐν μὲν ταῖς ἡσυχίαις καὶ ταῖς ἀσφαλείαις
αὐξανομένην καὶ διαμένουσαν, ἐν δὲ τοῖς πολέμοις δὶς ἤδη καταλυθεῖσαν, . . .

[Being concerned about our government not less than for the safety of the
whole city, and seeing that the democracy increases and endures in leisure and
safety, but in wars it has been twice lost. . . .] (Isoc. 8.51).[67]

Isocrates recognizes the natural opposition between τρυφή and war, but understands that, though sometimes necessary, war is not a desirable state:

ὅτε μὲν γὰρ ἐξῆν ἡμῖν τρυφᾶν, πλείους τοὺς πολέμους ἐποιούμεθα τοῦ δέοντος,
ἐπειδὴ δ᾽ εἰς ἀνάγκην καθέσταμεν ὥστε κινδυνεύειν, ἡσυχίας ἐπιθυμοῦμεν καὶ
περὶ ἀσφαλείας βουλευόμεθα.

[For when it was possible for us to live in *truphē*, we made more wars than we
needed to, and then when we are forced to risk fighting, we are eager for leisure
and we deliberate about our safety.] (Isoc. 6.51)

Thus the praise of war over peace in connection with τρυφή appears to be the
application of Roman views on the effects of *luxuria* to the Greek moral concept.
    Furthermore, in his comments, Manius Valerius did not just warn the Fa-
thers about their own potential despotism (Dion. Hal., *Ant. Rom.* 7.55.5–6). He
continued by repeating an identical anxiety regarding the masses:

αὐτὸν δὲ τὸν δῆμον, ἵνα μὴ τρυφᾷ τηλικαύτης ἐξουσίας γενόμενος κύριος, μηδ᾽
ὑπὸ τῶν κακίστων ἐκδημαγωγούμενος τοῖς κρατίστοις πολεμῇ· καὶ γὰρ ἐν
ὄχλῳ φιλεῖ γίνεσθαι τυραννίς,[68] φυλάξει τε καὶ οὐδὲν ἐάσει παρανομεῖν ὁ
διαφέρων φρονήσει ἀνὴρ δικτάτωρ ὑφ᾽ ὑμῶν αἱρεθείς,

[And as for the masses themselves, so that once they are in control of great
power they do not practice *truphē* nor, being led by the worst demagogues,
make war on the best men—for a tyranny loves to come into being in the
mob—a dictator, a man distinguished for his good sense who is chosen by you,

---

67. Cf. esp. Dion. Hal., *Ant. Rom.* 4.182; 5.73; 6.50.
68. We replace the raised dot of the critical editions with a comma.

will guard them and allow them nothing that is contrary to the laws.] (Dion. Hal., *Ant. Rom.* 7.56.2)

In these passages, τρυφή is the precursor to tyranny, when it arises either from the aristocracy or from the people. In the first case, the responsibilities of leading a nation at war prevent the elite from seeking the satisfaction of their own desires. Τρυφή is equally pernicious for the masses, but it functions somewhat differently among them. The common people, Valerius implied, currently lacked the power that would allow them to exhibit τρυφή. In addition, they also lacked a unity of purpose that would make their τρυφή dangerous to the Senate, unless they should come under the influence of "the worst demagogues." Thus, the seditious effects of τρυφή are, according to Dionysius, apt to manifest themselves at all levels of society. Measures must be taken against this harmful tendency, and the most effective is the mixed constitution developed by the *maiores*.

In many Greek writers of the Roman era, a common theme that we are tracing is that τρυφή leads to hubris, and thence often provokes destruction. In our opinion, this idea is a development of an older Greek concept under the influence of a Roman moralizing explanation for the growth of their empire. As such, the pattern fits when it pertains to cities of the distant past, especially those that endured catastrophic defeats. However, since the working of this process of decadence was thought to be nearly universal and inevitable, it must have a place in the history of Rome itself. But Rome was not, for Dionysius, in any danger of falling to an outside enemy. Thus, the theme must be altered, and the pattern of decadence offered here is the menacing shadow of tyranny and of civil dissension. Romans at the time of Augustus did not fear destruction, but they had very real reasons to dread civil war and tyranny. In addition to the shared, but distant, historical tradition of having expelled the tyrannical kings, more recently they had endured the tumultuous events of the Roman civil wars, where dictators arose one after another and the Republic suffered grievously. Only the presence of the *princeps* was sufficient to end the violence.[69]

Just as Dionysius integrates the concept of τρυφή with Roman beliefs about the consequences of too much prosperity, he exaggerates τρυφή in respect to its original meaning. It no longer denotes merely the presumption of being taken care of. Rather it refers to demands made beyond what is proper by people who have no business making demands in the first place. In a distinctively Roman

---

69. Fox 1993, 40–41.

way, it is linked to peace, something that he imputes is not good for Romans, rich or poor. Peace allows individual self-interest and self-indulgence to over-shadow concern for the good of the community and brings with it avarice, hu-bris, crime, and corruption. When expectations of entitlement extend beyond what one should demand in pursuing a humble, honest Roman lifestyle, those expectations become destructive, not of the physical city, but of its most funda-mental political institutions, by way of civil unrest.

We learn more about the implications of τρυφή in several passages pertain-ing to the struggle against Veii. At 9.16.6–7 Dionysius describes the Battle of Cremera from 478 BCE, including details of the exploits of Lucius Aemilius, the consul and victorious general. Afterwards, Aemilius distributed the plunder of this extraordinarily rich city:

καὶ ἐγένετο ἐν πολλῇ εὐπορίᾳ τὸ τῶν Ῥωμαίων στράτευμα ὡς ἐξ οὐδεμιᾶς ἑτέρας πώποτε μάχης. ἁβροδίαιτον γὰρ δὴ καὶ πολυτελὲς τὸ τῶν Τυρρηνῶν ἔθνος ἦν οἴκοι τε καὶ ἐπὶ στρατοπέδου, περιαγόμενον ἔξω τῶν ἀναγκαίων πλούτου τε καὶ τέχνης ἔργα παντοῖα πρὸς ἡδονὰς μεμηχανημένα καὶ τρυφάς.

[And so the army of the Romans came into great abundance as it had never before from any other battle. For the Etruscan people lived in luxury and were very wealthy, both at home and in the field, carrying with them beyond the necessities all kinds of items of wealth and craftsmanship that were devised for pleasure and *truphē*.] (Dion. Hal., *Ant. Rom.* 9.16.8)

The money came at a time when the public treasury was drained (9.15.1), and yet all the money was turned over to the soldiers. This theme, as well as the ac-count of the battle itself, is far more embellished by Dionysius than in the cor-responding passage of Livy (2.48–49).[70] Yet even here there are no direct conse-quences of the sudden onset of wealth offered in this passage.

In this context we may remember the related idea that arises very frequently in the works of Dionysius's immediate contemporary, Livy. Particularly in the context of the wars against Veii, Livy introduces the idea that wealth and luxury corrupt. According to Miles:

---

70. The only mention of money in Livy's account comes when the Fabii *gens* volunteers for this war, promising also to shoulder all its costs (Livy 2.48.9), while the battle itself is depicted quite differ-ently, as a brief affair that was decided before it even began, by a surprise cavalry charge (Livy 2.49.10). For quarrels over spoils in the early books of Livy, see Lintott 1972.

Both the failure of *pietas* and the conflict between patricians and plebeians during this period originate with questions of wealth, whether in the form of taxes, booty, land, or, eventually, the property of Veii. . . . More specifically, the power of wealth to distract Romans from their essential responsibilities emerges as an explanation for the failure of Roman *pietas*, when it occurs. This emphasis on the role of *luxuria* can be shown not only to be a unifying theme in Livy's narrative of Roman decline after Veii but also to express an original interpretation of that decline: where Livy's narrative can be compared with others', the emphasis on *luxuria* appears repeatedly as the result of his own modification of received tradition. (Miles 1995, 80)

While some scholars might find Miles's thesis overstated,[71] one cannot deny that Livy attributes great damage at Rome to the corrupting influences of luxury and avarice.

The situation at Veii in 392 BCE provided the setting for the beginning of that decline.[72] Set in the framework of civic disputes over money and public land, with a drained treasury and an expensive war on their hands, the conquest of "an extremely wealthy city" (*urbs opulentissima*, Livy 5.20.1, 21.17, 22.8) caused so much anxiety to the general, Camillus, that he offered prayers to avert the envy of any god or man who thought his luck excessive (Livy 5.21.14–16). His prayers were in vain: *idque omen pertinuisse postea eventu rem coniectantibus visum, ad damnationem ipsius Camilli, captae deinde urbis Romanae, quod post paucos accidit annos, cladem* ("to those afterwards deriving the meaning from the outcome, that omen seemed to pertain to the condemnation of Camillus himself, then to the capture and destruction of the city of Rome, which took place a few years later." Livy 5.21.16). Thus in Livy's account, the taking of so much war booty is connected with both the downfall of Camillus and the capture of the city of Rome. So it comes as no surprise that Dionysius, writing slightly later and well-aware of Livy's account, uses the wars against the same city of Veii to explicate the theme of destructive τρυφή. He is reinforcing the idea that the conquest of a major enemy and the resulting absence of external wars leads almost inevitably to civil stasis by means of ῥᾳθυμία and τρυφή.

In a remarkable statement set in his account of 455 BCE,[73] Dionysius makes

---

71. See Miles 1995, 80 n. 12, for other common interpretations.

72. Miles 1995, ch. 2, esp. 80–86. Cf. Feldherr 1997, 273–77; Lintott 1972, 630; Gowing 2009 (for Camillus in the *exempla* tradition).

73. Cf. Dion. Hal., *Ant. Rom.* 9.32.4, 37.1.

explicit this conjunction between peace and the moral decline that results in civil *stasis*:

ἐγκύκλιον γὰρ δὴ τοῦτο καὶ ἐν ἔθει ἦν ἤδη τῇ πόλει πολεμουμένῃ μὲν ὁμονοεῖν, εἰρήνην δὲ ἀγούσῃ στασιάζειν. τοῦτο συνιδόντες ἅπαντες οἱ τὰς ὑπάτους ἀρχὰς παραλαβόντες κατ᾽ εὐχὰς μὲν εἴ τις ἔξωθεν ἐπαναστείη πόλεμος ἐλάμβανον· ἡσυχαζόντων δὲ τῶν ἀντιπάλων αὐτοὶ κατεσκεύαζον ἐγκλήματα καὶ προφάσεις πολέμων, ἅτε ὁρῶντες διὰ μὲν τοὺς πολέμους μεγάλην καὶ εὐδαίμονα γινομένην τὴν πόλιν, διὰ δὲ τὰς στάσεις ταπεινὴν καὶ ἀσθενῆ.

[For this became the cycle and a habitual thing for the city, when it was at war, to be in harmony, but in peace to be embroiled in civil strife. And all those who entered the consulate, being aware of this fact, took it as the answer to their prayers if some foreign war should happen to arise. And if their enemies were not aggressive, they themselves made up complaints and excuses for war, since they knew that the city would be great and fortunate during wars, but base and weak during civil strife.] (Dion. Hal., *Ant. Rom.* 10.33.2)

This sentiment is similar to that expressed by Sallust, writing a few years earlier than Dionysius, in which the fall of Carthage proved to be a critical moment in the corruption of Roman morality. Where Dionysius's design differs from Sallust's in its optimism, perhaps the change in emphasis is best attributed to the distinction between their views of their own times: whereas Sallust was disillusioned under the reigns of dictators, Dionysius saw a new beginning under Augustus that promised great prosperity.[74] Whereas Sallust derives strife from tyranny and the ambition of high-ranking men, who in turn spawn lawlessness among their followers, Dionysius lived under a now-peaceful *princeps* and so focuses instead on the potential dangers of civil strife originating among the masses. There is no hint of softness associated with τρυφή. Rather peace, prosperity, and wealth lead to τρυφή, and thence to moral corruption, civil war, and dictatorship. This schema represents a distinctly Roman way of characterizing history, absent from the Greek sources.

---

74. Gabba 1991, 33: "It is equally clear that in Dionysius's reasoning, the new culture, the classicistic revival, corresponds to the principle of elite order, as opposed to the disorder supported by the masses." Cf. Fox 1993.

Strabo

The geographer Strabo, an Eastern Greek writing at the time of Augustus and Tiberius, uses the term τρυφή more than a dozen times. While its original Classical meaning is still evident, the influence of Roman ideas about decadence is also visible. Strabo offers the opportunity to identify in one author the two processes of decadence involving pernicious luxury. In one, τρυφή makes its possessors soft and unwarlike; in the other, it turns them hubristic and violent. The two processes are, as should be apparent, contradictory, and Strabo sensibly does not attempt to bring them together in the same passage.

Strabo is capable of using τρυφή in a sense that is neutral or even positive—the town of Baiai has hot springs, which are good for τρυφή and to cure disease (5.4.5)[75]—but he also follows the theme that τρυφή can cause weakness and effeminacy. A fountain at Halicarnassus has an ill-deserved reputation for turning those who drink from it soft. Strabo protests instead:

> ἔοικε δ᾽ ἡ τρυφὴ τῶν ἀνθρώπων αἰτιᾶσθαι τοὺς ἀέρας ἢ τὰ ὕδατα· τρυφῆς δ᾽ αἴτια οὐ ταῦτα, ἀλλὰ πλοῦτος καὶ ἡ περὶ τὰς διαίτας ἀκολασία.

> [The *truphē* of men seems to be caused by the airs or the waters, but these things are not the real cause of *truphē*, but rather wealth and a licentiousness lifestyle.] (Strabo 14.2.16)

Strabo here equates softness with τρυφή, and prefers a moral cause for the phenomenon to a geographical determinism. In particular, while the view that wealth may cause τρυφή is familiar to him, Strabo reverses the relationship which we might have expected to see between τρυφή and ἀκολασία. Here, it is not τρυφή, which causes a more generally immoral lifestyle, but a lax way of life that is explicitly identified as the αἴτια of weakness and effeminacy.

In the story of Tarentum, we get a clearer indication of the problems that come from enjoying too much τρυφή:[76]

---

75. So, for example, because of τρυφή, the Persian kings obtained their grain from one city, their wine from another, and their water from a third (Strabo 15.3.22).

76. For an excellent exposition of historiographical approaches, especially the use of *inventio*, demonstrated in the stories surrounding Tarentum, see Barnes 2005.

ἐξίσχυσε δ᾽ ἡ ὕστερον τρυφὴ διὰ τὴν εὐδαιμονίαν, ὥστε τὰς πανδήμους ἑορτὰς πλείους ἄγεσθαι κατ᾽ ἔτος παρ᾽ αὐτοῖς ἢ τὰς ἡμέρας· ἐκ δὲ τούτου καὶ χεῖρον ἐπολιτεύοντο. ἓν δὲ τῶν φαύλων πολιτευμάτων τεκμήριόν ἐστι τὸ ξενικοῖς στρατηγοῖς χρῆσθαι·

[Their later *truphē* prevailed because of their prosperity, so that they held more city-wide festivals each year than there were days. Because of this, they were governed badly. One indication of the bad governance is that they used foreign generals.] (Strabo 6.3.4)

Εὐδαιμονία leads to τρυφή and, though the exact nature of this quality is not specified in this passage, an inference is possible. The hyperbolic claim about the city's devotion to festivals perhaps reflects an anecdote from a tradition of popular moralizing, since no serious narrative of Tarentine history could have presented a city flourishing even a short time in a state of constant festivity, with all business and government duties being neglected. Yet this exaggeration gives a perfect rendition of τρυφή: everyone is celebrating and no one is minding the shop. Self-indulgence is put before common good. The result is bad government from sheer neglect. In particular, the Tarentines fail to take the lead in their own defense, and this detail confirms that the process of decadence depicted here entails a decline into effeminacy: desertion from military duties is a form of μαλακία.

Beginning with their wars against the Messapii and Leucani in the 330s BCE, the Tarentines were not fighting their own wars, but hiring others to do so. Later in the same passage, Strabo tells us that the Tarentines lost their freedom to Rome:

περί τε τὰ Ἀννίβεια καὶ τὴν ἐλευθερίαν ἀφῃρέθησαν, ὕστερον δ᾽ ἀποικίαν Ῥωμαίων δεξάμενοι καθ᾽ ἡσυχίαν ζῶσι καὶ βέλτιον ἢ πρότερον

[They were robbed of their freedom during the Hannibalic War. Later, having received a colony of Romans, they lived in peace, better than before.] (Strabo 6.3.4)

Tarentine τρυφή, it is implied, is at least partly the cause of their subjugation. Yet, in spite of the putatively harmful effects of the Tarentine lifestyle, someone unfamiliar with Roman history might be surprised to learn that, according to

Strabo's line of argument, the Tarentines lived in this state of τρυφή from the 330's, when they called in Alexander of the Molossi to fight the Messapii and Leucani, until they were taken by Rome in 209 BCE and then lived "better than before." It is difficult to see how harmful the τρυφή and endless festivity could have been for the Tarentines if they were able to abide in that state for 120 years. Yet Strabo's account only makes sense if one begins with the assumption that τρυφή is morally bad and being ruled by Rome is somehow morally uplifting.[77]

Elsewhere Strabo reaffirms the idea that τρυφή makes people easy to conquer and unwarlike. Twice he says the Etruscans were expelled from territory they had previously taken, the Po Valley (5.1.10) and then Campania (5.4.3). In the first instance he says they were driven out διὰ τὴν τρυφήν. In the second example, τρυφή led to softness (διὰ δὲ τὴν τρυφὴν εἰς μαλακίαν) and then conquest. After the Etruscans left, the prosperity of Campania harmed its own citizens and feminized the soldiers of Hannibal:

Καμπανοῖς δὲ συνέβη διὰ τὴν τῆς χώρας εὐδαιμονίαν ἐπ᾽ ἴσον ἀγαθῶν ἀπολαῦσαι καὶ κακῶν. ἐπὶ τοσοῦτον γὰρ ἐξετρύφησαν ὥστ᾽ ἐπὶ δεῖπνον ἐκάλουν πρὸς ζεύγη μονομάχων, ὁρίζοντες ἀριθμὸν κατὰ τὴν τῶν [συν]δείπνων ἀξίαν. Ἀννίβα δ᾽ ἐξ ἐνδόσεως λαβόντος αὐτούς, δεξάμενοι χειμαδίοις τὴν στρατιὰν οὕτως ἐξεθήλυναν ταῖς ἡδοναῖς ὥσθ᾽ ὁ Ἀννίβας ἔφη νικῶν κινδυνεύειν ἐπὶ τοῖς ἐχθροῖς γενέσθαι, γυναῖκας ἀντὶ τῶν ἀνδρῶν τοὺς στρατιώτας ἀπολαβών.

[And it happened that the Campanians, because of the fertility of the land, enjoyed equal shares of good things and bad. For they had so much *truphē* that they invited gladiators to dinner in pairs, determining the number by the importance of the banquet. And when Hannibal captured them, submitting easily and receiving his army in winter-quarters, they so womanized it with pleasures that Hannibal said that, though he was the victor, he risked being taken by his enemies, since he received back soldiers who were women instead of men.] (Strabo 5.4.13)

---

77. Strabo can also be maddeningly vague when he uses the term τρυφή, particularly in connection with bad government. Thus, at 17.1.11, a number of the Ptolemies rule badly, "having been corrupted by *truphē*" (ὑπὸ τρυφῆς διεφθαρμένοι), but the only specific example given is the last Ptolemy who was deposed after he held flute-playing contests in the palace. One cannot necessarily conclude that he was soft or effeminate, but perhaps that he neglected his duties.

Τρυφή is clearly a weakening force in this passage: the Campanians submit easily to Hannibal, and their further decline is then linked to pleasures that emasculate them in some vague manner. This is the single instance in Strabo of what seems to be explicitly feminizing τρυφή. Unlike, for example, the traditional picture of Sardanapalus, Strabo omits the descriptions of flowing garments, perfumes, soft beds, or painted faces, and concentrates instead on the unwarlike characterization of those who possess it.[78] This lack of specificity is an early sign of the trend that will eventually become noticeable in many authors; the original meaning of word τρυφή is beginning to fade. Instead of denoting, as we have seen, an attitude of expectation and entitlement, it is becoming a kind of all-purpose cliché for a lack of moderation more generally. In a usage that will be the norm for writers of the Empire, it becomes practically indistinguishable from terms such as ἀπόλαυσις ("enjoyment") and ἡδονή ("pleasure").

While Strabo associates the "bad" days of the Capuans with the height of their power and opulence, their share of good things occurred only later, when they were colonized by the Romans and accepted their submissive role, the opposite of τρυφή:

> νυνὶ μέντοι μετ᾽ εὐπραγίας διάγουσι τοῖς ἐποίκοις ὁμονοήσαντες καὶ τὸ ἀξίωμα φυλάττουσι τὸ ἀρχαῖον καὶ τῷ μεγέθει τῆς πόλεως καὶ κατ᾽ εὐανδρίαν.

> [Now however they live in prosperity, in harmony with their colonizers, and they guard the reputation they had of old in both the size of their city and in their manliness.] (Strabo 5.4.13)

Just as happened with the Tarentines, conquest by Rome made the Campanians into better people, by giving them in their capitulation a way of life somehow preferable to one marked by τρυφή and pleasure. But if life under Roman rule is superior, the excellence Rome bestows upon its subjects does not consist of independence or autonomy: they had that earlier and lost it, first to Hannibal and then to the Romans. Instead, it must be a more prosperous lifestyle (εὐπραγία) and a return to the virtuous simplicity (εὐανδρία) of their distant

---

78. In part this quote can be seen as an explicit allusion to Xerxes' famous remark in Herodotus, when Artemisia distinguished herself at Salamis: οἱ μὲν ἄνδρες γεγόνασί μοι γυναῖκες, αἱ δὲ γυναῖκες ἄνδρες ("My men have become women, and my women men," Hdt. 8.88).

ancestors. In this scheme, conquest by Rome allows the conquered to become true men, even though a necessary condition of that masculinity is subservience to Rome. Strabo thus constructs an argument to justify Roman rule based on the premise that it is morally better for the people who are being ruled, even if that construction rests on a paradox. Autonomy that comes with prosperity and τρυφή leads one to be womanly and unwarlike, but in servitude to Rome, one may enjoy manliness.

Yet in Strabo we see far more commonly the second thread of the τρυφή theme, that in which the possessor of τρυφή becomes violent and hubristic rather than unwarlike. In a pattern we have noted among the Latin writers, avarice serves a key function in this process, as the expectations and demands of such a person continue to grow out of control, until he takes what he desires by whatever means lay at hand. An example of this process is offered in Strabo's own voice at 7.3.7, where he identifies a corrupting influence of the modern way of life on the barbarian tribes, such as the Scythians. He shows the progression from a simple life of frankness and honesty to a life of τρυφή, pleasures, greed, and violence. That path leads directly through seafaring and retail trade:

ἁπλουστάτους τε γὰρ αὐτοὺς νομίζομεν καὶ ἥκιστα κακεντρεχεῖς εὐτελεστέρους τε πολὺ ἡμῶν καὶ αὐταρκεστέρους· καίτοι ὅ γε καθ᾽ ἡμᾶς βίος εἰς πάντας σχεδόν τι διατέτακε τὴν πρὸς τὸ χεῖρον μεταβολήν, τρυφὴν καὶ ἡδονὰς καὶ κακοτεχνίας καὶ πλεονεξίας μυρίας πρὸς ταῦτ᾽ εἰσάγων. πολὺ οὖν τῆς τοιαύτης κακίας καὶ εἰς τοὺς βαρβάρους ἐμπέπτωκε τούς τε ἄλλους καὶ τοὺς νομάδας· καὶ γὰρ θαλάττης ἁψάμενοι χείρους γεγόνασι λῃστεύοντες καὶ ξενοκτονοῦντες, καὶ ἐπιπλεκόμενοι πολλοῖς μεταλαμβάνουσι τῆς ἐκείνων πολυτελείας καὶ καπηλείας· ἃ δοκεῖ μὲν εἰς ἡμερότητα συντείνειν, διαφθείρει δὲ τὰ ἤθη καὶ ποικιλίαν ἀντὶ τῆς ἁπλότητος τῆς ἄρτι λεχθείσης εἰσάγει.

[For we think [the Scythians] are most straightforward and least mischievous, much more frugal and self-sufficient than we are. However, our way of life has encouraged a change for the worse for nearly all people, introducing *truphē* and pleasures and fraudulent dealings and much greed besides. Thus a great deal of this sort of evil has fallen even on the barbarians, and especially the nomads. For since they started following the sea, they have become worse, robbing and killing strangers and embracing in their many changes the extravagance and retail trade of those people. Although these things ought to incite them to civilization, instead they corrupt the morals and introduce an embroidery instead of the frankness that I mentioned just now.] (Strabo 7.3.7)

Here corruption is not a result of internal influences but of external contagion. Its source is the underspecified "our way of life" (ὅ γε καθ᾽ ἡμᾶς βίος). It is unclear whether this phrase refers to life under the Romans or merely a lifestyle less primitive and barbaric than heretofore. If the former, the passage is at odds with our previous discussion, since Roman influence improved the morals of the Capuans, but would have the opposite effect upon the Scythians. In any case, Strabo himself seems puzzled by this phenomenon: such a lifestyle, he says, might seem to lead them to ἡμερότης ("civilization" or "genteelness"), but in fact it does the opposite.[79]

This passage unambiguously makes τρυφή, in harness with πλεονεξία ("avarice"), a cause of hubristic behavior: the desire for more possessions makes the Scythians dishonest practitioners of outrageous lawlessness. In earlier Greek literature we have sometimes seen τρυφή and hubris combined in one person, but the causal relationship was usually lacking. This passage is significant because the causal relationship between τρυφή and hubris is spelled out plainly: though the word "hubris" does not appear, it is implicit in the acts of murder and robbery that are set out. But the next step in the Roman interpretation of τρυφή is still missing. According to Dionysius of Halicarnassus, the inevitable result of such τρυφή is civil strife or destruction, but here in Strabo, the τρυφή of the Scythians has no clear adverse effects for them, other than the corruption of morals itself. Scythian aggression is turned outward, toward the "stranger" on whom they prey.

On the other hand, Strabo makes the link between τρυφή, civic dissension, and eventual ruin explicit elsewhere. A straightforward illustration of this progression can be found in his depiction of the early government of Crete. Citing Ephorus, he claims that the greatest good that a state can enjoy is freedom (ἐλευθερία), because then property belongs to the individual and not to the ruler. Unlike the Tarentines and Campanians, the Cretans risk a kind of τρυφή that leads to disputes:

τὴν μὲν οὖν ὁμόνοιαν διχοστασίας αἰρομένης ἀπαντᾶν, ἣ γίνεται διὰ πλεονεξίαν καὶ τρυφήν· σωφρόνως γὰρ καὶ λιτῶς ζῶσιν ἅπασιν οὔτε φθόνον οὔθ᾽ ὕβριν οὔτε μῖσος ἀπαντᾶν πρὸς τοὺς ὁμοίους·

---

79. One wonders if Strabo has in mind Herodotus 1.155.4, where Croesus advised Cyrus to make the Lydians into shopkeepers if he wanted them not to rebel (discussed in Chapter 2, above).

[Harmony arises when dissension, which comes as a result of greed and *truphē*, is taken away. For those who live moderately and simply, there develops no envy or hubris or hatred toward those who are like them.] (Strabo 10.4.16)

A simple life eliminates avarice and τρυφή, which in turn cause hubris and civil strife. Believing this principle, the lawmaker established a Spartan-like regime, with common barracks and dining halls, and he set up a way of life centered around military training. Instead of the subjugation that brings improvement to morals, military discipline is proposed as the antithesis of τρυφή.[80]

The final two passages in Strabo that contain the word τρυφή are both significant because they link that concept unambiguously with destruction. The first is the story about Sybaris that we discussed briefly in Chapter 1. After affirming the good fortune (εὐτυχία) of that community such that it had twenty-five subject cities and could field an army of 300,000, he describes the end of Sybaris:

ὑπὸ μέντοι τρυφῆς καὶ ὕβρεως ἅπασαν τὴν εὐδαιμονίαν ἀφηρέθησαν ὑπὸ Κροτωνιατῶν ἐν ἡμέραις ἑβδομήκοντα· ἑλόντες γὰρ τὴν πόλιν ἐπήγαγον τὸν ποταμὸν καὶ κατέκλυσαν. ὕστερον δ᾽ οἱ περιγενόμενοι συνελθόντες ἐπῴκουν ὀλίγοι· χρόνῳ δὲ καὶ οὗτοι διεφθάρησαν ὑπὸ Ἀθηναίων καὶ ἄλλων Ἑλλήνων, οἳ συνοικήσοντες μὲν ἐκείνοις ἀφίκοντο, καταφρονήσαντες δὲ αὐτῶν τοὺς μὲν διεχειρίσαντο . . . τὴν δὲ πόλιν εἰς ἕτερον τόπον μετέθηκαν πλησίον καὶ Θουρίους προσηγόρευσαν ἀπὸ κρήνης ὁμωνύμου.

[However, because of their *truphē* and hubris, they were deprived of all of their prosperity by the Crotoniates within seventy days. For when they captured the city, they channeled the river over it and flooded it. Later, the survivors, who were few, united and resettled it. But in time, these people too were destroyed by the Athenians and other Greeks, who came as fellow-colonists with them, but despising them, killed them . . . and moved the city to another place nearby and called it Thurii from the name of a spring.] (Strabo 6.1.13)

So the Sybarites were destroyed not once, but twice. No cause is given for the second annihilation, and the first is explained merely by the expression ὑπὸ τρυφῆς καὶ ὕβρεως, as if in those few words we had a clear explanation of their faults. The phrase is used as an all-purpose formula for ill-doing that deserves

---

80. The Cretans also enjoyed a mastery of the sea (10.4.17), but it did not corrupt them as it did the Scythians. Presumably the Cretans were no mere tradesmen, but were themselves conquerors, and so the sea did not introduce them to pleasures and τρυφή, as it did the barbarians in book 7.

ruination. Since Sybaris did cease to exist in historical times, that city is a convenient paradigm for destructive τρυφή.

The final τρυφή passage in Strabo records the words of Calanus, a Brahman consulted by Onesicritus on behalf of Alexander. The Brahman told a story about the olden days, when food and drink presented themselves in abundance to people.

ὑπὸ πλησμονῆς δ᾽ οἱ ἄνθρωποι καὶ τρυφῆς εἰς ὕβριν ἐξέπεσον. Ζεὺς δὲ μισήσας τὴν κατάστασιν ἠφάνισε πάντα καὶ διὰ πόνου τὸν βίον ἀπέδειξε· σωφροσύνης δὲ καὶ τῆς ἄλλης ἀρετῆς παρελθούσης εἰς μέσον πάλιν εὐπορία τῶν ἀγαθῶν ὑπῆρξεν· ἐγγὺς δ᾽ ἐστὶν ἤδη νυνὶ κόρου καὶ ὕβρεως τὸ πρᾶγμα, κινδυνεύει τε ἀφανισμὸς τῶν ὄντων γενέσθαι.

[Because of abundance and *truphē*, men fell into hubris. And Zeus, hating that condition, destroyed everything and set up life based on toil. But as temperance and the rest of virtue came in the midst of them, again there began to be an abundance of good things. The affairs of men are already nearly now at a point of satiety and hubris, and there is the danger of the extermination of everything in existence.] (Strabo 15.1.64)

The pattern is the same as that in Pseudo-Scymnus: abundance and τρυφή lead to satiety and to hubris (the relationship between these two qualities is not further specified); the result is destruction by Zeus himself. Also noteworthy is the fact that abundance and τρυφή are contrasted with toil (πόνος), a circumstance that will become commonplace in subsequent authors.

In sum, we see that, by the writings of Strabo, the Hellenic concept of τρυφή has already undergone an evolution into a thoroughly Roman idea. The term is now rarely a good thing in and of itself, and is beginning to lose the more precise, original meaning of expecting others to take care of you. Rather, it is becoming a more vague cause of being incapable of defending oneself militarily: a person of τρυφή is so consumed with pleasures that he is easy to conquer. Conquest by Rome cures the τρυφή, and sets the afflicted back into a masculine way of life. But more commonly it makes one greedy and hubristic, leading to civil disputes and utter destruction. According to this Roman model, the best life is one of moderation without abundance but with honest toil.

Philo Judaeus

Philo assumes a distinctive tone within the corpus of Greek writers under Roman rule: he is chiefly an advocate for the culture and traditions of the Jewish community, but he is thoroughly Hellenized and writing under the influence of the contemporary system of rhetorical education in the first century of the Roman Empire. He probably lived from about 20 BCE to about 45 or 50 CE, born into a wealthy and influential Alexandrian family that was acquainted with emperors: he led a delegation to Caligula during conflicts between Jews and Greeks in Alexandria, a subject that he recounts in his essay, *Legatio ad Gaium*.[81] His brother Alexander was steward for Claudius's mother, Antonia, and was a friend of Claudius himself, who released him from the prison where Caligula had sent him.

Philo's culture is a blend of Judaism with Greek and Roman traditions. Within the framework of a very positive view of Rome, he openly admires many Greek writers, especially Plato, Zeno, Homer, Sophocles, and Euripides, but he does so from a position of cultural superiority.[82] He assimilates Greek philosophy with Jewish principles by assuming a scriptural derivation for the former, or at least a concurrent tradition. So when Philo writes about virtues and vices, his words may reflect either point of view, or a varied picture from within the two cultures.[83]

The majority of his work explicates Jewish life and scripture, and within this context his employment of the word τρυφή is frequent, more than fifty times in all. In many of his applications, he is heavily influenced by the Septuagint.[84] He quotes directly from Psalms 37:4, κατατρύφησον τοῦ κυρίου ("Have *truphē* in the Lord"),[85] and is certainly referring to Genesis 3:22–23, where Eden is called παραδείσου τῆς τρυφῆς, ("paradise of *truphē*"), when he refers to it in much the same language:[86]

---

81. Goodenough (1962) 1986, 2–4. The purpose of this treatise was to contrast the vices of the Romans with the virtues of the Jews and of God (Leisegang 1941).

82. A recent treatment of Philo's life and thought is Hadas-Lebel 2012, with bibliography, esp. ch. 7 on Philo's philosophy. Niehoff (2001) offers a lengthy discussion of Philo's identity within the three cultures. Goodenough (1938, ch. 4; [1962] 1986, ch. 3) argues for an anti-Romanism, which Niehoff (ch. 4) contests.

83. For his ethics (but no discussion of luxury), see Lévy 2009.

84. Hadas-Lebel 2012, 59–66.

85. *Plant*. 39; *Somn*. 2.242.

86. Cf. *LA* 1.96; *Cher*. 1, 12; *Plant*. 38; *Somn*. 2.242.

παράδεισος μὲν δὴ τροπικῶς εἴρηται ἡ ἀρετή, τόπος δὲ οἰκεῖος τῷ παραδείσῳ Ἐδέμ, τοῦτο δέ ἐστι τρυφή· ἀρετῇ δὲ ἁρμόττον εἰρήνη καὶ εὐπάθεια καὶ χαρά, ἐν οἷς τὸ τρυφᾶν ὡς ἀληθῶς ἐστι.

[And virtue is called paradise figuratively, and the suitable place for paradise is Eden, and this is *truphē*. And peace and comfort and delight are most suitable for virtue, in which things *truphē* truly abides.] (Philo, *LA* 1.45)

He expounds on this translation of Eden further at *Cher.* 12:

τοῦ μὲν οὖν ἀντιτεταγμένου παράδειγμα τὸ ἐπὶ τοῦ Κάιν εἰρημένον, ὅτι ἐξῆλθεν ἀπὸ προσώπου τοῦ θεοῦ καὶ ᾤκησεν ἐν γῇ Ναὶδ κατέναντι Ἐδέμ· ἑρμηνεύεται δὲ Ναὶδ μὲν σάλος, Ἐδὲμ δὲ τρυφή, τὸ μὲν κακίας κλονούσης ψυχὴν σύμβολον, τὸ δὲ ἀρετῆς εὐπάθειαν αὐτῇ περιποιούσης καὶ τρυφήν, οὐχὶ τὴν δι᾽ ἀλόγου πάθους ἡδονῆς θρύψιν, ἀλλὰ τὴν μετὰ πολλῆς εὐμαρείας ἄπονον χαρὰν καὶ ἀταλαίπωρον.

[Now the model of someone being placed face-to-face is what is said about Cain, that "he went out from the face of God and he lived in the land of Nod, which is opposite Eden" [Gen. 4:16]. Now Nod is interpreted as a disturbance, while Eden is *truphē*, so the one is a symbol of evil agitating the soul, and the other of virtue, which preserves comfort for the soul and *truphē*, not the shattering [*thrupsis*[87]] that comes from the irrational experience of pleasure, but a joy that comes with much comfort, free from toil and hard work.] (Philo, *Cher.* 12)

So τρυφή is a symbol of virtue, and stands in opposition to agitation and evil.[88] It is not associated with irrational pleasure, but rather with peace and freedom

---

87. The contrast here between τρυφή and θρύψις is telling. Τρυφή is an ease that brings comfort, while θρύψις reverts to its literal meaning, "broken into pieces." Yet Philo is not consistent: he names both terms in a list of vices at *Ebr.* 22.1. Philo employs θρύψις and compounds of θρύπτω sometimes physically (*Op.*131; *Aet.* 125; *Flac.* 71), sometimes metaphorically (*Her.* 201.5; *Mut.* 84.6), but most often as a clear vice (*Cher.* 92; *Op.* 164.5; *Post.* 181; *Plant.* 19, 159; *Ebr.* 22.6, 220.1; *Mig.* 111.3; *Her.* 77.5; *Somn.* 2.203.1; *Abr.* 136.3; *Jos.* 61.4; *Dec.* 122.2; *Mos.* 2.184.5; *Spec. leg.* 4.102). The equation of this term with the classical meaning of τρυφή is made clear by the context at *Somn.* 2.47.4 and *Ebr.* 22.1.

88. *LA* 1.64: ἣ χαίρει καὶ γάνυται καὶ τρυφᾷ ἐπὶ μόνῳ τῷ πατρὶ ("[Virtue] rejoices and brightens and has *truphē* in the Father alone"). Cf. *Virt.* 67. One can also have τρυφή in the dogma of the scripture (*Virt.* 99) and in the contemplation of the world, in obedience to nature, and in perfect harmony between oneself and His words (*Spec. leg.* 2.52).

from labor and worry (cf. *Flac.* 184). All these points of clarification are entirely consistent with the established sense of τρυφή: in the Septuagint, God will take care of the needs of the righteous.[89]

Tρυφή is coupled with wisdom,[90] as well as with divine reason and the idea of receiving everything good from God:

συμβολικῶς δέ ἐστιν Ἐδὲμ ὀρθὸς καὶ θεῖος λόγος, παρὸ καὶ ἑρμηνείαν ἔχει τρυφήν, ὅτι ἐνευφραίνεται καὶ ἐντρυφᾷ πρὸ τῶν ἄλλων ἀμιγέσι καὶ ἀκράτοις, ἔτι δὲ ἀρτίοις καὶ πλήρεσι κεχρημένος ἀγαθοῖς ὕοντος τοῦ πλουτοδότου θεοῦ τὰς παρθένους καὶ ἀθανάτους χάριτας αὐτοῦ.

[Eden is, symbolically, correct and divine reason, wherefore it has the meaning *truphē*, because it gladdens and has *truphē* more than everything else in that which is unmixed and pure, and it has enjoyed the perfect and full goodness of God, the giver of riches, who rains his virgin, undying graces on it.] (Philo, *Post.* 32)

Even this image of God raining down his graces is reminiscent of the etymological connotation of Eden, the abundance that comes with water in the desert.[91]

The image of τρυφή as the alleviation of thirst and hunger is one that occurs often in Philo. Moses commanded in Gen. 47:24 that a fifth part of the grain be stored up, as Philo explains in his discussion of the five senses, ὅπως ἑκάστη τῶν οἰκείων ἀνεπισχέτως ἐμπιπλαμένη τρυφᾷ ("in order that each of these [senses] have *truphē* by being filled without limit with suitable food," Philo, *Mig.* 204). Likewise, God honors his priests in many ways, including commanding that they be provided with the first-fruits of the wine, wheat, barley, oil, olives and fruit:

. . . ἵνα μὴ τἀναγκαῖα μόνον ἔχοντες αὐχμηρότερον ἀποζῶσιν, ἀλλὰ καὶ τῶν πρὸς ἁβροδίαιτον βίον εὐποροῦντες ἱλαρώτερον ἐξ ἀφθόνων τρυφῶσι μετὰ κόσμου τοῦ προσήκοντος.

---

89. *Praem.*146.4 portrays women who were formerly ἁβροδίαιτοι καὶ πανάπαλοι ("living luxuriously and being tender") because of their τρυφή, but who through their impiety and lawless inequity lost their comfortable lives, ἅμα ταῖς ψυχαῖς καὶ τὰ σώματα ἐξηγρίωνται ("at the same time they have become savage in their soul and in their body").

90. *Somn.* 2.242: ἐντρύφημα καὶ θεοῦ σοφία καὶ σοφίας θεός ("Wisdom is God's gratification [i.e., the satisfaction of the demands of *truphē*], and God is the gratification [*truphē*] of wisdom"); cf. *Cont.* 35.

91. See above (pp. 65–68).

[. . . so that they should not live too meagerly, possessing only the necessities, but rather that, abounding in the elements of a prosperous life (*habrodiaiton*), they should have *truphē* cheerfully and free from envy, in an arrangement that is appropriate.] (Philo, *Spec. leg.* 1.134)

It is not fitting that the priests live a life of bare subsistence, but rather God favors them with more than they need.[92]

The imagery is further developed when the most excellent people are chosen by God to serve him and are given as an honor

(1.303) . . . τὴν ἀέναον τῶν καλῶν πηγήν, ἀφ᾽ ἧς καὶ τὰς ἄλλας ὤμβρησεν ἀρετὰς καὶ ἀνέχεεν εἰς ἀπόλαυσιν ὠφελιμωτάτην, νέκταρος μᾶλλον ἢ οὐχ ἧττον ἀθανατίζον ποτόν. (304) οἰκτροὶ δὲ καὶ κακοδαίμονες ὅσοι μὴ τὸν ἀρετῆς πότον εὐωχήθησαν καὶ κακοδαιμονέστατοι διετέλεσαν οἱ εἰς ἅπαν ἄγευστοι καλοκἀγαθίας, παρὸν καὶ ἐνευφρανθῆναι καὶ ἐντρυφῆσαι δικαιοσύνῃ καὶ ὁσιότητι·

[(1.303) . . . the everlasting fountain of goods from which he showered the other virtues and in particular he poured forth what was most useful for enjoyment, a drink containing immortality, more than, or at least not less than, nectar. (304) But pitiable and ill-spirited are the men who have not feasted sumptuously on the drink of virtue, and ill-spirited they live entirely without tasting goodness, when it was possible for them to be gladdened and to have *truphē* in justice and piety.] (Philo, *Spec. leg.* 1.303–4)

Again, τρυφή is a gift from God, compared to a bounteous fountain and associated with enjoyment no less than with virtue, justice, and piety. It is a good thing to have your needs and wants provided for by God, and the unrighteous live ἄγευστοι ("without tasting"). Thus, true to his Jewish culture and traditional Greek linguistic usage, Philo employs τρυφή as an endowment from God in a manner consistent with the Septuagint.

Philo reflects his mixed heritage in other passages where τρυφή is not at all a gift of God, except perhaps to women, but rather is a softening agent that

---

92. For τρυφή being the fulfillment of needs, see also *Decal.* 117; *Virt.* 133; *Spec. leg.* 4.124; *Cont.* 74; *Jos.* 243. We may observe that the literal meaning of the adjective αὐχμηρός is "dry" or "drought-stricken." Thus Philo continues the association between τρυφή and rain as a symbol of the providential satisfaction of people's desires.

leads men away from virtue. This view stands in stark contrast both to the unified picture offered by the Septuagint of τρυφή as an endowment of abundance from God and to those passages from Philo that we have examined thus far. Thus the position derives not from Philo's Jewish background, but rather is a reflection of his contemporary pagan education in the teachings of Hellenistic philosophy, and represents an inconsistency that is characteristic of much of Philo's writing.[93]

A prime example of this other use of τρυφή can be found at *Somnium* 1.120–26, where Philo expounds on the meaning of Gen. 28:11, where Jacob sleeps with a stone for his pillow. The image is converted into an extended praise of asceticism as the path to virtue.[94] The author of Genesis, Philo explains, οὐ γὰρ ἀξιοῖ τὸν ἀρετῆς ἐπιμελούμενον ἁβροδιαίτῳ βίῳ χρῆσθαι καὶ τρυφᾶν ζηλοῦντα ("does not think it right that the man who is concerned with virtue should enjoy an easy life and pursue *truphē*," *Somn.* 1.121). Food, wine, excessive passions, and soft beds are fine for women:

αἷς ἡ φύσις ἐπέτρεψεν ἀνειμένῃ χρῆσθαι διαίτῃ, παρὸ καὶ τὸ σῶμα τοῦ μαλθακωτέρου κόμματος ὁ τεχνίτης καὶ ποιητὴς αὐταῖς εἰργάζετο.

[to whom Nature has bequeathed it to enjoy a looser way of life, since the Creator and Maker has fashioned their bodies too from a softer stamp.] (Philo, *Somn.* 1.123)[95]

Men in pursuit of virtue should seek a harder life (124), where ἐγκράτειαν, ὀλιγοδείαν, καρτερίαν ("self-control, being content with little, and endurance") are:

(1.124) ... χρημάτων καὶ ἡδονῆς καὶ δόξης κρείττους, σιτίων καὶ ποτῶν καὶ αὐτὸ μόνον τῶν ἀναγκαίων, ἐφ᾽ ὅσον μὴ νεωτερίζειν ἄρχεται λιμός, ὑπερόπται,

---

93. Inconsistency in his philosophy: Goodenough 1962; 1986, ch. 5–6. Lack of originality (1986, 94–95): "For he was not an original philosopher at all, and anything philosophic to be found in his writings can confidently be taken as genuine teaching of his environment. His task was to show that the best of Greek philosophic teaching was derived from, and got its highest expression in, the Torah, and his whole objective would have been lost had he been inventing anything especially novel. . . . I do not see in Philo one who was at all recondite in philosophical studies. . . . Always, it seems to me, we may assume that the philosophic elements in Philo were of the most obvious sorts and taken from contemporary presentations, oral or written."

94. For asceticism in the Latin authors in the second century CE, see Francis 1995.

95. Cf. *Mos.* 1.55. The theme of asceticism recurs once in Josephus in opposition to τρυφή at *AJ* 10.193.

πεῖναν δέχεσθαι καὶ δίψαν θάλπος τε καὶ κρύος καὶ ὅσα ἄλλα δυσκαρτέρητα ὑπὲρ ἀρετῆς κτήσεως ἑτοιμότατοι, ζηλωταὶ τῶν εὐποριστοτάτων, ὡς μηδ᾿ ἐπ᾿ εὐτελεῖ χλαίνῃ ποτὲ δυσωπηθῆναι, τοὐναντίον δὲ τὰς πολυτελεῖς ὄνειδος καὶ μεγάλην τοῦ βίου ζημίαν νομίσαι.(125) . . . τὸν βίον τοῦτον οἱ μὲν τρυφῶντες σκληροδίαιτον καλοῦσιν, οἱ δὲ πρὸς καλοκἀγαθίαν ζῶντες ἥδιστον ὀνομάζουσιν·

[(1.124) . . . stronger than money and pleasure and glory; those men despise foods and drink except only what is necessary so that hunger doesn't drive them to extremes; they are prepared to take hunger and thirst and intense heat and cold and whatever other things are difficult to endure in order to possess virtue; they admire the things most easy to obtain, so that they are not ever ashamed of a cheap cloak, but rather the opposite, they think an expensive one is a disgrace and a great loss in life. (125) . . . Those who enjoy *truphē* call this a hard life, but those living a noble life call it the most pleasant.] (Philo, *Somn.* 1.124–25)

Somnium 2.9 continues much the same theme, contrasting a life of τρυφή with the hard life of unadulterated goodness, where wants and needs are fulfilled only in a minimal way,[96] and associating τρυφή with the lifestyle of men raised among women. In praising a severe existence, Philo grants that women are designed by God to be taken care of, but that men of virtue should deny their physical wants insofar as they are able, to the point of condemning those who indulge themselves by fulfilling them.

Τρυφή is likewise censured in a variety of other passages. It is part of a flabby life (τὸν ὑγρὸν βίον, *Spec.* 2.240; cf. 2.99) and other people's customs (*Jos.* 44; *Cont.* 48; *Legat.* 168). It is included in a very long list of the attributes of personified Pleasure, who walks like a prostitute ὑπὸ τρυφῆς τῆς ἄγαν καὶ χλιδῆς ("from *truphē* and very great ornamentation," *Sac.* 21): jewelry, perfumes, makeup, and other physical charms, coupled with rashness, flattery, deceit, and all manner of falseness. These temptations she keeps stored up in order to bestow them on her followers: τούτους, ἢν ἐθέλῃς μοι συνοικεῖν, τοὺς θησαυροὺς ἀναπετάσασα χρῆσιν καὶ ἀπόλαυσιν τῶν ἐνόντων ἀφθονωτάτην εἰσαεὶ παρέξω ("Opening up these treasuries, if you want to abide with me, I will forever give you use and enjoyment of the things in them without envy."). It is telling that, in a departure from the tradition of the Septuagint, Philo

96. Cf. *Somn.* 2.48–55. At 55: τί δὲ . . . καὶ ὅσα οἱ ἐντρυφῶντες <τοῖς καθεστ>ῶσι νόμοις προσεξεῦρον σπουδάζομέν τε καὶ φιλοτιμούμεθα ("And why should we contend and desire the sorts of things that men who enjoy *truphē* find in addition to the normal things?").

can portray τρυφή as the cause of the typical degeneration that we see in the Roman tradition, from τρυφή to κόρος to ὕβρις, though in a confusing form. In a discussion of governments, Philo argues that individuals are as sheep, requiring the firm hand of a shepherd to govern them, so that they avoid both the lawless and violent behavior of ochlocracies and tyrannies, but also the scorn and hubris that is inherent in the governed who possess too soft a ruler.

τούτους μὲν <οὖν> θρεμμάτων, ἐκείνους δὲ κτηνοτρόφων οὐδὲν νομιστέον διαφέρειν· οἱ μὲν γὰρ τρυφᾶν ἐν ἀφθόνοις ὕλαις ἀναπείθουσιν, οἱ δὲ τὸν κόρον ἀδυνατοῦντες φέρειν ἐξυβρίζουσι.

[One must consider some to be no different from animals, and others no different from herders. For the ones persuade the governed to have *truphē* among unstinted resources, while the others, unable to bear their satiety, become hubristic.] (Philo, *Agr.* 48)

Thus, lenient and overgenerous rulers promote τρυφή in the people, while the people themselves are not content even with this overindulgence, but continue on to ὕβρις. [97]

In these contexts, Philo takes the degeneration no further, but elsewhere he makes explicit the connection between this sequence and the destruction of the laws. In *Moses* 2, Philo presents Moses as the embodiment of the best possible lawgiver, characterized by four principal virtues: humility, love of justice, love of virtue, and hatred of iniquity (τὸ φιλάνθρωπον, τὸ φιλοδίκαιον, τὸ φιλάγαθον, τὸ μισοπόνηρον, *Mos.* 2.9). He proves this status by contrasting Moses with other lawgivers:

(2.12) ὅτι δ᾽ αὐτός τε νομοθετῶν ἄριστος τῶν πανταχοῦ πάντων, ὅσοι παρ᾽ Ἕλλησιν ἢ βαρβάροις ἐγένοντο, καὶ οἱ νόμοι κάλλιστοι καὶ ὡς ἀληθῶς θεῖοι μηδὲν ὧν χρὴ παραλιπόντες, ἐναργεστάτη πίστις ἥδε· (13) τὰ μὲν τῶν ἄλλων νόμιμα εἴ τις ἐπίοι τῷ λογισμῷ, διὰ μυρίας προφάσεις εὑρήσει κεκινημένα, πολέμοις ἢ τυραννίσιν ἤ τισιν ἄλλοις ἀβουλήτοις, ἃ νεωτερισμῷ τύχης κατασκήπτει· πολλάκις δὲ καὶ τρυφὴ πλεονάσασα χορηγίαις καὶ περιουσίαις

---

97. This sentiment is echoed in the fragments of *Prov.* 2.12, preserved by Eusebius: τοῖς τῆς φύσεως ἀγαθοῖς ἐντρυφῶντες, ἐπ᾽ αὐτῶν μόνων οὐκ ἀξιοῦμεν ἵστασθαι, κόρον δ᾽ ὑβριστὴν ἡγεμόνα τοῦ βίου ποιησάμενοι ("having *truphē* in the good things provided by nature, [we citizens] do not think it right to stop at them alone, making satiety and hubris the guide of life"). Whether the wording belongs to Philo or Eusebius, we cannot say.

ἀφθόνοις καθεῖλε νόμους, τὰ λίαν ἀγαθὰ τῶν πολλῶν φέρειν οὐ δυναμένων, ἀλλὰ διὰ κόρον ἐξυβριζόντων· ὕβρις δ᾽ ἀντίπαλον νόμῳ.

[(2.12) That he is the best of all the lawgivers of all time anywhere, whoever existed among the Greeks or the barbarians, and that his laws are the best and truly the most godly, passing over nothing which they ought to address, this is the most manifest evidence: (13) if anyone should go over the laws of others using reason, he will find that they were set in motion from many pretexts, whether wars or tyrannies, or any other involuntary things, which fall upon them with a change of fortune. And often *truphē*, overflowing with abundance and unstinted surplus, has destroyed the laws, since the multitude was unable to bear the excessive goods, but instead grew hubristic through its satiety. And hubris is an adversary to the law.] (Philo, *Mos.* 2.12–13)

Here τρυφή sets in motion the same progression, to κόρος and then ὕβρις. But, instead of being caused by indulgent laws, the changes of fortune and accompanying prosperity lead to the destruction of the laws of other people, in direct contrast to Jewish law, which remains constant throughout time and alterations of fate (*Mos.* 2.14–44). Accordingly the same pathology of decadence from τρυφή to κόρος to ὕβρις that first occurs in extant writings in Ps.-Scymnus is repeated in this discussion of Moses the nomothete.

Because Philo uses κόρος quite frequently in relevant contexts, an examination of his evidence may allow us better to understand how this concept fits into the process of moral degeneration. From its first appearance in Homer, the basic meaning of κόρος is "satiety," and it is often applied to the alleviation of hunger or thirst. The term in this sense has no inherent moral connotations, and Philo sometimes employs it with just such a neutral meaning. More often, however, κόρος is found as part of a description of moral failing. The evidence for the meaning of κόρος in these passages is not entirely consistent, but a dominant sense does emerge. In descriptions of pernicious luxury, the term tends to indicate a "superabundance" of good things which is so pronounced that those who enjoy it lose their heads in overconfidence and self-importance. As a result, they feel themselves no longer bound by the usual rules and limits of society.

(161) τοιαύταις ὑφηγήσεσι τὰς διανοίας τῶν κατ᾽ αὐτὸν πολιτευομένων ἐξημερώσας ὑπεροψίας καὶ ἀλαζονείας, ἀργαλεωτάτων καὶ ἐπαχθεστάτων

κακῶν, διέζευξεν, ὧν ὡς μεγίστων ἀγαθῶν οἱ πολλοὶ περιέχονται, καὶ μάλιστα ὅταν πλοῦτοι καὶ δόξαι καὶ ἡγεμονίαι περιουσίας ἀφθόνους χορηγῶσιν. (162) ἀλαζονεία . . . περιφαίνεται . . . ἐν τοῖς μεγάλοις χορηγοὺς ὡς ἔφην ἔχουσι τούτου τοῦ κακοῦ πλούτους καὶ δόξας καὶ ἡγεμονίας, ὧν ὑποπλησθέντες καθάπερ οἱ πολὺν ἄκρατον ἐμφορησάμενοι μεθύουσι καὶ ἐμπαροινοῦσι δούλοις ὁμοῦ καὶ ἐλευθέροις, ἔστι δ᾽ ὅτε καὶ ὅλαις πόλεσι· τίκτει γὰρ κόρος ὕβριν, ὡς ὁ τῶν παλαιῶν λόγος. (163) διὸ παγκάλως Μωυσῆς ἱεροφαντῶν παραινεῖ πάντων μὲν ἁμαρτημάτων ἀπέχεσθαι, διαφερόντως δὲ ὑπεροψίας. εἶθ᾽ ὑπόμνησιν ποιεῖται τῶν μὲν ἀναφλέγειν τὸ πάθος εἰωθότων, πλησμονῆς γαστρὸς ἀμέτρου καὶ οἰκιῶν καὶ κτημάτων καὶ θρεμμάτων ἀφθόνου περιουσίας· γίνονται γὰρ εὐθὺς αὐτῶν ἀκράτορες, διαιρόμενοι καὶ φυσώμενοι.

[(161) By such directives he tamed the thoughts of those living under his guidance and unyoked them from disdain and pretension, most vexing and burdensome evils, which most people embrace as the greatest goods, especially when riches and reputation and high office supply them with unstinted resources. (162) For pretension . . . stands out among the great, who have, as I said, as supplies for this evil, riches and reputations and high offices; they become filled with these things just as those who pour down much unmixed wine become drunk and lose control against slaves and free men—even against cities. "Satiety begets hubris," as the ancient saying goes.[98] (163) For this reason, Moses, the All-Wise, expounding to his followers, told them to avoid all wrong actions, but especially disdain. And then he reminds them of the things which are accustomed to inflame that condition, the fullness of an immoderate belly and houses and possessions and masses of unstinted abundance. For from these things, people immediately become intemperate, lofty, and puffed up.] (Philo, *Virt.* 161–63)

Prosperity affects people in the manner of strong wine. It causes them heedlessly to overstep the boundaries of propriety. Κόρος, is, as it were, several drinks too many: unstinted abundance—to use one of Philo's favorite phrases—clouds the judgment of the prosperous and leads them to believe they are too important to be required to abide by laws and customs.

---

98. Philo quotes Solon (frag. 6.3–4 West); for Solon, the κόρος that leads to hubris is associated with the unrestrained acquisition of wealth, not its immoderate enjoyment. On the desiderative sense of this term in Archaic literature, see Balot 2001, 79–98; Anhalt (1993, 82–93) has a detailed discussion of κόρος and the "inherent interrelationship between satiety and insatiability" (82); cf. Gorman and Gorman 2010, 200 n. 35.

This function of κόρος, as it might unfold in a historical context, is well illustrated by the two falls of Sodom, both of which Philo explains as the result of the process that we are examining. The Sodomites' first catastrophe came at the hands of their political overlords, when the local governors decided not to pay the taxes they owed:

ἐπεὶ δὲ ἐκορέσθησαν ἀγαθῶν καί, ὅπερ φιλεῖ, κόρος ὕβριν ἐγέννησε, πλέον τῆς δυνάμεως φρονήσαντες ἀπαυχενίζουσι τὸ πρῶτον, εἶθ᾽ οἷα κακοὶ δοῦλοι δεσπόταις τοῖς ἑαυτῶν ἐπιτίθενται στάσει πιστεύσαντες ἢ ῥώμῃ

[But when they had become sated with good things, and, as often happens, satiety engendered hubris, then, thinking more of themselves than their power warranted, they first shook off the leashes from their necks, then, like wicked servants, they set upon their masters, relying on faction rather than strength.] (Philo, *Abr.* 228)

The overconfidence of the leaders of Sodom quickly met with the fate that we might expect. They were defeated by their erstwhile masters and either enslaved or slaughtered.

To this passage we may compare Philo's exegesis of the second, and more familiar, destruction of the Sodomites.

(133) ἡ Σοδομιτῶν χώρα, μοῖρα τῆς Χανανίτιδος γῆς, ἣν ὕστερον ὠνόμασαν Συρίαν Παλαιστίνην, ἀδικημάτων μυρίων ὅσων γεμισθεῖσα καὶ μάλιστα τῶν ἐκ γαστριμαργίας καὶ λαγνείας . . . (134) αἴτιον δὲ τῆς περὶ τὸ ἀκολασταίνειν ἀμετρίας ἐγένετο τοῖς οἰκήτορσιν ἡ τῶν χορηγιῶν ἐπάλληλος ἀφθονία· βαθύγειος γὰρ καὶ εὔυδρος οὖσα ἡ χώρα παντοίων ἀνὰ πᾶν ἔτος εὐφορίᾳ καρπῶν ἐχρῆτο· μεγίστη δ᾽ ἀρχὴ κακῶν, ὡς εἶπέ τις οὐκ ἀπὸ σκοποῦ, τὰ λίαν ἀγαθά. (135) ὧν ἀδυνατοῦντες φέρειν τὸν κόρον ὥσπερ τὰ θρέμματα σκιρτῶντες ἀπαυχενίζουσι τὸν τῆς φύσεως νόμον, ἄκρατον πολὺν καὶ ὀψοφαγίας καὶ ὀχείας ἐκθέσμους μεταδιώκοντες· οὐ γὰρ μόνον θηλυμανοῦντες ἀλλοτρίους γάμους διέφθειρον, ἀλλὰ καὶ ἄνδρες ὄντες ἄρρεσιν ἐπιβαίνοντες, . . . (136) εἶτ᾽ ἐκ τοῦ κατ᾽ ὀλίγον ἐθίζοντες τὰ γυναικῶν ὑπομένειν τοὺς ἄνδρας γεννηθέντας θήλειαν κατεσκεύασαν αὐτοῖς νόσον, κακὸν δύσμαχον, οὐ μόνον τὰ σώματα μαλακότητι καὶ θρύψει γυναικοῦντες, ἀλλὰ καὶ τὰς ψυχὰς ἀγεννεστέρας ἀπεργαζόμενοι, καὶ τό γε ἐπ᾽ αὐτοὺς ἧκον μέρος τὸ σύμπαν ἀνθρώπων γένος διέφθειρον.

[(133) The land of the Sodomites, part of Canaan, which later they called Syria-Palestine, was stuffed full with all kinds of wrongdoings, especially those arising from gluttony and promiscuity. . . . (134) And the cause of the excess in licentiousness was the fact that the inhabitants had access to an unstinted stream of resources, since the land had deep soil and was well-watered, and thus throughout the entire year produced abundant crops of all kinds. The familiar saying hits the mark: "The greatest source of evils is too much good." (135) Unable to bear satiety of such goods, skittering like animals, they shake the law of nature from their necks, pursuing quantities of unmixed wine, fine cuisine, and unlawful sexual acts. For not only did they go mad for women and destroy other men's marriages, but, although men, they even mount other men. . . . (136) Then, becoming accustomed bit by bit to submitting to womanly things, though born as men, they procure for themselves the woman's disease, an unbeatable evil; not only do they feminize their bodies with softness and decadence, but they also make their souls more ignoble, and corrupt the whole human race, at least as it pertains to them.] (Philo, *Abr.* 133–36)

This time it is not human enemies, but God himself, who destroys Sodom with a rain of fire.

This passage is particularly remarkable for the way in which Philo mixes the two processes of pernicious luxury to explain the moral decline at Sodom. Similarities between this description and the others that we have examined lead us to expect the Sodomites' offenses to be characterized as manifestations of hubris, the axiomatic consequence of τὰ λίαν ἀγαθά. But while the Sodomites in *Abr.* 133–136, like their compatriots at *Abr.* 228, shake themselves free of restraint (ἀπαυχενίζουσι), the expected hubris never materializes in explicit form. Instead, they become increasingly womanish. Indeed, the overconfidence and self-importance that arises from the land's great abundance does not induce the Sodomites to try to impose their will on others; rather it renders them passive (τὰ γυναικῶν ὑπομένειν) and weak (μαλακότητι). It is no wonder, then, that Philo omits any clear reference to hubris in his attempt to explain why the Sodomites' behavior was justly deserving of punishment from on high, while at the same time using an argument which, by its form and language, brings hubris to mind.

A final example shows that Philo may have sometimes given pernicious κόρος a different interpretation. Discussing Moses's provisions for the regulation of sexual behavior, Philo details the most egregious offenses against them:

ἀλλὰ γὰρ ἔνιοι τὰς Συβαριτῶν καὶ τὰς ἔτι λαγνιστέρων ἐπιθυμίας ζηλώσαντες
τὸ μὲν πρῶτον ὀψοφαγίαις καὶ οἰνοφλυγίαις καὶ ταῖς ἄλλαις ταῖς γαστρὸς καὶ
τῶν μετὰ γαστέρα ἡδοναῖς ἐνησκήθησαν, εἶτα δὲ κορεσθέντες ἐξύβρισαν—
ὕβριν γὰρ κόρος γεννᾶν πέφυκεν—, ὡς ὑπὸ φρενοβλαβείας λυττᾶν καὶ
ἐπιμεμηνέναι μηκέτ' ἀνθρώποις εἴτ' ἄρρεσιν εἴτε θηλείαις ἀλλὰ καὶ ἀλόγοις
ζῴοις, ὥσπερ ἐν Κρήτῃ φασὶ τὸ παλαιὸν τὴν γυναῖκα Μίνω τοῦ βασιλέως
ὄνομα Πασιφάην.

[Some people, rivaling the appetites of the Sybarites and those more lecherous
still, at first were conquered by fine cuisines and bouts of drunkenness and the
other pleasure of the belly and the parts beyond the belly. And then, becoming
sated, they committed hubris—for satiety naturally engenders hubris—so that,
with their wits astray, they went crazy and fell madly in lust no longer with human
beings, whether male or female, but even with brute beasts. This, they say, did
Pasiphae, the wife of King Minos, on Crete in olden days.] (Philo, *Spec. leg.* 3.43)

Here Philo apparently considers it reasonable to classify as hubris the act of forc-
ing oneself on "irrational animals." The precise meaning of κόρος is less clear.
Perhaps it is the same as in the previous examples, and the point is that increasing
indulgence in feasting, drinking, and sex (with other human beings) eventually
reaches such an extent (i.e., κόρος) that people feel superior to any restraint.
However, there is another possible interpretation. When justifying the death penalty for those guilty of zoophilia, Philo makes the following observation:

οἱ μὲν ὅτι ὑπὲρ τοὺς ὅρους ἀκρασίας αὐτῆς ἤλασαν εὑρεταὶ γενόμενοι
παρηλλαγμένων ἐπιθυμιῶν καὶ ὅτι ἡδονὰς ἀηδεστάτας ἐκαινούργησαν

[These people [must be executed] because they pushed beyond the limits of
intemperance itself, becoming inventors of different appetites, and because they
innovated pleasures most shameful.] (Philo, *Spec. leg.* 3.49)

Philo's emphasis on the novelty and innovation of this unlawful activity may
suggest that κόρος indicates satiety in the sense of "jadedness." On this view,
the subjects' continual dedication to pleasure causes them to partake fully of all
its available normal sources. As the effects of these practices grows less with
use, they look for new and varied entertainments and finally cross "beyond the
limits" (ὑπὲρ τοὺς ὅρους).

To summarize, in tracing the usages of τρυφή in Philo, we see the appearance of several different threads. First and most commonly, he presents the Jewish view, consistent with the Septuagint, that τρυφή represents the gift of abundance from God to the righteous. This positive sense accords with the meaning of τρυφή in Classical and Hellenistic sources, where the relevant concept is centered around an expectation that one's desires will be met. Second, Philo offers an opposing, ascetic philosophical model in which τρυφή and any kind of abundance can be fitting for a woman, but for a man must be seen in opposition to virtue. Finally, he reflects the twofold progression of decadence that we have identified in Roman authors: on the one hand τρυφή leads to a progression into satiety, hubris, and finally destruction; on the other, it brings about weakness, even effeminacy, with a subsequent loss of political independence. Furthermore, these two Roman patterns, are sometimes confused to a degree. Thus, Philo's evidence for τρυφή and pernicious luxury is perhaps more complex than that of any extant writer so far discussed.

Josephus

The Jewish historian Josephus adopts the Roman interpretation of pernicious τρυφή that had become commonplace by the end of the first century CE. Though he claims to have been thoroughly educated (*Vit.* 8),[99] his training in this regard must have been more Classical and Roman than Rabbinic. He is aware of the Classical implications of the word, but his understanding of it more commonly reflects the views of Strabo and Dionysius of Halicarnassus than those of either Philo or the Septuagint.[100]

The Classical meaning of τρυφή emerges clearly in several passages, particularly at *AJ* 2.88, where the Joseph of Genesis advises Pharaoh:

ὑπετίθετο καὶ συνεβούλευε φειδὼ τῶν ἀγαθῶν, καὶ μὴ κατὰ περιουσίαν αὐτοῖς χρῆσθαι τοῖς Αἰγυπτίοις ἐπιτρέπειν, ἀλλ᾽ ὅσα ἂν κατὰ τρυφὴν ἀναλώσωσιν ἐκ περισσοῦ, ταῦτα τηρεῖν εἰς τὸν τῆς ἐνδείας καιρόν, ἀποτίθεσθαί τε παρῄνει λαμβάνοντα τὸν σῖτον παρὰ τῶν γεωργῶν τὰ διαρκῆ μόνον εἰς διατροφὴν χορηγοῦντα.

---

99. The *Vita* tells us, *inter alia*, that Josephus, as a youth was praised by the chief priests for his knowledge of the laws, and that he painstakingly studied the three Jewish sects, the Pharisees, the Sadducees, and the Essenes (*Vita* 8–11).

100. For the relationship between Josephus and classical studies, see Chapman 2009.

[He was suggesting and recommending to him a sparing of the goods, and not to allow the Egyptians to use them for surplus; but as much as they might consume for *truphē* from the extra, so much he should conserve for the crucial time of need, and he was recommending that he take the grain from the farmers and stow it away, furnishing them with only that which was sufficient for subsistence.] (Josephus, *AJ* 2.88)

Τρυφή has its traditional sense of having one's needs and comforts seen to and more than satisfied by another, in this instance by Pharaoh, whom Josephus presents as "providing" (ἐπιτρέπειν) goods to the Egyptians for their enjoyment. At *AJ* 11.447, the king is sated by τρυφή and pleasure (ὁ μὲν τρυφῆς ἁπάσης καὶ ἡδονῆς ἀναπιμπλάμενος) administered by his attendants, while the False Alexander is distinguished at 17.333 by his rough hands which, had he been Alexander in truth, would have been soft, ὑπὸ τρυφῆς καὶ γενναιότητος ("because of *truphē* and nobility"). Thus τρυφή is sometimes depicted in a standard Classical Greek manner: being taken care of by others with an abundance beyond sufficiency, a normal attribute of kings.

On the other hand, Josephus shares with Roman authors the idea of a development from τρυφή to ὕβρις by way of greed:

(2.201) Αἰγυπτίοις τρυφεροῖς καὶ ῥαθύμοις πρὸς πόνους οὖσι καὶ τῶν τε ἄλλων ἡδονῶν ἥττοσι καὶ δὴ καὶ τῆς κατὰ φιλοκέρδειαν συνέβη δεινῶς πρὸς τοὺς Ἑβραίους διατεθῆναι κατὰ φθόνον τῆς εὐδαιμονίας. (202) ὁρῶντες γὰρ τὸ τῶν Ἰσραηλιτῶν γένος ἀκμάζον καὶ δι᾽ ἀρετὴν καὶ τὴν πρὸς τὸ πονεῖν εὐφυΐαν πλήθει χρημάτων . . . δεινῶς ἐνύβριζόν τε τοῖς Ἰσραηλίταις καὶ ταλαιπωρίας αὐτοῖς ποικίλας ἐπενόουν.

[(2.201) It happened that the Egyptians, being *trupheros* and indifferent toward toils and enslaved to other pleasures and especially to that associated with the love of profit, treated the Hebrews terribly because of envy of their prosperity. (202) For when they saw the race of the Israelites flourishing in the quantity of possessions through virtue and a favorable disposition toward toil . . . they committed hubris against the Israelites terribly and they contrived various hardships for them.] (Josephus, *AJ* 2.201–2; cf. *BJ* 1.524)

Here the τρυφή is not the direct cause of hubris. Rather, it is the characteristic that turns the Egyptians away from toils. As a result, the Israelites outstripped the Egyptians in prosperity. Thus, τρυφή contributes to the envy and "pleasure of avarice," which spur the Egyptians to their harsh treatment of the Hebrews.

When we search for signs of the Jewish tradition, we may notice a slight nod to the Septuagint, for Josephus could have been thinking about well-watered Eden when he describes the place Daphne as τά τε ἄλλα τρυφεροῦ καὶ πηγὰς ἔχοντος ("having the other things of pertaining to *truphē* as well as springs," *BJ* 4.3) or when he describes Solomon's new cities:

> . . . καὶ ἄλλας εἰς ἀπόλαυσιν καὶ τρυφὴν ἐπιτηδείως ἐχούσας τῇ τε τῶν ἀέρων εὐκρασίᾳ καὶ τοῖς ὡραίοις εὐφυεῖς καὶ νάμασιν ὑδάτων ἐνδρόσους.

> [. . . other [cities] suitable for enjoyment and *truphē* because they have mild weather and are fruitful in season and wet with streams of water.] (Josephus, *AJ* 8.153; cf. *AJ* 8.137)

Yet these passages probably reflect, not the Jewish tradition, but rather a familiarity with the practice represented by Diodorus Siculus, who often uses the word to describe lands that yield in abundance.

The reason we identify the Greco-Roman tradition here rather than the Jewish is that τρυφή *never* occurs in Josephus as the characteristic gift from God, and only rarely as a truly good thing, such as when, at *AJ* 11.67, the Jewish people celebrate the return to their homeland with seven days of feasting, after which they and their leaders travel back home μετὰ χαρᾶς καὶ τρυφῆς ("with delight and *truphē*"). In direct opposition to the scripture, Josephus portrays the wrath of God against the Jewish people precisely because of their τρυφή. The tribe of Dan turned away from military training and became farmers, and so were defeated by the Canaanites and forced to move to a place near Sidon. Once there:

> (5.179) τοῖς δ' Ἰσραηλίταις προύβαινεν ὑπό τε ἀπειρίας τοῦ πονεῖν τὰ κακὰ καὶ ἀπὸ τῆς περὶ τὸ θεῖον ὀλιγωρίας· μετακινηθέντες γὰρ ἅπαξ τοῦ κόσμου τῆς πολιτείας ἐφέροντο πρὸς τὸ καθ᾽ ἡδονὴν καὶ βούλησιν ἰδίαν βιοῦν, ὡς καὶ τῶν ἐπιχωριαζόντων παρὰ τοῖς Χαναναίοις ἀναπίμπλασθαι κακῶν. (180) ὀργίζεται τοίνυν αὐτοῖς ὁ θεὸς καὶ ἣν σὺν πόνοις μυρίοις εὐδαιμονίαν ἐκτήσαντο, ταύτην ἀπέβαλον διὰ τρυφήν.

> [(5.179) Evils befell the Israelites from their ignorance of toiling and because of their contempt of the divine. Having altered the entirety of their political order,

they turned themselves to living in accordance with pleasure and their private
will, so that they became occupied with the evils which the Canaanites were
used to practicing. (180) And therefore God became angry at them, and the
prosperity that they had acquired through many toils, this they threw away
because of *truphē*.] (Josephus, *AJ* 5.179–80)

Prosperity derives from toil, but is lost through τρυφή, which is opposed to toil.
The Israelites abandoned good laws and God became angry as a result.[101] Τρυφή
is not a gift that is being withdrawn, as in the Septuagint, but rather the cause
of God's anger and the subsequent conquest of the Israelites. This theme represents a substantial deviation from Jewish usage in the Septuagint and Philo, but
is entirely consistent with the Roman tradition.

Most common in Josephus is the proposal that we have already seen espoused by the early Latin authors as well as both Strabo and Dionysius of Halicarnassus, that τρυφή comes from peace and leads to the transgression of the
law and abandonment of good government. In Judges 1–2, the prophet tells the
story of the Israelites defeating the Canaanites, and the immediate dire consequences: the Israelites abandoned God, His covenant, and the judges appointed
by Him, and instead worshipped the gods of the Canaanites. As a result, God
was very angry and delivered them to their enemies to be plundered. Josephus
retells the same story, but with a completely different emphasis that reveals the
Roman tendency of his thought.

(5.132) καὶ μετὰ ταῦτα πρὸς μὲν τοὺς πολεμίους μαλακῶς εἶχον οἱ Ἰσραηλῖται,
τῆς δὲ γῆς καὶ τῶν ταύτης ἔργων ἐπεμελοῦντο. τῶν δὲ κατὰ τὸν πλοῦτον αὐτοῖς
ἐπιδιδόντων ὑπὸ τρυφῆς καὶ ἡδονῆς τοῦ κόσμου ὠλιγώρουν καὶ τῆς πολιτείας
τῶν νόμων οὐκέτ᾽ ἦσαν ἀκριβεῖς ἀκροαταί.

(133) παροξυνθὲν δ᾽ ἐπὶ τούτοις τὸ θεῖον ἀναιρεῖ, πρῶτον μὲν ὡς φείσαιντο
παρὰ τὴν αὐτοῦ γνώμην τῶν Χαναναίων, ἔπειθ᾽ ὡς ἐκεῖνοι χρήσοιντο πολλῇ
κατ᾽ αὐτῶν ὠμότητι καιροῦ λαβόμενοι.

(134) οἱ δὲ καὶ πρὸς τὰ παρὰ τοῦ θεοῦ δυσθύμως εἶχον καὶ πρὸς τὸ πολεμεῖν
ἀηδῶς πολλά τε παρὰ τῶν Χαναναίων λαβόντες καὶ πρὸς τοὺς πόνους ἤδη διὰ
τὴν τρυφὴν ἐκλελυμένοι.

---

101. Cf. *AJ* 6.34, where the children of Samuel abandon justice in favor of profit and, "inclining toward
truphē and an opulent lifestyle" (πρὸς τρυφὴν καὶ πρὸς διαίτας πολυτελεῖς ἀπονενευκότες), they
acted in opposition both to God and to Samuel.

(135) καὶ συνέβαινεν ἤδη τὴν ἀριστοκρατίαν διεφθάρθαι, καὶ τὰς γερουσίας οὐκ ἀπεδείκνυσαν οὐδ᾽ ἀρχὴν ἄλλην οὐδεμίαν τῶν πρότερον νενομισμένων, ἦσαν δὲ ἐν τοῖς ἀγροῖς ἡδονῇ τοῦ κερδαίνειν προσδεδεμένοι. καὶ διὰ τὴν πολλὴν ἄδειαν στάσις αὐτοὺς πάλιν καταλαμβάνει δεινὴ καὶ προήχθησαν εἰς τὸ πολεμεῖν ἀλλήλοις ἐκ τοιαύτης αἰτίας.

[(5.132) And after these things, the Israelites became soft regarding wars, and they devoted themselves to the land and its labors. When they thereby gained wealth, because of *truphē* and pleasure they neglected order and their constitution, and they were no longer exact disciples of the laws.

(133) And God, being angered by these things, reminded them first that they had spared the Canaanites contrary to his wishes, and then that the Canaanites treated the Israelites with much cruelty, when they had an opportunity.

(134) And they were despondent at the word they had from God but were sickened at the idea of war, since they were receiving many things from the Canaanites and had relaxed from toils on account of *truphē*.

(135) And it happened that the aristocracy had already been corrupted and they had not appointed a council, nor any other government of the sort they had been accustomed to have earlier, but rather they were bound to the fields by their love of profit. And because of great disregard of consequences, a terrible civil strife seized them again, and they were led into war against each other for the following reason.] (Josephus, *AJ* 5.132–35)

Instead of being angry at them for abandoning him for other gods, in accordance with the Septuagint, in Josephus's account God is angry because the Israelites spared the Canaanites and did not wish to fight further. A theme common to both accounts is the neglect of government and the laws, but the cause is radically changed: from idolatry to avarice and τρυφή.[102] As in Dionysius, the result of τρυφή is anarchy and the collapse of civil harmony.

---

102. In this passage, the process that makes the Israelites "soft in war" (πρὸς τοὺς πολεμίους μαλακῶς) is complex. Both ἡδονή and τρυφή play a part, but so too does the Israelites' devotion to agriculture. Josephus's explanation is in line with our interpretation of Classical Greek ideas about feminizing luxury. On this interpretation, τρυφή may lead to a loss of martial prowess inasmuch as it distracts its possessors from their military pursuits. In other words, excessive τρυφή may misdirect one's

There is a contradiction in Josephus in the relationship between τρυφή and toil, because τρυφή is first associated with the wealth obtained from the toil of farming and second with the profits acquired from the Canaanites, which relaxed them from both fighting and toil. There is also an obscure mingling of the two usual paths of pernicious luxury. In the first place, τρυφή and pleasure are associated with military weakness and the collapse of good government. As the passage progresses, we learn that this state of neglect, with the admixture of "heedlessness" and "the pleasure of avarice," brought about δεινὴ στάσις. At this point in the story, hubris is introduced, since the proximate cause (ἐκ τοιαύτης αἰτίας) of outright civil war was a gang rape by which a group of young men "glutted themselves with rape through the whole night" (δι᾽ ὅλης νυκτὸς ἐμπλησθέντες τῆς ὕβρεως, Josephus, AJ 5.146). We have already noted several times that it is rare for τρυφή to be blamed for effeminacy and hubris in the same context. Such a combination is made plausible here by the lack of any detailed elaboration about the Israelites' indulgent lifestyle: their pleasures kept them from attending to their civic responsibilities, but we hear nothing of the adoption of effeminate clothing, perfumes, or the like.

In his extensive discussion of the rape and subsequent war brought on by τρυφή (AJ 5.136–57; cf. Judges 19–20), Josephus omits the material from all the intervening chapters of Judges that contains the accounts of one attack against the Israelites after another. Thus Josephus takes a story from the Septuagint about abandoning God for idolatry and thereafter being punished by military conquest, and he transforms it into a tale with a moral that the Romans would approve: τρυφή is caused by turning away from war in favor of the pursuits of peace and the "pleasure of avarice," and so results in anarchy and civil war.[103]

To conclude, Josephus uses τρυφή often, but departs from the practice of Philo and the Septuagint, since he rarely presents it as a positive quality. Far

---

ἐπιμέλεια ("careful attention"). We see exactly this process here, where in order to indulge in τρυφή, the Israelites focus their attention (ἐπεμελοῦντο) on working their fields. This connection between farm work and feminization is significant, since it reinforces our claim that Greek tradition did not view a lifestyle marked by τρυφή as *necessarily* productive of such weakness. Rather, luxury was just a particularly enticing distraction from the proper focus of (a man's) ἐπιμέλεια. Certain styles of clothing, cuisine, etc. did not per se cause μαλακία, and, at the same time, the contrary lifestyle (e.g., field labor) could have that result even though it involves toil.

103. The opposition between fighting and the toil related to farming is reinforced at AJ 4.167, where the Canaanites take to raising livestock to avoid fighting and because αὐτοὺς μὲν βούλεσθαι τρυφᾶν ἀπόνως ("they wanted to have *truphē* without toil"), as if the agrarian life were a life of ease. Also at AJ 3.223, Josephus says that the laws were not being transgressed, μήτ᾽ ἐν εἰρήνη ὑπὸ τρυφῆς μήτ᾽ ἐν πολέμῳ κατ᾽ ἀνάγκην ("neither in peace because of *truphē* nor in war from necessity"), implying that τρυφή associated with peace is in itself a likely reason for transgression. Τρυφή is also set in opposition to warfare at AJ 7.133, *Vit.* 284, and *BJ* 4.592.

from being a gift from God, people are punished by Him for demonstrating τρυφή. Thus, the evidence examined suggests that Josephus represents a thoroughly Romanized approach to the idea of pernicious luxury.

Dio Chrysostom

Dio Chrysostom (died c. 120 CE) is an exemplar of the Second Sophistic, an educational movement distinguished by the revival of classical Greek rhetoric and values under the Roman empire. Yet in the case of τρυφή, Dio all but abandons the Hellenic tradition and unmistakably follows the moral ideal according to which τρυφή is universally a negative trait that necessarily corrupts its possessor and so is best forestalled in all circumstances.[104]

In the Hellenic tradition, τρυφή is an appropriate and expected trait of kings, since it helps establish their dignity and separates them from ordinary people. We have seen in Chapter 1 that the Persian royals in particular are often associated with the word, without harm to their masculinity or fighting prowess. Perhaps the paradigm example of the suitability of τρυφή for kings occurs in Isocrates' advice to Neocles, where the orator encourages him not to live ἀτάκτως ("without discipline"), but rather to embrace σωφροσύνη as an example to his people (Isoc. 2.31). A good reputation is more important than wealth. Yet, even then, it is fitting for a king to display τρυφή:

> τρύφα μὲν ἐν ταῖς ἐσθῆσι καὶ τοῖς περὶ τὸ σῶμα κόσμοις, καρτέρει δ᾿ ὡς χρὴ τοὺς βασιλεύοντας ἐν τοῖς ἄλλοις ἐπιτηδεύμασιν, ἵν᾿ οἱ μὲν ὁρῶντες διὰ τὴν ὄψιν ἄξιόν σε τῆς ἀρχῆς εἶναι νομίζωσιν, οἱ δὲ συνόντες διὰ τὴν τῆς ψυχῆς ῥώμην τὴν αὐτὴν ἐκείνοις γνώμην ἔχωσιν.

> [Have *truphē* in your clothing and in the adornment of your body, but be temperate, as befits those who rule, in your other habits, in order that those who look upon you will think that you are worthy of rule from your appearance, while those who are your companions will hold the same opinion in regard to these matters on account of the strength of your soul.] (Isoc. 2.32)

---

104. For the difficult subject of the putative conversion of Dio from rhetor to philosopher during his exile along with his relationship to emperors, see the discussion and bibliography at Whitmarsh 2001, 156–67. Bost Pouderon (2006, 2.358) refers to his philosophy as "un inévitable éclectisme" leaning heavily toward Stoicism. For his relationship to the New Testament, see Mussies 1972.

Thus, in Isocrates, τρυφή, in appearance at least, is both necessary to maintain a sufficient level of dignity and also entirely compatible with moderation and discipline in other aspects of one's life.

In particular contrast to Isocrates is the homily in Dio Chrys., *Or.* 1, where Hermes guides Heracles to view two different types of rulers.[105] Since this homily has its roots in the story attributed to Prodicus by Xenophon (*Mem.* 2.1.21–34), a comparison of the two passages is informative. In Xenophon's story, Heracles is met by two women, named Virtue and Vice or Happiness (Ἀρετή and Κακία or Εὐδαιμονία). Virtue is beautiful and pure and modest. Vice is τεθραμμένην μὲν εἰς πολυσαρκίαν τε καὶ ἀπαλότητα ("reared in fleshiness and softness"), and tries to exaggerate her appearance, but is not otherwise described negatively.[106] The two speakers have no attendants, but instead plead their own cases, with Virtue arguing for a noble life of toil, which is condoned by the gods and Vice promising pleasures without labor.[107]

In Dio's version, the story is far more intricate and relies on visual rather than verbal arguments. Heracles is led by Hermes to adjacent mountaintops on which the two women repose. The first woman, μακαρία δαίμων Βασιλεία, Διὸς βασιλέως ἔκγονος ("Blessed divinity Queen, offspring of the god-king," Dio Chrys., *Or.* 1.73), sits dignified, radiant, and still on a beautiful throne, holding a scepter made of something purer than gold or silver. She is attended by personified Justice, Good-Order, Peace, and Law, and surrounded by gold, silver, bronze, and iron, though she ignores the treasures in preference for the fruits and animals.

τὸ δὲ πρόσωπον φαιδρὸν ὁμοῦ καὶ σεμνόν, ὡς τοὺς μὲν ἀγαθοὺς ἅπαντας θαρρεῖν ὁρῶντας, κακὸν δὲ μηδένα δύνασθαι προσιδεῖν, μὴ μᾶλλον ἢ τὸν ἀσθενῆ τὴν ὄψιν ἀναβλέψαι πρὸς τὸν τοῦ ἡλίου κύκλον·

---

105. Dio gives advice to rulers in his first four orations, where he has eighteen passages linking kings with τρυφή, as well as in a handful of references elsewhere in his orations. Jones 1978, 115–22.

106. Dio deemphasizes the idea that τρυφή is linked to softness (μαλακ- or ἀσθεν-). Besides this passage, we see it in the context of τρυφή at 60.5, 60.8, 66.25. Softness is actually contrasted with τρυφή at 52.3: αὐτὸς δὲ ἐφαινόμην ἐμαυτῷ πάνυ τρυφᾶν καὶ τῆς ἀσθενείας παραμυθίαν καινὴν ἔχειν ("I appeared especially to be having *truphē* in myself, and to have a new consolation for my weakness"). The context is Dio's reflection on the tragedies to do with Philoctetes, and the use of τρυφή here brings to mind Cicero's pleasure at reading Theophrastus at Plut., *Cic.* 24.

107. Xenophon could have aptly used the word τρυφή in this instance, especially in the context where Vice offers Heracles a life where he uses the gains made by the labor of others (ἀλλ᾽ οἷς ἂν οἱ ἄλλοι ἐργάζωνται, τούτοις σὺ χρήσῃ). The fact that he does not may possibly be seen as further indication that the word did not have so many negative connotations in the fourth century BCE as it did by Dio's time.

[Her face was at the same time beaming with joy and sacred, so that all good men, looking upon her, would have good courage, but no evil man would be able to gaze upon her any more than a man with weak eyesight could look upon the orb of the sun. . . .] (Dio Chrys., *Or.* 1.71)

On the second peak, Hermes displays the lady Tyranny, a counterfeit of the Queen, sitting on a wobbly, but heavily adorned throne:

ἦν δὲ οὐδ᾽ ἄλλο οὐδὲν ἐν κόσμῳ διακείμενον, ἀλλὰ πρὸς δόξαν ἅπαντα καὶ ἀλαζονείαν καὶ τρυφήν, πολλὰ μὲν σκῆπτρα, πολλαὶ δὲ τιᾶραι καὶ διαδήματα ἐπὶ τῆς κεφαλῆς.

[There was nothing there that was not in disorder, but rather arranged for reputation and false pretense and *truphē*: many scepters and many tiaras and diadems on her head.] (Dio Chrys., *Or.* 1.79)

Tyranny scowls at everyone who approaches her, and embraces her gold stingily. She wears colorful clothing, but it is torn, and she alternates unpredictably between anger, suspicion, terror, grief, and joy. She is surrounded by attendants:

ἀλλ᾽ Ὠμότης καὶ Ὕβρις καὶ Ἀνομία καὶ Στάσις, αἳ πᾶσαι διέφθειρον αὐτὴν καὶ κάκιστα ἀπώλλυον. ἀντὶ δὲ Φιλίας Κολακεία παρῆν, δουλοπρεπὴς καὶ ἀνελεύθερος, οὐδεμιᾶς ἧττον ἐπιβουλεύουσα ἐκείνων, ἀλλὰ μάλιστα δὴ πάντων ἀπολέσαι ζητοῦσα.

[[Her attendants were] Savagery and Hubris and Lawlessness and Civil Strife, all of which destroy her and ruin her. And instead of Friendship, Flattery was present, servile and slavish, giving her advice no less than the others, and even more than the others being zealous to destroy her.] (Dio Chrys., *Or.* 1.82)

Her human followers are no less odious:

δεῦρο, ἔφη, θέασαι καὶ τὴν ἑτέραν, ἧς ἐρῶσιν οἱ πολλοὶ καὶ περὶ ἧς πολλὰ καὶ παντοδαπὰ πράγματα ἔχουσι, φονεύοντες οἱ ταλαίπωροι, παῖδές τε γονεῦσι πολλάκις ἐπιβουλεύοντες καὶ γονεῖς παισὶ καὶ ἀδελφοὶ ἀδελφοῖς, τὸ μέγιστον κακὸν ἐπιποθοῦντες καὶ μακαρίζοντες, ἐξουσίαν μετὰ ἀνοίας.

[He said, "Look here at the other [Tyranny], whom many men love and concerning whom they have many troubles of every sort, wretched men committing murder, sons frequently contriving against their fathers, fathers against
sons, and brothers against brothers, yearning for and congratulating that greatest evil, power with folly."] (Dio Chrys., *Or.* 1.76)

Dio has transformed the homily about Virtue and Vice into one about
good and bad rulers. Instead of simply praising a life of toil pleasing to the
gods, Dio stresses the attributes of a good ruler as justice and adherence to
proper laws. Where Xenophon contrasts a life of ease, living off the toil of
others, Dio emphasizes the abhorrent characteristics of Tyranny, starting
with her shabby and false appearance and extending into more significant
traits, such as savagery, hubris, murder, and lawlessness. Τρυφή is not particularly highlighted in this account—though it occurs many times elsewhere in his descriptions of autocrats—but it is an integral part of Tyranny's aim at deception.

Therefore, in Dio's view and in contrast to Isocrates', τρυφή even in appearance is incompatible with good rule. It is a characteristic of tyranny, coupled
with false countenance and lacking real substance. Finally, it is well to remember that savagery, hubris, lawlessness, civil strife, and especially flattery sur-
round and destroy this tyranny.

Similarly, τρυφή arises in connection to Dio's praise of good kings in *Or.*
3.2–8, but only as something to be avoided. Though he has the wherewithal to
live an easy life, a good ruler instead chooses to be virtuous. He delights in truth
rather than flattery. He is more equitable than the judges, more courageous
than the soldiers, kindlier to his people than a loving father. In addition, he is
ἔλαττον δὲ βουλόμενος τρυφᾶν τῶν μηδεμιᾶς εὐπορούντων τρυφῆς, ("less
willing to enjoy *truphē* than those who have no means of *truphē*," 3.5). A good
king sacrifices his own wants for the sake of his virtue and the well-being of his
people. For Dio, τρυφή has no place, even among sovereigns.

Dio cites Homer as an authority on this theme. In the dialogue of *Or.* 2,
Philip asks Alexander whether Homer did not dress his heroes finely. The response follows:

. . . οὐ μέντοι γυναικείαν οὐδὲ ποικίλην, ἀλλὰ πορφύρᾳ μόνον ἐκόσμησε τὸν
Ἀγαμέμνονα, καὶ τὸν Ὀδυσσέα δὲ μιᾷ χλαίνῃ τῇ οἴκοθεν. οὐδὲ γὰρ οἴεται δεῖν

Ὅμηρος τὸν ἡγεμόνα φαίνεσθαι ταπεινὸν οὐδὲ τοῖς πολλοῖς καὶ ἰδιώταις ὅμοιον, ἀλλὰ καὶ στολῇ καὶ ὁπλίσει διαφέρειν παρὰ τοὺς ἄλλους ἐπὶ τὸ μεῖζον καὶ σεμνότερον, οὐ μὴν τρυφῶντά γε οὐδὲ [σπουδάζοντα].

[. . . but not in womanly or embroidered [clothes], rather he dressed Agamemnon only in purple, and Odysseus has just one cloak from home. For Homer thinks that a leader should not appear to be low and dressed the same as the many private people, but in his clothes and his armor he should distinguish himself from the others in order to be greater and more august, but not have *truphē* or be zealous.] (Dio Chrys., *Or.* 2.49)

A leader should be prominent, but in a serious, not a foolish manner. Likewise Dio says that Homer mocks the Carian who went to fight in golden armor, καταγελῶν αὐτοῦ τῆς τρυφῆς ἅμα καὶ τῆς ἀφροσύνης ("laughing at him for his *truphē* and at the same time his thoughtlessness," *Or.* 2.51).

Another passage employs Socrates as the mouthpiece for a further contrast between good rulers and bad. A ruler who respects the laws and his citizens alike, taking care for their welfare and prosperity, is a true king:

(3.40) εἰ δὲ φιλήδονος καὶ φιλοχρήματος καὶ ὑβριστὴς καὶ παράνομος, αὐτὸν οἰόμενος αὔξειν μόνον, ὡς ἂν πλεῖστα μὲν χρήματα κεκτημένος, μεγίστας δὲ καὶ πλείστας καρπούμενος ἡδονάς, ῥαθύμως δὲ διάγων καὶ ἀπόνως· τοὺς δὲ ὑπηκόους ἅπαντας ἡγούμενος δούλους καὶ ὑπηρέτας τῆς αὑτοῦ τρυφῆς, (41) οὐδὲ ποιμένος ἐπιεικοῦς ἔχων ἦθος, σκέπης καὶ νομῆς προνοούμενος τοῖς αὑτοῦ κτήνεσιν, ἔτι δὲ θῆρας ἀπαμύνων καὶ φῶρας προφυλάττων, ἀλλ᾽ <αὐτὸς> πρῶτος διαρπάζων τε καὶ φθείρων καὶ τοῖς ἄλλοις ἐπιτρέπων, καθάπερ, οἶμαι, πολεμίων λείαν, οὐκ ἂν ποτε εἴποιμι τὸν τοιοῦτον ἄρχοντα ἢ αὐτοκράτορα ἢ βασιλέα, πολὺ δὲ μᾶλλον τύραννον καὶ λευστῆρα . . .

[(3.40) But if however he loves pleasure and money and is hubristic and lawless, thinking that only he need prosper, so that he possess as much money as possible and enjoy the greatest and most pleasures, passing through life easily and without toil, thinking all of his subjects to be slaves and servants to his *truphē*, (41) having the character not of a fit shepherd, providing shelter and law to his flocks, warding off the wild beasts and guarding them from thieves, but rather he is first to plunder and ruin them and to allow others to do so as well, just as if, I think, they were the spoils of the enemies. Not ever would I say that such a ruler is an autocrat or king, but much more I would call him a tyrant or an oppressor. . . .] (Dio Chrys., *Or.* 3.40–41)

Thus in Dio's orations, τρυφή is only associated with a bad king who "loves pleasure and money and is hubristic and lawless." This lawlessness is a reminder of the Roman theme of τρυφή leading to tyranny or anarchy and is without analogue in the Greek tradition.

Dio's τρυφή is opposed to toil, and leads sometimes to weakness rather than hubris:

(3.83) κατανοεῖ δὲ τοὺς μὲν πόνους ὑγίειάν τε παρέχοντας καὶ σωτηρίαν ἔτι δὲ δόξαν ἀγαθήν, τὴν δὲ αὖ τρυφὴν ἅπαντα τούτων τἀναντία. ἔτι δὲ οἱ μὲν πόνοι αὐτοὺς ἐλάττους ἀεὶ ποιοῦσι καὶ φέρειν ἐλαφροτέρους, τὰς δὲ ἡδονὰς μείζους καὶ ἀβλαβεστέρας, ὅταν γίγνωνται μετὰ τοὺς πόνους. ἡ δέ γε τρυφὴ τοὺς μὲν πόνους ἀεὶ χαλεπωτέρους ποιεῖ φαίνεσθαι, τὰς δὲ ἡδονὰς ἀπομαραίνει καὶ ἀσθενεῖς ἀποδείκνυσιν. (84) ὁ γὰρ ἀεὶ τρυφῶν ἄνθρωπος, μηδέποτε δὲ ἁπτόμενος πόνου μηδενός, τελευτῶν πόνον μὲν οὐκ ἂν οὐδένα ἀνάσχοιτο, ἡδονῆς δὲ οὐδεμιᾶς ἂν αἴσθοιτο, οὐδὲ τῆς σφοδροτάτης.

[(3.83) [The good king] realizes that toils offer health and salvation and also a good reputation, and *truphē* offers all the things opposite to these. Further, toils always make themselves lesser and easier to bear, while they make pleasures greater and less harmful, whenever those pleasures follow after toils. But *truphē* always makes toils seem more difficult, and it causes pleasures to waste away and renders them weak. (84) For the man who always has *truphē* and never engages in any kind of toil in the end can endure no toil at all, nor can he feel any pleasure, not even if it is extreme.] (Dio Chrys., *Or.* 3.83–84)

In this odd twist, Dio interprets τρυφή here to be detrimental even to the enjoyment of pleasure, an attribute usually coupled with τρυφή.[108] In an image reminiscent of Plato's Cave, toil makes further toil easier but also makes pleasures

---

108. The idea that τρυφή diminishes pleasure may be a reflection the process of decadence described the sequence πλοῦτος to τρυφή to κόρος to ὕβρις. If so, Dio may understand κόρος as a kind of jadedness or dissatisfaction with familiar pleasures, a meaning for which, as we have seen, there may be a trace of evidence in Philo, but which seems foreign to the original meaning of the traditional saying: τίκτει κόρος ὕβριν ("satiety engenders hubris").

felt more intensely, while τρυφή leaves its bearer with a kind of numbness, unable to bear work or feel pleasure.[109]

The peculiarity of this passage stands out, particularly in contrast to others such as 12.36, where humans also live in a kind of cave of denial, rejecting the true gods and erecting Pleasure as a replacement:

ὑπερφρονοῦσι τὰ θεῖα, καὶ μίαν ἱδρυσάμενοι δαίμονα πονηρὰν καὶ ἄλυπον, τρυφήν τινα ἢ ῥᾳθυμίαν πολλὴν καὶ ἀνειμένην ὕβριν, ἡδονὴν ἐπονομάζοντες, γυναικείαν τῷ ὄντι θεόν,

[They are despising the divine things, establishing instead one goddess who is grievous and without pain,[110] unloosing a certain *truphē* and much ease and hubris, calling her Pleasure, being a feminine god in reality.] (Dio Chrys., *Or.* 12.36)

The gods represent the opposite of τρυφή. In *Oration* 32.15, they give us everything that is good and useful—what in earlier times might have been called τρυφή—whereas evils derive from ignorance and τρυφή and ambition: διὰ γὰρ ἀνθρώπων ἄνοιαν καὶ τρυφὴν καὶ φιλοτιμίαν δυσχερὴς ὁ βίος καὶ μεστὸς ἀπάτης, πονηρίας, λύπης, μυρίων ἄλλων κακῶν ("Because of the ignorance of men and their *truphē* and ambition, life is difficult and full of treachery, wickedness, pain, and many other evils."). Thus Dio frequently connects τρυφή with kings who are corrupt rulers and with people who do not follow the true gods. From the gods come toil and virtue, while τρυφή arises from the lawlessness of selfish indulgence.

This theme of indulgence is also carried over into another of Dio's favorite themes, that of the role of oratory and the orator in society. Τρυφή is something that we have already seen linked to flattering oratory in Dionysius of Halicarnassus (esp. *Comp.* 23.37). Dio picks up this idea and elaborates on it at length, combining τρυφή frequently with the concept of deception (as he did with the personified Tyranny). *Oration* 33 begins with a long discourse in which Dio disparages eloquent, flattering speakers and people who follow them in search of false praise, and acclaims instead the speakers who criticize and rebuke their listeners in the manner of Archilochus or Socrates. He uses the term τρυφή

---

109. Τρυφή causes real weakness in one passage, at *Or.* 1.3, where Sardanapalus was in such a state of wretchedness from ἐξουσία and τρυφή that he would not leave his harem in order to fight.

110. Dio has chosen to use a contradictory phrase, meaning literally "oppressed by toil and without pain."

twelve times in this introductory material, conveniently illustrating the relationship between τρυφή and each of the participants in oratory:[111] the speaker who rebukes, the speaker who flatters, and the audience that generally wishes to be flattered. He begins by describing himself:

τί οὖν ἡμᾶς ἐλπίζετε ἐρεῖν, ἢ τί μάλιστα ἀκοῦσαι σπεύδετε παρὰ ἀνδρῶν οὐκ εὐτραπέλων οὐδὲ πρὸς χάριν ὁμιλεῖν εἰδότων οὐδὲ αἱμύλων οὐδὲ ὑπὸ τρυφῆς ἰόντων ἐπὶ τοὺς λόγους;

[What do you expect us to say? Why are you so eager to hear from men who are not nimble and do not know how to converse with men for the sake of favor, nor are wheedling, nor come to speak because of *truphē*?] (Dio Chrys., *Or.* 33.3)

He makes his position clear: he will not offer fawning, pleasant words in order to gratify his hearers.

He then contrasts the obsequious speakers with the better sort, such as himself:

(33.13) . . . ὅταν οὖν πρῶτον αὐτόν τινα ἴδητε κολακεύοντα ἐν ἅπασιν οἷς ποιεῖ καὶ χαριζόμενον ἐν τροφαῖς, ἐν ἐσθῆσι, καὶ περιιόντα ἀκόλαστον, τοῦτον οἴεσθε κολακεύσειν καὶ ὑμᾶς καὶ παρὰ τούτου προσδοκᾶτε λόγον ἡδύν, ὃν ὑμεῖς ἔπαινον ὀνομάζετε, τρυφῶντα δὴ παρὰ τρυφῶντος. (14) ὅταν δὲ αὐχμηρόν τινα καὶ συνεσταλμένον ἴδητε καὶ μόνον βαδίζοντα, πρῶτον αὐτὸν ἐξετάζοντα καὶ λοιδοροῦντα, μὴ ζητεῖτε παρὰ τοῦ τοιούτου μηδεμίαν θωπείαν μηδὲ ἀπάτην, μηδὲ τὸν δεξιὸν ἐκεῖνον καὶ προσηνῆ λόγον, ὃς δὴ μάλιστα διατρίβει περὶ δήμους καὶ σατράπας καὶ τυράννους.

[(33.13) Whenever you spot someone who foremost is flattering himself in everything he does and rejoicing in his livelihood and in his clothes, going around without discipline, know that that man will flatter you and expect a soft speech from him, which you label as praise, words of *truphē* from a man of *truphē*. (14) But whenever you see someone squalid and drawn, wandering around alone, who foremost is examining and abrading himself, do not seek from such a man flattery and deceit, nor that clever and soothing speech that especially wastes the time for the people and satraps and tyrants.] (Dio Chrys., *Or.* 33.13–14)

---

111. In chapter 31 he begins the discussion of the improbable topic at hand, the grunting noise that people make while sleeping or having sex, perhaps a metaphor for people who are slumbering through life indulging their pleasures. See the recent commentary on *Orations* 33–35: Bost Pouderon 2006 and her new Budé edition of *Orations* 33–36 (2011).

This image of the ascetic orator is a renewal of the theme touched on in Philo, in which τρυφή can be an undesirable trait of people who lack virtue (Philo, *Somn.* 1.120–26; 2.9; Josephus, *AJ* 10.193). It is associated not just with the concern for comfort that is characteristic of the Classical meaning of the word, but also with softness and lack of restraint. An orator with τρυφή is attempting to create a relationship with his audience whereby they think they are receiving τρυφή from him, when they are in fact being treated to empty words of adoration—τρυφῶντα δὴ παρὰ τρυφῶντος. In reality, the flatterer is the one receiving τρυφή from them in very concrete terms: he expects fine clothes and a sumptuous lifestyle.

The speaker who will advise on the path to true virtue lives a hard life, caring not for material possessions but for the possessions of the soul. He is not seeking τρυφή. He will not waste people's time with flattery. Instead, when Dio further depicts the more savage speaker in chapter 15, he is about to develop a comparison between that speaker and his audience, on the one hand, and Odysseus disguised as a beggar going among the suitors on the other. An orator who recognizes the terrible things in the world knows ὅτι μεστὰ πάντα πολεμίων καὶ ἐχθρῶν, ὅπου τρυφὴ καὶ ἀπάτη δυναστεύουσιν ("that everything is full of hostile men and enemies, wherever *truphē* and cheating hold sway," Dio Chrys., *Or.* 33.15). Dio taunts his audience, implying that they are those hostile men, unable to endure the words of such a speaker and likely to become annoyed with him.

οὐ γὰρ ὑμῶν παρεσκεύασται τὰ ὦτα δέξασθαι τραχεῖς τε καὶ στερεοὺς λόγους, ἀλλ᾽ ὥσπερ ἀσθενεῖς ὁπλαὶ κτηνῶν τῶν ἐν μαλακοῖς τε καὶ λείοις τραφέντων χωρίοις, ὁμοίως ὦτα τρυφερὰ ἐν κολακείᾳ τραφέντα καὶ λόγοις ψευδέσι.

[For your ears are not prepared to receive jagged, hard words. But just as the hooves of beasts raised in soft and level places become weak, in the same way your ears have become *trupheros* since they have been reared amidst flattery and lying words.] (Dio Chrys., *Or.* 33.15)

Finally he embroiders a lengthy parable of Odysseus and Troy. Odysseus represents the squalid speaker, coming ἐξ οὕτω λυπρᾶς καὶ ἀδόξου πόλεως ("from such a wretched and obscure city," Dio Chrys., *Or.* 33.22).

In contrast, in an extended depiction (33.19–21), Troy represents the audience that wishes to be flattered. At first, it seems a blessed place: great in size and extent of territory; with a large population and numerous of subjects and allies; rich in gold and bronze, and hence wealthy; possessing fertile soil and beautiful fields, mountains, and rivers; the people themselves were beautiful; their horses were swift, and their walls strong; and they were especially beloved of the gods. But all that ended:

ἀλλ᾽ ὅμως, ἐπειδὴ τρυφὴ καὶ ὕβρις εἰσῆλθεν αὐτοὺς καὶ παιδείας καὶ σωφροσύνης οὐδὲν ᾤοντο δεῖσθαι, πολὺ πάντων ἀτυχέστατοι γεγόνασιν. οὐχ ἡ σύμπασα χθὼν ταῖς συμφοραῖς αὐτῶν διατεθρύληται; καὶ οὐδὲν ὤνησεν αὐτοὺς οὔτε τῶν ἵππων τὸ τάχος οὔτε ὁ Ζεὺς οὔτε ὁ Γανυμήδης, ἀλλ᾽ ὑπ᾽ ἀνδρὸς ἐξ οὕτω λυπρᾶς καὶ ἀδόξου πόλεως ἀπώλοντο καὶ ἴσχυσεν ὁ τῆς Ἰθάκης πολίτης περιγενέσθαι τῶν ἐκ τοῦ Ἰλίου πάντων, καὶ τὴν εὐρυάγυιαν ἅπασαν πορθῆσαι καὶ ἀνελεῖν.

[But nevertheless, because *truphē* and hubris came to them and they thought that they had no need for culture or moderation, they became the most wretched people by far. Has not the entire earth been talked deaf about their misfortunes? For the speed of their horses did not profit them, nor Zeus, nor Ganymede, but they were destroyed by a man from such a wretched and obscure city. That citizen of Ithaca prevailed in gaining advantage over all the forces of Ilium, and he pillaged and plundered the entire city of wide-streets.] (Dio Chrys., *Or.* 33.22)

The destruction of Troy is caused by τρυφή and hubris and the abandonment of culture and moderation.[112] It is set in terms of wealth overcome by poverty and simplicity. The only reasoning offered is that prosperity leads to undisciplined behavior, which the gods hate:

οὐδὲ γὰρ οὐδ᾽ οἱ θεοὶ φιλοῦσιν ἔτι τοὺς ἀσελγεῖς καὶ ἄφρονας καὶ ἀκολάστους καὶ πρὸς ὕβριν ἐγκλίνοντας καὶ ῥᾳθυμίαν καὶ τρυφήν

[For the gods do not love licentious, outrageous, and undisciplined men, inclined toward hubris, laziness, and *truphē*.] (Dio Chrys., *Or.* 33.23)

---

112. Cf. *Or.* 11.63, where Agamemnon declares: εἶναι γὰρ τὴν μὲν πόλιν πλουσιωτάτην ἁπασῶν, τοὺς δὲ ἀνθρώπους ὑπὸ τρυφῆς διεφθαρμένους ("of all cities, [Troy] is the wealthiest, and the people there have been utterly destroyed by *truphē*").

So, he tells his audience, do not fawn over flattering speakers, pretending that prosperity is a worthy end in itself:

(33.25) τοὺς γὰρ ἀπείρους τρυφῆς καὶ πανουργίας, τούτους ἐγώ φημι πράττειν ἄμεινον. τί δ' αὐτῆς τῆς Ἰταλίας; οὐ Σύβαρις μὲν ὅσῳ μάλιστα ἐτρύφησεν, τοσούτῳ θᾶττον ἀπώλετο; Κρότων δὲ καὶ Θούριοι καὶ Μεταπόντιον καὶ Τάρας, ἐπὶ τοσοῦτον ἀκμάσασαι καὶ τηλικαύτην ποτὲ σχοῦσαι δύναμιν, ποίας πόλεως οὐκ εἰσὶ νῦν ἐρημότεραι;

(26) πολὺ δ' ἂν ἔργον εἴη πάντας ἐπεξιέναι τοὺς διὰ τρυφὴν ἀπολωλότας, Λυδοὺς πάλαι, Μήδους, Ἀσσυρίους πρότερον, τὰ τελευταῖα Μακεδόνας· οἳ νεωστὶ μὲν τὰ ῥάκη περιῃρημένοι καὶ ποιμένες ἀκούοντες, τοῖς Θρᾳξὶ περὶ τῶν μελινῶν μαχόμενοι τοὺς Ἕλληνας ἐκράτησαν, εἰς τὴν Ἀσίαν διέβησαν, ἄχρις Ἰνδῶν ἦρξαν. ἐπεὶ δὲ τὰ ἀγαθὰ τὰ Περσῶν ἔλαβον, τούτοις ἐπηκολούθησε καὶ τὰ κακά.

(27) τοιγαροῦν ἅμα σκῆπτρα καὶ ἁλουργίδες καὶ Μηδικὴ τράπεζα καὶ τὸ γένος αὐτῶν ἐξέλιπεν, ὥστε νῦν εἴ τις διέρχοιτο Πέλλαν, οὐδὲ σημεῖον ὄψεται πόλεως οὐδέν, δίχα τοῦ πολὺν κέραμον εἶναι συντετριμμένον ἐν τῷ τόπῳ. καίτοι μένει τὰ χωρία τῶν πόλεων ὧν εἶπον καὶ τῶν ἐθνῶν οἷα καὶ πρότερον ἦν καὶ τοὺς ποταμοὺς οὐδεὶς ἄλλοσε ἔτρεψεν, οὐδ' εἴ τι τοιοῦτον ἦν ἕτερον. ἀλλ' ὅμως ὧν ἂν πολυτέλεια καὶ τρυφὴ ἅψηται τούτοις οὐκ ἔστι πλείω χρόνον διαγενέσθαι.

(28) μὴ γὰρ οἴεσθε τοὺς κριοὺς μηδὲ τὰς ἑλεπόλεις καὶ τὰς ἄλλας μηχανὰς οὕτως ἀνατρέπειν ὡς τρυφήν, εἴτε ἄνδρα βούλεταί τις πεπτωκότα ἰδεῖν εἴτε πόλιν. οὐ ποταμός ἐστιν οὐδὲ πεδίον οὐδὲ λιμὴν ὁ ποιῶν εὐδαίμονα πόλιν οὐδὲ χρημάτων πλῆθος οὐδὲ οἰκοδομημάτων οὐδὲ θησαυροὶ θεῶν, οἷς οὐδὲν προσέχει τὸ δαιμόνιον· οὐδ' ἂν εἰς τὰς πόλεις τινὲς μεταφέρωσι τὰ ὄρη καὶ τὰς πέτρας ξὺν πολλῇ ταλαιπωρίᾳ καὶ πόνοις καὶ μυρίοις ἀναλώμασιν, ἀλλὰ σωφροσύνη καὶ νοῦς ἐστι τὰ σῴζοντα. ταῦτα ποιεῖ τοὺς χρωμένους μακαρίους, ταῦτα τοῖς θεοῖς προσφιλεῖς, ...

[(25) For people who are inexperienced of *truphē* and knavery, I say that these men do better. What of Italy itself? And did not Sybaris perish that much more swiftly by as much as it had *truphē*? And Croton and Thurii and Metapontum and Tarentum, though they came into such a great acme and held such a vast extent of power, what sort of city do they not now exceed in desolation?

(26) It would be a great task to recount in detail all those who have been destroyed by *truphē*. Long ago the Lydians and the Medes, and the Assyrians before them, and most recently the Macedonians. For men who only lately stripped off their rags and listened to their shepherds and made war on the Thracians for the sake of millet fields, these men were masters over the Greeks, they crossed over into Asia, and they ruled as far as the Indians. But when they took the goods of the Persians, bad things followed along with them.

(27) Therefore the scepters and purple robes and Median tables and the race itself disappeared at the same time, so that, if someone were to pass through Pella, he would not see any sign of a city, apart from a great deal of shattered pottery at that place. And yet the land of those cities remains, as I have said, and of the tribes, just as it was before, nor has anyone turned away the rivers, nor is anything else different. But nevertheless whatever extravagance and *truphē* have fastened onto, those things do not endure for very long.

(28) But do not think that rams and siege engines and other machines thus destroy anything as much as *truphē* does, whether one wishes to see an individual man fall or a city. There is no river nor plain nor harbor that makes a city fortunate, nor a multitude of wealth or of buildings, nor treasuries of the gods, which the divine honors not at all. Not even if some were to carry into the cities the mountains and rocks with much hard labor and toils and countless expenses. Rather moderation and the mind are what save. These things make those who use them blessed, these things make them dear to the gods, . . .] (Dio Chrys., *Or.* 33.25–28)

Τρυφή comes with hubris, but also with deceit and taking other people's goods; enjoying scepters, ornate clothing, feasts, wealth, buildings, and treasuries; and occupying a desirable geographical location. It is contrasted with moderation and mind, which are the things beloved of the gods. Most importantly, Dio expresses a view of τρυφή that is foreign to the Greek model, but harmonized with the Roman theme of destruction: τρυφή leads to hubris, excess, and then destruction, and all this happens because the gods do not love men of τρυφή.

Athenaeus

It seems only reasonable to conclude our discussion of Roman era authors with a very brief summary of Athenaeus, the person responsible for so many modern misunderstandings about the earlier sources. He wrote at or near the end of the second century CE[113] in a manner that is *sui generis*: though he works within the tradition of sympotic literature, his creation is far longer and less coherent than those of his predecessors.[114] Athenaeus has been characterized variously as a symposiast, a polymath, a lexicographer, and an antiquarian. The *Deipnosophistae* is described by one scholar as "a farrago of sources and sauces,"[115] and reads like an interminable listing of obscure references to foods and dishware, interspersed occasionally with moralistic themes such as gluttony, prostitution, and parasites.[116]

By far the most richly cultivated theme is that of τρυφή.[117] Though he refers to the term many times in passing throughout the work, Athenaeus is the only extant writer from antiquity to devote a discrete section of his work to τρυφή, in this case the entirety of Book 12. It quickly becomes apparent to his audience that he is not writing any kind of coherent history or lucid moralistic essay. Instead, he recounts anecdotes. If we examine the language he uses, we see a writer with his feet squarely in two worlds: his meaning of τρυφή is deeply rooted in the Classical world, but the language surrounding it illuminates a Roman tradition of near-constant, if light-hearted, disapprobation.[118]

Athenaeus uses as a starting point for the word τρυφή a typical Greek definition, characterized by the assumption of material things conducive to beauty

---

113. For his date, see Baldwin 1976; Zecchini 1989.

114. For Athenaeus's place within the context of sympotic literature, see Jacob 2001; König 2008, esp. 88–94. For recent work on Plutarch's *Table Talk*, see the essays in Klotz and Oikonomopoulou 2011.

115. Baldwin 1976, 42. He refers to the entire work quite aptly as a "brobdingnagian compilation" (21). The first Loeb editor, Gulick (1927–41), calls it "the oldest cookery-book that has come down to us," (viii) and says: "It would be hard to find a Greek work more diffuse in style or more heterogeneous in subject" (ix). Olson (2006–12), the recent Loeb editor concurs, describing it as "sprawling and oddly structured work, whose sheer mass threatens to overwhelm its modest literary pretensions" (ix).

116. For the narrative structure and role of the narrator, see Relihan 1993, 233–34. For the general purpose and structure of the *Deipnosophistae*, see: Braund 2000; Wilkins 2000b; Jacob 2000; Anderson 1997; Baldwin 1976. Braund and Wilkins 2000 contains many useful essays on specific topics and Wilkins 2000a, esp. ch. 6, approaches Athenaeus from the point of view of the role of food, especially luxurious food, in comedy. For a more positive interpretation of Athenaeus's cohesiveness, particularly in poetic quotations, see Danielewicz 2006.

117. Since his relationship to fragmentary writers has been discussed at length in Chapter 3, here we will restrict our comments to elucidating his place within the τρυφή tradition at Rome.

118. For the influence of Rome on Athenaeus, see Braund 2000.

and refinement, especially ornate clothing, jewelry, laborious hairstyles, cosmetics, and extravagant feasting. Thus the tables of the Sicilians were famous for luxury because they enjoyed fine fish (Athen. 12.518c). A subsection is devoted to people who, through τρυφή, became gluttons and grew morbidly obese (12.549a–550d). Aristippus reveled in perfumes, fancy clothing, and the company of prostitutes (12.544b). The Athenians in their heyday of τρυφή enjoyed purple cloaks and embroidered tunics. They wore gold ornaments in their elaborately done-up hair, and sat on stools provided by attending slaves (12.512b–c). The Samians were adorned with bracelets and carefully combed, long hair (12.525e), while the τρυφή of the Ephesians is illustrated by their garments, dyed violet, crimson, yellow, sea-green, or white, bearing intricate patterns, and decorated with gold beads: τούτοις πᾶσι χρῆσθαί φησι τοὺς Ἐφεσίους ἐπιδόντας εἰς τρυφήν ("They say that the Ephesians use all these things, giving themselves over to *truphē*," 12.529c–e).

Many of his anecdotes deteriorate into preposterous exaggeration, a feature conveniently illustrated by Athenaeus's long account of the τρυφή of the Sybarites (12.518c–522a), for the stories about them begin with the absurd and verge far into unreality. Their bath attendants were shackled so they couldn't walk too fast and thus scald the bathers with water that was too hot. They were legally obliged to announce their parties a year in advance, so that the women would have time to prepare their dresses. Roosters and loud craftsmen such as blacksmiths were forbidden within the city, since the resulting din might disturb their sleep. The Sybarites kept human dwarves as pets, taught their horses to dance, roofed over some of the roads that led to the country, and transported wine from their estates in pipes rather than casks.

This hyperbole, while entertaining, could be amplified to a violent pitch, often in disjointed accounts. Because of τρυφή, the Medes castrated their neighbors and made them into attendants (12.514d). The Lydians "went so far into *truphē*" (εἰς τοσοῦτον ἦλθον τρυφῆς) that they sterilized women and used them instead of male eunuchs (12.515d). The τρυφή of the Scythians was evident from the manner of dress and lifestyle of their leaders (περὶ τοὺς ἡγεμόνας αὐτῶν ἐσθῆτός τε καὶ διαίτης, 12.524c), but this regime led to inexplicable violence:

τρυφήσαντες δὲ καὶ μάλιστα δὴ καὶ πρῶτοι πάντων τῶν ἀνθρώπων ἐπὶ τὸ τρυφᾶν ὁρμήσαντες εἰς τοῦτο προῆλθον ὕβρεως ὥστε πάντων τῶν ἀνθρώπων εἰς οὓς ἀφίκοιντο ἠκρωτηρίαζον τὰς ῥῖνας·

[And especially enjoying *truphē*, they first of all men setting off into *truphē* went into so much hubris that they cut off the noses of all the men they came against.] (Athen. 12.524d)

Likewise the Tarentines "went so far into *truphē*" (εἰς τοσοῦτο τρυφῆς προελθεῖν) that they shaved their bodies bare, forced others to do the same, and wore diaphanous robes (12.522d). Shaving and transparent clothing impelled them somehow into outrageous hubris (ὑπὸ τῆς τρυφῆς εἰς ὕβριν ποδηγηθέντες). They destroyed the neighboring city of Carbina and set the captured women and children on public display naked for all comers to lust after.

Such cruelty was regularly punished with misfortune and even destruction. The Scythians suffered a series of disasters, and were stripped both of their prosperity and their hair (12.524e). The gods avenged the victims of the Tarentines: οὕτω δὲ τὸ δαιμόνιον ἠγανάκτησεν ὥστε Ταραντίνων τοὺς ἐν Καρβίνῃ παρανομήσαντας ἐκεραύνωσεν πάντας ("Thus the divinity, vexed that the Tarentines had ill-used the people of Carbina, struck them all with thunderbolts," 12.522e). The Colophonians delighted in elegant clothing and passed laws to financially support flute girls and other entertainers, but somehow this lifestyle led them to despotism and civil strife: τοιγαροῦν διὰ τὴν τοιαύτην ἀγωγὴν ἐν τυραννίδι καὶ στάσεσι γενόμενοι αὐτῇ πατρίδι διεφθάρησαν ("Accordingly, on account of the way they were carrying on, entering into tyranny and stasis, they were destroyed with the whole fatherland." 12.526c). The Iapygians began by wearing colored robes, cosmetics, and hair extensions, and proceeding to loot the temples of the gods, until they were struck by fire and copper raining down from the heavens (12.522f–523b). The Sybarites, who were the most extreme in their τρυφή, "ran aground on hubris" (ἐξοκείλαντες εἰς ὕβριν, 12.521d) and murdered the Crotonian ambassadors, before they were themselves utterly destroyed (διόπερ ἀνάστατοι ἐγένοντο καὶ διεφθάρησαν ἅπαντες, 12.521f).

Finally the Milesians were feminized by their τρυφή: ὡς δὲ ὑπήχθησαν ἡδονῇ καὶ τρυφῇ, κατερρύη τὸ τῆς πόλεως ἀνδρεῖον ("thus they withdrew into pleasure and *truphē*, and masculinity of the city flowed away," 12.523e). Yet, far from being soft and unwarlike, they fell into a brutal civil strife διὰ τρυφὴν βίου καὶ πολιτικὰς ἔχθρας ("because of the *truphē* of their lifestyle and political enmity," 12.523f). The popular party exiled the men of wealth, and then crushed their children under the feet of the oxen on the threshing floor. The oligarchs returned with a vengeance, tarring and burning both their opponents and their children.

If only a few of the people were actually wiped out by their τρυφή, we must remember that, throughout this account in book 12, the idiomatic language Athenaeus uses is nearly always disapproving in tone. We have discussed a number of these phrases in Chapter 3, so we will only review those conclusions here. We have seen people shipwreck on τρυφή with some frequency. People are destroyed (διαφθείρω) by it. They are notorious (διαβοήτος) for it, a term only used with vices in Athenaeus. They set off into it (ὁρμάω), excel in it (ὑπερβάλλω), and envy or rival each other in it (ζηλόω). No one can read book 12 of the *Deipnosophistae* and come away with the feeling that Athenaeus is praising a life of τρυφή. Τρυφή in Athenaeus is loosely faithful to the Classical meaning of the term, but it is commonly used in a derogatory manner that reflects the Roman historiographical tradition.

By 200 CE, it is normal and expected that τρυφή is a bad trait, harmful to those who possess it and dangerous for those nearby. Athenaeus's tangible contribution to the development of this concept is that he employs τρυφή as a kind of cliché for bad behavior. Usually, we have seen that τρυφή either makes one soft and therefore liable to be conquered or it is paired with hubris and violent behavior. Athenaeus regularly merges the two incompatible strands about τρυφή, transforming soft attributes like shaving into the violence and deliberate degradation of rape and mutilation. The stories he relates do not usually make much sense under close consideration, and Athenaeus feels no pressure to make them intelligible. He is not a historian or even a moralist. His sympotic genre is without strict rules, so much so that he can develop narratives that are as outlandish as he desires, combining stories in utter non sequiturs. He may make colossal leaps in logic and imply causality that the material simply will not bear. He does not have to explain anything, so neither need he refrain from relating anything, however eccentric. The result can be highly entertaining, but we cannot be surprised if it is incoherent.

Conclusion

By the time of our earliest extant Latin historical literature—Cicero, Sallust, and Livy—the theme of destructive luxury as a historical force is a commonplace Roman moral principle. With Rome's expansion and conquest of the Mediterranean world came an influx of wealth and opulence that had a debilitating effect on the manhood and moral fiber of the Roman people. To the Roman mind, the harmful effects of luxury could run two routes. Luxury defined as a life free from toil leads to softness and the corruption of the military spirit, and therefore to an enfeeblement that is easily conquered. On the other hand, luxury can initiate a desire for excess and a life devoted to obsessive self-indulgence. When an unrestrained desire for pleasure drives a person beyond the resources of one's own possessions, avarice leads to arrogance and violence. As a political and social force, this overweening attitude moves inevitably to civil strife, tyranny, and even destruction.

The Greek writers of the Roman era gradually adapted the Greek vocabulary of luxury to this quintessential Roman historiographical theme of moral deterioration in order to formulate a causative principle of decline and ruin in their own language. The theme is absent in Polybius, but it makes its first appearance in extant Greek a few decades later when Ps.-Scymnus lays out the essential, insidious sequence, that τρυφή leads to ὕβρις, thence to κόρος and ultimately to destruction. This pattern is reflected in Latin writing of the same generation—recall Cicero, *Rosc. Am.* 75: *ex luxuria . . . avaritia . . . ex avaritia . . . audacia, inde omnia scelera ac maleficia*—and the parallels suggest that this pathology of decadence was already well established and its vocabulary in common parlance in both languages.[119]

Unfortunately, we know almost nothing certain about the steps through which τρυφή became a concept powerful enough to explain the destruction of Sybaris, and how the theme of pernicious luxury became familiar enough to Greeks that Ps-Scymnus could use it without elaboration. We have very little directly transmitted evidence from what we see as the crucial period for the development of the idea. Nonetheless, there is some reason to suppose that τρυφή as a politically or historically significant phenomenon was to be found in the ambit of Greek writers such as Stoic philosophers Panaetius and Posidonius. While both are noteworthy for the liminal position they occupied—both were greatly influenced by, and had great influence upon, prominent Romans of their day—it is the latter who deserves special attention here.[120]

---

119. We over-simplify here to make our claim clear: Roman concerns about the ill effects of luxury were incorporated into the Greek concept of τρυφή, which previously had been of some interest to moralists but of little historiographical importance. The process by which this hybridization took place was no doubt complex, involving the interplay of Roman and Greek ideas and traditions, rather than the mere recasting of a Roman view in Greek words.

120. Posidonius, for example, knew personally and was familiar with the historical writings in Greek of P. Rutilius Rufus (Posid., test. 13 EK = Cicero, *Off.* 3.10). This Roman (*cos.* 105 BCE) seems to have written about the theme of frugality versus prodigality in Roman politics: Athen. 6.274c–e, drawing on Rutilius's own *History* of Rome (πάτριος ἱστορία), relates how he was one of only three men at Rome who abided by the sumptuary strictures of the *lex Fannia*. Very few fragments of Rutilius re-

Posidonius (c. 135–c. 51 BCE), from the Syrian city of Apamea but later a citizen of Rhodes, was a famous polymath who, among his other works, wrote a *History* in fifty-two books. This work began where Polybius finished (146/45 BCE) and apparently left off sometime in the 80s. It survives only in fragments, but these contain what may be plausible traces of a role played by pernicious luxury. For example, "the virtues of the old Romans" seems to have been a topic discussed in several places.[121] From this fact we can assume, although the evidence is less clear, that Posidonius contrasted the morality of previous generations with later decadence.[122] In addition, scholarship on the *History* emphasizes Posidonius's concern for explicating causes.[123] Accordingly, one might expect that the fragments of the Stoic might shed some light on the development of the causal nexus that formed around τρυφή.

Posidonius's treatment of the Sicilian slave revolt of c. 136–132 BCE offers tantalizing hints that the *History* may have explored the workings of τρυφή as a cause of events. According to Posidonius, the servile war broke out in part because of the depredations of a certain Damophilus. We can suggest with some confidence that Posidonius described Damophilus's character in terms of τρυφή: Athen. 12.542b (Frag. 59 EK), τρυφῆς . . . δοῦλος ἦν καὶ κακουργίας ("he was a slave of *truphē* and evil-doing").[124] His τρυφή was instantiated by his custom of driving around his estates in four-wheeled carts with a large retinue of attendants. Damophilus was also a man of violence, whose harshness toward

---

main, and the only one that directly addresses immorality is cast entirely in Athenaean framing language. See above, page 222.

121. Under this rubric Edelstein and Kidd (1989, 234–35) classify fragments 265 EK (Athen. 6.273a–b), 266 EK (Athen. 6.274a), and 267 EK (Athen. 6.275a). Kidd (1988b, 914) sees that idea of early Roman frugality, justice, and piety as important for Posidonius: "The *History* was a long book, and this was a common theme running through it."

122. The relevant evidence is almost entirely from Athenaeus and is subject to the usual reservations. For example, a Posidonian doublet reminds us that apparent moral implications of a fragment may be due to Athenaeus rather than the original: Athen. 5.210e (frag. 62b EK) discusses the extravagance of "everyone in Syria" without criticism in connection with the topic φιλοδείπνων βασιλέων ("kings who love dinner parties," 5.210c). The same quotation recurs in Book 12 with a different interpretation: Athen., 12.527e (frag. 62a EK) Ποσειδώνιος δ' ἐκκαιδεκάτῃ Ἱστοριῶν περὶ τῶν κατὰ τὴν Συρίαν πόλεων λέγων ὡς ἐτρύφων γράφει καὶ ταῦτα ("Posidonius too, speaking in the sixteenth book of his *Histories* about the cities of Syria and how they displayed *truphē*, writes the following").

123. Malitz 1983, 409–28; Kidd 1989; Hahm 1989, with bibliography at 1326 n. 2.

124. Athenaeus is fairly reliable when he quotes a source for a lexical usage. Here his focus is on Posidonius's expression "slave of *truphē*." In addition, certainly similarities of diction between Athen. 12.542b and Diodorus's discussion of the same episode (34/35.2.34) are too close to be accidental. On the other hand, an explicit mention of τρυφή by Posidonius is not confirmed by Diodorus. Thus it remains only a hypothesis that Posidonius made the rebellion a consequence of pernicious luxury.

his slaves finally drove them to rebel. Details come from Diodorus Siculus, who drew on the account of Posidonius. Damophilus's emulation of "Persian *truphē*" is followed by the familiar stages of decadence: Diod. Sic., 34/35.2.35, τὸ μὲν πρῶτον κόρον ἐγέννησεν, εἶθ᾽ ὕβριν, τὸ δὲ τελευταῖον ὄλεθρόν τε αὐτῷ καὶ συμφορὰς μεγάλας τῇ πατρίδι ("[Damophilus's uncultured way of life] first generated satiety, then hubris, and finally destruction for himself and great misfortunes for his country"). It is tempting to see Posidonius, the great aetiologist, behind this explanation.[125] However, since this sequence could be the contribution of Diodorus or even of the Byzantine excerptor, it would be doubly imprudent to insist that Posidonius presented, and perhaps even analyzed, τρυφή as a historical force.[126]

No matter how the idea originated, the subsequent Greek prose authors integrate the theme of pernicious luxury into their texts with increasing consistency and consequence. In justifying Roman rule and the prosperity of the Augustan principate, Dionysius embraces the Roman ideals about the ruinous effects of luxury and the dangers inherent in peace. Mollifying luxury is absent in his work. Instead, the dangers he warns against are the potential hazards of moral corruption leading to civil strife. Strabo incorporates both strands of the argument while at the same time blurring the meaning of τρυφή. In its softness, it may make a people easy to conquer, but, in a convoluted argument, by that very conquest that people is restored to masculinity. However, like most Roman authors, Strabo's more usual thesis is that τρυφή makes a people hubristic and therefore prone to civil strife and even subject to divine punishment.

The Jewish writers unmistakably demonstrate the transformation of the neutral or advantageous Greek idea of τρυφή into the Roman concept of destructive luxury. In harmony with early Greek uses, the Septuagint holds τρυφή as an unfailingly beneficial trait, the gift of abundance from God unto the righteous whereby all their wants and needs are fulfilled. Philo generally continues

---

125. This pathology of decadence is given more general explanatory scope at Diod. Sic., 34/35.2.25–26; the slave revolt struck the majority of people by surprise (ἀνελπίστως καὶ παραδόξως), but: τοῖς δὲ πραγματικῶς ἕκαστα δυναμένοις κρίνειν οὐκ ἀλόγως ἔδοξε συμβαίνειν. διὰ γὰρ τὴν ὑπερβολὴν τῆς εὐπορίας ... ἅπαντες σχεδὸν οἱ τοῖς πλούτοις προκεκοφότες ἐζήλωσαν τὸ μὲν πρῶτον τρυφήν, εἶθ᾽ ὑπερηφανίαν καὶ ὕβριν ("for those, on the other hand, able to judge each thing prudently it seemed to occur not without reason. For, because of the excess of resources ..., nearly all those advanced in wealth were zealous first for *truphē*, then for arrogance and hubris").

126. Kidd (1988a, 294–95) notes that "the verve, vividness and social analysis" of the excerpts from the *Bibliotheca* point toward a close reuse of Posidonius, but he adds that "there is still no control over the possible extent and fidelity of this use" of the *History* by Diodorus.

with that Jewish interpretation of the idea, but he also exhibits a contrary, ascetic view of τρυφή rooted in Hellenistic philosophy. Finally he presents evidence of the twin Roman patterns, in which τρυφή can lead to the loss of political independence because of softness or it can march along in the determinative path from τρυφή to excess and hubris, and on to ruin. In the writings of Josephus, τρυφή has utterly lost its original, favorable characterization and has been turned on its head: it is now only viewed in a thoroughly Roman light as a lifestyle that is punished by God.

By the second century CE, in the writings of Dio Chrysostom and especially Athenaeus, the concept of τρυφή is both thoroughly Romanized and also stripped of much of its original, very precise meaning. It is now more usually a generic vice and often appears in a list of other vague moral shortcomings, such as pleasure, extravagance, and a degenerate lifestyle characterized by wine, women, and song. It can be feminizing or it can be hubristic, or it can be a bizarre and convoluted combination of the two, whereby the affected person becomes weak and therefore commits acts of outrageous violence. A life devoted to τρυφή rarely ends well. In the Greek writers of the Roman Era it has become a moral truism that τρυφή necessarily results in moral depravity.

Conclusion

It may be illuminating to conclude this examination of the historiographical valorization of luxury by returning to the example with which we began. At the height of its prosperity, the Archaic city of Sybaris suffered catastrophe. This turn of events constitutes perhaps the most notorious instance of the phenomenon of corrupting luxury.

Σύβαρις, Ἀχαιῶν ἐπιφανὴς ἀποικία,
δέκα μυριάδας ἔχουσα τῶν ἀστῶν
σχεδὸν περιουσίᾳ πλείστῃ τε κεχορηγημένη·
οἳ δὴ παρεξαρθέντες οὐκ ἀνθρωπίνως
αὔτανδρον ἐξέφθειραν ἐπιφανῆ πόλιν,
τἀγαθὰ τὰ λίαν μὴ μαθόντες εὖ φέρειν.
. . . .
τρυφὴν δὲ καὶ ῥᾴθυμον ἑλομένους βίον
χρόνῳ προελθεῖν εἰς ὕβριν τε καὶ κόρον,

[. . . Sybaris, the famous colony of the Achaeans, possessing nearly one hundred thousand townspeople and furnished with a great deal of wealth. Exalting themselves as human beings should not, they destroyed their famous city and all its people, for they had not learned to handle good fortune well. . . . but choosing *truphē* and the easy life, in time they advanced to hubris and excess.]
(Ps.-Scym. 340–45, 348–49)

[handwritten note: belief of truphe leading to destruction]

The fate here ascribed to the Sybarites is paradigmatic of the Greek view as reconstructed in the scholarship. According to this view, great prosperity is an

427

inducement to τρυφή, which is thought to be a kind of self-indulgent weakness or womanishness; τρυφή leads naturally and inevitably to acts of contemptuous violence (hubris) which, in their turn, bring accompanying misfortune and even disaster. The importance of this process for Hellenistic historiography was emphatically stated by Passerini in his seminal study:

> . . . τρυφή che è l'origine di una conseguente ὕβρις (Questo concetto è assai importante e lo troviamo constantemente applicato: di ogni uomo o Stato, che viva nella τρυφή, vengono riferite, dopo i tratti che caratterizzano quella, le azioni inspirate da ὕβρις, che presto o tardi ne causano la rovina. . . .) (Passerini 1934, 44)

The accuracy of this statement has not, as far as we are aware, ever been called into question. Thus, a recent work can speak of "die verweichlichende, unhellenische Tryphe," and describe its morally corrosive effects in a manner completely consonant with Passerini's view:

> Überdruss und Glück führen mächtige Menschen und reiche Völker zur Hybris, und diese wiederum führt unvermeidlich zum Verderben. . . . Bei allzu reichen oder mächtigen Menschen . . . führt Tryphe natürlich zu Exzessen und hat eine entsprechende göttliche Bestrafung zur Folge. (Tsitsiridis 2008, 70–71)

Although these formulations of the *communis opinio* seem to explain and to be justified by Ps.-Scymnus's treatment of the fall of Sybaris, our arguments have shown that the prevailing view is wrong in several regards.

In the first place, as used in the Classical and Hellenistic periods, τρυφή does not indicate a particular state or degree of opulence. More specifically, it does not designate excessive consumption, as often assumed.[1] Rather, it is a psychological disposition or attitude, principally the expectation that one's wants will be seen to by others. The meaning is most easily apparent when the word is used outside of the realm of wealth and physical comfort. Thus, Demosthenes, criticizing the habitual reluctance of the Athenian assembly to listen to unpopular policy recommendations, can describe this attitude as an instance of τρυφή.

---

1.   Thus Bollansée 2008, 405. Bonfante (2011b, 19) prefers "luxurious excess" and "ostentatious display."

νῦν δὲ δημαγωγοῦντες ὑμᾶς καὶ χαριζόμενοι καθ᾽ ὑπερβολὴν οὕτω διατεθήκασιν, ὥστ᾽ ἐν μὲν ταῖς ἐκκλησίαις τρυφᾶν καὶ κολακεύεσθαι πάντα πρὸς ἡδονὴν ἀκούοντας

[But as things now stand, excessively using demagoguery on you and indulging you, they have so disposed you that in meetings of the Assembly you show *truphē* and court flattery, hearing only things that please you.] (Dem. 8.34)

In a similar fashion Socrates characterizes an interlocutor who refuses to answer Socrates' questions until Socrates has answered his:

—Κἂν κατακεκαλυμμένος τις γνοίη, ὦ Μένων, διαλεγομένου σου, ὅτι καλὸς εἶ καὶ ἐρασταί σοι ἔτι εἰσίν.
—Τί δή;
—Ὅτι οὐδὲν ἀλλ᾽ ἢ ἐπιτάττεις ἐν τοῖς λόγοις, ὅπερ ποιοῦσιν οἱ τρυφῶντες, ἅτε τυραννεύοντες ἕως ἂν ἐν ὥρᾳ ὦσιν, καὶ ἅμα ἐμοῦ ἴσως κατέγνωκας ὅτι εἰμὶ ἥττων τῶν καλῶν· χαριοῦμαι οὖν σοι καὶ ἀποκρινοῦμαι.

[—Even blindfolded, Meno, a person could tell from the way you act in conversations that you are beautiful and are still pursued by lovers.
—What do you mean?
—Because your conversation consists of nothing but commands, just as those do who show *truphē*, insomuch as they act the tyrant as long as they are in bloom. And perhaps also you are using against me the knowledge that I am a pushover for beautiful boys. So I'll indulge you and answer.] (Plato, *Meno* 76b–c)

We emphasize that these two passages are not anomalous; rather they capture the essential meaning of τρυφή, one that is evident in practically every securely attested Classical or Hellenistic occurrence for which a clear sense is able to be discerned.

For this reason, the usual descriptions of the pernicious effects of luxury involve the most basic misunderstanding. Explanations of this process see τρυφή as a certain kind of moral deficiency, namely "softness" or "effeminacy." If by these characteristics is meant the quality of one who is submissive and prone to be overborne by the will of others, then these interpretations are very wide of the mark. The two passages just quoted make it clear that when τρυφή indicates the imposition of the concerns of one person upon another, it is the possessor of τρυφή who occupies the dominant position in the relationship. Thus both the Athenian *demos* and the boy, Meno, expect to enforce their will. It makes no sense, therefore, to associate τρυφή per se with effeminacy as a symbol of weakness and compliance.

The second misconception in the standard treatment of decadence is that the Greeks believed that this process of corruption was an unavoidable consequence of a life of τρυφή, somehow inherent in human nature ("di ogni uomo o Stato . . . presto o tardi"; "führt unvermeidlich . . . führt Tryphe natürlich"). More accurately, τρυφή is itself a morally ambivalent characteristic. Its status as virtue or vice largely depends on external circumstances. An attitude of confident expectation may be appropriate for those of high sociopolitical status. Accordingly, Isocrates recommends to Nicocles, a Cypriote king, that he show τρυφή in his outward appearance so that the public may consider him "worthy of his office" (ἄξιον τῆς ἀρχῆς, Isoc. 2.32). More dramatically, in Lagid Egypt, τρυφή appears as an official appellation for the beneficence of the monarchy, expressing verbally, as the cornucopia did iconographically, the rulers' opulence as a resource from which the people's needs might be satisfied. This same environment prompted the authors of the Septuagint to select τρυφή as the translation of the name Eden, a symbol of the provision of human comforts through divine providence. They regularly choose, moreover, to use τρυφή to indicate the special relationship between the Hebrews and their God: if they would properly keep the faith, they could be confident that God would provide.

Τρυφή, then, could be ranked among virtues. What is more, even when the term is negatively charged and understood to be the first step on an path to degeneracy, the process did not function as is generally presented in the scholarship. This observation comprises the next of our departures from the received view.

Although τρυφή in and of itself does not denote weakness or effeminacy, this quality could, under suitable conditions, lead to moral or physical enervation. At a theoretical level, Plato offers a model in the *Republic's* discussion of political evolution. On this view, the leaders of a ruling oligarchy, being too intent on making money, neglect their own fitness and the upbringing of their sons:

διατιθέασιν . . . ἆρ᾽ οὐ τρυφῶντας μὲν τοὺς νέους καὶ ἀπόνους καὶ πρὸς τὰ τοῦ σώματος καὶ πρὸς τὰ τῆς ψυχῆς, μαλακοὺς δὲ καρτερεῖν πρὸς ἡδονάς τε καὶ λύπας καὶ ἀργούς;

[Don't they dispose the young men to show *truphē* and be averse to toil, both with respect to body and soul; don't they make them soft at enduring both pleasures and pains, and lazy?] (Plato, *Rep.* 8.556b–c)

As a result, the rich rouse the contempt of the lean and hard-bodied men of lesser means, who become intent on revolution.

It should be evident that Plato's theory does not directly illuminate our excerpt from Ps.-Scymnus. Plato focuses on a phenomenon that is internal to the polis and on a process that is necessarily limited to a small segment of a society. Such an extreme degree of τρυφή is only available to the richest elite. Furthermore, the effect of τρυφή that Plato hypothesizes is dependent on close familiarity and, indeed, face-to-face contact. The collapse of the oligarchy is set in motion when the common man finds himself "stationed in battle next to the rich man, raised in the shade, with a strangely fleshy body" (παραταχθεὶς ἐν μάχῃ πλουσίῳ ἐσκιατροφηκότι, πολλὰς ἔχοντι σάρκας ἀλλοτρίας, *Rep.* 8.556d). Thus, Plato's theory of political development does not seem to provide the basis from which historians might have derived a general rule of causation.

If we move next to the evidence of historical narrative itself, material explaining exactly how τρυφή might lead to weakness, loss of nerve, and military collapse is meager. We have shown that even in Herodotus, where the feminizing effects of luxury are said to play a major role in his presentation of the defeat of the Persian invasion, there is little foundation for assuming the presence of this concept. Perhaps the best candidate for a description of the relevant process in the *Histories* is the story of Ionian behavior at the Battle of Lade. Here, the Ionians withdrew from a harsh regime of training imposed by their general and in the subsequent battle purposely played the coward; the result was their defeat by the Persian navy. Although the word τρυφή does not appear, the attitude exhibited by the Ionian rank and file—the selfish insistence that their concerns be served—is consonant with examples of τρυφή from other authors. However, as was the case for Plato, this passage does not offer a plausible pattern from which a widely applicable concept of enervating decadence might be derived. While it is sometimes suggested that a relatively lax way of life was responsible for the Ionians' willfulness, the key to their behavior as Herodotus presents it was rather a perceived lack of a shared self-interest among segments of the Ionian forces. A significant portion of the navy did not believe that its concerns and welfare were the same as those of its leaders. Thus, although the Ionians' attitude certainly led to a collapse of morale and a military defeat, any connection with opulence or lifestyle is contingent and ad hoc. The story tells us nothing precise about how to understand the evolution of decadence at Sybaris.

In spite of the strikingly narrow compass of the phenomena described in these two passages—and we are aware of no fuller treatments before the Roman period of τρυφή as a historical force—it might be possible to extrapolate from them an underlying moral principle. Ignoring divergent details and generalizing broadly, one could suggest the existence of a belief that the attitude represented by τρυφή, whether induced by wealth or other circumstances, was attended by dangerous consequences when it distracted its possessor from the efforts needed for physical fitness and military competence or when it led one to neglect the concerns of the community while preferring individual gratification. A moral precept of such a level of abstraction is not particularly interesting. Nor would it contribute, as general as it is, to efforts to contextualize the words of Ps.-Scymnus, for it has no relevance to the crucial step in that chain of decadence: the movement from τρυφή to hubris.

In the course of this study, we have frequently made the point that, throughout antiquity, τρυφή could be presented as a stage in two distinct moral pathologies: one leads to softness and martial cowardice and another culminates in acts of outrageous violence. We have also emphasized that scholars have regularly ignored this distinction, treating any example of pernicious τρυφή in the sources as a manifestation of a single phenomenon and a straightforward concept. Thus, they imagine a process of moral corruption that progresses from riches to τρυφή and μαλακία to κόρος to hubris to destruction. It is to highlight this misconception one last time that we have reexamined the rather thin evidence for a feminizing τρυφή. Not only does the evidence reveal that this sort of τρυφή is an extremely banal concept. It also indicates that such τρυφή is almost universally devoid of any important connection with hubris.

It is very difficult to find, before the Roman period, solid evidence of any historically significant case of τρυφή producing acts of hubris. A rare example comes from Isocrates (*Paneg.* 150–53). The orator seeks to explain the military incompetence recently displayed by the previously fearsome Persians. He offers a solution that he considers "not unreasonable" and "likely." The Persians have been undone by the steeply hierarchical nature of their society. The elite have been raised to expect their comforts to be attended to by their inferiors (τὰ μὲν σώματα . . . τρυφῶντες, 151). This attitude, acceptable at home, where the common people are "trained for servitude" (πρὸς δὲ τὴν δουλείαν . . . πεπαιδευμένος, 150), is disruptive when the Persians go to war. Thus, when abroad, they "live haughtily, scorning their allies" (ὑπερηφάνως ζῶντες, τῶν μὲν συμμάχων καταφρονοῦντες, 152). Isocrates' evidence is to be found in recent campaigns, where the Persians withheld the pay from those fighting on their behalf and "treated those fighting beside them in Cyprus with greater hubris than they had shown their prisoners" (τοὺς δὲ μεθ᾽ αὑτῶν εἰς Κύπρον στρατευσαμένους μᾶλλον ἢ τοὺς αἰχμαλώτους ὕβριζον, 153).

Any attempt to interpret this passage as an instantiation of a general belief about pernicious luxury would face serious difficulties. Most importantly, the process of decadence that afflicts the Persians arises from special circumstances—it is narrowly based on a combination of enjoyment of great wealth and despotic oppression—and it is of extremely limited application, taking effect by causing rifts in the relationship of the Persians with their allies. Once again, pertinence to the story of the fall of Sybaris seem very tenuous.

Thus, our examination of the idea of corrupting luxury in the Classical literature, undertaken in Chapters 1 and 2, constitutes an argument that this idea was of no particular historiographical importance in that period. We should not attempt to understand the case of Sybaris with reference to a long-standing tradition about the harmful ramifications of a sumptuous lifestyle, since such a tradition did not exist in Greek times.

Chapters 3 and 4 make this point doubly clear. There we investigated the fragmentary evidence, primarily in order to evaluate the significance of pernicious luxury in Hellenistic writers. Chapter 3 details the problems with relying on Athenaeus as a cover text for source material on τρυφή. Chapter 4 applies the methods and conclusions developed in that study. We believe that the result is a demonstration that the apparent prominence of corrosive τρυφή as a historical force in the works of Hellenistic authors owes more to manipulation of the originals by Athenaeus than to the genuine importance of this theme. Our arguments on this question are lengthy and complicated. Here we will add one last consideration.

The *Deipnosophistae* contains a good many quotations in which τρυφή appears as a step toward hubris. We claim that in every case the connection was probably made by Athenaeus. The methods we advance to support this view make up what we hope will be the most widely useful result of this book. Nonetheless, let us for the moment set aside skepticism and assume, *argumenti causa*, that Athenaeus's presentation accurately represents the original lines of thought. These are the clearest examples from Book 12 of Athenaeus:

- Lydians: move from unspecified τρυφή to sterilizing women (515d–e, authority of Xanthus)
- Lydians: move from τρυφή in building shade gardens to group rape (515e–f, Clearchus)
- Sybarites: move from τρυφή in excessive feasting to murder of embassy (521d, Phylarchus)
- Tarentines: move from τρυφή in removing body hair to group rape (522d–e, Clearchus)
- Iapygians: move from τρυφή in wearing cosmetics to robbing temples (522f–523b, unspecified)
- Milesians: move from unspecified τρυφή to murdering children (523f–524a, Heraclides)
- Scythians: move from τρυφή (unspecified, but connected to dress) to mutilation (524c–d, Clearchus)
- Cotys: moves from τρυφή in banqueting to the murder of servants and his wife (531e–f, Theopompus)
- Peisistratids: move from excess in partying and playing the horses to oppressive rule (532f, Idomeneus)
- Dionysius II: exhibits τρυφή in scattering rose petals to make a comfortable place for rape (541c–e, Clearchus)

With the exception of the story of Dionysius the Younger, these passages all display a striking randomness. Apparently, the writers in question found plausible a process by which practically any manifestation of τρυφή—from depilation to playing the horses—could lead to any sort of violent act. Nor have we elided any material that would make the relationship of cause and effect clearer. The lack of any reasonable connection between the stages of moral degeneration is a feature of all these passages. Thus, we feel that the pattern revealed by these quotations does not allow the reconstruction of an underlying theory of pernicious luxury that could be taken seriously by the authors or their readers. In our opinion, this incoherence is not accidental; it is not the result of careless abridgement of intermediate steps clearly laid out in the originals, for our study of Classical and Hellenistic texts has not revealed what those step could possibly be. Rather, we are reinforced in our conclusion that the connections which we see here were drawn by Athenaeus, who juxtaposes disparate material for humorous effect.

While a painstaking investigation of the Classical and Hellenistic materials cannot reveal an explanatory context for Ps.-Scymnus's description of the end of Sybaris, the opposite is true in sources written from the first century BCE onward. Thus, in Chapter 5, we discuss the evidence for the ways in which the idea of pernicious luxury developed and flourished in the Roman period. Elaborate references to the idea that *luxuria* and related concepts are responsible for important historical trends and events appear in Cicero, Sallust, and Livy, to name only the earliest. When the Roman understanding of pernicious luxury is taken up by Greek authors, we finally meet with powerful *comparanda* for the interpretation of Sybarite decadence. Philo, writing of the difficulties faced by great lawgivers, explains:

πολλάκις δὲ καὶ τρυφὴ πλεονάσασα χορηγίαις καὶ περιουσίαις ἀφθόνοις καθεῖλε νόμους, τὰ λίαν ἀγαθὰ τῶν πολλῶν φέρειν οὐ δυναμένων, ἀλλὰ διὰ κόρον ἐξυβριζόντων

[And often *truphē*, overflowing with abundance and unstinted surplus, has destroyed the laws, since the multitude was unable to bear the excessive goods, but instead grew hubristic through its satiety.] (Philo, *Mos.* 2.12)

Elsewhere, Philo adds more details: if the attitude of τρυφή becomes excessive through its demands being continually met, its possessor develops contempt for the concerns of others (ὑπεροψία). This process is compared to becoming drunk, and it culminates in being glutted (κόρος) with τρυφή and contempt as if with too much wine. At this stage, those affected lose all self-control and turn in violence against free and slave alike, and even against whole cities. Thus does "satiety beget hubris."[2]

Philo is able to illustrate his analysis from the pages of history:

μεγίστη δ' ἀρχὴ κακῶν, ὡς εἶπέ τις οὐκ ἀπὸ σκοποῦ, τὰ λίαν ἀγαθά. ὧν ἀδυνατοῦντες φέρειν τὸν κόρον ὥσπερ τὰ θρέμματα σκιρτῶντες ἀπαυχενίζουσι τὸν τῆς φύσεως νόμον . . .

[The familiar saying hits the mark: "The greatest source of evils is too much good." Unable to bear excess of such goods, skittering like animals, they shake the law of nature from their necks . . .] (Philo, *Abr.* 134–35)

Hence the destruction of Sodom.

---

2.   Solon, frag. 6.1 West. Cf. Philo, *Virt.* 161–63.

The verbal similarities suggest that Philo is illustrating the paradigm that is reflected in our passage from Ps.-Scymnus, and we may infer that the geographer understands Sybarite decadence in something close to the way in which Philo pictures it. However, for us, the details of the portrayal of pernicious τρυφή are not as important as the setting in which we find it in an author of the Roman era. Our research has led to the realization that there are no extant sources predating Ps.-Scymnus (that is, about 100 or 90 BCE) that may serve as good analogues for the sequence of destructive luxury. In addition, one should not ignore the fact that Philo's rather extended treatments of the degenerative effects of opulence occur as explanations for events that were, even for him, ancient history. These two observations point to our final and overarching conclusion: we maintain that Ps.-Scymnus offers the first solid evidence for pernicious luxury as an accepted force of historical causation because it was a relatively new idea. Our reading of the sources indicates that this idea was a creation of the Roman period and a reflection of Roman concerns. It was accepted by Greek thinkers, harmonized with traditional moral beliefs centered around the concept of τρυφή, and presented to a Greek-speaking audience that was adopting the Roman outlook on luxury. Invested with a new historical significance, τρυφή was available to give a novel twist to events of the Greek past and was widely adopted for this purpose.

If we return to the specific instance of the destruction of Sybaris, we can likewise be confident that no source earlier than the first century BCE shows particular interest in details of Sybarite history or connects τρυφή with the fall of the city. We cannot link the complex of ideas reflected in Ps.-Scymnus, Diodorus, and Strabo to enemies of Sybaris seeking to justify its destruction and must therefore seek another explanation for these passages. The Diodorus passage may give some indication of what this explanation might be. After Diodorus has introduced the topic of Sybarite wealth and population, he goes on to relate in some detail the events leading to the destruction of Sybaris (Diod. Sic. 12.9.2–10.1). The Sybarite tyrant Telys drove into exile five hundred of the richest of the city's citizens. These men took refuge at Croton as suppliants at the altars. Telys then demanded their surrender; refusal meant war. The Crotoniates were cowed by the power of Sybaris and were on the point of yielding when Pythagoras spoke on behalf of the exiles. The philosopher persuaded the people of Croton to accept war rather than give up the refugees. The famous Olympic victor Milo, dressed in the costume of Heracles, led one hundred thousand Crotoniates against the three hundred thousand Sybarites. After the rout, the victors killed all the enemy who fell into their hands. They took the city and left it a desert.

The appearance of Pythagoras in this story is of obvious importance, and it is widely agreed that this tradition bears a Pythagorean stamp. We would certainly accept this view. However, for most scholars "Pythagorean" in this instance means "Crotoniate" as well, and a date in the early- or mid-fifth century is thought most appropriate for its point of origin.[3] This interpretation is now revealed as untenable. The fragments of Timaeus do not, as is generally maintained, indicate that that historian had any information about, or interest in, the fall of Sybaris. Without Timaeus to serve as lynchpin in a chain of evidence leading back to the decades immediately after the events of 510, the Pythagorean coloring of this set of passages points to a very different matrix for their creation: the neo-Pythagoreanism of the Hellenistic period.

The idea of τρυφή begetting a catastrophic hubris was, we are told, a favorite of the Pythagoreans,[4] who drew attention to the occurrence of this pathology in Sybaris in order to justify its destruction at the time of Pythagoras's residence in Croton. Sybaris's decadent condition was illustrated with suitable examples of its τρυφή and hubris. This seems correct as far as it goes. However, because a causal relationship between τρυφή and hubris cannot be established from evidence earlier than the story of the fall of Sybaris itself in Ps.-Scymnus (c. 100 BCE), the tradition on the final days of Sybaris looks to have originated sometime in the last decades of the second century. The years in question saw a great upsurge of interest in Pythagoras due in large measure to his identification by the Romans as an "Italian" philosopher, and one who exerted influence on the Romans' own development. Add to this fact the Roman emphasis on the political effects of luxury, and the circumstances were right for the sequence πλοῦτος, τρυφή, κόρος, ὕβρις and ἀπώλεια to appear and to be set in opposition to Pythagoras's own moderation and restraint. The war between Sybaris and Croton became an object lesson in the practical superiority of Pythagorean sobriety.

---

3.   Mele (1984, 33) calls the tradition "crotoniate e pitagorica" and thinks its creation to be unlikely after the foundation of Thurii.

4.   See Cozzoli 1980, 136–37 and Talamo 1987. Concerning Pythagoras at Croton, Pompeius Trogus says: *laudabat cotidie virtutem et vitia luxuriae casumque civitatium ea peste perditarum enumerabat* ("Every day he used to praise virtue and he would detail the evils of luxury and the fall of cities destroyed through that disease," 20.4.1). The words of Iamblichus have the same purport: διὰ ταῦτα δὲ καὶ τὴν τοιαύτην διαίρεσιν ἐποιεῖτο, ὅτι τὸ πρῶτον τῶν κακῶν παραρρεῖν εἴωθεν εἴς τε τὰς οἰκίας καὶ τὰς πόλεις ἡ καλουμένη τρυφή, δεύτερον ὕβρις, τρίτον ὄλεθρος ("For this reason he would make the following analysis: that *truphē* was the first of evils accustomed to slip into families and cities; the second was hubris; the third, destruction." Iamblichus, *Vit. Pyth.* 30.171).

The tale of Sybaris's deserved end, and other similar stories, were, we suggest, composed to provide the telling example.

It is not difficult to imagine how the story could have taken shape. Herodotus tells us that Telys was tyrant of the Sybarites at the time of the decisive war with Croton. Furthermore, relating the adventures of the physician Democedes, Herodotus characterizes the Crotoniates as stubborn in the face of demands by a greater power. Democedes, escaping by guile from the clutches of Darius, whose court physician he had unwillingly become, took refuge in his native Croton. When agents of the king arrived in Croton to demand the return of Democedes, the citizens were split by their fear of Darius, but refused to surrender the fugitive.[5] Threatening war, the Persians returned home. Democedes remained and married the daughter of the athlete Milo (Hdt. 3.136–37). These suggestions present in Herodotus are elaborated according to a familiar pattern. The plot of the fall of Sybaris is essentially the same as that of Aeschylus's *Suppliants*, with Pythagoras as protagonist in place of Pelasgus.[6] Although our recreation of the seminal stage of the tradition is altogether speculative and meant to serve merely *exempli gratia*, the parallel between Democedes and the *Suppliants* on the one hand and the five hundred wealthy Sybarites and Pythagoras on the other must arouse suspicions. In any case, there seems to be almost no detail in Diodorus's narrative on the conflict between Croton and Sybaris—apart from the names of Telys and Milo,[7] both present in Herodotus— which could not be concocted.

The arguments that undercut the historicity of the story of Telys and the five hundred exiles also pertain to the tantalizing data on the Sybarite empire, which served as the jumping off point for this investigation. Diodorus and Strabo tell of the city's huge population, prodigality with citizenship, and its four subject tribes and twenty-five subordinate poleis. Although in the immediate context Diodorus does not mention τρυφή and its *sequelae*, Strabo explicitly says that Sybaris was lost ὑπὸ τρυφῆς καὶ ὕβρεως and we have seen that a

---

5. In Herodotus's brief discussion of the war between Sybaris and Croton we may also find a hint of the structure of the tradition as given in Diodorus: a certain Callias, an Elian seer, escaped from the hostility of Telys and found a place at Croton (5.44).

6. Del Corno (1993, 12–13) sees a connection between the story in Diodorus and the *Suppliants*. However, for him, it is the events at Sybaris, having taken on great importance, which Aeschylus reflects, perhaps unconsciously, in his tragedy: "Successiva di qualche decennio agli avvenimenti, la trilogia eschilea delle *Danaidi* . . . proiettava nell'evento storico la voce possente di una sanzione universale" (13).

7. And, of course, the information that Milo was six times an Olympic victor. This detail was available from a tradition that had nothing to do with Sybaris.

comparison of these passages with Diodorus 10.23 and Ps.-Scymnus 337–60 establishes their common origin in a tradition that emphasized the progression from πλοῦτος to τρυφή to ὕβρις. It is therefore of great significance to note that both Sybaris's πολιτῶν τριάκοντα μυριάδας and generosity with its citizenship (Diod. 12.9) have been identified precisely as exemplifying this "theory of decadence."

Camassa has argued convincingly that the figure of three hundred thousand citizens is a symbol of Sybarite excess, indicating the disproval felt by the Greek world for the lavish way in which Sybaris granted citizenship, a right that most other cities granted "con una parsimonia che rasenta l'avarizia."[8] According to our interpretation, the connection that Camassa draws between these "facts" and "la classica struttura triadica τρυφή-ὕβρις-κόρος" constitutes a *prima facie* reason to doubt their historical value.[9] This reason receives some support from Diodorus's wording. The expressions ἐπὶ τοσοῦτο προέβησαν ὥστε and τοσοῦτο διήνεγκαν ὥστε, used to emphasize precisely the details in question, are reminiscent of the phraseology associated with τρυφή in Athenaeus. This similarity gains added significance when we notice that the quoted material comes immediately after we are told that the Sybarites enjoyed a καρποφόρον χώραν ("a productive countryside"), since in several other passages Diodorus follows a description of the fertility of the χώρα with an indication of the resultant τρυφή.[10] In view of these factors, we consider Diodorus's information on the extended population of the Sybarites to be no more secure than is that on the fall of Sybaris.

Strabo's view, having as it does the same origin, is no better. Where Diodorus explains the large population of Sybaris in political terms, Strabo sets out its geographical dimensions. The geographical tradition had at its disposal the names of a number of πόλεις Οἰνώτρων ("cities of the Enotrians") in the neighborhood of Sybaris; from such information may have arisen the four tribes and twenty-five cities under the sway of Sybaris.[11] It is in any event suspicious that,

---

8. Camassa 1989, 8.
9. Camassa 1989, 6. For his part, Camassa doubts the historicity of the figure of 300,000, but accepts as genuine the extensive granting of citizenship. Furthermore, he suggests that this information reached Diodorus and Strabo from Antiochus via Timaeus, and Ps.-Scymnus via Ephorus; the different lines of transmission would perhaps explain why Ps.-Scymnus has 100,000 instead of 300,000.
10. Especially Diod. Sic. 3.42 and 5.10, where words from the διαφέρειν family likewise occur.
11. Stephanus of Byzantium lists the names of sixteen such cities, of which nine are attributed to Hecataeus of Miletus: (with attribution) Arinthe, Artemision, Erimon, Ixias, Menekine, Kossa, Kyterion, Malanios and Ninaia; (without attribution) Brystakia, Drys, Patrykos, Siberine, Setaion, Temese and Pyxis. Some incuse coins have been connected with certain of these communities (coins bearing the

if we include Sybaris itself, Strabo's geographical subdivisions of the Sybarite empire add up to thirty, each perhaps with a hypothetical population of ten thousand.

We are not in a position to fix with any precision the source of the tradition reflected in Strabo and Diodorus. The *Quellenforschung* on these passages has put forward Ephorus and Timaeus as the two most likely authorities. However, we have seen that the presence of the τρυφή-ὕβρις complex here means that it is unlikely that either Ephorus or Timaeus was the direct source for the tradition. On the other hand, the parallel between the wording of Strabo and Diodorus and that of Athenaeus suggests that both the geographer and the historian had recourse to the same kind of moralist tradition that seems to have provided Athenaeus with his immediate source for historical examples of τρυφή. Elsewhere, too, in Diodorus and Strabo the mark of this moralizing intermediary may be identified.

Both authors tell of the debilitating effect suffered by Hannibal's army from its stay among the riches of Campania:

Ὅτι ἡ τοῦ Ἀννίβου δύναμις πολὺν χρόνον τῆς τῶν Καμπανῶν εὐδαιμονίας ἀπλήστως ἐμπλησθεῖσα μετέβαλε ταῖς ἀγωγαῖς εἰς τοὐναντίον· τρυφῆς γὰρ συνεχοῦς καὶ μαλακῆς εὐνῆς καὶ μύρων παντοίων καὶ παντοίας τροφῆς πολυτέλεια τὴν μὲν ἀλκὴν καὶ συνήθη τῶν δεινῶν ἐξέλυσεν ὑπομονήν, τὰ δὲ σώματα καὶ τὰς ψυχὰς εἰς γυναικώδη καὶ τρυφερὰν διάθεσιν μετέστησεν.

[Hannibal's force, after insatiably taking its fill of the Campanians' prosperity for a long time, changed its way of life to the opposite. For extravagance of continual *truphē* and soft bedding and all sorts of perfume and a variety of food undid their strength and accustomed endurance of hardships. It changed their bodies and their souls to a womanly disposition of *truphē*.] (Diod. Sic. 26.11.1)

Καμπανοῖς δὲ συνέβη διὰ τὴν τῆς χώρας εὐδαιμονίαν ἐπ᾽ ἴσον ἀγαθῶν ἀπολαῦσαι καὶ κακῶν. ἐπὶ τοσοῦτον γὰρ ἐξετρύφησαν ὥστ᾽ ἐπὶ δεῖπνον ἐκάλουν πρὸς ζεύγη μονομάχων, ὁρίζοντες ἀριθμὸν κατὰ τὴν τῶν [συν]δείπνων

---

lettering *Sirinos-Pyxoes, Pal-Mil, Ami,* and *So*), but the location of these sites remains a matter of conjecture; see Rutter 1970, 172; Lepore 1980, 1332–36; Ronconi 1993, with bibliography; and Greco 1993, 460–65.

ἀξίαν. Ἀννίβα δ᾽ ἐξ ἐνδόσεως λαβόντος αὐτούς, δεξάμενοι χειμαδίοις τὴν στρατιὰν οὕτως ἐξεθήλυναν ταῖς ἡδοναῖς ὥσθ᾽ ὁ Ἀννίβας ἔφη νικῶν κινδυνεύειν ἐπὶ τοῖς ἐχθροῖς γενέσθαι, γυναῖκας ἀντὶ τῶν ἀνδρῶν τοὺς στρατιώτας ἀπολαβών.

[And it happened that the Campanians, because of the fertility of the land, enjoyed equal shares of good things and bad. For they had so much *truphē* that they invited gladiators to dinner in pairs, determining the number by the importance of the banquet. And when Hannibal captured them, submitting easily and receiving his army in winter-quarters, they so womanized it with pleasures that Hannibal said that, though he was the victor, he risked being taken by his enemies, since he received back soldiers who were women instead of men.] (Strabo 5.4.13)

A common origin is not unlikely for the two passages. The Diodorus passage comes to us through a Byzantine excerptor, and so is less trustworthy. In the Strabo, we see a permutation of the idiom familiar from Athenaeus: ἐπὶ τοσοῦτον ἐξετρύφησαν ὥστ᾽. . . . Taken together, the passages on Campania and Sybaris constitute sufficient reason to posit that the two authors' interest in τρυφή may have led them to draw upon a second- or first-century moralist compilation.

Was the theme of pernicious luxury commonplace in the Hellenic world and, in particular, was the city of Sybaris destroyed because of its luxury? In spite of the frequent claims by scholars, the evidence for the unusual wealth of Sybaris is not robust. Archeology offers scant proof and the matter is not attested explicitly in the literary sources before the first century BCE. By the same token, the supposedly weighty impact of the destruction of Sybaris on the psyche of the rest of the Greek world is open to doubt. Herodotus 6.21, the only solid evidence regularly offered in support of this view, admits of another interpretation. The idea that the τρυφή of the Sybarites was a cause of their deserved destruction does not appear before Ps.-Scymnus. There is no good evidence for this view in Timaeus or any other Hellenistic historian. Accordingly, there is no support for the theory that the τρυφή-ὕβρις complex was associated with Sybaris by the Crotoniates in the aftermath of the fall of Sybaris. No early τρυφή tradition developed, later to spread abroad via Antiochus of Syracuse, carrying genuine Sybarite and Crotoniate historical information with it. Diodorus 12.9.1

and Strabo 6.1.13 contain no reliable data about Archaic Sybaris. The features of the "empire" of the Sybarites must be established through other means; the literary sources shed no light.

We must also stress once more our methodological conclusion. In the course of pursuing the development of the idea of pernicious luxury, we have laid out a philological method that we believe should be employed in the future by anyone using the fragments of authors that are preserved in any later cover text or epitomizer. One cannot simply lump these citations in with directly transmitted sources, assuming that they share equal validity and correctly represent the views and wording of the original author. Instead, the cautious scholar must go through a series of steps to determine more about that accuracy. First, one should examine the vocabulary of the fragment horizontally, or synchronically, to determine the frequency and idioms of usage within the cover text and within contemporaneous works. Next one must examine the vocabulary vertically, or diachronically, to determine the frequency of use over the course of centuries. It is important to look beyond mere occurrences in order to identify changes in meaning and nuance. Also, within the fragment collections of a given author, one should look for odd coincidences: for example, if every discussion that has moral significance is preserved in a very few "quotes" all derived from a single cover text, and all of the other fragments, often numbering in the hundreds, have ethnographical and historical details with no moral implications, one must consider the possibility that the moral overtones were added by the later transmitter and were not prominent in the original.

In the end, the evidence collected in this way may be difficult to interpret, and one must make a judgment call: perhaps three uses in the Classical era are enough to justify assigning a word to a Hellenistic author, but the hundreds of occurrences in the Roman era may weigh against it. Whatever the decision of the individual scholar, the evidence should be evaluated openly and in detail. It is not enough to characterize a cover text as "generally reliable" and leave it at that. All of these steps represent a laborious process, made simpler and more difficult at the same time by digital search engines. One must find and examine thousands of passages, focusing on any discrepancies. Evolving technology will continue to put at our disposal greater amounts of information about the relationship between fragments and cover texts, making their interpretation certainly more complex and hopefully more precise.[12] For example, in the near

---

12. For the application of digital tools and procedures specifically to the problems raised by fragments,

future, we will have the ability to specify and classify features of a work based
on computer analyses of digitized texts that have been syntactically analyzed.
At any rate, all promising processes of analysis must be engaged in order to establish the credibility of any fragment that is transmitted to us indirectly.

We will say a last word about a question that may occur to any reader who has
followed us at great length through this difficult and complex material: is the
subject we have chosen worth the effort? Can it matter, to those who are not
specialists in the relevant disciplines, whether the idea that certain choices in
lifestyle—preferences of cuisine or costume or kind of entertainment or type of
sexual practice—can change the course of history originated in the sixth century BCE or in the first? Is it of any importance whether it was a creation of the
Greeks or of the Romans? We think the answer is an emphatic "yes," and we
hope the reader will agree. Even today, the authority of the ancients is invoked,
as in a *New York Times* op-ed piece, to support the proposition that "wealth and
power lead to affluence and luxury. Affluence and luxury lead to decadence,
corruption and decline."[13] If we are going to allow the concept of pernicious
luxury a place in our political discourse and influence in our decisions, we
should be aware that it is not certainly a discovery of "Greek genius," derived
from a keen observation of the unrolling of history in many cultures, a Natural
Truth, in other words; rather, that it may be an artifact of the Roman perspective, developed to address concerns of imperial expansion. This possibility
should condition the weight that we allow the concept to have in our judgment.
It is, we suggest, a distinction that truly makes a difference.

[handwritten marginal note: idea of luxury remains after 2000 years]

---

see the work of Monica Berti (2013). More generally, Greg Crane's Open Philology Project (Crane,
forthcoming) at the University of Leipzig is spearheading the effort to generate, promulgate, and
analyze new data on world heritage languages such as Greek and Latin. The announcement of the
project is at Crane 2013.

13. Brooks 2009. For general studies on the influence of the morality of wealth after 200 CE, see Brown
2012 and Berry 1994.

Bibliography

Alty, John. 1982. "Dorians and Ionians." *Journal of Hellenic Studies* 102: 1–14.

Ambaglio, Delfino. 1990. "I Deipnosofisti di Ateneo e la tradizione storica frammentaria." *Athenaeum* 78: 51–64.

Ampolo, C. 1993. "La città dell'eccesso: per la storia di Sibari fino al 510 a.C." In Stazio and Ceccoli 1993, 213–54.

Anderson, Graham. 1997. "Athenaeus: The Sophistic Environment." *Aufstieg und Niedergang der römischen Welt* 2.34.3: 2173–85.

Anhalt, Emily Katz. 1993. *Solon the Singer: Politics and Poetics*. Lanham, MD: Rowman & Littlefield.

Arnott, Geoffrey. 2000. "Athenaeus and the Epitome: Texts, Manuscripts and Early Editions." In Braund and Wilkins 2000, 41–52.

Asheri, David. 2006. *Erodoto "Le Storie" Libro IX: La battaglia di Platea*. Rome: Mondadori.

Asheri, David, and Virginia Antelami. 1988. *Erodoto "Le Storie" Libro I: La Lidia e la Persia*. Rome: Fondazione Lorenzo Valla and Mondadori.

Asheri, David, Alan Lloyd, and Aldo Corcella. 2007. *A Commentary on Herodotus Books I–IV*. Edited by Oswyn Murray and Alfonso Moreno. Translated by Barbara Graziosi et al. Oxford and New York: Oxford University Press.

Asheri, David, and Silvio M. Medaglia. 1990. *Erodoto "Le Storie" Libro III: La Persia*. Translated by Augusto Fraschetti. Rome: Fondazione Lorenzo Valla and Mondadori.

Astin, Alan. 1978. *Cato the Censor*. Oxford: Clarendon Press.

Ayo, N. 1984. "Prolog and Epilog. Mythological History in Herodotus." *Ramus* 13: 39–42.

Bakker, Egbert J., Irene J. F. de Jong, and Hans van Wees, eds. 2002. *Brill's Companion to Herodotus*. Leiden, Boston, and Cologne: Brill.

Baldwin, B. 1976. "Athenaeus and His Work." *Acta Classica* 10: 21–42.

Balot, Ryan K. 2001. *Greed and Injustice in Classical Athens*. Princeton, NJ: Princeton University Press.

Barnes, Christopher L. H. 2005. *Images and Insults: Ancient Historiography and the Outbreak of the Tarentine War*. Historia Einzelschriften 187. Stuttgart: F. Steiner.

Baron, Christopher A. 2011. "The Delimitation of Fragments In Jacoby's *FGrH*: Some Examples from Duris of Samos." *Greek, Roman, and Byzantine Studies* 51: 86–110.

Baron, Christopher A. 2013. *Timaeus of Tauromenium and Hellenistic Historiography*. Cambridge and New York: Cambridge University Press.

Bernhardt, Rainer. 2003. *Luxuskritik und Aufwandsbeschränkungen in der griechischen Welt*. Historia Einzelschriften 168. Stuttgart: F. Steiner.

Berry, Christopher J. 1994. *The Idea of Luxury: A Conceptual and Historical Investigation*. Cambridge: Cambridge University Press.

Berry, D. H. 2004. "The Publication of Cicero's *Pro Roscio Amerino*." *Mnemosyne* 57: 80–87.

Berti, Monica. 2013. "Fragmentary Texts: Quotations and Text Re-Uses of Lost Authors and Works." Accessed July 16. http://www.fragmentarytexts.org.

Bichler, Reinhold. 2011. "Ktesias spielt mit Herodot." In Wiesehöfer, Rollinger, and Lanfranchi 2011, 21–52.

Bischoff, Heinrich. (1932) 1965. "Sinn des letzten Kapitels." In *Herodot: Eine Auswahl aus der neueren Forschung*, edited by W. Marg, 681–87. 2nd edition, revised and enlarged. Munich 1965. Originally published as "Der Warner bei Herodot." Ph.D. diss., University of Marburg, 1932.

Bockmuehl, Markus N. A., and Guy G. Stroumsa, eds. 2010. *Paradise in Antiquity: Jewish and Christian Views*. Cambridge and New York: Cambridge University Press.

Boedeker, Deborah. 1988. "Protesilaos and the End of Herodotus' *Histories*." *Classical Antiquity* 7: 30–48.

Boedeker, Deborah. 2009. "No Way Out? Aging in the New (and Old) Sappho." In Greene and Skinner 2009, 71–83.

Bollansée, Jan. 2008. "Clearchus' Treatise *On Modes of Life* and the Theme of *Tryphè*. *Ktema* 33: 403–11.

Bonfante, Larissa, ed. 2011a. *The Barbarians of Ancient Europe*. Cambridge and New York: Cambridge University Press.

Bonfante, Larissa, ed. 2011b. "Classical and Barbarian." In Bonfante 2011a, 1–36.

Bost Pouderon, Cécile. 2006. *Dion Chrysostome: Trois discours aux villes ("Orr."), 33–35)*. 2 vols. Salerno: Helios.

Bowie, Angus, ed. 2007. *Herodotus. Histories. Book VIII*. Cambridge and New York: Cambridge University Press.

Bowra, Cecil M. 1941. "Xenophanes, Fragment 3." *Classical Quarterly* 35: 119–26.

Bowra, Cecil M. 1957. "Asius and the Old-Fashioned Samians." *Hermes* 85: 391–401.

Bowra, Cecil M. 1970. "Xenophanes and the Luxury of Colophon." In *On Greek Margins*, 109–21. Oxford: Clarendon Press.

Braund, David. 2000. "Learning, Luxury and Empire: Athenaeus' Roman Patron." In Braund and Wilkins 2000, 3–22.

Braund, David, and John Wilkins, eds. 2000. *Athenaeus and His World: Reading Greek Culture in the Roman Empire.* Exeter: University of Exeter Press.

Bréchet, Christophe. 2007. "Du 'grand livre' homérique aux *Deipnosophistes*: exploration d'un *continuum*." In Lenfant 2007a, 321–40.

Brooks, David. 2009. "The Next Culture War." *New York Times*, September 29, 2009, A39.

Brown, Peter. 2012. *Through the Eye of a Needle: Wealth, the Fall of Rome, and the Making of Christianity in the West, 350–550 AD.* Princeton, NJ: Princeton University Press.

Brown, Truesdell. 1958. *Timaeus of Tauromenium.* Berkeley and Los Angeles: University of California Press.

Brunt, Peter. 1980. "On Historical Fragments and Epitomes." *Classical Quarterly* 30: 477–94.

Bugno, Maurizio. 1999. *Da Sibari a Thurii: la fine di un impero.* Naples: Centre Jean Bérard.

Burton, R. W. B. 1962. *Pindar's Pythian Odes: Essays in Interpretation.* Oxford: Oxford University Press.

Cairns, Douglas L. 1996. "Hybris, Dishonour and Thinking Big." *Journal of Hellenic Studies* 116: 1–32.

Camassa, Giorgio. 1989. "Sibari polyanthropos, II." *Serta Historica Antiqua* 2: 1–9.

Camassa, Giorgio. 1993. "I culti." In Stazio and Ceccoli 1993, 573–94.

Canfora, Luciano, ed. 2001. *Ateneo, I Deipnosofisti: i dotti a banchetto.* 4 vols. Rome: Salerno.

Carter, John. 1992. Review of Sacks 1990. *Classical Review* 42: 34–36.

Cassio, Albio C. 1985. "Two Studies on Epicharmus and His Influence." *Harvard Studies in Classical Philology* 89: 37–51.

Cassuto, Umberto. 1984. *A Commentary on the Book of Genesis. Part Two: From Noah to Adam.* Jerusalem: Magnes Press.

Chapman, Honora. 2009. "Josephus." In Feldherr 2009, 319–31.

Clarke, Katherine. 1999. *Between Geography and History: Hellenistic Constructions of the Roman World.* Oxford: Clarendon Press.

Classen, J., and J. Steup. 1919. *Thukydides.* 5th edition. Vol. 1. Berlin: Weidmann.

Cobet, Justus. 1971. *Herodots Exkurse und die Frage der Einheit seines Werkes.* Historia Einzelschriften 17. Wiesbaden: F. Steiner.

Collard, Christopher, ed. 1975. *Euripides' "Supplices."* Groningen: Bouma's Boekhuis.

Connolly, Joy. 2009. "Virtue and Violence: The Historians on Politics." In Feldherr 2009, 191–94.

Connor, W. Robert. 1968. *Theopompus and Fifth-Century Athens.* Washington, DC: Center for Hellenic Studies.

Corcella, Aldo. 1984. *Erodoto e l'analogia.* Palermo: Sellerio.

Cornell, Timothy J. 1986a. "The Formation of the Historical Tradition at Rome." In Moxon, Smart, and Woodman 1986, 67–86.

Cornell, Timothy J. 1986b. "The Value of the Literary Tradition Concerning Archaic Rome." In *Social Struggles in Archaic Rome*, edited by Kurt Raaflaub, 52–76. Berkeley: University of California Press.

Cornell, Timothy J. 2003. "Coriolanus: Myth, History and Performance." In *Myth, History, and Culture in Republican Rome: Studies in Honour of T. P. Wiseman*, edited by David Braund and Christopher Gill, 73–97. Exeter: University of Exeter Press.

Cozzoli, Umberto. 1980. "La τρυφή nella interpretazione delle crisi politiche." In *Tra Grecia e Roma: temi antichi e metodologie moderne*, 133–46. Rome: Istituto della Enciclopedia italiana.

Crane, Greg. 2013. "The Open Philology Project and Humboldt Chair of Digital Humanities at Leipzig." Posted April 4. http://sites.tufts.edu/perseusupdates/2013/04/04/the-open-philology-project-and-humboldt-chair-of-digital-humanities-at-leipzig.

Crane, Greg. Forthcoming. "Open Philology." http://openphilology.org/.

Croissant, Francis. 1993. "Sybaris: la production artistique." In Stazio and Ceccoli 1993, 539–59.

Dalby, Andrew. 1996. *Siren Feasts: A History of Food and Gastronomy in Greece*. New York and London: Routledge.

Dalby, Andrew. 2007. Review of Bernhardt 2003. *Classical Review* 57: 164–65.

Danielewicz, Jerzy. 2006. "Poetic Quotations and Discourse Strategies in Athenaeus." *Eos* 93: 116–30.

Davidson, James. 2009. "Polybius." In Feldherr 2009, 123–36.

Davies, John Kenyon. 1981. *Wealth and the Power of Wealth in Classical Athens*. New York: Arno Press.

Del Corno, Dario. 1993. "L'immagine di Sibari nella tradizione classica." In Stazio and Ceccoli 1993, 9–18.

Denniston, John Dewar, and Denys Page, eds. 1957. Aeschylus *"Agamemnon."* Oxford: Clarendon Press.

Desmond, William. 2006. *The Greek Praise of Poverty: Origins of Ancient Cynicism.* North Bend, IN: University of Notre Dame Press.

DeVries, Keith. 1973. "East Meets West at Dinner." *Expedition* 15: 32–39.

DeVries, Keith. 2000. "The Nearly Other: The Attic Vision of Phrygians and Lydians." In *Not the Classical Ideal: Athens and the Construction of the Other in Greek Art*, edited by Beth Cohen, 338–63. Leiden and Boston: Brill.

Dewald, Carolyn. 1997. "Wanton Kings, Pickled Heroes and Gnomic Founding Fathers: Strategies of Meaning at the End of Herodotus' Histories." In *Classical Closure: Reading the End in Greek and Latin Literature*, edited by D. H. Roberts, F. M. Dunn, and D. Fowler, 62–82. Princeton, NJ: Princeton University Press.

Dover, Kenneth J., ed. 1968. Aristophanes' *"Clouds."* Oxford: Clarendon Press.

Drews, Robert. 1962. "Diodorus and His Sources." *American Journal of Philology* 83: 383–92.

Duff, Tim E. 1999. *Plutarch's "Lives": Exploring Virtue and Vice.* Oxford: Clarendon Press.

Earl, D. C. 1961. *The Political Thought of Sallust.* Cambridge: Cambridge University Press.

Eckstein, Arthur M. 1995. *Moral Vision in the "Histories" of Polybius.* Berkeley: University of California Press.

Edelstein, I, and I. G. Kidd, eds. 1989. *Posidonius,* vol. 1: *The Fragments.* 2nd edition. Cambridge and New York: Cambridge University Press.

Edwards, Catharine. 1993. *The Politics of Immorality in Ancient Rome.* Cambridge and New York: Cambridge University Press.

Erbse, Hartmut. 1992. *Studien zum Verständnis Herodots.* Berlin and New York: De Gruyter.

Evans, Rhiannon. 2011. "Learning to Be Decadent: Roman Identity and the Luxuries of Others." In *Australasian Society for Classical Studies* 32 *Selected Proceedings,* 1–7. Accessed Oct. 22, 2012, http://www.ascs.org.au/news/ascs32/index.html.

Feldherr, Andrew. 1997. "*Caeci auaritia*: Avarice, History, and Vision in Livy V." In *Studies in Latin Literature and Roman History,* vol. 8, edited by Carl Deroux, 268–77. Bruxelles: Latomus.

Feldherr, Andrew. 2009. *Cambridge Companion to the Roman Historians.* Cambridge and New York: Cambridge University Press.

Finglass, Patrick J., ed. 2007. *Sophocles "Electra."* Cambridge and New York: Cambridge University Press.

Fisher, Nicolas R. E. 1992. *Hybris: A Study in the Values of Honour and Shame in Ancient Greece.* Warminster: Aris & Phillips.

Flashar, Hellmut, trans. and comm. 1972. *Mirabilia. Aristoteles Werke in deutscher Übersetzung* 18.2–3. Berlin: Akademie-Verlag.

Flory, Stewart. 1987. *The Archaic Smile of Herodotus.* Detroit, MI: Wayne State University Press.

Flower, Michael. 1994. *Theopompus of Chios.* Oxford and New York: Clarendon Press.

Flower, Michael, and John Marincola, eds. 2002. *Herodotus "Histories" Book IX.* Cambridge: Cambridge University Press.

Fornara, Charles. 1983. *The Nature of History in Ancient Greece and Rome.* Berkeley: University of California Press.

Fornara, Charles. 1992. Review of Sacks 1990. *Classical Philology* 87: 383–88.

Forsdyke, Sara. 2001. "Athenian Democratic Ideology and Herodotus' *Histories.*" *American Journal of Philology* 122: 329–58.

Forsythe, Gary. 1999. *Livy and Early Rome: A Study in Historical Method and Judgment.* Stuttgart: F. Steiner.

Fox, Matthew. 1993. "History and Rhetoric in Dionysius of Halicarnassus." *Journal of Roman Studies* 83: 31–47.

Fraenkel, Eduard, ed. (1950) 1962. *Aeschylus "Agamemnon."* 3 vols. Oxford: Clarendon Press.

Francis, James A. 1995. *Subversive Virtue: Asceticism and Authority in the Second-Century Pagan World*. University Park: Pennsylvania State University Press.

Gabba, Emilio. 1991. *Dionysius and the History of Archaic Rome*. Berkeley: University of California Press.

García Quintela, Marco Virgilio. 2002. "La destrucción de Síbaris y la mitopoyesis pitagórica." *Dialogues d'histoire ancienne* 28.2: 19–39

García Quintela, Marco Virgilio. 2010. "La destrucción de Síbaris y la política pitagórica." *Athenaeum* 98.2: 365–88.

Garvey, A. F., ed. 2009. *Aeschylus "Persae."* Oxford: Clarendon Press.

Geddes, A. G. 1987. "Rags and Riches: The Costume of Athenian Men in the Fifth Century." *Classical Quarterly* n.s. 37.2: 307–31.

Geffcken, Johannes. 1892. *Timaios' Geographie des Westens*. Berlin: Weidmann.

Georges, Pericles. 1994. *Barbarian Asia and the Greek Experience: From the Archaic Age to the Age of Xenophon*. Baltimore: Johns Hopkins University Press.

Gomme, A. W. 1956. *A Historical Commentary on Thucydides 2–3*. Oxford: Clarendon Press.

Godley, A. D., trans. 1921. *Herodotus*. London: Heinemann.

Goodenough, Erwin R. 1938. *The Politics of Philo Judaeus: Practice and Theory*. New Haven, CT: Yale University Press.

Goodenough, Erwin R. (1962) 1986. *An Introduction to Philo Judaeus*. 2nd edition, reprinted. Oxford: Blackwell. Reprinted Lanham, MD: University Press of America.

Gorman, Vanessa B. 2001. *Miletos, the Ornament of Ionia: A History of the City to 400 B.C.E.* Ann Arbor: University of Michigan Press.

Gorman, Robert J., and Vanessa B. Gorman. 2007. "The Τρυφή of the Sybarites: A Historiographical Problem in Athenaeus." *Journal of Hellenic Studies* 127: 38–60.

Gorman, Robert J., and Vanessa B. Gorman. 2010. "*Truphē* and *Hybris* in the *Peri Biōn* Of Clearchus." *Philologus* 154: 186–206.

Gowing, Alain M. 2009. "The Roman *Exempla* Tradition in Imperial Greek Historiography: The Case of Camillus." In Feldherr 2009, 332–47.

Grandjean, Catherine, Anna Heller, and Jocelyne Peigney, eds. 2013. *À la table des rois: Luxe et pouvoir dans l'oeuvre d'Athénée*. Tours, France: Presses universitaires François-Rabelais de Tours; Rennes, France: Presses universitaires de Rennes.

Granger, Herbert. 2007. "Poetry and Prose: Xenophanes of Colophon." *Transactions of the American Philological Association* 137: 403–33.

Greco, Emanuele. 1993. "L'impero di Sibari: Bilancio archeologico-topografico." In Stazio and Ceccoli 1993, 459–85.

Greco, Emanuele, et al. 2004. "Sibari 2004." *Annuario della Scuola Archeologica di Atene* series 3a, 4.2: 823–40.

Greco, Emanuele, et al. 2005. "Sibari 2005: campagna di scavo a Casa Bianca settembre-dicembre." *Annuario della Scuola Archeologica di Atene* series 3a, 5.2: 1001–66.

Greco, Emanuele, et al. 2006. "Sibari 2006: campagna di scavo a Casa Bianca aprile-settembre." *Annuario della Scuola Archeologica di Atene* series 3a, 6.2: 1025–94.

Green, Peter, trans. and comm. 2006. *Diodorus Siculus, Books 11–12.37.1: Greek History 480–431 B.C.—the Alternative Version.* Austin: University of Texas Press.

Green, Peter, trans. and comm. 2010. *Diodorus Siculus: The Persian Wars to the Fall of Athens; Books 11–14.34 (480–401 BCE).* Austin: University of Texas Press.

Greene, Ellen, and Marilyn B. Skinner, eds. 2009. *The New Sappho on Old Age.* Washington, DC: Center for Hellenic Studies.

Greenfield, Jonas. 1984. "A Touch of Eden." In *Hommages et Opera Minora. Vol. IX: Orientalia J. Duchesne-Guillemin Emerito Oblata,* 219–24. Leiden: Brill.

Gronewald, M, and R. W. Daniel. 2004. "Ein neuer Sappho-Papyrus." *Zeitschrift für Papyrologie und Epigraphik* 147: 1–8.

Gruen, Erich. 1992. *Culture and National Identity in Republican Rome.* Ithaca, NY: Cornell University Press.

Gruen, Erich. 2011. *Rethinking the Other in Antiquity.* Princeton, NJ: Princeton University Press.

Gulick, Charles B., ed. and trans. 1927–41. *Athenaeus "Deipnosophistae."* London: W. Heinemann; New York: G. P. Putnam.

Guzzo, Pier Giovanni. 1976. "Tra Sibari e Thurii." *Klearchos* 8, no. 69–72: 28–64.

Guzzo, Pier Giovanni. 1981a. "Vie istmiche della Sibaritide e commercio tirrenico." In *Il commercio Greco in Tirreno in età arcaica,* 35–55. Salerno: Università degli Studi di Salerno.

Guzzo, Pier Giovanni. 1981b. "Scavi a Sibari, II." *Annalidell'Istituto universitario orientale di Napoli. Sezione di archeologia e storia antica* 3: 15–27.

Guzzo, Pier Giovanni. 1982. "La Sibaritide e Sibari nell' VIII e nel VII sec. a. C." *Annuario della Scuola Archeologica di Atene* 44: 237–50.

Guzzo, Pier Giovanni. 1992a. "Sibari." *Atti et memorie della Società Magna Grecia* 3a.1: 121–53.

Guzzo, Pier Giovanni. 1992b. "Sibari e la Sibaritide: Materiali per un bilancio della conoscenza archeologica." *Revue archéologique* 3–35.

Guzzo, Pier Giovanni. 1993. "Sibari: Materiali per un bilancio archeologico." In Stazio and Ceccoli 1993, 51–82.

Guzzo, Pier Giovanni. 1997. "Thurii e la Sibaritide." *Ostraka* 6.2: 379–84

Guzzo, Pier Giovanni. 2003. "Sul mito di Sibari." *Babesch* 78: 221–23.

Hadas-Lebel, Mireille. 2012. *Philo of Alexandria: A Thinker in the Jewish Diaspora.* Translated by Robyn Fréchet. Studies in Philo of Alexandria 7. Leiden and Boston: Brill. Originally published as *Philon d'Alexandrie: Un penseur en diaspora.* Paris: Fayard, 2003.

Hahm, D. E. 1989. "Posidonius' Theory of Historical Causation." *Aufstieg und Niedergang der römischen Welt* 2.36.3: 393–435.

Hall, Edith. 1989. *Inventing the Barbarian: Greek Self-Definition through Tragedy.* Oxford: Clarendon Press.

Hall, Edith. 1993. "Asia Unmanned: Images of Victory in Classical Athens." In *War and Society in the Greek World,* edited by John Rich and Graham Shipley, 108–33. London and New York: Routledge.

Hammerstaedt, Jürgen. 2009. "The Cologne Sappho: Its Discovery and Textual Transmission." In Greene and Skinner 2009, 17–40.

Harrison, Thomas. 2000. *Divinity and History: The Religion of Herodotus*. Oxford: Clarendon Press.

Hartog, François. 1988. *The Mirror of Herodotus: The Representation of the Other in the Writing of History*. Berkeley: University of California Press.

Heinen, Heinz. 1983. "Die *Tryphè* des Ptolemaios VIII. Euergeres II: Beobachtungen zum ptolemäischen Herrscherideal und zu einer römischen Gesandtschaft in Ägypten (140/39 v. Chr.)." In *Althistorische Studien [Festschrift for Hermann Bengtson]*, edited by Karl Stroheker and Gerold Walser, 116–28. Wiesbaden: F. Steiner.

Hellmann, Fritz. 1934. *Herodots Kroisos-Logos: Neue Philologische Untersuchungen 9*. Berlin: Weidmann.

Hengst, Daniël den. 2010. *Emperors and Historiography: Collected Essays on the Literature of the Roman Empire*, edited by D. W. P. Burgersdijk and J. A. van Waarden. Leiden and Boston: Brill.

Herington, J. 1991. "The Closure of Herodotus' *Histories*." *Illinois Classical Studies* 16: 149–60.

Hoffmann, Wilhelm. 1936. "Der Kampf zwischen Rom und Tarent im Urteil der antiken Überlieferung." *Hermes* 71: 11–24.

Hoffmann, Wilhelm. 1942. *Livius und der zweite punische Kreig*. *Hermes* Einzelschriften 8. Berlin: Weidmann.

Holger, Thesleff. 1986. "Notes on the Paradise Myth in Ancient Greece." *Temenos* 22: 129–39

Hornblower, Jane. 1981. *Hieronymus of Cardia*. Oxford and New York: Oxford University Press.

How, W. W., and J. Wells, eds. 1936. *A Commentary on Herodotus*. 3rd edition. 2 vols. Oxford: Clarendon Press.

Hunt, P. 1998. *Slaves, Warfare, and Ideology in the Greek Historians*. Cambridge and New York: Cambridge University Press.

Husson, Geneviève. 1988. "Le paradis de délices (*Genèse* 3, 23–24)." *Revue des études grecques* 101: 64–73.

Immerwahr, Henry R. (1966) 1981. *Form and Thought in Herodotus*. APA Monograph Series 23. Ann Arbor: University of Michigan Press.

Isaac, Benjamin H. 2004. *The Invention of Racism in Classical Antiquity*. Princeton, NJ: Princeton University Press.

Isager, Jacob. 1993. "The Hellenization of Rome: *Luxuria* or *Liberalitas*?" In *Aspects of Hellenism in Italy: Towards a Cultural Unity?*, edited by Pia Guldager Bilde, Inge Nielsen, and Marjatta Nielsen, 257–75. Copenhagen: Museum Tusculanum Press.

Jacob, Christian. 2000. "Athenaeus the Librarian." In Braund and Wilkins 2000, 85–110.

Jacob, Christian. 2001. "Ateneo, o il Dedalo delle parole." In *Ateneo, I Deipnosofisti: i dotti a banchetto*, vol. 1, edited by Luciano Canfora, xi–cxvi. Rome: Salerno.

Jacob, Christian. 2013. *The Web of Athenaeus*. Edited by Scott Fitzgerald Johnson. Translated by Arietta Papaconstantinou. Washington, DC: Center for Hellenic Studies.

Jacoby, Felix. 1913. "Herodotos, der Historiker von Halikarnass oder Thurioi." *Real-Encyclopädie der classischen Altertumwissenschaft* n.s. supplement 2: 206–519.

Jones, C. P. 1978. *The Roman World of Dio Chrysostom*. Cambridge, MA: Harvard University Press.

Kallet-Marx, Lisa. 1993. *Money, Expense, and Naval Power in Thucydides' History 1–5.24*. Berkeley: University of California Press.

Kallet, Lisa. 2001. *Money and the Corrosion of Power in Thucydides: The Sicilian Expedition and Its Aftermath*. Berkeley: University of California Press.

Kebric, Robert. 1977. *In the Shadow of Macedon: Duris of Samos*. *Historia* Einzelschriften 29. Weisbaden: F. Steiner.

Kidd, I. G. 1988a. *Posidonius*, vol. 2.1: *The Commentary; Testimonia and Fragments 1–149*. Cambridge and New York: Cambridge University Press.

Kidd, I. G. 1988b. *Posidonius*, vol. 2.2: *The Commentary; Fragments, 150–293*. Cambridge and New York: Cambridge University Press.

Kidd, I. G. 1989. "Posidonius as Philosopher-Historian." In *Philosophia Togata: Essays on Philosophy and Roman Society*, edited by Miriam Griffin and Jonathan Barnes, 38–50. Oxford: Clarendon Press.

Kidd, I. G. 1997. "What is a Posidonian Fragment?" In Most 1997, 225–36.

Kleibrink, Marianne. 2001. "The Search for Sybaris: An Evaluation of Historical and Archaeological Evidence." *Babesch* 76: 33–70.

Klotz, Frieda, and Katerina Oikonomopoulou, eds. 2011. *The Philosopher's Banquet: Plutarch's "Table Talk" in the Intellectual Culture of the Roman Empire*. Oxford: Clarendon Press.

König, Jason. 2008. "Sympotic Dialogue in the First to Fifth Centuries CE." In *The End of Dialogue in Antiquity*, edited by Simon Goldhill, 85–113. Cambridge and New York: Cambridge University Press.

Kurke, Leslie. 1992. "The Politics of ἁβροσύνη in Archaic Greece." *Classical Antiquity* 11: 91–120.

Lanfranchi, Giovanni B. 2011. "Gli *Assyriaka* di Ctesias." In Wiesehöfer, Rollinger, and Lanfranchi, 2011, 175–223.

Lardinois, André. 2009. "The New Sappho Poem (*P. Köln* 21351 and 21376): Key to the Old Fragments." In Greene and Skinner 2009, 41–57.

Lateiner, Donald. 1986. "The Empirical Element in the Methods of Early Greek Medical Writers and Herodotus: A Shared Epistemological Response." *Antichthon* 20: 1–20.

Lateiner, Donald. 1989. *The Historical Method of Herodotus*. Toronto: University of Toronto Press.

Leisegang, H. 1941. "Philon." *Realencyclopädie der classichen Alterstumswissenschaft* 39: 1–50.

Lenfant, Dominique. 2001. "De Sardanapale à Élagabal: les avatars d'une figure du pouvoir." In *Images et représentations du pouvoir et de l'ordre social dans l'Antiquité*, edited by Michel Molin, 45–55. Paris: De Boccard.

Lenfant, Dominique, ed. 2004. *Ctésias de Cnide. La Perse. L'Inde.* Paris: Les Belles Lettres.

Lenfant, Dominique, ed. 2007a. *Athénée et les fragments d'historiens.* Paris: De Boccard.

Lenfant, Dominique. 2007b. "Les 'fragments' d'Hérodote dans les *Deipnosophistes.*" In Lenfant 2007a, 43–71.

Lepore, E. 1980. "L'*Italía* dal 'punto di vista' ionico: tra Ecateo ed Erodoto." In *PHILIAS CHARIN: miscellanea di studi classici in onore di Eugenio Manni*, 4: 1329–44. Rome: Bretschneider.

Levick, Barbara M. 1982. "Morals, Politics, and the Fall of the Roman Republic." *Greece and Rome* 29: 53–62.

Lévy, Carlos. 2009. "Philo's Ethics." In *The Cambridge Companion to Philo*, edited by Adam Kamesar, 146–71. Cambridge and New York: Cambridge University Press.

Lewis, John David. 2008. *Solon the Thinker: Political Thought in Archaic Athens.* London: Duckworth.

Liébert, Yves. 2006. *Regards sur la* truphè *étrusque.* Limoges: Presses Universitaires de Limoges.

Lind, L. R. 1972. "Concept, Action, and Character: The Reasons for Rome's Greatness." *Transactions of the American Philological Association* 103: 235–83.

Lind, L. R. 1986. "The Idea of the Republic and the Foundations of Roman Morality." *Studies in Latin Literature and Roman History*, edited by Carl Deroux, 5–34. Collection *Latomus* 4. Brussels: Latomus.

Lintott, Andrew. 1972. "Imperial Expansion and Moral Decline in the Roman Republic." *Historia* 21: 626–38.

Llewellyn-Jones, Lloyd. 2010. "Introduction." In *Ctesias' "History of Persia": Tales of the Orient*, edited by Lloyd Llewellyn-Jones and James Robson, 1–87. London and New York.

Lloyd, Alan. 1989. *Erodoto "Le Storie" Libro II: L'Egitto.* Translated by A. Fraschetti. Milan: Fondazione Lorenzo Valla.

Lloyd, Alan. 1990. "Herodotus on Egyptians and Libyans." In *Hérodote et les peuples non-Grecs*, edited by Walter Burkert, Giuseppe Nenci, and Olivier Reverdin, 215–53 (with discussion). Entretiens sur l'Antiquité classique de la Fondation Hardt 35. Geneva: Fondation Hardt.

Lombardo, Marie. 1983. "*Habrosyne* e *habrá* nel mondo greco arcaico." In *Modes de contacts et processus de transformation dans les sociétés antiques: Actes du colloque de Cortone (24–30 mai 1981)*, 1077–1103 Pisa: Scuola Normale superiore; Rome: École française de Rome.

Longley, Georgina. 2012. "Thucydides, Polybius, and Human Nature." In Smith and Yarrow 2012, 68–84.

Maisonneuve, C. 2007. "Les 'fragments' de Xénophon dans les *Deipnosophistes.*" In Lenfant 2007a, 73–106.

Malitz, J. 1983. *Die Historien des Posidonius.* Zetemata 79. Munich: C. H. Beck.

Masaracchia, Agostino. 1977. *Erodoto "Le Storie" Libro VIII: La battaglia di Salamina*, 2nd ed. Milan: Fondazione Lorenzo Valla and Mondadori.

Mastrorosa, Ida. 2006. "Speeches 'Pro' and 'Contra' Women in Livy 34, 1–7: Catonian Legalism and Gendered Debates." *Latomus* 65.3: 590–611.

McGing, Brian. 2010. *Polybius' "Histories."* Oxford: Clarendon Press.

McGing, Brian. 2012. "Polybius and Herodotus." In Smith and Yarrow 2012, 32–49.

Mele, Alfonso. 1984. "Crotone e la sua storia." In *Crotone. Atti del ventitreesimo Convegno di studi sulla Magna Grecia*, 9–87. Tarentum: Istituto per la Storia e l'Archaeologia della Magna Grecia.

Meyer, Terry Matthew. 2009. "Diodorus Siculus: Τρυφή and Historiography in the *Bibliotheca*." MA thesis, University of Nebraska–Lincoln.

Miles, Gary. 1995. *Livy: Reconstructing Early Rome*. Ithaca, NY: Cornell University Press.

Millard, Alan R. 1984. "The Etymology of Eden." *Vetus Testamentum* 34: 103–106.

Moles, John. 1996. "Herodotus Warns the Athenians." *Papers of the Leeds International Latin Seminar* 9: 259–84.

Moore, J. M. 1965. *The Manuscript Tradition of Polybius*. Cambridge: Cambridge University Press.

Most, Glenn W., ed. 1997. *Collecting Fragments / Fragmente sammeln*. Aporemata 1. Göttingen: Vandenhoeck and Ruprecht.

Moxon, I. S., J. D. Smart, and A. J. Woodman, eds. 1986. *Past Perspectives: Studies in Greek and Roman Historical Writing*. Cambridge and New York: Cambridge University Press.

Munson, Rosaria. 1988. "Artemisia in Herodotus." *Classical Antiquity* 7: 91–106.

Mussies, Gérard. 1972. *Dio Chrysostom and the New Testament*. Leiden: Brill

Nagy, Gregory. 1990. *Pindar's Homer: The Lyric Possession of an Epic Past*. Baltimore: Johns Hopkins University Press.

Nenci, Giuseppe. 1983. "Tryphé e colonizzazione." In *Modes de contacts et processus de transformation dans les sociétés antiques: Actes du colloque de Cortone (24–30 mai 1981)*, 1019–30. Pisa: Scuola normale superiore; Rome: École française de Rome.

Nenci, Giuseppe. 1989. "Un nuovo frammento di Clearco sulla *tryphe* Iapigia (Athen., 12, 522f–593b)." *Annali della Scuola normale superiore di Pisa* 19: 893–901.

Nenci, Giuseppe. 1998. *Erodoto "Le Storie" Libro VI: La battaglia di Maratona*. Milan: Fondazione Lorenzo Valla and Mondadori.

Neville, J. 1979. "Was There an Ionian Revolt?" *Classical Quarterly* 29: 268–75.

Nichols, Andrew. 2011. *Ctesias: "On India" and Fragments of His Minor Works*. London: Bristol Classical Press.

Niehoff, Maren. 2001. *Philo on Jewish Identity and Culture*. Tübingen: Mohr.

Olson, S. Douglas. 2006–12. *Athenaeus "The Learned Banqueters."* 8 vols. Cambridge, MA, and London: Harvard University Press.

Palm, Jonas. 1955. *Über Sprache und Stil des Diodoros von Sizilien*. Lund: Gleerup.

Parmeggiani, Giovanni. 2007."I frammenti di Eforo nei *Deipnosopistai* di Ateneo." In Lenfant 2007a, 117–37.

Passerini, A. 1934. "La ΤΡΥΦΗ nella storiographia ellenistica." *Studi italiani di filologia classica* 11: 35–36.

Paulas, John. 2012. "How to Read Athenaeus' *Deipnosophists*." *American Journal of Philology* 133: 403–39.

Pearson, Lionel. 1987. *The Greek Historians of the West: Timaeus and His Predecessors*. Atlanta, GA: Scholars Press.

Peigney, Jocelyne. 2013. "Un modèle 'homérique' du banquet royal?" In Grandjean, Heller, and Peigney 2013, 39–66.

Pelling, Christopher. 1979. "Plutarch's Method of Work in the Roman *Lives*." *Journal of Hellenic Studies* 99: 74–96.

Pelling, Christopher. 1985. "Plutarch and Catiline." *Hermes* 113: 311–29.

Pelling, Christopher. 1997. "East is East and West is West—Or Are They? National Stereotypes in Herodotus." *Histos* 1: 51–66. Accessed June 12, 2012, http://research.ncl.ac.uk/histos/documents/1997.04PellingEastIsEast5166.pdf.

Pelling, Christopher. 2000. "Fun with Fragments." In Braund and Wilkins 2000, 171–90.

Pohlenz, M. 1937. *Herodot: Der erste Geschichtschreiber des Abendlandes*. Leipzig and Berlin: Teubner.

Powell, Enoch. 1938. *A Lexicon to Herodotus*. Cambridge: Cambridge University Press.

Pownall, Frances. 2004. *Lessons from the Past: The Moral Use of History in Fourth-Century Prose*. Ann Arbor: University of Michigan Press.

Raaflaub, Kurt. 1987. "Herodotus, Political Thought, and the Meaning of History." *Arethusa* 20: 221–48.

Raaflaub, Kurt. 2002. "Philosophy, Science, Politics: Herodotus and the Intellectual Trends of His Time." In Bakker, De Jong, and van Wees 2002, 149–86.

Rainey, Froelich. 1969. "The Location of Archaic Greek Sybaris." *American Journal of Archaeology* 73: 261–73.

Rawlinson, George, trans. 1942. *Herodotus*. New York: Modern Library.

Redfield, James. 1985. "Herodotus the Tourist." *Classical Philology* 90: 97–118.

Reinhold, Meyer. 1970. *History of Purple as a Status Symbol in Antiquity*. Collection Latomus 116. Brussels: Latomus.

Relihan, Joel C. 1993. "Rethinking the History of the Literary Symposium." *Illinois Classical Studies* 17.2: 213–44.

Rodríguez-Noriega Guillén, Lucia. 2000. "Are the Fifteen Books of the *Deipnosophistae* an Excerpt?" In Braund and Wilkins 2000, 241–43.

Roller, Matthew. 2009. "The Exemplary Past in Roman Historiography and Culture." In Feldherr 2009, 214–30.

Romano, Alba Claudia. 2003. "*Luxuria/luxuries*." *Revista de estudios clásicos* 31: 13–23.

Romeri, Luciana. 2013. "Luxe ou sobriété? L'érudition comme solution." In Grandjean, Heller, and Peigney 2013, 23–38.

Ronconi, Lucia. 1993. "Ecateo e le poleis degli Enotri." *Hesperia* 3: 45–51.

Rood, Tim. 2012. "Polybius, Thucydides, and the First Punic War." In Smith and Yarrow 2012, 50–67.

Roskam, Geert, and Luc van der Stockt, eds. 2011. *Virtues for the People: Aspects of Plutarchan Ethics.*" Leuven: Leuven University Press.

Rubincam, Catherine. 1987. "The Organization and Composition of the Diodoros' *Bibliotheke.*" *Classical Views* 31: 313–28.

Rubincam, Catherine. 1998. "Did Diodorus Siculus Take Over Cross-References from his Sources?" *American Journal of Philology* 119.1: 67–87.

Russon, G. 1988. "Le Paradis de délices (*Genèse* 3, 23–24)." *Revue des Études grecques* 101: 64–73.

Rutter, N. Keith. 1970. "Sybaris—Legend and Reality." *Greece and Rome* 17: 168–76.

Rutter, N. Keith. 1973. "Diodorus and the Foundation of Thurii." *Historia* 22: 155–76.

Sacks, Kenneth. 1990. *Diodorus Siculus and the First Century.* Princeton, NJ: Princeton University Press.

Sacks, Kenneth. 1994. "Diodorus and His Sources." In *Greek Historiography*, edited by Simon Hornblower, 213–32. Oxford: Clarendon Press.

Sancisi-Weerdenburg, Heleen. 1987. "Decadence in the Empire or Decadence in the Sources? From Source to Synthesis: Ctesias." *Achaemenid History* 1: 33–45.

Sandridge, Norman B. 2012. *Loving Humanity, Learning, and Being Honored: The Foundation of Leadership in Xenophon's "Education of Cyrus."* Washington, DC: Center for Hellenic Studies.

Sartori, Franco. 1960. "Il problema storico di Sibari." *Atene e Roma* 5: 143–63.

Schepens. Guido. 1997. "Jacoby's *FGrHist*: Problems, Methods, Prospects." In Most 1997, 144–72.

Schepens. Guido. 2007. "Les fragments de Phylarque chez Athénée." In Lenfant 2007a, 239–61.

Schultze, C. 1986. "Dionysius of Halicarnassus and His Audience." In Moxon, Smart, and Woodman 1986, 121–41.

Schütrumpf, Eckart 2008. *Heraclides of Pontus: Texts and Translation.* New Brunswick, NJ: Transaction Publishers.

Schütrumpf, Eckart. 2009. "Heraclides, *On Pleasure.*" In *Heraclides of Pontus: Discussion*, edited by W. Fortenbaugh and E. Pender, 69–91. New Brunswick, NJ: Transaction Publishers.

Shaw, Brent. 1975. "Debt in Sallust." *Latomus* 34: 187–96.

Shrimpton, Gordon S. 1991. *Theopompus the Historian.* Montreal and Buffalo, NY: McGill-Queen's University Press.

Sinclair, Robert K. 1963. "Diodorus Siculus and the Writing of History." *Proceedings of the African Classical Association* 6: 36–45.

Smith, Christopher, and Liv Mariah Yarrow, eds. 2012. *Imperialism, Cultural Politics, and Polybius.* Oxford and New York: Oxford University Press.

Sniezewski, Stanislaw. 2001. "The Concept of Roman History in Livy: Philosophical, Religious, and Moral Aspects." *Eos* 88.2: 341–50.

Spagnoli, Emanuela. 2006. "Cultura materiale a Sibari: officine e maestranze." *Annali dell'Istituto Italiano di Numismatica* 52: 281–88.

Spawforth, A. J. S. 2012. *Greece and the Augustan Cultural Revolution*. Cambridge: Cambridge University Press.

Spoerri, Walter. 1979. "Hippys, von Rhegion." *Der kleine Pauly* 2.1179–80.

Stazio, Attilio, and Stefania Ceccoli, eds. 1993. *Sibari e la Sibaritide: atti del trentaduesimo Convegno di studi sulla Magna Grecia; Taranto–Sibari, 7–12 Ottobre 1992*. Tarentum: Istituto per la Storia e l'Archaeologia della Magna Grecia.

Stelluto, Sonia. 1995. "Il motivo della τρυφή in Filarco." In *Secondo miscellanea filologica*, edited by Italo Gallo, 47–84. Naples: Arte tipografica.

Stronk, Jan P., ed. and trans. 2010. *Ctesias' "Persian History": Part 1, Introduction, Text, and Translation*. Düsseldorf: Wellem.

Stylianou, P. J. 1992. Review of Sacks 1990. *BMCR* 02.06.19. Accessed January 13, 2012, http://bmcr.brynmawr.edu/1991/02.06.19.html.

Sulimani, Iris. 2008. "Diodorus' Source-Citations: A Turn in the Attitude of Ancient Authors Towards their Predecessors?" *Athenaeum* 96.2: 535–67.

Swain, Simon. 1990. "Hellenic Culture and Roman Heroes in Plutarch." *Journal of Hellenic Studies* 110: 126–45.

Talamo, Clara. 1987. "Pitagora e la TRUFH/." *Revisti di filologia e di instruzione classica* 115: 385–404.

Thomas, Rosalind. 2000. *Herodotus in Context: Ethnography, Science, and the Art of Persuasion*. Cambridge: Cambridge University Press.

Thompson, Wesley E. 1985. "Fragments of the Preserved Historians—Especially Polybius." In *The Greek Historians: Literature and History. Papers Presented to A.E. Raubitschek*, 119–39. Saratoga, CA: ANMA Libri.

Tronson, A. 1984. "Satyrus the Peripatetic and the Marriages of Philip II." *Journal of Hellenic Studies* 104: 116–26.

Tsitsiridis, Stavros. 2008. "Die Schrift ΠΕΡΙ ΒΙΩΝ des Klearchos von Soloi." *Philologus* 152: 65–76.

Tsumura, David Toshio. 1989. *The Earth and Waters in Genesis 1 and 2: A Linguistic Investigation*. Sheffield: Sheffield Academic Press.

Ussher, Robert Glenn, ed. 1973. *Aristophanes "Ecclesiazusae."* Oxford: Clarendon Press.

Van der Stockt, L. 1999. "A Plutarchan *Hypomnema* on Self-Love." *American Journal of Philology* 120: 575–99

Van Groningen, B. A. 1960. *La Composition littéraire archaïque grecque*, 2nd edition. Amsterdam: Noord-Hollandsche.

Van Hoof, Lieve. 2010. *Plutarch's Practical Ethics: The Social Dynamics of Philosophy*. Oxford: Clarendon Press.

Vasaly, Ann. 2009. "Characterization and Complexity: Caesar, Sallust, and Livy." In Feldherr 2009, 245–60.

Vattuone, Riccardo. 1991. *Sapienza d'occidente: il pensiero storico di Timeo di Tauromenio*. Bologna: Patrone editore.

Venturini, Carlo. 1979. "*Luxus* e *auaritia* nell'opera di Sallustio (osservazioni e problemi)." *Athenaeum* 57: 277–92.

Walbank, Frank W. 1957–79. *A Historical Commentary on Polybius*. 3 vols. Oxford: Clarendon Press.

Walbank, Frank W. 1992. Review of Sacks 1990. *Journal of Roman Studies* 82: 250–51.

Walbank, Frank W. 2000. "Athenaeus and Polybius." In Braund and Wilkins 2000, 161–69.

Walbank, Frank W. 2002. *Polybius, Rome, and the Hellenistic World*. Cambridge: Cambridge University Press.

Walsh, P. G. 1963. *Livy: His Historical Aims and Methods*. Cambridge: Cambridge University Press.

Waters, Kenneth. 1971. *Herodotos on Tyrants and Despots: A Study in Objectivity*. Wiesbaden: F. Steiner.

Wehrli, Fritz. 1969. *Clearchus*. Die Schule des Aristoteles, vol. 3. Basel: Schwabe.

West, Martin L., ed. 1987. *Euripides "Orestes."* Warminster: Aris and Phillips.

Wheeldon, M. J. 1989. "'True Stories': The Reception of Historiography in Antiquity." In *History as Text: The Writing of Ancient History*, edited by Averil Cameron, 33–63. London: Duckworth.

Whitmarsh, Tim. 2001. *Greek Literature and the Roman Empire: The Politics of Imitation*. Oxford: Clarendon Press.

Wiater, Nicolas. 2011. *The Ideology of Classicism: Language, History, and Identity in Dionysius of Halicarnassus*. Berlin and New York: De Gruyter.

Wiesehöfer, Josef, Robert Rollinger, and Giovanni B. Lanfranchi, eds. 2011. *Ktesias' Welt / Ctesias' World*. Wiesbaden: Harrassowitz.

Wilkins, John. 2000a. *The Boastful Chef: The Discourse of Food in Ancient Greek Comedy*. Oxford: Clarendon Press.

Wilkins, John. 2000b. "Dialogue and Comedy: The Structure of the *Deipnisophistae*." In Braund and Wilkins 2000, 23–37.

Wilkins, John. 2008. "Athenaeus the Navigator." *Journal of Hellenic Studies* 128: 132–52.

Yarrow, Liv Mariah. 2006. *Historiography at the End of the Republic: Provincial Perspectives on Roman Rule*. Oxford: Clarendon Press.

Zancani Montuoro, Paola. 1980. "La fine di Sibari." *Atti della Accademia Nazionale dei Lancei* 35: 149–56.

Zancani Montuoro, Paola. 1982a. "I vini di Sibari e Thuri." In *APARXAI: Nuove ricerche e studi sulla Magna Grecia e la Sicilia antica in onore di Paolo Enrico Arias*, edited by L. Besche, et al., 559–62. Pisa: Giardini.

Zancani Montuoro, Paola. 1982b. "Sibari sul Teutranto." *La Parola del passato* 37: 102–108.

Zanda, Emanuela. 2011. *Fighting Hydra-Like Luxury: Sumptuary Regulation in the Roman Republic*. London: Bristol Classical Press.

Zecchini, Giuseppe. 1987. "La conoscenza di Diodoro nel tardoantico." *Aevum* 61: 43–52.

Zecchini, Giuseppe. 1989. *La cultura storica di Ateneo*. Milan: Vita e pensiero.

Zepernick, K. 1921. "Die Exzerpte des Athenaeus in den Deipnosophisten und ihre Glaubwürdigkeit." *Philologus* 77: 311–63.

Index Locorum

Index Verborum Graecorum

σωφροσύνη/σώφρων: 58, 65n121, 285, 304,
   316, 373n62, 386, 388, 407, 416–17

ταλαιπωρία/ταλαίπωρος: 23n40, 87, 88, 104,
   135–37, 143n144, 237, 355, 390, 402, 409,
   417
τοιοῦτος ἦν: 191n83, 202, 270n56, 271, 273–75,
   278n72, 313, 362, 364
τρυφή
   beneficial: 65–74, 351–57, 389–92,
      402–4
   corrupting: 326–345, 357–426, 433–36
   defined: 2, 34–46, 61–66, 401–2, 419–20,
      428. See also τρυφή: entitlement
   entitlement, attitude of: 2, 35–43, 54, 57n111,
      58, 59n114, 60, 62n119, 63, 71–74, 198,
      205, 257–58, 332n10, 336, 370–78, 384,
      394, 402, 432
   gift of God: 65–74, 389–92, 401
   leads to hubris and excess: 4, 22–25, 41–43,
      46, 75, 78, 147, 287, 327–28, 332, 335,
      342–44, 373–81, 385–87, 395–400,
      402–3, 412n108, 421–23, 425–26, 432–
      36
   leads to softness: 2, 4, 20n33, 43, 49–65, 70,
      75, 77–78, 80–94, 221, 222, 235, 326–28,
      332, 340–43, 346, 349, 352, 361, 371,
      381–85, 392–95, 399, 405, 408, 415,
      422–23, 425–26, 432, 440
   oratory and: 413–15. See also flattery

presumption, attitude of. See τρυφή:
   entitlement
punished by God: 395–407

ὕβρις/ὑβρίζω: 22–26, 42, 51–52, 57–58, 78, 85,
   93, 94n40, 106, 213, 224, 233–35, 242n3,
   243–44, 248–50, 252, 255, 259, 285,
   292n102, 293–94, 320n157, 324, 335, 344,
   348, 355, 362, 373, 375, 386, 388, 395–402,
   409–413, 416, 421, 423, 425–28, 433, 435,
   437, 439–41
ὑπερβάλλω/ὑπερβολή: 135, 141, 211,
   229–31, 258–60, 278n74, 307–8, 311–13,
   317, 346–47, 352, 355–57, 422, 425n125,
   429
ὑπερηφανία/ὑπερήφανος: 51–52, 61n117, 211,
   425n125, 433

φθονέω/φθόνος/ἄφθονος: 37, 49, 50n99, 93–
   94, 133, 285, 347, 386, 402
φιλοπότης: 183n68, 304, 306

χλιδή: 18, 20n35, 27–30, 74, 178, 191, 201–2,
   205–7, 284, 317, 394
χορηγία: 233, 243–46, 262, 267, 354–55, 395,
   398, 435

ψίλωσις: 248–49

ὡς ἔνεστι: 279

Index Nominum et Rerum

Achaeans: 8, 12n12, 16, 17n26, 21–23, 162, 427

Achaeus (governor of Asia): 215

Acragantini. *See* Agrigentinum (Acragas)/ Agrigentines

Aeschylus. *See* the Index Locorum

Agamemnon: 48–50, 160, 170–71, 411

Agatharchides of Cnidus: 180n63, 293n104. *See also* the Index Locorum

Agrigentum (Acragas)/Agrigentines: 188–89, 203–4, 352–54, 356, 358

Alcibiades of Athens: 63–64, 190, 208–9

Alcisthenes of Sybaris, cloak of: 7n2, 13n13, 22n39, 201–2

Alexander of Troy (Paris): 28, 29, 36, 42

Alexander the Great: 180n63, 225, 231n157, 355, 361, 364–65, 388

Anaximenes of Lampsacus: 222–23, 307

Androcydes of Cyzicus: 217

Antiochus of Syracuse: 10, 15–17, 439n9, 441

Appian: 327n1, 369n51

Aristides: 276–77

Aristippus of Cyrene: 195n88

Aristophanes. *See* the Index Locorum

Aristotle: 18, 20–22, 56, 59n114, 131, 185–87, 192, 214, 245, 275–77, 282–84. *See also* the Index Locorum

arrogance: 41, 61n117, 106, 211, 328, 331–32, 334, 338, 343, 351, 423, 425n125

Artemisia (ruler of Halicarnassus): 95–98, 100, 116nn82–83, 384n78

asceticism: 392–94, 401, 415, 426

Assyrians: 130n104, 130n106, 131, 279–81,

290n96, 361–64, 418. *See also* Sardanapalus; Ninyas; and Semiramis

Astyages (King of Media): 56, 84n22, 124, 129

Athenaeus (character in the *Deipnosophistae*): 152–53

Athenaeus (author): 3, 10, 13n13, 18, 20, 146–239, 240–325, 419–422.

categories of citation: 155–57, 174n51, 183–89

compositional drift (the "Pelling Principle"): 170n44, 189–95, 228, 277, 302, 317–22

diction. *See* Athenaeus, formulae of expression

epitome, *Deipnosophistae* as: 150n12; 157n28

formulae of expression: 212–38, 239

fragmentary writers and: 3–4, 240–326

framing language: 170n45, 190n78, 195–212, 218–34, 239, 241, 268, 278n74, 288, 291n100, 303–4, 311, 314–16, 423n120

Homer, use of: 157–71

intermediate source for: 195n89, 204n101, 267n47

methods of citation: 3, 155–82

motion, verbs of: 216–18, 224–25, 233n163, 237n174, 243, 247–53, 255, 346–47, 420–21

novelty as a goal: 149–55, 166, 182, 191–92, 195, 234, 256, 265

paraphrases original sources: 155–57, 159–64, 169, 174n51, 183–94, 196n59, 198n92, 200, 202n99, 203–6, 209, 211, 217, 220–21, 223, 232, 234, 236, 238–39,